THE MASTER MUSICIANS

BERG

SERIES EDITED BY R. LARRY TODD

THE MASTER MUSICIANS

Titles Available in Paperback

Bach • Malcolm Boyd

Bartók • Malcolm Gillies

Berlioz • Hugh Macdonald

Beethoven • Barry Cooper

Brahms • Malcolm MacDonald

Britten • Michael Kennedy

Bruckner • Derek Watson

Chopin • Jim Samson

Grieg • John Horton

Handel • Donald Burrows

Liszt • Derek Watson

Mahler • Michael Kennedy

Mendelssohn • Philip Radcliffe

Monteverdi • Denis Arnold

Mozart • Julian Rushton

Musorgsky • David Brown

Puccini • Julian Budden

Purcell • J. A. Westrup

Rachmaninoff • Geoffrey Norris

Rossini • Richard Osborne

Schoenberg • Malcolm MacDonald

Schubert • John Reed

Schumann • Eric Frederick Jensen

Sibelius • Robert Layton

Richard Strauss • Michael Kennedy

Tchaikovsky • Edward Garden

Vaughan Williams • James Day

Verdi • Julian Budden

Vivaldi • Michael Talbot

Wagner • Barry Millington

Titles Available in Hardcover

Bach • David Schulenberg

Beethoven • Barry Cooper

Byrd • Kerry McCarthy

Carter • David Schiff

Chopin • Jim Samson

Debussy • Eric Frederick Jensen

Elgar • Robert Anderson

Handel • Donald Burrows

Liszt • Derek Watson

MacDowell • E. Douglas Bomberger

Mozart • Julian Rushton

Musorgsky • David Brown

Puccini • Julian Budden

Rossini • Richard Osborne

Schoenberg • Malcolm MacDonald

Schubert • John Reed

Schumann • Eric Frederick Jensen

Schültz • Basil Smallman

Richard Strauss • Michael Kennedy

Strauss • Laurenz Lütteken

Stravinsky • Paul Griffiths

Tallis • Kerry McCarthy

Tchaikovsky • Roland John Wiley

Verdi • Julian Budden

THE MASTER MUSICIANS

BERG

BRYAN SIMMS

CHARLOTTE ERWIN

OXFORD

UNIVERSITY PRESS

OXFORD
UNIVERSITY PRESS

Oxford University Press is a department of the University of Oxford. It furthers
the University's objective of excellence in research, scholarship, and education
by publishing worldwide. Oxford is a registered trade mark of Oxford University
Press in the UK and certain other countries.

Published in the United States of America by Oxford University Press
198 Madison Avenue, New York, NY 10016, United States of America.

Library of Congress Cataloging-in-Publication Data
Names: Simms, Bryan R., author. | Erwin, Charlotte Elizabeth, 1948– author.
Title: Berg / Bryan Simms, Charlotte Erwin.
Description: New York : Oxford University Press, 2021. |
Series: Master musicians series |
Includes bibliographical references and index. |
Identifiers: LCCN 2020027710 (print) | LCCN 2020027711 (ebook) |
ISBN 9780190931445 (hardback) | ISBN 9780190931469 (epub) | ISBN 9780190931476
Subjects: LCSH: Berg, Alban, 1885–1935. | Composers—Austria—Biography.
Classification: LCC ML410.B47 S49 2021 (print) | LCC ML410.B47 (ebook) |
DDC 780.92 [B]—dc23
LC record available at https://lccn.loc.gov/2020027710
LC ebook record available at https://lccn.loc.gov/2020027711

DOI: 10.1093/oso/9780190931445.001.0001

1 3 5 7 9 8 6 4 2

Printed by Sheridan Books, Inc., United States of America

Contents

Preface

He had a beautiful face, a smiling, almost mocking mouth, great warming eyes that always looked straight at you. Most of the many photographs that survive do him small justice: they are always a little stiff, a little too beautiful, a little posed, never quite as human as he was—they have neither the twinkle in the eye which we all remember nor the suffering that we also knew so well.

THOSE WHO KNEW ALBAN BERG OFTEN RECORD THE SAME TRAITS that Hans Heinsheimer did in this recollection.[1] Berg was an attractive person, someone who drew people to him and won their lasting affection. But beneath the courteous, affable and somewhat shy exterior, a complex and restless spirit resided. His student Theodor Adorno characterized him in a different way—as a man whose person was the stuff of his art, his music: "Berg's empirical existence was subordinate to the primacy of creative work; he honed himself as its instrument, his store of life experiences became solely a means of supplying conditions that would permit him to wrest his oeuvre from his own physical weaknesses and psychological resistance."[2]

This book will portray Alban Berg from both of these perspectives, man and musician. While the two are intertwined in the careers of all major composers, they are tied especially tightly together in the case of Berg, who continued the romantic's inclination to encode thoughts about his life—both inner and outer—in musical form. Our study of Berg's life is based on contemporary documents and reminiscences of those who knew him, also on the discoveries about him that are found in the large scholarly and analytic literature written since his death in 1935. By using these sources we hope to elucidate the forces that shaped his personality, career, and artistic outlook. A distinctive feature of the book will be an assessment of the role of Berg's wife, Helene Nahowski Berg, in his life and work and her later quest to shape his artistic legacy in the forty-one years of her widowhood.

The book also contains a concise study of the music itself. All major works are described and analyzed, with attention to their history, form, style, and expressive intentions. Whenever possible Berg's own analyses of his music—some of these new to the literature—will be brought into play. These discussions will show how Berg's music continually evolved to reflect his personal circumstances and changing artistic outlook and how it was a product of its time and place, beginning in the waning years of the Habsburg Monarchy, maturing under the influence of Arnold Schoenberg and the *Wiener Moderne*, and finally reaching its most fully realized state as a distinctive amalgamation of old and new in an environment when outright experimentation in music had lost favor. Given the especially close connection between Berg's life and the content of his music, the biographical and analytical sections are juxtaposed, although, for ease of reference, they retain a measure of separation as signaled by subheadings. The goal of the book is to provide reliable information on the composer and his works that will be of use to anyone wanting to know about him and his music. Although some moderate amount of technical terminology is used in the study of the music, there is enough non-technical discussion for the book to be accessible to all inquisitive readers.

Our first objective has been to record as accurately as possible the important events in Berg's life. Our responsibility as biographers requires us also to go beneath the surface of Berg's life to seek explanations for events and for the thoughts and motivations that surround them. To do this, we introduce, as needed, a measure of conjecture and theory. Our attempt to explain has led us to explore Berg's complex relations with Arnold Schoenberg and Karl Kraus, whose authority in artistic judgments and historical interpretations he accepted as indisputable fact. Also his relations with his family, especially with his wife, whose impact on his personal life has been underscored in recent years by the documentary studies of Herwig Knaus. These relations were a factor in Berg's creative life and a cause for the slow and often sporadic pace of his composing. Berg's interest in pseudo-science and his attraction to numerology will be investigated as they relate to his compositions and to his view of his own fate. It is our hope that Berg's personality will come into ever sharper focus as the events of his life and his responses to them are told. The Alban

Berg we have come to know lived in two worlds—one of the everyday and one almost entirely rooted in imagination and fantasy. Just how these two worlds interwove makes Berg's life story endlessly fascinating.

The biographical part of the book is built on a close study of thousands of documents from Berg's personal library that now make up the Fonds Alban Berg at the Österreichische Nationalbibliothek, as well as relevant documents from the Alban Berg Stiftung (Vienna), Wienbibliothek im Rathaus, Morgan Library (New York), New York Public Library, Library of Congress, and Bayerische Staatsbibliothek (Munich), among other repositories. We are grateful to the staffs of these institutions for their assistance in supporting our study. Our knowledge of the composer's life has been enriched also by recent editions of the composer's complete known correspondence—with Arnold Schoenberg, Theodor Adorno, Erich Kleiber, Hanna Fuchs-Robettin, Soma Morgenstern, and, most importantly, with his wife, Helene. Volumes of the Quellenkatalog zur Musikgeschichte by Herwig Knaus and Thomas Leibnitz containing Berg's letter drafts, notes, and miscellaneous writings have been indispensable. The critical reports to installments in the Alban Berg Sämtliche Werke have provided us with new and detailed information on the history of Berg's compositions and writings. The majority of our primary sources are in German, and unless otherwise noted, the translations offered in the text are our own. When published sources originally appeared in German, we have consulted the German version. Reliance on the published translations of others has been noted.

We are deeply grateful to those who have assisted us in the completion of this project. The generous advice given by Dr. Regina Busch at the Alban Berg Stiftung has been invaluable to us, as has assistance from others at the Stiftung including Dr. Daniel Ender, Dr. Jonas Pfohl, Manuel Strauß, Klaus Lippe, Sabrina Kollenz, and Dr. Ingrid Schraffl. Eike Feß from the Arnold Schönberg Center provided valuable assistance to us. Eika Bernauer gave advice on some difficult translations. We especially thank those who have read and commented on passages from the book: Professor Janet Schmalfeldt; Cornelia Hamilton, M.D.; Paul Z. Bodnar, M.D.; and Allison Parelman, PhD. For her willingness to read the entire manuscript and offer much helpful editorial guidance, we owe special thanks to Karen Baart.

Abbreviations

(see the Bibliography for full publication data)

AMB   *"Immer wieder werden mich thätige Geister verlocken"*:
        Alma Mahler-Werfels Briefe an Alban Berg und seine Frau
        (Vienna, 2008)

ABS   Alban Berg Studien (Vienna)

BBF   *Alban Berg Briefwechsel mit seiner Familie*
        (Wilhelmshaven, 2016)

BSB   *Briefwechsel Arnold Schönberg—Alban Berg,* 2 vols.
        (Mainz, 2007)

BStaB   Bayerische Staatsbibliothek (Munich)

BW   *Briefwechsel Alban Berg—Helene Berg: Gesamtausgabe*
        3 vols. (Wilhelmshaven, 2012–14)

ISCM   International Society for Contemporary Music
        (Internationale Gesellschaft für Neue Musik)

ÖNB   Österreichische Nationalbibliothek (Vienna)

ÖMZ   *Österreichische Musikzeitschrift*

PMPD   *Pro Mundo-Pro Domo: The Writings of Alban Berg*
        (New York, 2014)

QMG   Quellenkataloge zur Musikgeschichte, vols. 29, 34, 35
        (Wilhelmshaven, 2004–06)

WBR   Wienbibliothek im Rathaus

Alban and Helene Berg. Courtesy of the Alban Berg Stiftung (Vienna)

Music in the Twilight of the Habsburg Empire

OR A COMPOSER LIKE ALBAN BERG WHO CAME OF AGE IN THE CITY at the close of the nineteenth century, Vienna was a place of artistic brilliance and opportunity. It was widely recognized in these years as the world's music capital, home to Brahms, Bruckner, Mahler, Wolf, and the waltz king Johann Strauss. The Vienna Philharmonic Orchestra played in the "Golden Hall" of the Musikverein, whose bright and crystalline acoustics made it then, as now, the best auditorium in the world to hear the details in symphonic music. In 1869 a new theater for the Court Opera was opened, the first of the major public buildings constructed on the Ringstrasse during the great urban renewal of Vienna that continued for the remainder of the century. A broad repertory of German, French, and Italian operas was performed at the Opera, including classic and modern works. Berg attended the Opera regularly, racing to the cheapest seats or standing room at the top of the theater, the "fourth balcony," where he met other young and aspiring musicians and first laid eyes on Helene Nahowski, whom he married in 1911.[1] Giuseppe Verdi arrived at the Opera in 1875 to conduct his Requiem and *Aida*. "What a good orchestra and what good choruses!" he exclaimed. "And how manageable they are, and they let themselves be led correctly. To sum up, a performance that, all things considered, will never be heard again!"[2]

Vienna was also a center for musical scholarship and learning. Near the end of the century the modern discipline of musicology was

Berg. Bryan Simms and Charlotte Erwin, Oxford University Press (2021). © Oxford University Press.
DOI: 10.1093/oso/9780190931445.003.0001.

created in part by the theory of style analysis advanced by Guido Adler at the University of Vienna, and several of Adler's doctoral students in the subject—including Anton Webern, Paul Pisk, Egon Wellesz, Erwin Stein, and Heinrich Jalowetz—became close friends of Berg and fellow students of Arnold Schoenberg. The Conservatory of the Gesellschaft der Musikfreunde (after 1909, Akademie für Musik und Darstellende Kunst) attracted young musicians from around the world. A whole generation of young composers—Gustav Mahler, Erich Wolfgang Korngold, Jean Sibelius, Alexander Zemlinsky, Franz Schmidt, Franz Schreker, and Hugo Wolf, among many others—learned music theory and composition there in classes taught by Robert Fuchs. They came together with a heady self-consciousness, a belief in the importance of their calling, and a pride in writing down their profession as "Komponist."

The great flowering of modern music and the other arts around 1900 may in retrospect seem perplexing at a time when the Habsburg Empire was led by an antiquated government, stricken by national rivalries, and plagued by social ills and unrest. The romantic preoccupation with love and death took on a deadly realism in Vienna, where suicide was common and prostitution overt and widespread. Still, music flourished—not on account of the frictions that propelled the other modern arts—but sustained instead by distinctive traditions within the outwardly placid Viennese society itself. The first of these factors was the presence of a large audience committed to the arts, a middle class with a consciousness about living in the "City of Music." In his classic account of growing up in Vienna, *The World of Yesterday*, Stefan Zweig observed a special "urge toward culture" among his neighbors. "An artist always feels most at ease and at the same time most inspired," Zweig wrote, "in a place where he is valued, even overvalued. Art always reaches its zenith where it is important in the life of an entire nation."[3] Leon Botstein has pointed to the "phenomenal growth in numbers of individuals engaged in music" in Vienna of this time, a music public not just involved as listeners but active participants as pianists, singers in choral groups, and chamber players. The outcome, Botstein concludes, was an audience so knowledgeable that it could anticipate, follow, and recall the important elements in a musical work.[4] In a lecture given in 1930 Arnold Schoenberg looked back wistfully to this earlier time and to the level of sophistication in music among the Viennese:

> I come from a time when there were still amateurs in music who were able to retain a melody—even one by Brahms—after only one hearing. This was a time when musicians could listen once to a canon and know how many voices it had, about its structure, plan, and other such facts; they could hear a variations piece, for example, and not have a momentary doubt about what was going on in it.[5]

This special interest in music and in the arts in general was stimulated by the growth and relative affluence of the Viennese middle classes. The population of Vienna exploded at the end of the century, growing from about 700,000 in 1880 to 2 million in 1919, although these numbers are in part inflated by the incorporation of Vienna's outer suburbs into the city limits. Berg's parents are examples of this demographic phenomenon. His father, Conrad Berg, immigrated to Vienna from Bavaria in 1868, opened a successful bookstore in the central city, married the daughter of a local jeweler, had four children, bought a summer house in the country, and installed a pipe organ in his residence. The Bergs typified the Viennese rising bourgeoisie of the time, who were devoted to achieving a comfortable standard of living through business and an orderly family life, enriched by an interest in art, literature, and music.

Stefan Zweig also underscores the role of Vienna's large Jewish population in the support of the arts. "Without the constant interest of the Jewish bourgeoisie as stimulation, at a time when the court was indolent and the aristocracy and the Christian millionaires preferred to spend money on racing stables and hunts rather than encouraging art, Vienna would have lagged as far behind Berlin artistically as Austria did behind the German Reich in politics."[6] Berg's whole intellectual life was conducted largely among Jewish artists whom he admired and with whom he was delighted to interact. Berg's idols included Arnold Schoenberg, Peter Altenberg, Karl Kraus, and Gustav Mahler—all Jews—so too such trusted friends as Erwin Stein, Theodor Adorno, Soma Morgenstern, Willi Reich, and Joseph Polnauer.

Another consideration behind the thriving culture for music in Vienna at the time was the coalescing of groups of artists into "circles," each consisting of an artist-teacher and his students or followers, and each providing a "one for all and all for one" system of support. A composer's circle was reliably present at concerts, ready to cheer and, if necessary, do battle with the philistines in the audience. Following a performance of Bruckner's Symphony No. 3 by the Vienna Philharmonic Orchestra in 1899, the composer's circle rose up against the apathy of the audience. The critic Eduard Hanslick, who did not care for Bruckner's music, dutifully noted in his review the "stamping, raging, and screaming" of Bruckner's circle at the symphony's conclusion. Schoenberg's close-knit group was equally devoted and engaged. At concerts of Schoenberg's music, his circle, led by the husky Polnauer, formed an exuberant cheering section with no patience for those daring to whistle or boo. Things came to a head in the "scandal concert" at the Musikverein in March 1913, when the audience erupted in protest during the performance of a song by Berg. The police were summoned and the remainder of the concert canceled. It seems inconceivable to us in the present day that a work of serious music—one with dissonant rather than triadic harmonies—could bring an audience to blows, but such was the importance of music to the Viennese of that period. Although Berg struggled with Schoenberg's demands on his personal life, his rise in the musical world would be hard to imagine without Schoenberg's influence.

Edward Timms has observed that circles in different artistic disciplines often overlapped. Artists of different stripes assembled at the tables of Vienna's coffee houses to exchange ideas and encourage their mutual instinct for experimentation.[7] Near to his residence in Hietzing, Berg met friends at the Café Gröpl, and at the Löwenbräu Bierhalle in the central city he sat with Karl Kraus, Gustav Klimt, and Adolf Loos, among others. The emergence of a *Wiener Moderne* around 1900 could not have occurred without this tradition of social and artistic exchange. On a personal level more than a musical one, Berg relished his contacts with writers and artists. He formed a lifelong friendship with Adolf Loos, Peter Altenberg, and Erhard Buschbeck, among others, and Karl Kraus became one of his idols. A keen interest in modern literature was a characteristic of all in Schoenberg's circle. Schoenberg himself confessed to being led toward the atonal style in music by his attempt to match the mysterious "tone" that he heard in the new poetic language of Richard Dehmel and Stefan George. "It's good to let poetry lead you back to music," he advised Berg.[8] Berg first contemplated a career as a writer, wrote poetry and drama himself as a youth, and as a composer brought modern developments in poetry into his music. Berg and Egon Wellesz, for example, were the first composers to set the aphoristic prose-poems of Peter Altenberg to music.

A crucial element of Viennese culture before World War I that supported artists in their experiments was a general optimism about the future. Stefan Zweig remarked, "In those days this faith in uninterrupted, inexorable 'progress' truly had the force of a religion."[9] A belief in the future was especially important for Vienna's musical modernists. If their new harmonic language was whistled down by contemporary audiences, then it would surely be understood and applauded by those in generations to come. In his *Harmonielehre* of 1911, Schoenberg reiterated his hopes for the future: "Certainly we must not be satisfied with our time. But not because it is no longer the good old times, gone forever, but because it is not yet the better, the new times of the future."[10] The Viennese had reason to be confident in the future of music: the era of Beethoven and Schubert, for example, had been followed by the era of Brahms, Bruckner, Dvořák, and Mahler; the operas of Wagner and Verdi had followed upon those by Mozart and Rossini. It seemed self-evident that the great music of the present would lead in the future to new works of equal or superior greatness.

The Viennese belief in the future was complicated by a division in musical taste among audiences and critics across Europe. It separated traditionalists from "progressives," or *Fortschrittler* as they were called, and the split came sharply into focus in Viennese musical life by century's end. The division began to appear in the years following Beethoven's death in 1827. Both progressives and traditionalists looked to Beethoven as their point of origin. The classical-minded traditionalists such as Mendelssohn sought to preserve the principles of form and balanced, restrained expression found in Beethoven's early and middle period works. Progressives like Franz Liszt found models on which to build in Beethoven's later works in which classical restraint and proportions were exceeded and where an intensified musical expression could lead beyond the music itself into the realm of "programs" drawn from literature and the picturesque. "My only ambition as a musician," wrote Liszt, "has been and shall be to hurl my lance into the infinite expanse of the future."[11]

By mid-century the division between the two camps had widened with the ascendancy of Liszt and Richard Wagner to a position of leadership among the progressives. The traditionalists looked then to Vienna as a safe haven for their values. Their leader was Johannes Brahms, who moved to Vienna permanently in 1865, wanting, as he put it, "to drink my wine where Beethoven drank his."[12] A strongly supportive circle soon developed around Brahms, including the influential music critics Eduard Hanslick and Max Kalbeck, pedagogues including Robert Fuchs, and prestigious patrons such as Theodor Billroth.

At the same time Vienna was home to an intensely progressive faction of composers, including Anton Bruckner, Gustav Mahler, and Hugo Wolf, and bitter tensions flared up between the two camps, with accusations that often overlooked the elements of tradition and modernism in the music of both parties. Brahms in 1885 reassured his friend Elisabet von Herzogenberg that she was right to doubt the artistic merit of Bruckner's Seventh Symphony: "About his things there is no going back and forth—they are beyond discussion. The man himself likewise. He is a poor, deranged person whom the clerics of St. Florian have on their conscience."[13] The progressives responded by inflammatory attacks on the Viennese traditionalists. In an article in the *Bayreuther Blätter* written shortly after the appearance of Brahms's Symphonies No. 1 and 2, Wagner found that such music had a "viscous sort of melody." Wagner continued, "what heretofore was prepared as quintets and the like is now served up as symphony: with little chips of melody, like tea made from hay and used tea leaves, such that no one knows what he is sipping although it is called 'genuine' in an attempt to pass off world weariness as a thing of pleasure."[14] Even in Vienna itself, Brahms was relentlessly attacked by Hugo Wolf in articles written for the *Wiener Salonblatt*. Following a performance of Brahms's Symphony No. 3 in 1884 by the visiting Meiningen orchestra, Wolf wrote disparagingly:

> The arrival of Brahms's F major Symphony threw a wet blanket over the happy mood that followed the jubilant tones of [Weber's] *Freischütz* Overture. The symphony by Herr Dr. Johannes Brahms is in part an able and meritorious work; but as a Beethoven no. 2 it turns out quite badly because the one thing that we expect from a Beethoven no. 2—originality—is entirely missing from the one by Dr. Johannes Brahms. Brahms is an epigone of Schumann and Mendelssohn and as such he exerts the same measure of influence on artistic history as did the late Robert Volkmann. That is to say, Brahms has just as little significance as did Volkmann, which is to say none at all.[15]

With the passing of Brahms in 1897, Dvořák in 1904, and Grieg in 1907, the traditionalists were left with no composer of like stature, no one who could compete with a rising generation of younger progressives. Feeling no restraint, some of the *Neutöner* moved musical style far into the future by creating a strikingly new harmonic language that was soon designated by the term "atonality." The word itself has always been treacherous, often misunderstood, and frequently rejected by composers. But it was used approvingly by others, including Alban Berg, to describe their own compositions.[16] The term and the phenomenon behind it are needed for an assessment of Berg's originality as a composer and the critical reaction to his music. The term "atonal" began to appear in music criticism around 1910, at first to describe harmonic innovations in Schoenberg's recent music. The first to use the term in this way was Schoenberg's student Egon Wellesz in an article of 1911, in which Wellesz pointed to the abandonment of the traditional distinction between consonant chords (harmonies based on the triad) and dissonant ones (non-triadic harmony) as the main characteristic of the new style. Regarding Schoenberg's Piano Pieces, Op. 11 (1909), Wellesz wrote: "They are atonal and remove the concept of dissonance."[17] Wellesz's definition is similar to Schoenberg's own statements about his music composed after about 1907. Schoenberg pointed to the pervasive presence of dissonant harmony as the most distinctive feature of such works. "Dissonances are used like consonances and a tonal center is avoided," he wrote.[18] Schoenberg never settled on a term to describe the new harmonic idiom, but he rejected "atonal" as pejorative and imprecise in meaning.

Atonality was not a "revolutionary" development, not the property of Viennese musicians per se, nor the invention of any single figure. It was instead an international phenomenon appearing in the first decade of the twentieth century in music by leading progressive composers— Richard Strauss in Berlin, Béla Bartók in Budapest, Alexander Scriabin in Moscow, Charles Ives in New York, and Arnold Schoenberg and Alban Berg in Vienna, among many others. It built upon harmonic innovations in the music of the preceding generation of composers: Liszt, Wagner, Mahler, Bruckner, also Brahms.

Many of the progressive composers readily accepted the term atonal to describe the new harmony. "Music of the present day tends decisively toward atonality," wrote Béla Bartók in 1920. "But it is not correct to conclude that the tonal principle is completely the opposite of the atonal principle. The latter is instead the outcome of a gradual development that took its departure from the former."[19] Bartók found the atonal principle in full force in music in which the twelve tones of the chromatic scale were used as though equals. In such music none of these tones was a priori distinctive or functional: for example, none could be construed as a tonic, dominant, leading tone, or "accidental." With this as a principle of tonal equality, the functional harmonic progressions of tonality—the harmonic syntax that previously allowed for the establishment of a central keynote or tonic—were not present.

The term atonality was quickly taken in a different and pejorative direction by journalists and used as a blanket term by which to suggest the absence of all musical values in modern works. Berg argued strongly against this mistaken use of the word in his radio dialog "What Is Atonal?"[20] Here he reiterates that the term is valid to describe the harmonic idiom of many modern works that "cannot be related in harmonic terms to a major or minor scale." This idiom, Berg continues, rests on the pitch resources of the full chromatic scale and "new chords" derived from it. But Berg dismisses the pejorative use of the term that was increasingly attached to modern music: "The opponents of this music hold to [the word] with great persistence so as to have a single term to dismiss all of new music by denying, as I said, the presence of what until now has comprised music and thus to deny its justification for existence."[21]

An especially misleading application of the term atonal at the time—which continues to the present day—labeled modern music categorically as either tonal or atonal. Bartók in 1920 had cautioned against this naive and uninformed dichotomy. Modern harmony, he said, could profitably mix or alternate the principles of tonality and atonality. Some composers in the atonal movement—Schoenberg, for example—practiced just the "radical exclusion" of triadic harmony that Bartók questioned. "The simple chords of the earlier harmony," Schoenberg wrote, "do not appear successfully in this environment. . . . I believe they would sound too dry, too expressionless."[22] But for most of the progressive composers of the early century, a mixing of atonal and tonal harmony was preferred. The merger of the tonal and atonal principles proved to be one of Alban Berg's major achievements in music.

A confidence in the future that had long nourished music in Vienna began to erode as World War I approached, and it would then be shattered by the disastrous outcome of the war for both Germany and the Empire. Six hundred years of Habsburg sovereignty came to a ruinous end in 1918, and the new rump state to be called "Austria" began the arduous process of becoming a democratic republic. Vienna's breakthrough into modernism now seemed at best an anomaly, at worst a doomed failure. A new pessimism descended upon German culture. In his 1917 polemic *Futuristengefahr* (The danger of futurism), Hans Pfitzner dismissed the optimism expressed by Ferruccio Busoni in his prewar *Sketch of a New Esthetic of Music*:

> Busoni fondly hopes for a future with everything for Western music and sees the past and present as a hesitant beginning, a preparatory stage. But what if this isn't right? Maybe we have already passed some high point or *the* high point? What if our last century or century-and-a-half was actually the heyday of Western music, its height, its true time of brilliance that will never come again and will be followed by a decline, a decadence, as in the time following the heyday of Greek tragedy? My view tends much more in this direction.[23]

The loss of confidence in the future about which Pfitzner spoke was an indication that Vienna as a center for the modern arts had begun to wane. Berg strongly sensed this change from optimism to pessimism: in his later years, he spoke out ever more frequently condemning the musical culture in Vienna—his once beloved home city. His sarcastic message to the conductor Erich Kleiber in 1925 is typical:

> Allow me to congratulate you heartily that for the time being nothing has come of your Vienna Opera opportunity! If one has the insight into the musical conditions in this city—this second Bucharest—as I do, then with all genuine friendship for you, I can only *warn* you against an involvement with this sinking ship. And it's sinking unstoppably! I say this regardless of my *personal* regret in not having you here.[24]

Berg's life would coincide with this turbulent period of change—from opportunity and optimism to ultimate disaster. His environment inevitably shaped his thinking and impelled his artistic creations. But more than for most composers, Berg's music reveals his life as much as his life determined his music. It is in the music that we find the truest and most intimate map of the inner dimensions of that life.

Two Viennese Families

Alban Berg. Born 1885 in Vienna. School diploma. Piano instruction at home. First attempts at composing in 14th year. Autodidact until 19th year. Two years in civil service. From 1904 to 24th year exhaustive instruction in theory and composition with Arnold Schoenberg. Since 1910 teacher in areas of music theory and composition. Preparer of piano arrangements (for Schoenberg's Gurrelieder, Mahler's Eighth Symphony, four hands, Schreker's opera Der ferne Klang, among others), writer of music theory (guides, thematic analyses of Schoenberg's works, etc.). Married in 1911. Military service 1915–18. After that rehearsal coach with the "Society for Private Musical Performances in Vienna"—founded and led by Arnold Schoenberg from 1918—whose mission is to give weekly concerts solely of modern music.[1]

WHEN ALBAN BERG WROTE THIS ASSESSMENT OF HIMSELF IN 1921 he was thirty-seven years old and had only fourteen more years to live. It was his first published statement about himself and what he had accomplished in music. Like all of his later self-assessments it is terse and understated, at the same time pointing confidently to what he considered important in his life—his studies with Schoenberg, his marriage and military service, and a modest number of musical activities and achievements.

Berg's self-effacing presentation of himself seems baffling for a composer who by 1921 had completed works of such imagination and originality as to become classics in the history of modern music—the

Berg. Bryan Simms and Charlotte Erwin, Oxford University Press (2021). © Oxford University Press.
DOI: 10.1093/oso/9780190931445.003.0002

Piano Sonata, the String Quartet, the Altenberg Songs, the Orchestra Pieces, and an opera, *Wozzeck*, nearing completion. But these works were still little known, and Berg had not found a way to bring himself out of the shadow of his teacher, Arnold Schoenberg, or to escape from Schoenberg's readiness to keep him on hand as a permanent student. What circumstances of life led a composer of such genius to remain so long in obscurity?

Berg's Early Life

Albano Maria Johannes Berg was born on 9 February 1885, in his family's genteel residence on the Tuchlauben in Vienna's inner city.[2] Berg never used the name "Albano," a variant of the name of his godfather, Baron Alban von Salzgeber.[3] He had two older brothers—Hermann (1872–1921) and Karl, called Charly or Charley (1881–1952)—and also a younger sister, Smaragda (1886–1954). Berg's mother, née Johanna Braun (1851–1926), was the daughter of a Viennese goldsmith, Franz Braun, who supplied jewelry to the Habsburg court. Hermann Watznauer, a family friend and Berg's first biographer, described her in these terms:

> She had a command of English and French as well as German, was exceptionally well-read, and fond of music. She understood the artistic value of the pictures and objects of plastic art, which were to be found in abundance and variety among the ecclesiastical devotional pieces [in her husband's shop]. She had the happy temperament of the typical, healthy, true Viennese woman.[4]

Berg's future wife, Helene Nahowski, remembered her mother-in-law as "a good-natured, cheerful lady, very attached to the good life, and extremely amenable to the use of alcohol. For me she was a charming dear."[5]

Watznauer described Berg's father, Conrad Berg (1846–1900), as "thoroughly correct and refined. . . . He spoke little, but one nevertheless had the feeling that he took a lively part in social intercourse."[6] Conrad Berg grew up in Nuremberg, moved to Vienna in 1868, and became a successful businessman who ran a book and art dealership and from 1895 an export-import firm that served as the Vienna branch office of the Geo. Borgfeldt Co., an import house in New York. This firm played a large role in the life of the Berg family. Borgfeldt founded his company in New York in 1881, bringing in specialty goods from throughout

Europe—china, glassware, dolls and toys, and furnishings of all kinds. The company experienced phenomenal growth, soon opening branch offices throughout the United States and abroad. Their home office occupied nearly an entire block of Manhattan at Washington Square. In 1886 Berg's eldest brother Hermann, thirteen years older, emigrated permanently to America, acquired American citizenship—changing his name's spelling to "Herman"—and worked for Borgfeldt as a buyer. His greatest coup was finding an early version of the teddy bear—a stuffed toy bear made by the Richard Steiff Co. that was exhibited in Leipzig in 1903. Herman immediately ordered 3,000 to be sent to New York, although at about the same time a similar toy bear was being made by an American company. Charly Berg also worked for the Borgfeldt Co. in Vienna and later founded his own export-import business. He was musical, a singer with a special interest in the music of Wagner.

Berg was closest to his sister, Smaragda. She had been—according to many sources—one of the 2,000 piano students of the famed pedagogue Theodor Leschetizky, and she later worked as an accompanist, piano teacher, and rehearsal pianist at the Vienna Opera, where she formed a close friendship with singers including Anna Mildenburg and Marie Gutheil-Schoder. She also frequented Vienna's cafés and cabarets and was much admired by Peter Altenberg, among other writers. Following a brief marriage in 1907 to Adolf Freiherr von Eger—son of the director of Austria's Southern Railway—her lesbianism came into the open in liaisons with the cabaret *diseuse* Marya Delvard, the actress Erika Stiedry, and (briefly) her own sister-in-law, Alice Berg. Her attraction to Helene Nahowski—her future sister-in-law—will be discussed later in this chapter.

The Bergs lived an affluent life typical of the Viennese upper-middle classes near the end of the nineteenth century. In addition to their success in the world of business, they were patrons of art, literature, and music. They installed in their residence a pipe organ purchased from the old Burgtheater when it was razed in 1888. Anton Bruckner, a customer at Conrad Berg's bookshop, came to their residence to play on this instrument. In 1894 the Bergs purchased a large house and adjacent property on the Ossiachersee in Carinthia, which they christened "Berghof" and used as a summer residence. After 1900, following the death of Conrad Berg, the Berghof was opened to paying visitors, among them so many executives from Borgfeldt that the Berg children jokingly called it the "Borgfeldthof."

The principal existing records of Alban Berg's personal life before about 1900 are his school reports.[7] Following five years of elementary school, 1890–95, he entered the Oberrealschule at Vienna's Schottenbastei in a seven-year program whose curriculum emphasized the sciences, modern languages, history, and religion. The Austrian Realschulen were intended to prepare the children of the middle classes for lucrative careers in industry and commerce. The curriculum differed from that of a Gymnasium mainly in the absence of instruction in Greek and Latin, although both study programs led to the *Matura* examination, which qualified students to attend university. For the first five years, 1895 to spring 1900, Berg had good if unexceptional grades. His schoolwork then began to suffer as he developed an indifferent attitude, followed by outright scorn for his schooling and his instructors. This attitude is displayed in his earliest existing letters written to school chums. In March 1900 he wrote to his friend Johannes Huber:

> Just think, Hans, in the first semester report I got an F in German. How humiliating for a poet like me! But I'm sure that next time I'll get at least a C. Last Monday in math we had 6 problems and I got 5 of them right, while Bing, sitting next to me, was looking on my paper. When the director [Franz Wallenstein, who was also the mathematics instructor] saw this he said to Bing: "Bing, you'd better not look on Berg's paper. It'll be bad if you do, and *you won't find much there anyway*." On Wednesday he read out the grades: "Berg C, Bing D. Now I see why you looked on Berg's paper!"[8]

Berg's father died from heart failure on 30 March 1900, shortly after the letter to Huber was written. His death marked the beginning of a period of great stress for the fifteen-year old Alban and for others in the Berg family. Alban's schoolwork then steepened its decline, as his episodes of poor health, absences, and failing grades increased and he too stooped to the cheating that was widespread in his school. Before the end of the sixth year (1901–02) he dropped out of school entirely and had to repeat that level in 1902–03. At the end of that year he could not take his examinations—"for reasons of health" according to his school report. The second semester of his seventh year was disastrous, as he failed German and mathematics and was forced to repeat the entire grade in

1903–04. During this final year he apparently had no hesitation to ask his school friend Paul Hohenberg to write three of his assigned essays. In May 1904 he passed his *Matura* examinations; for the German examination he—or someone of his acquaintance—wrote, ironically, on the theme "Knowledge is Power."

Berg's outlook on his schooling was immature and lacking in self-discipline, but these attitudes were common at the time, especially among youth who, like Berg, had already shown a precocious talent in the arts. Ernest Newman's description of Wagner's elementary education might well be suited to Berg: "At school he applied himself very casually to the subjects that did not interest him, while he appears to have made no exceptional progress in those that did, because of his congenital inability to learn except in his own way."[9]

Following the death of Conrad Berg in March 1900, many luxuries earlier available to the Berg family disappeared. According to Austrian law, the settlement of an estate is controlled by a local court, which compiles an inventory of assets (the so-called active legacy) and debts weighing against it (the "passive" legacy). Both can then be passed on to next-of-kin. The court probates any existing wills, makes provisions for minor children, and finally distributes property to heirs.[10] Conrad Berg's personal indebtedness was modest, amounting to 7,047 kronen — roughly equivalent to $1,400 at the time—but debts accruing to his business increased the total liability of his estate to 38,348 kronen ($7,670). Johanna Berg agreed to pay off this amount herself, "to keep the memory of her husband clear," with the help of money received from her son Herman, the Borgfeldt Co., and benefits from a life insurance policy. A portion of this last sum was set aside for the younger children. Johanna and Herman Berg were appointed joint guardians of Alban while a minor, and Johanna also received funds from Marie von Bareis, Berg's godmother, to help with his education. Johanna took over the ownership and management of the bookstore, but she had to do without income from Conrad's lucrative export-import business, which was dissolved.

Following his graduation from Realschule in 1904 and given the family's limited financial prospects, Berg obeyed his mother's wish for him to seek regular employment as an accountant in the Austrian civil service. In October of 1904 he began a one-year unpaid training program, and at the same time he enrolled at the University of Vienna in a course in accounting and finance. (He also began his musical studies with Schoenberg at this time, to be discussed in the next chapter.) In the summer of 1905 he passed an examination in accounting and began to receive a modest salary for his work. But in October 1906 he resigned, much to his mother's chagrin. According to Watznauer, Berg found his office work to be deadly boring, and the Bergs were aware that their financial outlook was about to improve dramatically. In 1906 Berg decided on music as his profession, and he threw himself totally into his studies with Schoenberg.

The improvement in the financial condition of the Bergs came when Johanna Berg received a large inheritance from her aunt, Julie Weidman. She and her husband, Josef Weidman, were among Vienna's wealthiest and most prominent couples, and they died only months apart in 1905. The active estate was valued at 2.5 million kronen (about $506,000 at the time), and it consisted primarily of real estate: eight rental houses, half of a villa in Hietzing (where the Bergs resided from 1905 to 1908), and a large estate on seven acres of land called "Stock im Weg" in nearby Ober St. Veit. Johanna Berg was the sole heir and received the entire estate upon its settlement in August 1907. Berg was then hired by his mother to manage the rental properties, which were soon mortgaged, then gradually sold off, leaving Frau Berg the owner only of the Berghof, and in 1920 it too was sold.

Most of what is known about Berg's early adolescence after 1900 comes from the recollections of and Berg's correspondence with his first biographer, Hermann Watznauer (1875–1939).[11] Watznauer met the Bergs in 1898 at the residence of a neighbor and was then welcomed into the Berg family, with whom he formed a warm friendship. He was especially attracted to Alban—fourteen years old at the time and ten years younger than Watznauer. They shared common interests in music, literature, and art, and they could share their frustrations over difficulties both had encountered in school. Watznauer's homosexuality may also have played a role in this attraction, although Watznauer always handled this inclination with discretion, and Berg showed no apparent interest in homosexual experimentation despite a deeply emotional closeness to Watznauer that continued for some five years after Berg's father died.

According to Watznauer, Conrad Berg asked him, shortly before his death, to take over as the young man's mentor when he passed away.

Watznauer readily complied, and he proved to be a true and devoted lifelong friend to Alban. By profession Watznauer was an engineer, but he was also a writer, an avid reader, a singer, and an artist. His avocation was working with young men and boys in the context of clubs, in which the higher things of life—literature, music, art, and nature—were discussed and promoted.[12] He relished debate, in which he engaged with Berg, bringing him into long discussions about aesthetics and literature. Watznauer was especially attentive to Berg's earliest song compositions. He made calligraphic copies of most of them, sang them himself, and recorded their dates—with varying degrees of accuracy—in his notes and later in his biography.

Berg's relationship with Watznauer reached a peak of intensity in 1903 and 1904, and it is documented by some one hundred pages of letters that Berg wrote to him during these years, documents that strikingly reveal Berg's personality during this critical developmental period.[13] (Berg did not preserve Watznauer's letters to him from the same time although some still exist in copies made by Watznauer himself.[14]) Two important topics emerge in Berg's letters: the fragile state of his emotional development and his remarkably precocious involvement with literature.

The loss of his father in 1900 likely triggered many of Berg's emotional problems in the ensuing years. Berg's known writings and correspondence scarcely mention his father. This silence may well stem from a feigned lack of involvement or glib attitude about a deceased parent, which is a common defense mechanism among bereaved children.[15] Berg's only significant reference to his father comes in a letter to his friend Paul Hohenberg dated 27 October 1905, shortly after Hohenberg had lost his own father. Berg writes:

> I know myself the grief in losing one's father, so I can empathize most warmly and sincerely. You may be able to take a measure of comfort in thinking that it was a blessing for your father to be freed from his suffering, a comfort that I did not have in those difficult days since all that kept coming to my mind were my father's last words spoken before a new and final attack: "I think it's going to pass!"[16]

For an adolescent the death of a parent is often accompanied by failures in school, moody and depressive episodes, bouts of ill health, feelings of guilt and self-loathing, and a recurring fear of isolation and abandonment.

These all characterize Berg and his psychological state following his father's death, and they persisted into his early twenties. They are expressed most emphatically in his letters of 1903 and 1904 to Watznauer, to whom he revealed his innermost thoughts. "My future is very cloudy, and so is my mood. If I could only be happy!" is a recurring theme. Berg is even more explicit in a letter of 20 November 1903. Here he says that he fell into a depressive state—accompanied by violent headaches—after Watznauer had left a Berg family gathering. He continues:

> You left us on Thursday and after the high spirits, as always with me, doldrums followed. The old misery that clings to me like a plague laid hold of me again. I had a few things to do that were quickly finished, and then I went to the piano. I wanted to keep the first impression that Hofmannsthal's poem awakened in me, "Hörtest du denn nicht hinein":

. . . We went to bed and I lay there with a heavy heart. I had that feeling of uneasiness and could only ask, "Oh, let it slowly pass! Be soft and quiet and still!" And then I fell asleep, thinking piously into eternity- -. When I reawakened later, I really thought that my final hour had arrived, so fearfully did it occupy my mind. It was as though a half-burning mass of lead was in my head and on every movement it beat against my skull trying to blast free. That's what it seemed like. Now that I'm much better I can only dimly recall it all, and every attempt to describe it is as weak as trying to describe music! Then I tried not moving, hoping that it would subdue the pain. I stared as though paralyzed into the darkness. . . .[17]

Berg's letters to Watznauer from 1903 and 1904 reveal a knowledge of literature that is astounding in its breadth for his teenage years. The letters suggest Berg's inclination to make writing his profession, a goal that was encouraged by Watznauer. Berg comments with insight into writings by classic authors—especially Goethe, Grillparzer, and, most of all, Ibsen—and his readings increasingly embraced modern figures including Karl Kraus, Peter Altenberg, Otto Weininger, August Strindberg, Charles Baudelaire, and Frank Wedekind. The essays and satires of Karl Kraus (1874–1936)—with their mordant commentaries upon contemporary Viennese life—helped to shape Berg's own outlook and his polemical writing style. At about the time that he was writing his massive letters to Watznauer and possibly at Watznauer's suggestion, Berg was compiling a series of notebooks with citations from his readings; these were provided with subject indexes as though for future reference. The notebooks, each titled "Von der Selbsterkenntnis" (On self-knowledge), contain more than 1,100 citations, drawn from about 230 authors, plus a few of Berg's own aphorisms.[18]

One of the principal themes in Berg's citations is the nature of women, on which his views were strongly influenced by his literary diet, including the misogynist writings of Nietzsche and Weininger. He doubts that the ideal woman exists, one who is the "proper 'woman of Nature'," that is to say, truthful. In an often-cited ten-page letter to Watznauer of 1906 he dilates on the character of Nora from Ibsen's *A Doll's House*, whom he sees as a "normal" woman: pleasant and frivolous but also given to deceit. When her deceptions are discovered, she walks out on her marriage at the end of the play, by which she transforms herself into a higher being, a denouement that Berg termed purposely "unrealistic": "Ibsen wants to show us how the doll of the first two acts—and all the world's dolls—*should* transform themselves in an idealistic sense if not a realistic one."[19] In the real world, Berg claims such a woman may never be found. Quoting from Ibsen's *Lady Inger of Östrat* he writes:

> "I hope that when I go out into the great, wide world, I am approached by a noble, lovely young woman, who beckons me, who shows me the path to glory! But no! Young women approached me, but such a maiden was not among them"—up to now only this holds true.[20]

The interpretation of Nora also illustrates Berg's attempt to view his own life through a literary lens. In his later correspondence with Helene Nahowski, he repeatedly identifies himself with Wagnerian heroes—Tristan, Stolzing, Siegfried—ready to do battle with the Melots, Beckmessers, and Alberichs around him.[21]

During the period 1903–04 Berg began to write poetry and works of fiction, which were exercises that he may have considered first steps toward a career as writer. Some of Berg's poems reveal the same depressive state that haunted his letters to Watznauer.

A poignant undated example follows:

Der schwere Tag bricht an:	The heavy day dawns:
Halt fest! Halt fest!—	Hold fast! Hold fast!—
Luftleer der Raum,	Space a vacuum,
restlos die Zeit:	time a void:
Wer schwankt,	Who does not stagger,
Wer wankt da nicht	who does not stumble
nach äusserer Begier	toward distant desire
und greift nach Armen,	and grasp for arms
die da fassbar sind	that are held out there,
und lebt kein Leben,	and live no life
stirbt keinen Tod—.	and die no death—.
Halt fest! Halt fest!	Hold fast! Hold fast!—
Der schwerste Tag bricht an.	Dawns now the heaviest of days.
Die Uhr bei meinem Bett	The clock by my bedside does
steht still	not move.
und zeigt die Stunde an, die nie	It points to an hour that never
vergeht.	goes past.
Was nützt's, dass ich in Zeiger	What's the use of pushing its hands
greifen,	ahead
und Räder drehn	or turning its dial
und Federn und Spiralen spannen	or winding up its springs and coils.
will:	
Die Uhr steht still!—	Time stands still!—
Rathlos mein Kopf in Kissen sinkt	My head sinks helplessly into the
	pillow
und schluchzt:	and I sob:
Die Zeit! Die Zeit!	Time! Time!
Die Zeit steht still;	Time stands still:
ich trat da in die Ewigkeit,	I move toward eternity
dieweil ich schlief,	while I sleep,

und meine Hand,	and then my hand
die Räder rücken,	moves the dials,
in Zeiger und Spiralen greifen will,	the springs and coils,
erstirbt,	dying away,
fällt auf mein Herz zurück,	falling back to a heart,
das nicht mehr schlägt.	that beats no more.
Was bin ich noch?	So what am I?
Was soll ich noch?	What am I to be?
die Uhr, die nicht mehr geht,	A clock that does not work,
die Hand, die nimmer fleht,	a hand of no use,
der Kopf, der rathlos räth,	a head with no thought,
Ein Herz, das still steht—:	a heart that does not beat:—
Ein Mensch ins Jenseits späht—	A man who gazes into the beyond—[22]

Berg's two principal fictional writings of this period that still exist are "Hanna"—he described it as "a long love epic"—and an incomplete and untitled play that is now known as the "Bergwerk" or "Mining Drama."[23] Both are dark and contorted tales. In the folk-like "Hanna" the well-to-do farmer Franz loves the maiden Hanna. Her father, a forester, is killed in a hunting accident, whereupon Franz takes in both Hanna and her mother. The mother wrongly believes that Franz intends to marry her and plans her wedding. On the night before the ceremony the despondent Franz contemplates suicide. Before carrying this out, he confronts Hanna and confesses his love for her. They are seen by the mother, who in a jealous rage burns the house down with all in it.

Berg completed one act of his "Mining Drama" and left behind an outline for four additional acts. The play is set in a mining town in the modern day, in which deadly accidents mingle with violent conflicts among the company staff. Berg's "Mining Drama" was written at a time when he was absorbed by the writings of Ibsen, and his fragment is modeled on themes and techniques from Ibsen's *Ghosts* (1881). Berg's drama adapts the main theme of *Ghosts*—a view of heredity by which disease, antisocial behavior, and immorality are passed from one generation to another, haunting those in the present day like ghosts. Berg's characters are plainly based on those in Ibsen's model.

In addition to his precocious taste for literature and talent for composition during his adolescence, Berg also showed skills as an artist, especially in drawing. He studied drawing during his years in Realschule, and throughout his life, Berg drew and painted for his own pleasure and relaxation. An example is a drawing of a scene in Nuremberg (Figure 1.1) that Berg entered on a postcard of June 1899 to his friend Johannes Huber.[24] Berg also designed the covers, in a *Jugendstil* manner, for his earliest musical publications.

Figure 1.1   Berg, ink drawing, 1899. Courtesy of the Austrian National Library

The Specter of Ill Health

Following his father's death when he was fifteen—and for the remainder of his life—Berg was plagued by ill health, especially by severe asthmatic attacks. The impact of asthma on Berg's life was deep and persistent. The early stages of the illness are recorded in his courtship letters to Helene Nahowski, especially during the summer months when he and his family were in the country, where such attacks were most acute. During the summers of 1907 through 1909 he devoted himself reluctantly to cure regimens designed to foster weight gain and strengthening, since his gangly appearance caused the Nahowski parents to think him weak and unwell and thus a poor suitor for their daughter's hand. In 1907 and 1908 he reported to Helene from the Berghof that he was ill, but he did not mention asthma specifically.[25] The next year, in 1909, he reported in detail on severe asthma attacks. They typically came on at night, and he would lie awake for hours struggling to breathe. As a result of this stress, his nerves and digestion suffered and his mood became despairing.

> How could it be otherwise, when it is long past midnight, when the first cock crows, still to be sitting up in bed and, bathed in sweat, struggling and struggling to breathe in enough air for the body's functions, and then by day to hear that there is nothing wrong with me. It's just nerves; ah, this is something nasal, just eat more, etc. etc.[26]

He reported to Helene on the medicines he was then taking, and the list is astonishing: aspirin, lactose, codeine, sodium iodide, morphine, cocaine solution, California fig syrup (a laxative), menthol with paraffin oil, Pyramidon, Arsenferratone, and Schiffsmumme beer.[27] Berg confessed that this was enough medicine both to cure and to kill him, and the list is an early indication of his tendency to overmedicate himself, which would ultimately have disastrous consequences. To Helene he also related having accidentally taken an overdose of morphine that brought on hallucinations. Writing at 5:30 AM he describes another attack, "being unable to breathe since 1:30, and all the morphine in the world can't give me any sleep because every time that I start to fall asleep from exhaustion, in that moment I start up because in my drunken stupor I forgot to breathe three times as fast and would then strangle."[28]

These nightmarish accounts, plus Berg's heavy reliance on medication, prove the gravity of his condition and the high level of stress and anxiety it brought with it, including a genuine fear of death. The severe recurring asthma may have triggered in Berg what is today defined as somatic symptom disorder, which is an individual's extreme focus on physical symptoms such as pain or fatigue that causes significant emotional distress. A clear instance of such distress is offered in Berg's letter to Watznauer, quoted above, about the "burning mass of lead" in his head. A related psychological condition is illness anxiety disorder, formerly known as hypochondriasis, which Theodor Adorno ascribes to Berg in a 1955 memoir.[29] The latter condition is characterized by a fear that one may become seriously ill, and clearly the two conditions can easily be confused. It is without a doubt true that the physical and psychological condition of asthma was at the root of Berg's lifelong health problems.

At the time that Berg's asthma struck, doctors had little to offer on this illness. On one occasion Berg was treated by Sigmund Freud, who was vacationing on the Ossiachersee near the Berghof. Freud suggested a cure in Meran. (Berg later reported to Theodor Adorno on Freud's failure to treat him successfully.[30]) In fact, asthma was and still is incurable and in Berg's time its symptoms were not easily treatable. In his case, the night occurrences were typical and the seasonal incidents at the Berghof suggest an allergy-induced condition made worse by his smoking. Berg explained as much to Schoenberg (also an asthma sufferer) in a letter of 1912:

> For my asthma I went to a professor in Vienna, since I was experiencing it there after a day spent outdoors. His opinion is that it is a nervous irritability or an oversensitivity of the mucous membranes. The mucus membranes of the nose are extremely irritated by pollen in the air, which causes sneezing, congestion etc. as well as hay fever. As a remedy there is an antidote created from the pollen itself, which when ingested into the nose really provides relief. This remedy doesn't work for the effects on the mucus membranes of the trachea and the bronchial tubes, and there is simply no remedy other than to avoid the places where fields and woods are. All of which explains why I never have asthma in Vienna, why I have signs of it in Hietzing, but out in the country I immediately have bad attacks, no matter whether it's here at the Berghof or in Styria or at the base of the Rax (in Prein) or in the Wachau

or the Tyrol. The doctor thinks by the sea would be good, but I can't manage that for monetary reasons.[31]

In 1909 Helene forcefully advised Berg to give up all medicines along with coffee, tea, and alcohol, in favor of walking in the fresh air, although in the case of a pollen-induced allergy this activity might have exacerbated his condition. So much was Alban trying to please Helene that he humbly confessed to treating himself successfully one asthmatic night with coffee, a remedy suggested to him by his mother's friend, Marie von Salzgeber.[32] Berg was probably unaware that caffeine, a bronchodilator, had been known as an asthma treatment since the nineteenth century.[33] Berg's daily use of coffee and tea, especially the latter, throughout his life suggests that he continued to find some mild relief for his breathing problems from these drinks.

Berg was inclined to attribute asthma and his other illnesses to psychosomatic or nervous causes. He mentions this in a letter of 12 August 1916 to his wife—the only letter to her, incidentally, that so much as mentions his father:

> So it is that in the last 10 or 20 years (maybe even 30) I have gotten sick only after some turmoil, grief, or bad experience. So too in recent years there has scarcely been turmoil, some great vexation, grief or the like that did not immediately lead to some illness, etc., in some part of my body. Like the serious rheumatic attack that I had suddenly after Papa's death, which after 1, 2 years just as suddenly went away despite my leading the same life and having the same living conditions.[34]

In a letter to Webern of 1913—at a time when Webern was undergoing psychoanalysis—Berg speculated that his asthma attacks might be linked to the subconscious. He wrote:

> I still don't know if perhaps suggestion or something from the "subconscious" may be partly to blame. But all the same the illness is in such cases undoubtedly still present. Perhaps the illness appears when one wants to be ill, even if this desire resides in the subconscious and goes against one's outward willpower. Even when one is well, he may not want to be.[35]

Berg's admission of an inner compulsion toward illness ties him, in Adorno's words, to "that generation of artists who felt the ailing Tristan to be a model." Adorno also comments that Berg "may have enjoyed the euphoric aspects of illness."[36] Certainly the development of psychology and psychiatry in Vienna in the late nineteenth and early twentieth centuries sparked popular interest in the origins and significance of disease, not least among the artists and literati of the day. It has been confirmed that some forms of asthma can have a psychosomatic origin coinciding with depression or emotional distress, and Berg's belief was no doubt reinforced by reading Otto Weininger's *Über die letzten Dinge*, a work that he owned, in which Weininger asserts, "Every sickness has mental causes."[37]

The Marie Scheuchl Affair

On 4 December 1902, Marie Scheuchl, a thirty-two-year-old domestic servant earlier in the employ of the Berg family, gave birth to a baby girl, whom she named Albine. A year later Alban Berg, then eighteen years old, admitted in a note to being the father: "It is hereby confirmed," he wrote on 8 December 1903, "that I am the father of the child Albine, born on 4 December 1902, and that I will never evade the obligations that this entails."[38]

Whatever obligations Berg had in mind in 1903 were left obscure. His confession was written after he had received from Marie a diary that described her pregnancy and the birth of her child and also a picture of their infant daughter (both now lost). But Berg was slow to respond directly to her. Probably at some point in 1904 he wrote a long, rambling letter to her that he left undated and unsigned. It reads in part:

> I have before me two things: your diary and Albine's little picture. Oh, when I see this dear countenance—I want her with me to kiss it—and hold her in my arms.—You asked if I would love her?—She is my own flesh and blood—and even if my flesh and blood is unworthy and miserable, you have transformed them through this child and made them adorable. Oh, if I only had her here beside me. . . . But, no, I am nearly gripped with dread of myself, that I, miserable one, might touch this innocent angel and besmirch it—! Oh! There is no consolation left for me. . . . Should something happen that is important for me to know (for example, some legal issue or the health of you and Binchen), then send me an anonymous

postcard with *question marks* on it. That will alert me that a letter is waiting for me at the post office, no. 7272.[39]

This document, wandering as it does between the mundane and emotional, shows Berg's uncertainty and self-absorption in dealing with crises. There is no mention of practical matters such as financial support for Marie and his daughter, no ideas for their future, and no thoughts on how he should continue to be involved with them. There is no profession of love or even fondness that he might feel for Marie herself. Berg's emphasis is instead on his emotions, mainly his "anguish," and to a lesser extent on Marie's burdens. Berg is also secretive about the affair, suggesting that others in the family, probably including his mother, did not know of his involvement. Nothing is said about receiving support from members of the Berg family who may have known the true circumstances. The letter is also striking for its lack of focus—at one moment Berg declares himself a scoundrel who has brought anguish upon himself; the next moment he passes along casual information about how he likes to compose his letters in bed.

The diary and photo that Marie sent to Berg in 1903 are not known to exist, nor are there any known letters from Marie to Berg. But a measure of contact continued to exist between the two. Berg received two additional studio photographs of his daughter taken about 1906 or 1907 by the Viennese photographer August Kühnel. Berg used one of these images to make a watercolor drawing of his daughter (shown in Figure 1.2), and he then probably gave the photo to his sister, Smaragda. Her nephew Erich Berg found it among her papers after her death in 1954.[40] Berg and Smaragda may later have sent an amount of money to Marie to support her in a business opportunity, although there is no evidence that Berg's mother ever knew details of the affair.

Information about Berg's daughter came into the open in 1979, following inquiries made by Erich Berg, who was researching a biography of his uncle. According to several of Albine's relations, Marie placed her daughter in an orphanage, where she remained until 1906, when Marie married a local brush maker, Karl Manninger, who adopted the child. The family then lived alternately in Vienna and Graz where Albine attended public schools. In March 1922 Albine married Walter Wittula, an employee of Austria's Southern Railway, and the couple continued to

Figure 1.2   Berg's daughter, Albine, ca. 1902–03 and his water color drawing made
from a photograph. Courtesy of the Alban Berg Stiftung and from Erich Alban Berg,
Alban Berg: Der unverbesserlicher Romantiker: Alban Berg 1885–1935 (Vienna: Österreichischer
Bundesverlag, 1985), 126

live in Vienna and Graz. Albine worked as a librarian in Perchtoldsdorf (a Vienna suburb) and was a secretary there for the writer Maria Grengg. Berg gave Albine a ticket to the Vienna premiere of *Wozzeck* in 1930, and she had at least one face-to-face meeting with him at about this time. Albine died childless in 1954 and is buried beside her mother in the Südwestfriedhof in Vienna-Hetzendorf.

Following a 1999 rebroadcast of the BBC documentary "The Secret Life of Alban Berg,"[41] other relatives came forward with documents and information.[42] Albine was said to have had a sensitivity to art, and she sat as a model for the Virgin Mary in a wood carving by the sculptor Hans Domenig.[43] An especially provocative photograph of Albine is one taken by her husband and dated 1930, which unmistakably shows her walking beside the Casa Mahler in Venice.[44] Alma Mahler and Franz Werfel resided at Alma's villa in Venice in spring of 1930, but no evidence has come to light that Alma met the Wittulas, and there are no references in her correspondence with Berg of any sort about the existence of his daughter.

Virtually every author who has discussed Berg's connection to Marie Scheuchl has speculated on its relation to his music, but there is no concrete evidence for any such relationship. Almost certainly the character Marie in *Wozzeck*—the innocent woman with an illegitimate child, scorned by society—would have awakened Berg's memories of Marie Scheuchl. Douglas Jarman has proposed that Berg's choice of a Carinthian folk tune for use in the Violin Concerto came from its ribald text, where a young man tells of being in bed with "Miazale," a dialect name related to "Mizzi," this sometimes a nickname for Marie.[45] But in Berg's single known reference to her—the letter of ca. 1904—she is called "Marie," not "Mizzi." Several authors point to Berg's choice of poetic texts for his songs of 1902–04, whose topics most often deal with emotional distress and lost love. Almost certainly, these choices reflect Berg's depressive and hyper-emotional state of mind during his teenage years, but none of the poems suggests a direct connection to his illegitimate daughter.

The available evidence suggests that the Scheuchl affair had its greatest impact on Berg in his later relationship with his wife, Helene. Given his keen interest in parenthood, Berg might have hoped for some measure of open social contact with his daughter, but this would not have been accepted by Helene, and it remained one of the many issues that Berg did not discuss with her. According to Erich Berg, Albine attended Berg's funeral after which she came to the Bergs' Hietzing residence and introduced herself to Helene. Only then did Helene learn of the existence of her husband's daughter, and, before being unceremoniously shown to the door, Albine may have given Helene the letter of 1904 and statement of paternity. Shortly afterward, on 2 January 1936, Helene wrote to Watznauer, "Could you please come by as soon as possible, in the morning at 9:00 AM, and bring along things handwritten by Alban (1901–1904). This is a very urgent matter, and I'll tell you more later."[46] Very likely Helene wanted to compare Berg's early handwriting with the documents provided by Albine, to be convinced of their authenticity. Helene may then have realized that the thirty-year presence of Berg's daughter—so near but so far away—was a great frustration in his childless marriage and one cause for his gradual emotional estrangement from his wife. Helene softened toward Albine in later years, as far as to bequeath her a sapphire and diamond ring in her will of 1946.[47] In the end Helene outlived Alban's daughter by more than twenty years.

The Marie Scheuchl affair did not diminish Berg's youthful attraction to other women. In a letter to Watznauer dated 16 July 1903, he mentions his relationship with "S. S." Nothing definite is known of her identity, although Rosemary Hilmar asserts that in September 1903, an unhappy love affair with the daughter of a certain "Baumeister Stiasny" brought Berg to the brink of suicide.[48] Such thoughts are also mentioned in Willi Reich's 1963 biography, probably based on information from Watznauer. Berg's letters from 1903 and 1904 express feelings of adolescent angst, but there is no mention there of contemplating suicide.

Berg at this time was also strongly attracted to Frida Semler, an American teenager, daughter of a Borgfeldt executive, who visited the Berghof in the summers of 1903 and 1904.[49] Although "Miss Frida," as Berg referred to her, later remarked that her friendship with Berg was purely platonic, Berg's letters to Watznauer during these years show a more amorous inclination on his part. During a thunderstorm in August 1904, the two ran into the rain to experience nature in all of her fury, during which Berg's attention was most riveted by Frida's wet and skimpy clothing. He wrote to Watznauer:

We were freezing as the icy wind blew over our soaked bodies, especially Frida's, whose very airy clothing (2 pieces of underwear, a *very* décolleté dress with sandals and no hosiery) left her wet to the skin. We went back full of enthusiasm for such splendor. In the house everyone was having their afternoon nap—those poor blind people.[50]

Berg could hardly have remained indifferent to Frida. She was a year younger than he, fluent in German, and her pictures show her to be highly attractive—Berg proved readily susceptible to feminine allure. She could match him as a reader, and even then she was herself an ambitious writer of drama and poetry. She was also high-spirited, with a mind of her own about literature, and she had no reluctance to contradict Berg's tastes. After they had read Ibsen's *The Master Builder*, Frida declared that the work was "confused in thought," its characters "sickly in nature." These remarks triggered a petulant tirade from Berg in a letter to Watznauer, although Berg admitted that Frida's many admirable qualities made him hold his tongue in her presence. Berg renewed his contact with Frida Semler in 1907 and 1908, when they struck up an informative exchange of letters in which Berg gives details about his studies with Schoenberg and his evolving tastes in literature, now concentrated on modern writers, especially Oscar Wilde and Frank Wedekind.[51]

Frida returned to Vienna in September 1908, shortly after she graduated from Wellesley College, and she renewed her contact with Berg. But Berg was by then zealously pursuing another woman whom he had met a year before, Helene Nahowski, whom he would later marry and whose influence shaped not only his life and work but also the management of his legacy for forty years following his death. Documents now available concerning the Nahowskis establish that family's consequential role in Berg's personal and artistic life.[52]

The Nahowski Family

When he met Helene Nahowski in the spring of 1907, Berg was living with his mother and sister in the stately villa inherited from Aunt Julie Weidman at 6 Hietzinger Hauptstrasse in the fashionable Vienna suburb of Hietzing. Down the street at Maxingstrasse 46, Helene's family occupied an equally elegant residence. The house was purchased in 1885 by Helene's parents, Franz and Anna Nahowski, with funds provided to

Anna by Emperor Franz Joseph with whom she was engaged in a liaison that had begun ten years earlier. A few months after Franz and
Anna moved in, on July 29, a daughter was born there and christened
Helene Caroline. It was subsequently rumored that Helene was the natural daughter of the emperor. If Franz Joseph was her father, the emperor
made not the slightest hint in that direction.[53]

The house on Maxingstrasse directly faced the western wall of
Schönbrunn Park, which was breached not far from the Nahowskis'
frontage by a small door through which the emperor came to visit Anna
at her villa. Their affair had begun through a chance encounter in the
park in 1875 when Anna, aged sixteen, was in the early months of an arranged and unhappy marriage. It continued through Anna's divorce and
remarriage nine years later to Franz Joseph Nahowski and was terminated
abruptly by the emperor following the death of Crown Prince Rudolf,
in January of 1889. Anna Nahowski compiled two diaries which recount
her affair with the emperor and include additional biographical material.
The diaries, now published in two separate editions, are the principal
source for the Nahowski family history during the years of Anna's involvement with the emperor and, in less detail, as far beyond as 1921.[54]

Helene was the Nahowskis' third child and third daughter. The oldest
child, Carola, born in 1877, was Anna's daughter by her first marriage.
The second daughter, Anna—nicknamed Annschi, Antschi, or Fips—was
Franz Nahowski's child, born out of wedlock early in 1883. The paternity of these two daughters has never been disputed, and the chronology
offered in Anna's diaries is consistent with this assumption. A fourth child
and only son, Franz—called Franzl and later Frank—was also rumored to
be the emperor's child, but according to the diaries he was born twelve
months after the last meeting of Anna and Emperor Franz Joseph, thus
ruling out the emperor's paternity. Helene's imperial paternity is neither
proved nor ruled out by the diaries. The name of her father on her birth
certificate is Franz Nahowski.[55]

Although Helene's paternity and her view of it remain open to question, the affair of her mother and Emperor Franz Joseph determined to
a large extent the circumstances of her childhood and upbringing. The
family had money and rose in the course of time from the middle to
upper-middle class. The villa on Maxingstrasse was the outward symbol
of this transformation. In a strange congruency, Alban Berg was to prowl

the street before Helene's house in the early days of his infatuation much as the emperor did, dodging surveillance, in the time of his relations with her mother.

Helene's mother, Anna Nahowski (1859–1931), was born in Vienna to the basket and wickerwork manufacturer Franz Nowak (1821–71) and his wife, Karoline, née Zehetner (1823–1903). Following Franz Nowak's early death, Karoline was eager to marry off her eldest daughter, and when Anna was not yet fifteen Karoline chose a husband for her, Johann Nepomuk Heuduk (also spelled Heuduck), a manufacturer of silk ribbon. Heuduk was a compulsive gambler who fell steadily into debt and finally bankruptcy, and the marriage ended in a divorce after four years.[56]

Anna met Franz Nahowski in 1879 shortly after her divorce. As father-in-law, he was to play a large role in Alban Berg's life, beginning with his adamant opposition to Alban and Helene's courtship. Nahowski (1849–1925) was born in Biala, which was a German-speaking island in an ethnically Polish region within the province of Galicia. In 1919, after the breakup of the Habsburg Empire, he was issued a passport stating that he was a Polish citizen.[57] When he met Anna, Franz Nahowski was a bachelor and an employee of Austria's Southern Railway in an administrative capacity. In the early days of their courtship, he wrote Anna treacly love poems that reveal a side of his personality otherwise not evident in his unsympathetic relations with future family members. One such literary endeavor follows:

Pallas-Athene küsste Deine Stirne,	Pallas Athene kissed your brow
Als Du den Kinderschuhen kaum entstiegst	When you had scarce outgrown childhood's shoes
Apollo lehrte Dich das Saitenspiele	Apollo taught you to play the strings
So, dass Erato Du und Polyhymnen besiegst.	So you could surpass Erato and Polyhymnia.
Und Aphrodite selbst, erkennet neidlos,	And Aphrodite herself, without envy,
Die Kerze Deiner Schönheit an;	Acknowledged the candle of your beauty;
Sie überlässt Dir ihren Zaubergürtel,	She bequeathed to you her magic girdle
Der Deinen Zauber kaum erhöhen kann	Which scarce has power to increase your magic.[58]

Anna developed a burning passion for Franz Nahowski that overrode her fidelity to the emperor, whom she still continued to see. Although details are not recorded in the diaries, it is clear that Nahowski came to an accommodation concerning the emperor, probably because of the money involved, which Anna turned over to him after they were married. Because Anna was divorced, remarriage within the Catholic Church was forbidden, so both Anna and Franz converted to Protestantism and were finally married on 28 May 1884, in Pressburg (now Bratislava). Consequent to the parents' conversion, the younger children, Helene and Frank, were raised in the Protestant Church. Helene was baptized in the Reformed Church in central Vienna known historically as the Dorotheerkirche. Franz Nahowski was later to insist that Alban Berg convert to Protestantism and marry in the Protestant Church in case a divorce would be needed later.[59] After her marriage in 1911 Helene converted to Catholicism and Alban reconverted, and they were remarried in the Roman church in 1915. Although Berg was generally indifferent to organized religion, Helene's attachment to the church was strong and increased following Alban's death. Her spiritual quest outside of Catholic orthodoxy will be discussed in later chapters.

Franz Nahowski's professional and personal lives were troubled. His wife's diaries relate that he was fired from his job at the Southern Railway for failure to report for duty after he was transferred to Ala on Lake Garda in Italy. He later sued the railroad over his pension rights and lost his case.[60] In his marriage he was jealous and sometimes violent. After drowning his sorrows in drink, he abused his wife psychologically and sexually. Anna suffered at least two miscarriages, and it is possible that they were precipitated by Nahowski's rough sexual behavior. She writes in her diary:

> My husband torments me with his jealousy, torments and persecutes me with his lovemaking. . . . [A]fter such an act I am swimming in blood. Quickly Grohmann [the midwife] and Dr. Reith. . . . I needed 3 weeks to recover, Nahowski is completely broken. He kneels repeatedly at my bed, he begs me for forgiveness, kisses my hands and weeps. I am so weak, my hand strokes him again and again over his head, how inescapable is this love to which I have fallen victim. . . . What I have taken on myself, that I must bear—no one can help me.[61]

Helene was born into this environment of domestic strife and abuse. It is plausible to conclude that Anna wished fervently for Helene to be the emperor's daughter, given what was by then her desperation over her marriage. It is often said about Helene that she was secretly proud of being an emperor's daughter, but this assumption is almost certainly false. She spoke publicly about the rumor of her parentage only once, in 1947 in response to an article in the journal *Der Turm* by Bruno Walter in which he reflects on personalities whom he met at the home of Alma Mahler and Franz Werfel: "The most interesting of the musicians was Alban Berg, the composer of *Wozzeck*," says Walter. "I got to know him as a curious and introverted person. His wife, the natural daughter of Emperor Franz Joseph, was a smart, soulful woman, entirely devoted to her husband."[62] Helene requested a retraction of the paternity claim from the editor, which was made in a subsequent issue of *Der Turm*: "I kindly request that you correct the statement that I am a natural daughter of Emperor Franz Joseph. This is erroneous and not in keeping with the facts."[63]

Whatever the facts about Helene's paternity, there are hints in the diaries about Helene's special status in her mother's eyes. Helene was noted to be her favorite and most like her. She describes her as a "healthy, well developed child, not a screamer like Annschi."[64] Helene is the only child, according to the diaries, that Anna ever brought to the attention of the emperor on one of his visits. She showed him a photo of her with a musical toy. His only comment: "Already musical."[65] Finally there is the matter of Helene's name. Her mother plainly chose it with reference to the emperor's birthday, which was on August 18, St. Helena's day.

Anna Nahowski's contact with the emperor ended when Helene was three years old, although according to the diaries Franz Nahowski's jealous rages and his infidelities persisted long after. Nahowski also turned away from his daughter Helene, and their relations became more and more strained. Possibly Nahowski feared Helene was after all not his daughter and persecuted her as a result. A letter written by Helene to her father, undated but from her early adulthood, offers a painful glimpse into the father-daughter relationship. It begins by remarking on how ridiculous it is that two people who live together should have to write letters because they can't have a reasonable conversation. She concludes:

I have so often felt such bitterness in my heart when I have seen you chatting in such a friendly manner with Anna and Franzl—and I was shut out like a criminal. Do you think that doesn't hurt? How often have I then wanted to ask you to tell me very simply the reason for treating me so, why it is me especially that you don't like. You don't know me. I certainly do have failings, and I won't make myself out better than I am; but worse than the others I'm not! And since I am no longer a child and think perhaps more seriously and more maturely than other girls of my age, so I believe I have the right to receive from you an open and sincere answer to my question. You owe it to me.[66]

The Nahowski family's internal strife, no matter how well covered up, affected family life in all its aspects. Despite a posh home, a summer villa in Trahütten in Styria, and many cultural and educational advantages, the Nahowski children clearly bore scars that were in some respects disabling in later life. For Helene, the issues of her own marriage, particularly her iron-clad notion of fidelity, must be understood against this troubled family background.

The paucity of specific information about Helene's childhood and upbringing as compared to that available for her siblings leads inevitably to the conclusion that she destroyed documents pertaining to her early life. Such a deliberate act would have a bearing on her attitude toward her parents and could be seen as a dismissal of their importance in her life or even a display of hostility. There are no extant records concerning Helene's education other than a short biographical note with the remark that she received a "normal" education.[67] Her parents sent all of the other children to good schools. The eldest daughter, Carola (1877–1946), distinguished herself as an artist and illustrator. She studied with Kolomon Moser at the Kunstgewerbeschule attached to the Österreichisches Museum für Kunst und Industrie (today known as MAK). In her career, during which she worked as an artist, fashion illustrator, and designer, she was often identified with the Klimt school.[68] She became an early member of the Vereinigung bildender Künstlerinnen Oesterreichs (Union of Austrian women in the fine arts), founded in 1910, and exhibited in a number of their shows under the name Carola Nahowska.[69] Referred to as Carola Heuduck in family letters, and sometimes by the nickname James, Carola occupied an atelier in a house adjacent to the Maxingstrasse residence in neighboring Weidlichgasse. She never married and died on 6 June 1946, at the age of 68.[70]

More is known about the relationship of Helene Berg to her sister Anna (1883–1973) from Anna's extensive correspondence.[71] These two sisters were two and a half years apart in age. According to her mother's diaries, Annschi spent three years at the convent school of Sacré Coeur in Pressbaum, about twenty kilometers west of Hietzing. School records confirm that she entered in the fall of 1894, when she would have been eleven years old, and left at the end of 1897. Although the school claims to have no record concerning Helene, she may also have attended Sacré Coeur or possibly another convent school. Both she and Alban later refer to her time in the *Kloster* (convent).[72] However, a second short biographical sketch of Helene states that she attended "Volksschule und Bürgerschule," both public schools (primary and secondary), the latter essentially equivalent to the Hauptschule.[73]

Helene's brother, Frank Nahowski (1889–1942), represented the family's greatest sorrow. A talented artist and strikingly handsome, he became more and more mentally unstable, until he was placed under his father's guardianship in 1917 and finally declared legally incompetent due to mental illness, understood to be schizophrenia, in 1930. Alban Berg became Frank's guardian in 1931 after both parents were deceased.[74] Frank was perceived to be effeminate and probably also homosexual. Berg's sister, Smaragda, recognized this fact and alluded to it in a letter written to Helene after she had become smitten with her in 1907. Smaragda commented on Helene's siblings and had this to say about her only brother:

> Franzl, the third daughter, is a picture-pretty fellow (girl, I mean) whose face I love because it is truly beautiful and because I feel a great pity for him. When I see him blush like a virgin, "I am gripped by the whole misery of mankind!" Why?! Dear, I could tell you why, but I think I'm the only one of you all who can truly understand it.[75]

In the midst of this stressful family life, what transpired with the young Helene? How did she cope with her parents' marital conflict, her father's hostility, and her brother's mental instability? There is little documentation from her youth to shed light on these questions, but indications begin to emerge later in her marriage and in her long widowhood. From letters and other writings, it is clear that Helene was well educated and well read in her youth. She wrote poetry, and three of her lyrics were set to music by her first important suitor, Paul Kammerer. In later years Alban routinely encouraged her in her literary pursuits. But above all, it was music that drew her. In one of the few expressive letters she wrote to Alban during their courtship, she stated:

> I am passionate about two things, music and nature! I can become as ecstatic over a beautiful landscape as I can by listening to good music. The same great, unfulfilled longing comes over me for something grand, beautiful, splendid— it is a feeling that one can neither grasp nor express.[76]

In a short biographical note written years later, Helene briefly described her musical education as composed of piano study and training as a young dramatic soprano ("jugendlich-dramatische Sängerin").[77] She began vocal studies in 1903 under the tutelage of the renowned Wagnerian singer Marianne Brandt (1842–1921), Wagner's first Kundry in 1882 at Bayreuth. When Helene began her voice lessons, Brandt had long since retired and returned to Vienna to teach. She was selective in her choice of students, and Helene's acceptance by Brandt points to her talent and high potential for the operatic stage. Helene described her lessons with Brandt as the happiest working hours imaginable.[78] Brandt showed great affection for Helene, writing her many cards and letters from 1903 through the last year of her life, addressing her as "liebe Kleine" or later "liebstes Helenchen." She established a friendship with the entire Nahowski family and frequently inquired after Frank's health.

Brandt held musical "Matinées" in the Bösendorfer-Saal in central Vienna at which her students sang, and Helene is named as a performer in a newspaper account of one of these, on 27 April 1904. One of her accompanists, Tony Colbert, recalled her singing in a letter to Marianne Brandt: "I heard Fräulein Nahowska sing twice in your productions and was both times delighted with her secure performance and musical sensitivity, in intonation as well as rhythm."[79] In the following year, 1905, Helene sang lieder by Schumann, Grädener, and d'Albert, along with "Elsas Traum" ("Einsam in trüben Tagen") from *Lohengrin* in a benefit concert at the health resort in Rohitsch-Sauerbrunn (today Rogaška Slatina in Slovenia). Her fellow voice student Mizzi Fink, who was by then launched on a successful stage career, congratulated her on her public acclaim from this appearance:

> I read with pleasure about your success. Fräulein Brandt told me about it. I can well imagine that you were enthusiastically cheered. Young, beautiful and a truly sweet, wonderful voice; dear heart, what more do you need?[80]

Charting Helene's vocal studies through Brandt's letters alone is difficult, but a thread emerges concerning constant health problems. Helene was often unwell and missed lessons. Along with the usual colds, Brandt refers in a letter of 1904 to swelling (*Geschwulst*) and urges Helene to take especially good care of herself in view of an upcoming performance.[81] In later years, Helene referred to having a goiter, and she underwent a throat operation in 1927, so there is reason to believe that the throat problems had a physical basis.[82] By 1907, it seems, Helene had given up the voice lessons following persistent throat ailments. A revealing letter from Brandt at this time casts some doubt on whether her teacher believed the problems were physical:

> Dearest Helenchen: If I had not had the *joy* of teaching you for more than two years and if I did not know that during this entire time you had virtually no difficulties with your throat, then I might believe that all the cures you are now undertaking for it are necessary. But since I know from experience that your throat is as healthy as any can be, so I expect that it will again be just as healthy if you give it *a complete rest* for a period of time!!![83]

Helene Nahowski and Paul Kammerer

Helene's difficulties with singing came to a head at the time of another crisis in her life, a failed love affair with Paul Kammerer, a brilliant Viennese scientist and musician. Marianne Brandt was wise enough to grasp the connection, as implied in a letter to Helene's father early in 1906, when she identified Helene's problem as depression:

> Dear Sir: Helene's lack of energy [*Atonie*] is emotional! Throughout the past winter I have sensed in her a psychological depression! Her natural sunny cheerfulness disappeared, as if under a gray fog! I did not intrude on her trust and do not know the cause, but in the course of years I have become knowledgeable about human beings and I am seldom mistaken: body and spirit are closely bound, one suffers with the other. Maybe a cure for the body will

also strengthen her emotions and make her happy again! I hope so from the bottom of my heart, for I love this highly gifted child as if she were my own, and I feel with her her suffering and joy!

Be assured of my highest regards, yours devotedly, Marianne Brandt.[84]

In 1904, at the age of nineteen Helene Nahowski met and fell in love with Kammerer, at the time a doctoral student in zoology at the University of Vienna. Earlier he had attended lectures on music history by Guido Adler and Maximilian Dietz at the University of Vienna and had studied counterpoint under Robert Fuchs at the Vienna Conservatory.[85]

Like many aspiring composers at the outset of a career, Kammerer wrote mainly songs, which he eagerly offered to Viennese singers, badgering them for readings and performances. From his mother he learned of the singing of Helene Nahowski, and he contacted her to ask her to read through a selection of his works. In time-honored fashion, music and love came together for Kammerer. In a letter to Helene written a few months later, he recalled their first meeting:

> My generally rather negative mood took a huge upswing when we read through my simple song "Jugend." The melody is plain, and you sang it well at sight. But I still wasn't convinced. And while I found your voice strong and powerful in the performance of the Mascagni song—almost too much for the room—now I heard its sweetness, and I was won over. . . .
>
> Psychologically speaking, the remaining history is quickly told. When we saw each other for the fourth time, my life took on a new content; when we saw each other for the fifth time, I knew that I loved you.[86]

After the initial revelation of his love for Helene, Kammerer became a relentless suitor. Within months, he had mentioned marriage: "*Even today I am positioned to offer my wife a comfortable existence, if not a lavish one,*" he assured her in a letter of 18 July 1904. He continued:

> Dear Helene, what have you done to me! Can an inclination be so powerful, a yearning be so torturous? Before now I didn't know that it could! I have already experienced love in my life, and I know that this is love and not just infatuation. . . . For the future, *I will work for you.* What I have achieved since knowing that I love you—it is not little despite the short time—I have done for Helene! And if you will not love me, then I will still live only for you. . . .[87]

Helene soon fell equally in love with the talented and spirited young composer and scientist. Her budding relationship with Kammerer was looked on favorably by her parents and siblings, given Kammerer's lively nature, outstanding academic credentials, and bright professional future. Even before the completion of his dissertation in June 1904, he was appointed research assistant at Vienna's new Biologische Versuchsanstalt (Experimental biology institute), located in the Prater and called the "Vivarium," where he carried out his research through the breeding of various types of lizards and amphibians. The original direction of his research—supporting ideas advanced earlier by the Chevalier de Lamarck that under certain conditions species could inherit acquired characteristics—was promising for a future university appointment. This varied and distinguished background appealed to Franz Nahowski, signaling bright prospects for his daughter's future in a way that he later found so bleakly absent in Alban Berg.

The known compositions by Paul Kammerer consist of twenty-four pieces, mainly songs for voice and piano that were composed from approximately 1903 to 1906.[88] Eight of the songs were published by Simrock in Berlin in 1906 (*Acht Gesänge für eine Singstimme mit Begleitung des Pianoforte*), the only music by Kammerer ever to be published.[89] The works in this collection show him to be a gifted composer in the progressive lieder style of the day. The texts that he chose create a narrative cycle that may well dramatize Kammerer's relationship with Helene, which in 1906 had reached a peak of intensity, and Kammerer's music projects this distressed narrative with great insight and poignancy. The collection begins with "Danke, lieber Sonnenstrahl!" (the poem is by Gustav Przibram) and the music expresses the bliss of nature. It is followed by Evers's "Jugend," in which a boy and girl discover love amid dreams spun beneath nature's benevolent wing. The third piece of the cycle uses Helene's poem "Tänzerin," in which the subject betrays a deep sadness beneath her exuberant exterior.

Tänzerin	The Dancing Girl
Wie jauchzen und klingen die Geigen,	How the fiddles rejoice and resound,
wie hell erschallt dein Gesang;	how brightly your song rings out;
du drehst dich lustig im Reigen,	you turn merrily in the round dance,

Nur die Augen blicken so bang.	and only your eyes betray distress.
Und die Bogen schneller streichen	And the strings bow faster
und du jubelst hinaus dein Juchhe,	and you cry out 'hurrah!'
Nur um die Lippen, die bleichen,	only your pale lips
zuckt es wie verhaltenes Weh.	tremble with suppressed woe.

—Helene Nahowska

This is followed by "Bettlerliebe," where the boy tells of his hopeless feelings of inadequacy. In "Stilles Lied," the fifth song, the idyll of love is dispelled, and the speaker wanders aimlessly into the distance. He thinks back bitterly in Lenau's poem "An . . ." and finally returns to nature in "Abendrot" and "Ruhetal" to yearn for rest and oblivion.

Whether Paul Kammerer intended to press his suit with the *Acht Gesänge* or whether the cycle bears witness to a hopeless passion is not clear. But for reasons unknown, he suddenly broke off his relationship with Helene at about the same time that the collection was published, in 1906. To make matters worse, Kammerer in the spring of 1906 married Felicitas Theodora von Wiedersperg. She came from a distinguished and aristocratic German-Bohemian family and was also an amateur singer who had offered to read some of Kammerer's songs. According to her daughter, Maria Lacerta Finton, it was (again) love at first sight, but now with no hesitation on Wiedersperg's part as had been the case earlier with Helene.

There is no existing correspondence between Helene and Kammerer from this time, although the events of 1906 were plainly devastating for Helene and cast her into a deep depression whose severity caused anxiety for her parents and siblings. She later spoke of her feelings in a letter to Alban Berg:

Do I have to tell you more about my love for Paul? Since you are so good at preaching and have the makings of a confessor, listen up: "It was once upon a time." Do I have to begin again and tell the long story, a story with so many unhappy memories? Let me be brief. I was so in love with Paul that I will never feel that way about anyone again. This love perished, killed by many unwept tears. It died from a cold and gruesome fate—a great love—died a bitter and disgraceful death. From that day on I became a different person.[90]

Berg's Courtship of Helene Nahowski

While still reeling from her abandonment by Kammerer, Helene met another talented young composer of songs, Alban Berg. Helene's nephew Erich Berg told the story of how she met him:

> In the spring of 1907 we see this beanstalk of a young man—so strikingly similar in appearance to Oscar Wilde—promenading for hours before the house. He would disappear around the corner just as his beloved, accompanied by a lady who was presumably her mother or by her brother, emerged from the house. These promenades became so conspicuous that the brother, Frank, said to his sister, "We have to help this man." He put on Helene's hat and a veil, and when Alban next appeared he saw the "girl" lightly wave to him from the bay window. Despite this help, Alban could not find the courage to speak to her at the next opportunity. So Frank again had to play the deus ex machina. He went out with the dog and when Alban came around the corner, the dog snarled at him. Frank apologized and got him into a conversation, then invited him into the large family garden that lay on the far side of the street opposite the villa. They sat on a stone bench, talked about this and that, and took pleasure in one another. Then Frank used some pretext to run over to Helene and yelled, "Hey, I've got him!" Then he and his sister returned to the garden, and the ice was broken. The date was Good Friday [March 29] 1907.[91]

Even before this date Berg had apparently contacted Helene, who later recalled that he had sent her two of his songs—"Fraue, du Süße" and "Fromm"—before they met. Beginning almost immediately after their first encounter at the end of March 1907, Berg began to pour out letter upon letter to Helene. This was the beginning of an extraordinarily large and valuable correspondence between the two, which by the time of Berg's death in 1935 would occupy more than 2,200 pages in the recently-published critical edition.[92] The huge size of the letter exchange came in part from long periods when the two were apart, also because the writing of lengthy letters to Helene became for Berg virtually a compulsion by which he created a relationship that was partly real and partly imaginary. Their correspondence is the principal source of information about Berg's adult life, and it is one of the most detailed and richest such resources in the entire history of music. Helene preserved most but not all of Berg's letters. Some pages are missing and Helene erased and crossed out many passages. Many of Helene's letters to Berg—far fewer in number and generally more objective in tone—were not preserved or were destroyed following Berg's death. The complex history of early editions of the letters will be discussed in a subsequent chapter.

Berg's letters to Helene during their courtship revive many of the themes and much of the rhetoric of his earlier letters to Watznauer, and these would be repeated again in the letters of 1925–34 to his paramours Hanna Fuchs-Robettin and Anny Askenase.[93] In letter after letter Berg bombards Helene with expressions of passionate love and desperate yearning. The letters are afloat in self-pity, expressions of dejection and self-doubt, garrulous overstatement, threatening, bullying, and pleading. As with the letters to Watznauer, the early ones to Helene take on a *Sturm und Drang* tone, as though Berg had again placed himself in a literary world, as he had done in his Nora letter, but now with far more urgency and emotion. In these writings, Helene, like Hanna Fuchs later, seems scarcely to exist as a real person, figuring far more as an abstraction upon whom Berg acts out a passion that is modeled on *Tristan und Isolde* among other fictional works. George Perle has described Berg's letters—both to Helene and to Hanna—as those of "a perpetual adolescent, the letters of one who cannot free himself, who does not wish to free himself, from the painfully acute sensitivity, the intense self-consciousness, the anxiety and perfectionism of youth."[94]

Underlying all of the emotion and bombast of the courtship letters are, however, rationally motivated currents, one of which is Berg's attempt to win Helene over to his world view. This required formulating his vision for his future life, which he hoped to share with her. Although Berg is less than systematic in this effort, certain themes arise that are key to understanding his narratives of identity. One such theme addresses the artist's way of life, which must be based in a spiritual, as opposed to a material, realm. This idea is of course not new, and Berg certainly found it embedded in his early reading and after 1907 confirmed within the Schoenberg circle. In the summer of 1909 Berg traveled from the Berghof to Bayreuth—thirteen hours by train—to hear *Parsifal*, an excursion paid for by his brother Herman.[95] He returned strongly affected by the magical world of Wagner's music and the power of the imagination that could create it. His own imagination, he boasted to Helene, was exceptional. While others need—he sarcastically noted—picture postcards to jog their imaginations, he can conjure up images of nature, even far-off places, with no difficulty. In his world of imagination he is freed to embrace the highest in everything, including love.

> My imagination [*Phantasie*] is so great, I have the beauties of the whole world within me, so that a well-drawn tree on a picture postcard is enough to awaken within me the vision of all these beautiful places, to bring before me the splendor of a North German larch forest, the proud towering trunks of dead trees high on the mountain, the tangled enormity of a primal Indian forest, and much, much more. And so in all things!! . . . For I am driven everywhere toward the highest, most exalted, the ultimate: I must know every note that has been composed and brings us closer to the highest things, attainable only at their highest—Strauss, Mahler, Schoenberg, Debussy; and I can't rest until I have absorbed this into myself. So it was with *Parsifal*—! I had to obtain the most splendid woman—*you*, Helene—and I have attained her—just in this way I would not rest until I had made the most splendid beauties of nature my very own—and that can only be done through imagination![96]

Playing with the dichotomy between real and imaginary, as he had done in the Nora letter, Berg argued for the "reality" of his life of the mind, which had none of the illusions of a dream.

> I've experienced myself enough brutal encroachments into my own created world. But note: a world created, not just dreamed about. And that is the difference that I've already spoken about: Not that I lead a life of fantasy, but that I lead a life that is beautiful, expansive, elevated as fantasy is . . . Thus brutal reality cannot affect me, I can set my own higher, holier, more beautiful, self-created reality against it.[97]

By delineating his own reality of the mind and fixing his identity within it, Berg sought to woo Helene to his cause and to show that Kammerer's science was part of a lesser reality. He would return to this theme many times in their married life. Having been raised, like Berg, in an environment of material comfort and upper-middle-class values, Helene had to struggle to break free from the path her parents anticipated for her. In this same summer of 1909 she wrote that in the face of family pressure she felt herself to be a cripple, to be driven forward against her will to an unknown goal. Berg explains again that their destination cannot be material things, like Kammerer's salamanders or his brother Herman's fancy cars.

> But on the other hand, there is still a goal, a "where to" for us, and if it has not yet opened up for you, nevertheless you are on the path to finding it. It is the way that leads past all the external worldly goals, up to a perfection of our soul in all its humanness—to the only right, worthy, highest, most ideal existence . . . past all the petty goals of the world, this miniature world, past all the gas stations, past the swamps in which one fishes for toads and honors, and leaves all that aside, having only one thing in sight—to become a good, noble, righteous human being.[98]

In the manner of many converts, Helene—far more than Berg—was to live out these ideal precepts in her marriage and with striking fidelity after her husband's death.

Impediments to Berg's courtship arose from the very start. Helene was away with her parents for most of the spring and summer of 1907, first to Bogliaco on Lake Garda near Verona, then at the family retreat in Trahütten in Styria. Helene was still apparently in despair over the Paul Kammerer affair, and she had several suitors in addition to Berg. A more formidable barrier was Helene's father, who immediately and forcefully disapproved of Alban as a suitor for his daughter. Berg had none of Kammerer's qualifications— no university degree and no bright prospects for the future. Franz Nahowski would not allow Alban into the family residence and did all in his power to keep the two apart. For a long time Berg could write no letters directly to Helene (brief picture postcards were acceptable), so he relied on help from Helene's siblings to bring his letters to her and to arrange for the couple to meet.

Another complex issue for Berg arose when his sister, Smaragda, fell passionately in love with Helene at the same time that he did. Smaragda and Alban were soul mates, and Alban was fully knowledgeable and accepting of his sister's lesbianism. But, at least briefly in 1907, they were jealous rivals for Helene's attention. Smaragda had married Adolf von Eger in April, 1907, at about the same time that she first met Helene, but the marriage was dissolved by the end of the year. While Berg was away on a trip to Dresden from 28 June to 2 July, Smaragda wrote Helene a long love letter in which she shrewdly suggests that for Helene to reject her homosexual advances might also mean a break in the relationship with Alban. Smaragda writes:

> You know, what you see as something peculiar in my personality is nothing more than a dark secret that resides in my essence and inner nature. Unfortunately I can't tell you more about it now, not quite yet. If I did *our* relationship with you might immediately break off, and for me this is a terrible thought. You don't know how attached I am to you, how I yearn for you. An unfortunate creature like me cannot be so lavish with the loss of love. . . .
>
> How I would like to confide every detail to you, my dear, but that's scarcely possible in a letter, and I know you too briefly to be able to judge whether you can or want to understand me, and I don't want to lose you now because I am so terribly lonely———
>
> When I saw you for the first time, even then I had the unconscious feeling that this blond-haired girl would have meaning for my life, and now I see clearly that it is so. You have entered my life at its unhappiest moment, and your appearance can signify for me a renewal of life—or death! I don't think I can ever do without you. With a single kiss I would be able to say so much more to you, but you are away. When I close my eyes I can conjure up your image. Can you do that with me too? If so you must be very fond of me! . . . I love only you. Give me your trust as I give you all of mine. Farewell, write soon and at length. I yearn for news from you. Be deeply kissed by she who loves you, *Smaragda.*[99]

Helene was neither notably attracted nor repelled by Smaradga's declaration, and she tried to reassure Alban of her detachment from any such relationship following upon the Kammerer debacle. She wrote to him on August 13:

> But now to something important, so pay attention. You have read my letter to Smaragda. Did I come out and say that same-sex love was degenerate? And did you not tell me candidly that I gave the impression of being a sick, degenerate person? People would laugh in my face if I tried to explain the logic of that! I don't recall writing anything to your sister that could upset you. Smaragda is such a charming creature, I think, to whom everyone would be good, everyone would take to her. Let's call it a love of beauty! Now, little Alban, are you put at ease?[100]

In addition to his letters, Berg communicated with the object of his affections through his songs. In their choice of text, several of the songs composed in 1907 and 1908 seem to be explicitly addressed to Helene and intended to communicate Berg's emotional state to her during a period when their contact was restricted by Helene's father, much as Robert Schumann in 1840 communicated with Clara Wieck through his songs. In "Schilflied" (1908) the dejected poet takes comfort when he imagines that he hears the beloved singing; in "Die Nachtigall" (spring 1907) Helene is likely the child of nature whom the nightingale's song has thrown into confusion. In "Traumgekrönt" (August 1907) she comes to him in a dream, "like a song from a fairy tale." In "Läuterung"—a work played for Schoenberg in November 1908 for which no complete manuscript exists—the speaker has been purified by his emotionally painful encounter with the beloved.

Berg continued to send copies of these personalized compositions to Helene. In an undated letter, he speaks rapturously about hearing her read through two of his songs:

> The beauty of your voice, the all-embracing expression in your delivery, the compassion and sympathy—all of this left me speechless with emotion and joy. And, Helene, I was nearly angry when you mentioned such trivia as "intonation" after the *entirety* made such an artistic and humanly rounded and perfect impression. *Whoever sings as you do* and listens as I do can joyfully and *proudly* declare: I will be an *artist*! So now I am thanking you in writing, a thousand times so—not for the two songs, no! Instead for the feeling that you awakened in me, that I love a woman who has *art* within and *that one* art—music—that is everything to me and which builds for me the most beautiful bridges to nobler humanity.[101]

There is no evidence that Helene ever sang Berg's songs in public. Also, in Berg's correspondence with Helene from this time there is an almost complete absence of discussions about his compositions, whether songs or other works. Nothing is found in the letters about his choice of texts, interpretive issues, their relation to the song literature, or about technical aspects of song composition. Unlike Kammerer, Berg did not engage with Helene—an accomplished and devoted musician—in the creation of his music. Helene was painfully aware of her exclusion from

Berg's creative life. She later wrote: "I have often been saddened that you haven't let me participate in it [your music] even a little. If I now perhaps lack a correct understanding for your recent music, my path to it will be *love*! *I believe in you!*"[102] By 1907 Berg had become absorbed into Schoenberg's all-male circle of composers, and women existed on the periphery of the circle, primarily as performers or as muses. Also, Berg's songs from 1907 had begun to evolve toward an unfamiliar, modernistic style, one increasingly remote from the Wagnerian and post-Wagnerian music that Helene had in her repertory and most admired.

Despite Kammerer's marriage, the rivalry between him and Berg only intensified from 1907 to 1909. Soon after his marriage in 1906, Kammerer went through periods of estrangement from his wife, during which he tried to reestablish contact with Helene and again persuade her to sing his music. Berg's jealousy boiled over as Helene remained susceptible to his charms. At New Year in 1909, Berg sent a greeting card (Figure 1.3) showing a man sitting dejectedly beside a lady who sings music on which Berg has written the name "Kammerer."

In fact, Berg's relationship with Helene during these years was haunted by Kammerer's presence, and his response to it became increasingly personal and vitriolic. Kammerer is an idée fixe that Berg identified with everything that held him back and defeated him. To Helene, he repeatedly erupts with disdain for Kammerer's scientific thinking, his academic success, university degree, correctness in writing, orderly life, good health, outward success and prominence, and especially his music—all accomplishments that Berg lacked except for the last.

Berg's ridicule of Kammerer became ever more heavy-handed. In his letters to Helene, Berg compares himself to the heroes of Wagner's operas while Kammerer is cast in the roles of Albrecht, Mime, or other Wagnerian "Schwarzalben." In a letter of 2 August 1909, Berg writes:

> I have long stopped, or had to stop, leading a correct life, a life according to rules. And I'm suited less and less for the world of the Kammerers and the Drills ["Drill" was Berg's derisive nickname for Helene's father], where everything happens according to the strictures of an academic education. . . .
> Here's a day from the life of a great academic [Kammerer] after solving the puzzles of the world in kindergarten:

Figure 1.3 Berg's New Year's Card, 1909, ÖNB, F21.Berg.1581/1909/114. Courtesy of the
Austrian National Library

6:35 precisely, take the tram back to Hütteldorf

7:02–7:15, read one of his own articles in the *Journal of Frog Legs and Scholars'*
Bellies

8:10–9:27, supper

9:28–9:39, practice dancing to [Kammerer's song] "Der Traumbild"

10:00 precisely, get into bed in his underpants

10:01–10:45, sex

10:46, the first snore of the correct and righteous man

And so on, day after day.[103]

The turning point in Berg's relationship with Helene came in January of
1909, when she visited Kammerer for the last time. Afterward she wrote
to Berg:

I should not have gone to Paul's on Sunday because I knew how it would hurt you, but I went anyway . . . There I felt a great desolation and boredom and regret that I had lost an entire afternoon. Could this be the same person who once was so close to me, who impressed me so much, and whom I loved more than anything? I sought in vain for a bridge between then and now, but he remained someone else. A stranger? No, something worse (or better!)—someone alien, whose glance aroused not the slightest desire to come closer to him.[104]

Soon after this final encounter with Kammerer, Berg and Helene became unofficially engaged. But the problem of opposition from Helene's father remained, although her mother had come to support her engagement. After making his intentions of marriage known, Berg wrote on 28 July 1910 a twenty-four page "defense" letter to the elder Nahowski in which he attempted to address Nahowski's objections to him.[105] In this often cited letter Berg resorts to the "logic of a courtroom," as he forcefully addresses the accusations made by Nahowski concerning his intellectual inferiority, poverty, ill health, and the "immorality" within his family. Berg's courtroom tactic was to compare himself to Arthur Lebert, who was then engaged to Helene's sister, Anna, with her father's approval, although Lebert was generally despised by both Alban and Helene. Berg's rebuttal is subtly argued. Music is at least as secure a profession, he says, as is Lebert's grinding wheel factory, and when his training is complete he can find regular employment as a theater conductor or in a conservatory. His health and stamina are actually sound despite his being high-strung and excitable. Berg's family is distinguished in every way, he says, and his sister's lesbianism, although her family's "desperate sorrow," is untypical of the Bergs as a whole.

The skillfully argued letter predictably fell on deaf ears. At the end of it, Helene later wrote: "Papa *never* read the letter. He would never approve! There were such angry scenes—yes, he threatened not even to come to the wedding of my sister with Lebert. But that was our last 'act of obedience.' In May of the next year we were married. Mama helped us to reach our goal."[106]

The day before her wedding, Helene wrote Alban this letter:

My dearest and closest! Tomorrow is our wedding day. With you I will take the path into the "land of marriage" with complete confidence and the best of intentions. I will ever be your companion, lover, and support, from here to eternity. I willingly and gladly give up what I pursued during my maiden years with such beauty, happiness, and hope—*my own* modest "artistry." I will efface my own self and be only for you. Now we will remain together *always!* Amen.[107]

Berg at the time may not have realized how literally Helene would honor these vows.

The wedding of Alban and Helene Berg took place on 3 May 1911 in the Evangelische Kirche on the Dorotheergasse. A few weeks before, Berg, born into the Catholic Church, converted to the Nahowskis' confession, the Reformed branch of Protestantism, at the insistence of Franz Nahowski. Thirty years later, Helene penned a letter to her long-departed husband, in which she recalled their wedding day: the mixed weather, the shabby taxi they rode in to the church, the witnesses, the fact that she did not listen to the lofty words of the minister. "I breathed in the cool, gentle scent of the flowers on the kneeler, in which our entwined hands rested, and I knew that our marriage was sealed long before in Heaven."[108] On the day after the wedding, Paul Kammerer—the specter that haunted Berg's entire courtship—wrote his final letter to Helene:[109]

> My dear Helene,
>
> With all my heart I wish you the best for the future.
>
> In addition to caring for your soul, which you have taken as your main goal, do not neglect caring for your health (provided that you will accept advice from me). Because a healthy soul can only exist in a healthy body. The spiritual cannot be separated from the physical, and when this seems to have happened, really it is only an illusion, an unhealthy illusion. . . .
>
> So this is what I wish for you above all else: a complete restoration of your still frail nerves, as you have put it. You have already shown that you understand this, it seems to me, by caring for and uplifting the health of your husband. Please give him my best wishes too. —Paul

Berg's resentment for Kammerer eased with time, and they saw each other occasionally at the residence of Alma Mahler. Although scornful of his scientific work, Berg was attracted to ideas in Kammerer's widely read *Das Gesetz der Serie* (The law of seriality, 1919). Here Kammerer attempted to account for chains of coincidences by pseudo-scientific reasoning, holding that a cluster of related events might not be accidental but an outcome of processes that transpire beneath the realm of perception. Berg's interest in this idea is apparent in a letter to Helene in which he notes parallel events in Schoenberg's life.[110]

Following World War I, Kammerer's career ran seriously aground as his methods and experimental results were questioned in the scientific literature. A crisis arose in 1926 when he was accused in the journal *Nature* by the American herpetologist G. Kingsley Noble of falsifying certain of his earlier experimental data, an accusation that Kammerer could not fend off due to the loss of most of his experimental specimens during the war. As the scandal over these accusations was brewing, Kammerer was offered a professorship at the Communist Academy in Moscow, which he initially accepted. But depressed over the prospect of moving alone to Russia and probably equally over the allegation of scientific fraud, Kammerer committed suicide on 23 September 1926.[111]

Berg's marriage in May 1911 marked a turning point in his life, a moment for optimism and a sign that his life was now on the right track. Like Siegfried and Stolzing, he had won a beautiful maiden to be his bride, and he had completed his "exhaustive instruction in theory and composition" with brilliant results. As the couple moved to their new residence at 27 Trauttmansdorffgasse in Hietzing, they could be confident that prospects for the future were bright.

Berg's Musical Apprenticeship, 1899–1911

ALBAN BERG GAVE 1899 TO 1911 AS THE DATES OF HIS APPRENTICE-ship as a composer.[1] His first compositions, he wrote, came during his fourteenth year (1899), and he chose the year 1911 to mark the end of his formal study of music, although Berg often put forth such dates as approximations that had meaning for him beyond simple chronology. His earliest compositions are juvenilia that reveal his instinctive musical talent; later, under the tutelage of Arnold Schoenberg, he quickly mastered traditional musical forms and styles. By the end of his apprenticeship Berg had emerged as a composer of originality, one with a distinctive and advanced formal and expressive identity. Throughout his apprenticeship Berg composed mainly songs and pieces for piano and chamber ensemble. In a typically self-conscious fashion, he signaled the end of his apprenticeship with major compositions, Opp. 1–3, in each of these three categories. In these works Berg's mature musical personality is evident, and they also represent his training at Schoenberg's hands and his belief in the artistic path on which Schoenberg traveled.

The groundwork for Berg's career as a composer was laid during his early family life, in which music, literature, and art were prized and encouraged. Berg's parents were typical of middle-class Viennese families in their attention to the arts, while at the same time striving to provide a high standard of living through work and business. Conrad and Johanna Berg encouraged artistic development among their children and especially the practice of music in their home. According to the recollections

Berg. Bryan Simms and Charlotte Erwin, Oxford University Press (2021). © Oxford University Press.
DOI: 10.1093/oso/9780190931445.003.0003

of Berg's friend and mentor Hermann Watznauer, Berg and his sister, Smaragda, received piano lessons from the sister's governess, Ernestine Götzlich, who also organized household singing and skits with music. All of the Bergs sang, Smaragda and Alban accompanied them at the piano, and the playing of four-hand arrangements was a regular activity. Smaragda later became a professional pianist and teacher, and Berg a competent pianist who occasionally played the instrument in public.

When Berg began to compose in 1899, he was likely guided by Fräulein Götzlich and spurred on by his friend Watznauer, but his own curiosity drove his musical explorations. A valuable resource for him at this time was a copy of the new *Spemanns Goldenes Buch der Musik*, given to him by Watznauer in 1900. Berg fondly recalled the value of this book for the remainder of his life. The 900-page, encyclopedic "Golden Book" opens with words fictitiously attributed to Beethoven: "Music is a form of revelation higher than all wisdom and philosophy." Berg often repeated this phrase in his early writings, and the thought may have lured him away from his earlier literary inclinations and toward the power of music. The Golden Book introduced Berg to the history of music and to rudiments of music theory, notation, and harmony. Armed with this source he began to compose simple pieces for piano, then songs for voice and piano, which were performed in the Berg household.

At the same time that his desire to compose grew, Berg familiarized himself with the standard literature of song and opera by playing through scores, and with Smaragda he played a large number of orchestral and chamber works arranged for four hands, marking the beginning of his lifelong delight in four-hand playing. In 1904 Berg wrote out an inventory of the works he had played in this way, adding comments about them.[2] More than eighty composers are represented in his list, with music by Brahms and Dvořák most frequently cited. Berg's remarks about the pieces are the words of an opinionated youth who is discovering music for the first time. About Mozart's *The Magic Flute*, he writes: "The overture delightfully perky. The overture to Act 2 is nice but certainly not Wagner or Meyerbeer."[3] Brahms's *Deutsches Requiem* proved to him the rightness of Beethoven's dictum: "This is music!," Berg exclaimed. "Truly a higher form of revelation!"

Berg's future in music was far from assured. His mother continued to run her husband's bookstore after his death in 1900, but the family's income was much reduced. Consequently, Johanna Berg did not favor music as a profession for her son Alban, despite his eagerness and apparent talent. Berg was obedient to the wishes of his mother, and upon graduation from Realschule in 1904, he began an apprenticeship in the civil service of Lower Austria. Johanna Berg apparently had no objections to her son's continuing his musical activities, which in October of 1904 entered a new and far more structured phase at the hands of Arnold Schoenberg.

Studies with Schoenberg

Berg's student Willi Reich was the first to tell the often related story of how his teacher came to study music with Schoenberg.[4] At the same time that Berg began an apprenticeship in accounting in October 1904, his siblings saw an announcement of courses in music to be given at Eugenie Schwarzwald's Lyceum in the Wallnerstraße. Arnold Schoenberg was to teach the basic class, in harmony and counterpoint; Alexander Zemlinsky, a more advanced class in form and instrumentation; and Elsa Bienenfeld gave instruction in music history. Berg's brother Charly then secretly took five of Alban's songs to Schoenberg, who accepted Berg into his Schwarzwald class and also met him occasionally for private instruction. For two years Schoenberg provided the lessons gratis to his impecunious student. "It was a pleasure to teach him," Schoenberg recalled.

> He was industrious, eager, and did his best in everything. And like all the gifted young people of that time he was soaked in music, lived in music. He went to all operas and concerts and knew them all; at home he played piano four hands and was soon reading scores. He was enthusiastic and uncritical, receptive to the beautiful whether old or new, whether music, literature, painting, sculpture, theater, or opera.[5]

Another story—one that is almost certainly false although often repeated—comes from the memoirs of Alma Mahler. Berg, according to Alma Mahler, was wavering between Schoenberg and Hans Pfitzner as a teacher, and he turned to Schoenberg only after missing a train to Strasbourg to meet Pfitzner.[6] The anecdote may actually concern Anton Webern rather than Berg, since Webern consulted with Pfitzner for lessons shortly before turning to Schoenberg.[7]

Berg probably knew little about Schoenberg in 1904, either as composer or teacher. Schoenberg had only recently returned from a three-year sojourn in Berlin, and in 1904 he had few musical publications or performances. His reputation was beginning to grow as a composer in the progressive style of the period associated with Mahler, Strauss, and Wolf, and he had several acquaintances in Vienna who spoke to his excellence as a teacher. Thanks to recommendations from Guido Adler, professor of musicology at the University of Vienna, Schoenberg attracted several doctoral students to his Schwarzwald class, including Anton Webern, Egon Wellesz, and Heinrich Jalowetz. But enrollment in the class was small, and it was abandoned after a single year, whereupon Berg and other, more advanced, students continued their lessons privately in Schoenberg's residence.

Schoenberg's teaching and personality were magnetic forces for most of his students. Almost all of them recognized his extraordinary skill as a teacher, but the personal dimension of his relations with them—often remote, demanding, and highly critical—produced differing reactions. John Cage, who studied with Schoenberg from 1935 to 1937 in the United States, recalled that his teacher kept him in a "permanent state of failure." Other students, including Anton Webern, Erwin Stein, and Alban Berg, formed a near fanatical bond with their teacher. What Webern confessed to Schoenberg in 1911 expressed Berg's sentiments equally well: "I believe that the disciples of Jesus Christ could not have felt more deeply for their Lord than we do for you. God protect you."[8]

Egon Wellesz recalled the atmosphere during his lessons with Schoenberg:

His room with piano looked out on an unfriendly, gritty courtyard. Even in the winter the window was open, and Schoenberg—just as in his self-portrait—bent over, hands behind his back, paced restlessly around the room, smoked one cigarette after another, and blurted out explanations of his theories in his dark and somewhat hoarse voice. In a heavy Viennese dialect, he spoke in incomplete sentences separated by pauses. It was as though he was talking aloud to himself until, as if awakening from a kind of trance, he again spoke to the student. When he wanted to play an example at the piano, he would nervously strike every chord over and over. He considered the study of harmony, counterpoint, and fugue only as preparatory for the young musician, who after completing these studies could move on to composition. He emphasized that every good musician, even those lacking creative talent, could master the practice of theory. But instruction in composition, which aimed at the development of creative talent, could only begin when the student had fully mastered theory.[9]

Schoenberg's teaching conformed to standard nineteenth-century German musical pedagogy.[10] For a beginner like Berg instruction started, as Wellesz noted, with music theory, covering rudiments, harmony, and counterpoint including fugue. These subjects occupied Berg for three years, from fall 1904 to spring 1907. Berg then began to study composition per se, and for this subject Schoenberg used the established method of *Formenlehre*, the study of form. Hugo Riemann describes the aims of this traditional discipline:

> The study of form begins above all with a consideration of the artful spinning out of motives. At first the scope of this procedure is small, then gradually more and more extended, i.e., it begins with a demonstration of how a small musical piece (like an *Albumblatt*, song, or dance) is normally put together and ends by referring broadly to the layout of works of larger size (a sonata movement). Much of what more generally concerns the study of composition— such as musical rudiments, harmony, and counterpoint—is assumed to have been already covered.[11]

For his teaching of composition, Schoenberg had consulted standard textbooks on the subject. A copy of Adolph Bernhard Marx's encyclopedic *Die Lehre von der musikalischen Komposition* (1837–47) was in his private library, and he also relied on Heinrich Bellermann's *Der Kontrapunkt* (1862). Schoenberg probably also drew upon Johann Christian Lobe's *Lehrbuch der musikalischen Komposition* (1850–67), a copy of which was in Berg's personal library, and Berg later cited writings by Hugo Riemann and Ludwig Bussler as authorities on theoretical issues.[12] Schoenberg's teaching was also shaped by his own instruction at the hands of Alexander Zemlinsky and by a close and independent study of the German musical classics. Schoenberg did not provide instruction in performance and music history, and Berg made no advanced study in these areas.

Berg's first year at the Schwarzwald school focused on the study of harmony with an introduction to counterpoint.[13] From the fall of 1905, when the subject turned explicitly to counterpoint, Berg's lessons were conducted privately at Schoenberg's residence in the Liechtensteinstraße. During this year Schoenberg's curriculum was based mainly on Heinrich Bellermann's *Der Kontrapunkt*, whose text closely agreed with Johann Fux's classic method from the *Gradus ad Parnassum* (1725) that German composers had used since the time of Haydn. Schoenberg follows Bellermann by having a student progress from the simplest of forms— two-part counterpoint based on a cantus firmus—to multi-voice fugues, the most complex of forms. Bellermann's course of study moves through the five (sometimes six) species in two, three, and four voices, with musical examples in the church modes taken directly from Fux. For these exercises Schoenberg gave Berg new canti firmi in major and minor, replacing Bellermann's and Fux's modal examples. Berg also practiced modulations around the circle of fifths, the making of cadences, arranging chorales, and composing short polyphonic compositions for piano, chamber ensemble, and chorus.[14]

The year 1906–07 was devoted to imitation and fugue, during which Berg composed a series of canons to texts drawn from Goethe, more chorale arrangements, keyboard inventions, and instrumental and choral fugues of increasing complexity.[15] In the nineteenth century and early twentieth, fugue remained a viable if minor genre of composition, supported by the rediscovery and romanticization of the music of Bach and Handel and by the fugal compositions of Beethoven, Mendelssohn, Brahms, and Reger. Still, the stronghold of fugue was in the area of music education, where it was viewed as a necessary discipline for the aspiring composer, regardless of what use it might later have. Treatise after treatise covering counterpoint and fugue came into print during this period, directed toward a booming educational market. Schoenberg's teaching of fugue relied on methods drawn from several such textbooks, mainly Bellermann's *Der Kontrapunkt* and Adolf Bernard Marx's *Lehre*. Ulrich Krämer has argued that Schoenberg's approach to fugue was also indebted to the teaching of Robert Fuchs, with whom Alexander Zemlinsky, Schoenberg's own mentor, had studied the subject. Berg's study materials conform to the topics addressed in these sources: canonic imitation, fugue in ever larger numbers of voices, invertible counterpoint and its use in fugues with multiple themes. Berg proved to be especially gifted in counterpoint, as Schoenberg recalled: "I could do counterpoint with him in a manner rare among my pupils."[16]

Berg culminated his three-year study in music theory with his earliest extended composition, a *Fugue with Two Themes for String Quintet with Piano Accompaniment in the Manner of a Realized Continuo.*[17] This was performed, together with three of Berg's songs, at his first important public appearance as a composer, a concert of music by Schoenberg's students on 7 November 1907. The pieces that Berg chose to present show the two faces of his music during this phase of his apprenticeship. On one hand is the *Fugue,* a study piece based on Schoenberg's teaching and German fugal theory of the later nineteenth century. It imitates existing styles and forms and makes a limited attempt at originality or personalized expression, although it is a remarkably intricate and accomplished work in light of Berg's mere three years of serious musical study. In the songs, on the other hand, Berg aimed at a greater originality and distinctive musical identity. Although he showed his songs to Schoenberg for advice, they were not part of Schoenberg's curriculum, and in them Berg was freer to express modern ideas in harmony and form with a more personal stamp. The most advanced of the songs on the 1907 concert, "Traumgekrönt," will be discussed shortly.

Berg's *Fugue with Two Themes* adheres to the overall form posited by Marx and other German writers on fugue of the nineteenth century. This consists of three connected parts distinguished by keys, each part termed a *"Durchführung,"* or "carrying through," of thematic material. The first *Durchführung* is equivalent to what in English is called a fugal exposition; it remains in the home key and alternates tonic and dominant harmonies in the interchange of subjects and answers. The second *Durchführung* moves without pause into more distant tonal regions, and the third returns to the home key and presents the themes in stretto, augmentation, and other such variants. Marx was especially keen on fugues in five voices and also—as in Berg's *Fugue with Two Themes*—fugues with non-fugal accompaniment.

Berg's *Fugue with Two Themes* has almost all of the features that Marx describes. The two themes mentioned in the title are the subject and countersubject, bracketed in Example 2.1. Marx uses the term "double fugue" for a work of this type. The exposition, or first *Durchführung,* extends to m. 17. Here each of the five voices has its first complete statement of the subject and countersubject, and a sixth entrance is added in the two violas playing in thirds, something explicitly recommended

Example 2.1   *Fugue on Two Themes*, mm. 1–9 (Piano omitted), from ÖNB, F21.Berg.35–36

by Marx. Following the exposition the second *Durchführung* begins as the music moves, without pause, into new tonal regions. This middle *Durchführung* ends at m. 42 with a half cadence in C major, signaling a return to the tonic and the beginning of the third part of the fugue. Here Berg presents his subject and countersubject in stretto and, from m. 58, in augmentation.

Some aspects of Berg's fugue deviate from Marx's model. The work contains no episodes—contrasting passages with no full statement of the subject—and this deprives the piece of the variety that Marx recommends. The exposition of Berg's fugue is also highly unusual in that the space between entrances of subjects and answers continually expands. The answer in Viola II in m. 3 follows the beginning of the subject by eight quarter-note values. The following entrances come after ten, twelve, and sixteen such values. This may be one of the "ingeniosities" that Schoenberg recalled in the work some thirty years later. He wrote:

> And I would like to mention a five-part double fugue for string quintet that was overflowing with ingeniosities. But I could see already to what lengths he could be pushed: when the fugue was ready I told him to add a piano accompaniment in the manner of a continuo. Not only did he execute this with all excellence, he found ways of adding a further host of minor devilries.[18]

Following the concert on 7 November 1907, Berg wrote to his friend Frida Semler, assuring her that his music had "scored a great success." "I can safely say," he continued, "that my Fugue was the hit of the evening although other things were at a far higher level. But that's the way it is with the public! I saw this clearly with my three songs. Certainly the best one ("Traumgekrönt") did not please while the weakest ("Nachtigall") delighted everyone."[19]

After the concert Berg graduated from the study of music theory to that of composition per se, and for two years Schoenberg's pedagogy in this area remained strict and systematic. In Schoenberg's traditional form-based approach to the subject, the student composed instrumental pieces that progressed from small and simple forms to larger and more complicated ones.[20] Berg's study pieces of this type were mainly for piano and for string quartet or quintet, some for chorus. At first Berg's attention was drawn to the creation of simple eight-measure themes and phrases in which motivic variation is the principal means of musical expansion. He then moved on to writing minuets and scherzi, larger sets of variations, adagios, and finally to whole movements in sonata form—the highest and most challenging formal archetype.

Toward the end of his period of study with Schoenberg, from fall 1909, Berg was freed to take a more independent direction as a composer, although Schoenberg's strict form-based teaching remained with Berg for the rest of his creative life. Even in his later atonal and twelve-tone compositions, Berg was guided by the traditional formal archetypes that he learned under Schoenberg, and in his own analyses of these works he almost always points to their presence. His composing at the end of his period of study continued on the three main tracks that he had pursued since 1907: songs, piano pieces, and chamber music. Each of the three culminated in a graduation piece—the Piano Sonata, Op. 1; Four Songs, Op. 2; and String Quartet, Op. 3—that Berg felt confident to have published as his earliest mature works.

For Berg's future as a composer, the impact of Schoenberg's teaching went far beyond training in composition. Berg quickly accepted Schoenberg's underlying philosophy about all of music and its historical unfolding. He was by nature susceptible to Schoenberg's ideologies: he quickly developed an unwavering belief in Schoenberg's artistry and an absolute certainty that his teacher could never err in artistic matters. "To the end of my life a student of Schoenberg," he declared in a note written in 1924. A good bit of Berg's susceptibility to Schoenberg's ideology about music came from two tendencies. The first was an inclination to see, in high contrast, right versus wrong in artistic expression. Second was Berg's readiness to idolize a few individuals—Schoenberg at their head—and to accept without question their moral and cultural authority. Berg had little tolerance for alternative tastes in art or diverging outlooks among his acquaintances, and he often took a dogmatic tone in his discussions with Helene Nahowski during their courtship. Schoenberg's authoritarian posture, his clear-cut ideas and dictatorial manner reinforced this inclination and gave Berg a rationale with which to identify what was good and bad in the world of music and what direction his own development had to take.

Very soon after beginning study with Schoenberg, Berg's tastes in music changed to align with Schoenberg's ideas. No longer did he point to pieces like Grieg's *Autumn Overture* and Smetana's *Dalibor* as favorite works—as he did in a letter to Watznauer of 1903—but now to compositions by Mahler, Strauss, and Schoenberg as the masterpieces of the present. In May 1906, Berg and Watznauer joined Mahler, Schoenberg, and other students in Graz for the Austrian premiere of *Salome*, conducted by Strauss himself. The audience for the triumphant performance included celebrities from far and wide, including Giacomo Puccini and an aspiring teenage artist from Linz, Adolf Hitler. A year later Berg accompanied Helene to the Vienna premiere of *Salome* at the Deutsches Volkstheater. "Thinking of *Salome* makes me dizzy," he wrote to her.[21]

Schoenberg's knowledge of music was deep but also constrained by his rigid ideology. Important music for him was German music from Bach to Mahler. By an intense first-hand study of this repertory Schoenberg found common formal archetypes and an organic unity based on development and variation, and these were the elements that his students had to master and repeat. These classical forms and formal procedures would in the future, Schoenberg held, be expanded by the need for originality, but they were ideas that could never be outdated or ignored. The direction for this future expansion could only be a continuation of evolutionary patterns seen within this relatively small repertory itself. Since triadic tonality, for example, played an ever weaker role in later nineteenth-century German music, it was preordained that traditional tonality in music of the future would ultimately play no role. Schoenberg's outlook on music could not accommodate alternative ideas in modern music that even at the turn of the twentieth century were beginning to attract attention. Debussy's bypassing of motivic development, Bartók's exploration of the musical resources found in primitive folk song, Satie's music of simplicity, or Ives's abandonment of unified design in music held little interest or importance for him.

Berg's Early Songs

Both before and after he began his studies with Schoenberg, Berg devoted himself to composing songs—short works for voice and piano using lyric poetry of the nineteenth and twentieth centuries. He began to write them in 1901, at age sixteen, before he had begun to study music seriously. Berg performed his earliest songs in his home, playing piano to accompany amateur singers including his sister, Smaragda, his brother Charly, and acquaintances including Hermann Watznauer. Watznauer had a keen interest in Berg's songs. He made calligraphic copies of many of them and recorded in his diary Berg's progress as a song composer.[22] Berg's production of songs increased during the period 1904–07, when he studied music theory under Schoenberg, to whom he brought the songs for advice, although they were not part of Schoenberg's curriculum. After graduating to the study of composition in the fall of 1907, his writing of songs dwindled as he became more engrossed by the complex forms associated with instrumental music.

By the end of his apprenticeship in 1911, Berg had composed about eighty-five songs in all.[23] After 1911 he made only a few additional efforts in this genre. He tried his hand at orchestral songs in the Altenberg

Songs, Op. 4 (1912), but these highly original works brought such sharp criticism upon him from Schoenberg that Berg all but abandoned song composing. In 1925 he recomposed Theodor Storm's poem "Schließe mir die Augen beide," a text that he had used in an early song and which in 1925 became his first experiment with twelve-tone composition. Although they have received relatively little attention in the literature on the composer, Berg's early songs deserve careful study. They document his earliest musical instincts and gradually reveal distinctive compositional techniques and an original musical personality.

At some point, possibly as early as 1906, Berg began to put his song manuscripts in order. He retrieved one copy of each and placed these in an approximate chronological sequence. He made at least two attempts at numbering them chronologically, the more complete sequence running from no. 1 ("Heiliger Himmel") to no. 65 ("Viel Träume"). The manuscripts were then placed into two binders to which Berg added tables of contents which match the numbering on the manuscripts. Later, he enlarged the content of the second binder with songs that he composed from 1906 to 1908, these given numbers that run from 66 ("Der milde Herbst") to 81 ("Läuterung"). Berg apparently placed the two compilations, which are the most comprehensive and authoritative sources for his early songs, in Helene's custody since she attached a note to them saying that Berg had "turned them over" to her.

Well after Berg's death in 1935, Helene Berg declared that the music in the two songbooks should be neither performed nor even seen by anyone, and that this was Berg's wish. She wrote in the first binder: "Examination is not permitted! *Book 1 and 2* [contain] songs that Alban Berg composed as autodidact, which he intended to destroy. He turned them over to me *only* with the stipulation that they never be published. They may never be made available for examination. Helene Berg."[24]

Helene Berg's insistence in this matter is confusing and may have stemmed from her misinterpreting a passing remark made far earlier by her husband. There is not a single recorded statement written by Berg himself saying that the early songs were not to be studied, performed, or published—and least of all destroyed. In fact, all available evidence suggests the opposite: that Berg was proud of the songs both in their own right and for how they documented his early development as a composer. He made multiple copies of many of them or had others, especially Watznauer, do so, and early manuscript copies are now scattered throughout libraries and private collections worldwide. His nephew Erich Berg was equally skeptical about Helene's idea. In his 1985 biography of Berg his nephew wrote:

> In reading the legions of letters to his wife, friends, publisher, and others I could find no reference to the idea that Berg had strictly forbidden the publication of his youthful songs. I will assume that he expressed this wish to Helene Berg viva voce. But the fact that Berg repeatedly sent several of these piano songs to friends like Frida Semler and Hermann Watznauer and had no opposition to their being performed in public then and there also speaks against it, as does the fact that the cycle *Sieben frühe Lieder*—orchestrated 25 years later and in 1927 [*recte* 1928] first performed in Vienna's Musikverein with Claire Born as soloist and Robert Heger conducting—was drawn entirely from the "songs of youth." Even more telling is Arnold Schoenberg's judgment concerning these autodidactic compositions of Alban Berg. These prompted him to take on Berg as a student without charging a fee.[25]

The dating of Berg's early songs is mostly uncertain. The composer entered dates on few of his song manuscripts, and relatively few others can be confidently dated by references that he made in contemporaneous correspondence. The main source for dates is found in Berg's first biography, a fragmentary work compiled by Hermann Watznauer, who drafted the biography in 1927–29 based on earlier diary notes.[26] Berg himself examined the biography for accuracy, and he also provided dates for many of the earliest songs on a preliminary questionnaire sent to him by Watznauer.[27] But even Berg himself sometimes gave unreliable dates for his music. His memory for dates seems to have been imprecise, possibly intentionally so, as dates (like other numbers) gradually took on for him more symbolic than documentary value.

Prior to beginning his study with Schoenberg in October 1904, Berg had composed about thirty-three of the eighty-five songs. Two of these are duets, one is a melodrama, and the remaining ones are for solo voice and piano. A few fragmentary songs not placed in the two songbooks may also date from this period. The songs are fairly uniform in style and typical juvenilia at a time when song was the most alluring avenue for amateur musical expression. In these small works Berg shows himself to be aware of and ready to copy the romantic German lieder style as practiced by a host of nineteenth-century composers. Those who have studied the songs have compared them to lieder by Schubert, Schumann, Wolf, Mahler, Tchaikovsky, Grieg, Schoenberg, Strauss, and Brahms, among others.[28] Berg's choice of texts—including poetry by Franz Evers, Otto Julius Bierbaum, Heinrich Heine, Friedrich Rückert, Emanuel von Greif, and Rainer Maria Rilke—is typical for the genre. Berg also used poetry by his youthful friends Frida Semler and Paul Hohenberg, and some of his choices of texts may reflect the moods—ranging from elation to depression—that haunted him during his teenage years.[29]

A handsome and typical example of this first group of songs is Berg's "Am Abend," which Watznauer dates 1903. The poem by Emanuel von Geibel was repeatedly used by song composers of the nineteenth century, including Anton Bruckner, Max Reger, Eduard Lassen, and Adolf Jensen. The first of three stanzas is shown in Example 2.2. Like many of the earliest songs, it is melodious and expressive, its vocal line tending toward declamation, but it is plainly the work of an untrained composer. The notation in Berg's manuscript is often incorrect—there is no use of key signature and accidentals appear in an irregular and sometimes redundant manner. The song is not unified in tonality as it wanders from F major to C major and ends with a sudden shift to minor. Berg instinctively places Geibel's three stanzas into a ternary form, but one that remains irregular in key and uncertain in its reprise.

The aspect of "Am Abend" that is most typical of the earliest songs is that it could equally well stand as a solo piano piece simply by dispensing with the voice, whose melody is entirely present in the right hand. This similarity of the early songs to piano pieces was later exploited by Berg during the compositional phase of his studies with Schoenberg, which began in 1907. At this time Schoenberg turned Berg mainly to piano music to develop his command of ever larger formal archetypes, and Berg returned to several of his songs to rewrite them explicitly as piano pieces. He then corrected their irregularities and eccentricities and made them conform to Schoenberg's pedagogical principles. "Am Abend" was one of those to be reused. In his revision Berg makes the song into a regular "small ternary form" A-B-A (also called a "song form"), which in Schoenberg's teaching was one of the simplest formal archetypes for instrumental music. The A-section (mm. 1–8) is the same as in the song's first stanza. The middle B-section is entirely rewritten to add more

Example 2.2 "Am Abend," mm. 1–8, from ÖNB, F21.Berg.2

variety in rhythm and melodic contrast, and the piano version ends with a simple return to the A-section in the home key of F.[30]

During his study of harmony and counterpoint, from about fall 1904 to fall 1907, Berg composed a second group of approximately forty-one songs—the largest outpouring of compositions during any comparable period in his life. Stimulation from his lessons with Schoenberg and with the musicians whom he had befriended among Schoenberg's other students—Anton Webern, Erwin Stein, Karl Linke, Heinrich Jalowetz, and others—is the likely cause for this upswing in his creative output. Berg's study of Schoenberg's own early songs, which had begun to appear in print shortly before, also provoked him to bring a more advanced harmonic and formal thinking into his music at the same time that his composition lessons adhered strictly to traditional models.

The songs of this group are polished in form and style, and they avoid the eccentric and amateurish features of the earlier songs. They alternate in style from relatively simple and traditional works to others that are nontraditional in harmony and tonality, more tightly unified by motivic development, and more reliant on special contrapuntal patterns.

Berg entered a third phase of song composing around 1907, when he began to study composition per se with Schoenberg. The year 1907 also marked the beginning of his long and turbulent courtship of Helene Nahowski, whom he married in May 1911. Although fewer in number than before, Berg's songs from 1907 to 1910 take on special and distinctive features: a continued enrichment of harmony by the increased use of dissonant, nontriadic chords; more extended whole-tone passages, chromatic density, and a greater reliance on motivic development as a principle of construction. Most of the texts of these later songs, composed just before he met Helene or with her explicitly in mind, explore Berg's Tristanesque imagination, the introspective and morbid aspects of which he poured out to Helene in impassioned letter upon letter from the very start of their relationship.

Seven Early Songs (1907)

Berg's second and third phases of song composition are well represented by selections that he retrieved in 1928 to be published as *Sieben frühe Lieder (1907)* (*Seven Early Songs 1907*). Berg's path toward this publication was long and complex. His composition of traditional lieder had come to an end in 1909–10, toward the end of his period of study with Schoenberg, and for years thereafter he showed little interest in his early songs. A reassessment of them that ultimately led to the *Seven Early Songs (1907)* began in 1917, when he selected ten songs to be handsomely copied to present to Helene on their sixth wedding anniversary.[31] He chose these ten:

1. Die Sorglichen (Gustav Falke)
2. Schließe mir die Augen beide (Theodor Storm)

3. Nun ziehen Tage [Sommertage] (Paul Hohenberg)
4. Die Nachtigall (Theodor Storm)
5. Liebesode [Selige Nacht] (Otto Erich Hartleben)
6. Im Zimmer (Johannes Schlaf)
7. Schilflied (Nikolaus Lenau)
8. Nacht (Carl Hauptmann)
9. Traumgekrönt (Rainer Maria Rilke)
10. Leukon (Johann Gleim)

Berg's selection seems to have been guided by the songs' relevance to Helene—ones that were inspired by her, sung or praised by her, or with texts that referred to her or to their courtship. Their poetry expresses the happiness of love, pleasant dreams, and the beauty of nature. Musically the songs are diverse. Some are tuneful, simple in harmony, and repetitive in form. Others are experimental in harmony and at the leading edge of lied composition of the day as found in songs by Schoenberg, Reger, and Pfitzner.

Berg's interest in his early songs again revived around 1925, at the beginning of his infatuation with Hanna Fuchs. It is likely that Berg went back to his songs at this time to reexperience the passionate sentiments that led to their creation, hoping to find those same feelings with Hanna as muse. In 1925 he chose an early song, "Schließe mir die Augen beide," that was closely associated with his courtship of Helene to recompose using a twelve-tone method and to allude subtly to Hanna Fuchs by numbers and pitch letters.[32] In his *Seven Early Songs (1907)*, Berg attempts to relive his past, to blend his bygone and present emotional states, and to use Helene as an outward symbol of a new and secret passion.

In 1927 or 1928 the conductor Paul von Klenau asked Berg to orchestrate a selection of early songs for a radio broadcast, and Berg willingly complied. The broadcast was to take place on 18 March 1928, and in an announcement in *Radio-Wien*, three orchestrated songs were listed: "Liebesode," "Im Zimmer," and "Die Nachtigall." In a letter to Schoenberg of 30 March 1928, Berg mentions that Klenau had performed five of his orchestrated songs with the Vienna Symphony Orchestra, so Berg must have increased the number from three to five at the last moment. The singer on that occasion was Wanda Achsel-Clemens, whose enthusiasm for the songs prodded Berg to have them published.

For this purpose, Berg orchestrated two additional songs, bringing the total to seven, this number having some special meaning for him. Rudolf Stephan has suggested that the number seven for his collection was awakened by the 1926 publication of Mahler's *Sieben Lieder aus letzter Zeit* (Seven recent songs), a collection of songs that is closely related to those of Berg also in orchestrational style.[33] Judging from notes and lists that he entered in several manuscripts, Berg had differing ideas about which songs to orchestrate and what order to put them in.[34] All that he considered came from the collection of ten made for Helene in 1917, and Berg's lists also show a consciousness of the succession of keys and alternating slow and moderate tempos. Berg also apparently wanted to intersperse harmonically experimental songs with more traditional ones. The content of the poetry must also have been in his mind, since he later stressed that the songs formed a dramatic cycle.[35]

Berg finally settled on these seven songs to revise, orchestrate, and publish:

1. Nacht, *Sehr langsam*, A major
2. Schilflied, *Mässig bewegt,* F minor
3. Die Nachtigall, *Zart bewegt*, D major
4. Traumgekrönt, *Langsam*, G minor
5. Im Zimmer, *Leicht bewegt*, B♭ major
6. Liebesode, *Sehr langsam*, F♯ minor
7. Sommertage, *Schwungvoll*, C minor

Berg always included the parenthetical "1907" in the title of the publication, although the songs were composed between 1905 and 1908. The date may have been another of Berg's symbolic uses of numbers and dates, agreeing with the number of songs that he chose to include and the year that he first met Helene. Berg dedicated the collection to Helene when it was published in 1928, possibly to reassure her in light of his dalliance with Hanna Fuchs.

The texts of the *Seven Early Songs (1907)* outline a narrative of blissful love, experienced as in a dream. The musical cycle begins with "Nacht" (Example 2.3). The song's opening is striking, a depiction of a magical world lit by moonlight whose mysterious aura is translated at first solely by whole-tone chords and lines. Later these glide into more familiar, extended triadic progressions, then back into whole-tone regions. Berg,

Example 2.3 "Nacht," mm. 1–5

like virtually all progressive composers at the turn of the twentieth century, explored the whole-tone scale as a resource with which to expand diatonic harmony and to add a new expressive color to music.
Debussy was then best known for such explorations, and Berg (far more
than Schoenberg) was very familiar with his music even at this early period. German progressive composers of the day—Schoenberg, Strauss,
Reger, and Pfitzner among others—were not far behind their French
contemporaries. Berg had already experimented with whole-tone
passages in earlier songs like "Traurigkeit," but they are far more pervasive in "Nacht."

A model for Berg's song "Nacht" may have been Hans Pfitzner's song,
"An den Mond," Op. 18, published in 1906, just at the time that Berg
began to experiment with whole-tone harmony. Berg at this time closely

studied Pfitzner's music and was susceptible to its new ideas. Later, in a 1920 polemic, he found Pfitzner's ideas and music worthy only of derision, but this was not his viewpoint in 1907. In summer of that year he wrote to Helene Nahowski placing Pfitzner explicitly among the greatest figures in music and literature—Altenberg, Wedekind, Strauss, and Ibsen—all of whom had the capacity to "create such divinely ideal thoughts."[36] In "An den Mond" Pfitzner, like Berg later, associates the color of whole-tone harmonies with the image of moonlight: the opening notes of his song (Example 2.4), again like Berg's, come entirely from a single whole-tone scale. In m. 7 Pfitzner's augmented chords are gently transformed into triads, E minor then E♭ as whole-tone lines continue to circle above. At the conclusion of the lengthy song, the music settles on an E-minor triad, which dimly suggests a tonic chord.

In many other ways Berg's "Nacht" occupies the frontiers of tonality. Berg restricts harmonic progressions in the key of A (ostensibly the tonic) to the middle of the song, leaving the beginning and end remote from

Example 2.4   Hans Pfitzner, "An den Mond," mm. 1–8

the home key. All of the tonic A-major chords are decorated by the tone
F♯ and all dominant chords are altered to become augmented triads. The
song contains a pervasive thematic development reminiscent of earlier
songs such as "Das stille Königreich," as at the reprise in mm. 27–28
where the theme returns simultaneously in the piano and (inverted) in
the voice.

"Schilflied," the second song of the cycle, returns to a more familiar
late-romantic ambience, with wisps of whole-tone harmony still present. The 6/8 rhythm gives the work a pastoral flavor, which agrees with
Lenau's text. "Die Nachtigall," the third song, is the simplest and most
traditional of all. It is followed by the highly complex "Traumgekrönt,"
which is the centerpiece of the cycle, a position that for Berg always
signaled special importance. The text by Rilke spoke to Berg's intense
infatuation with Helene Nahowski and his interest in poetic expression involving dreams. On her name day, 18 August 1907, Berg wrote
to Helene and quoted the entire poem, the setting of which he had just
completed "with a beating heart."[37]

Example 2.5 "Traumgekrönt," mm. 1–6

Example 2.6 "Liebesode," mm. 1–4

"Traumgekrönt" contains all of the distinctive traits seen in Berg's most advanced songs of 1907–08. As seen in the opening of the song in Example 2.5, it makes ample use of whole-tone passages that delay the appearance of triadic harmony; it begins far from the tonic G minor and major, which is firmly established only at the very end; it is intensely unified by recurrences of the small motive F♭–E♭–B♭–A heard at the beginning; and its main theme (voice in mm. 1–3) recurs with contrapuntal complexity, as in a canon at the reprise in mm. 15–18. Berg's harmonic experiments in the song are held in place by its traditional strophic form.

"Im Zimmer" arrives as the fifth song and with it comes a return to the relative simplicity of "Die Nachtigall." In the final two songs of the cycle, "Liebesode" and "Sommertage," Berg shifts again to his experimental mode. "Liebesode" begins with a four-measure motto-like phrase over a whole-tone chord and ends with a full cadential progression in the home key of F♯ minor (Example 2.6). Berg used a similar motto-like gesture to open his Piano Sonata, Op. 1. The opening phrase of "Liebesode" also announces a motive in the right hand, G♯–E–E♯, that reappears in an endless variety of shapes in each measure of the song, and the work is developmental from beginning to end. "Sommertage" is similar to "Liebesode." Berg largely ignores the strophic structure of the poem and replaces it with a continual development of a small initial motive.

For the 1928 publication of the *Sieben frühe Lieder (1907)*, Berg made numerous refinements to the early songs. He added metronome markings, rewrote some melodic and accompanimental passages, and added many nuances for the performers. The orchestrations that he created in 1928 show Berg's great originality and skill in the expressive handling of the orchestra. He calls on a small orchestra—woodwinds in twos and threes, four horns, one trumpet and two trombones, celesta and harp, percussion, and strings. The full orchestra is used only in the first and last songs. In the other five, the instrumentation changes, in each case geared to a specific sound that Berg wanted for these texts. "Die Nachtigall" uses strings alone, divisi in nine parts; "Im Zimmer" dispenses with the strings altogether. Berg's orchestration for the songs has much in common with that of Mahler's *Sieben Lieder aus letzter Zeit*, a collection containing the five Rückert songs plus two earlier *Wunderhorn* songs. It was republished by Universal Edition in 1926, shortly before Berg began to orchestrate his early songs. Mahler also uses a small orchestra whose instrumental makeup changes in each song. Berg, like Mahler, completely avoids the German romantic style of orchestration that he had earlier used, with its blended sound achieved by doubling important lines across different choirs of the orchestra. Here Berg is closer to the understated and nuanced French style of orchestration of the late nineteenth century, with virtually no exact doublings, unexpected combinations of instruments, delicate percussion effects, and generally soft dynamics. To expand the sonority of his orchestra Berg relies on extended playing techniques—different types of pizzicati, flutter tonguing (especially in the flutes), and prolonged muted effects in the brass. Although Berg also published the *Seven Early Songs (1907)* with piano accompaniment in 1928, most listeners will find the orchestrations to be the definitive versions, among the greatest orchestral songs in the late romantic style.

The premiere performance of the *Seven Early Songs (1907)* was given by the orchestra of the Gesellschaft der Musikfreunde on 6 November 1928, conducted by Robert Heger with the soprano Claire Born. The songs were well received by critics, although some wondered if they signaled Berg's uncertainty about his contemporaneous embrace of atonality. For Julius Korngold the songs were a symptom of just such nostalgia among modernist composers of the 1920s. In the *Neue freie Presse* Korngold wrote:

> Berg has our sympathy, even the Berg of 1928, on account of an artistic personality that is ever serious, full of character, and free from all speculative posturing. All the more sympathetic when he does not disavow the Berg of 1907. Perhaps we see in this reaching back a symptom of the unmistakably broad regrouping within the atonal-linear-New Objectivity-constructivist world of thought.[38]

Theodor Adorno wrote repeatedly about the *Seven Early Songs (1907)* and insisted that they could not be seen as a "back to . . . " retrospective, but were instead a subtle reminiscence of voices from the past:

> Expressive music, yes, but whose voice speaks? Certainly not the self-glorifying, violently erotic voice of Wagner, although the urge toward night in these songs plainly comes from him; nor the private voice, a world unto itself, of Brahms and Schumann; nor the voice of grieving nuance that clearly evokes Debussy. It is instead the voice of an adolescent who knows all this, learned it from his parents from childhood on, burdened himself with it in his own speech. It is not only genetic but intentional. What part of the man he would later become that is communicated in these songs is less important than how he disguises himself with the accents of his forebears—uncertain, inquisitive, like a soft tuning fork stealing in behind them and echoing their sounds. The dominant affect of Berg's early songs is *shyness*, and just as it does in poetry that barricades itself behind its outward form, such adolescent shyness reveals the romantic foreground far more readily than through any stylistic, historical ancestry. Schumann and Wagner are cited here like a sixteen-year-old who shies away from giving the name of his beloved, concealing it in the great names of history, in Heloise, Ophelia, or Botticelli's *Primavera* allegory.[39]

Four Songs, Op. 2

Berg's final group of piano lieder consists of four works composed, according to Berg, in 1908 and 1909, although some were probably completed in the early months of 1910. These were the first songs that Berg chose to have published, in July 1910 at his own expense, and his first group of songs constructed as a unified cycle in both text and music. Like Opp. 1 and 3, the Four Songs were graduation pieces, a culmination of his six years of study with Schoenberg and decade-long cultivation of the genre of song. In style they sit astride Berg's transition from tonality to atonality, and they represent a clearer statement than ever before of his personal idiom, although their originality builds upon the harmonic and formal thinking evident in earlier works such as "Nacht" and "Traumgekrönt." They form a confident profession of allegiance to the musical evolution proclaimed by Schoenberg, for whom atonality— understood as a removal of the structural distinction between consonant and dissonant harmony and a supplanting of diatonic pitch resources by the full chromatic—was an inevitable step leading beyond the late romantic language of composers like Pfitzner, Reger, or Strauss.

The suffering Tristanesque mood that hung over Berg's courtship of Helene Nahowski and found expression in many of his songs of 1907 and 1908 reaches a climax in the Four Songs. The texts create a narrative cycle reminiscent of Tristan's dream in Act 3, but with a distinctly personal meaning for Berg and his future wife. In the first song, set to Friedrich Hebbel's "Schlafen, schlafen, nichts als schlafen," the speaker welcomes the arrival of sleep, akin to death, as a refuge from life.

Schlafen, schlafen, nichts als schlafen!	Sleep, sleep, only to sleep.
Kein Erwachen, keinen Traum!	No awakening, not a dream!
Jener Wehen, die mich trafen,	Those woes that assailed me—
Leisestes Erinnern kaum,	hardly the slightest recollection.
Daß ich, wenn des Lebens Fülle	So when life's bustle
Nieder klingt in meine Ruh',	comes down to stir my rest,
Nur noch tiefer mich verhülle,	I'll cloak myself more firmly
Fester zu die Augen tu!	and close my eyes the tighter!

While the poetry of Hebbel was often used by lieder composers of the nineteenth century, the remaining three songs, on poetry from Alfred Mombert's *Der Glühende* (Aglow), were a daring choice. The eighty-seven verses in the 1902 edition of *Der Glühende*—the source used by Berg—are all first-person prose poems that explore the inner world of the speaker, with a dreamlike irrationality that borders on surrealism. No coherent narrative runs through the poems, although references to death, nature, loneliness, love, and dreaming recur prominently.

In songs two and three—"Schlafend trägt man" and "Nun ich der Riesen Stärksten überwand"—the speaker overcomes obstacles to reach a homeland, guided by a magical white hand.

Schlafend trägt man mich	I am carried in sleep
In mein Heimatland.	to my homeland.
Ferne komm' ich her,	I come from afar,
über Gipfel, über Schlünde,	over peaks and valleys,
über ein dunkles Meer	over a dark sea,
In mein Heimatland.	to my homeland.
Nun ich der Riesen Stärksten überwand,	Now I overcame the strongest giants,
mich aus dem dunkelsten Land heimfand	and from the most distant land found my way home,

an einer weißen Märchenhand—	led by a magical white hand—
Hallen schwer die Glocken.	The bells toll heavily
Und ich wanke durch die Straßen	and I stumble through the streets
schlafbefangen.	overcome by sleep.

In the fourth song, "Warm die Lüfte," the treachery of day returns as the speaker glimpses a forlorn lover in emotional distress.

Warm die Lüfte,	The air is warm,
es sprießt Gras auf sonnigen Wiesen.	the grass sprouts on sunny meadows.
Horch! —	Listen! —
Horch, es flötet die Nachtigall.	Listen, the nightingale warbles.
Ich will singen:	I will sing:
Droben hoch im düstern Bergforst,	High above in the dusky mountain forest
es schmilzt und glitzert kalter Schnee,	the cold snows melts and glitters.
ein Mädchen in grauem Kleide	A girl in gray attire
lehnt an feuchtem Eichstamm,	leans on a damp oak—
krank sind ihre zarten Wangen,	her tender cheeks are pale,
die grauen Augen fiebern	her gray eyes glare
durch Düsterriesenstämme.	through the dark, giant tree trunks:
"Er kommt noch nicht. Er läßt mich warten" . . .	"He is not coming. He abandons me" . . .
Stirb!	Die!
Der Eine stirbt, daneben der Andre lebt:	One dies while the one beside lives on:
Das macht die Welt so tiefschön.	That makes the world so deeply beautiful!

Berg's choice of this text may well be an oblique reference to Helene and her unhappy love affair with Paul Kammerer, which remained in 1909 and 1910 as a major theme in Berg's letters to his future wife. This reading is reinforced by the following poem in *Der Glühende*—not included in Berg's cycle but certainly known to Helene—where the girl's anxiety has been alleviated by the passing of time: "Now look: the snow is past, your suffering is off and away." The Four Songs were dedicated to Helene in their first printing in 1910. Mombert's final thought in "Warm die Lüfte"—"Die! One person dies while the one beside lives on. That makes the world so deeply beautiful"—is not closely related to Berg's narrative and can be read in different ways. Mombert may have intended it in a Schopenhauerian sense, suggesting the futility of individual life and the beauty of the collective and enduring species.

The texts of Berg's Four Songs refer repeatedly to sleep and dreams, underscoring the composer's lifelong interest in these topics. The meaning of dreams is explored in literature that Berg admired, and it plays a large role in most of Wagner's operas, including *Tristan*. Berg had studied the theory of dreams proposed by Sigmund Freud—with whom Berg and his family were personally acquainted—in Freud's *Interpretation of Dreams* (1899). Berg comments on aspects of Freud's dream theory in a letter to Schoenberg dated 21 August 1911, and, in an undated note probably from about the same time, he tries his own hand at a psychoanalytic interpretation of a dream in which he ascends a narrow, stone-lined stairway, finding in the dream a reference to sexual relations with his wife and to her brother's homosexuality.[40]

Berg apparently did not begin to compose the four songs with the idea of the unified cycle that he ultimately created. The third song, "Nun ich der Riesen Stärksten überwand" was composed first, in the summer or fall of 1908. The creation of a cycle began later, when Berg added "Schlafend trägt man" to create a closely related song pair. The two poems are adjacent in Mombert's poetic collection. Later still he expanded the pair into a four-song cycle by adding "Schlafen, schlafen" and, last of all, "Warm die Lüfte."

The narrative of the poetry is reinforced by distinctive musical materials that are shared by all four songs. Despite this cyclicism, Berg had no objection to having the songs published or performed separately. He had "Warm die Lüfte" published by itself in 1912 in Vasili Kandinsky's almanac *Der blaue Reiter*, and he proposed having the pair "Nun ich der Riesen Stärksten überwand"—"Schlafend trägt man" appear in a 1914 song anthology of Universal Edition, a project that never came to fruition.

"Nun ich der Riesen Stärksten überwand," the first song composed, is close in style to the progressive idiom of songs from summer 1908, such as "Sommertage" and "Das stille Königreich." The song introduces a syncopated rhythmic motive in mm. 3–4 (right hand) that Berg brings back in each of the four songs (Example 2.7). Rhythmic motives became trademark features of almost all of Berg's later works, such figures

Example 2.7 "Nun ich der Riesen Stärksten überwand," mm. 3–4 (right hand)

Example 2.8 "Schlafend trägt man mich," mm. 1–4 (Piano only)

usually asymmetric as here. Although triads play a role in the work's sonority—the song begins by outlining an A♭-minor chord and ends on an E♭ harmony—there is no strong sense of key. It is not surprising that in Berg's earliest sketches for the song, no key signature is present, and the later addition of a signature of seven flats is so irrelevant to the music that it probably had a symbolic rather than musical meaning.[41]

"Schlafend trägt man" was the second song composed and paired with "Nun ich" to form the core of the larger cycle. In the opening measures of the song Berg again experiments with chords and their progressions that arise by coherent intervallic patterns rather than by rules from tonal harmony. The bass line in the first four measures moves through seven tones by ascending fourths or descending fifths, from B♭ to E, with each tone supporting a whole-tone chord with the same intervals equivalent to that of a French sixth chord (see Example 2.8). Motives from the opening are developed throughout the song and at the end the whole-tone chords over ascending fourths from the opening return in diminution. The song ends on a whole-tone French sixth chord with E♭ in the bass. This mimics an E♭7 chord that "resolves" to the A♭-minor harmony that begins the next song and links the two together. As in "Nun ich," Berg chooses a key signature—six flats—that is largely irrelevant to the music, especially so since he attaches an accidental to virtually every note.

Probably in 1909 Berg expanded upon his song pair with a third song, "Schlafen, schlafen," that functions as an introduction to the cycle that Berg by then had in mind. Superficially at least, this song has the appearance of a late-romantic lied in D minor, as though Berg wanted to ease his listeners gradually into a harmonic environment in which tonality would gradually evaporate. D-minor chords are heard at the beginning and end, and some other chords in the key of D minor are briefly touched on. As in the reprise of "Das stille Königreich," figures from the opening return freely reversed in order.

Toward the beginning of the song, Berg fleetingly introduces another formal pattern that he would take up more extensively in the final song. This occurs most clearly in the two chords that straddle the barline between mm. 8–9 (see Example 2.9). The bass moves by descending fifth and all upper voices descend chromatically. The two chords that result are the two forms of what Elliott Carter later termed "all-interval" tetrachords, that is, four-note chords in which tones can be paired off to form each interval class.[42] The all-interval tetrachords are often encountered in Berg's early atonal music, also in that of Schoenberg and Webern.

"Warm die Lüfte" concludes the cycle, and here Berg completes the movement from tonality to atonality. No vestiges of tonality remain in the final song, no key signature, no triads at the opening or closing, no functional harmonic progressions nor priority accorded to any diatonic scale. In place of these traditional principles of organization, Berg relies all the more on those ad hoc patterns with which he had experimented in earlier songs and which now contribute to a distinctive and personal musical style. Whole-tone passages continue to attract attention, as in the

Example 2.9 "Schlafen, schlafen, nichts als schlafen!" mm. 8–9 (Piano only)

Example 2.10   "Warm die Lüfte," mm. 20–22 (Piano only)

piano's dramatic *martellato* in m. 17, and high points of the song coincide with the recurrence of the basic rhythmic motive, as in the bird-song figure in mm. 4–6. A contrapuntal figure resembling a wedge, often seen in Berg's music, is found in mm. 20–22 (Example 2.10). Here the pattern that created all-interval tetrachords in "Schlafen, schlafen" is stretched out to three measures. The outer voices move in contrary motion, each progressing by a single interval type: ascending fourths in the bass and descending semitones in the soprano. (Virtually the identical figure was later used by Debussy in the fourth of his *Six épigraphes antiques*, mm. 29–32.)[43] Another wedge pattern appears at the song's climax in m. 15, as the pianist sweeps the hands apart by glissandi on the white and black keys, creating a figure that contains all twelve tones.

"Warm die Lüfte" is often cited as Berg's first fully atonal composition, although manuscript evidence suggests that it was composed just after the first movement of the String Quartet, Op. 3. These two works mark the beginning of Berg's lifelong commitment to the atonal harmonic style and its implicit "liberation" of dissonance. On a copy of the printed score of the songs given to Alma Mahler (Figure 2.1), Berg extolled dissonant harmony as a path to higher meaning:

> Dissonances? . . . Why not these restraints too, since they give music and love, friendship and nature their true worth, and really everything that has any life—even sensuality itself—is pointless, if lacking these painfully dear restraints.

Certainly this transformation in Berg's musical language around 1908–09 reflects his study of and admiration for Schoenberg's music and Schoenberg's ideas about musical evolution. But we cannot assume that Berg in any sense copied Schoenberg's approach to atonality. The

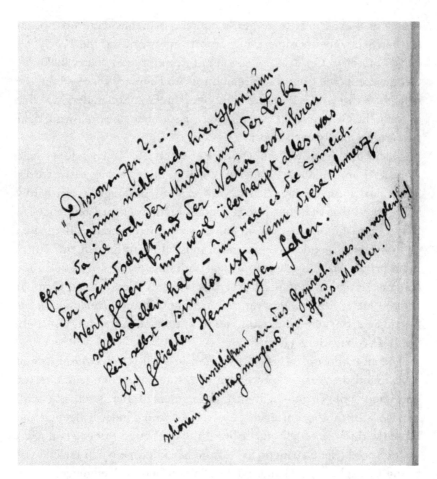

Figure 2.1 Berg's note on dissonance. Courtesy of the Bavarian State Library, Mus.
ms. 17487

earliest atonal songs by the two composers were created at about the
same time, and they are distinct in style and compositional approach. In
his early atonal music Berg relied more than Schoenberg on structures
and methods, including wedges, symmetries, chords with special intervallic content, and lines moving by fixed intervallic patterns. Schoenberg
relied more on instinct and intuition as a guide. In his 1911 *Harmonielehre*
Schoenberg praised the power of the unconscious mind in the creation of music. "The artist's creative activity is instinctive. Consciousness
has little influence on it. . . . He is merely the instrument of a will
hidden from him, of instinct, of his unconscious."[44] Furthermore, Berg's

early atonal experiments are nearly contemporaneous with those of his teacher. Schoenberg's earliest fully atonal large work was the *Book of the Hanging Gardens*, Op. 15, a collection of fifteen songs to poetry by Stefan George composed from about March 1908 to February 1909—about the same time, that is, that Berg was composing his Four Songs. Berg was able to study the George songs carefully only in summer 1914, following their publication in July of that year.[45]

Much has been written about Berg's efforts to encode Helene Nahowski in the Op. 2 songs as well as in his other early works. Such ideas must be approached with caution, although it can hardly be doubted that the Four Songs contain highly personal references to Berg's courtship. Even early in his musical apprenticeship, Berg used pitch letters as a code to represent in musical terms himself and others in his private life. His correspondence with Helene from 1907 and 1908 contains several such musical excerpts. He ends a letter of 30 October 1908 to Helene by quoting the "Desire" motive from *Tristan und Isolde* (Example 2.11), which he transposes so as to contain the notes A–B♭–B♮ (*A–B–H*, Alban-Berg-Helene).

Theodor Adorno, in his contribution to Willi Reich's *Alban Berg* of 1937, found the A–B♭–B♮ succession in "Nun ich der Riesen Stärksten überwand" (m. 5) and held that it represented Berg's alliance with Helene.[46] But the occurrence to which Adorno alludes is fleeting and buried within a larger chromatic line. In all likelihood, Adorno contrived the idea for Helene's benefit, to reassure her at a time when Helene was trying to explain the Hanna Fuchs affair to herself. References to the key of D minor—made by inserting D-minor triads in songs one and three—are equally suspect as to their relevance to Helene. In his letters of 1907 and 1908 to her, Berg repeatedly associates her with this key. She is his "most splendid D minor symphony," he exclaims in an early letter. "The most splendid D minor chords of your beautiful soul rang out in all magnificence," he says in a letter of 16 July 1909.[47] But the key of D

Example 2.11   Wagner, *Tristan und Isolde*, "Desire" motive

minor does not appear in any of the songs of 1907 and 1908 preceding
the Four Songs, Op. 2, including those whose texts most clearly suggest contact with Helene. The key has far stronger associations with
Schoenberg and others in his circle of composers—especially Zemlinsky
and Webern—all of whom used it repeatedly in their late tonal music
and continued to allude to it in their early atonal works. Although Berg
probably wanted Helene to find herself in the songs, his references to
the key may have arisen from a far deeper emotional involvement—
with Arnold Schoenberg—the object of Berg's "holy and inconceivable
love," as he described it to Webern.[48] If pitch letters are actually symbolic
references in the Four Songs, they point to Schoenberg more than to
Helene. The ostinato A–E♭ pair (*A–Es* in German, A̲rnold S̲choenberg)
in "Warm die Lüfte" (mm. 6–8), the musically irrelevant key signatures
in "Nun ich" (suggesting A♭ minor, or *As*) and "Schlafend trägt man"
(suggesting E♭ minor, *Es*) may well be Berg's allusions to Schoenberg.
Berg had made a similar juxtaposition of the notes A and E♭ in his
early song "Er klagt," which begins squarely in A major and ends in
E♭ major.[49] The song was composed shortly after Berg began to study
with Schoenberg. At the climax of "Warm die Lüfte" in mm. 18–19,
the singer declaims the non-pitched word "Die!," which Berg notates
A against the piano's B♭ (*A—B* in German), thus reinforcing the notion
that he is the speaker at this impassioned moment. Berg's correspondence from 1910 and 1911 shows that Helene was a prize that had then
been won; Berg was freed to focus on Schoenberg—a far more complex
and powerful force within his psyche. The use of codes and the duality
of symbolism in the Four Songs—a surface level that exists simultaneously with a deeper and more private, inward dimension—would in the
future characterize Berg's music.

Music for Piano

At about the same time that Berg was writing his last songs he was
also composing for piano, guided by Schoenberg's ever more challenging
curriculum. After a few early piano pieces originating around 1899 or
1900, Berg did not again compose for the instrument until 1905, then in
the context of study pieces under Schoenberg's tutelage. As part of his instruction in counterpoint, Berg wrote polyphonic inventions and fugues
for piano.[50] He then used the piano to gain experience with longer

forms associated with classical instrumental music, beginning with short themes and pieces that have the character of minuets, scherzi, waltzes, and adagios. In 1907 and 1908 he moved on to the still more complex challenge of theme-and-variations form, composing several such works for piano, string quartet, and other chamber groups.

Berg's principal accomplishment in his study of theme-and-variations form is his *Twelve Variations on an Original Theme* in C major for piano, completed in 1908 and performed in Vienna on 4 November 1908 in a concert of works by Schoenberg's students. Even among Berg specialists the *Twelve Variations* is little known. There is still no performing edition of the work, no commercial recording, and scant discussion in the technical literature. Some writers have seen it as a mere student's assignment, unworthy of attention. For George Perle it is "puerile" and "an utterly derivative academic exercise by a diligent but inexperienced student who has not yet learned how either to correct or to avoid some elementary crudities in harmony, rhythm and instrumental writing."[51]

A close study of the piece does not support Perle's assessment.[52] The *Twelve Variations* is the work of a remarkably gifted and advanced student composer who has a broad knowledge of the classic variations literature. Although it is not primarily a work of self-expression or originality, it is an ingenious copy of an existing style and filled with invention, with touches of whole-tone harmony and contrapuntal wedges that hint at Berg's emerging musical identity. It contains no "elementary crudities" in harmony, rhythm, and pianism. In a review in the *Neues Wiener Journal* following the 4 November concert, Elsa Bienenfeld made a more perceptive assessment: "Berg's Variations, fine and rich in melodic invention, splendid in pianism, point to a strong compositional talent."[53] Still, Berg himself must have recognized that the *Twelve Variations* lacked a personal voice. He never distributed the work nor had it played after 1908, and it was first published in Hans Redlich's 1957 study of the composer, using a manuscript loaned to Redlich by Berg's widow.[54]

In Schoenberg's teaching, the classical theme-and-variations was the penultimate lesson in the study of composing in classical forms, just short of the highest challenge of sonata form.[55] For the student, the first necessity was to obtain a usable theme, which could be drawn from a popular melody, from the works of another composer, or made up by the student anew. In Berg's existing study materials there are sixteen original themes, some with variations attached, some not. The most important feature of a usable theme was simplicity, Schoenberg said, in the persistence of a few motives and in basic slow-moving harmonies, regular phrasing, and uncluttered texture.

Berg's theme for the *Twelve Variations* (Example 2.12) has just this degree of simplicity: it is unified by recurrences of basic motives and it is laid out in two eight-measure phrases that together create a classic thematic pattern that Schoenberg called a *Satz*, "sentence." The harmonies move slowly through basic chords in the key of C, and the rhythms and texture are uncomplicated although pregnant with developmental possibilities that Berg explores in the variations that follow.

In these variations Berg again closely adheres to Schoenberg's ideas about classical form. According to Schoenberg, the variations should differ in character, tempo, meter, mode, and occasionally key. Berg's variations are largely the same in overall form and key but strongly differentiated in character. Variation 5 is in C minor, and Variation 9 moves to F major although here, as in related passages in variations by Beethoven and Brahms, Berg cleverly brings in fragments of his theme untransposed. Strict counterpoint is appropriate in the variations, says Schoenberg, and Berg's Variations 3 and 6 are canons while invertible counterpoint is a feature of Variations 5 and 9.

Example 2.12   *Twelve Variations on an Original Theme*, **theme**

Example 2.13   *Twelve Variations*, syncopation in theme, mm. 9–13

Berg makes the theme recognizable by a resourceful exploration of its constituent motives, which are shuffled about in ever changing configurations. Two basic motives—the descending line E–D–C in m. 1 and the chain of fourths C–G–A–E in m. 15 (bracketed in Example 2.12)—return in every variation, often in disguise and differently positioned. More subtle are Berg's variations upon rhythms and meters found in the theme. One example occurs in mm. 9–13, where the two lines in the right hand are separated in meter by an eighth-note value, creating a syncopation that is shown schematically in Example 2.13. The syncopation is reconceived in several of the variations that follow. In Variation 11, for example, it returns in m. 17 with different values and a different configuration of motives. As the left hand descends chromatically, the right hand takes on a variant of the chain of fourths, creating a typical Bergian wedge in which each voice moves in contrary motion through a single interval type. The passage is shown schematically in Example 2.14.

Schoenberg also stressed the importance in each variation of the presence of a "motive of the variation." This is a short figure, derived from some underlying feature of the theme, which is brought to the surface and developed, lending that variation an additional measure of unity with the work as a whole. An example of Berg's adaptation of this principle is seen in Variation 7, in the sweeping septuplet figures that recur throughout (Example 2.15). The origin of the figure is in the second half of the theme, right hand, in the slow stepwise motion spanning an octave, C to C.

Berg's *Twelve Variations* ends with a virtuosic twelfth variation, marked "Finale." Like the Finale of Brahms's *Haydn Variations* this one follows upon the preceding eleventh variation without pause and dispenses with the form of the theme. Berg's Finale is a climactic fantasia on earlier motives: the two basic motives intertwine in ever more complex ways,

Example 2.14   *Twelve Variations,* syncopation in Variation 11, m. 17

Example 2.15   *Twelve Variations,* from Variation 7

and sequence—introduced in mm. 9–14 of the theme—leads the development far afield harmonically. A climactic reprise of the opening measures arrives majestically at m. 52, intensified by whole-tone motions that had been hinted at in the theme. A coda from m. 63 gives the chain-of-fourths motive an emphatic last word.

Piano Sonata, Op. 1

Following the performance of his *Twelve Variations* in November 1908, Berg focused his attention on sonata form, the highest and most challenging classical formal archetype in Schoenberg's teaching, with which Berg had tentatively experimented in earlier fragmentary works.[56] In the early twentieth century, the genre of the piano sonata itself had taken on an association as a student exercise more than an avenue for original composition. Although one-movement piano "sonatas" continued to attract the attention of Russian modernists such as Scriabin, most of the leading progressive composers of the day—including Stravinsky, Prokofiev, and those in German lands—wrote traditional piano sonatas primarily as student projects.

During this phase of his training Berg was still closely under Schoenberg's supervision, and his first assignment was to draft isolated passages within traditional sonata form—main theme groups, transitions, and developments—without attempting to connect these into a complete movement. He referred to these fragmentary exercises as Sonatas I–V.[57] Nos. I and II were left as brief sketches of themes. Nos. III–IV are longer although still incomplete, and Sonata V, the most extended of the fragments, was completed up to the recapitulation. After Sonata V Berg was ready to move on to a complete sonata-form movement, and he kept Sonatas I–V on hand as sources for several later compositions.

The Piano Sonata, Op. 1, was Berg's sixth in his series of sonata-form exercises. Although he always gave the date 1908 for its creation, it is far more likely that it was composed in the spring and summer of 1909, at the same time that he was also working on the songs of Op. 2 and the String Quartet, Op. 3.[58] The Piano Sonata was published in July 1910, at the same time as the Four Songs, Op. 2, both at Berg's own expense. Following their publication Berg wrote to Webern to complain about the "vexation and effort" that it cost him to bring the two pieces into a publishable form.[59] Neither this nor any of the fragmentary sonatas extends beyond a single movement. Berg's student Joseph Polnauer recalled Berg saying that he had planned to add a slow movement and finale to the one-movement Piano Sonata but, when no additional ideas came to him, Schoenberg advised him to consider the work complete as it was.[60] There is no confirmation of this anecdote in writings by Berg or Schoenberg, and the one-movement form ties it all the more closely to its origin as a study piece.

In the Piano Sonata Berg is much freer from classical models and from Schoenberg's traditional formulations than he was in the *Twelve Variations*. While adhering superficially to Schoenberg's ideas about sonata form and to its traditional parts, the Sonata reveals Berg's adoption of a distinctive approach to the form in which contrasting key and thematic areas and triadic harmony are diminished in importance and continual thematic and motivic variation increased. As in the other culminating student works—Four Songs, Op. 2, and String Quartet, Op. 3—in his Sonata Berg forges his own harmonic language in which chords in the key of B minor, ostensibly the tonic key, are far outnumbered and outweighed by chords that are not part of normative tonal harmony, including fourth chords and harmonies derived from whole-tone scales. The dissonant first chord of the piece—C♯–G–B–F♯ —has special importance, as Berg brings it back in different configurations at important moments throughout the movement, using it as an element of harmonic reference. Berg uses the same four-note chord to end the first movement of his String Quartet, Op. 3, and in various configurations the chord is prominent in his later music, including *Wozzeck* and *Lulu*.

Berg's independent harmonic thinking is joined to an expansion of the classical formal model. The traditional sonata-form movement consists of stable passages that alternate and contrast with others that are unstable. The stable areas, such as those in which the main and subordinate themes are introduced, usually maintain a single key, lay out themes in strict form, and reach a definite cadence at their end. The unstable passages modulate in key, present thematic ideas in free form, and function as elaborations or connectives. Berg's sonata forms differ from this traditional profile in that they are far more unstable and developmental from beginning to end, with few clear-cut contrasts among themes, few sustained tonal regions and few clear points of demarcation within the form. The main parts of the form are separated mainly by changes in tempo, sometimes by fleeting references to harmonies in the primary or related keys, and by a phenomenon that Schoenberg termed "liquidation." This occurs in passages at the end of structural units in which motives are reduced to minimum content, losing their distinctive features. An example from Op. 1 is at the end of the exposition, mm. 54–55 (Example 2.16). Here the bass and middle voices drift downward chromatically while the top line repeats a simple three-note figure in sequence. The motives make no further demand for development, which signals the approach of a new section.

Prior to a performance of the Piano Sonata by Eduard Erdmann at the Donaueschingen Festival in 1921, Berg wrote a rudimentary analysis of the form of the work.[61] Here he notes that its melodic dimension

Example 2.16 Piano Sonata, Op. 1, liquidation of motives, mm. 54–55

Example 2.17 Piano Sonata, Op. 1, mm. 1–4

is influenced by whole-tone and quartal harmonies and that the piece
has the familiar three parts of a sonata form: exposition, development
(*Durchführung*), and reprise. The exposition has four parts, Berg says: a
main group of themes (*Hauptsatz*), subordinate theme (*Seitenthema*),
closing group (*Schlußsatz*), and coda—these four parts beginning at
mm. 1, 29, 38, and 49. Berg does not further divide the "main group,"
but his earlier fragmentary sonatas all show an A–B–A' pattern in this
region that is also evident in Op. 1, with each of the three parts marked
by a change of tempo. Part A (its opening phrase is shown in Example
2.17) states and works out the main thematic material; B (mm. 11–16)
introduces contrasting though subtly related figures, and A' (16–28)
stands in place of the familiar transition, here alluding developmentally
to motives from both A and B and leading to a new theme in a slower
tempo at m. 29.

Berg recognizes only a single "subordinate theme," in mm. 29–37,
possibly limiting it to these measures because they reveal a distant

relation to the relative major key of D, a relation absent from what follows.[62] The closing group works out a motive from mm. 38–39 and ends in m. 48 not in a contrasting key but over a dominant chord in the home key of B minor. This introduces the coda of the exposition (mm. 49–55), which prepares for the return to the opening by reiterating its dotted first motive. Berg's development and reprise follow the general order of events in a classical sonata form but with little other relevance to that model. The music of the development freely reshapes earlier motives with ever denser counterpoint and sequence, rising to a climax in m. 91, as the opening chord, transposed, resounds *ffff*, then dwindles away as the reprise approaches. The events of the exposition (except for the transition, which is removed) recur in the reprise, generally at their original level of pitch but otherwise transformed by continual development.

For years following its publication in July 1910 and premiere performance on 24 April 1911 in Vienna, the Piano Sonata had limited success among pianists and critics. There were few performances, and the work itself seemed to confuse audiences by its mixture of styles and oddity of form. After a performance by Erwin Schulhoff in Prague in 1919, one reviewer wrote:

> Alban Berg's Sonata is a work that comes more from intellectual than emotional necessity. It travels on the road of compromise: it has neither the lyricism or pathos of his teacher Schoenberg (*Pelleas*) nor the abstraction from life and pathologically hysterical condition that Schoenberg put forth, as in *Pierrot lunaire*.[63]

After about 1919, as Berg's reputation had begun to grow and the Sonata had been taken up by such leading performers as Edward Steuermann and Eduard Erdmann, the work began to attract more positive attention. Fritz Windisch reviewed a performance by Erdmann for the *Berlin Mittagszeitung* on 1 April 1919 in terms that prefigure the work's general acceptance in the 1920s and later:

> Berg travels on his own paths. His own ideas ferment and brew in his works, convulsively breaking through forms into which they were crammed. Brilliant ideas in the invention of new sounds and harmonies. The most potent seeds promise a fruitful maturity. . . .[64]

String Quartet, Op. 3

In Schoenberg's teaching, string chamber ensembles, along with piano, were the preferred media in which to develop a command of classical forms. In the theory phase of his studies (1905–07) Berg composed fugues and short pieces for string quartet and quintet, and in the early years of his study of composition he composed several theme-and-variations sets, as well as other character works, for strings. In 1908 or 1909, as his Four Songs, Op. 2, neared completion, Berg began a more ambitious project: a string quartet that would stand as the third and by far the most original graduation piece of his apprenticeship. Schoenberg exercised less oversight of the String Quartet than of the Piano Sonata or the preliminary Sonatas I–V, on whose drafts he wrote out extended alternate versions following what Berg had written. There are no such markings on drafts of the String Quartet, where Berg was largely on his own, freed from the need to adhere strictly to classical forms and free to follow his own instinct for musical originality.

Berg gave the date 1909–10 for composing the String Quartet, which agrees with the evidence in other sources. In a letter to Webern dated 30 May 1910, he says that the first movement was then complete and had been read through by a quartet, but the work was otherwise still unfinished.[65] By the summer of that year he had added a second movement, leaving the quartet with an unusual two-movement form, the first movement generally slow and introspective, the second alternating moments of strident aggressiveness and calm.[66] Both the String Quartet and Piano Sonata received their first public hearing on 24 April 1911 in Vienna, the quartet played by an ensemble led by the violinist Fritz Brunner. The work was first published in 1920 by the Robert Lienau-Carl Haslinger firm, again with Berg paying for the engraving. In 1921, possibly an outcome of the emphasis on piano arrangements in the concerts of the Society for Private Musical Performances, Berg made a four-hand arrangement of the String Quartet, which was published first in 2007. In 1925 a revised version was published by Universal Edition.

In the early twentieth century the string quartet genre flourished among composers of all nationalities and both progressive and conservative allegiances. Numerous professional quartets were in existence. In

Vienna the leading ensemble was the Quartett Rosé, founded by Arnold Rosé in 1882 and widely esteemed for a repertory of both classical and modern works. Other Viennese quartets led by Gottfried Feist, Fritz Brunner, and Hugo Gottesmann also took an interest in modern music. Although the genre itself had strongly classical associations, new quartets by Debussy, Bartók, Reger, Pfitzner, Zemlinsky, Webern, and Schoenberg were taking quartet writing into new areas of expressivity, harmony, and form.

Schoenberg's Second Quartet (1908) is the closest antecedent of Berg's Op. 3, although Schoenberg's work is generally more conservative than Berg's except for the presence of voice in its last two movements. Schoenberg's first movement displays a straightforward sonata design with fleeting references to the key of F♯ minor and with whole-tone passages and quartal harmony marking important junctures. In his Second Quartet Schoenberg preserves the order of thematic events associated with sonata form, with each section set off by a change of tempo and prepared by motivic liquidations. Berg followed this strategy in Op. 3. In his Second Quartet Schoenberg expands upon basic motives by a concentrated and continuous development, and he uses special playing techniques, such as bowing on the bridge and tremolo, to create contrasts. Berg again follows Schoenberg in his treatment of the string instruments, although he goes considerably further with such colorism than does Schoenberg. Schoenberg's Quartet is, like Berg's, cyclic in the return of themes from the first movement in later movements.

The first movement of Berg's String Quartet, composed only slightly after Schoenberg's Second Quartet, takes a far bolder step into the future of music by fully embracing atonality. Like the contemporaneous song "Warm die Lüfte," the Quartet has no vestiges of traditional tonality. Its harmony is pervasively dissonant, using chords outside of the vocabulary of tonal harmony; its pitch field is uniformly chromatic with no priority accorded to diatonic scales; there are no framing triads, no sporadic functional harmonic progressions, and no consistent assertion of a tonal center.[67]

Berg's embrace of the atonal style around 1910 was a daring move that would shape and define his whole future as a composer. Recall from the discussion in the Introduction that "atonality" at first referred to a harmonic practice broadly shared by progressive composers beginning in the first decade of the twentieth century. Berg quickly put the term atonal into his own vocabulary, and, for his own music, he associated it with other unorthodox ideas such as the abolition of traditional rhythm and meter. In a letter to the Dresden pianist Erwin Schulhoff of 19 June 1919, Berg wrote, "My later things, which of course I consider more mature and successful, are all atonal, and although they use bar lines—which I have kept in for *practical* reasons, for ensemble playing or works with conductor—they are fully freed from regular rhythm, that is, they are arhythmic."[68]

It would have been unthinkable for Berg not to have hastened toward atonal harmony in his own compositions. His unquestioning belief in Schoenberg's artistic authority was a primary reason; also, atonality represented a broad movement in which most progressive composers throughout the world were participating—Stravinsky and Scriabin in Russia, Bartók in Hungary, and Ives in New York—not to mention friends such as Webern closer to home. Still, the atonal style was a provocative harmonic innovation that increased the distance between composer and audience, composer and critic, composer and performer, even between composers themselves. Many of the progressive figures of the older generation, including Strauss, Debussy, and Mahler—all held in the highest esteem by Berg—were quietly unsympathetic or openly dismissive of the new style. After hearing Schoenberg's Chamber Symphony, Op. 9, in 1907, Mahler remarked: "I don't understand his music, but he's young and perhaps he's right. I am old and I dare say my ear is not sensitive enough."[69] The "old" Mahler was forty-six at the time.

The confusion over and impreciseness of the terms atonal and atonality only increased in the 1920s and 1930s as triadic harmony, diatonic pitch fields, and tonal centers returned to favor among leading modernist composers. The terms at this time became a handy cudgel for music critics—as well as politicians—to attack a variety of modernist directions in music, associating "atonal music" by whatever definition as a product of degeneracy, Bolshevism, and other assaults upon the spirit of the German folk. Many former allies of the Viennese modernists then dismissed atonality as something contrary to natural musical laws. In a 1935 lecture the conductor Bruno Walter—highly respected by those in Schoenberg's circle—dismissed music of the atonalists as an error: "In place of things that are natural, their music is artificial, something made by a manikin, an abstract speech in tone. This speech cannot be understood or believed in since its creators base it on something intellectual. What they create may be clever or bold, but it can never be felt musically."[70] In his 1937 *Unterweisung im Tonsatz* (*The Craft of Musical Composition* in its English version) Paul Hindemith rejected atonal, or non-triadic, music as a dead end. Hindemith writes:

> Music, as long as it exists, will always take its departure from the major triad and return to it. The musician cannot escape it any more than the painter his primary colors, or the architect his three dimensions. In composition, the triad or its direct extensions can never be avoided for more than a short time without completely confusing the listener.[71]

The controversy surrounding atonality was heightened in part by a tendency among its early critics to see it as a uniform style, when in fact it was almost always in flux and constantly reformulated by a composer's individual tastes. In his String Quartet Berg hewed to Schoenberg's interpretation, that composers in the new style needed to banish all vestiges of earlier harmony. In his *Harmonielehre*, written at the same time as Berg's String Quartet, Schoenberg spoke of his "aversion to recalling even remotely the traditional chords" in the new style. Compared to the new dissonant harmonies—vast in number, "full and sumptuous"—triads seemed "cold, dry, and expressionless."[72]

The music of the first movement of the String Quartet refers to a sonata-form design, but here it is even less applicable to the organization of the music than in the Piano Sonata. What remains of the traditional form is an exposition of main motivic and thematic material at the outset, contrasting or distantly related motives introduced somewhat later (m. 41), and a recognizable reprise of these themes toward the end (m. 105). No other clear markers of traditional sonata form remain—no repeated exposition, no contrasting key areas, no distinguishable transitions from one key area to another. The music is all essentially motivic development, stated with a continually changing expressive profile and surface design.

Berg left no analytic outline of the work, and Theodor Adorno's detailed analysis from 1937 has been adopted and refined by most later
writers.[73] In the first movement Adorno finds vestiges of the main parts
of sonata form—exposition (mm. 1–80), development (81–104), reprise (105–87)—although he concludes that the form itself has been
"liquidated" and largely replaced by a continual process of developing
variation in which all themes and motives grow from a few initial
shapes and rhythms. The first phrase of the exposition (Example 2.18)
shows Berg's new thinking. The movement opens not with a traditional
theme, instead with a composite of small gestures that will later undergo
development—whole-tone figures, lines moving in fourths, wedges of
different types, and distinctive rhythmic figures. These are continually
splintered into particles, Adorno says, then reassembled into new forms.

Example 2.18   String Quartet, Op. 3, movement 1, mm. 1–8

Example 2.19   String Quartet, Op. 3, movement 2, mm. 1–3

The atmosphere of the second movement changes dramatically, its mood more unstable as it ranges from the strident, aggressive opening (Example 2.19) to peaceful middle passages. Its form is more complex than the first movement's and further from any classical formal archetype. Berg made good use of his opportunity to hear a quartet read through the first movement in 1910 by calling in the second movement for unusual bowings and special effects, by which he expands the coloristic differentiations of a medium that tends to be uniform in sound. Adorno, like most later analysts, finds a mixture of elements from sonata and rondo in the movement, but all that is clearly left over from sonata form is an exposition of motives at the outset and their reprise at m. 151. The opening theme returns in rondo fashion at mm. 48, 61, 151, and 223, but little else about the movement resembles a genuine rondo. Some motives dimly recall the profile of motives from the first movement, and the opening motive from that movement returns explicitly in mm. 168 and 227.

In the absence of tonal harmony in the String Quartet, Berg continues to experiment with alternative harmonic principles. An example is in a passage in Violins I-II in the second movement at mm. 34–38, which is repeated in mm. 91, 177, and 218. The figure, given schematically in Ex. 2.20, shows Berg again using harmonies that arise and interrelate by common intervallic patterns. The progression is generated by a familiar Bergian wedge in which the outer voices move in contrary motion, each through a single interval (here semitones); the inner voices descend chromatically. The progression has an additional measure of symmetry since

Example 2.20   String Quartet, Op. 3, movement 2, mm. 36–38 (Violins)

each of the first four chords has the same intervallic content, only symmetrically inverted from one chord to the next. This relationship can be
seen by comparing the notes of the first chord with those of the second.
The first has the tones E♭–E–G–B, in a compact scalewise order. The
intervals separating these tones are reversed, or "inverted," in the second
chord, F♯–F–D–B♭ and the alternation of the two inversionally related
forms continues until the pattern is broken on the final chord. This last
harmony is a transposition of the chord (with identical vertical spacing)
that ends the Piano Sonata and (with different spacing) that ends the first
movement of the String Quartet.

Berg always assured Helene that she was the inspiration for the
String Quartet, although he mentioned this to no one else. When it was
published in 1920, its dedication was "to my Helene," and following its
highly successful performance in 1923 in Salzburg, Berg wrote to her to
describe the occasion: "It was artistically the most wonderful evening
of my life, and I am full of sorrow that you couldn't experience it, you
who have spent at my side so many sad decades artistically, you to whom
the Quartet relates as much as to me, the one to whom it completely
belongs."[74] In later years, Helene told friends that the Quartet depicted
the difficulty of her courtship in light of opposition from her father.
"Love speaks from it, also the jealousy and outrage over the injustice
done to us and to our love."[75] Writers looking for symbols of Helene in
the work have pointed to the frequent pedal tones on the note D in the
second movement (although similar pedals occur also on other notes).

For years Berg's String Quartet had few performances, but it eventually proved to be the pivotal work in the composer's breakthrough to
international prominence.

★★★

The completion of the String Quartet marks the end of Berg's apprenticeship. Shortly afterwards, his life took a new turn: he married Helene Nahowski in May 1911 and in August of that year Schoenberg unexpectedly and suddenly fled from Vienna after an ugly quarrel with a neighbor. He later resettled in Berlin and did not hesitate to ask Berg to pack up his entire Vienna apartment and to oversee the lawsuit that he initiated against his former neighbor. Schoenberg turned over his small composition class to Berg, which launched Berg's career as a distinguished teacher. Berg now faced an uncertain future. Where would he turn as a composer? Would he flourish as an artist or wilt with Schoenberg's absence? How could he make a living for himself and his bride? These questions will be addressed in the next chapter.

A Struggle for Recognition, 1911–15

B Y THE TIME THAT HE COMPLETED HIS FORMAL MUSICAL STUDY IN 1911, Berg had composed the highly original Opp. 1–3 and was poised for a brilliant rise in the world of modern music. But his prospects and productivity as a composer were then to descend into a dark period from which he would need more than ten years to extricate himself. There were many factors in Berg's decline—his lack of self-confidence, the distractions posed by obligations to his family, his mobilization during World War I, and his wife's illnesses, among others. Berg also struggled with his relationship with Schoenberg. Berg was emotionally unable to separate himself from Schoenberg, and he willingly accepted his former teacher's demands for menial and time-consuming tasks, regular and subservient personal contact, continuing financial support, and negative remarks that threatened Berg's belief in himself as a composer. Schoenberg was not inclined to release Berg from his role as a student, and his presence—so stimulating for Berg's creative spirit during the student period—after 1911 became a hindrance in Berg's development as a composer.

The pattern for Berg's future relationship with Schoenberg was set immediately after Berg's wedding. In the summer of 1911, after a brief honeymoon in Payerbach-Reichenau, Berg was swamped by family obligations, Helene's poor health, and the moving of his residence first to the Nahowskis' house in the Maxingstrasse, then to a permanent apartment on the Trauttmansdorffgasse nearby. For a few days he failed to call

Berg. Bryan Simms and Charlotte Erwin, Oxford University Press (2021). © Oxford University Press.
DOI: 10.1093/oso/9780190931445.003.0004

upon Schoenberg, which brought upon him Schoenberg's wrath, and the incident cast Berg—twenty-six years old at the time—back into in an adolescent's emotional panic. He wrote to Anton Webern:

> It was just dreadful. My attempts to answer his scornful accusations, to explain my dilemma failed miserably because I was so upset and because I couldn't justify my behavior for these 10 days in mere words. . . . I swear to you by the sanctity of our art, by my wife's very life, that despite the peculiarity of my actions there was not a shred of coldness, indifference, or lack of interest toward Schoenberg. The anguish that I had already suffered for my apparent negligence was not enough to avoid his embitterment and scorn—anguish, as I said, that I experienced even before Schoenberg told me directly of his anger with me. Not enough that there could be no better way to express the holy and inconceivable love that I feel for him than by this anguish. Perhaps you won't understand me because I'm struggling with words when I suffer from doubts and eternal questions. Perhaps someday these feelings will emerge in tones.[1]

Emotional attachments between a younger and older adult such as Berg's with Schoenberg are now better understood than in the past, when such relations were often seen as a young person temporarily reaching out to a "father figure." Their origin in Berg's case could be found in his adolescence, in all likelihood triggered by the death of his father when Berg was fifteen. He entered then into an emotional attachment with an older man, Hermann Watznauer, who took over his father's role as mentor and friend, someone always ready to support the young Berg, to be there for him for reassurance. Cindy Hazan and Phillip Shaver, who have studied such adult attachments in a romantic context that also has relevance to non-sexual relationships among adults, have called this type of attachment "secure."[2] The two partners of a secure attachment have reliably warm and open contact, mutual responsiveness, and a positive feeling about themselves.

Around 1906, as his commitment to music deepened, Berg transferred his need for attachment to Schoenberg, redefining his relationship with Watznauer as a normal friendship. Berg soon found that the new attachment would not be secure, as it had been with Watznauer, but instead what Hazan and Shaver call "anxious-preoccupied." In this type of relationship the subject (the one reaching out for attachment) fears abandonment, believes that the other figure does not value him, and feels inferior and doomed to failure. He blames himself for such feelings, which bring on agonizing mood swings. Hazan and Shaver found a recurring pattern of behavior in such subjects, a pattern that Berg also exhibited. Some incident provokes anxiety in the subject, and he seeks closeness to the partner. But the partner responds negatively, which increases the subject's insecurity and sends him back to an ever more urgent appeal for closeness. After several such cycles through the pattern, a temporary balance is reached until the cycle is again triggered by some new anxiety. Since the attachment is in part a psychosis—a circumstance beyond the control of the subject—he is unable to break the cycle on his own. Berg's attachment to Schoenberg was also reinforced by the cult-like mentality of other Schoenberg students, especially Webern.

Shortly after Berg's appeal to Webern in August 1911, Schoenberg suddenly left Vienna and in September resettled in Berlin.[3] Schoenberg's absence from Vienna might have allowed Berg to right his emotional ship and return to composing, but Schoenberg would not allow it. Instead, he made Berg his unpaid secretary, factotum, and scapegoat, assigning him to pack and oversee the moving of his Vienna residence, to oversee a lawsuit that Schoenberg had initiated against a former neighbor, to negotiate on his behalf with Universal Edition, to run a fund-raising effort for his benefit, to proofread musical scores and parts, and to proofread and index his *Harmonielehre*, among many other such tedious services. Schoenberg was well aware that Berg could not refuse him in any of these duties, and Berg was left with little time or energy for composing.

In the time that he had and given Schoenberg's distance, Berg dared to experiment with new musical resources in his Altenberg Songs, Op. 4, and Clarinet Pieces, Op. 5, works whose new ideas deviated sharply from the music that Berg had composed under Schoenberg's eye. But these works and other gestures toward independence would be scornfully attacked by Schoenberg, declared "worthless" by him, with a devastating effect on Berg's self-confidence and emotional equilibrium.[4]

Before the War: 1911–14

Berg's emotional distress at Schoenberg's hands was balanced by his marriage, which for more than ten years was happy and filled with mutual support. A few months after their wedding the Bergs set up housekeeping in Hietzing, at Trauttmansdorffgasse 27, not far from Helene's family residence and where Helene would live until her death in 1976. (The building is now owned by the Alban Berg Foundation.) The ground-floor apartment was secured for them by Helene's mother, Anna Nahowski, who generously furnished it at her own expense.[5] In these early years Alban and Helene developed an intimacy focused largely around their health and well-being. They hoped for a child but did not produce one, and Helene's health in this connection was a constant theme, somewhat obliquely treated in their letters. Later, Berg would admit that Helene's poor health had for years stood between him and her.[6] In these years the Bergs were financially constrained, a situation that later improved. Alban's income was small, and he relied on a yearly allowance of 700 kronen from his mother to see him through. Helene earned an annual interest of 4,000 kronen from her dowry, which was invested in commercial shares.[7] Living conditions became more difficult during the First World War, but while food was rationed, the extended Berg and Nahowski families came through without serious privation, thanks in part to their agricultural holdings at the Berghof and at Trahütten. Relations within and between the families were often strained and became more so as the years progressed, leading to a crisis in 1919 that will be addressed in a later chapter.

The principal source for the interpretation of the Bergs' marital relationship is the critical edition of the complete existing letters between Alban and Helene.[8] These documents offer a telling insight into the personalities and viewpoints of the writers, Alban's in the early marital years still full of ardor and emotion, Helene's practical and matter-of-fact. A peculiarity of the letters following their marriage is the plethora of pet names that the couple employed for each other, which amount to, for Helene, something over eighty, and for Alban, over ninety.[9] Many of these names come from Austrian dialect or colloquialisms and remain obscure. Others are obvious, such as the first applied to Alban during their courtship, *Zwerg* (dwarf), referring ironically to his height. In a comparable vein was the sobriquet *Floh* (flea). (By way of comparison, the tall Emperor Franz Joseph signed his letters to his wife as "Klein," or simply "Kl.") Helene early became *Pfersch* or *Pferschel* (peach or little peach), and this remained Berg's favorite name for her. After their marriage they never referred in their letters to each other by their given names, thereby building an elaborate set of peculiar forms of address that served as a species of secret language and upon which changes were often rung to add special nuance, much of which is lost on the external reader. Helene writes to Alban as *Sualchen*, but also as "Liebes, liebes, liebstes Sualchen, Swilli Schuslin Puffi," eventually abbreviated to "SSS.P." At times Alban was *Stinko* when he failed to bathe, Helene *Swipel*, and the codename for the wished-for baby was *Swipelinchen* (or *Swipilinchen*). Helene's family also used nicknames, some friendly, others derisive. Alban and Helene both referred to Franz Nahowski as "Drill." By her family Helene was addressed as Len or Lenchen, although her sister Carola addressed her commonly in letters as "liebe Bergin." Carola herself was often called "James." But it was Alban and Helene who took to an extreme the eccentric Viennese nickname practice.

The many coded names used by Alban and Helene Berg are evidence of a fantastic facade of endearments that seem intimate but masked some relational issues, perhaps functioning as a means of dancing around difficult topics such as health or sex. Aside from Alban's recurring asthma, use of alcohol, and lack of money, Helene's health problems were the chief source of stress between them. Berg sometimes mentioned Helene's illnesses in his letters to others, including Schoenberg, and he often used— and probably exaggerated—her various indispositions as an excuse to evade some task that Schoenberg hoped to impose on him. Undoubtedly Alban's time and energy were routinely taken up with worry and frustration over Helene's condition.

It is difficult in retrospect to be certain what her fundamental ailments were, and since she lived to be ninety-one years old, it is tempting to conclude that her illnesses were partly imaginary, although no less painful or disruptive. She may have suffered from an autoimmune disorder, of which there are many types. She mentions once in a letter to Alban that she had a serious illness as a child, which she called a kidney disease and which may have triggered something more complex. She recounted this episode in terms of pain, both physical and psychic:

> I often reflect on why since my childhood I was destined to suffer so much pain. From my kidney disease onward, for which I was punished for 2 years (the angst of this punishment!), by the setbacks on account of my siblings (who rudely and tactlessly humiliated me without end), up to the struggles on your account. This was a series of sad experiences and bitter disappointments![10]

In later life Helene continued to complain of kidney pain. She was also thought to be chronically anemic and was taking iron pills for this condition before her marriage.[11] Certainly she had dysmenorrhea—extremely painful menstrual periods—a common condition whose cause is still not well understood according to the medical literature. Her menstrual period—always referred to as her "Unwohlsein" (unwellness)—is a continuing topic in letters (all such references were struck by Helene in her edition of the letters in 1965). Her condition routinely made her unable to travel or be active as she was often confined to her bed for a day or two with severe cramps and sometimes headaches, nausea, and vomiting. Alban appears unusually involved in this matter, given the amount of discussion and advice he devoted to it. Helene's symptoms may point to additional gynecological problems that could have played a role in her infertility.[12] Helene's letters to her husband are filled with references to painful conditions, which she described variously as rheumatism, gout and "nerve pain," again possibly caused by an underlying but non–life-threatening disorder. Helene believed that she had a nervous system disorder, which she described to Paul Kammerer as "frail nerves." She had headaches and "buzzing" in her head, pain in her legs, palpitations and lack of appetite. She was prone to nightmares and sleepwalking, at which times she sometimes injured herself. Alban insisted that she take sedatives such as Validol or Adalin to avoid such accidents. It is likely that Helene's matrix of ailments included psychological components, and it is not difficult to understand how these could have developed in her youth within the context of her dysfunctional family and especially the strained, sometimes abusive relations between her parents.

The preoccupation with Helene's health by both partners over many years can seem like an affectation. Was Helene after all really ill? Her insistence on nervous ailments such as "nerve fever" (Nervenfieber) and "nerve pain" reflects the vogue of neurasthenia around the turn of the twentieth century. This condition, essentially "weak nerves," was usually ascribed by the medical profession, including the eminent German-Austrian psychiatrist Richard von Krafft-Ebing, to an overstimulation of the nervous system occasioned by modern urban life.[13] It was typified by fatigue, weakness, anemia and eating disorders, but there were other manifestations such as insomnia and headaches. Neurasthenia (Nervenkrankheit in German) was not categorized as a mental illness, and this distinction was important for those who wished to elude any such stigma.

In the case of women, the most common sufferers under this malady, neurasthenia became aestheticized by turn-of-the-century artists in the figure of the *femme fragile*. A counterpoint to the better known *femme fatale*, this was a provocative image found in both literature and the arts across Europe and prominently in the Vienna of the Secession. It was characterized visually by a marked bodily thinness, languor, pallor, and affective reserve.[14] Under these externally expressed vulnerabilities lurked a suppressed and possibly decadent eroticism. In real life the *femme fragile* was often found, as Helene Berg frequently was by the 1920s, among the voluntary patients at private clinics, usually designated sanatoria, where well-to-do women sought treatment for a range of maladies, often unspecified *Frauenkrankheiten* (women's diseases), which may have included psychological components. It is plausible that Helene's illnesses and her periodic immersions in sanatorium culture cast her in her own mind, and perhaps even more dramatically (and ambivalently) in her husband's, as a *femme fragile*. Her many attempts at cures become one front in Alban Berg's increasingly self-conscious battle against the malign forces that would destroy the beautiful, idealized life the Bergs had promised themselves at the time of their marriage.

In the early years of their marriage, Berg's letters reveal a nascent frustration with Helene's health that would eventually cause an estrangement between them. Berg traveled alone to Amsterdam in 1914—Helene remaining behind due to poor health—and there he saw the sun set brilliantly over the sea while the moon was in the sky. But Helene was not there to see it!

> I'm in such despair, more than ever—this *must* change—you must do *everything* to get your nerves healthy! In short, you must *live*—and not do what you actually do, which is to busy yourself *with* life. . . . Believe me, you must do *everything, everything*, my Pferschel, to get *well* and to be able to *live*![15]

The Bergs' struggles with health came to a point of crisis in their common desire for parenthood. They both asked—with a hint of accusation—whose fault it was that no pregnancy had occurred, and this question hovered persistently in the letters during the early years of their marriage. Alban never revealed his fathering of a daughter at age

seventeen, but given this proof of his potency, for him Helene's reproductive health, or lack thereof, was the issue. Alban longed for a child, despite his claim in his "defense letter" to Helene's father of 1910 that they
intended to "prevent" pregnancy (*verhüten*).[16] This statement does not accurately represent Berg's later thoughts. To his wife he wrote urgently on
the subject, several times during his military service when Helene was at
Trahütten for lengthy periods:

> A time must surely come when we can live together there [in Trahütten] in
> blissful peace, where my health will be restored more quickly than you think,
> along with my ability to work. These almost too beautiful hopes and dreams
> will support me in the bitter weeks ahead, and I beg, beg my Pferschel to
> stand by me by doing everything possible to get well and strong. For to give
> all these hopes and goals a deeper meaning for the future one thing is still
> needed—needed—you know it too—a Swipilinchen.[17]

Such thoughts persist in Berg's letters to Helene. In a letter of 8 June 1921
he assures her that he is building up his strength: "I eat very well and will
have gained weight when you come back; and then—the Swipel—do
you think about this all the time, as I do??!!."[18] After 1921 there is no further mention of Swipilinchen or childbearing in their correspondence,
and the silence signals another step toward the estrangement that beset
their marriage at a later time.

During the wartime period, despite its many prolonged separations,
Alban and Helene spoke feelingly about their connection to each other.
A letter from Helene in August 1916 struck Alban deeply. She wrote:

> You see, I feel more and more clearly that we two belong together—and that
> heaven has given us a happiness in our marriage that blots out everything else.
> I often imagine the two of us in a shabby little boat (which people would
> ridicule), driven far, far from shore (where those that we love and to whom
> we have only offered friendship have given us only disappointment and pain)
> to a beautiful, better world, *our world*, that no one can take away from us![19]

Alban responded to this letter, with its claim of a perfect intimacy in
the face of all misunderstanding and misfortune, with ardor and with
exaggerated gratitude. It was the most beautiful letter he had ever received, he wrote, and he "swam in a sea of happiness":

With this letter, which I will always carry with me, you have made me end-lessly happy. It means more to me—after 5½, no, almost 10 years—than you can know or could when you wrote it. For you can't know what has se-cretly pained me so in these last years, *so secretly* that it has not even success-fully entered the forum of my own logic and understanding, never mind being expressed aloud. I don't want to disrupt this deep, holy atmosphere into which your letter has in one stroke sent me. . . . I'm going to put out the light and—I'm almost tempted to pray.—But that is not necessary: my thoughts today are themselves a great prayer of thanks for this *one hour in the evening* in which my good spirit (you, of course) has saved my deeply oppressed *soul* and my guardian angel (who is maybe the very same as my good spirit), my *life*.[20]

Alban's secret fear was not explained in any ensuing letter that survives. Given the context of the two letters in which it arises, it must relate to his marriage and to a deep but not fully suppressed doubt that he was not worthy of Helene, and that she could not come to love him as he loved her or to believe in him as an artist and thus in their common des-tiny. Her words on the "shabby little boat" quelled this fear, as he eagerly grasped the meaning of her metaphor and that the two of them were bound in a union that no misfortune could shake or destroy. Helene's view of her marriage was to continue in this vein, but by the mid-1920s, Berg's need for emotional rejuvenation drove him to seek connections with other women.

Berg's Work for Schoenberg

In a letter of late November 1915, Berg listed for Schoenberg the things that had kept him from accomplishing more as a composer. He mentions "various fund-raising campaigns, concert arrangements, reading the final proofs for the *Harmonielehre*, publication of the *Arnold Schonberg* mon-ograph (which, in fact, rested almost entirely on my shoulders), all the work for *Gurrelieder* (proofreading of score and parts, the two guides, the performance), vocal scores for the two songs from the F♯-minor Quartet, the partial four-hand reduction of Mahler's VIIIth Symphony, [and] transpositions of Strauss songs."[21] Schoenberg must have noticed that vir-tually all of these distractions were undertaken on his behalf, mostly at his command, and none with significant compensation.

"Fund-raising campaigns" were cited first on Berg's list. Beginning in 1909, Schoenberg several times asked Berg for loans, which were readily granted. When Schoenberg fled from Vienna in August of 1911, Berg and other former students believed—wrongly as it turned out—that their teacher was in dire financial straits in his exile, and five of them, Berg and Webern included, pooled their resources to send him 1,000 kronen to tide him over. Berg also hatched a plan, in which other students joined, to support Schoenberg for a longer term. Karl Linke drew up an appeal to be printed and sent to prominent figures in the arts, asking for their signatures as an expression of support for Schoenberg. These could then be used to raise funds from wealthy Viennese donors. The appeal was sent around on September 1, 1911, and it read:

> Appeal [*Aufruf!*]
>
> The students and friends of Arnold Schoenberg consider it their duty to make his plight known. He has not done so himself out of shame, so we are going over his head to call for help. The thought that this artist should founder over the common necessities of life has made us speak out. The catastrophe came upon him with unexpected speed, and long-range help would arrive too late. At the time that these lines are being written, Schoenberg is living with no means of support in a village near Munich. This appeal is being sent with the intention of raising money from lovers of art. We ask you to support this prospective action by your signature. Reply as soon as possible to Alban Berg, Vienna, XIII., Trauttmansdorffgasse 27.[22]

More than forty prominent figures in music and the arts responded with their signatures—Richard Strauss, Peter Altenberg, Arthur Schnitzler, Bruno Walter, Julius Korngold, among others—and some like Strauss and Korngold immediately added a financial contribution. But the subsequent appeal to donors produced relatively small results. Still, Berg continued to work tirelessly to raise money, and the resulting "Schoenberg Fund" contributed sporadically to Schoenberg's benefit for several years. From 1912 Schoenberg also received a stipend from the Gustav Mahler Stiftung, which Schoenberg expected Berg to coordinate, sending him angry reproofs if there was any delay in his receiving money.

Those in Berg's family were indignant at Schoenberg's financial manipulations. Berg's sister Smaragda wrote to Alban: "He can't *demand* that a person live in a sewer pipe and eat onions so that he can keep his 6-room apartment! You all—his friends—have just spoiled him so as not to lose his favor, and now that the war prevents you from doing that he is indignant. A blood sucker . . . !"[23] Helene had similar thoughts: "I'd just like to know what we're supposed to do for him. Since my relatives happen to have money, are we supposed to put him on a pension? Probably so! And we're absolutely obligated to eat beans, like the Weberns! That's what he thinks! Sweetheart, it's really sad that such a great and significant person, whom we must *love* and *honor* because of his overwhelming mind, acts in other ways that are so ugly. And we're just supposed to be patient and get over it, right?"[24] Despite such pleas, Berg was helpless in freeing himself from Schoenberg. "You yourself know, Dear Herr Schoenberg, that I am always conscious of, and never want to be conscious of anything but to be your student. To follow you in every respect, knowing that everything I do in *opposition* to your wishes is wrong."[25]

In his list of activities sent to Schoenberg in 1915, Berg also mentions his making of piano arrangements. The craft of piano arranging was an important exercise within Schoenberg's circle. Schoenberg gave out his works to his advanced and former students to be arranged for piano, just as Alexander Zemlinsky had done for him during his own student period and Berg would later do with his students including Gottfried Kassowitz, Willi Reich, and Fritz Heinrich Klein.[26] This was an opportunity to earn a bit of money from Schoenberg's publisher, Universal Edition. For Emil Hertzka, director of Universal Edition, piano scores of operas, oratorios, and symphonies had a far larger market than did full scores, and Hertzka sometimes called on an experienced craftsman like Josef Venantius von Wöss to make these arrangements, or, less expensively, on students recommended by Schoenberg and others. Hertzka had no hesitation to make an arrangement into a group project, asking one person to revise or continue the work of another until a useable score was obtained. The identity of the arrangers was often omitted from the subsequent publication. Berg's piano arrangements originating after 1911 are summarized here:

Arnold Schoenberg, *Pelleas und Melisande*. Fragmentary piano arrangement, four hands, ca. 1911. Unpublished (manuscript in ÖNB, F21.Berg.97).

Franz Schreker, *Der ferne Klang*. Piano-vocal score (Acts 2-3), two hands, completed April 1911. Publication: Universal Edition no. 3096, 1911. Act

1 was arranged by another musician, possibly Josef V. von Wöss, and subsequently revised by Berg. An "Erleichterte Ausgabe" of Berg's version by
Ferdinand Rebay was published by Universal Edition no. 3096-5369, 1912.

Gustav Mahler, Symphony no. 8. Partial piano arrangement, four hands,
completed December 1911–January 1912. Publication (with no reference to
Berg): Universal Edition no. 3390, 1912.

Arnold Schoenberg, *Gurre-Lieder*. Piano-vocal score, two hands, completed
January 1912. Publication (February 1912): Universal Edition no. 3696, 1912.
Four songs from *Gurre-Lieder* in Berg's piano-vocal score were published in-
dividually by Universal Edition, 1912–14.

Arnold Schoenberg, Second String Quartet, Op. 10, movements 3 ("Litanei")
and 4 ("Entrückung"). Piano-vocal score, two hands, completed ca. July 1912.
Publication: Universal Edition, nos. 6862–6863, 1921.

Arnold Schoenberg, Chamber Symphony Op. 9. Piano arrangement, four hands,
completed ca. 1915. Unpublished (manuscript in ÖNB, F21.Berg.91).

Berg's first important assignment from Hertzka was to complete the
vocal score of Franz Schreker's opera *Der ferne Klang*, whose first act had
already been prepared by some other arranger, possibly Wöss.[27] Hertzka
published the piano score in 1911, naming Berg alone as the arranger,
although he found Berg's version to be too difficult for the piano, a
complaint that haunted all of Berg's later arrangements. When Schreker's
opera proved successful on German stages beginning in 1912, Hertzka
then hired Ferdinand Rebay to revise and simplify Berg's score, and
Rebay's version was also published in that year.

We can assess Hertzka's complaint about excessive difficulty in Berg's
arrangement by looking at a brief passage in the orchestral Prelude to
Act 2 of *Der ferne Klang*. Example 3.1 shows (a) Schreker's scoring for the
passage, (b) Berg's reduction, and (c) Rebay's simplified version. Given its
four contrapuntal lines and many notes, Berg's version is hard to play, but
for the skillful pianist it provides an ingenious translation of Schreker's
colorful music for the raucous Venetian dance hall that opens Act 2 of the
opera. Berg does not just reduce Schreker's score, instead, he reinterprets
it and revises its harmonic dimension to preserve and enhance the dramatic spirit of the music and to heighten the harmonic implications
of the score. In the left hand he reiterates a fourth chord, B–E–A–D,
throughout the passage, something only hinted at in Schreker's score,
and he keeps as many of the colorful grace-note figures as possible. In

Example 3.1   (a) Franz Schreker, *Der ferne Klang*, Act 2 Prelude, mm. 26–28

(b) Berg's reduction of (a)

(c) Rebay's simplified version of (b)

Rebay's simplification, all such expressive details and reinterpretations are removed, making the part far easier to play, but pedestrian in musical content. Even when making arrangements, Berg aimed to create a sophisticated musical substance, never a purely practical object. He spoke to his objectives in a letter to Hertzka of September 1912:

> Let me take this opportunity to say something about my piano scores in general. In your eyes they are too difficult. But here it is a question of arranging completely new, unknown, and unperformed works. Such arrangements must be more difficult than those for older works that are well-known and often played. Compare the difficult but wonderfully beautiful *early* piano scores of Wagner's works, especially those by Bülow and Liszt, with the more recent, easy ones by Kleinmichel or Klindworth (his "simplified versions"). With the latter there is an approximation of the sound that is *by then* well-known, or, for example, a finger exercise in one hand and a single-line theme in the other to substitute for a *familiar* though more complicated passage in a polyphonic and resounding large score. In an *early* piano score there can be no such approximations, omissions, or substitutions.[28]

Berg's piano-vocal arrangement of *Gurrelieder* was one of many tasks that Berg took on as a willing labor of love for Schoenberg's music, an expression of his lifelong and unshakeable belief in Schoenberg's leading role in the development of modern music. It was followed by Berg's prodigious assistance in the premier performance of *Gurrelieder*, which took place in Vienna's Musikverein on 23 February 1913. Shortly after the publication of Berg's piano-vocal score for *Gurrelieder* in February 1912, Franz Schreker announced his intention to perform the mammoth cantata in Vienna with his Philharmonic Chorus. Berg then worked tirelessly to make the performance a reality. He helped to raise money for it, wrote a lengthy guide to the work, conducted rehearsals with the chorus, and, most importantly, wrote out and corrected parts. In a letter of 3 November 1912, he explains to Webern why he had devoted himself to such a project:

> I would never have undertaken this work if I did not believe in its great importance and without which the performance (in February) will probably not come off. And no one could help me with it because no one knows the work as I do, no one who could correct the errors in the parts in comparison

to the score (misspelling of notes coming especially from transposing). But what an enormous job![29]

The Scandal Concert

The triumphant success of *Gurrelieder* in Vienna in February 1913 was followed only weeks later by one of the low points in Berg's career in music. This occurred at an orchestra concert sponsored by Vienna's Akademischer Verband für Literatur und Musik, an organization then under the leadership of the writer Erhard Buschbeck that promoted modern music and new ideas in literature. Buschbeck was an enthusiastic supporter of music by those in Schoenberg's circle, and Berg acted as his musical advisor. In 1912 Buschbeck proposed an orchestral concert in which Schoenberg would conduct his own Chamber Symphony and *Pelleas und Melisande*. Schoenberg responded positively to the plan but proposed a different program:

> I've decided to change the program: I'll do the Chamber Symphony (with orchestra) and at most two orchestral songs ("Natur" and "Sehnsucht") if you can find a singer (maybe Frau Gutheil?). By way of contrast, Webern's Orchestra Pieces [op. 6] and a classical work (perhaps the *Eroica* or the *Tristan* Prelude plus Brahms's Haydn Variations). My reasons: 1) I especially want to perform Webern's Orchestra Pieces (I'd like to do something by Berg, but there would not be enough rehearsal time); 2) I don't want so much of my own music to be played in Vienna, at least not in special concerts as opposed to subscription concerts; 3) the seven rehearsals might not be enough for both the Chamber Symphony and *Pelleas* while they would be adequate for this program; 4) I want to draw public attention to my conducting because I'd someday like to get a conducting position, something I've wanted for more than 15 years so as to be able to make music.[30]

A few weeks later, Schoenberg again rethought the program to bring in music by Berg, although Berg still had little experience as a composer for orchestra. Schoenberg knew that he was working on orchestral songs to poetry by Peter Altenberg, and he wrote to Berg on 7 January 1913: "Do you have 1–2 fairly short (fairly easy?) orchestra songs for mezzo soprano? I may do them in the Akademischer Verband orchestra concert if it's on 30 March. For on that day Frau [Marya] Freund would participate (for free!)."[31] Berg was quick to respond: "Your card made

me happier than I can say," he exclaimed. He then sent Schoenberg a full
score of the five Altenberg Songs, which he had completed the previous
summer. On January 14 Schoenberg wrote back about the songs:

> They seem (at first glance) remarkably well and beautifully orchestrated.
> I find some things disturbing at first, namely the rather too obvious desire to
> use new means. Perhaps I'll come to understand the organic interrelationship
> between these means and the requirements of expression. But right now it
> troubles me.[32]

Berg tried to allay Schoenberg's reservations about his "new means":

> I'm more receptive to the new sounds created by precisely these new means,
> hear them everywhere, even where it might be possible without them, and
> thus I employ them because I don't know anything else! Perhaps my mode
> of expression is like that of a child who hears so many foreign words at home
> that he uses them all the time, even when he hasn't quite mastered German
> yet. But at least I cherish the hope that the child uses the foreign words
> correctly.[33]

On 20 January 1913, Schoenberg informed Berg that two or three of
his Altenberg Songs would appear on the forthcoming program, with
Marya Freund making the final selection. But, unknown to Berg, Freund
refused to sing any of Berg's pieces—"not beautiful," she told Schoenberg.
Schoenberg informed Berg that he would have to find another singer,
and at the eleventh hour he settled on Alfred Boruttau, who was to
sing the role of Klaus Narr in the forthcoming premiere of *Gurrelieder*,
despite Berg's belief that the Altenberg Songs were for a woman. The
concert finally took place on 31 March 1913, in the Golden Hall of the
Musikverein, with this program:

Webern, Six Orchestra Pieces, Op. 6

Zemlinsky, Four Maeterlinck Songs, Op. 13, nos. 1, 2, 3, 5

Schoenberg, Chamber Symphony, Op. 9, arranged for strings and ten solo
winds

Berg, Orchestra Songs on Picture Postcard Texts by Peter Altenberg, Op. 4,
nos. 2–3[34]

Mahler, *Kindertotenlieder*

No longer would Berg's music be heard among works by students. Now it was to stand beside those of composers whom he held to be the very greatest in modern music.

The program contained pieces in two sharply different styles. Those by Schoenberg, Zemlinsky, and Mahler were in the progressive idiom that would have been familiar to audiences in 1913 and supported by many despite their modernistic elements. Those by Webern and Berg were different, written in a style that was pervasively dissonant, miniaturist in dimension, with no presence of a key or easily followed themes or formal archetypes, and no familiar harmonies. Their pieces could not be heard or assessed like the other works, and in all ways they were unfamiliar to the typical audience that came to the Musikverein in 1913. Viennese audiences were just then in a mood to bring down music that they found odd or unpleasing. Two weeks earlier the Viennese premiere of Schreker's *Das Spielwerk und die Prinzessin* at the Hofoper had produced a great eruption in the audience between the "frenetic applause" of Schreker's supporters and the whistling of his detractors.

The concert on March 31 was an even greater fiasco. Hissing and whistling greeted the selections by Webern, and laughter erupted during Berg's Altenberg Songs. The battle was on, as the audience divided into factions at war with each other, with the music largely forgotten. Punch-ups erupted in the audience and face slaps (*Ohrfeigen*) resounded in the hall. Finally the orchestra felt sufficiently threatened to leave the stage, Mahler's songs were canceled, and police cleared the hall. Many of Berg's friends were in attendance at this important concert, and they were spoiling for a fight with the philistines. From the loge Webern cried out, "Throw the scum out of here!" Hermann Watznauer reported: "The exciting thing was that I was sitting in the cheap seats in the middle of the mob and roaring like a bull! . . . Never in my life have I participated in something so exciting!" He assured his old friend Berg that his name would now be known everywhere.

The press had a field day in reporting the "scandal concert," which was described in newspapers throughout the empire, often with comic sarcasm.[35] "12 Dead, 20 Wounded, 110 Missing," was the headline in the *Neues Wiener Journal* on 8 April. Even serious critics who supported the progressive music of the day had only derision for the pieces by Webern and Berg. Writing in the *Neues Wiener Journal*, Elsa Bienenfeld praised Schoenberg's Chamber Symphony, but she had this to say about the works by Webern and Berg:

> That Schoenberg would energetically apply himself to the compositions of his students on this occasion was as lovely on a human level as it was unjustified on an artistic one. The Six Pieces for Orchestra by Webern, even more Berg's two orchestral songs on Altenberg picture postcards, were either calculated experiments that entirely misfired or the grotesque expression of an utter lack of ability.[36]

Richard Specht—a staunch supporter of progressive music from the time of Mahler—was outspoken in his rejection of the works by Webern and Berg:

> It is inconceivable that the person who created such a noble and lofty work as the *Gurrelieder* could champion such faltering experiments as these tragicomic "Picture Postcards" by Berg, except as a kindly human gesture of gratitude extended to two of his fanatically devoted students. . . . Even sympathy for them and my honest pleasure in their youthful and serious experimentation cannot make me—even with the danger of seeming unprogressive—see them as martyrs to a good cause. Because here was an eruption of indignation coming not only from the instincts of indolent philistines but also from those well-intentioned. A red line separates the impulse toward innovation and the striving for things preposterous. A calf having five feet is not original but a monstrosity.[37]

The review that most upset Berg was the one that appeared in the Viennese journal *Die Zeit* on April 2. A critic identified as "B.G." wrote:

> Herr Webern and Herr Berg have affirmed from the beginning a measureless devotion, a sort of adoration, for their teacher, to a degree that not even Richard Wagner had from his most enthusiastic disciples. Since both of them are affluent, they had long expressed their devotion by according material support for Schoenberg, who was going through hard times. . . . Schoenberg felt it his duty to repay his disciples by using his influence to have their works performed, despite his own very low opinion of their music. He repeatedly stated this viewpoint, specifically as regards the works that were on the program.[38]

The reviewer was plainly in error on several facts—certainly Webern was not "affluent" and Schoenberg was eager to have Webern's Orchestra Pieces on the program. But there was much truth in what the reviewer said about Berg. He had, after all, given money to Schoenberg in the recent past, and his Altenberg Songs were not held in high esteem by his teacher. It is also probably true that Schoenberg scheduled the Altenberg Songs primarily as an expression of thanks for Berg's work for him in the recent past.

The review in *Die Zeit* touched a raw nerve in Berg's psyche when it suggested that there was duplicity in Schoenberg's attitude toward him as a composer. Berg protested to *Die Zeit*, demanding that they publish this correction: "In today's issue of *Die Zeit* (morning edition), in the article 'Scandal in the Concert Hall,' it says that I long supported Schoenberg materially. This is completely untrue. I have never supported Schoenberg materially. Quite the opposite, Schoenberg for years provided me with lessons gratis."[39] Berg's statement is untrue, and it could not have been the thing about the review that most upset him, which was instead the assertion that Schoenberg did not value Berg's Altenberg Songs and placed them on the program only as a sop for Berg. Berg urgently wanted Schoenberg to contest this assertion: "What are *you* going to do, dear Herr Schoenberg? Are you going to refute the various statements in this article? We assume so!"[40] Schoenberg never asked for a correction of the review in *Die Zeit*.[41]

The concert on March 31 proved damaging not only to Berg but also to Schoenberg and the Akademischer Verband. After the concert, membership in the Verband dwindled and it soon went out of existence. For Schoenberg it diminished his hopes for a career as an orchestra conductor, and for many years after the concert Schoenberg harbored resentment toward Berg. In a 1928 article following the stormy Berlin premiere of Schoenberg's Orchestra Variations, Berg wrote in the *Neues Wiener Journal* that innovative music will always produce scandal. "Is that in itself so terrible? Are we to contrive to keep people from expressing disapproval if they feel moved to do so? I don't think so. Every person in the public eye, everyone who creates for the public, must put up with public criticism, provided that it does not go beyond an expression of approval or disapproval."[42] When Schoenberg read Berg's article it must have awakened his memories of 1913, and he wrote angrily on his copy of it:

I do *not* hold this opinion. I find applause and whistling equally offensive and degrading. Above all to the composer who has no desire to be judged by his contemporaries, the falsity of whose judgments will be corrected only fifty years later. And no less by those audiences who should be cautious about letting their lack of judgment lead to impertinence that reveals their cowardice and irresponsibility. Who wants to be held accountable to a jury that issues death sentences whose injustice is plain to everyone?[43]

Berg as Writer

As his prospects as a composer waned in the years following the devastating events of 1913, Berg reluctantly turned to writing on music as a possible occupation—this despite his skepticism about its value. Like his idols Schoenberg and Karl Kraus, he viewed musical journalism with contempt, and he found popular writing on music—such as that done by critics like Richard Specht and Paul Stefan—to be trivial. He had no training in writing about the history of music, and writing detailed musical analyses—for which Berg had great insight—had few prospects for publication. Still, critical writing was highly valued within Schoenberg's circle, which was a group distinguished by superior academic and intellectual credentials and included many influential critics and essayists.

Berg's first musical writing appeared in a monograph on Schoenberg that Berg, together with other students, put together in 1911. The impulse for the project came from an abrasive review in the *Illustriertes Wiener Extrablatt* of a student concert on 24 April 1911, in which the critic, Paul Stauber, concluded, "It is apparent that not just incompetent but also talented young people are being pushed by unconscionable speculators along a false path that leads neither toward art nor culture. The sharpest protest imaginable must be lodged against the postponed carnival that took place last Monday."[44] Outrage against the review was widely felt among Schoenberg's students, and a book-length tribute was launched to counter the falsity of Stauber's assessment.

Berg eventually took over as the main editor and organizer of the volume, which was titled *Arnold Schönberg* and published by the Munich firm of R. Piper in February 1912. The book contains articles on Schoenberg's music, his *Harmonielehre*, and his paintings, and it closes with nine tributes from former students attesting to Schoenberg's excellence as a teacher.

The last of the tributes was by Berg, his first published writing. In this short article Berg intended to take a "broad viewpoint," as he told Webern in a letter of January 1912, and he does so by using a fulsome hyperbole to describe his teacher. Berg portrays Schoenberg as a type of god—miraculous, infinite, messianic, beyond time. Berg later may have found the tone of the article excessive since he told his student Willi Reich that he did not wish to have it reprinted in Reich's journal *23: Eine Wiener Musikzeitschrift.*[45] After receiving a copy of the book Schoenberg confided his feelings about it to his diary: "I find myself spoken about too effusively," he wrote. "I am too young for such praise, I have still achieved too little, completed too little. . . . But on the other hand I was so overwhelmed by the great love that it expressed that it made me happy, to the extent that something like that can make one happy."[46]

Berg's next opportunity to write posed a greater challenge. In November 1912, following a recommendation from Schoenberg, Emil Hertzka asked Berg to write a guide, or "Führer," to *Gurrelieder*, to coincide with its premiere performance only a few months away. The guides were typically brochures intended to give the general audience background information on a composition, provide the text of a vocal work, and illustrate its important themes. While Berg had a keen interest in musical analysis, he was dismissive of superficial or journalistic writing about music, the type that typically appeared in concert guides. Following Hertzka's offer, he wrote to Schoenberg to express contempt for the "dreadfulness and *irrelevance* of such analyses."[47] Schoenberg answered Berg on 4 December. He agreed that the typical analyses were "abominable," but he urged Berg to accept Hertzka's offer all the same, and he recommended that Berg limit his work to "a list of the most important themes, in the order of the individual sections. . . . So: in a loose aphoristic form! That would certainly be something new."[48]

Berg could not bring himself to follow Schoenberg's recommendation for a mere list of themes in a loose aphoristic form, and he returned instead to his original idea of a deep and comprehensive account of the music in which themes were presented in all of their "developmental, variational, formal aspects," with extensive information about harmony, tonal plan, counterpoint, and orchestration, and with absolutely no poetic language or hermeneutics. The elements of *Gurrelieder* would be viewed strictly as recurring musical objects, with no reference outside of their own form and place in an abstract language.

Remarkably, Berg completed his complex analysis—eighty-four pages in length, illustrated by some 450 lines of the most intricate musical examples—in the space of about seven weeks, while during the same period attending *Gurrelieder* rehearsals and correcting the many errors in the work's parts. On 1 February he sent the eighty-seven musical examples for Parts I and II of the Guide ahead to Universal Edition, and Hertzka finally saw how much longer Berg's Guide had become than he had anticipated. He contacted Schoenberg, who replied on 3 February supporting Berg's work despite its unwieldy length. "He is very intelligent and conscientious," Schoenberg said about Berg, "and I have confidence that he does nothing superfluously."[49]

Berg made no reduction, either in the number of musical examples or in the text, and Hertzka had no alternative but to publish it in full, with an instrumentation list and Jens Peter Jacobsen's complete text added at the beginning. On 22 February, a day before the premier performance, 2,000 copies of Berg's Guide were delivered to Universal Edition.

Even within Schoenberg's circle, reaction to Berg's Guide was muted. Webern quipped to his friend that it was a "mountain guide" (*Bergführer*). On 10 March Schoenberg wrote to Berg about it in the coolest of terms: "Sometimes you overstate the case a bit. And I'm afraid you often claim something is new when that can scarcely be proved! But it's definitely a very interesting piece of work."[50] For a reprise of *Gurrelieder* scheduled for 27 March 1914 in Vienna, Hertzka again approached Berg, asking this time for the creation of a shortened version of the earlier Guide, a list of themes with verbal commentary reduced to a minimum. After considerable hesitation, Berg agreed to Hertzka's proposal, and in December 1913 he began to make the "short edition" of his Guide. Most of the front matter from the earlier edition was carried over into the new version, Berg added a brief notice concerning Jacobsen's treatment of the legends of Gurre, and he reduced the earlier analysis to a reprinting of selected musical examples and a formulaic accounting for their other occurrences in the work. The large edition of Berg's guide was destined to have only a modest sale; its first press run numbered 2,000 copies, and it was reprinted once (again with 2,000 copies) in 1921. The short edition—for which Berg always had disdain—had an excellent market, with 34,595 copies printed between 1914 and 1929.[51]

Five Orchestral Songs to Picture Postcard Texts by Peter Altenberg, Op. 4 (1912)

Near the completion of his studies with Schoenberg, Berg turned toward orchestral composition as a new area for development.[52] Schoenberg's curriculum did not address orchestration per se, and Berg learned instead by studying and arranging the scores of Mahler, Schreker, and Schoenberg, among others. Although at first he expressed uncertainty over his command of the orchestra, Berg soon became a master of this part of his craft. In May of 1911 he mentioned to Webern that he had begun a passacaglia for orchestra, perhaps taking his cue from Webern's own orchestral Passacaglia, Op. 1 (1908). Berg drafted about one hundred measures of the passacaglia in short score before putting the project aside.[53] Its opening theme (Example 3.2), in a free D minor, touches on all twelve tones and in this respect is a forerunner of the twelve-tone materials in the Altenberg Songs and the passacaglia theme in *Wozzeck*, Act 1.

Early in 1912 Schoenberg again prodded Berg to turn to orchestral composition. "How's your composing?" Schoenberg inquired. "You never mention it. You should see to it. Perhaps a few songs for the time being!! Perhaps orchestral songs!"[54] Berg immediately picked up on the idea and completed an orchestral song on a text by Peter Altenberg. On March 10 he sent its score to Schoenberg for his advice, adding that additional Altenberg songs were to follow.

Even as a teenager, Berg was an enthusiastic reader of literature by the Viennese writer Peter Altenberg (1859–1919). Altenberg had burst upon Vienna's literary world in 1896 with a collection of miniatures, *Wie ich es sehe* (As I see it).[55] Like his later books, it was a compilation of "little things," as Altenberg called them—prose poems, aphorisms, sketches, narrations—many of which had been published earlier in magazines and journals. Altenberg's vignettes had a disarming simplicity and immediacy, freshness of form and insight, and for his subjects he dwelled on the beauties of nature and the presence of women as stimulants for

Example 3.2   Passacaglia (1911), theme

art, stressing visual impressions that were expressed with a minimum of mediation or contrivance. "So are my little things literature?," he asked. "Not at all. They are extracts, extracts from life. The life of the soul and coincidences of the day, boiled down to 2–3 pages, rid of the fat, like beef in the stewpot."[56] "I invent nothing," he added later, "so I am neither writer nor poet. Life brings everything to me and all I have to do is not falsify what I have received."[57]

According to Hermann Watznauer, Berg met Altenberg in 1906, probably through Smaragda Berg, who had fallen in with Altenberg's circle of café and cabaret habitués.[58] Probably in the early months of 1910 Berg introduced the poet to his fiancée, Helene Nahowski, who immediately charmed Altenberg and inspired him to write several sketches in her praise.[59]

Given their prose structure, Altenberg's writings were a rare and unusual choice as song texts, although they are akin to the prose poems by Alfred Mombert that Berg had used for his Op. 2 songs. Earlier, around 1906, Berg had set three of Altenberg's poems to music, and Egon Wellesz—a fellow student of Schoenberg—had used Altenberg's "Wie ein Bild" in a song published in 1909.[60]

For his Altenberg Songs of 1912, Berg chose five passages from Altenberg's anthology *Neues Altes* that appear under the heading "Texte nach Ansichtskarten" (Picture postcard texts). Altenberg was an avid collector of picture postcards and photographs—mainly those depicting scenes from nature and portraits of women, both clothed and nude. He called his collection a "poor man's gallery" and used it to stimulate his poetic imagination. Altenberg's "Picture Postcard Texts" are mainly aphorisms on subjects favored by the writer: artistic inspiration from nature, the soul of women, spiritual enrichment following emotional turmoil, and the role of the artist. There are no known pictures from Altenberg's collection that definitely correspond to the texts that Berg chose, although Gert Mattenklott has published selections from Altenberg's picture collection (now at the Galerie St. Etienne in New York) that may be similar to the ones studied by the poet.[61]

Berg placed Altenberg's brief texts in an order that created a poetic cycle, much as he had done with the prose poems that he used in Op. 2. Here, as there, the speaker is the inner self, which discovers parallels with the natural world in the first two poems, "Seele, wie bist du schöner" and "Sahst du nach dem Gewitterregen." The storms of nature must be endured to refresh the soul, says the poet.

Seele, wie bist du schöner, tiefer, nach
  Schneestürmen—.
Auch du hast sie, gleich der Natur—.
Und über beiden liegt noch ein trüber
  Hauch, wenn das Gewölk sich schon
  verzog!

O Soul, how more beautiful, how
  deeper you are after snowstorms—
You have them too, just like nature—
And over both lies a darksome breath
  when the clouds move off!

Sahst du nach dem Gewitterregen den
  Wald?!?
Alles rastet, blinkt und ist schöner als
  zuvor—.
Siehe, Fraue, auch du brauchst
  Gewitterregen!

Did you see the forest after the
  thunder shower?
Everything rests, gleams, and is more
  beautiful than before—.
Look, woman, you also need thunder
  showers!

But nature cannot ultimately rescue the tortured soul. A peripeteia is reached in the third song, "Über die Grenzen des All," as the speaker mutters, "suddenly it's all over!" Recall the word "Die!" in Berg's "Warm die Lüfte," which is spoken, as is the line here, rather than sung.

Über die Grenzen des All blicktest
  du sinnend hinaus;
Hattest nie Sorge um Hof und Haus!
Leben und Traum vom Leben—
  plötzlich ist alles aus—.
Über die Grenzen des All blickst
  du noch sinnend hinaus—!

Across the limits of the universe you
  gazed out contemplatively;
without care for home or hearth!
Life and dream of life—
  suddenly it's all over—.
Across the limits of the universe you
  gaze out contemplatively—

In the final two songs, "Nichts ist gekommen" and "Hier ist Friede," the soul finds no remedy for its anguish except to live on in desolate isolation.

"Nichts ist gekommen, nichts wird
  kommen für meine Seele—.
Ich habe gewartet, gewartet, oh,
  gewartet—.
Die Tage werden dahinschleichen—.
Und umsonst wehen meine
  aschblonden seidenen Haare um
  mein bleiches Antlitz—."

"Nothing has come, nothing will come
  for my soul —.
I waited and waited—.
The days are stealing past—
And for nothing does my ash blond,
  silken hair waft over my pale
  countenance—."

Hier ist Friede—. Hier weine ich mich aus über alles. Hier löst sich mein unermeßliches unfaßbares Leid, das meine Seele verbrennt. Siehe, hier sind keine Menschen, keine Ansiedlungen. Hier tropft Schnee leise in Wasserlachen—.	Here is peace—. Here I weep over everything. Here dissolves the immeasurable ungraspable anguish that burns my soul. Look, there are no people here, no settlements. Here snowflakes drop softly into pools of water—.

Berg continued to compose his Altenberg Songs during his summer retreat at the Berghof in 1912, and he completed the cycle of five, according to a letter to Schoenberg, in October of that year. The premiere of two of the songs at the "scandal concert" in March 1913 has already been discussed, and, given the large size of the orchestra that Berg specifies and Schoenberg's sharp criticism of the songs, Berg made no further efforts to have a full performance during his lifetime. In a letter to Schoenberg dated 20 July 1913, Berg says that he came close to destroying the songs, but certainly this was spoken only out of deference to Schoenberg's criticism. Berg never wavered in his belief in the value of any of his music. He made a piano-vocal score of nos. 2–5 in January 1913, prior to the performance in March, although he held that the complex first song could not be reconceived for piano. In 1917 he arranged "Hier ist Friede" for piano, harmonium, violin, and cello as a present to Alma Mahler, and in 1921 he had his piano-vocal arrangement of this song published in the Dresden art journal *Menschen*.[62] Also around 1921 he contemplated making a chamber orchestra arrangement of the entire cycle, which he announced in the repertory list that he assembled in November of that year for a prospectus of the Society for Private Musical Performances. Such an arrangement was never carried out.

As with the songs of Op. 2, the Altenberg Songs form a cycle in music as well as in text. Even more than in the earlier songs, the Altenberg cycle is knit together by an intricate development and recurrence of themes and motives, especially in the first and last numbers, as well as in other gestures toward a large symmetry. Like the poems that he takes from Altenberg, Berg's songs are miniatures, the entire cycle of five numbers having a duration of about ten minutes. In these musical moments Berg adopted a style, often termed "aphoristic," that had been used by

Schoenberg in his Three Pieces for Chamber Orchestra (1910) and Six
Little Piano Pieces, Op. 19 (1911), and by Webern in works such as the
Movements for String Quartet, Op. 5 (1909).

A close study of the music of the Altenberg Songs will show the many
"new means" that Schoenberg found questionable in the works. Here
Berg experiments freely with new compositional ideas that were unavailable to him during his study period under Schoenberg. These include
new thinking about harmony—twelve-tone lines and chords constructed
and used in systematic ways, experimentation with octatonic scales, and
the association of dissonant chords on the basis of related interval content. Berg experiments with new formal plans based on symmetries,
cyclic recurrences, and miniaturistic dimensions. He explores complex ostinati without unified meter or rhythm, and he refines his earlier
practices involving contrapuntal wedges and chords and lines based on
fourths and whole tones. Most important of all is Berg's expansion of
the deep structure of his music by the covert use of related pitch and
rhythmic configurations that periodically come to the musical surface,
there taking on contrasting designs. In this way the songs take on a multidimensional unity that maintains—for all their artifice—an emotionally
expressive representation of Altenberg's texts. The innovative thinking
in the Altenberg Songs continued to be developed in Berg's later works
leading to *Wozzeck* and *Lulu*.

In the first song, "Seele, wie bist du schöner," which was probably
the last one composed, Berg is at his most original and experimental,
and for the analyst the song is a rich field for study. Although the song
has many features of his earlier works—passages based on whole-tones,
themes made from chromatic wedges, and motives containing chains of
fourths—it introduces new compositional strategies by which the entire
song cycle is unified on a deep level. Earlier, Berg's technical trademarks
were ad hoc processes applied only sporadically within a work, but here
their presence is relevant to entire sections and to a unity of the entire
cycle. Douglas Jarman has described Berg's processes as "precompositional,
apparently abstract, schemes" that gradually replaced subjective choice in
Berg's compositional method.[63]

In form, the song has two contrasting parts, the first for orchestra
(mm. 1–19), the second with voice (20–38). The orchestral part produces
a great cloud of sound that vividly depicts the snowstorm of the text. It

masses and rises to a climax at m. 15, then collapses into a liquidation of motives that signals the approach of the second part. Given the expanded percussion section (including triangle, cymbals, and tamtam) and the presence of six keyboard and mallet instruments, the sound of this opening part recalls, perhaps inadvertently, that of a gamelan ensemble.

The blur of sound may seem random in construction but it is in fact a product of Berg's newly systematic approach to composing. At the outset of the first part, several important motives are stated simultaneously, each multiplied into a complex heterophony, and all moving at first by ostinato. None of the motives has the same duration or a regular meter or rhythm. From m. 5 the music intensifies in volume, as all of the motives move upward by sequence, reaching a climax on the downbeat of m. 15. Some of the motives in the sequential passage ascend by semitone, others by whole tone, the one in Clarinets II and III by an expanding pattern of 1, 2, 3, 4, 5, 6, and 7 semitones. Within this tangle of motives lie hidden figures that rise to the surface in later songs of the cycle. One example is the ascending sequential pattern of a motive first heard in mm. 1–5. Its first statement (G–E–F–B–A), which is doubled in the winds, strings, and percussion, is shown schematically in Ex. 3.3. The motive itself has less importance later than does the pattern of intervals through which it ascends. This pattern is shown in the example by the upward stems on the notes G–A♭–B♭–C♯–E, the first pitches of the motive as it rises sequentially. These tones are brought together as a chord in m. 14 (labeled A in the example) that moves to the climactic and closely related chord B in m. 15. Later in the cycle, the pitch set G–A♭–B♭–C♯–E comes to the surface as a motive, and it becomes the principal theme in a passacaglia in song no. 5. At the conclusion of the fifth song, chords A and B are restated in reverse order amid other gestures that reinforce the palindromic form of the cycle as a whole.

Example 3.3 "Seele, wie bist du schöner," sequential pattern, mm. 1–15

Example 3.4   "Seele, wie bist du schöner," Viola, mm. 9–15

Beneath the cloud of motives, a longer theme emerges in the violas from mm. 9 to 15. It is a compound melody made at first from two contrapuntal strands that move by semitones outward in a contrary motion beginning on the tone C. The contrary motion underlying the theme creates a contrapuntal wedge akin to that contained in the main theme at the beginning of the String Quartet, Op. 3. By its end the theme touches on all twelve tones (see Example 3.4), which forecasts an element of twelve-tone chromaticism that is worked out systematically in songs no. 3 and 5.

The second part of "Seele" differs from the first by a slower tempo, a far thinner texture, and by new motives (although a few motives from the first section persist). The voice enters with its first tone hummed with lips closed, then open, "like starting and finishing a breath," as Berg instructs. For Adorno the voice enters "as if out of a pre-musical realm," creating a continuum with the opening orchestral music. The orchestra again rises to a climax in m. 29, then quickly dwindles into a liquidation that leaves mere splinters of earlier motives.

The second song, "Sahst du nach dem Gewitterregen," is the shortest of the five, a mere eleven measures. It has a rounded form, as the opening theme in the voice (Example 3.5) returns at m. 10, there in canon with the solo strings. Harmonically, the song is notable as Berg's first major study in octatonic pitch organization. Like the whole-tone scale, the octatonic scale—eight notes that alternate half and whole steps—was used by progressive composers to increase the chromatic flavor of their music. It was employed especially by Russian composers from the time of Rimsky-Korsakov, and it was revived in works by Debussy and Ravel and in an atonal context in music by Stravinsky, Scriabin, and Bartók.

Example 3.5 "Sahst du nach dem Gewitterregen," mm. 1–3

Ein wenig bewegt

Sahst du nach dem Ge - wit - ter - re - gen den Wald!?!

Example 3.6 "Sahst du nach dem Gewitterregen," octatonic formations

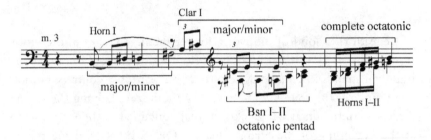

It has relatively little relevance to the music of Schoenberg. Given its symmetric structure, the scale has no a priori keynote and is only susceptible to three distinct transpositions before replicating itself; it is thus an example of what Olivier Messiaen later called a "mode of limited transposition."

Berg, like most composers who used octatonicism in atonal music, freely and quickly shifts among the three transpositions of the scale, drawing four- and five-note figures from one transposition or another. Except for a few whole-tone figures, every important harmony in the second song is a four- or five-note subset of an octatonic collection of pitches. The most distinctive octatonic chord of all, very prominent throughout "Sahst du nach dem Gewitterregen," is sometimes called the "major/minor tetrachord," a four-note figure made from notes of a common triad with both major and minor thirds.

An example of how this and other octatonic harmonies arise in the orchestral music is shown in Example 3.6, which contains the wind and brass music in mm. 3–5. A major/minor tetrachord first occurs in Horn I in mm. 3–4, echoed immediately in Clarinet I while the bassoons play a five-note octatonic configuration. The horns in m. 5 state a full eight-note octatonic collection, divided into two diminished chords. (Any two different diminished chords will fill out an octatonic scale, hence its designation by jazz musicians as the "diminished" scale.) It may well be that Berg's experiment with octatonic harmony, so remote from Schoenberg's own harmonic practices, was one of those "new means" that disturbed Berg's teacher when he first examined Berg's songs. In his later music Berg continued to make at least passing use of octatonic pitch fields.[64]

The third song, "Über die Grenzen des All," is the centerpiece of the arch-like cycle and with its simple ABA form it is the most clearly symmetrical of the five individual pieces. Berg often favored ternary or arch-shaped forms in his earlier music, but from this point the symmetry is created more systematically than ever before, it tends toward palindrome, extends to multiple aspects of structure, and is far-reaching in respect to the meaning of the music. The creation of large formal symmetries would be for Berg a standard procedure from this point forward. The song begins with a sustained twelve-tone chord played softly by twelve solo winds and brass. The notes from lowest to highest have the order C♯–A♭–D–G–B♭–E♭–F♯–A–C–E–F–B (Berg's placement of white-key tones together, here at the top of the chord, would be characteristic of his later twelve-tone music). The use of the complete chromatic was Berg's way of projecting the idea of the text, "Across the limits of the universe. . . ." Every four beats, each tone is taken by a different instrument, giving the chord a subtly changing color. Berg undoubtedly took this orchestrational idea from Schoenberg's third Orchestra Piece, Op. 16, where a five-note chord changes color in a similar way. Beginning in m. 6, the notes of the twelve-tone chord drop out one by one, from lowest to highest, until only the tone B remains in Clarinet I. At the reprise from m. 18, the voice repeats its initial theme while the orchestral chord is reassembled in the order that it was earlier disassembled, beginning with the note C♯ and ending with B.

The fourth song, "Nichts ist gekommen," is delicately orchestrated for a somewhat reduced ensemble emphasizing high-register and soloistic playing. At m. 10 the xylophone and voice introduce the motive shown in Example 3.7, which arose in the first song as an intervallic pattern within a sequence (G–A♭–B♭–C♯–E, cf. Example 3.3). This motive will then dominate the next song.

Example 3.7 "Nichts ist gekommen," mm. 11–13, Xylophone and Voice

The final song of the cycle, "Hier ist Friede," is a portrait of a hollow state of peace occupied by a soul in utter desolation. Berg uses the historical term "passacaglia" to describe its form, suggesting that the piece will consist of continuous variations on a theme first stated in long values in the bass. The passacaglia form had been brought to its greatest heights in the baroque period, and it kept its appeal in the late nineteenth and early twentieth centuries in a freer and more modern guise in works by Reger, Zemlinsky (Third Symphony finale), and Brahms (Fourth Symphony finale).

Berg begins his passacaglia in a traditional fashion with a somber theme laid out in long values in the bass, in triple meter (A in Example 3.8). The theme is made from the aforementioned five-note figure that played a background role in the first song and a motivic role in the fourth song. After m. 5 there is little that is true to the baroque model. The next five measures contain two themes brought back from the first song (B and C in Example 3.8), and materials from the third song are imported later. Theme B is a barer version of the viola theme from the first song (seen in Example 3.4), its twelve-tone content now more apparent with the earlier pitch redundancies removed. This theme and the use of the twelve-tone chord in song no. 3 show Berg in 1912 seeking a systematic approach to the use of the full chromatic collection of tones. In the atonal music of this time by many in Schoenberg's circle, full chromatic pitch fields are common, often used for emphasis or to mark climaxes, but Berg in 1912 was the first to explore methods by which to generate and apply the twelve tones systematically.

Example 3.8 "Hier ist Friede," principal themes

Example 3.9 "Hier ist Friede," mm. 52–53

Berg does not label the placement of the variations in his passacaglia, but in the *Menschen* piano score of 1921 he inserts a double bar every five measures, implying that there are nine variations, each about five measures in length beginning at m. 10. In these passages the three main themes return in intricate and ingenious variations that account for virtually every tone in the complex score.[65] In the final two variations (mm. 45–55) the voice falls silent while the orchestra returns to the somber spirit of the opening as its motives evaporate. The ending reinforces the large palindromic form of the whole cycle by restating materials from the beginning of song no. 5 in a reversed and palindromic order. One of the most provocative of these palindromes is the return of the main theme A with its notes transposed and in reverse order (Trombone III, mm. 51–52, Example 3.9). In passages such as this Berg takes an intuitive first step toward his later twelve-tone method.

Berg's scoring in the Altenberg Songs adheres to an essentially German, or blended, style of orchestration, by which important lines are usually doubled by instruments from several different choirs. The score reveals an enormous sensitivity to special colors inherent in the large orchestra, created by unusual combinations and by extended playing techniques. The treatment of some instruments—loud passages for muted trombones, for example—makes the score sound distinctly like that of *Wozzeck*. At the same time, the score has some notations that leave Berg's intentions for the players unclear, such as changes of clef in cellos, horns, and violas where it is uncertain what register the part should occupy. The orchestration has many examples of what Schoenberg in his *Harmonielehre* termed "tone color melody" (*Klangfarbenmelodie*). This, Schoenberg wrote, is a melody-like line made from changing timbres, these having the capacity to capture "the illusory stuff of our dreams." Berg would continue to refine his orchestrational style in the Orchestra Pieces of Op. 6.

Four Pieces for Clarinet and Piano, Op. 5 (1913)

Before Berg returned to orchestral composition, he created one of his least known and least studied works, the Four Pieces for Clarinet, Op. 5. They were written in April and May of 1913, shortly after the debacle of the scandal concert, and nowhere in his correspondence does Berg explain why he chose the combination of clarinet and piano nor what circumstances led him to compose the work. As with the Altenberg Songs, these pieces are miniatures, all four lasting less than eight minutes, but unlike the Altenberg Songs, they lack the intricate motivic development and recurrence that characterizes those works. Many who have studied the clarinet pieces find a sonata cycle implied by their tempos (moderate, slow, scherzando, slow), and a resemblance to Schoenberg's Six Little Piano Pieces, Op. 19, has often been noted. In those and a few other works from 1909 and 1910, Schoenberg experimented with a miniaturist style that banished themes and motives. He described it in a letter to Ferruccio Busoni from August 1909: "I strive for complete liberation from all forms, from all symbols of cohesion and of logic. So away with 'motivic working out,'" he wrote. "My music must be *brief*. Concise! In two notes: not constructed but '*expressed*.'"[66] This description might also serve for Berg's clarinet pieces, and the connection with Schoenberg's Op. 19 is reinforced by a few motivic figures common to the two works. Berg had studied Schoenberg's pieces Op. 19 as early as 1911, and he told his teacher that he found them "incredibly beautiful."

Berg's four pieces each have a different character, ranging from the improvisatory no. 1 to the somber no. 2 to the whimsical no. 3. All four have great freedom from regular rhythm, meter, or stable tempo. "We have long since dispensed with the bar line, which would place melody and phrasing in chains," Berg wrote to Erwin Schulhoff. "Take a look at my old clarinet pieces, or at Schoenberg's *later* works. In these the bar lines [*Takt*] could just as well be eliminated."[67] As in the Altenberg Songs, Berg explores new sounds from both clarinet and piano by extended playing techniques, especially trills, tremolos, flutter tonguing, and "echo tones" for the clarinet. In the piano part of the fourth number Berg employs a device first used by Schoenberg in his Piano Piece, Op. 11, no. 1, by which the keys of a chord in the right hand are silently held down to release the dampers. The same notes are then sharply struck in a lower register, which causes the right-hand chord to sound with a glassy shimmer.

Each of the four pieces ends softly, drifting away over quietly re-peated chords, and each piece that follows begins also softly and tenta-tively, as though awakening from sleep. Plainly Berg wanted there to be connections between the four numbers, but in the absence of motivic recurrence and development he had to experiment with a new way to interrelate them. He does this by bringing back in each piece certain constellations of tones that return hidden beneath highly contrasting sur-face appearances.[68] The basic collection is heard at the outset of no. 1, presented in the brief figure in the clarinet (Example 3.10). Its defining feature is not the motive in which it is found or the order of its notes, in-stead its total content of pitches—C–E♭–E–G–A♭–A—these notes placed, for purposes of comparison, in a compact scalewise order. The set of tones recurs at the beginning of each of the following three pieces. In no. 4 its notes are pared down to a five-note subset presented as chords; in no. 3 the tones are transposed; and in all appearances the basic set is reconfigured on the surface or motivic level. A subtle reappearance

Example 3.10   Piece for Clarinet and Piano, no. 1, Clarinet, m. 1

C E♭ E G A♭ A

Example 3.11   Piece for Clarinet and Piano, no. 2, Clarinet, mm. 2–4

of the basic collection is found in the clarinet part at the beginning of no. 2 (Example 3.11). The basic set recurs straightforwardly in the second bracketed phrase, and the six notes in the first phrase, in addition to sharing five tones with the basic phrase, have an abstract similarity with the basic phrase since the two have the same total intervallic content.[69]

The Clarinet Pieces had few performances during Berg's lifetime. They were published in 1920 by Robert Lienau after Berg had paid for their engraving, and they began to receive attention following a performance by Edward Steuermann and Karl Gaudriot at a concert on 23 October 1920 of the Society for Private Musical Performances. The concert was in honor of the visiting Maurice Ravel, who had great praise for the works that he heard by Schoenberg, Berg, and Webern. Ravel took a copy of the Clarinet Pieces back to Paris, where they were performed in June 1921 by the Société Musicale Indépendante. A review of the concert in *Le Ménestrel* drew a parallel between the pieces and miniaturistic literary forms:

> It is difficult to arrive at a clear judgment of the Four Pieces for piano and clarinet by M. Alban Berg after a single hearing. These pieces pertain to that literature, both in poetry and in music, that has spread throughout the world: pieces called "miniatures," "sarcasms," "bickering" [*criailleries*], "haikus." In them, brevity must correspond to an abridgment and compression, which this performance—though very correctly done by Mlle Suzie Welty and M. J. Guyot—did not allow us to perceive.[70]

Berg wrote to Helene after reading the review: "The critic spoke respectfully but without a correct understanding."[71]

Three Orchestra Pieces, Op. 6 (1914–15)

Following the conclusion of his studies with Schoenberg, Berg contemplated writing a symphony, a genre which, together with opera, posed the greatest challenge for a composer. During the winter months of 1911–12 he foresaw the symphony along the lines of one by Mahler, with voice or boys' chorus, and he contemplated drawing on Balzac's *Séraphita* for a text. But these aspirations were opposed by Schoenberg, who told Berg to take on an easier task, an orchestral suite of character pieces. Throughout the summer of 1913 Berg wavered between the two ideas, feeling a "necessity" behind the symphony and little enthusiasm for a suite. In March of 1914 he met Schoenberg in Amsterdam for the premiere of his teacher's Orchestra Pieces, Op. 16, and at this time Schoenberg's impatience with Berg boiled over. He told Berg that his recent works like the Altenberg Songs and Clarinet Pieces were "worthless" and "insignificant," and that a suite should be presented to him for his fortieth birthday in September.[72]

Berg of course did as he was ordered. When he returned to Vienna he set to work on an orchestral suite and soon settled on three character pieces of moderate length: a *Präludium*, a waltz movement that he titled *Reigen* (Round Dance), and a March. The first and third were completed in the spring and summer of 1914 and sent to Schoenberg by the time of his birthday on 13 September. *Reigen* was completed in 1915 and sent on in August of that year, just before Berg began his wartime military service.

In his Three Orchestra Pieces Berg found an ingenious way to comply with his former teacher's commands while still asserting his own will as a composer. In notes that he wrote for the first complete performance—on 14 April 1930 in Oldenburg, Johannes Schüler conducting—Berg revealed that the suite was actually a symphony in disguise.[73] The *Präludium* was its first movement; *Reigen* combined a scherzo and a slow movement, and the March was the symphonic finale. In his Orchestra Pieces Berg calls for an enormous orchestra and creates an intense unity and complexity of materials that characterize symphonic composition, not a loosely formed and lighter suite of character pieces as Schoenberg expected. Berg's model for this symphony was not Schoenberg, instead Gustav Mahler, the greatest master of the symphony at the end of the romantic period. In a letter to Helene, Berg admitted that the pieces arose at Schoenberg's command after hearing Schoenberg's Op. 16 in Amsterdam. But his own pieces—Berg insisted on this with an edge in his voice—would not resemble those of his teacher: "mind you, *not* modeled on his. They are utterly different from them!"[74] At last Berg was in rebellion against his overbearing former teacher. He later told Schoenberg that he had composed the Orchestra Pieces "in the manner you desired," but Schoenberg must certainly have seen that these enormously difficult works were not at all what he had ordered; rather, they were a declaration of independence. Schoenberg's control over Berg—at least as a composer—was now to wane.

Most who listen to Berg's Orchestra Pieces first note their great density and complication in texture, counterpoint, harmony, and form, and their similarity in gesture and expression to the symphonies of Mahler. This is quite the opposite of the light spirit normally found in "character pieces" even though the second piece plainly alludes to a waltz and the third to a march. Much about the Orchestra Pieces shows Berg in the same experimental frame of mind that he displayed in the Altenberg Songs. He returns to ideas that he had used in those earlier pieces—a coloristic treatment of the orchestra, twelve-tone chords and lines, and complex ostinati—and he adds to them several new compositional strategies and formal innovations. Even more than in the Altenberg Songs, the Orchestra Pieces are connected by shared themes and motives, which exist in a state of continual and far-reaching development as often occurs in Mahler's symphonies. The traditional formal archetypes that guided Berg during his studies with Schoenberg are little in evidence, replaced instead by symmetrical designs.

The *Präludium* is the shortest and simplest of the three pieces. In a letter to his student Josef Schmid, Berg described its form in these terms:

> The lst piece is called *Präludium*. Inadvertently it became an effort to write something symmetrical, i.e., the form can be explained approximately like this:

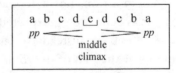

Of course, not slavishly so. It came out this way accidentally.[75]

Example 3.12 Präludium, rhythmic motive, m. 9

Example 3.13 Präludium, mm. 15–19

The piece begins mysteriously, almost primitively, with soft percussion sounds and pentatonic harmonies coming from intervals of the fourth. Gradually, motivic ideas emerge, then themes leading to extended melodies, all closely interrelated on the basis of small pitch cells and developing variations. At m. 9 Berg introduces an element that will play a prominent role in most of his remaining works. This is a syncopated rhythmic figure (shown in Example 3.12), scored unmistakably for trombone, playing softly at the very top of its range, and tamtam. The figure returns in the *Präludium* to mark structural junctures, and it is also developed like a motive throughout this and the two remaining pieces.

The main melodic material in the *Präludium* appears at m. 15 in a quicker tempo with a Mahler-like expressivity (Example 3.13). As Berg explained to Schmid, the music then rises to a climax (m. 36) where thirty-six orchestral lines fill an oversized score. The music then gradually thins out, and from m. 42 to the end returns to the opening materials in a freely reversed order, finally "disintegrating like dust," as Adorno put it.

Reigen (Round dance) is Berg's title for the second piece. Robert Falck and others have drawn a parallel between its form and that of Arthur Schnitzler's sex comedy of the same title, although Berg had relatively little interest in Schnitzler's plays, and the title might refer instead to the dance-like character of the music and its rounded form. Like the *Präludium*, *Reigen* has a symmetrical plan. It begins with an *alla breve* introduction where themes and motives from the *Präludium* reappear in new configurations. At m. 20 the music moves into a slow triple-time waltz whose melody is based on earlier motives and pitch cells (Example 3.14).

Example 3.14 *Reigen*, mm. 20–23

The middle of the piece from m. 42 is developmental, and virtually every section from this point introduces some innovative compositional process. The music gradually masses into a climax at m. 66 on a twelve-note chord made from intervals of the fourth. From mm. 83 to 94, where the waltz themes return, Berg superimposes multiple ostinati, like those used in the first Altenberg Song, here producing a texture of enormous complexity. Gradually themes from the *alla breve* introduction invade the triple-time waltz, producing a polymeter worthy of Charles Ives. *Reigen* ends with the entire orchestra softly intoning the rhythmic motive from the *Präludium*, after which the muted brass softly sustain a C-major triad, played "as from afar."

The Orchestra Pieces end with a March—the most complex piece that Berg ever composed. Mosco Carner held it to be "organized chaos," while Theodor Adorno deemed it "*terra incognita.*" Adorno told Berg that it sounded like a piece by Schoenberg and another by Mahler played at the same time, adding that Berg seemed pleased by this description.[76] Beneath its stunning complication lies a powerful, even demonic, expressivity. Much about it is plainly inspired by Mahler's symphonies. It begins with a grim funeral march as does Mahler's Fifth Symphony. The impetuous music that follows recalls the finale of Mahler's Sixth Symphony in which a march is repeatedly derailed by music having an eerie tranquility and a presentiment of doom, these moments exploded by massive stretti and outbursts punctuated by blows of a hammer. There is an especially close parallel between the end of Mahler's Sixth Symphony and Berg's March. In his symphony Mahler used an idea that he probably discovered in the finale of Tchaikovsky's Sixth Symphony by which the eerie stroke of the tamtam suggests the moment of death.[77] In both works a funereal equale in the trombones is next heard. Berg creates a similar figure at m. 155 (Example 3.15).

The form of Berg's March is very free, unstable in tempo, with march-like episodes crystallizing at mm. 50, 91, and 136, each in a different

Example 3.15   March, mm. 155–59 (condensed score)

tempo. In his letter to Schmid, Berg described the piece as an irregular A B A song form:

> The March has gotten quite big, but it has no formal similarity to those of Mahler. Basically it is again a three-part song form: Part 1; Part 2 with elements from the first part mixed in, and a great intensification to the reprise of Part 1. This [reprise] of course contains new shapes in addition to various elements from Part 1, and in form it is *quite different* from Part 1, giving rise after all to a beginning and conclusion like the middle section [Part 2?] (so somewhat like a two-part song form).[78]

We can only guess what Berg may have meant by this description. The main theme is probably the one heard in Violin I in mm. 6–8 (Example 3.16). Typically, the theme is a variant of those heard in the earlier pieces. Almost certainly, the reprise following the "great intensification" comes at m. 126, where the original tempo is reestablished and where the main theme returns. Berg's Part 2 may begin at mm. 53 or 92—new tempos mark both places. Mark DeVoto, who has studied the thematic form of the movement in detail, concludes that "the Marsch really reflects none of the classical forms so central to other works of Berg, but rather only a series of episodic sections set off from each other by changes in texture or tempo."[79]

Performances of the Orchestra Pieces have been rare. Berg made an eight-hand arrangement of them around 1920 for use by the Society for Private Musical Performances, and his autograph full score was published in facsimile by Universal Edition in 1923, part of his agreement with this publisher for the rights to *Wozzeck*. On 5 June 1923 Webern conducted the first two pieces at a concert in Berlin, and the reviews were mixed. Conservative critics like Max Marschalk dismissed them out of hand in a review in the

Example 3.16   March, main theme, mm. 6–8

Vossische Zeitung, but other critics found promise in them. In the *Deutsche allgemeine Zeitung* Walter Schrenk wrote with a perceptive insight:

> From Berg we heard two Orchestral Pieces from Op. 6, "Präludium" and "Reigen." Whoever comes upon them unprepared will, I fear, not get much from them. But it must be said that a quite distinctive and independent gift is heard. Berg is not a composer who relies on a teeming inspiration. Instead music wrestles its way out of him with difficulty. It trickles down, as it were, from the orchestra, which is handled with a sophisticated ability. It doesn't bloom, instead develops only slowly, as though having difficulty freeing itself from the heaviness of its thought. But it is a music of inward perception, coming from a diverse richness in rhythm—and, above all, it has line.[80]

Berg later refined and lightened the orchestration prior to the first complete performance of the work, in Oldenburg in April 1930, and this "new version" was published in a study score in 1954, edited by Hans Apostel. Berg approved of performances of the first two pieces, omitting the March, as was done when Webern conducted the work in 1923. Orchestras of the present day could make a great discovery by bringing these enigmatic and brilliant works into their repertory.

On 2 August 1915—two weeks before reporting for military duty— Berg sent off to Schoenberg the remaining movement, *Reigen*, of the Orchestra Pieces. Just before reporting for duty he purchased a copy of Georg Büchner's play *Wozzeck*, which he had seen staged a year before and which immediately attracted him as a prospective operatic text. He contemplated *Wozzeck* as his next major composition, but with it he faced considerable uncertainty. He had no experience with operatic composition and no idea how long the war would last. How would these circumstances affect his creative spirit and his prospects for the future?

4

The War and Its Aftermath, 1914–20

T HE DECLARATION OF WAR BY THE HABSBURG MONARCHY UPON Serbia on 28 July 1914 took many in Austria by surprise. Schoenberg was vacationing in Bavaria in the company of Vasili Kandinsky. Helene Berg had just returned from a month-long cure in Karlsbad and had moved with her husband to Trahütten for their summer retreat. There Alban's zest for composing fully revived. In addition to progress on the Orchestra Pieces he had begun to contemplate an opera based on Georg Büchner's play *Wozzeck*. But as Europe descended into all-out war and the Monarchy suffered repeated military disasters, Berg's prospects for the future again darkened.

Patriotic Enthusiasm

Berg at first supported the war and was ready to serve in the emperor's military, which he then did honorably for the duration of the conflict. Initially he shared the exhilaration that artists and intellectuals throughout German lands felt for the war. The writers whom Berg most admired were nearly unanimous in their support for it. In an open letter to Hugo von Hofmannsthal, Hermann Bahr wrote:

> Every German, whether at home or in the field, now wears a uniform. This
> is the tremendous fortune of this moment. May God preserve us! Nothing
> more can now distract us; once again we are on a single great German road.
> It's the old road of the *Nibelungenlied*, of the minnesingers and mastersingers,

Berg. Bryan Simms and Charlotte Erwin, Oxford University Press (2021). © Oxford University Press.
DOI: 10.1093/oso/9780190931445.003.0005

our mystics, our German baroque, Klopstock and Herder, Goethe and Schiller, Kant and Fichte, Bach, Beethoven, and Wagner. We had all split up on our own paths, but these took us into a thicket. Now to our great fortune we have been brought back together on the proper way.[1]

Austrian musicians, including those in Schoenberg's circle, were highly patriotic and confident that German cultural superiority would translate into military superiority. In the Foreword to his 1915 edition of Beethoven's Piano Sonata, Op. 111, Heinrich Schenker belligerently extolled the preeminence of everything German:

> Therefore, let the German nation, the most able on earth, endowed with talents and capabilities richer than even the Greek and the Roman, ascend the throne, and demand that the lesser finally learn to comprehend and gratefully appreciate their dimensions. Whether they like it or not! And in case the lesser, in order to learn at all to receive the benefits, should at first have to be coerced, even have to be punished like a child by its father—so be it![2]

Schoenberg was outraged to read the remarks made by Maurice Maeterlinck, widely reported in the Viennese papers, in which Germans troops were deemed barbarians for their actions in Belgium. In a letter to Zemlinsky of 25 October 1914, Schoenberg commented on Maeterlinck: "Now we should just let our guns do the talking and whoever can't wield them should crawl into a corner and try not to be seen."[3] Webern wrote to Heinrich Jalowetz on 4 September 1914, "I have only a single wish—to meet the enemy. To get to Lemberg! Dear God!"[4]

Predictably, Berg fell in line with such ideas. In a remarkable letter to Helene written on 31 December 1914, he declared the war to be a necessity:

> It's probably understandable that my thoughts turn again to the war, which now frightens me twice, three times more since I see that it will last much, much longer. It's unimaginable to me that the purpose of this war could be fulfilled more quickly. The task of purification! Certainly not *yet*. Things are still the way they were. There are still people, families, cities where they just don't see what the war is about. Where this corruption—by which I mean this aggregate of philistinism, greed, stupidity, mercantilism, journalism, laziness, egotism, petulance, deceit, hypocrisy, and what not—where this corruption is not in the slightest improved. . . . Yes! The war must go on. There's

still not a trace of purification in the last decade's old trash. If the war ended *today*, I tell you, Pferschl, in a fortnight the old corrupt conditions would be right back.[5]

Here Berg displays the naive idealism and unquestioning readiness to follow authority that haunted him throughout his life. The frame of mind revealed in the letter had already arisen in his fury at those who did not share his values and his unconditional surrender to the ideas of others whom he idolized. One of these was Karl Kraus, and Berg's letter parrots the content and style of Kraus's lectures that Berg had recently attended. Kraus's early wartime writings, such as the widely read "In dieser grossen Zeit" (In these great times, 1914), were not overtly anti-war but were instead cynical and subtly ironic critiques of a society led to war by deceitful journalists and greedy businessmen, those "sitting at the cash register of world history," as Kraus put it.[6]

By war's end in 1918, Berg's enthusiasm for the conflict had long since disappeared, and he more and more accepted Kraus's strident critique of its causes. In a letter to Erwin Schulhoff of 27 November 1919, Berg lists those responsible for the misery that the war had produced: the press, cap-italism, militarism, and Jewry.[7] His mention of Jewry is highly uncharac-teristic of Berg and reflects an idea taken obediently from Kraus. It would soon disappear from Berg's writings. Berg also endorsed the post-war ideas of Schoenberg, who could never abandon a belief in German cultural su-periority. Just after the war, French writers led by Romain Rolland asked intellectuals throughout Europe to sign on to a "declaration of the mind" that demanded artists to abandon nationalism. "We honor truth alone," Rolland wrote, "free, frontierless, limitless, without prejudices of nations or castes. It is for humanity that we work, for humanity *as a whole*."[8]

Rolland's declaration had many supporters in German lands, including Schulhoff, who had served in the German military during the war and was seriously wounded. Following the war he campaigned for Rolland's cause and wrote to many leading composers to ask for their participation. Berg responded that he was sympathetic to Rolland's ideas but could not endorse the declaration because Schoenberg and Kraus, among others, had refused to do so. Schoenberg had responded angrily to Schulhoff's appeal:

> I must speak out that I do not share your opinion over this impious interna-tionalization of art. Even before the war, the greatest German composers were

pushed aside and virtually every "modernist" was proud to take his modernism from Debussy while wanting nothing to do with me or Mahler. . . .
Are we now to lose our hegemony in music too? Certainly art is a common
inheritance of all nations, but if this common inheritance is to be spread
equally everywhere, then we Germans will have to give our music away
with nothing in return. The victors even before the war treated us differently: taking much from us that they lacked and giving back abundantly of
waste that we didn't need. I'm not for a politics of art but I must repeat what
I have often said. When I think of music, I think only of German music![9]

Schulhoff scornfully sent a copy of Schoenberg's letter to Berg, but
Berg even then could not question the ideas of his former teacher. Ten
years later, in his "Lecture on *Wozzeck*," Berg dutifully regurgitated
Schoenberg's last sentence: "The music of *Wozzeck* does not stray
from this path of German music—and when I think of music pure and
simple it is the only one, the only one that I find to be music at all."[10]
Schoenberg's idea may have lingered in Berg's mind as late as 1934, when
he dedicated his opera *Lulu* to Schoenberg. "Like all my works," Berg
wrote to Schoenberg, "it is indigenous to the realm of that most German
of music." Schoenberg was surely aware of the irony of Berg's words in
1934 when being "German" had expanded its meaning from a matter of
nationality and culture to one of race.

Men in Austria could be conscripted into the army until age forty-
two, and Berg was called for a physical examination in November 1914.
He was then declared unfit for military service, but after a second examination in June 1915, he was ordered to report for duty, which he did on
16 August 1915. He enlisted in the infantry as a "one-year volunteer," an
option available to those who had passed the *Matura*. After a year of active
service beginning at the lowest rank of *Gefreiter* (private), the one-year
volunteers could advance to the reserve officer corps. Following a short
training period in nearby Hütteldorf, he was taken in early October to
the Reserve Officer School in Bruck (twenty-five miles from Vienna) for
more intensive training.

Berg's Conscription

Berg's physical condition—never robust and never suited to the rigors of
military life—soon deteriorated, and within weeks of his arrival he was

taken to a military hospital in Bruck with a severe respiratory condition that was diagnosed as bronchial asthma with emphysema and chronic bronchitis.[11] The doctors there referred him to a "superarbitration" board in Vienna that acted on recommendations for sick leave and medical reassignment. After reviewing his papers, the board found him fit for office duty (*Hilfsdienst*) or for guard duty (*Wachdienst*). These two forms of service were very different, guard duty far more stressful and physically demanding than office duty. At first Berg was placed on guard duty at a barracks in Vienna, and his grueling service regularly entailed more than thirty hours of continuous work every two days.

His health again deteriorated, and he descended into a state of depression and panic. Later he told Schoenberg that he felt "degraded to the point of self-loathing," and in the draft of a letter to Karl Kraus he recalled that thoughts of suicide had come to him at this time.[12] His principal hope was to be reassigned from guard duty to a lighter type of work, the so-called *Hilfsdienst*, normally a secretarial or desk job. He argued that his one-year volunteer status entitled him to such a position, and his argument succeeded. On 26 January 1916 his superarbitration report was emended to stipulate solely "auxiliary service as clerk, office work," not guard duty. In April he was assigned to clerical work at a military base in Bisamberg, a northern suburb of Vienna, where runaway soldiers were sent. Berg witnessed their punishment:

> Their arms are crossed and tied behind the back, the arms then hoisted up on a tree so that the prisoner can only stand on his toes. When he can do that no more, he hangs until he faints from the pain. The barracks are atop a remote hill, reachable only by walking for an hour up a path through a sea of dust and excrement. It is surrounded by pickets and barbed wire, and we can leave only on Sundays. The barracks are wooden shelters that outdo any description. Completely lice-ridden. There are straw sacks on the ground that we are supposed to clean. The housekeeping is deplorable, and the toilets, or better latrines—I'll have to tell you about these in person.[13]

In mid-April Berg's prospects again improved as he was assigned to the Vienna War Ministry, and in May to "Division 10," which dealt broadly with war preparedness and planning. He put in long hours in his support position and served with distinction, receiving several promotions, finally to the rank of sergeant (*Zugsführer*).

How was it that Berg was moved into a relatively safe and comfortable desk job for the remainder of the war? There are no records that definitively explain his good fortune, but it is very likely that it came from the intervention (*Protektion*, as it was called) on his behalf by someone in a position of authority. Berg had several acquaintances who might have argued for him, the most likely one being his brother Charly, who was already stationed at the War Ministry. In a letter of 12 November 1919, Charly reminded Alban that it was he who had "offered him a position at the War Ministry."[14] A much more colorful explanation comes from Soma Morgenstern, a writer and friend of the Bergs from 1923 on. In his memoir *Alban Berg und seine Idole*, Morgenstern writes:

> Alban was mustered in 1915 and drafted into the military. Helene was very concerned about his health and she attempted to exploit the relationship of her mother to the court. At first her mother demurred but finally approved of a petition to His Majesty. Both awaited the outcome with great anxiety, and they secretly hoped for a favorable result for the appeal. To their great surprise, His Majesty invited Helene Nahowska for an audience. The Emperor promised the young petitioner to ask his aide, Duke Paar, to do something in the matter. Evidently the Emperor arranged the audience out of curiosity about his daughter. We can assume that he was very pleasantly surprised, because none of his archduchesses—certainly not the well-liked Gisela—were nearly so comely as Helene. I was curious to know if he sent her something. "Oh no," she said, "that cheapskate?" Alban added, "He was as big a tightwad as Helene. If she were a born Nahowska, she wouldn't be that stingy. The Poles aren't stingy." Still, he had her and her Papa to thank for a transfer to a special ministry service following his military training. He spent the whole war there—a life insurance policy that is not to be underestimated.[15]

The truthfulness of Morgenstern's anecdote is highly questionable. In the earlier days of his reign, Franz Joseph was famous for giving brief audiences to his subjects, often more than one hundred in a single day. But by the spring of 1916 these had ended and the emperor had withdrawn into his apartments in the Hofburg and Schönbrunn, making almost no public appearances, suffering poor health, and wrestling with depression over the progress of the war. Rumors had spread by this time that the emperor had descended into senility or perhaps had died, which he did only months later, in November 1916. The detailed records of the emperor's meetings in 1915 and 1916 now found in Vienna's Haus-, Hof-, und Staatsarchiv contain no mention of Helene Berg, and most of Morgenstern's statements about Helene in his memoir are equally questionable and arguably demeaning.

For the remainder of the war, Berg's life in Vienna returned more or less to normal. He and Helene formed a friendship with Alma Mahler, which grew out of mutual concern over the prospects of Schoenberg, for whom Berg continued to be a dedicated advocate and partial factotum. Berg and his wife frequented Mahler's soirées in Vienna and visited her often at her mountain retreat at Breitenstein near Semmering. The experience of Mahler's luxurious lifestyle with its rich artistic milieu was a welcome treat for the Bergs, given wartime shortages, and entrée into Mahler's circle gave Berg an opportunity to make and to hear music and to meet important people in Viennese musical life. At first the somewhat prudish Helene was troubled by Alma's notorious relations with men, and she referred to Alma acerbically in her letters to her husband as a succubus and hussy (*Luder*). Later these terms of opprobrium disappear as a closer friendship was formed.[16] Alma Mahler's many letters to the Bergs have survived; those with Helene continued until Alma Mahler's death in 1964, long into Helene's widowhood. To some degree Alma exploited Helene, as Schoenberg exploited Alban, to run errands and perform personal services like taking care of her daughters on occasion. With these girls—Anna and Manon Gropius (called Mutzi)—Helene developed a closeness that was expressed in birthday presents, gifts of chocolate, and other treats. Helene found her husband's relations with Alma a bit too close for her comfort, which explains why she herself maintained a presence with Alma, despite the insults that the latter was prone to deliver. The later correspondence between the two women documents Alma's genuine concern for Helene after Berg's death and her readiness to help Helene in her precarious financial condition in 1936 and in her long struggle to establish the Alban Berg Foundation.

Berg provided valuable assistance to Alma Mahler in 1923 and 1924 in the preparation of materials for the premiere performance of Gustav Mahler's Tenth Symphony. The work was left incomplete at the time of the composer's death in 1911, and in 1923 Alma called upon her future son-in-law, Ernst Krenek, to create a performing score based on the materials that Mahler left behind. Krenek prepared a score for two movements—an

Adagio and a scherzo-like movement headed "Purgatorio"—the only parts that he thought reconstructible with reasonable authenticity.[17] In an article in the *Musikblätter des Anbruch* in December 1923, Alma declared that the two movements had been virtually completed by Mahler himself and were then ready to be performed. Their authenticity, she wrote, would be shown by a forthcoming facsimile edition of the sources—an idea that Berg had proposed to her in the previous summer.[18] Alma then turned over Krenek's work to Franz Schalk, who was to conduct the Viennese premiere performance with the Vienna Philharmonic Orchestra. But Schalk found many of Krenek's readings to be deficient, especially in orchestration, and he added revisions to Krenek's score. Alma then turned to Berg to check the accuracy of Krenek's work against Mahler's manuscripts. Berg familiarized himself with Mahler's score drafts, closely examined Krenek's readings as well as Schalk's revisions, and, with his customary thoroughness, produced a lengthy and insightful critique of Krenek's score of the Adagio movement.[19]

During the war years Berg also renewed his teaching, for which he had great talent and devotion. He had begun his work as a teacher in the summer of 1911, taking on several of Schoenberg's students when Schoenberg left Vienna for Bavaria. Berg adopted Schoenberg's form-based pedagogy, which began with "theory" (harmony, counterpoint, and fugue) and continued to composition per se (which for Berg included instruction in form and orchestration). Those who studied with both Schoenberg and Berg usually found Berg to be the more patient and encouraging teacher. Gottfried Kassowitz (1897–1969) was one of these students, and he later recalled Berg's teaching in comparison to Schoenberg's:

> Alban Berg was *the* true teacher of all those in Schoenberg's circle. He lacked neither love nor empathy nor patience with his students. He taught harmony according to Schoenberg's method, and from the very beginning looked through all of my compositions and urged me to bring them in whenever I later hesitated. When reviewing them he noted every bit of epigonal thinking; when he saw this he would go to his library, take down a score and show me that the idea had already been done much better by this or that master. With a somnambulistic certainty he identified everything not carried through, not relevant to the overall work. . . . Berg concentrated more [than Schoenberg] on melodic construction, rhythmic refinements, large formal

proportions and the relation of content to form. He never used his own works as models.[20]

With more advanced students, like Theodor Adorno, Berg's teaching was based on a freer discussion and review of compositions during which Berg made observations that were relevant to his own compositional thinking. Adorno recalled:

> In order to get an idea of what it was like to study with him one must have a sense of his particular brand of musicality. Even as a teacher he responded slowly, almost broodingly, his strength was that of intellectual imagination and an acutely deliberate command of the possibilities, as well as a strong original fantasy in all compositional dimensions; not one among the newer composers, not even Schoenberg or Webern, was so much the antithesis of the ideologically puffed-up musician of that period as he was. Usually he would take a long time looking at what I brought him and then come up with possible solutions, particularly for passages where I had reached an impasse. He never smoothed over difficulties or skirted them with facile answers, but always hit the nail on the head: he knew better than anyone that every properly composed measure represents a problem, a choice between evils. Systematically he cultivated in me a feeling for musical form, inoculated me against what is insufficiently articulated, against idle activity, above all against mechanical, monotonous rudiments in the midst of compositional materials cut loose from their moorings. . . . The main principle he conveyed was that of variation; everything was supposed to develop out of something else and yet be intrinsically different. Unlike Schoenberg he had little use for stark juxtapositions. . . . He firmly distinguished between two kinds of composition: symphonic, dynamic, richly organized music and that which, possibly using one of Schoenberg's terms, he called the "character piece," in which, ideally, a single strongly defined trait serves to set it apart from what follows.[21]

As Schoenberg had done, Berg often called upon his students to assist him in chores such as proofreading, making of arrangements, writing program notes, and running errands.

Superstition and Pseudo-Science

The events of the war and Berg's anxiety about his future propelled him to an engagement with mysticism and the occult. During his courtship,

Berg had labored to convince Helene about the idealistic world in which he lived, a world that eschewed the material in order to realize the highest goals of the mind and spirit. Although Berg had little interest in or instinct for organized religion, he did not argue for any unorthodox beliefs—unorthodox as seen against his Roman Catholic upbringing—nor did he reveal any notable superstitions in the normal sense of the word. But by 1914 Berg had begun to interest himself in certain of the occult currents of the day, and this interest had an impact on his music at that time and later.[22] This preoccupation was not particularly idiosyncratic, as Douglas Jarman has pointed out, but was common throughout Europe in Berg's time.[23] In his classic account of Viennese life at the turn of the century, *The World of Yesterday*, Stefan Zweig points to an interest in the occult among the Viennese as "extravagant and uncontrolled," whose branches he enumerates as theosophy, anthroposophy, somnambulism, spiritualism, palm-reading and graphology, to which he might have added astrology and numerology.[24]

Strands of thought from several of these movements appear in Berg's writings and musical works throughout his life. They appealed above all to his imaginative, intuitive mind; they were the stuff of magic and of hidden meanings in which he delighted, along with more mundane activities like puzzles and acrostics. Things hidden or yet to be revealed touched his artistic sensibility as he, like other modernists, strove to find new forms of expression for inner meanings. In all that he distilled from contact with occult movements or practices, there lingers a whiff of skepticism and of irony, the latter often directed at himself, as for example his speculations on what form his own reincarnation might take, perhaps, he wrote to Helene, that of a dog because of his fidelity.[25] Berg's excursions into mystical or quasi-mystical belief systems can be puzzling, but they provide a means of teasing out some of the complexities in Berg's personality and in his approach to his art.

Related to his interest in the occult was Berg's notion that fate and predestination played a decisive role in his life, especially when he faced adverse circumstances. He found such ideas in the literature that he admired, especially the writings of Balzac and Strindberg. "Balzac always allows the figures in his books to form themselves upon events. They are modelled by the hand of fate as clay is moulded by the potter," writes Zweig.[26] Strindberg's *Blue Book*, which Berg closely read, allies the idea of fate, or predestination, to the idea of correspondences in the world—numerical relationships and quantities that seem to underlie reality. Like Strindberg, Berg thought that he had glimpsed the mysterious working of fate in recurrences, cycles, and symmetries of events in his own life that he thought coincided with certain numbers. Berg construed these sorts of occurrences as flashes of insight from a higher reality, and his working of numbers and patterns into his music became a type of signature.

In 1909 Berg underlined the following passage from the *Blue Book*: "There must be secret laws that guide our fate, and they can only be secret."[27] He marked up another page with Strindberg's explanation of karma, which is taken from theosophy: one's present incarnation comes from an earlier state of being according to the hand of fate, which the individual is obligated to bear for a lifetime.[28] While Berg's understanding of fate drew upon theosophy's focus on karma and reincarnation, he was in no sense a practicing theosophist, even less so than Schoenberg, who dallied with this philosophy off and on.

Other writings besides those of Strindberg that may have influenced Berg's views on determinism around this time are Otto Weininger's *Über die letzten Dinge* (Concerning last things, 1904) and Freud's *Zur Psychopathologie des Alltagslebens* (The psychopathology of everyday life, 1907).[29] Both embrace the idea that nothing happens by chance and there is no such thing as coincidence. Paul Kammerer's *Das Gesetz der Serie* (1919), mentioned in a previous chapter, also builds upon a theory of the periodicity of related events, and Berg's susceptibility to such ideas is apparent in his remarks to Helene.[30]

Berg's fatalism came to be expressed most overtly in his fascination for numbers. Number superstition has a long history in both intellectual and popular culture, and it enjoyed wide currency in Austria during the run-up to World War I.[31] Berg at some point decided that his fateful number was 23, and he first calls attention to it in a letter to Helene of 27 January 1914. His hotel room in Prague is no. 69, he writes, "which is three times 23!"[32] For believers in number mysticism, 23 has long been an object of attraction. Julius Caesar was said to have been stabbed twenty-three times, Shakespeare died on 23 April, and so forth. After settling on the importance of this number in his life, Berg typically thought back to earlier times to try to recall important and usually dire events that occurred on a 23rd day. Wasn't it on 23 July years before when he had his first asthma attack? In her later recollections, Helene Berg wavered between 1900 (shortly after his father died) and 1908 (when he was twenty-three years old) as the correct year.[33]

Berg's belief in the fateful importance of 23 was strengthened in the summer of 1914, when he read Wilhelm Fliess's *Vom Leben und vom Tod: Biologische Vorträge* (On life and death: Lectures on biology).[34] Fliess (1858–1928) was a curious and contentious figure: an otolaryngologist who wanted to make biology a more exact science by laying a mathematical or physical foundation for it, although his theories are often far outside the realm of science. In the first lecture of *Vom Leben und vom Tod*, Fliess summarizes his intentions:

> What I intend to bring forward for you today is the proposition that all of life progresses according to an inner mechanism that is part and parcel of the living organism itself. This mechanism is just the same for man, animal, and plant; it bears witness to our hour of birth with the same certainty as that of our death.[35]

Fliess based his ideas on copious observations of his patients, also of plants and animals, and on a variety of statistics, and he concluded that important events in all life forms occur in durations of twenty-three and twenty-eight days. "In every living organism," he wrote, "there are two periodic processes that return in 23 and 28 days. These are the rhythms of life—they are the pulse of birth, development, illness, and death." His sweeping theory about the periodic nature of all forms and aspects of human, animal and vegetable life was based on an interpretation of the female menstrual cycle, which he found to vary between 28 and 23 days. This led to his identification of 28 as the female number and 23 as the male number, since he argued that both sexes had some aspects of the other within them.[36] Fliess also held views concerning the significance of biological symmetry and right- and left-handedness and its relation to gender and to artistic and creative ability.

From his biological observations, Fliess made a string of bizarre conclusions, the strangest of which was the idea of a functional connection between the nose and the genitals, especially in women. Although outlandish, many of his ideas were taken seriously. He was a friend and confidant of Freud until about 1900 when they parted company over disagreements on scientific method. Freud still gave Fliess a measure of credit: "A bit of truth lurks behind every popular lunacy," Freud told him.[37] The concepts of bisexuality and periodicity were taken up by Otto Weininger and Hermann Swoboda, and Fliess sued both men for plagiarism, implicating Freud in the betrayal of his intellectual property. Freud later dubbed Fliess paranoid.[38] Paul Kammerer refuted Fliess's ideas on periodicity and the numbers 23 and 28 at length, concluding that there was no causal connection between symmetry and gender or between left-handedness and artistic ability, nor did the number 23 have any biological significance.[39] It is unlikely that Berg followed the debate over Fliess's priority on the matter of periodicity and bisexuality, given his antipathy to things scientific and to Kammerer in particular.

Berg soon brought his ideas about fate and numbers to Schoenberg's attention. In a letter of 10 June 1915 he explained why his actions often vexed his teacher:

> I will calmly characterize it as: *my fate*. That fate, which for years now has always made me appear disagreeable to you, if not through my own doing, then nevertheless *in association with events* that cause you annoyance. I remain unshaken in my firm belief in this fate—I could write a book on the subject; but even more interesting is the fact that it always involves a fateful number. The number 23![40]

Berg backed up his belief by citing some recent occasions when the number played a role, ranging from a telegram number to Alma Mahler's street address. Schoenberg's advice was that, while everyone had a special number (he himself was superstitious about the number 13), Berg should not allow himself to become bound by any such figure.[41] Berg returned to the subject in his letter of 20 June, wherein he reiterates that 23 "has always played a crucial role in my life and (since it seems as immutable and as unavoidable as the events it accompanies), I designate it as fateful, instead of just calling it significant."[42]

Related to their interest in numerology, the Schoenberg circle dabbled in astrology. A serious approach to this subject was taken by Dr. Oskar Adler, a close friend of Schoenberg's and an excellent violinist who regularly played and socialized with the circle members and participated in the Society for Private Musical Performances. Based on a series of lectures given in the years 1928–35, Adler published a multi-volume *Einführung in die Astrologie als Geheimwissenschaft* (Introduction to astrology as secret knowledge) in Vienna in 1935.[43]

Berg had sufficient interest in the subject to send a photo of himself to Fritz Werle, who was compiling a collection of artists' horoscopes. Berg's horoscope and photo appeared in Werle's publication in 1926.[44] Berg also sent photos of his hands to a palm reader, Marianne Raschig, who then published the hand photos and her analysis of Berg's and other prominent artists' hands in 1931.[45] Notes on astrology and a few horoscopes may be found in Helene Berg's papers, some of which are tucked into her books on anthroposophy.[46] There is little if any evidence that Berg took astrology or palm-reading seriously except as a matter of curiosity.

Certainly the most bizarre incident in Berg's flirtation with the occult is found in his correspondence with Günther Marstrand, who wrote to Berg in 1929 to inform him that, on the basis of similar handwriting, he believed him to be the reincarnation of Emperor Charles V (1500–88). Marstrand described himself as a student of Rudolf Steiner and an occultist with "a certain instinct for karmic threads that allow me to find the connection between various personalities."[47] Berg played along, in return asking Marstrand for his opinion on numerology and astrology, about which the latter offered nothing of note. Marstrand's presumption reached a peak when he proposed that Berg write an opera on his libretto that traced a thread of reincarnations from Brutus to Charles the Bold to the explorer Robert Scott. Robert Schumann was an embodiment of Scott, Marstrand contended, but this was not part of the libretto. At this point Berg dropped the correspondence.

Of most importance is the impact of Berg's occult thinking on his music. In addition to the use of number in both a symbolic and an architectonic manner, Berg also increasingly used musical forms of a circular or palindromic design. These are described in the musical discussions in this book, and their presence has been linked to Berg's occult interests by many Berg specialists. Theodor Adorno characterized Berg's attraction to mirror and retrograde forms as "anti-temporal," but he explained them in artistic as opposed to metaphysical terms, linking their static quality to Berg's visual imagination rather than the normally dynamic requirements of music.[48] Robert Morgan and Douglas Jarman, among others, have debated the meaning of Berg's circularities. Jarman convincingly relates circular motion to Berg's fatalism; Morgan links the practice to Nietzsche's idea of eternal recurrence.[49]

Postwar Burdens

As the war neared its end in the fall of 1918, conditions of life throughout Austria descended into chaos. Alban and Helene both claimed to have contracted Spanish flu during a pandemic that killed millions worldwide. Berg's mother reported on riots in the town of Villach near the Berghof, where stores were looted as food became unavailable.[50] Stefan Zweig recalled conditions in Vienna: "Two starving and freezing millions crowded the capital alone. . . . There was no flour, bread, or oil; there appeared to be no solution other than a revolution or some other catastrophe."[51] Berg's military service ended on 5–6 November 1918, six days before an armistice between the Allied Powers and Germany ended the war. "I am again a person!" he exclaimed to his friend Erhard Buschbeck. "Those were years of suffering and humiliation at a low rank, not composing a single note," he complained to Erwin Schulhoff. "Oh, it was so terrible that today—despite literally freezing and having nothing to live on—I am *happy* in comparison to then."[52]

In the summer of 1918, as the war ground to an end, Berg learned of Schoenberg's idea to found a "Society for Private Musical Performances" (Verein für musikalische Privataufführungen). The new organization would continue the work of a similar society that Schoenberg had helped to create in 1904—the Organization of Creative Musicians (Vereinigung Schaffender Tonkünstler)—which sponsored performances of modern works in Vienna, where public access to new music was notoriously limited. In an announcement of the objectives of this earlier organization, Schoenberg stressed the need for repeated performances of complex new works: "Only by regular performances of new works will it be revealed whether an interest for the products of the present day can be stimulated and kept alive within musical circles."[53]

Schoenberg hired Berg to be a manager of the new organization, which proved to be virtually a full-time job from its first concert in December 1918 until its demise in 1921. Berg wrote prospectuses and, at least in part, twenty-nine newsletters (*Mitteilungen*) to Society members.[54] He was also one of the authorized rehearsal coaches (*Vortragsmeister*), and he served on the Society's governing board. In the first of his yearly prospectuses, he stated rules of the organization: works were presented only following extensive rehearsals and these were often given repeated hearings, there could be no applause or booing, no reviews of works could be published, and attendance at concerts was open only to Society members.[55] No one style of modern music was given priority, and works by Claude Debussy and Max Reger proved to be the most often heard.

Berg's involvement with the Society brought him a small income and a measure of attention as a composer, since his Piano Sonata, Four Songs, Four Clarinet Pieces, and *Reigen* from his Orchestra Pieces (in his arrangement for eight hands) were performed at Society evenings. He, like others in Schoenberg's circle, made other arrangements for use by the Society, including a version of Johann Strauss's waltz *Wein, Weib und Gesang* for piano, harmonium, and string quartet.

Berg's work for the Society again diverted his attention away from composing. An additional distraction arose in the fall of 1919 in the form of a full-scale family crisis over the Berghof. This grew into a drama— Helene Berg dubbed it the "Berghof Catastrophe"—that involved larceny, embezzlement, accusations of slander and conspiracy, and legal actions that threatened to derail Berg's entire future as a composer.

The trouble over the Berghof began to brew shortly after war broke out in 1914, and it was at the beginning essentially financial in nature. Alban, his mother, and siblings had always formed a close-knit group, ready to offer each other financial assistance and other forms of support. Even at the age of thirty, Berg continued to receive an allowance, or "appanage," from his mother, partly in return for his continuing management of her property and finances, partly so that he could pursue his musical career. A large part of Johanna Berg's income came from the Berghof. Far more than a summer retreat, the Berghof was an extensive, self-supporting property that required year-round management. In addition to a large house and several outbuildings there was farmland and pasture for animals, along with fishing on the bordering Ossiachersee and a small forestry operation that yielded extra income. Agricultural production over and above that required for maintenance could be sold for a profit. A guest house with a tavern was run during the summer months. The whole operation required reliable personnel in a variety of roles and at the top a competent manager working under the family's supervision. Shortly after war was declared, management of the Berghof was disrupted. The farm's work horses were requisitioned and the farm manager was conscripted.[56] Farm products were soon subject to quotas. The government seized all milk beyond that supplied by two cows per farmer; butter became a luxury item and was not to be had by most people. Widespread hunger quickly became a fact of life in the major cities throughout the empire as farm production fell off. A shortage of agricultural manpower persisted throughout the war years.

Berg made two trips to the Berghof in November and December 1914 to sort out war-related problems and to hire a new manager. But his own wartime service precluded a return to the property until 1919. What little summer vacation he received from the War Ministry he spent in Trahütten in Styria with Helene, who preferred her own family's summer retreat to the Berghof. Helene's failure to fall in with the Berg family norm of gathering in the summer at the Berghof caused tension with the Berg family, and her reserve over family relations contributed to the Berghof crisis, as will be seen.

In the last year of the war, 1918, Johanna Berg resided at the Berghof for long periods to escape the shortages that plagued Vienna. She was joined there that year by her son Charly, his wife Stefanie (called Steffy) and their young son, Erich. Charly took over the management of the Berghof after receiving a furlough from his military service for agricultural duty. In late summer, Helene Berg made a rare trip from Trahütten to the Berghof to visit her mother-in-law, but soon thereafter Stefanie Berg faulted her for failing to pay for her food. This food quarrel is one indication that the Bergs did not think that Helene, with her family money, was doing enough to contribute to the family welfare. Helene did not let the accusation pass unchallenged.

The strain over worsening finances rose even higher at this time when Alban asked his mother for a raise in his allowance, which she granted but with a measure of resentment that also involved Helene. Alban remained a "problem child," and she was not optimistic, she wrote, about a future of "Componiererei"—literally, fooling around with composing. "You can't live in penury, that I must concede," she wrote to Alban. "And you have only *me* who can provide for you because we can't depend on *Helene*, who won't touch any of her money. That we—Charly and I—work all the time to bring in money and to maintain our assets, this you know already."[57]

Charly had no talent or interest in running a farm, and the failing conditions at the Berghof came to Alban's attention in fall 1919 when he and his sister Smaragda received anonymous letters from Villach warning them of nefarious goings-on at the Berghof. Alban and Helene investigated by suborning the Berghof servants—the housemaids Julianne Scheubeutel and Julie (Julchen) Achatz—in a spying operation. Helene wrote to Julie:

> Dear Julchen, Many thanks for your good letter and also for the proof sent by Julianne of your loyalty. I haven't forgotten you, Julchen, and will keep my promises. As soon as better times come for Vienna and the Viennese I will think of you! Your various reports interested us greatly. [58]

In October of 1919 the family, except for Herman, met at the Berghof, where accusations of conspiracy, theft, freeloading, and greed were hurled, not only among the Bergs but also among their spouses. Two of Helene's letters to Julchen had been intercepted by Charly or Stefanie and became evidence of a surveillance campaign conducted against them by the "Hietzinger," that is, Helene and Alban. To make matters worse, Johanna Berg, under the influence of Charly and Stefanie, had changed her will to make Charly the Berghof's permanent manager, while the other children would share only in whatever slender profit the property might produce. After an especially heated exchange involving the inheritance of his mother's jewelry, Alban filed a lawsuit for slander against Stefanie. Charly then erupted in outrage in a twelve-page letter to Alban in which he denounced his brother in the strongest terms:

> Yes, as long as anyone can remember, your character has been one of inconsiderate egotism bound to a total weakness of willpower. Your most fervid wish from your days of youth onward has been to get others to take care of you. When you gave up your work in the civil service you didn't want to go to work as a Kapellmeister, instead you weaseled your way into Mama's affairs. You have shirked every opportunity to make money, to become a productive member of society, to stand on your own two feet. And the result has always been that Mama has had to keep you afloat. Even your marriage became a binding obligation [bindender Zwang] on Mama, and the old lady,

as always naive in financial matters, willingly sacrificed without realizing that her monthly allowance was for you only a welcome refuge from having to work. . . . I don't question the beauty of a life in art, *but you should enjoy it at your own expense, not at that of others to the end of your days.*[59]

Following this vehement outburst, Alban wrote to his brother Herman to give a lengthy account of the Berghof situation, his "complete break" with Charly, and especially the unfairness of his mother's change of will:

If at the time of Mama's death the capital and the [Vienna] house no longer exist and only the Berghof survives, on which Charly can live comfortably his whole life, the others, without recourse, will receive maybe a couple 100 kronen profit. Even on an excellently run farm a profit can be exactly zero. . . . Thus a single person in the family becomes essentially a sole heir.[60]

Believing that they had been evicted by Alban and Helene, Charly and his family abandoned the Berghof in late December 1919, and Alban went there alone to take his brother's place. He would remain at the Berghof for four months, and the bitterness over the event was never to heal. In a strongly accusatory letter written to Helene in June 1965, Erich Berg thought back forty-six years to that moment:

The five to eight days that the three of us spent in that shabby Gasthof Six on the church square in Villach before going home, while Alban was already moving into the Berghof, remains with me a sharply painful memory. Papa and the rest of us were left literally staring into the void. But even then we did not suspect the forthcoming fate of the Berghof [its sale], and your secret plan was a real masterpiece.[61]

Alban saw things differently. During his months on the farm he poured out his misery to Helene in almost daily letters. His motivation in staying at the Berghof, he reiterated, was the need to repair his mother's finances, with which he had long been involved as manager of her Vienna properties, as well as to rectify the management crisis—all of this in his mind for the good of his family. He first defended himself to his mother, who had echoed Charly's accusations concerning his lack of a profession:

I am not going to the Berghof just because "I have no proper employment in Vienna" nor because "I am receiving no appanage"! Quite the opposite! Let me be specific (to prevent any misinterpretation later on):

1. In Vienna *I have proper employment.* Specifically, my position with the Society [for Private Musical Performances], which is continuing; 3 students; and your business affairs, which cost me 1 or 2 half days per week.

2. In light of this—even without your allowance—I make 850 K. (Kassowitz pays 300 K., Jelinek 50, Watza 100, the Society 400 K.). Also I have five more installments coming from the Bareis and Herman funds [set up in 1900], so 1250 K. monthly, which will continue at least until May. I'm not even including the *continuing* payments I get from Universal Edition: in the same mail [as your letter] I received a new assignment—writing a Guide to Schoenberg's *Pelleas* for January!!! . . .

3. Helene understandably will not be coming to the Berghof (among other reasons, just now she is negotiating with the American embassy for the export of models of children's clothes, which promises to pay off handsomely).[62]

Alban's reference to Helene's burgeoning profession, which never attained any significance, was more than likely an excuse to cover up her real feelings about the Berg family and her wish to separate herself—and her money—from their quarrels.

Berg remained at the Berghof until April 1920, in company with his mother, Smaragda, and Smaragda's companion, May Keller. His letters to Helene give a vivid picture of the deplorable state of affairs there and the hard physical labor that was needed to make the property again profitable. Charly has stolen over 300 pounds of food staples, he reports, along with sausage, crates of potatoes, the four best laying hens, and almost all kitchen utensils.[63] More particulars were later added in a strongly worded letter to his mother, drafted mainly by Alban for Helene to send. The letter goes into detail about the wretched condition of the animals, the poor harvest, and the deplorable condition of the farm equipment. The conclusion of the letter is that neither Charly nor Mama Berg can run the Berghof, and Alban and Helene are not prepared to do so. Finally, Helene explains that she has no intention of becoming a farmer's wife:

> I know for sure that I am, in spite of my millions, a modest middle-class woman, and even stretch to be that and, if we kept the Berghof, would even then be only a simple farmer's wife . . . and my life, like that of the boy who runs the farm, would be shaped accordingly.[64]

Helene's reference to her "millions" suggests that the Bergs felt they had some claim on the Nahowski family money. In a tax appeal in 1912, Berg reported Helene's dowry as totaling 100,000 kronen in securities, which yielded about 4,000 kronen a year in income.[65] Insinuations from Johanna, Charly, and Stefanie Berg about her miserliness drove Helene further away from the Berg family. She defended herself in a letter from February 1920 to Herman, also partially drafted by Alban. Helene begins with an attempt to justify "my conduct and especially that of my family." Her family, she continues, has been puzzled over the Bergs' treatment of Alban, and the crowning blow was the accusation from Charly and Stefanie that she and Alban had actually squandered Mama Berg's money.

> The opposing party [Charly and Stefanie], who could not do enough to throw dirt on Alban, asserted in the presence of Mama, May and Smaragda that the "Hietzinger have squandered Mama's assets." I don't know if you are aware of what sort of lie that is. . . . Then the unbelievable happened: Mama remained silent concerning this outrageous lie; she actually seemed to welcome it! To me, who number among the "Hietzinger," this was too much! On the advice of my parents, I withdrew, deeply hurt and insulted from such crass unfairness. My parents did the same, as this slander of their daughter and Alban, the squandering of Mama's assets, unrefuted by Mama Berg, fell also upon them.[66]

Johanna Berg finally, after many painful scenes and recriminating letters, recognized that the state of the Berghof property had declined to the point that selling it was the only realistic choice. Her change of heart may have been effected by Herman, who responded to the crisis by fully taking Alban's side and dismissing Charly as a rogue and weakling. Johanna acknowledged Charly's failure—although she preferred to blame Stefanie—and again rewrote her will. The Berghof sale to a consortium of four Italians was finally concluded on 24 April 1920, for the sum of 1.25 million kronen.[67] Johanna used part of the money to purchase a house in Küb in the Semmering. She put the property in the name of her daughter, Smaragda, with whom she and May Keller shared its occupancy in the summer months.[68]

A Change of Profession

In the turmoil of trying to find a solution to the Berghof problem, Alban's mind kept going back to his abandoned profession and his family's continuing incomprehension concerning his musical career. This crushing realization was for him the ultimate blow of the Berghof catastrophe—that his family never would fully understand or support him emotionally or intellectually. On this topic he repeatedly unburdened himself to Helene during the months at the Berghof:

> It is astonishing, the complete obtuseness concerning my livelihood and my career! Even Herman, who really in the most touching way wishes me well, really thinks that my greatest good fortune would be to manage the Berghof. I truly think he has forgotten that I have a profession and a calling![69]

He sounded the same note a month later:

> They [Mama, Smaragda and May] think now that I don't *want* to be here, although I've told them X number of times that it is not that, it is a pure *impossibility for me*, even with the *very best* income and the best *material* conditions, yes, even if *you* were here, I cannot be a farmer after 35 years of being Alban Berg! This Alban Berg would cease to exist in the moment that he gave up everything else to be the manager of the Berghof. These people don't understand this (as they don't understand German, because they don't understand my letters).[70]

While he wrote and spoke vehemently to Helene and to his family about his musical calling, during the months at the Berghof, Berg was in fact forced to reassess his whole future occupation and livelihood. For him composing was always a deeply felt necessity, but at the age of thirty-five he had earned virtually nothing doing so, and the wolf was at the door. He was stung by his brother's accusations of his freeloading as well as by Schoenberg's repeated pressure to spend his time writing about music rather than composing it.

As always, Berg could not say no to his former teacher, and writing pushed composing ever more aside. In May 1918, while at work in the War Ministry, he had written a short "thematic analysis" of Schoenberg's Chamber Symphony, Op. 9.[71] The analysis was far more modest than the *Gurrelieder* Guide of 1913 and was limited mainly to a list of themes. But Berg's originality as an analyst of music is apparent in his insight into the work's large-scale organization, in which he recognized the presence of a hybrid form that intertwined the four movements of a symphony with the sections of a single sonata form. This plan had been used in works by

Franz Liszt, among others, in the nineteenth century, but in 1918 it was still virtually unmentioned in the analytic literature.[72]

In March 1920 Berg made the painful decision to change his profession and become a freelance writer on music and consultant for publishers. Composition would be secondary, done only during summer vacations as time permitted. He explained his plan in a letter to Webern:

> I would like to devote myself, as I have already told you, to "writing about music," also to make piano scores etc., to write on Schoenberg's works after all that. I think I'll be able to accomplish something in this. . . . This is work that will be permanent and not just occasional. In this way I think steady advancement will be possible. I almost forgot—I would give lessons as often as possible. Composing? Yes, that would be nice. Maybe during one or two summer months![73]

Berg had many projects in mind in 1920 for his new career. He planned to contribute articles on music theory to the *Musikblätter des Anbruch,* a new journal on modern music published by Universal Edition. He wanted to write polemics in which he could imitate the edgy style of Karl Kraus, also concert guides and studies of the music of Schoenberg, on which he was then recognized as an authority. In December 1919 he had received a request from Emil Hertzka of Universal Edition to write another short concert guide, this time to Schoenberg's tone poem *Pelleas und Melisande*, which Berg completed in short order. In the following spring he expanded the guide into a longer *Thematic Analysis* that shows the work's major themes integrated into a hybrid symphonic form, akin to the one he had found in Schoenberg's Chamber Symphony. Berg neatly accounts for the programmatic element of Schoenberg's tone poem by inserting quotations from Maeterlinck's play at relevant points in the analysis. In June 1920 Universal Edition published the earlier, short version of Berg's study but rejected the later version as too long for publication.[74]

In his new occupation Berg most wanted to write polemics directed at critics of modern music. These would be similar to the polemics of Karl Kraus, which he eagerly read in Kraus's journal *Die Fackel*. Berg wrote two such essays in the spring and summer of 1920: "Die musikalische Impotenz der 'neuen Ästhetik' Hans Pfitzners" (The musical impotence of Hans Pfitzner's *Neue Aesthetik*), which appeared in the June 1920 issue of the *Musikblätter des Anbruch*, and "Wiener Musikkritik" (Vienna's music criticism), which was first published in 1963.[75]

In the first of these Berg launched an assault on Hans Pfitzner's recent book *Die neue Aesthetik der musikalischen Impotenz: Ein Verwesungssymptom?* (The new aesthetic of musical impotence: A symptom of decay?).[76] Pfitzner (1869–1949) was widely respected as a composer and conductor, and Berg had long counted him as one of the greatest contemporary composers.[77] After Berg and his wife attended a series of three concerts in Vienna in February 1916 devoted to Pfitzner's music and conducting, Berg wrote to him, "from the depths of our hearts we thank you for these unforgettable evenings."[78] But as World War I wore on, Pfitzner's trenchant German nationalism and distress at the state of modern German music increased, and he began to write broad and exaggerated condemnations of modern trends that, in his view, were dragging German music downward. In his widely read polemic *Futuristengefahr* (The danger of futurism, 1917), Pfitzner forcefully dismissed the modernist ideas of Ferruccio Busoni.[79] Busoni had forecast a future for music that would outstrip its past, provided that it was freed from hidebound rules.[80] For Pfitzner an untested future for music filled with unproven innovations was unsettling, according too little respect for the greatness of German composers of the past. Schoenberg had entered the dispute by taking Busoni's side in an essay "Falscher Alarm" (False alarm) that contested Pfitzner's position.[81] Although Schoenberg found it politic to leave the essay unpublished, Berg could be assured that an attack on Pfitzner would have Schoenberg's support.

Still, Pfitzner was an odd choice as the object of Berg's polemic, which may have been provoked by hearsay and misunderstandings. While managing the Berghof in February 1920, Berg received a report from Helene on a visit with Maria and Franz Schreker: "By the way, [Schreker] told me that Pfitzner has written an outrageously nasty book about modern music, *against Mahler, Schoenberg, and himself!*"[82] In fact Pfitzner does not mention Mahler, Schoenberg, or Schreker in his *Neue Aesthetik*, and Schreker was probably repeating what he had recently read in a short notice in the journal *Melos*. Here the editor, Hermann Scherchen, strongly denounced Pfitzner's book. "That an artist of Pfitzner's standing," wrote Scherchen, "could call out Paul Bekker but actually have Mahler, Busoni, Schreker, and Schoenberg in mind . . . cannot be too strongly condemned."[83]

Pfitzner has little to say about modern music in his *Die neue Aesthetik*, although at the end he laments a decline in musical culture in comparison to the greatness that once was. "*Quiet* music is no longer composed," he writes. "The piano sonata has died out. Whoever nowadays says that he finds a song by Adolf Jensen beautiful is disgraced. But the madhouse kitsch of a Cyril Scott or other futurists is taken seriously."[84]

Pfitzner was also skeptical about the value of musical analysis in discussions of aesthetics. Inspired ideas are beyond analysis, he asserts, products instead of an irrational process based on pure feeling. As an example Pfitzner cites the melody of "Träumerei" from Schumann's *Kinderszenen*, which, he says, has no strikingly distinctive structural features but still engages the emotions of the listener, with no intervention from reason or analysis. In contemplating such a melody, Pfitzner concludes, the listener can only exclaim, "How beautiful!"[85]

Berg might readily have agreed with most of the ideas in Pfitzner's book. He certainly would have agreed with Pfitzner's view on the superiority of German music, which is a recurrent topic in Berg's writings, and Berg also often lamented the degraded taste in music among contemporary audiences. But Berg had no sympathy with Pfitzner's many eccentricities and exaggerated hostilities: his view of the pervasive decline of German culture, his hopeless pessimism about the present and future, or his blatant anti-Semitism.

In his attack on Pfitzner, Berg adopts subtle polemic strategies inspired by the writings of Karl Kraus.[86] He begins with an expression of respect for Pfitzner, only later holding him up to ridicule. He then quotes extensively from an isolated passage in the middle of Pfitzner's text concerning Schumann's "Träumerei," glossing each quotation and piling argument upon argument against Pfitzner's viewpoint. He then turns to technical analysis—his strong suit as a writer—to reveal motivic features in Schumann's melody that are rich, ingenious, and outside the norm, all suggesting a special aesthetic quality in the melody. Near the very end of the essay, Berg arrives at his main point. If structural ingenuity, richness, and going against the norm promote a sense of beauty in Schumann's melody, then these features can also suggest the presence of beauty in modern music, making such works potent rather than impotent. Berg says that he is ready to analyze melodies by Mahler and Schoenberg with this goal in mind, but limited space allows him only to cite a counterexample from the modern repertoire. The unnamed work that he produces is the opening of Pfitzner's own song "Nachts," Op. 26, no. 2 (1916), which had recently been performed by the Society for Private Musical Performances. The music has none of the special qualities that Berg had just observed in "Träumerei": its phrasing is entirely in two-measure units, the texture and rhythm are unvaried, the voice line is melodically sterile, and the harmonies move sluggishly. Under his quotation from Pfitzner's song, Berg tauntingly adds the exclamation, "How beautiful!" Berg ends his essay with a polemical flourish, restating Pfitzner's empty description of Schumann's melody, now applied to Pfitzner's own music.

Berg's article had a mixed reception among his acquaintances. Heinrich Jalowetz wrote to Berg to ask: "Can we exhaust the essence of an art by using the means of a conceptual language, an art whose means of expression has just the advantage that it is *not* conceptual?"[87] Alma Mahler strongly took the side of her friend Pfitzner, and she wrote to Helene, "All of the quotes from Pfitzner show *him* to be right. Music is something unexplainable, above all melody. It's not A B C D, X, Y, Z. Does Alban really think that something can be explained in this way—or anything at all?"[88] In the 1926 edition of his *Neue Aesthetik*, Pfitzner himself addressed Berg's article. "Having certain people instruct me about inspiration makes me think of the hospital trainee telling the woman who has just given birth how to get through labor. Who should deal with aesthetics? One can only testify to what one has experienced."[89]

Berg followed up on the Pfitzner article with a related polemic attacking selected musical journalists. Displeasure with music critics and their writings was strongly felt throughout Schoenberg's circle, especially by Berg, whose letters are filled with expressions of vexation over the negative and superficial coverage that their new music received in the press. In the summer of 1920, Berg began to research the new article by collecting newspaper clippings with ideas that seemed to him to be glaringly defective. At first he chose three of these—a concert review by Julius Korngold in the *Neue freie Presse*, a book review by Elsa Bienenfeld in the *Neues Wiener Journal*, and a diary notice by Max Kalbeck from the *Neues Wiener Tagblatt*. Berg quickly dropped the Kalbeck article from his essay and concentrated on the remaining two. As he did with Pfitzner, Berg chose large targets for his polemic. Korngold (1860–1945) was the principal music critic for the *Neue freie Presse*, Vienna's largest paper, and his reviews were known for their broad knowledge and erudition, devotion to the classic masters, openness to the progressive music of the period of Richard Strauss and Gustav Mahler, and vitriolic intolerance for such later developments as atonality and the New Objectivity of the 1920s. Elsa Bienenfeld (1877–1942) was the leading music critic for the *Neues Wiener Journal*, a respected tabloid founded in Vienna in 1893. Her caustic review of the Altenberg Songs following the scandal concert of 1913 may still have been in Berg's mind when he chose her as one of his targets.

In "Vienna's Music Criticism" Berg follows the Krausian model deployed in the Pfitzner article. He quotes extensively from his sources, refuting their every thought from multiple angles, and he uses witty puns to satirize his subjects. His method in this article is to point out the factual inaccuracies in the two feuilletons and their sloppy grammar: if these writers make repeated gaffes in such basic mechanics, how could their fair-mindedness or judgments about new music be trusted?

As he was planning "Vienna's Music Criticism" during the summer of 1920 Berg agreed to take on editorial work for the bimonthly journal *Musikblätter des Anbruch*. In late June he signed a contract with the publisher, Universal Edition, to run the Vienna office of the journal. The position, which was to begin on September 1, was largely managerial: assisting the principal editor, Otto Schneider, to assemble articles and musical supplements, proofreading, attending to correspondence, and the like. But very quickly Berg realized that he was not suited to this type of work. In late September he resigned from the position, citing poor health as the reason, although he continued to do freelance editorial work for *Anbruch* for several years.

With the composition of *Wozzeck* in full swing by 1920, Berg's interest in writing waned. In a letter to Kassowitz he compared writing about music to composing *Wozzeck*: "How disgusting the former seems to me compared to the latter. But it has to be."[90] Berg leaped at the chance to write a book on Schoenberg's music when an offer was made to him in November 1920. Earlier, in January of that year, Schoenberg had recommended him to the E.P. Tal Verlag for such a book, but Berg could not accept due to the Berghof crisis. In November another opportunity arose when he was contacted by the Otto Halbreich Verlag in Munich with an offer to write a short book on Schoenberg. Berg readily accepted and hoped to focus on Schoenberg's entire musical oeuvre "to show its seamless development."[91] Over a period of years Berg compiled copious notes for the project, but he was never able to bring it to completion.[92]

By 1920 the factors that had long stalled Berg's progress as a composer were finally past. Given resources from their families, the Bergs were spared much of the deprivation that plagued Austria after the war. Berg's relations with Schoenberg were on a more even keel than earlier, and he had assembled his own circle of devoted students. He was ready now to push forward on the work that would make him an international celebrity: the opera *Wozzeck*.

Wozzeck

BERG'S EIGHT-YEAR JOURNEY TOWARD THE COMPLETION OF HIS FIRST masterpiece, the opera *Wozzeck*, began in May 1914. Georg Büchner's play *Wozzeck* was given then at Vienna's Residenzbühne by a visiting company from Munich's Court Theater, with the celebrated actor Albert Steinrück in the title role. Berg attended two performances and immediately saw in the play material for an opera. Composing an opera had long been in his mind. When his Altenberg Songs neared completion in 1912 he wrote to Schoenberg: "If only I had a suitable text for the theater," he lamented. "I was already considering Strindberg's *Chamber Plays*, and now that you suggest Strindberg that of course seems all the more compelling."[1] Berg said nothing more about an opera based on Strindberg's five *Chamber Plays* although Strindberg's writings remained for several years in Berg's mind as an alternative to Büchner's play for operatic use.

Operatic Plans and Uncertainties

When Berg first contemplated setting Büchner's drama in 1914, far-reaching changes within the operatic genre itself were underway. By temperament Berg was closest to the nineteenth-century German and Wagnerian operatic model, but he was also well acquainted with the broader operatic repertory. As a youth he regularly played four-hand opera scores with his sister, and throughout his life he attended works of all sorts staged at the Vienna Opera. His keen interest in new operas

Berg. Bryan Simms and Charlotte Erwin, Oxford University Press (2021). © Oxford University Press.
DOI: 10.1093/oso/9780190931445.003.0006

was nurtured by a careful study of scores and stagings. Before the Vienna premiere of Paul Dukas's *Ariane et Barbe-Bleu* in April 1908, for example, Berg wrote to Helene about the "thousands of splendid passages" that he had found when he studied the work at the piano and which he had heard when he attended rehearsals and finally witnessed when he attended several consecutive performances.[2]

Modern works that signaled new directions for the genre especially drew Berg's attention. He was very familiar with Debussy's *Pelléas et Mélisande* (1902), whose libretto was an abbreviated, unadapted version of the play by Maurice Maeterlinck. It created a model for "literary opera," of which the *Wozzeck* libretto is a later example. During his student years, when he contemplated a career as writer, Berg had tried his hand at creating a libretto of this type. He chose Franz Grillparzer's play *Die Ahnfrau* (The ancestress), which he abbreviated with minimal adaptation, although he never composed music for the resulting libretto.[3]

Berg was also alert to new ideas on operatic form. Maeterlinck's play *Pelléas et Mélisande* consists of a series of tableaux, which Debussy connects by symphonic interludes in his opera, as did Berg later in *Wozzeck*. An important development in operatic form that began to appear in works around the time of World War I was the return to operatic numbers—arias, duets, ensembles, choruses—whose closed forms were an alternative to Wagnerian continuity. Richard Strauss's *Ariadne auf Naxos* (1912) is an early example, and works of the 1920s in the neoclassical vein continued in this Mozartian direction. Although Berg often expressed disdain for neoclassicism, in *Wozzeck* (and even more in *Lulu*) he made concessions to its emergence in operatic form. In harmonic language Berg was influenced by Strauss's *Salome* (1905), which maintained much of the rich orchestration, complex intertwining of leitmotives, and through-composed form of Wagnerian opera but brought to it a higher level of dissonance, moments of atonality, and a scandalously erotic text.

Despite his initial enthusiasm in 1914 for *Wozzeck*, Berg for years made little concrete progress on his operatic plans. His attention was still absorbed by the Orchestra Pieces, which he would complete only at the end of July 1915. His student Gottfried Kassowitz recalled that Berg sketched two scenes of the opera shortly after seeing the 1914 staging, but studies of the opera's musical manuscripts have not confirmed this recollection, which was recorded fifty-four years after the fact.[4] More than a year elapsed before Berg purchased a copy of Büchner's play, and it is questionable that he would have begun even preliminarily to sketch music without a text at hand.[5]

During the war years Berg's confidence that he had found the right subject for an opera faltered, and he contemplated giving up on *Wozzeck* and trying another text. His fading self-assurance at this time increased when Schoenberg told Berg that his *Wozzeck* project was doomed to fail. Gottfried Kassowitz had this recollection:

> When Berg had been working on *Wozzeck* for some time, he became quite despondent. When I asked him why, he told me that he had just spoken with Schoenberg about *Wozzeck* and that Schoenberg had said that it could never lead to anything good. Why? Because "Wozzeck" was an anti-musical and unsingable name! Berg was so under Schoenberg's thumb that he was actually wavering. But the splendid material soon exerted so much power that it won him back.[6]

After completing the opera, Berg remarked to his wife that Schoenberg "tried to take away all my pleasure in it."[7]

At this time of self-doubt, Berg returned to his longstanding interest in the plays of August Strindberg and wrote extensive notes and drafts for an alternative operatic text of his own that he titled "Nacht (Nokturn)." After telling friends that he was planning an opera on *Wozzeck*, Berg evidently was reluctant to mention the alternative plan, although he talked about it briefly in a letter of 28 February 1917 to Erhard Buschbeck. After thanking Buschbeck for sending him an almanac on modern writers, Berg continued:

> Also many other names in the almanac I have long known and admired (including the fabulous Büchner, whose Wozzek I for years thought of composing until an equally old idea for an opera, let's call it, in recent times again attracted me).[8]

"Nacht" is an incomplete and fragmentary text—Berg called it a "monodrama"—whose drafts came to light only in 2006.[9] Berg dated one page of the fragments "winter 1915/16," but it is certain that he continued to add materials to it through the early months of 1917, at which point he put it aside permanently and returned to *Wozzeck*. The monodrama focuses on a single character, designated "He," who plainly represents Berg himself. As he falls asleep at night, aided by the use of alcohol, he confronts the Other, a figment from his own subconscious mind. He engages the Other in a philosophical discussion based on ideas from the books in his library. He experiences a dream filled with memories that lapse into erotic nightmares. Gradually his sleep lightens as he imagines a ramble in the mountains, moving from dense forests to pastures to snowy heights. Images from the mountain journey were to have been conveyed through silent film. Morning arrives at last and the monodrama ends.

Much about "Nacht" resembles the plays of August Strindberg, especially *Jacob Wrestles*. This play is also a monodrama in which the protagonist, an autobiographical representation of the author, speaks with an "Unknown One"—probably the principal model for Berg's Other. The texts of Schoenberg's *Erwartung* and *Die glückliche Hand* also have much in common with "Nacht." *Erwartung*, whose full score proofs Berg had read in 1915, is also a monodrama that explores its protagonist's psyche in a nightmarish trek through a forest that lasts from night to morning.

By the summer of 1917 Berg's interest in his Strindbergian text had waned, and he decided once and for all to return to *Wozzeck*. He announced this in one of only three letters written to Schoenberg in that year. "I'm working again on the composition of the drama *Wozzeck* by Büchner, which I've been planning for more than 3 years," he wrote tersely.[10] Later in his career, Berg chose 1917 as the year when his work on *Wozzeck* began, and as always the date was largely symbolic. There was little significant progress on the opera in 1917, but it marked the time when his decision about the subject matter was resolutely made and when he took another small step toward independence from Schoenberg.

From Play to Libretto

The *Wozzeck* that Berg saw in May 1914 consisted of a string of short, unconnected scenes beneath which a grimly realistic story is acted out. Wozzeck is an impoverished soldier, a lowly orderly for an overbearing officer and a guinea pig for experiments by an egotistical doctor. All that he has in the world is his common-law wife, Marie, and their child. Marie proves unfaithful with the virile Drum Major, who then boasts to Wozzeck of his conquest and thrashes him for good measure. In a demented rage Wozzeck stabs Marie to death, then drowns in an attempt to wash off the blood. The next morning, children, joined by Marie's child, rush off to see her corpse.

The drama *Wozzeck* was reasonably well known in Viennese literary circles in 1914. Karl Emil Franzos—a Viennese journalist and writer of short stories and travel vignettes—had published a series of feuilletons in the *Neue freie Presse* in 1875 on Georg Büchner, including selected scenes from an untitled play that Franzos called "Wozzeck."[11] At the time of his death in 1837, Büchner left the play in an incomplete state in several manuscript fragments, which his brother Ludwig turned over to Franzos. In 1879 Franzos brought out a new "critical, complete edition" of Büchner's writings including a complete *Wozzeck*.[12] Although Franzos was not a literary scholar, he assured his readers that his edition was scrupulously true to what Büchner had left behind. He explained:

> This work contains the text of the manuscript presented with literal faithfulness. Any passage that was so illegible that I could only guess at its content rather than being certain about it has been left out rather than resorting to guesswork. . . . The ordering of scenes was certainly a difficult matter since there was absolutely nothing to go on. I took content into consideration but whenever possible I also applied another, aesthetic viewpoint. *Wozzeck* consists of two elements—the grotesque and the tragic—and I tried to group these so that the former would not impair the effect of the latter.[13]

For forty years after 1879, Franzos's version of the play was the only one known, and his assurances of its fidelity to Büchner's manuscripts were accepted as fact. As the reputation of the play grew, new editions appeared, all until 1920 adhering to Franzos's text. An edition of 1909 made by Paul Landau changed the order of a few of Franzos's twenty-six scenes to make the play unfold more logically, setting aside Franzos's separate groupings of "grotesque" and "tragic" scenes. Landau's version—reprinted in 1913 by the Insel-Verlag under the title *Wozzeck–Lenz: Zwei Fragmente*—was the principal source used by Berg for his operatic libretto, which he revised as he composed.[14] The *Wozzeck* that the composer saw on stage in 1914 used the same version, and the prompt book made by Arthur Rundt, the director of that staging, shows that scenes that he omitted from that production were in almost all instances the same ones that Berg later omitted from his libretto.[15]

The early stagings of *Wozzeck* renewed interest in the life and works of Georg Büchner (1813–37). He was trained in biology and medicine, and at the time of his death, at the age of twenty-three, he was lecturer in anatomy at the University of Zurich. During his student days he had earned a reputation as a revolutionary eager to bring his political and socialist viewpoints into his literary works. His approach to imaginative writing was to convert vivid accounts of historical events into fiction, often quoting or paraphrasing his sources directly. "The dramatist is in my view nothing other than a historian," he wrote to his family in 1835.

> But he is superior to the latter in that he *re-creates* history: instead of offering us a bare narrative, he transports us directly into the life of an age; he gives us characters instead of character portrayals; full-bodied figures instead of mere descriptions. His supreme task is to get as close as possible to history as it actually happened.[16]

History for Büchner was bleakly deterministic, unsusceptible to improvement by individual actions or even revolutionary causes. After studying the French Revolution for his first work, the play *Dantons Tod*, he wrote to his fiancée:

> I felt as though utterly crushed by the hideous fatalism of history. I find in human nature a terrible sameness, in human circumstances an ineluctable violence vouchsafed to all and to none. Individuals are but froth on the waves, greatness a mere coincidence, the mastery of geniuses a dance of puppets, a ridiculous struggle against an iron law that can at best be recognized but never mastered.[17]

Before his death in a typhus epidemic in 1837, Büchner could bring his last work, *Wozzeck*, only to a preliminary state. Its manuscripts consist of a hodge-podge of short scenes—some brief fragments of only a few sentences, others seemingly complete, some comic or grotesque, others tragic in content—all drafted as working copies having no title, the characters assigned multiple names, and no clear order.[18] To find a historical model for this work, Büchner consulted several accounts of women murdered by deranged men. He relied mainly on a case in Leipzig of an impoverished former soldier, Johann Christian Woyzeck, who in 1821 stabbed his lover to death in a jealous rage after seeing her consort with other men. To determine Woyzeck's sanity, a Leipzig court appointed a physician, Johann Christian August Clarus, to examine the prisoner and report on his mental competency.[19] Clarus issued lengthy and detailed reports describing Woyzeck's earlier life including his history of hallucinations and hearing voices—one telling him to stab his lover to death. Despite these findings, Clarus found Woyzeck to be mentally competent, and on 27 August 1824, the prisoner was executed in Leipzig by beheading. The Woyzeck case continued to attract attention in the medical literature. Clarus's reports were published and despite a subsequent debate over his judgment and expertise, Büchner freely draws upon Clarus's documents in his play.

Berg in 1914 immediately saw in *Wozzeck* the material for an effective and innovative operatic text. Although the content of Büchner's play was plainly unusual for opera—filled with passionate social criticism, pessimism, and a deranged murderer as the central character—grotesque themes had begun to appear in modern operas that Berg admired, including Strauss's *Salome* and Schoenberg's *Erwartung*. In a letter of 1918 to Webern, Berg expressed uncertainty over dealing operatically with a play made from disjunct tableaux, but he saw an effective model in Debussy's *Pelléas et Mélisande*. "Of course, I was attracted by the idea of having orchestral interludes connect four or five scenes into each *single* act," Berg wrote. "(You'll find something similar in Debussy's *Pelléas*!)."[20] Berg had seen *Pelléas* staged at the Vienna Opera in May 1911, and he was more familiar with Debussy's music than others in Schoenberg's circle.

Berg's initial idea for the libretto was to use almost all of the scenes in the Franzos-Landau version. In a notebook following the date of 17 February 1916, he lists twenty-three of Franzos's twenty-six scenes and places them into four acts, a very different conception of the opera from the one that later evolved.[21] *Pelléas* was on his mind also at this early time: on a following page of the notebook he lists the number of acts, scenes, and scene changes that he foresees in his opera in 1916 and places these beside the comparable numbers in Debussy's opera.

Berg's attraction to the play *Wozzeck* increased during his years of military service in part because he saw his own plight mirrored in the character Wozzeck. "There's a bit of me in him," he told Helene in 1918, "since I have been spending these war years just as dependent on people I hate. I have been in chains, sick, captive, resigned, humiliated."[22] In fact, Berg brought a good bit of himself into his libretto through small changes that he made to the Franzos-Landau text. An example occurs in Act 1, scene 4, where Wozzeck is examined by the Doctor. The Doctor is angry after having seen Wozzeck relieve himself against a wall outside, a natural urgency that might cast doubt on the Doctor's theory of free will. Berg changes pissing into uncontrollable coughing, an ailment all too familiar to Berg himself. Asthmatic symptoms appear even more explicitly in the staging instructions that Berg gives for the Captain in Act 2, scene 2, when the Doctor tells the Captain that he will soon suffer a stroke. In an asthmatic panic, the Captain wheezes, becomes breathless, coughs uncontrollably until the Doctor pounds on his back. Berg may have seen parallels between the Doctor—a man concerned only with the scientific theories that will make him famous—and the doctors who examined him during his military service. But Berg's changes in Landau's text suggest that the caricature is directed primarily at Dr. Paul Kammerer, Berg's nemesis of old. In Landau's text, the Doctor says that he cannot let the illness of a mere human being upset him, as he would if one of his laboratory specimens were failing. The Doctor uses the obscure term *Proteus* for such a specimen, which Berg changes to the familiar term *Molch*, salamander. (Kammerer's dissertation was a study of salamanders.) At the end of the scene, the Doctor goes over things that Wozzeck should be doing, and to the list Berg adds, "catching salamanders," just as Kammerer did on his outings with Helene years before.

Berg had new concerns over his libretto as the opera neared completion. He had been using the Franzos-Landau "critical edition" of Büchner's *Wozzeck*, but questions about this edition were then being raised. The Berlin literary scholar Hugo Bieber, in a 1914 article "Wozzeck und Woyzeck," was the first to report on the connection between the play and the 1821 murder trial of Johann Christian Woyzeck and Clarus's reports on Woyzeck's symptoms of insanity.[23] Bieber's study left no doubt that Franzos had misread the name of the title character (in old German handwriting, the letters y and z are similar in appearance).

A broader critique of Franzos's text would soon follow. In 1918 Büchner's manuscripts were acquired by the Leipzig publisher Insel-Verlag and opened to scholarly study. A 1919 article on the play caused Berg unease. It was written by the prominent literary scholar Georg

Witkowski and contained a forceful attack upon the entire authenticity and value of Franzos's edition. After retranscribing the manuscripts for "Woyzeck," Witkowski found that Franzos's edition had none of the "literal faithfulness" to the sources that its author had claimed. "It is more accurate to say," Witkowski wrote, "that Franzos was stunningly untrustworthy in his omissions, changes, reorderings, and—worst of all—adding his own freely invented passages to try to increase the effect." Franzos was like a clumsy art restorer, Witkowski said accusingly, working with a masterpiece that he did not understand. "He falsified the large conception by painting it over, sweetening it up, casting an all too glaring light into its dark corners, misrepresenting its effects, and in these ways severely damaging Büchner's artistry. What we have had until now as *Woyzeck* can only be thought of as a poor copy."[24]

Witkowski followed up on this article by producing a new critical edition of *Woyzeck*—the title that the spoken play has had to this day. Berg acquired Witkowski's edition, probably in 1921 as he was at work on the end of Act 2, scene 4, and he made a few changes in wording there to conform to Witkowski's readings. But what was he to do with more than half of the opera composed to Franzos's "poor copy"? Berg decided to stay with Franzos—except for the spelling of the title, which he provisionally changed to "Woyzeck." Berg may have feared that even that title could be claimed by Insel-Verlag as copyrighted. In 1922 he wrote to all of the publishers who had an edition of Büchner's play to ask about copyright, and he received an especially reassuring reply from Franzos's publisher, J.D. Sauerländer: "For my part I have no longer rights to Büchner's works," Sauerländer wrote.[25] Berg then changed the title back to "Wozzeck," to agree with Franzos's spelling, which is how the opera is now distinguished from the spoken play *Woyzeck*.

Berg must also have recognized that his opera was in no way diminished by Franzos's lack of fidelity to Büchner. After all, it was Franzos's version that filled him with enthusiasm when he saw it presented in 1914 and that later inspired him to compose. He may have seen less of the gripping theater in Witkowski's authentic version than what we now admire in the opera's libretto. Berg must also have recognized the greater continuity and coherence that Franzos had brought to Büchner's highly fragmented work in comparison to Witkowski's version. Berg spoke to the necessity of these elements in a letter of 1925 to Hanns Heinz Ewers, who had sent him a text to consider as an operatic subject. "For me the main thing is *theater*," Berg explained. "The drama itself must go forward so that one breathlessly awaits its continuation."[26] One way that Franzos achieved this degree of continuity and coherence in the drama was to order the scenes on the large scale in three groups: the first he described as expository, then development, and finally "catastrophe."[27] Berg often used just these terms to describe the scenes that he placed in his three acts. Berg also reinforced Franzos's gestures toward coherence by the addition of extensive staging instructions into his libretto that contribute to a realistic and unified impression. Berg's lighting instructions, for example, suggest a logical elapse of time for an action covering parts of five consecutive days.

Imagine that Berg had not used as his final scene the starkly poignant vision of Marie's child mindlessly riding his hobby-horse off to see his mother's corpse—a scene written entirely by Franzos—and had used instead Büchner's comparable scene:

> Karl [Idiot] (holding the child in his lap). He fall in d'water.
> Wozzeck: Boy, Christian.
> Karl. He fall in d'water.
> Wozzeck (trying to cuddle the child, who turns away and cries). Good God!
> Karl. He fall in d'water.
> Wozzeck. Little Christian, here's a toy soldier. Got you a toy soldier.
> Karl (staring away).
> Wozzeck. Hop! Hop! Wet.
> Karl (jubilant, running off with the child). Hop! Hop! Wet! Wet![28]

The opera might have been a lesser masterpiece if Berg—with his great instinct for theater and music—had not embraced Franzos's less authentic but theatrically superior version. Theodor Adorno later spoke with insight into this matter:

> The more faithfully the Büchner philologists restore Wozzeck, or Woyzeck, as they call it, the paler and worse it becomes; now they are even claiming to have found that Wozzeck does not drown and other things—while Franzos' edition, the "false" one, the Wozzeck set by you, remains eternally beautiful and not to be improved on by any philology, or hopefully spoilt by the professors. Because: this is the one that burst in upon history, and it is

not the abstract "work-in-itself" that lives, but only the historical-dialectical Wozzeck, namely yours![29]

Berg responded enthusiastically to Adorno's thoughts: "I absolutely agree with what you say about literary historicism."[30]

In his lectures, articles, and interviews about *Wozzeck*, Berg was inclined to focus on its music more than on its libretto.[31] Most often he deferred to other authorities as to its literary meaning, rather than stating his own interpretation. In an interview of 1930, Berg probably recalled his military service when he pronounced that the drama was not about poverty so much as an individual's subjugation, which might afflict people from all walks of life. "*Wozzeck* is no 'we-poor-people' play," Berg insisted. "What happened to Wozzeck can happen to anyone who is subjugated by others and cannot defend himself."[32] Berg also approvingly recommended a socialist interpretation of the opera that appeared in a 1926 article on *Wozzeck* by Alexander Landau. Landau found that Berg's opera brought the individual dilemma of the characters to a universal and collective level that made it more relevant to social issues:

> The man Alban Berg calls out his harrowing *ecce homo*, and this *ecce homo* now suddenly applies not to Wozzeck but to all of suffering humanity. There is but a single sin—poverty. There is but a single crime—hunger. The listener cries out, "Who is responsible?" For neither music nor text bring him answers or a solution.[33]

"I could endorse virtually every word by this author," Berg commented about Landau's article.[34]

Berg also approved of a biblical interpretation of the character Wozzeck by the literary critic Otto Brües in a 1929 article. Brües compares Wozzeck to Job: "It doesn't matter whether the sufferer accepts his dire misfortunes, like Job, and thus acknowledges God, or, like Woyzeck, rebels and atones by his death. In the end it is God who triumphs."[35] Brües's interpretation "agrees uncannily with what I wanted to say," Berg adds.[36]

A *Wozzeck* Chronology

During his long period of work on *Wozzeck*, Berg settled into a method of composing that he would use in all of his later works. With a few exceptions (as during his push to complete *Lulu* in the winter of 1933–34), he composed only during his summer retreats in the mountains of Styria and Carinthia, when he could clear his mind and focus solely on the work at hand. The remainder of the year was given over to revising works, making full scores or piano scores, copying parts, teaching, travel, and the like.

Most opera composers obtained a complete libretto before beginning to compose, but Berg revised his text scene-by-scene as he was composing. The earliest "composing" of a new work was often a purely mental exercise. Berg mentions this in a 1923 letter to Helene: "I worked mentally on the Chamber Concerto and doing so I solved in the most advantageous way an important passage that I've racked my brains over for weeks."[37] Such detailed thinking through of a new work was usually facilitated by verbal outlines and written formal plans that normally preceded composition per se. These plans take many different forms. For *Wozzeck* the earliest datable sketches (made in February 1916) consist of lists of scenes from the play that Berg wished to retain in the opera.[38] Some of the verbal plans contain fragmentary musical notations, and these often resemble analyses of the work that Berg had provisionally in mind. Such plans helped to guide him in organizing details in the music. Later came the sketching of short and isolated passages—lines, chords, or rhythms— these sometimes merged into continuity drafts, normally worked out at the piano. Later still came the creation of the *Particell*—a condensed score on two or more staves, usually with orchestrational annotations. The first page of the *Particell* for *Wozzeck* is shown in Figure 5.1. The layout of the *Particell* is often similar to that of the piano-vocal score, although in some passages the instrumental part expands beyond two staves. Berg's students normally made his piano-vocal scores. Fritz Heinrich Klein prepared the piano score for *Wozzeck* (one scene was done by Gottfried Kassowitz) under Berg's close supervision using the *Particell* as a model.

Except for a few early sketches and verbal plans, Berg's real composing of the opera began in 1918.[39] During a six week furlough from the War Ministry in the summer of that year, he finally completed entire scenes, probably those later situated as Act 2, scene 2, and Act 1, scene 2, judging from materials entered in the earliest of his *Wozzeck* sketchbooks.[40] But even in 1918 he was still uncertain about the larger form and style that the opera would take, still undecided about how many scenes he would use, and still experimenting with musical ideas that he later abandoned. He

Figure 5.1 *Wozzeck, Particell,* Act 1, scene 1, ÖNB, F21.Berg.14. Courtesy of the Austrian National Library

tells Webern that the music will alternate "normal operatic scenes using thematic development with others without themes, like Schoenberg's *Erwartung* (understand—not imitating its style, only in form!). Then song forms, variations, etc."[41] He adds that melodrama—speech-like vocal music accompanied by orchestra, as in the *Sprechstimme* in Schoenberg's

Pierrot lunaire—would play a large role and be used exclusively for the parts of the Doctor and Captain. *Sprechstimme* ultimately played a lesser role in the work, and Berg later revised much of the music for the Doctor and Captain to change declamation into singing.

Work on *Wozzeck* resumed in the summer of 1919. At that time Berg finalized the overall form for the work—choosing fifteen scenes to be placed symmetrically into three acts—and in less than four weeks in July he was able to complete the remaining four scenes of Act 1. But in August his progress was interrupted by having to copy parts for his Orchestra Pieces, Op. 6, for prospective performances in Dresden and Prague. He returned to the opera a year later, during the summer of 1920, concentrating on Act 2. He wrote to Kassowitz on 9 July 1920 that the scenes of Act 2 would resemble a four- or five-movement symphony, and on 9 August he reported that three scenes were completed (probably 1, 3, and 5).

Berg again took up *Wozzeck* in June 1921, this time with far fewer distractions than ever before. The Berghof had been sold during the previous year, and Berg's financial worries were largely relieved by an inheritance from his brother Herman, who had died in Florida from a stroke in February 1921. Johanna Berg inherited about one-third of Herman's sizeable estate, and she used these assets to create accounts, kept in dollars and overseen by the Geo. Borgfeldt Co., for her surviving children.[42] This guaranteed Alban and Charly, following Johanna's death in December 1926, capital of $13,000 each plus 6 percent interest per annum. Smaragda got an additional $5,500. For the Bergs, the American funds were a godsend since Austria soon experienced a devastating inflation that made assets denominated in kronen virtually worthless.

During the month of July 1921, Berg remained in Vienna while Helene was taking a cure in Hofgastein, and he then completed the long and complex tavern scene (Act 2, scene 4). On July 25 he traveled to his Trahütten retreat and there picked up the thread of composition. He remained in Trahütten until basic compositional work on the opera was finally completed, around October 7, whereupon he and Helene returned to Vienna.

On 13 October Berg traveled to Traunkirchen to show the complete *Particell* draft to Schoenberg, who immediately recognized the work's importance. Schoenberg wrote straightaway to Emil Hertzka of Universal

Edition, advising him to put the work under contract. "This is an *opera*! Genuine *theater* music!," Schoenberg exclaimed. "Everything is flawlessly done, as though Berg had never composed anything but theater music."[43] Later in October Berg resumed his work for the Society for Private Musical Performances, although its financial condition was weak and it ceased giving regular concerts in December. Berg was at last free to make final revisions in the opera's *Particell* and to begin its orchestration. In a letter of 2 June 1922 to Schoenberg he confided that *Wozzeck*—he had returned to this spelling of the title—was then, after eight years, at an end: "*Wozzeck* is now at least *entirely* finished. There are two identical, handsomely bound scores. The piano-vocal score is also largely completed and in a few weeks awaits only my revisions."[44]

On Schoenberg's recommendation, Emil Hertzka began to negotiate with Berg for publication and performance rights to the new opera. But Hertzka balked at paying to engrave the piano score, so Berg decided to have this done at his own expense and to publish the work privately.[45] He dedicated the score to Alma Mahler, who had sent him 10,000 kronen at Christmas in 1919, a time when Berg's finances were at a low ebb. Additionally Berg had received a loan from May Keller to defray the printing costs, and in June 1923, to repay the loan, Alma Mahler sent him an additional 7 million kronen.[46] As an expression of gratitude, Berg gave her the *Particell* of the work (she would later return it to Helene Berg). Alma responded to Berg's gift by presenting him with an autograph score draft of the first three movements of Mahler's Ninth Symphony.

Berg received the printed piano scores just before Christmas, 1922. He was then prepared to launch an elaborate plan to make the opera known and to bring it to the stage, a strategy that will be described in the next chapter.

The Music of *Wozzeck*

"By opera I understand drama that is reinforced by means of music. This is the sole artistic objective that guided me in composing *Wozzeck*."[47] Berg's statement is strikingly affirmed by a close study of his music for the opera. It has many of the components of traditional opera: powerfully expressive orchestral passages, vocal styles ranging from aria to recitation, melodramas where the orchestra accompanies speaking, and motives that mirror the development of characters. Detailed analysis of the pitch and rhythmic organization in the work reveals additional dramatic symbols of an extraordinary subtlety and intricacy that project the drama on deeper levels. Every page of the *Wozzeck* score contains figures—some relatively obvious, others virtually imperceptible—that express and symbolize Büchner's text. Berg believed in the importance of the extraordinary deep structure of the work, and he was confident that its features would eventually be known and studied. In 1923 he wrote to Fritz Klein, who had drafted a detailed analytic guide to the opera:

> Personally I would be very happy to know that you have written your study in all of its detail, because who else will know everything that you do. Even I myself forget about most of those musical details, relationships, and intentions in a matter of months, and who else could find even half of them? So I place great value on having everything that I have hidden away in this music settled for the future. Someone someday will want to know these things.[48]

Many features of the music of *Wozzeck* had appeared earlier in the Altenberg Songs and Orchestra Pieces. The harmonic idiom remains generally atonal, and Berg's distinctive and complex style of orchestration is still evident. Other familiar features reappear: lines and chords made from whole tones or fourths, contrapuntal wedges, twelve tone lines and chords, complex ostinati, symmetric organization, palindromes, and favored dissonant harmonies. But much is new. For the first time Berg was dealing with a complex and lengthy dramatic work, one with memorably diverse characters, and scenes that range from comic to grotesque. To capture these contrasts, Berg's bypasses the uniformity of musical style found in his earlier works and instead mixes together music of contrasting types: simple triadic harmony with great splashes of dissonance, tonality with atonality, bel canto singing with speaking and declamation.

A starting point for studying the music of *Wozzeck* is Berg's own description of it. This took the form of articles, interviews, and, most important, a "Lecture on *Wozzeck*" that Berg delivered beginning in 1929 to coincide with early performances of the work.[49] Here Berg stresses the unity and closure, in both the large and small dimensions, by which the music gives coherence to the brief scenes. On the large scale, he points to a loosely symmetric organization for its three acts, comparing the whole to a "three-part song form," ABA. Additionally, he ends each act on the same nearly-whole-tone harmony F–G–A–B–C♯–D, which functions like a tonic chord in earlier music. On the smaller scale of the individual scene, Berg points to his use of "old forms"—a suite, passacaglia, chorale harmonization, fugues, and variations, among others—whose patterns bear analogies to the dramatic content.

The forms that Berg created in *Wozzeck* are summarized in an outline, or "scenario," drawn up by Berg's student Fritz Mahler under the composer's supervision and sent out with the first copies of the piano-vocal score. It is shown in Table 5.1 in a somewhat simplified version.[50]

Table 5.1   *Wozzeck*: Formal Design

act	*scene*	*setting*	*form*	*m.*
1. Five character pieces	1	Captain's room	suite	1–
	2	Open field	rhapsody on three chords / hunting song	201–
	3	Marie's room	military march / lullaby	320–
	4	Doctor's study	passacaglia theme & twenty-one variations	488–
	5	Street by Marie's room	Andante affetuoso (quasi-rondo)	656–
2. Symphony in five movements	1	Marie's room	sonata (first movement) form	1–
	2	City street	fantasy / fugue on three themes	171–
	3	Street by Marie's room	largo [A B A']	367–
	4	Tavern garden	scherzo	412–
	5	Barracks guard room	rondo with introduction	737–
3. Five inventions	1	Marie's room	on a theme [variations–fugue]	3–
	2	Path by the lake	on a note	71–
	3	Tavern	on a rhythm	122–
	4	Path by the lake	on a six-note chord	220–
	—	Epilogue (interlude)	on a key	320–
	5	Street by Marie's room	on a steady eighth-note rhythm	372–

Plainly, Berg wanted to call attention to the presence of these traditional forms. Their appearance in the music, however, is far from simple or straightforward. In some instances, such as Andres's hunting song in Act 1, scene 2, the simple strophic design is immediately apparent; elsewhere, as in the sonata form in Act 2, scene 1, the music has a dimmer resemblance to the classical formal prototype. An analogy with a few features of an irregular sonata form can be found in the score but the musical design could just as well be described in some other way. In other cases still, as in the "inventions" of Act 3, scenes 2–5, no traditional form is present.

Why was Berg so insistent that the opera contains these familiar forms? First of all, the presence of traditional musical forms was the most basic element in Berg's narrative about his own music. Such forms constituted the Schoenbergian "idea" of his music, a deep and timeless principle that it shared with all great music, far exceeding the importance of surface elements that characterized its style. Harking back to his training in *Formenlehre* under Schoenberg, Berg relied on the traditional musical forms to focus his musical thoughts—regardless of how different from these archetypes a composition might ultimately become. In many cases, the form label was probably attached to a scene after it had been composed, much as Berg described the form of the March of Op. 6 as an ABA song form. In such cases the designated forms were approximations often far distant from the music itself. Since the forms were part of the deep structure or idea of the work, they were not necessary to a listener's understanding of it: "There should be no one in the audience who will notice the diverse fugues and inventions, suites, and sonata movements, variations, and passacaglias," he wrote.[51]

In *Wozzeck* a reference to traditional forms was also Berg's way to account for its many musical recurrences. These have analogies with the recurrences in traditional musical forms, which in turn correspond to recurrences and parallel situations as the drama unfolds. Büchner's play is filled with repetitions and parallelisms that suggest recurring musical patterns. Some are brief phrases like "ein guter Mensch," "wir arme Leut," and "eins nach dem andern" that return like musical themes and motives; others are larger narrative elements, such as Wozzeck's recurring hallucinations and quotations from the Apocrypha, which return like sectional repetitions in music. Berg used musical forms to interrelate subtly related scenes in the drama, such as the interaction between

Example 5.1   Act 1, scene 1, mm. 4–5, Captain's motive

Sehr mäßige Viertel

Marie and the Drum Major in the seduction scene (Act 1, scene 5) and between Wozzeck and the Drum Major in the barracks scene (Act 2, scene 5). He casts both scenes as free rondo forms with shared motives.[52] Berg must also have been aware that the novelty of an opera made from traditional forms would attract attention at a time when Wagnerian through-composition in opera was becoming a cliché. The strategy was a success. In the first article to call widespread attention to the opera, the conductor Ernst Viebig wrote: "It is in the *form* of the piece that the composer opens up new paths. . . . Perhaps the road to a truly 'musical opera' lies here—away from music drama."[53] A sampling of ways in which Berg's music reinforces Büchner's drama is found in the following survey of its scenes.

Act 1. Berg described the scenes of Act 1 as "character pieces" depicting the five main figures who interact with Wozzeck. Like Franzos, he called the scenes an "exposition" within the drama. The first scene focuses on the Captain, who is parodied pitilessly. In a sketchbook note, Berg described him as a "nobody—mediocre ability to dissemble, i.e., to seem like something more."[54] The scene begins with Wozzeck shaving the Captain, who is identified by the motive in Example 5.1. Amid his ludicrous philosophizing he chides Wozzeck for rushing about, being always on edge and stupid, and lacking morality for having a child out of wedlock. His tenor voice leaps shrilly into the high register or breaks into falsetto, much like that of Herod in Strauss's *Salome*. At last Wozzeck responds, in a passage that Berg termed an aria. "We poor people!" he exclaims (Example 5.2). We cannot afford morality and have only our flesh and blood, he continues. The "Wir arme Leut" figure is Wozzeck's principal motive, and its symbolism resides not only in its melodic shape but also in its total pitch content, D♯–E–G–B. This set of tones recurs in various configurations and transpositions throughout the opera when the focus is on Wozzeck.[55]

Example 5.2   Act 1, scene 1, m. 136

As the Captain darts from topic to topic—unable to develop a coherent thought—the music passes through sections that are distinct in
surface design and orchestration. This sectionalism may have led Berg
to describe the scene as a suite, although that term tells us little about
the music. As always, there are many subtle symbolic gestures. Much of
Wozzeck's impassioned aria is accompanied by twelve-tone lines in the
orchestra, possibly symbols of the universality of his plight. Twelve-tone
figures often arise in the opera, especially when Wozzeck is involved. In
the first scene they are generated by spinning out different successions
of major and minor thirds, a procedure that Berg would use to generate
twelve-tone or nearly-twelve-tone lines in all of his later works (especially in the Violin Concerto). Two examples of the technique from the
first scene are shown in Example 5.3. The first pattern could be construed
as a succession of three diminished seventh chords, and this arrangement
returns verticalized at the climax of the Epilogue of Act 3 at m. 364 (see
the example). In the Lecture Berg said that the Epilogue contained "the
important musical shapes relating to Wozzeck."[56]

In scene 2 Andres and Wozzeck are cutting wood in a field outside
of town, and Wozzeck senses that the place is cursed. Heads roll here
at night, he says, the work of Freemasons. The earth is hollow and you
can hear footsteps below, he tells Andres, whereupon he has apocalyptic visions—flames shooting from earth into the heavens while brass
instruments blare from below. Andres tries to dispel Wozzeck's fears with
a carefree hunting song. As night falls, a military tattoo heard from afar
calls the soldiers back to their quarters.

The music for scene 2 alternates between a depiction of Wozzeck's
fearful visions and stanzas of Andres's cheerful, folkish song. In a 1954
letter to Hans Redlich, Helene Berg insightfully describes her husband
as a "specialist" in music for demonic scenes.[57] Here Berg creates an
uncanny mood by his choice of chords and by unusual orchestrational

Example 5.3 Acts 1 and 3, twelve-tone lines and chord

mm. 136–37

C♯ E G B♭ D F A♭ B E♭ G♭ A C
semitones: 3 3 3 4 3 3   3 4 3 3 3

m. 147

C♯ A F♯ D♯ B G♯ F D B♭ G E C
4 3 3 4 3 3 3 4 3 3 4

Act 3, m. 364

E♭ F♯ A C E G B♭ D♭ F A♭ B D
3 3 3 4 3 3 3 4 3 3 3

effects. The central recurring elements in the scene are three chords (A, B, and C in Example 5.4), which return throughout the scene in various combinations, incomplete forms, and transpositions. In a sketch, Berg labeled the three chords "Nature."[58] The chords reappear later in the opera when Wozzeck again tells of his visions. George Perle has noted that the voice leading that connects the chords gives them a rightness when sounded in succession.

Berg's orchestration also contributes to the eerie mood. Developing ideas used in Opp. 4 and 6, he creates unusual instrumental combinations and indicates extended playing techniques whose sounds suggest

Example 5.4 Act 1, scene 2, mm. 201–04

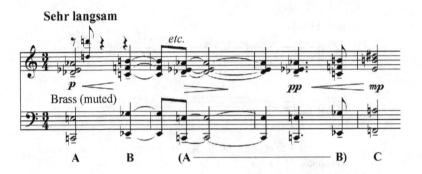

Wozzeck's anxiety. These include muted playing in the brass (especially the trombones), *col legno* passages in the strings, flutter tonguing in winds and brass, and the hard, penetrating sound of the xylophone (probably inspired by its use in Strauss's *Salome*, also used prominently by Berg in the March from Op. 6).

Andres is Wozzeck's foil, and the contrasting character of their music is apparent in the juxtaposition of stanzas of his light-hearted hunting song with Wozzeck's dark episodes. Folk songs such as Andres's are frequent in Büchner's text, and in the Lecture Berg explained how he distinguished folklike music (and characters) from their atonal surroundings:

> This includes a preference for four-measure phrases and a symmetric construction of periods, bringing in major and minor thirds and also fourth chords, and also using a melody in which the primitive whole-tone scale and the perfect fourth play a large role. . . . So-called polytonality is another such primitive harmonic means of composition.[59]

The opening phrase of Andres's song (Example 5.5) shows the "primitive whole-tone scale and the perfect fourth," and in the military march that opens scene 3 (Example 5.6) the melody is in thirds. Polytonality arises as the upper parts outline C major against a "false bass" suggesting C♯ major below. The march music is later used as a symbol of the Drum Major.

Scene 3 follows immediately in the timeline of the plot, as the evening's military tattoo continues to sound. The band marches past Marie's room in town as she watches from inside, talking with her neighbor Margaret, who stands at her window. Marie is absorbed by the march and by the

Example 5.5   Act 1, scene 2, mm. 213–16

Example 5.6   Act 1, scene 3, mm. 334–35, military march

dashing Drum Major at its head. When Margaret notices her wandering eye, insults are traded and Marie slams the window shut. She takes her child sadly into her arms and sings him to sleep with a lullaby. As the march fades away she sinks into a reverie only to be awakened by Wozzeck rapping at the window. Excitedly he tells her of his visions (accompanied by the "Nature" chords of the previous scene). "I'm on to lots of things!" he exclaims, then hurries off to the barracks. Marie is left alone in the darkness, gripped by fear. "We poor people!" she laments.

Music for the scene has the same three parts as the text: a military march (m. 326), Marie's lullaby (363), and the episode after Wozzeck arrives (427). The middle section of the scene is dominated by Marie's motives, which form an interrelated complex of chords and lines that refer both to her and to her child. Four of these are shown in Example 5.7. The first passage in the example (m. 363) begins an introduction to the lullaby, the second (m. 371) is the opening of the lullaby, and the third and fourth (mm. 415 and 425) come from later in the scene. Intervals of the

Example 5.7   Act 1, scene 3, Marie's motives

fourth—symbols of Marie's simplicity and naturalness—appear plainly in her melodic lines and chords (as in the fourth chords marked C). Chords A and B, often transposed and reconfigured, are very prominent in this scene and later when Marie or her child are involved.

The last part of the example shows Berg's ingenious musical depiction of Marie's central place in the drama. The child has fallen asleep, and Marie is "lost in thought." At m. 415 in the example, the fourths of the lullaby continue in the bass as the upper voices dwindle to open fifths A–E. As she drifts off in the music that follows, the march is still in her mind while chord B wafts dreamily in the harp and celesta. Finally, at m. 425 (see the example), the symbols of her external world are banished by sleep and she arrives at her very essence, represented by the open fifths brought forward from m. 415, played *ppp* in the strings in multiple registers and now with the tritone F–B in the bass. In a sketch Berg labeled this motive as Marie's "waiting," and Adorno recalled Berg saying that it was his favorite moment in the work.[60]

The dyad F–B is heard throughout the score—too frequently to be associated with any one character—but its presence often coincides with basic and fateful realities in the drama. Looking ahead, the music of Marie's waiting at m. 425, with its F–B ostinato in the bass, is quoted by Berg at the very end of his opera *Lulu*, most likely to draw a parallel between Marie and the dying Countess Geschwitz. Harmony A formed in m. 425–27 is a fundamental symbol of Marie.[61]

Scene 4, which presumably takes place on the next day, is a character study of the egotistical Doctor, who pays Wozzeck a pittance as a research subject for diet experiments. During his physical examination Wozzeck blurts out his visions: a frightful voice has spoken to me, he confides, and mushrooms have formed circles on the ground. At this the Doctor is ecstatic: Wozzeck is being driven mad by his diet, and now the Doctor is sure that his theories will make him immortal.

The scene contains twenty-one variations on a twelve-tone theme, and Berg labels it a passacaglia although it has little relation to that historical form. The theme is present in each variation, constantly reconfigured, as the music closely illustrates the text. The Doctor's principal motive (Example 5.8) plays only a slight role, as it is heard as a mere fragment a single time, in the thirteenth variation (m. 562–63). There is much recurrence of earlier motives. When the Doctor gives Wozzeck an extra penny for his good progress toward insanity, Wozzeck cries out "Ach Marie! Marie! Ach!," realizing that he can give the money to her. At this, her motives from Example 5.7 flood back, and we will recall this moment all the more poignantly near the beginning of Act 2.

Scene 5 takes place again in the street by Marie's door where, as evening gathers, the Drum Major returns to find Marie. He postures before her, and she is smitten by his manliness. He grabs her, she struggles briefly, then goes inside with him. "What's the difference," she says. The curtain falls on Act 1 as the orchestra sounds the opera's pseudo-tonic chord F–G–A–B–C♯–D.

Act 2. Berg described the five scenes of Act 2 as a symphony in five movements. The first, or "jewelry" scene, has a free sonata-form design, and here Berg repeats some features of his earlier tonal sonata form

Example 5.8 Act 1, scene 4, mm. 562–63, Doctor's motive

movements, such as an exposition with three themes (m. 7, 43, 55), each with a different character and tempo. Guided by parallel situations in the text, Berg adds a reprise of the three themes at m. 60, by which he imitates the traditional repeat of a sonata-form exposition. In the development section that follows from m. 96, Wozzeck discovers earrings given to Marie by the Drum Major, but he lets it pass because he has come to give her the money that he has earned from the Captain and Doctor. In a memorable passage (Example 5.9), Marie receives the money while a few strings quietly play a sustained C-major triad, something unique in the opera. In the Lecture Berg comments wryly about the triad: "How could the objectivity [*Sachlichkeit*] of money, which is at issue here, be better represented?"[62] Surely Berg meant this ironically: money is not the issue at all in this passage, instead Wozzeck's desperate affection for Marie, to whom he gladly gives what little he has. Still, the same triad is used in *Lulu* Act 1, when Lulu gives money to Schigolch, and we also recall the magical emergence of the chord at the end of *Reigen*. Wozzeck then rushes off as a second reprise of the exposition begins (m. 128), which extends through the following interlude.

Scene 2 opens with a comic encounter between the Captain and Doctor. The Captain hails the Doctor as "Herr Coffin Nail," whereupon

Example 5.9   Act 2, scene 1, mm. 116–21

Example 5.10   Act 1, scene 2, mm. 273–74, Wozzeck's motive

the Doctor observes that the Captain may soon suffer a stroke. If you're lucky, you'll be paralyzed only on one side or maybe lower down. In a panic, the Captain sobs that at his funeral people will at least say, "Er war ein guter Mensch"—He was a good man. The mood changes when Wozzeck rushes by. He is mercilessly taunted by the two about Marie's infidelity, and he can only respond that she is all that he has in the world. "And you would make a joke of it?" he asks.

Berg described the music for the scene as a fantasy (m. 171) and fugue on three themes (from 286), with coda (345). The three themes are those of the Captain and Doctor (Examples 5.1 and 5.8) and a new theme for Wozzeck (Example 5.10). The final chord of the last of these is the transposed "Wir arme Leut" harmony, consistently a representation of Wozzeck. The fugue has three brief imitative expositions on the principal themes interspersed with episodic developments.

In scene 3 the drama moves quickly toward its tragic conclusion. Wozzeck confronts Marie in the street to accuse her of "a sin so wide and deep that its stench would smoke the angels out of heaven." Marie dissembles briefly, then resists. "What of it!" she says. "Better a knife in my body than your laying a hand on me!" At the mention of a knife, Berg introduces a chromatic wedge (Example 5.11) that will return grimly in Act 3. Marie rushes to her room as the music swirls in nearly-twelve-tone circles while Wozzeck mutters, "Man is an abyss that makes you dizzy to look into."

In this central scene of the opera, which alternates largo and agitato tempi, Berg divides the orchestra into a chamber group and the remaining tutti. The chamber orchestra has the same fifteen instruments that Schoenberg used in his Chamber Symphony, "a small tribute to my teacher and master," as Berg said in the Lecture. We can only wonder

Example 5.11   Act 2, scene 3, mm. 395–96, knife motive

what Schoenberg may have thought of a reference to him in a scene of such bitter strife between a man and his unfaithful partner. To sharpen the conflict of their encounter, the small orchestra accompanies Wozzeck, the large orchestra Marie.

Scene 4, set in a crowded tavern garden late at night, is the opera's longest and most complex scene. In the Lecture Berg compared its form to that of the scherzo movements of Schumann's symphonies, but the similarities are slight. The scene begins with dancing to a slow Ländler accompanied by a *Heuriger* band placed on stage, while drunken apprentices sing away. Their singing continues in an interlude following the Ländler, which Berg called a "trio." The next dance number is a waltz during which Wozzeck arrives and sees Marie and the Drum Major dancing. "See him pawing her body, and she laughs at it!" After the waltz ends, another "trio" begins during which a male chorus sings a hunting song. The band then strikes up the same Ländler as before. One of the apprentices climbs on a table to deliver a drunken sermon on the goodness of God's creation, accompanied by a "chorale" played by the tuba in the band. Berg used the term "chorale" here and later not to refer to a sacred melody, but instead to any theme that is used as a cantus firmus, presented normally in long values, usually in the bass, and the subject of a free harmonic arrangement. As the band tunes up before playing the waltz again, an Idiot approaches Wozzeck: "I smell blood!" he declares. "Blood? Blood. Blood!," Wozzeck screams as the waltz begins and then continues through the ensuing interlude.

A scene that combines dancing with dramatic development reminded Berg of similar scenes in other operas. In Act 1 of Weber's *Der Freischütz*, villagers joyfully dance a waltz at an inn while Max stands outside cursing his fate. At a grand ball in Don Giovanni's castle in the finale of Act 1 of Mozart's opera, villagers dance a stately minuet while Don Giovanni maneuvers Zerlina into a side room. In Act 3 of Strauss's *Der Rosenkavalier*, Baron Ochs brings the disguised "Mariandl" into a room at an inn for a tryst while waltzes are heard from another room. Berg refers to each of these forerunners toward the beginning of this scene (mm. 429, 439, and 442).

More than anywhere else in the opera, Berg in this scene experiments with abstract compositional devices and patterns that are not directly related to the drama. The most elaborate of these involves a complex series of ostinati in which repeated rhythmic patterns create their own irregular meter, different from that of the notated meter.[63] In this Berg develops an idea that he had used earlier at the beginning of the first Altenberg song and in *Reigen*. Additionally, several of the ostinati are linked as variations upon a long series of harmonies. These underlie the initial ostinato (mm. 447–55) and they return, at least in part, in later ostinati (456–80 and 643–49 in retrograde). With notes horizontalized, the series of chords also forms the tuba "chorale" in 605–33.

Given the many contrasting and recurring sections within this and other scenes throughout the opera, Berg looked for ways to connect sections with a smooth fluidity of tempo. To do so he resorted to a device that Elliott Carter later called "metric modulation." In this procedure an irregular subdivision of the beat in one section (e.g., an eighth-note within a triplet) becomes a regular subdivision in the next section while keeping its same duration, thus producing a smooth transition to a new pulse. An example in this scene is found in mm. 455–56 at the juncture of the first two ostinati. The first of these is notated in 3/4 with the beat divided into eighth-note triplets, and the tempo gradually slows to the quarter note at 54. The eighth-note value within the triplet keeps its duration and becomes a normal eighth in 4/4 time, producing a new tempo of about 80. The relationship is shown schematically in Example 5.12. Metric modulations will be used by Berg prominently in all of his later works.

Scene 5 occurs late on the same evening in the barracks, where Andres and Wozzeck share a bunk amid other sleeping soldiers whose snoring creates an unearthly chorus. Wozzeck cannot sleep and asks Andres if he too heard voices from out of the wall and had a vision of a gleaming

Example 5.12 Act 2, scene 4, mm. 455–56, metric modulation

knife. The quiet is shattered when the Drum Major bursts in to brag about the woman he has just had: "Breasts and thighs, all good and firm!" he relates. Andres asks who she is and the Drum Major tells him to ask Wozzeck. Wozzeck whistles impudently, whereupon he is attacked by the Drum Major, who beats him to the floor. "What a man I am!" he declares as he leaves. Wozzeck collapses on his bunk, muttering "one after another" to a transposition of the pseudo-tonic harmony that closes each act. The soldiers return to their bunks, "one after another," as Berg writes into the score, and a tense quiet returns. Just before the curtain falls, the harp sounds a hushed, menacing low B natural, left over from the cadential harmony.

Berg called the music of the scene after the Drum Major enters a "rondo marziale," in which the returning elements are motives associated with the Drum Major. The snoring chorus forms an introduction, and here the "Nature" chords of Act 1, scene 2, return, as before to accompany Wozzeck's hallucinations. Here as elsewhere, Berg constructs the rise and fall of the curtain with the same care as the music. He instructs that the curtain should remain up for a time at the end of the scene, then fall; the same two durations are to be duplicated before and during the rise of the curtain for Act 3, scene 1, creating a continuity that bridges the disjunction with the opening of the next act.

Act 3. In this final act Berg largely abandons his references to traditional forms and constructs each scene (and the final interlude) instead as "inventions" that dwell persistently on some single musical element. The first scene—placed in Marie's room late at night—is an "invention on a theme," which Berg works out as a theme with variations ended by a double fugue. Marie reads from the Bible about the forgiveness of sinful women, alternating these readings with emotional outbursts. Using a text that Berg brought in from a different scene in the Franzos-Landau edition, she then sings to her child a grim folk tale, nostalgically in the key of F minor: "There once was a poor child who had no father or mother. Everything was dead and there was no one in the world, and he wept and went hungry day and night because he had no one in the world." Finally, Marie cries out for God's mercy.

In his Lecture, Berg stressed the "architectonics" of the music for this scene, pointing to a strictness of form to which the number seven contributes. He said:

> The principle of the first scene is that of a varied theme. The strictness of its architectonics (I purposely choose this word) involves a two-part theme, with antecedent and consequent phrases, that covers seven measures; the theme has seven variations and then a double fugue made from two subjects drawn from the two parts of the theme, each with seven notes.[64]

Berg never explained why he chose the number seven or what deeper meaning it may have had for him, but it initiates a conception about musical structure based on certain numbers; Berg returned to this thinking in all of his later compositions.

The first part of the theme is serene and diatonic, corresponding to Marie's pensive reading from the Bible (Example 5.13a); the second part, coinciding with her despairing outbursts, has three simultaneous thematic strands, all dissonant and chromatic (Example 5.13b). The four phrases then underlie all of the thematic content for the remainder of the scene. Berg derived the first phrase, transposed and in augmentation, from a fragmentary piano piece, a "Clavierstück" in F minor, that he had composed ca. 1908 (Ex. 5.14).[65] When Marie begins to sing her once-upon-a-time folk tale to her child in Variation 5, Berg brings in additional music from the Clavierstück (from mm. 18–21), material explicitly in F minor, including its key signature. By shifting from atonality to tonality at this moment, Berg finds a powerful way to make his music reinforce the drama.

Scene 2, the murder scene, is the climax of the tragedy. Late at night Wozzeck and Marie walk on a dark forest path by a lake. Marie is gripped by fear as Wozzeck hints broadly about his intentions. After a long silence, the moon rises blood red, and Wozzeck stabs her to death, crying out, "If not I then no one else!" Silently he rushes away. The scene is an invention on the tone B, which is present in every measure as a symbol of Wozzeck's murderous obsession that gripped him starting at the end of

Example 5.13   Act 3, scene 1, (a) mm. 4–6; (b) 7–9

Example 5.14   Berg, *Clavierstück* in F minor (ca. 1908), mm. 14–17

Act 2. In the few measures before Marie's death, her important motives from earlier in the opera rush past: "the most important moments of her life," Berg said in the Lecture, "as is said about the instant of death."[66]

The scene change music that follows, only fourteen measures in length, is one of the most ingenious and riveting passages in the opera. Here the tone B, the unifying element in the scene just ended, continues to sound in two great crescendos. Within them Berg subtly introduces the unifying elements of the next two scenes: a rhythm that will dominate scene 3 and a chord that will be ever-present in scene 4. As the orchestra sounds the first crescendo on a unison B, the brass enter at points

Example 5.15   Act 3, interlude 2–3, mm. 109–14

that create the rhythm seen in Example 5.15. The rhythm is duplicated a quarter value later by entrances of the woodwinds. The crescendo ends on the six-note chord that is central to scene 4.

In scene 3 Wozzeck arrives at a tavern where an out-of-tune piano bangs out a polka in the rhythm established in the preceding interlude. This rhythm is then treated like a theme or motive, continually repeated throughout the scene in ever changing shapes.[67] Berg later said that the scene should have a "demonic madness," and this may refer to Wozzeck's fully schizophrenic state. He takes on the identity of other characters, singing a folk song to the melody and harmony of Marie's lullaby from Act 1, then impersonating the Drum Major by using his motives and announcing that he is spoiling for a good fight. But when blood is seen on his arms people crowd around him to demand an explanation. "Am I a murderer?" he screams and rushes out.

In scene 4 Wozzeck returns to the lake to find the knife he left behind. He throws it into the lake, wades in to wash off blood, and drowns. Just then two people happen by—Büchner calls them simply "townsfolk" and Berg cleverly changes them to be the Doctor and Captain. Speaking in melodrama, they hear someone drowning, do nothing to help, then hurry off. Music for the scene consists of an invention on the hexachord heard earlier at the end of the great crescendo (see Example 5.15). The harmony is present in every measure in changing configurations. From m. 267—as Wozzeck sinks further into insanity and drowns—the chord undergoes a series of transpositions, then returns to its original form, played as softly as possible by six solo strings, as the curtain falls.

During the change of scenery before the final scene of the opera, Berg inserts a passionate orchestral "Epilogue" in which he speaks out with his own voice about Wozzeck's fate. In his Lecture he says:

> It is to be construed as a confession by the composer, who has stepped outside of the theatrical action; indeed, as an appeal to the audience, inasmuch as they represent mankind. From a musical standpoint this final orchestral interlude contains a thematic development of all the important musical shapes relating to Wozzeck.[68]

Berg marks the Epilogue as a personal statement by beginning it with one of his own earlier compositions—the main theme of the fragmentary Sonata IV in D minor from ca. 1908. Berg retains its original key and key signature (Example 5.16). The middle part of the Epilogue returns to atonal harmony and brings in themes representing Wozzeck and the forces that shaped his life, with Marie now poignantly absent.

The brief, grotesque text for scene 5—the shortest of the opera—was written entirely by Franzos. The morning after the murder, children are playing by Marie's door, and one yells to her child, "Hey, your mother's dead!" They all run off to see the corpse, Marie's child absentmindedly following on his hobby-horse. The music is an invention on a steady eighth-note rhythm, and it is filled with Marie's motives and her other symbols. As the curtain slowly falls before an empty stage, the motion continues mechanically, finally stopping on the cadential chord but with no sense of conclusion. The implication is that Wozzeck's fate is simply an episode in a tragic cycle, destined to be continued in his hapless child.

Example 5.16   Berg, Sonata IV (ca. 1908), theme

Wozzeck on Stage

Berg took a keen interest in all details of how *Wozzeck* should be staged. In the score he included extensive staging directions with attention to lighting, time of day, and blocking. He had traditional views about set design, at a time when symbolic and non-realistic staging was increasingly imported into theatric and operatic productions. Berg explained some of his ideas in a letter to Erich Kleiber prior to the 1925 Berlin premiere:

> In general I did not imagine what is called an "expressionistic" decor. In my view we can easily do with mere hints about the various rooms, taverns, and interiors. But with the outdoor images we will need a definite realism. For example, in the "open field, city in the distance," or the "street at Marie's door" (a few alley trees, one lighting fixture), "tavern garden," "forest path by the lake." These are scenes that must be recognized for what they are immediately even by the unsophisticated viewer. Other scenes, for example the tavern in the last act can well enough be designed so as to drift past the viewer with only a specter of realism. That's also how it was *composed!*[69]

Berg elaborated on his ideas about a proper staging for the opera in instructions titled "A Few Remarks on Staging the Opera *Wozzeck*," drawn up in 1930 to be sent out by Universal Edition with the rental of parts.[70] Here Berg defines the general mood that he intended in *Wozzeck* as relaxed rather than tense or frantic, generally soft rather than loud, and he gives much practical advice for the orchestra, conductor, and singers. He reiterates the need for realism in the outdoor scenes and a certain abstraction for those indoors. He also underscores the need for making the time of day obvious and lighting effects precise. Most of all he demands that the staging precisely coincide with the dramatic symbolism within the music. As an example, he writes of the murder scene of Act 3:

> Wozzeck murders Marie by "stabbing the knife into her neck" *only once* (m. 103). Everything following (mm. 104, 105, and 106) relates *musically* only to *Marie* and to her death. There may be no additional butchery enacted by Wozzeck.[71]

Berg had little sympathy with *Regietheater*—an approach to theater and opera in which a director reconceives the staging. Should Wagner stagings be modernized, Berg was asked. "How else?," he replied.

But if you mean by "modernization" to put on *Tristan und Isolde* as New Objectivity, and do *Siegfried* in tie and tails, and *Die Meistersinger*—where the connection of verse and industry (it need not be just the shoe business) is easily maintained—as *Zeitoper*, then the answer to your question is *no*.[72]

Wozzeck represented the culmination of Berg's long struggle for the recognition of his music and his greatness as a composer. In it he demonstrated the capacity of atonality to express a wide range of emotions and dramatic complexities. He showed that shifting from atonal harmony to passages plainly in a key was a powerful dramatic device, one that did not "impair the effect," as Schoenberg predicted.[73] Once and for all, he declared his artistic distance from Schoenberg by forging an original musical style not driven by ideologies or existing models but by his unique instinct for a music whose dramatic content could grip and hold the imagination. Berg was now prepared to make his way as a leading figure in the world of modern music.

6

International Acclaim, 1923–25

B Y NEW YEAR 1923 *Wozzeck* WAS FINALLY COMPLETED AND PUBLISHED, and Berg's confidence in himself as a composer had risen to its highest level ever. He was certain that the opera was an important work: Schoenberg had praised it after all, and Berg could confidently tell Emil Hertzka of Universal Edition of his "rock solid belief in its success (despite the opera's innovations) and in its lasting value."[1] The new year would hold great importance for Berg, as he finally rose to a position of prominence in international modern music. But his successes were still clouded by uncertainties: the health of both Berg and his wife continued to decline, prompting a slow but relentless deterioration in the couple's marriage. Artistically Berg had to contend with a new method of composing that he felt compelled to adopt and a new spirit in postwar music that threatened his rising esteem.

Wozzeck Triumphant

Despite the distractions of Helene's ill health, Berg in 1923 devoted himself fully to his career. Early in that year he launched an astute and multifaceted plan to bring *Wozzeck* to the stage. He first sent out copies of the self-published piano score to journal editors, conductors, and theater directors. He also offered copies of the score for sale, each priced at 150,000 kronen (equivalent to about $2.50 at this time of runaway inflation), although he later admitted that few were ever purchased. Recognition of the opera soon followed. In the April 1923 issue of *Die*

Berg. Bryan Simms and Charlotte Erwin, Oxford University Press (2021). © Oxford University Press.
DOI: 10.1093/oso/9780190931445.003.0007

Musik, a widely read Berlin journal, Ernst Viebig wrote a glowing assessment of *Wozzeck*, to which the music of Marie's lullaby from Act 1 was added as a supplement. "In this score absolute musical forms and the demands of the libretto find the perfect fusion," Viebig wrote. "Perhaps the road to a truly 'musical opera' lies here—away from music drama."[2] Berg was ecstatic over Viebig's article: "Everything correctly stated, as if I had dictated it to him," he told Helene. "I didn't think it possible that a person by himself could see all that I intended with Wozzeck—morally, theatrically, musically, etc."[3]

Viebig's article set in motion a remarkable series of events that carried Berg in short order from obscurity to prominence in the world of modern music. "After fifteen years at a standstill," he exclaimed to Helene, "my career is now taking giant strides forward."[4] On 13 April, shortly after the Viebig article appeared, Berg concluded negotiations with Universal Edition for rights to *Wozzeck*. The publisher agreed immediately to issue the libretto under separate cover, to produce performing materials for the opera, and to publish the Orchestra Pieces in a facsimile edition.[5] This investment by Universal Edition virtually ensured that a staging of *Wozzeck* would soon materialize.

In August, Berg's reputation advanced further when the Gustav Havemann Quartet performed his String Quartet, Op. 3, at a chamber music festival of the International Society for Contemporary Music in Salzburg. Berg was present at the festival and reported on it to Webern: "By the way, my reviews were good, really quite good. The performance was such that the right impression could be taken from it easily. It was especially good in sound and in clarity."[6] Berg added that the Havemann ensemble planned to perform the work elsewhere in Europe and that Paul Hindemith had expressed interest in it for his Amar Quartet.

During the festival, Hermann Scherchen proposed to Berg that he prepare a suite of excerpts from *Wozzeck* for Scherchen to conduct in a forthcoming orchestra concert in Berlin. Berg readily complied. He had many ideas about which passages to choose, and he finally settled on three excerpts that focus on the figure of Marie: the military march followed by Marie's lullaby from Act 1, the Bible scene from Act 3, and the drowning scene toward the end of the work. Although Scherchen's Berlin performance did not materialize, he conducted the premiere of the "Three Fragments for Voice and Orchestra from the Opera *Wozzeck*" in Frankfurt in June 1924, and its rousing success there made a staging all the more likely.

By the summer of 1924 Universal Edition had several possibilities for the premiere of *Wozzeck*. They chose the most prestigious of these, which came from Berlin's Staatsoper Unter den Linden and its new musical director, Erich Kleiber. Ernst Bachrich (assisted by Berg) had played excerpts from the piano score of the opera for Kleiber during a visit to Vienna in November 1923, and Kleiber then assured the publisher that he would stage the work. But he gave no specific date, and only in May 1925 did Kleiber assure Berg that the opera would appear during the 1925–26 season. After several postponements, the date for the premiere was set for 14 December 1925.

Berg traveled to Berlin in November of that year to be on hand for rehearsals, and he wrote to Helene: "*Wozzeck* is something really great!" he exclaimed. "I never dreamed I could find such understanding as a musician and dramatist as I am finding with Kleiber," he continued.[7] A close and lifelong friendship between Berg and Kleiber began at this time. But as the *Wozzeck* premiere neared, the Berlin Opera had descended into a state of crisis during which a variety of personal rivalries threatened not only the *Wozzeck* premiere but Kleiber's position. In late November Max von Schillings, the intendant of the Berlin Opera and a firm supporter of Kleiber, resigned in a dispute with the Ministry of Culture, and rumors circulated that Kleiber had exhausted the resources of the Opera by expending over one hundred rehearsals on *Wozzeck*. (Kleiber later said that no more than fifteen orchestral rehearsals took place.[8]) Despite the great difficulty of the music, the artistic staff at the Opera had come to believe in the new work, as Kleiber later reported: "I can only say that the entire orchestra of the Berlin opera, the soloists, chorus, and everyone else collaborating on the artistic side to bring off the performance, myself included, were from one rehearsal to the next ever more inspired by the work, shaken by it actually."[9] H.H. Stuckenschmidt attended the dress rehearsal on 12 December and wrote:

> Stefan Wolpe and I had tickets given to us by Kleiber. All of the Berlin music critics were there; Paul Stefan had come from Vienna, Erich Steinhard from Prague. Next to me sat a young man with glasses with a piano score. We talked, and he introduced himself as Dr. Wiesengrund-Adorno from Frankfurt. We

knew each other's writings. From the sound of the orchestra alone, by the end of the first act of the rehearsal we were all fascinated. By the end of the second there was general acclamation. This mixed with angry cries of protest and whistling when Kleiber and Berg appeared before the curtain. But the success by the end was overpowering.[10]

The first performance was equally successful, and it vaulted the composer to international recognition. Lengthy articles about Berg appeared in newspapers in New York and London, and in German papers the major critics were mostly full of praise for the new work. Much was made of the absolute musical forms in the opera and of the aptness of Berg's music to Büchner's drama. "It is difficult to account for the extraordinary accomplishment and uniqueness of this work in a review," wrote Stuckenschmidt for the *Thüringer allgemeine Zeitung*. He continued:

> Berg's creation for this text of a music that could not only stand up to it but enormously intensify it—revealing its dark corners and deepest states of mind, and, most importantly, with no sacrifice in dramatic conception or musical coherence—shows an ingenuity that places him immediately beside the most outstanding musical dramatists of the present day. . . . The performance was not only the greatest sensation of this season but also an event of significance for the entire history of dramatic music.[11]

Theodor Adorno recalled Berg's mixed feelings following the triumphant occasion: "The night of the premiere of *Wozzeck*, Berg, without any affectation, acted deeply upset by its success. He thought that music that could immediately appeal to the public had to have something wrong with it."[12]

Despite the Berlin triumph, other theaters were at first hesitant to attempt a modern work of such difficulty and massive orchestral requirements. A year elapsed before the next new staging. This was in Prague, where audiences were familiar with modern music through the efforts of conductors there including Alexander Zemlinsky and Otakar Ostrčil but where the modern arts were often viewed through a strongly nationalistic lens. In November 1926 "Vojcek" was staged at Prague's National Theater, using a Czech translation and conducted by Ostrčil. Although the first two performances were acclaimed by most in the audience, the third performance was interrupted by an organized resistance from pro-fascist elements, after which the city government forced the work to be removed from the repertory.[13] Opposition to the opera had been stirred up by reviews such as the one in the journal *Čech*, where Emanuel Žák wrote:

> Last Thursday at the National Theater an example of Bolshevik "art" was given, a musically and textually perverse piece by the Berlin Jew Berg. The dragging-out of such a piece onto our national stage was an example of unbounded impertinence and an arrogant provocation of music and of our art-loving nation.[14]

This was Berg's first encounter with organized and politicized opposition to his music, something that later had a drastically damaging effect on his career. Žák's description of the work as "Bolshevik" and Berg as a Jew returned to plague Berg following the rise of the Nazis in the 1930s.

Leningrad (now St. Petersburg) was the next city to take on *Wozzeck*. Russia had shown an openness to modern Western music—especially in Leningrad—since the early 1920s, when it was promoted there by the influential musicologist and composer Boris Asafyev and by the Association for Contemporary Music (ASM). *Wozzeck* premiered at Leningrad's State Academic Theater of Opera and Ballet (formerly the Mariinsky Theater) on 13 June 1927, conducted by Vladimir Dranishnikov, and Berg traveled nearly seventy hours by train to attend the first performances. "I was celebrated in a way that I have never been before," he wrote to Soma Morgenstern. "The *Wozzeck* performance was really a sensation for Petersburg, in purely artistic, not political, terms."[15] During his time in Leningrad he met many Russian composers, including Dmitri Shostakovich.[16]

A turning point for the history of *Wozzeck* on stage came in March 1929, when the work was performed at the Landestheater in Oldenburg, a city of a mere 55,000 inhabitants. Under the conductor Johannes Schüler it was shown that the opera could be performed successfully in provincial theaters with a manageable number of rehearsals. For Oldenburg, Berg asked his friend Erwin Stein to revise the orchestration by reducing the winds and brass from fours to threes, and before the premiere in Oldenburg Berg first gave his "Lecture on Wozzeck," which he subsequently repeated in eleven cities.[17]

The premiere of *Wozzeck* in Vienna on 30 March 1930, conducted by Clemens Krauss, held special importance for Berg. He saw to it that many of his friends and family, also his daughter Albine Wittula, would receive complimentary tickets. Although Berg never had the close artistic relationship with Krauss that he did with Kleiber, he was very satisfied with the performance and gratified by its successful outcome in his home town. The only dark cloud was a long and vitriolic review written by Julius Korngold—Berg's nemesis of old—in the *Neue freie Presse*. Korngold rejected every aspect of the work's harmonic and vocal language. He wrote:

> If there is such a thing as "atonal" music, it is found in Berg: a music that cannot be construed or deduced given its fanatic attachment to chromaticism—in both vertical and horizontal dimensions. . . . More than anywhere we have here "negative composing," as we once called it, with its conscious dethrone-ment of the evolving tonal system and rejection of tonal relationships and a tonal center.[18]

Berg defended himself against Korngold's distortions in a version of his "Lecture on Wozzeck," which he ironically retitled "The 'Atonal Opera'" and presented on 15 May at Vienna's Kulturbund.[19] On 23 April he con-tinued his battle with Korngold in a carefully scripted "conversation" on Radio Wien with the critic Julius Bistron, titled "What Is Atonal?"[20] Here Berg argued that atonal music differed from traditional German music only in its harmonic language. All other features, he insisted, were deeply rooted in traditional laws and established forms.

On 19 March 1931 the Philadelphia Grand Opera, in collabora-tion with the Philadelphia Orchestra and the Curtis Institute of Music, presented the American premiere of *Wozzeck*, with Leopold Stokowski conducting an opera for one of the few times in his career. The per-formance proved to be a landmark for musical culture in the United States. In a country with conservative tastes and limited experience with musical modernism, *Wozzeck* was a sensation. Interest in the opera had been keen following a performance of the *Wozzeck Fragments* by the New York Philharmonic under Erich Kleiber in October 1930. After Kleiber's performance, in a lengthy article in the *New York Herald Tribune*, Lawrence Gilman praised the opera lavishly: "Like Debussy in his *Pelléas*, Berg sought to touch by delicate antennae the rim of sensibility and to probe the depths of consciousness."[21]

As the Philadelphia premiere neared, the excitement rose. The Pennsylvania Railroad arranged for a special train to take New Yorkers to Philadelphia for the event, with George Gershwin (who had met Berg in Vienna in 1928) among their number. The performance "attracted what was probably the most brilliant audience that has gathered for a musical occasion in any American city this winter," wrote Olin Downes in the *New York Times*. After the premiere Downes—someone usually critical of musical modernism—assessed the new work in flattering terms:

> The opera had an astonishing success, astonishing in view of its extreme modernity, its alternate crass realism and nightmarish fantasy, its unpleasant lack of all compromise with pleasing convention. . . . This score employs any and all methods that serve its purpose, but always it goes sheer, direct to the point of the situation, and sometimes, most effectively, there is a moment of silence. You may hear the military band approaching, the crackling and cutting of the wood for the captain's fire, feel the approach of darkness and find reflected in the instruments the sulphurous sky of the field scene, and the setting of the sun. Or you will feel the blinding, insane thought of murder in Wozzeck's brain, and may be conscious, with weird distinctness and psychology of effect, of bubbles rising in the pool into which Wozzeck's body has sunk. All these things are synthesized and reflected as in a transparent mirror by "Wozzeck's" score. And finally, and in the last analysis, this score, at the moments of emotional crises, is beautiful.[22]

Lawrence Gilman had similar thoughts in his review for the *New York Herald Tribune*:

> The layman, if he can accustom himself to a doubtless indisposing idiom, will find in this music a bitter and a piercing loveliness, a piercing intensity, a compassionate wisdom of the heart, a suffusing tenderness, often intolerable, which reveals Berg for what he is: a poet, a man of torturing sensibility, a pitiful humanitarian, even (let us whisper it!) a shameless romanticist—a social and spiritual rebel, no less than an aesthetic one.[23]

On 24 November Stokowski brought the Philadelphia troupe to present *Wozzeck* at the Metropolitan Opera in New York, after which Olin Downes again wrote on the work with knowledge and insight:

> If this were mere Zolaism, it would be trite and ugly. The themes are touched with nobler things—with emotion, tenderness, pity. And perhaps those who

find little music in it will remember such moving passages as the interludes between the second and third scenes of the first act, the scene of Marie reading the Bible, the interlude which precedes the last act, when Berg writes melodically and in a mood of poignant beauty. In other pages he is not the lyrist or compassionate poet of humanity. He is Wozzeck himself, and we then know Wozzeck's terrors of the strange things afoot in the twilight, his premonitions which he cannot explain, of the evil that dogs him, his hallucinations, his murderous revolt. This is the psychological and emotional quality of the music.[24]

The Continuing Quest for Health

In the 1920s during the composing of *Wozzeck* Berg continued to struggle with poor health. In the fall of 1920 he suffered asthma attacks of such severity that he had to spend several weeks in a sanatorium. But during the period up to 1925 it was Helene's persistently bad health that caused him the greatest concern. He describes her condition in a letter to his brother Herman of February 1921:

> Helene is not at all well. The year-long neglect of her chronic gout condition has made this worse, which reminds me vividly of the time when you, dear Herman, had such bad rheumatism. . . . Something must be done this summer, if we are not to risk seeing Helene permanently chained to her bed in one or two years.[25]

The prospect of Helene's succumbing to a crippling disease made the Bergs explore cures at clinics where up-to-date medical treatments were offered. Helene had extensive experience of cures before her marriage. She accompanied her mother and sister Anna to a number of health resorts, Meran in the South Tyrol in 1902 and then on Lake Garda in 1907.[26] In 1908 she spent the entire summer in the South Tyrol again at mineral baths in two locations, Mitterbad and Rabbi.[27] Her last letter to Alban from this long tour vividly describes the heady spa culture she experienced:

> I'll be able to tell you a lot when I come back to Vienna: about the different circles I moved in, from the entertainers up to the so-called highest society! From military and Polish Jews, and aristocrats and landowners and from lady celebrities and the demimonde—from the affairs of honor [Ehrenhändel] in

which I became involved—in short, from a life—breathless—full of vain brilliance and unease—Oh! How I long finally for true peace . . . [28]

In 1910 Helene undertook a cure in Tobelbad near Graz and another
after her marriage in 1914 at the fashionable Bohemian spa, Karlsbad.
With Berg's urging she took five lengthy cures between 1921 and 1925.
During these periods she received a traditional restorative treatment with
an emphasis on rheumatic and nervous ailments, and in 1923 a psychoanalytic component was added. Each of the cures required Helene to be
away from home for three to four weeks, and the letters written during
her absences provide the clearest view of what these medical programs
offered and how both Helene and Alban responded to them. They also
chronicle the difficulties of separation and the resulting stress imposed on
Berg's work—as well as on his marriage.

The popularity of spa cures—normally undertaken by urban dwellers
who traveled to a location known for delivering health benefits, typically
from waters—was high during the nineteenth and well into the twentieth centuries in both Europe and America.[29] Balneotherapy—bathing
in mineral-rich water or mud—was a long-established practice, as was
the somewhat overlapping practice of hydrotherapy, the drinking of mineral waters. These modalities were frequently prescribed to relieve the
pains of arthritis and rheumatism, and for this reason they were a logical
fit for Helene Berg. Beside bathing in and drinking the local waters, cure
regimens of Helene Berg's day typically included massage, prescribed
diet, exercise, and rest. There was also the dubious lure of the spa social
culture, as Helene detailed in 1908, with its distracting interaction with
other cure participants, along with musical and other entertainments for
those so inclined. Presided over by qualified doctors, these programs were
the forerunners of modern health tourism, and they attracted largely affluent members of society.

Helene's cure regimen from the Wildbad Sanatorium in Tobelbad in
1910 has been preserved.[30] It prescribed water baths (at 95°F), sunbathing,
massage, resting, and gymnastic exercise. Additional therapy included
Zandergymnastik, one of a number of mechanical interventions offered
at sanatoria, in Helene's case involving vibration of the hands and feet.[31]
Helene's weight is recorded as 152 pounds: not underweight for her
height, despite her husband's later admonitions for her to eat more.

At Karlsbad in 1914 Helene was under the care of Dr. Rudolf Kolisch, the father of the violinist of the same name and of Schoenberg's second wife, Gertrud. In the summers of 1921 and 1922 Helene went to Hofgastein (now Bad Hofgastein) near Salzburg, for extended treatment. Helene's letters to her husband suggest that she found such cure regimens unpleasant and agreed to them only at her husband's insistence. Writing on the train, she reproached her husband: "That was a sad departure, I cried. Why are we doing this to each other? You should by all means have come with me! Now you are stuck in hot, stinking Vienna."[32] Alban answered, paraphrasing *Wozzeck*: "Why are we doing this to each other? Because we are poor people." He continues: "This is not a frivolous matter. How long have we thought about the possibilities? You must get *well*. So you have to take a cure. This costs time and money, of which we have precious little. I have to complete a work, so that in the fall I can begin to earn again."[33] The two competing objectives—Alban's urgent need to complete *Wozzeck* and to find a successful treatment of Helene's chronic maladies—are consistently woven through the Bergs' personal relations for the period between 1921 and 1925.

The 1921 cure set a pattern for the next years as Helene found fault with most aspects of her cure, in particular with her doctors. Their correspondence shows that Berg's insistence on the treatments came in part from the couple's infertility. Towards the end of her 1921 cure, Helene believed that she had done her best to strengthen her body, and for there to be a Swipelinchin Alban would now have to improve his own health.[34] Alban knew otherwise about his potency but did not enlighten his wife, and his letters continue in his long-standing mode of sacrificial suffering during her absences. The letters project a multilayered drama generated by a cultish preoccupation with health and all the reasons why robust health and parenthood kept eluding them.

During the 1921 cure in Hofgastein Helene met Dr. Johann Wengraf and his wife, Alice, who introduced her to the study of anthroposophy, the new philosophical-social movement founded by Rudolf Steiner. Helene began to take "lessons" from Alice on this subject. She wrote to Alban: "Their teachings are interesting. . . . She teaches it in Vienna. I am to read this journal *Dreigliederung des sozialen Organismus* (The threefold social organism) and then discuss it with her, and she will teach me about her world view. But is this necessary? I already have art, and here we need no translator!"[35]

Alice Wengraf found that Helene, despite her doubts, had a special aptitude for anthroposophy, and her lessons continued after returning to Vienna. But during her time with the Wengrafs in 1921, Helene seemed nonchalant about anthroposophy, possibly thinking that her husband would not have taken this brand of metaphysics seriously. Still, anthroposophy became central to Helene's thinking during her long period of widowhood, when she reconstructed her life and her marriage along new spiritual lines.

During Helene's 1922 stay at Hofgastein, Alban remained in Vienna to complete the score of *Wozzeck*, and his letters to her are filled with reassurance and extravagant gratitude for her sacrifice for the sake of his career. He writes:

> Pferschi, to whom can I give thanks for *Wozzeck* other than you!!! You who gave me the inner and outer peace for five years. The peace without which I could not have composed one measure! And which no person on earth other than you can give me or take from me. . . . Yesterday when I wrote to Mama how I owe *Wozzeck* to you (intellectually to Schoenberg, financially to Jeanette [his mother], emotionally to you) I said among other nice things about you—you who accompanied me through the hell of military service as if it were stroll—that you showed me the path to the heaven of creation. And I say this now: all paths with you are paths to heaven, even the one we are now on, rich with disappointments.[36]

In late March of 1923 Helene went again to Karlsbad for about four weeks. Again Alban declared that he was suffering as much as she was:

> I am so sad, and so sad in a way that I haven't been for years. This morning was so horrible as the train rolled away and I saw less and less of you! Only then did the desire to travel [with you] diminish and then I felt the pain of separation with such vehemence that my heart was in my throat. . . . Never have I felt so abandoned as now! No, no, never again![37]

In Karlsbad Helene's disgust with her doctors took on new substance. Her doctor, named Klemperer, had been recommended to the Bergs by the prominent music critic Ludwig Karpath.[38] After a number of uneventful visits, Klemperer assaulted her:

> This morning I was at the doctor's. Never again will I go there! The lout embraced me, squeezed me and kissed me on the breast and then twice

on the face! I was so astonished, I was completely frozen! Thankfully I was dressed! Only when I got out into the anteroom did I break down in tears, and I cried all along Parkstrasse and the Promenade until I reached home. People were looking at me, I now realize. I was so miserable.[39]

Helene wrote to Karpath about this incident, and she then received a letter of apology from him. Dr. Klemperer heard too from Karpath, and he sought Helene out, terrified of repercussions to his practice, but he also thought Helene had exaggerated the whole encounter. He then fell to his knees, begging her to pardon him, which she refused to do.[40] After this Klemperer wrote a formal letter of apology.

The incident brings to the fore the strongly gendered practice of medicine at this time, especially at spas, where patients were often predominantly women and doctors exclusively male. Helene objected to having to disrobe for a doctor. Whether this level of modesty was normal at that time for women in the context of a doctor's visit is difficult to assess, and it probably varied by patient and practice. Certainly Dr. Klemperer's insulting behavior set Helene's cure back. She told Alban she felt sick as a result of this episode. Alban related the incident to Alma Mahler who, while sympathetic, remarked that Helene should be proud that the doctor found her so attractive.[41]

During her stay in Karlsbad in 1923, Helene's mother turned over to Alban the diaries that recorded her earlier affair with Emperor Franz Joseph.[42] Certainly the Bergs knew of the existence of these documents and had heard rumors of Anna Nahowski's affair, but neither Alban nor Helene had been allowed to read the diaries before 1923. They came as a revelation to Berg, and it is no coincidence that Anna chose to show them to him during Helene's absence. He wrote to his wife:

> Yesterday evening Mama gave me that certain diary [*das gewisse Tagebuch*]. It's much, much more interesting and it reads like a novel involving three characters—Mama, the Emperor, Papa—that couldn't have been conceived even by the boldest imagination. I have read few things that have affected me so. I read non-stop until midnight and couldn't sleep afterward for a long time. I don't know why Mama won't show it *to you*. Except for one or two erotic pages out of some 200, there is nothing that would offend you. On the contrary, there are countless things that clarify the whole situation.[43]

Shortly afterwards Anna also showed Berg the second diary.[44] She clearly wished her son-in-law to vet the diaries before she permitted Helene to see them. Her reservations revolved around at least two contentious matters, the possibility of Helene's illegitimacy and the shocking treatment meted out to Anna by her husband in the course of her affair. For Berg the diaries "clarified the whole situation," by which he probably meant Franz Nahowski's antisocial temperament, his coolness toward Helene, and Helene's feelings of estrangement from him and others in her family. Although Berg gives no hint to her in his letter, he may also have divined that Helene's nervous and emotional problems, her insecurity, possessiveness, and jealousy, derived from a more complex family situation than he had previously acknowledged. As to her paternity, he makes no statement, and the subject never arises in any of the extant letters between them. No one seems to have addressed openly the question of whether Helene's psychological and physical issues could have come from a fear of being illegitimate or simply being cut off from any relationship with a loving father. Given Berg's powers of insight on relational complexities, the diaries may have given him reason to view his wife's ill health as essentially psychosomatic in origin and in need of psychological as well as physical modes of treatment.

His new viewpoint is evident in his choice of the Sanatorium Parsch outside of Salzburg for a cure beginning in November 1923. The clinic had been recommended by a Viennese doctor, Wilhelm Wiesel, and it was known for its use of psychoanalysis in the treatment of symptoms. The sanatorium was run by Dr. Bernhard Schwarzwald, a specialist in nervous diseases, women's illnesses, and heart disease.[45] Helene described Schwarzwald at first as "an unsympathetic, intellectual Jew," and she dismissed the clinic as a place for rich hystericals who want to be distracted by psychoanalysis—a preliminary stop on the way to the madhouse, she says. "Why have you done this to me?" she wrote accusingly to Alban.[46] At the first consultation the doctor told her that she had no rheumatism and that her problems were instead psychological. Schwarzwald questioned the happiness of her marriage and worked his way around to unfulfilled sexual desires. She reported this to Alban with heavy cynicism:

> "How were your glands when you were first in love etc.?" An aggravating session, I feel defiled. . . . After dinner I had diarrhea and colic (after brussels

sprouts at lunch). Since these are merely *psychological* reactions, they have no meaning. . . . I have *terrible* nerve pain. Pains in the lower back and legs (unfulfilled sexuality!!!) . . . In the afternoon not a wink of sleep because of pain.[47]

At first Alban urged Helene to persist in her treatments and, to spare her nerves, cultivate an indifference to the people and the surroundings at the clinic. Ultimately he recommended that Helene stop her psychoanalytic sessions entirely and come home early. If they were in need of psychoanalysis, they could go to Sigmund Freud or Alfred Adler, both of whom "we have known well for years."[48] Their marriage, he reassured her, was the very best. When Helene did not stop her psychoanalytic sessions, he became uncharacteristically irritated, unleashing his fury over the whole notion of psychiatry, calling it "bestial," "crack-brained" and a "prostate-driven science."[49]

Berg's views on psychoanalysis were shaped by Karl Kraus. In the pre-World War I decade Kraus was a sharp critic of psychoanalysis, although he admired Freud's frankness on sexuality and his stand against moral hypocrisy. But Kraus roundly condemned the misapplication of Freud's methods by his followers, many of them less scientifically conscientious and less skilled than their teacher. The danger to patients of irresponsible treatments led Kraus to formulate his most famous aphorism on this theme: "Psychoanalysis is the disease for which it purports to be the cure."[50] Berg no doubt knew that some people had been treated successfully, for example Webern, who went through a course of psychoanalysis with Alfred Adler in 1913 that cured him of his intense anxiety over conducting.[51] When it came to Helene, Berg's feelings were plainly mixed. Psychoanalysis seemed worth a try, but when she fell into the hands of a harsh and authoritarian practitioner such as Dr. Schwarzwald, he could only believe that her sessions would make her worse, not better. Further, the analytical probing suggested that Berg's marriage was in part a failure, and he would not at this time accept this conclusion.

Helene's reaction to the treatment at the Sanatorium Parsch has subtle pointers to her later state of mind. Despite her professed outrage, she may perversely have found something of interest in psychoanalysis and fallen into the situation, described by Kraus, in which the patient paradoxically takes pride in her own symptoms ("*Symptomenstolz*").[52]

Despite her distaste for her doctor, she continued to see him, and her persistence could have been a passive-aggressive way to punish Alban for insisting on this form of cure. The gender issue may again play a role. Helene's letters suggest that her doctor exploited women, yet she appears to have given in to his masculine authority. After a week at the clinic, Helene received permission from a second doctor to end the treatment and return to Vienna. Berg reported to Schoenberg that her condition was so bad that he would have to devote himself to her exclusively so that she could recover at home in complete seclusion. He added that he would not give up until Helene was well and they "could lead a life like other people."[53] Unless Berg was wildly exaggerating her condition, Helene—despite her familiarity with the spa experience—returned from the Parsch cure a confirmed *femme fragile*.

The cures paused until the spring of 1925, when Helene went to the local Park Sanatorium in Hacking near Hietzing, where Berg had earlier gone during his asthma episodes in 1920. While she was at the clinic, Berg traveled to Prague for a performance of his *Wozzeck Fragments*. There he stayed with Herbert and Hanna Fuchs-Robettin, thereby inaugurating a new phase in his emotional life that will be discussed in the following chapter.

New Directions in Postwar Music: Neoclassicism and Dodecaphony

Berg's rise to prominence in the 1920s coincided with a test of his artistic convictions. The Schoenbergian ideology about modern music was one of Berg's most deeply held beliefs: atonality and an expansive use of dissonance were evolutionary necessities, music had undergone a steady progress toward greater complexity, and the leaders in this evolution were German musicians headed in the present day by Schoenberg. But following World War I this ideology was called into question by a change of taste in modern music. A new style arose—most often termed "neoclassicism" or "New Objectivity" by critics of the time—that had far less of the complexity that characterized the music of Berg or Schoenberg. The new style mixed together elements of old and new, popular and serious, and it had a lightness and wit absent in music of the Schoenberg school. Many composers and critics spoke up to support the new taste and, by implication, to cast doubt on the future relevance of the older notion of modernism with which Schoenberg and Berg were associated. Igor Stravinsky, the most prominent composer in the new spirit, dismissed Schoenberg's modernism as a relic of an antiquated German culture:

> I respect the achievements that he has brought to today's music, although I go in an entirely different direction. But I find his mentality and his aesthetic principles to be unsupportable. He reminds me of an Oscar Wilde in contemporary music, or of a German romantic. He is closely linked with the development of German music—he seems to me like a disguised Brahms.[54]

After hearing Schoenberg's Serenade, Op. 24, at the 1925 Festival of the International Society for Contemporary Music in Venice, Erich Steinhard, editor of the journal *Der Auftakt*, wrote that it "sounded despairingly aged." "This Serenade is a non-music," he continued, "that is entirely avoided by all musical young people, with the exception of a small Viennese circle. It is out of date."[55] In his article "Musik in der Gegenwart" (Music of today, 1925), Ernst Krenek rejected Schoenberg's artistic ideology, holding that it was irrelevant to audiences of the present. To reengage people with modern music, it must become simpler, Krenek wrote. It must turn away from chromatic density and return to the tonic–dominant relation and the resources of diatonic scales. "We want to live, look life in the face, and say yes to it with a passionate heart." Krenek concluded. "Then we will suddenly have art and not know how it happened."[56]

Schoenberg leapt to his own defense in articles and lectures, even in compositions that satirized the new style. He lashed out at Krenek's ideas, suggesting that Krenek was at home with pimps and whores in his appeal for a lighter music.[57] In the text of his choral *Satire* Op. 28, no. 2, he belittled Stravinsky as the "little Modernsky," and in the Foreword of the score he reviled those who "nibble at dissonances and still want to be modern."[58] Although Berg was more open-minded about music of the 1920s than was his teacher, he also ridiculed many products of the new taste. After hearing new music at the Salzburg ISCM Festival in 1923, he wrote to Webern:

> Even Milhaud, Bliss or Honegger etc. were weak and unpleasant. And the others! Janissary music or solemn psalmody—these were the only things from

these people. It even colored works by the German composers. By the end of the festival I just couldn't take any more of this type of humor (false basses) and tortured non-melodic muddling through. Despite being unpleasant, it had one good outcome—raising my self-esteem! We can feel good. We're masters by comparison.[59]

Berg had not written a substantial journal article since 1920, but in 1924 he came to Schoenberg's defense against the neoclassicists with a polemic titled "Warum ist Schönbergs Musik so schwerverständlich?" (Why is Schoenberg's music so difficult to understand?).[60] It was published in the September 1924 issue of the *Musikblätter des Anbruch*, an issue honoring Schoenberg's fiftieth birthday. Although ostensibly an effort to explain the difficulties in Schoenberg's music, using his teacher's First String Quartet as an example, the article is mainly an attack upon the neoclassicists. The difficulties of Schoenberg's music—with its asymmetrical phrases, dense counterpoint, and motivic concentration, among other features—are in fact a great virtue that places this music at a higher artistic level than that of composers who want to be "modern but not extreme" and who aim for music "with easy appeal." Schoenberg's music, Berg concludes, assures "the supremacy of German music for the next fifty years."[61]

Despite such assurances, the rise of neoclassicism put Berg on the defensive and made him look to his circle—especially Schoenberg, Webern, and himself—as the righteous few against the many. In July 1922 he wrote to Webern: "More than ever I sense the unity of us three—this despite our obvious differences. But never before have I felt so strongly our separation from all other music that is being composed nowadays."[62]

At the same time that the neoclassicists were challenging Schoenberg's position in the world of modern music, Schoenberg himself was creating a new approach to composing that—like neoclassicism—was a product of the postwar spirit. After World War I, Schoenberg was one of several composers who searched for rules and systems to control the compositional process in the absence of tonality and to organize the full chromatic spectrum of tones that had become fully and equally available in the atonal style. During the period from 1913 to 1923, Schoenberg completed few new compositions and dwelled instead on theories and experiments with new approaches to composing that were attuned to the rule-based spirit of the postwar years.

In his period of research Schoenberg focused first on a new process of variation upon a melody-like line—a procedure that will be termed "serialized variation." In this procedure the notes of an entire melodic phrase—Schoenberg called it a "basic shape"—would stay together as an integral unit and continually recirculate in transposed, inverted, or retrograded forms. The tones in the basic shape created a "row" that might reappear in lines or be concealed when distributed into a contrapuntal texture and contribute in this way to a multi-dimensional unity within an atonal composition.

The systematic deployment of the full field of twelve tones was a later stage in Schoenberg's compositional experiments. Earlier, he had used twelve-tone lines, chords, or constellations in a sporadic and informal way, especially at the beginning of a work or at a point of climax, where he often saturated the music with the full chromatic. By the early 1920s, Schoenberg's interest in devising a method for the use of the twelve tones was spurred on by other musicians, including his students Berg and Webern, who were conducting related compositional experiments. One of his competitors was Berg's student Fritz Heinrich Klein (1892–1977), who in 1921 composed a chamber orchestra piece, *Die Maschine*, that uses twelve-tone lines and chords with mechanistic, serialized recurrences.[63] Klein's ideas were partly original, partly taken from elsewhere in the modern musical literature, many from Berg. The principal line in *Die Maschine*—Klein called it a "model" rather than a theme—has twelve-tones (it is bracketed in Example 6.1a). At the outset of the work the model is repeated as an ostinato in which the recurring rhythm spans 4½ beats. Since no rests are added, the repetitions of the twelve-tone figure coincide neither with the recurring rhythm nor with the bar lines. This irregular rhythmic and metric element is similar to the ostinati that Berg constructed in *Wozzeck*, Act 2, scene 4. Klein varies his twelve-tone model by keeping its notes together as a unit with a fixed order, then transforming it as a whole by retrogression (Example 6.1b), inversion (Example 6.1c), transposition, or a combination of these.[64]

Much about *Die Maschine* predates Schoenberg's use of serialized variation upon a twelve-tone basic shape. Berg told Schoenberg that Klein's piece was "very interesting," and Klein sent Schoenberg a copy of the

Example 6.1   Fritz Heinrich Klein, *Die Maschine*, twelve-tone ostinati

work when it was published in 1923. Although Schoenberg claimed that he had never looked at the piece, some of Klein's ideas recur in passages from Schoenberg's Serenade, Op. 24.

In a letter to Klein of 22 May 1924, Berg questioned the "lack of thematic development" in *Die Maschine*, to which Klein responded that thematic development was not intended. Berg's attention was drawn not so much to Klein's serialized variations as it was to his use in *Die Maschine* of a twelve-tone chord—the "mother chord" as Klein called it—whose notes were separated by eleven different intervals (Example 6.2). Berg's fascination with the mother chord was probably increased by its symmetry, since the notes from bottom to top are the same as those from top to bottom when transposed to the tritone.[65] Berg brings in Klein's mother chord at the end of the Chamber Concerto, and his more extensive adoption of it and other ideas formulated by Klein will be discussed in a later chapter.

Berg was well informed about Schoenberg's new compositional methods. In 1922 and 1923 Schoenberg lectured to a group of students about his new principles, and in a letter of 31 March 1923, Berg told Helene that "he wants to show me all the secrets in his *new* works."[66] The main work that Schoenberg showed to Berg on that occasion in March was almost certainly the Serenade, Op. 24, which Schoenberg had

Example 6.2   Klein, *Die Maschine*, "mother chord," m. 75

completed in that month. Its seven movements present a cross-section of the composer's compositional experiments just before he settled on his mature twelve-tone method.

Would Berg adopt Schoenberg's new method in his own future works? Unhesitatingly he did so, despite having achieved such satisfying results with the eclectic and freely atonal language of *Wozzeck*. The shift to a new method was not done only out of allegiance to his former teacher. Berg had already used aspects of Schoenberg's method—working with twelve tone lines and chords, varying motives by inversion and retrograde motion, for example—although he did so in a sporadic and unsystematic manner. And Berg, like many highly gifted composers, must have felt the need for control and restriction in the creative process, the need for a structure that was generally absent in the freely atonal style. Stravinsky spoke to this need when he wrote, "The more art is controlled, limited, worked over, the more it is free . . . . I have no use for a theoretic freedom."[67] It is likely that the freedom implicit in the atonal style had run its course for Berg, as it had also for Schoenberg, and he too looked to impose a new layer of restraint upon himself that Schoenberg's method made available. Berg spoke to this search for limits:

> The chromatic scale is entirely (indeed *excessively*) regular and undifferentiated, so if one composes unreservedly with all twelve tones, one must have a way to give them differentiation, which is just what the "row" does. There may be other ways . . . , but this is *one* way, specifically one leading Wagnerian

chromaticism onward within the realm of German music, just as Bach's diatonicism derived from music in the church modes.[68]

Ultimately Berg would follow Schoenberg's method only to a limited extent: he gradually made up a distinctive twelve-tone method having a measure of resemblance to Schoenberg's but remaining his alone. Certainly mastering this new method slowed him down and periodically cast him into despair, but Berg overcame its impediments to create such masterpieces as the *Lyric Suite* and the opera *Lulu*.

Chamber Concerto

Schoenberg's fiftieth birthday was looming in September 1924, and Berg would need a major work to dedicate to his teacher on that occasion, just as his Orchestra Pieces had been in 1914 and *Lulu* would be in 1934. Schoenberg had advised Berg to compose a piano concerto or a piece for wind ensemble, and in March 1923 Berg began a work that would honor his teacher's ideas, but with enough differences to show that he was now making his own artistic decisions. Instead of a piano concerto, Berg began a double concerto for piano and violin accompanied by an unusual chamber orchestra of winds and brass. The work would be dedicated to Schoenberg and it would also be a programmatic tribute to Schoenberg's circle, especially to its three leading figures: Schoenberg, Webern, and Berg. Earlier Berg had shown no interest in programmatic instrumental music, and his turn to the genre in the Chamber Concerto may have been a reaction against the neoclassicists, among whom program music was out of favor for its romantic ethos. Berg's approach to programmaticism was both symbolic and descriptive: outwardly it would reside in the pervasive presence of things in threes—symbols for the threesome of Schoenberg, Webern, and Berg—and it would use motives made from the musical letters of those three names. Berg had earlier made a passing and playful use of themes containing his own initials A B (A–B♭), possibly Helene's initials H B (B–B♭), and those of Arnold Schoenberg (A–E♭). But here the artifice is more extensive and laid out for all to see. Berg begins the score with the marking "Aller guten Dinge . . . " (All good things . . .), the maxim completed musically in a five-measure passage for three instruments, each playing a theme made from the musical letters of the names Arnold Schönberg

Example 6.3   Introductory motto with names

(A–D–E♭–C–B–B♭–E–G), Anton Webern (A–E–B♭–E), and Alban Berg
(A–B♭–A–B♭–E–G) (Example 6.3). Berg may have been influenced in
creating these musical ciphers by a similar practice in piano music by
Robert Schumann, which Berg had studied while preparing his Pfitzner
essay. The main theme of Schumann's *Variations on the Name Abegg*, Op. 1,
is close to Berg's personal cipher.[69]

Berg explained how the number three appears in the work in an
"Open Letter" to Schoenberg, published in the journal *Pult und Taktstock*
in February 1925.[70] Here Berg points to the concerto's three movements,
three instrumental groups (piano, violin, winds), three-fold formal
dimensions, and numbers of measures that are multiples of three, among
many other such representations of this number. He summarizes these
in a "tabular overview" (Figure 6.1) that also shows the presence of the
traditional forms that Berg always cited when describing his music. The
chart has a number of curious mistakes, which often arise when Berg
uses numbers or dates. For example, the division of the B section of the
Adagio into passages with 12, 36, and 12 measures should read 12, 39,
and 9. Although not mentioned in the Open Letter, Berg also uses the
number 5 prominently in the work, perhaps an allusion to Schoenberg's
fiftieth birthday.

Tabular Overview

I	Thema	Var 1	2	3	4	5	Number of bars:
Thema con Variazioni	in the basic shape		in retrograde	in inversion	in retrograde inversion	basic shape	
	exposition	lst reprise	|------------------- development -----------------| 2nd reprise				
	bars: 30	30	60	30	30	60	240
II	----------------------Ternary----------------------			----------------------Retrograde ----------------			
Adagio	A1	B	A2 inversion of A1	A2	B mirror form of preceding B	A1	480
	bars: 30	12–36–12	30	30	12–36–12	30	240
III (= I plus II)	Introduction (cadenza for violin & piano)	⦂ Exposition			Development ⦂	2nd reprise or coda	960
Rondo ritmico with introduction			*(da capo)*				
	bars: 54	96			79	76	305 480
	|------------------------- Repetition: 175 -----------------------|						175

Figure 6.1   Berg's "Tabular Overview" of the Chamber Concerto

Berg concludes his Open Letter by implying that the work has an even deeper dimension of programmatic reference in addition to its formal subtlety:

If it were known how much friendship, love, and world in human and spiritual references I have smuggled into these three movements, the adherents of program music—if there are any left—would be delighted, and the representatives and defenders of the "New Classicism," and "New Objectivity," the "linearists," "physiologists," the "contrapuntists," and the "formalists" would fall upon me in indignation at such "romantic" tendencies—if I did not make them aware that they too, if they wanted to look, would have their hearts' desire.[71]

Sketches for the Chamber Concerto provide many hints about the programmatic references that Berg "smuggled" into the concerto. In one sketch—probably made in the summer of 1923—he outlines a programmatic content for the three movements (Table 6.1).[72]

Table 6.1   Berg's programmatic sketch of the Chamber Concerto

chamber concerto		
1st movement	2nd movement	3rd movement
Friendship	Love	World
scherzoso theme:	Adagio	sonata form
A.S., A.W., A.B.	Ma	world
5 variations		life
1. piano Steu[ermann]		kaleidoscopic
2. waltz ~~me~~ / Kolisch		
3. blocks Polnauer		Rondo Rhythmico
4. races ~~Web[ern]~~ / Stein		
5. canons: others (who follow & try to overtake)		

The sketch suggests that the first movement, subtitled "Friendship," would have a lighthearted theme containing the Schoenberg, Webern, and Berg motives. The theme is followed by five variations, each associated with a figure from Schoenberg's circle: first the pianist Edward Steuermann, next the violinist Rudolf Kolisch, then Josef Polnauer, Erwin Stein, and finally students who try to overtake the others. As seen in the outline, Berg had second thoughts about whom these variations would represent. The second movement, subtitled "Love," was associated with Schoenberg's wife, Mathilde. The third movement, "World," would present a kaleidoscopic vision of life, and Berg had second thoughts about its design, first contemplating a sonata form, later a rondo, and ultimately composing a movement with features of both.

Typically, Berg adhered only partially to his early outline in the music that he later composed. The scherzoso theme of the first movement contains the three name motives, and the first variation is a virtuosic study for piano, Steuermann's instrument. The fifth variation shows students trying to overtake others by canons in the winds in which the space between entrances steadily diminishes. The "kaleidoscope" in the finale refers apparently to Berg's ingenious formal scheme for that movement, in which fragments from the first two movements are reassembled with a sonata-rondo form suggested by recurring rhythmic rather than melodic figures.

The most provocative part of the program sketch is for the Adagio middle movement, "Love," beneath which Berg abbreviates the name Mathilde.[73] This was apparently intended as a private gesture on Schoenberg's behalf—it was not explained in the Open Letter. The movement was probably conceived as an expression of a loving relationship between Schoenberg and his wife, Mathilde, and on one page of sketches Berg enters the terms "tender, melancholic, romantic" to describe the music that he had in mind.[74] Toward the beginning of the Adagio movement Berg introduces a motive made from the musical letters of the name Mathilde, A–B–D–E, and he shadows it with a secondary figure that he labels "Melisande" in his sketches. The "Melisande" figure, which begins with a twelve-tone row, has a passing resemblance to Melisande's motive in Schoenberg's *Pelleas und Melisande*.[75] The Mathilde and Melisande motives are shown on their first occurrence in mm. 260–64 (Example 6.4), the Mathilde figure played quietly in the muted trumpet, the Melisande expansively in the oboe.

We can only guess what Berg may have intended by the apparent comparison of Mathilde Schoenberg to Melisande. It was probably meant to reassure Schoenberg, finding in his wife a quiet and delicate innocence. But as so often happened in Berg's contact with Schoenberg, the outward gesture conflicts with a more complex reality. The actual relationship between Arnold and Mathilde Schoenberg had little of the affection contained in Berg's idealized musical portrait, as their marriage was periodically turbulent. Their wedding on 18 October 1902 had been a necessity given Mathilde's advanced state of pregnancy, and a few years later, in 1908, her affair with the painter Richard Gerstl burst into the open, leading to Gerstl's suicide and triggering similar thoughts in Schoenberg.

Example 6.4   Adagio, Melisande and Mathilde themes

For the sake of their two children, the marriage continued, although there is evidence that Mathilde persisted in promiscuous behavior.

The Bergs were dragged into one such incident early in 1920 when Mathilde developed an attraction for one of Schoenberg's students, Hugo Breuer. Helene described in strong language Mathilde's efforts to enlist her assistance in gaining the young man's attention:

> She asked me to call Breuer and tell him that I have something important to give him. This is to lure him over here because otherwise he wouldn't come if he knew he would meet her. She told me that without embarrassment! She wants to force a meeting, wants to get him here and rape him on my sofa! This woman must be crazy![76]

Berg cautioned Helene about offering Mathilde any such assistance:

> I would advise you *no longer* to provide such services for Mathilde. You could get yourself into the most nightmarish situation. If it were to get out, a hussy like her could impute to you some sort of complicity to partly excuse herself. Tell her calmly of your misgivings, that you have learned about her passions from me but at the same time you would be helping her to betray Arnold. In your role as wife of one of his best friends, you simply cannot be part of such an utterly hostile action against him. It would be tantamount to a gigantic offense against me, and in such matters I could take no pleasure. Really, the whole business makes you want to puke![77]

Schoenberg was well aware of Mathilde's actions, which she did little to hide. She told Helene that Schoenberg had "meddled" into her contact with Breuer and "frightful scenes" between them had ensued. During the incident, the Schoenbergs' eighteen-year old daughter, Gertrud, attempted suicide by taking a large overdose of the sedative Bromural.

Schoenberg's resentment against Mathilde only increased in the years following 1920. In October 1922 he began to compose the Sonnet movement of his Serenade, Op. 24, in which he chose a Petrarchan text that certainly reflected upon his relationship with Mathilde:

> Oh, that I might find relief from that resentment against her. She who assails me by glance and speech alike, and, causing greater suffering still, turns away and hides from me her sweet and evil eyes. Thus she gradually consumes and saps the feeble, fretful essence of myself.[78]

At about the same time in 1922, Schoenberg wrote a poetic "Requiem" in which he again exteriorizes his feelings of betrayal: "Pain, rage yourself to a standstill. Grief, lament until you are weary!"[79]

In September 1923 it became apparent that Mathilde was suffering from a serious illness. At first it was diagnosed as a gallbladder inflammation, but shortly after, cancer of the adrenal gland was discovered, and at the age of forty-six Mathilde died —on 18 October, twenty-two years to the day after her wedding. Schoenberg was extremely distraught by the turn of events, which unleashed in him a tangle of conflicted feelings. He later confided to Berg that Mathilde's ghostly presence continued to haunt their residence. Everyone in their circle was aware of Mathilde's weaknesses and transgressions, and there was an outpouring of sympathy for Schoenberg and a sense that the hand of fate had somehow again interceded in the affairs of the Schoenberg circle. The Adagio was conceived as an idealized tribute to Schoenberg and Mathilde—a portrait of how their marriage should have been; after her death it became a solemn representation of the power of fate, which seemed to have played a cruel role in the Schoenbergs' lives together.

To represent the idea of fate, Berg used musical symbols to which he would return in his later works. On the large scale, he represents fate in the Mathilde movement by a palindromic design that is far stricter than the free symmetries found in such earlier works as the third Altenberg Song, the Präludium of the Orchestra Pieces, or passages from *Wozzeck*. Berg's tabular overview outlines the symmetries that he created: the movement begins with an ABA′ form that is then restated in reverse by which the order of some its elements—mainly tones in principal lines and a few other striking figures from before—recur in a reversed order. At the midpoint of the palindrome at mm. 358–63 Berg again shows the special skill that he had revealed in *Wozzeck* for evoking a demonic presence. As the tempo stalls and dynamics are reduced to a whisper, the piano grimly intones twelve pedal C sharps. The muted brass state a twelve-tone constellation with the Mathilde motive at its top, arriving at a diminished seventh chord at the very midpoint. Everything is then reversed, the rising lines descending and Mathilde's name spelled backwards. Berg instructed the engraver to center this moment of reversal between facing pages, and he made the four measures of music on either side of the divide exactly palindromic. After these passages, the palindrome becomes free and sporadic. Douglas Jarman has interpreted such formal reversals in Berg's music as "symbols of negation" and representations "of Berg's view of man as a helpless creature unable to alter his preordained fate and unable to break out of the tragic and absurd dance of death within which he is trapped."[80] Theodor Adorno adds: "Nothing could capture more drastically the sense of hopeless confinement than the circular closed form."[81]

Another important symbol of fate that Berg brings to the Adagio is a short rhythmic motive that occurs ominously before and, in retrograde, after the center point of the movement (Example 6.5). Recall that Berg had used similar, recurring rhythmic figures in earlier works, notably in the Orchestra Pieces, but here for the first time he associates a rhythmic motive with programmatic meaning, much as Mahler did with the "tragedy" rhythm in his Sixth Symphony.[82] Berg instructs that the motive is to be played loudly and precisely, making it plainly audible within the complex texture. In the score Berg marks the most obvious occurrences of the main rhythm with the notation RH~.

The third movement begins with a fifty-four measure "introduction"—a stormy cadenza for violin and piano that leaves an impression of incoherence. Constantin Floros argues plausibly that the music represents Schoenberg's disarray in the period following Mathilde's death, a reading supported by the return to and subsequent treatment of his name motive.[83] This erupts in a fury in the lowest register of the piano as a pickup leading into the cadenza. Berg then created the "kaleidoscope" of life that the finale was to embody by making the music out of bits and pieces from the first two movements.

Example 6.5 Adagio, main rhythmic motive

Berg dated the completion of the Chamber Concerto 9 February 1925, his fortieth birthday, and its orchestration continued to occupy him until the following July. The work was published in December 1925 by Universal Edition in a facsimile of Berg's handsome manuscript, and Fritz Heinrich Klein was put to work preparing a two-piano version that was published in 1926. But performances of this immensely difficult composition were slow to materialize. Only in March 1927 was the work heard in public, first in Berlin, then in Zurich and Vienna. Berg was especially pleased by the Vienna performance, conducted by Webern with winds from the orchestra of the Vienna Opera and with Rudolf Kolisch and Edward Steuermann as soloists. A week before the Vienna performance Webern had reported to Berg about the work's difficulty:

> I'm convinced that a great deal turns on how well the conductor knows the score. And I also think that it won't depend so much on small alterations (*Retouchen*) as on the conductor's understanding of the dynamics that appear in the score. And the tempi! Yes, really knowing the work! And that's not so easy, especially with one of yours. You see, by now even you yourself do not know so precisely what's in the score as the performers must know it. I think I know it.[84]

The concert, sponsored by Vienna's Verein für Neue Musik, received little attention in the press and what appeared was unusually skeptical and hostile, out of keeping with Berg's recent success with *Wozzeck*. A sympathetic review by "O.R." appeared in the *Reichspost*:

> Dr. Anton Webern conducted a technically splendid rendition of Alban Berg's Chamber Concerto, with Ed. Steuermann and Rudolf Kolisch supported by a wind band from the Staatsoper. The constructivist and mathematical design—almost rigidly symmetric—might be cited as the essence of this atonal work were it not for an audible impression that revealed that its real core springs from an extraordinarily artistic imagination. The ingenious scaffolding gives it a firm support in the absence of guidelines from traditional artistic practice. Without it this realm of tones would drift into the infinite and lose artistic value.[85]

For a 1935 concert organized by Universal Edition to honor Berg's fiftieth birthday, the violinist Dea Gombrich was enlisted to play the

Adagio movement of the Chamber Concerto using Klein's piano accompaniment. Berg was always ready to have the movement performed separately in this way, which he praised as a "very congenial arrangement for violin and piano. The piece is a completely self-contained Adagio lasting 15 minutes."[86] But Berg then went further with a new idea for the movement by adding a clarinet part to those for violin and piano. According to Gombrich's recollection, Berg went through the piano version with a colored pencil to indicate which notes the clarinet should play, and he later added further revisions on the same music.[87] The trio arrangement was played several times in 1935 and 1936, and it was published by Universal Edition in 1956, from a copy made presumably by Erwin Stein.[88]

The Chamber Concerto is an enormously complicated work whose demands on the players to produce an accurate and coherent impression have caused it to be rarely performed. Complication and artifice seem to have been among Berg's objectives in the concerto, much as they were in the Orchestra Pieces, in both cases tributes to Schoenberg. In the Open Letter he says that the concerto exhibits "virtuosity and brilliance" not only for the performers but also for the composer.

The work has three thematically related movements played without pause, similar to the integrated multi-sectional form of Schoenberg's Chamber Symphony. (Berg allowed each of the first two movements to be played separately by providing an ending for them in the Appendix to the published score.) The soloist in the first movement is piano, violin in the second, and both in the third. As part of his public tribute to Schoenberg, Berg uses a few of Schoenberg's twelve-tone and serial techniques, such as themes made from the twelve tones and these themes or whole sections varied by inversion, retrograde, or both. Berg also refers to other works by Schoenberg, most importantly to his Chamber Symphony, Op. 9. Still, the "twelve-tone" apparatus of the Chamber Symphony is superficial, primarily a tribute to Schoenberg and expression of support in his new compositional direction.

Like the third movement of Schoenberg's Serenade, the first movement consists of a theme with five variations. The variations maintain the proportions of the theme although they differ in character, ranging from the virtuosic runs in Variation 4 to a slow waltz in Variation 2 to the stumbling rhythms of Variation 3. Multiples of three abound: the light-hearted theme is contained in a line that runs on for thirty measures, passed from instrument to instrument. It is divided into three sections of fifteen, nine, and six measures, each in a different tempo whose metronome markings have three as a factor. The three name motives appear toward the beginning of the theme and recur in each variation. Several twelve-tone segments arise in the theme, the principal one being Schoenberg's motive in mm. 3–5, which is stretched to twelve-tones by a four-note prefix in the English horn.

As Berg observes in his tabular overview, the thirty-measure "basic shape" returns in a fairly strict retrograde as the principal line in Variation 2, in inversion in Variation 3, and in a retrograde of the inversion in Variation 4. The similarity with Schoenberg's twelve-tone techniques as they existed in 1923 is otherwise slight. The accompanying material in Berg's variations is free and developmental, and this allows him to make witty allusions to Schoenberg and his music. An example arises in Variation 2 (Example 6.6), where a passage within the retrograded theme in the trumpet moves through fourths. It is shadowed developmentally by fourths in the horn that make a clear allusion to the horn theme in fourths from Schoenberg's Chamber Symphony.

Berg reported to both Schoenberg and Webern that he had completed the first movement around 1 September 1923 and was moving on to the second movement, the Adagio. Before returning to Vienna from Trahütten on 21 September Berg probably composed the beginning of the

Example 6.6 Thema scherzoso con variazioni, mm. 98–100

movement, then put it aside, returned to it in March of 1924, following the death of Mathilde Schoenberg, and completed it in May of that year.[89] The principal melodic material in the Adagio derives from a succession of five themes, each a "basic shape." Some coincide with twelve-tone rows while one has fewer than twelve notes and in others there are notes repeated. The first two themes appear in section A1 (see Figure 6.1), and these are inverted from m. 331 in A2. The other three basic shapes occupy section B. Following the midpoint of the movement at m. 361, the shapes return in reverse order, with tones stated in retrograde and retrograde inversion, although maintaining aspects of their original thematic character.

The third movement is a technical tour de force in which Berg brings back and combines thematic and harmonic material from the two preceding movements. He adds two rhythmic motives that function like main and subsidiary themes in a sonata-form design, an idea used by Schoenberg in the finale of his Serenade.[90] Berg divides the body of the movement following the introduction into an "exposition" followed by a "development." The whole passage is framed with repeat signs—the only use of an exact sectional repeat in his music after the Piano Sonata, Op. 1. The appearance of repeat signs is again a tribute to Schoenberg, who used them for the only time in his entire mature oeuvre in the March of the Serenade. Schoenberg had earlier dismissed the use of repeats in modern music, and he returned to them in the Serenade as a parody of the emerging neoclassical style. As the music moves to a climax at mm. 775–80, the piano thunders out the notes of Klein's mother chord (Example 6.7), transposed and arranged as a line rather than a chord per se, probably to suggest that composing with twelve-tone rows lay in the future of the Schoenberg circle.

Example 6.7   Rondo ritmico, mm. 775–80

★★★

The completion of the Chamber Concerto marks a new stage in Berg's creative life. More than in his earlier works he brings into it an image of himself. The outer features of his self-portrait are presented for all to hear; the inner ones carefully hidden from view. From this point Berg's music becomes a form of "autobiography," to use Constantin Floros's term.[91] For Theodor Adorno the musical self-portraits were like puzzles: "This is the riddle of Berg's music," Adorno wrote. "We could scarcely describe it more simply or accurately than by saying that it resembled him."[92] At the same time, the Chamber Concerto is a preparatory step toward future twelve-tone composition. Berg's challenge was now to bring the same degree of personal expression to his music within a new method of composing.

Berg's parents: Conrad and Johanna. Courtesy of the Alban Berg Stiftung (Vienna)

Alban, Charly, and Smaragda Berg. Courtesy of the Alban Berg
Stiftung (Vienna)

Alban Berg and his siblings: Herman, Charly, and Smaragda (seated). Courtesy of the Alban Berg Stiftung (Vienna)

Franz and Helene Nahowski. Courtesy of the Alban Berg Stiftung (Vienna)

The Berghof (2017 photo). Collection of the authors

Paul Kammerer. Courtesy of the Library of Congress

Helene and Alban Berg on their wedding day. Courtesy of
the Alban Berg Stiftung (Vienna)

Arnold Schoenberg. Courtesy of the Arnold Schönberg Center (Vienna)

Hanna Fuchs-Robettin. From the collection of Dorothea Robetin

Ružena Herlinger, ca. 1925, Courtesy of Carleton University,
Archives & Special Collections

Villa Nahowski, Trahütten (photographed in 2017). Collection of the authors

Secret Programs with Twelve Tones, 1925–27

FOLLOWING THE RESOUNDING SUCCESS OF *Wozzeck*, BERG'S REPUTA-
tion soared, and his works were introduced to audiences throughout
the world. The concert culture of New York is an example of this explosive change. Before 1925 there were virtually no public performances
there of any music by Alban Berg.[1] Within a few years after 1925, his
String Quartet, *Wozzeck Fragments*, Chamber Concerto, and Piano Sonata
were performed by leading musicians in prominent New York venues,
and Berg was featured in articles in major New York newspapers. But
his new-found acclaim was jeopardized by a change in European musical culture and taste during the 1920s. Berg—like all composers in that
period—had to decide which of several competing directions he would
follow. In early works such as the String Quartet, he had adhered to
Schoenberg's ideology of what music at that time should be: in a uniform
style characterized by pervasive dissonance, counterpoint, and chromaticism, with little on the surface to remind the listener of any previous style.
In *Wozzeck* Berg went in another direction, combining Schoenbergian
atonality with elements brought forward from tonal music—passages
overtly in a key, triadic harmonies, quotations from his earlier music, and
diatonic melodies. Given the acclamation accorded to *Wozzeck* in 1925,
the rightness of his distinctive blend of old and new seemed confirmed.

In adopting a mixed style, Berg was far more in tune with the general direction of modern music in the 1920s than was Schoenberg.
The neoclassicists, with Stravinsky at their head, composed music that

Berg. Bryan Simms and Charlotte Erwin, Oxford University Press (2021). © Oxford University Press.
DOI: 10.1093/oso/9780190931445.003.0008

incorporated and called attention to styles of earlier music, placing them in a modern harmonic and rhythmic context. If he adopted Schoenberg's twelve-tone method of composing, Berg would have all the more difficulty in balancing multiple styles. In addition to coping with the shifting landscape of modern music, he was confronted in the mid-1920s by personal dilemmas. He was facing middle age and his marriage was approaching a crisis, caused in part by Helene Berg's persistent illnesses, in part by Berg's need for new emotional incentives. Given these realities, Berg would struggle to find inspiration to compose under the weight of mounting personal and artistic adversity.

The Hanna Fuchs Affair

On 20 May 1925 Alexander Zemlinsky was to perform Berg's *Wozzeck Fragments* with the Philharmonic Orchestra of Prague as part of a modern music festival. Berg traveled alone to Prague to attend—Helene was again taking a cure at a clinic in a Vienna suburb—and in Prague he found himself a musical celebrity: "The musical life of the whole world is surging around me so that my brain is on fire," he wrote to Helene. "I've already talked with a hundred people I know, talked in every language (my Quartet is being played in Moscow!), and I feel quite respected and famous."[2]

For his trip to Prague Berg had received an invitation from Herbert Fuchs-Robettin to stay with him and his family in their villa in the posh suburb of Bubeneč.[3] Fuchs-Robettin was a wealthy industrialist married to Hanna Werfel, Franz Werfel's sister. When Berg arrived on 15 May he was soon captivated by the luxurious lifestyle of his hosts and beguiled by their two young children. "My hosts spoil me," he wrote to Helene. "Room with hot water, glorious view, Roger & Gallet soap, roll-down blinds so that you can sleep with the windows open at night."[4] There were wonderful dinners and an excellent wine cellar, along with a private car at his beck and call. In short, he experienced all of the ample amenities that he so plainly lacked in his own life.

Out of this charmed sojourn in Bubeneč sprang Berg's consuming passion for Hanna Fuchs-Robettin, the golden-haired queen in this fairy-tale episode. He bore this passion for the remaining ten years of his life, and without doubt it provided a critical impulse for his late creative works. Fifteen letters from Berg to Hanna have survived but none to him from her, and he never refers to having received any. His infatuation found its most ardent expression in five long and desperate letters in 1925 and 1926, after which it subsided into a resignation bolstered by vows of undying fidelity through the last letter, from December 1934, written just a year before his death. It is clear from the letters that the relationship was never consummated: Berg—adopting his most Parsifal-like identity—speaks in one letter, "we renounce and thereby deny fulfillment to the holiest desires of both body and soul."[5]

During the years of his attachment to Hanna Fuchs, Berg continued to affirm his fidelity to Helene, meanwhile addressing Hanna as his only and eternal beloved. How this situation came about is one of the most tantalizing riddles of Berg's life story, given the unflinchingly honest character so often ascribed to him by others and also by himself. A number of factors came into play in the launching of his passion and its continuation; among these were Hanna's seductive and controlling personality, the aiding and abetting of the relationship by third parties, foremost among them Alma Mahler and Franz Werfel, and not least the wearisome tale of Helene Berg's illnesses and her ever-increasing jealousy and possessiveness. As Berg began to break free creatively from Schoenberg's restrictive views following the completion of *Wozzeck*, he also strove to loosen the chains that had bound him to Helene for so long. In this case, Berg's straying from his own avowed principles may be understood as a bid for an emotional fulfillment, an escape from subservience, which he had sought for years and which was, at least in his own view, necessary for creative achievement to continue for the next (and last) decade of his life.

The story of Berg's "affair" with Hanna Fuchs is well known.[6] The discussion here will serve to draw the different elements of the affair together and to place the episode in the context of Berg's life and career as a whole prior to an examination of the musical works that followed upon it. The catalyst for the affair may well have been Alma Mahler. She invited Alban and Helene to a gathering at the home in Prague of Franz Werfel's parents to coincide with a performance on 11 December 1924 of Mahler's Tenth Symphony.[7] Though not certain, it is very probable that Helene Berg was with her husband on this occasion since she later appeared well informed about Hanna and knew her by her nickname, Mopinka. The invitation to Berg from Herbert Fuchs-Robettin for the following spring likely stemmed from this gathering where the couples became acquainted. It is also clear that Helene did not miss the signals of admiration for the attractive and flirtatious Hanna Fuchs at this first encounter, and her suspicions, jealousy, and subtle machinations took shape accordingly.

While Berg was in Prague with the Fuchs-Robettins, Helene arranged to take a cure near home, in the Hacking sanatorium. Details of the cure program are lacking, but it is noteworthy that she chose to undertake a cure just at the time of her husband's trip to Prague. In the letters during their separation there is an undercurrent of strain, mainly over Helene's present state of health and whether or not she would be able to travel to Prague for the concert. The matter was undecided when Berg left home, and in the end Helene did not come. Berg also complained that Helene did not write, and he was in the dark about her plans. When she finally did write, she held out the hope that she still might come and wondered if she could sleep on the Fuchs-Robettins' sofa.[8] This latter remark is certainly disingenuous. Berg responded that any plan for Helene to travel to Prague would be so stressful for her that it would be a "crime" against her poor nerves.[9] The letter exchange over whether Helene would come to Prague or not takes on the aspect of a charade, since it is unlikely she intended to come but wanted Alban to think that she might. Meanwhile he dutifully reported on the official events in Prague, which culminated in the performance of his *Wozzeck Fragments* on Wednesday, 20 May. He took the train home the next day.

Berg's emotional state during and after the Prague visit—or at least the state in which he imagined himself—is best understood from his secret letters to Hanna. He was aided in the delivery of these by his then-student Theodor Adorno, who described his role as *postillon d'amour*.[10] The letters reveal that Berg again, as in the days of his courtship of Helene, had placed himself as an actor in a fantasy world. This is plain from the first of the private letters in which Berg takes on the identity of a succession of romantic figures from his literary and operatic worlds. He is Tristan helplessly in love with Isolde, Beethoven writing to the Immortal Beloved, Amfortas suffering a wound that will not heal, Alwa finding art in the sensual body of Lulu, Parsifal renouncing the flesh.[11] The letter is long, rambling, and somewhat contradictory, and by sending it, Berg violated an agreement with Hanna not to exchange any secret communications. Its tone is self-dramatizing in the extreme, despairing, and, finally, openly calculating concerning how the relationship might be sustained through sporadic contact in the guise of ordinary friendship. Berg writes:

> I am no longer myself since this greatest of events. I have become a madman staggering about with an ever-pounding heart, to whom everything, yes everything that once moved him, that brought him either joy or pain—from the purely material to the most spiritual things—has become completely indifferent, inexplicable, even hateful. The thought of my music is as burdensome and ludicrous to me as every morsel of food I am forced to choke down. One thought alone animates me, one desire, one longing: you! And in what numberless shadings: from the highest heights of human bliss to the lowest, most abysmal depths of human despair, my never-resting fantasies gallop to and fro, day and night. . . . And all this because of you, my one and only, glorious Immortal Beloved![12]

Like Beethoven in the letter to his Immortal Beloved, Berg enters into a full-blown metadiscourse on the distant beloved. He argues, didactically and perhaps with a degree of sophistry, that their bond is eternal, not temporal, and thus morally defensible. It can only be compared to that of Tristan and Isolde or Pelleas and Melisande, he says, and—perhaps imagining himself a Knight of the Holy Grail—he assures Hanna that their love has been consecrated by a renunciation of the flesh:

> Each of us has, after all, also obligations to the other and to self. To simply negate these obligations by lying to ourselves would be fraud and treason to ourselves. And since we are willing, in spite of everything, to renounce (and what a heaven on earth I thereby renounce! If one thinks about it but for a moment, one's heart threatens literally to tear asunder—)—since, then we nonetheless renounce, and thereby deny fulfillment to the holiest desires of both body and soul, I maintain that we do no wrong in loving each other eternally.[13]

Despite these protestations that his love existed most profoundly on a spiritual plane, Berg falls readily into a description of Hanna's physical charms. He praises her eyes, her "heavenly mouth," her "rosy heels," "the warm, sweet mystery" of her armpits, her way of walking and dressing, "the manner in which you transmute an erotic, lascivious fashion into unobtrusive noblesse"—these terms virtually quoting Alwa's praise of Lulu in Wedekind's *Pandora's Box*, a work that Berg had long admired. Clearly, Hanna did not hide her sexuality.

At the conclusion of this first private letter Berg declares that the hand of fate has been at work, since he unwittingly enshrined Hanna in his earlier music, by the notes H (in German the pitch B) and F as they occur in the Chamber Concerto and the String Quartet, Op. 3. Berg then proposes a new piece, a second quartet, that will be wholly dedicated to her.

Berg returned to Prague and to the Fuchs-Robettins six months later on his way to Berlin for rehearsals for the *Wozzeck* premiere. Two letters to Helene reveal that "Mopinka" was a topic between them. The first of these was written in the train, and on its envelope Helene later wrote, "This letter is important! It proves Alban's fidelity!"[14] It did not, as Helene well knew. In her 1965 edition of Berg's correspondence to her, Helene made sure to include the letter, which reads in part:

> I am really reluctant to reassure you about Mopinka. Maybe just this one thing: my main character trait is fidelity. In a previous incarnation I was surely a *dog* and will be one in a later incarnation (so starting again from the beginning!) who will die of distemper if I sin against fidelity: fidelity to *you*, but also to *myself*, to *music*, to *Schoenberg* (who makes it really hard)— . . . So how, with such a conservative disposition, *could* I not, and to you *more than ever*, be *true and remain so forever*, my Goldchen!! Believe me—as I believe it of you.[15]

Berg did not stop in Prague on his way home, nor did he on his return to Berlin for the *Wozzeck* premiere, but he was back in Prague in 1926, for the Prague premiere of *Wozzeck* under Otakar Ostrčil at the Czech National Theater on 11 November. Helene joined him there, and they did not stay with the Fuchs-Robettins, as Berg's three letters to Hanna from this time period reveal. This visit seems to have brought the Hanna infatuation to a crisis point. Only two short postcards from Alban to Helene survive from 1926, and it is possible that Helene destroyed the remaining correspondence for that year.[16] Berg wrote the first card on the day that he left for Prague, 6 November 1926. It reads in part: "Pferschel, think kindly of me and *only* good things. I have only *one* goal in Prague: a good Wozzeck performance. And only *one* expectation: to lay it at your feet act by act on Monday and Tuesday."[17] In Helene's 1965 edition, she removed the words "in Prague" from the card and attached its text as a postscript to a letter written from Berlin a year earlier, on 5–6 December 1925. This alteration can only have been done on purpose, to erase any link to that painful time in Prague in 1926 and to stress Berg's faithfulness to her—something she knew by this time to be false.

Berg arrived in Prague two days before Helene, whereupon he again saw Hanna and reignited his passions. On the night of his arrival he made a solitary nocturnal foray to Bubeneč for a "night of madness," about which he wrote deliriously to Hanna in another secret letter:[18]

> After hours of marching (hours, because of the dark, and lied to by innocent enemies, I had repeatedly gone astray), I made it to Bubeneč after midnight—to you—to you—to you—and when at last I found the house and walked around all four of its sides—finally, finally stumbling through meadows, saw your windows, and even these serving to seal you off hermetically from the outside world—I could have screamed, with a scream such as the world has never heard, your name—the one, the only—HANNA— . . . Having now, around three o'clock, gotten back to the misery of my lonely hotel room, I am drinking the cognac your husband gave me, knowing only too well how badly I would need it, and wander on—and on—and on through the night—what a night—what a night of madness. "Madness"—so be it!![19]

The madness was, of course, generated completely in his imagination, with the aid of alcohol, and his words resemble those of a besotted adolescent. He resumes the letter on the next morning in a more rational tone, pleading pathetically for ways to bring about more meetings after Helene had arrived. Could Hanna invite them for supper? Could they see a movie together? Would they have supper at the Zemlinskys, could Alma suggest that they stay on for a few days in Prague?

It is hardly to be imagined that anyone—least of all Helene—missed what was going on with Alban in the fall of 1926, and he confessed as much to Hanna, citing "scenes" with Helene over his desire to remain longer in Prague. Still in Prague, he wrote a letter to Herbert, part confession, part exoneration, in which he asserts that his veneration of Hanna flows from the same feelings he has for Herbert himself (clearly a fabrication), and then he refers to his unswerving fidelity in his almost twenty years of marriage (in fact he had been married then for fifteen years).

> No individual who halfway knows me could think me capable of risking the happiness of a marriage like mine—even for the sake of the most

all-consuming passion. Perhaps only my music, which mirrors my character more fully than do either my letters or my conversation, can convince you of both: my deep friendship and admiration for you, Mr. Fuchs, and my unwavering fidelity to my wife.[20]

Two days later Berg found himself writing to Hanna in full contravention of his letter to Herbert: "Will we again, like this time, have to tell each other: as yet there is not the slightest hope that our love will have the consummation that belongs by rights to it alone? A consummation, to be sure, that I cannot even begin to imagine, but in which I nonetheless believe with unshakable, holiest confidence." As if to underscore the irrationality, even the duplicity of his behavior, he returns to the madness theme.

> I fear the resolve to be reasonable is a ridiculous undertaking. It cannot succeed! But then, it is enough that I intend it. The madness comes all by itself. The state that already beset me during the nights in Prague, from the night when I roamed about your sleeping house, all the way to these last ones, when I try to drown this raging, ever-returning orchestrion of my thoughts about you in alcohol—such a state may appear quite normal to me: to all others it is sheer madness.[21]

No letters from Berg to Hanna survive from the year following the 1926 crisis. They resume in 1928 with Berg's repeated vows of undying faithfulness. In a letter of 7 June 1928 Berg mentions that Hanna had confessed to her husband concerning her exchange with him.[22] She must have cooled toward him, Berg thinks, yet he has held fast to his love for her: "But my love remains, although everything else that goes to make it up be buried alive—it is strong and sweet and aching, as in that second when I clasped your hand for the first time—and kissed it—and when—."[23]

Whatever Hanna Fuchs represented in Berg's emotional and creative mind is present to a degree in all the works of his final decade, 1925–35. In the end, it is not surprising that Berg, like many other composers in middle age, sought erotic inspiration with a younger woman which then led to a renewed level of productivity. Haydn's affair with Luigia Polzelli or Wagner's with Mathilde Wesendonck are well-known examples. Wagner is perhaps the best model for Berg, since he imported his passion into his work, most plainly in *Tristan und Isolde*. The events in Prague and Berg's subsequent letters to Hanna underscore the composer's unusually complex intertwining of his life and music. They also mark the beginning of Berg's sense of a divided life, which dogged him for his remaining years. Hanna was not held in high regard by those in Berg's circle, which provides further evidence that his attachment to her may be seen as an illusion. Those who knew her describe her as an elegant and attractive socialite and charming hostess but intellectually shallow, egocentric and domineering. Theodor Adorno described her later to Helene as "a bourgeoise through and through, who was once touched by the chance to be different, yet without being herself able to fulfill it. And he [Berg] was, besides everything else, a thousand times too astute not to see that she was not his equal, as clearly as he saw that you were his equal."[24] Soma Morgenstern remembered her more prosaically as "a sexy lady [*eine scharfe Dame*], not my type."[25] Her daughter-in-law, Lesley Fuchs-Robetin, described her in later years as a still beautiful, proud woman with a violent temper.[26] Anna Mahler, Alma's daughter, recalled her reaction to news of the death of her brother, Franz Werfel: "She had this fit of rage, the most tremendous I've ever seen anyone have. And her main target of that rage was *God*. That God had been able to do *this* to her although she had kept her vow to stop smoking!"[27]

A Return to Composing

Following the tumultuous two weeks in Prague, Berg arrived home in Vienna on 21 May, and with Helene he then traveled to Bavaria to pay a lengthy visit to the Danish conductor Paul von Klenau. "I am soaking my nerves," he confessed to Adorno on 18 June, "which are improving daily, in water and air."[28] In July the Bergs returned to Vienna, and Alban finally completed a full score fair copy of the Chamber Concerto—he symbolically dated it 23 July. The Bergs then took up their traditional summer residence in Trahütten. But the presence there of the Leberts, Berg's in-laws, prevented the relaxed atmosphere that Berg needed to work, so he and Helene returned to Vienna where Berg pondered his options as a composer. There was no doubt that he would take up Schoenberg's new compositional method—composition with twelve-tone rows—and do so more extensively than the token gestures made in the Chamber Concerto.

Soon after completing *Wozzeck* Berg had thoughts of composing a second opera and had begun to search for a suitable subject. But for the time being he put aside his operatic explorations until he had honed his skills in the new way of composing. He decided on several smaller works that would allow him to develop his own version of Schoenberg's method that could reinforce and facilitate his existing compositional priorities. In this way Berg could reaffirm his allegiance to his teacher and, by adapting the method to his own artistic personality, he would maintain a measure of independence.

He thought first of composing songs, much as he had done in 1907 during the euphoria of meeting Helene. In late July he wrote to Hanna: "I would most like to write songs. But how could I? The words of the texts would betray me."[29] Again attempting to relive his courtship of Helene, he mentions composing a string quartet that would be secretly programmatic. "Its four movements would reenact everything I went through from the moment I entered your house," he told Hanna.[30]

In September the Leberts vacated the villa in Trahütten, and the Bergs returned there for Alban to compose. On September 21 he reported his progress to Adorno:

> Now I'm composing a song, an occasional composition. It's for a portfolio in Hertzka's honor on the 25 years of U. E. Two songs on facing sheets of music paper, both on the same text. The first in C major composed almost 25 years ago; the 2nd composed today in the strictest style of 12-tone composition (tone rows!). So *25 years of U.E.*! But the latter is giving me little joy, although it is progressing relatively easily. *Too easily*, I fear! Then, however, I want to return to real composing, and I am still thinking a great deal about the quartet suite. Then perhaps a symphony next, since I will surely never find an opera text![31]

The "occasional" song mentioned to Adorno was his second setting of Theodor Storm's poem "Schließe mir die Augen beide." Ostensibly, the song was composed as a tribute to Emil Hertzka. Berg made a fair copy of both songs, adding this greeting:

> Twenty-five years of Universal Edition—equivalent to the enormous distance that music has traveled from tonal composition to composition "with 12 tones," from the C major triad:

to the "mother chord" (the 12-tone chord discovered by Fritz Heinrich Klein, which also contains all 12 intervals):

It is the everlasting merit of Emil Hertzka to have been the only publisher to have gone this distance from its very beginning. To him are dedicated the following two songs (on one and the same text by Theodor Storm), which should illustrate this development. They were composed—one toward the beginning, the other at the end of the quarter century 1900–1925—by Alban Berg.[32]

The date of the earlier version of the song is uncertain, although Berg's remark to Adorno that it was composed "nearly twenty-five years ago" suggests a date of 1901 or 1902. Berg then likely revised the song in 1907 as a tribute to Helene, whom he had recently met, and now in 1925 he returned to it in his attempt to revive his Tristanesque fantasy world of

1907. In a letter to Webern dated 12 October, Berg reports that the song was then completed:

> I sent in a love song that in text was entirely unrelated to the [Hertzka] tribute, actually two songs on *the same* text, one quite old and one quite new. I just composed the latter one here, my first attempt at strict twelve-tone, row composition. But in this art unfortunately I am not as far along as you, so for now I can't say much on my current work on the string quartet. . . . It's a lot of trouble for me.[33]

George Perle has assessed the song as a twelve-tone "compositional exercise" and a study for the string quartet, which agrees with Berg's description of it to Adorno and to Webern.[34] Its soprano line has little of the lyricism of Berg's other vocal writing, leaping ecstatically over sevenths, ninths, tenths, and one augmented twelfth. In 1955 Willi Reich told Helene that Berg did not want either version of "Schließe mir" in his "collected works" (*Gesamtwerk*).[35] It is unclear what Reich meant by this because Berg seemed eager to have the two songs known. In 1929 he turned them over to Reich to be published as a supplement to Reich's article "Alban Berg," which appeared in the February 1930 issue of the Berlin journal *Die Musik*. Still later, in 1932, Berg sent the two songs to Henry Cowell to be published in the American periodical *New Music*, although the songs were never to appear there.

For "Schließe mir" Berg developed a hybrid twelve-tone method that was indebted to several other composers as well as using his own earlier compositional devices. Berg had already sporadically used twelve-tone lines and chords, these arising mainly as extra-musical symbols as in "Über die Grenzen des All" or the Doctor's passacaglia theme in *Wozzeck*. Now he added ideas that he culled from Schoenberg's lectures on twelve-tone composition and from his study of Schoenberg's Opp. 23–26. To these he brought in concepts developed by his student Fritz Heinrich Klein, and possibly ideas taken from music by Webern and a Viennese contemporary, Josef Matthias Hauer. He would continue to use and to refine this hybrid method in all of his later compositions and ultimately make it his alone.

Berg learned of Klein's theories by reading the lengthy Foreword to Klein's Piano Variations, Op. 14 (1924).[36] Klein's piece consists of variations not on a theme but on what Klein calls a "model"—a jagged line

Example 7.1   Fritz Heinrich Klein, Variations, Op. 14, "model"

made from horizontalizing the tones of his mother chord. The mother chord, as has been noted, has all twelve notes separated by eleven different intervals. For the model of his Variations Klein placed the notes of the chord into the arch-shaped line seen in Example 7.1.

The model creates an all-interval tone row that has numerous special characteristics. The row is inversionally symmetrical in its succession of intervals—the first interval A–G♯, for example is an inversion (D–E♭) of the last interval; the second interval (G♯–E) inverts the next to last (B♭–D), and so forth. This means that there are no distinct retrograde forms of the row as a whole: any retrograde can be duplicated by transposing the original row. Of particular interest to Berg was the appearance in the model of familiar chords among its segments, for example, minor triads as notes 2–3–4 and 9–10–11. The notes of the two hexachords can be reordered as major scales on E and B♭. Every second note within these hexachords forms a chain of fourths or fifths, relating the row to Berg's longtime use of such successions. Given these features in Klein's model, Berg discovered an adaptability of dodecaphony to elements of tonal music and to his own earlier works. He explained this in a letter to Adorno: "As far as the 12-tone technique is concerned," he wrote, "the most conspicuous thing about it, I would say, is the fact that it does not at all exclude tonality (intentional tonality–not simply chance tonality)."[37] Here and elsewhere Berg uses the term "tonality" in a way unlike its usage by most musicians of the present day, for whom tonality is a syntax that governs all melodic and harmonic motions in a work to produce a unity based on a central tone and the major or minor triad built upon that tone. For Berg "tonality" resided not in a pervasive syntax but in surface elements, especially triadic harmonies, even if these appear only sporadically.

In the piano part of the song Berg generally has tones enter one by one, and he prolongs some of them to create chords by a type of finger pedaling. This is an effect that Berg may have taken from his study of twelve-tone music by his Viennese contemporary Josef Matthias Hauer,

Example 7.2   Josef Matthias Hauer, Piano Etude, Op. 22, no. 2, mm. 1–4

who called the effect "sustaining of melody tones" (*Liegenlassen der Melodietöne*).[38] An example is seen at the opening of Hauer's Piano Etude, Op. 22, no. 2 (1922–23), shown in Example 7.2. Hauer's etude consists of a succession of loosely related twelve-tone rows that he called *Bausteine*, "building blocks," a term that Berg also used in later sketches of ways to use twelve-tone rows. The first of Hauer's blocks is deployed with his typical pedaling effect. At the end of the first stanza of "Schließe mir" in mm. 10–11, the pedaling produces the entire mother chord as a verticality when read from top to bottom.

A closer study of the music will show how Berg reshaped these existing notions of twelve-tone music for his own purposes and applied them to later works in a distinctive manner. The basic tone row in "Schließe mir" is Klein's model transposed down a major third (Example 7.3). This transposition makes the diatonic content of the two hexachords all the more obvious, as it segregates them into groups of white and black notes, similar to the twelve-tone chord that Berg had used in "Über die Grenzen des All." Berg emphasized this white note/black note separation in all of his later twelve-tone works. The transposition also makes F and B (H in German), Hanna Fuch's initials, prominent as boundary tones. In choosing such a row, Berg allies himself with Klein, not Schoenberg. Schoenberg favored rows with a variety of intervals—not too many or

Example 7.3   "Schließe mir die Augen beide," version of 1925, basic tone row

too few of any one type. In a lecture of 1951 Schoenberg remarked, "I have been told that Alban Berg was aiming for a set which contained every possible interval. One must possess Alban Berg's genius in order to escape all the difficulties that such a set would offer."[39]

The entire vocal line of "Schließe mir" consists of five consecutive statements of the basic row, the notes given rhythms that agree with words of the poem. Berg maintains Klein's arch-shaped registral placement of tones in the first and fifth statements in the voice; in between, the contour of the row is freely changed. The row is not itself used as a theme. It lacks melodious character, and the melodic phrases in the song do not coincide with any of its five statements. Berg later explained that in his music a tone row was comparable to a major or minor scale for the earlier composer, that is, a collection of notes that could stand behind the foreground of themes, motives, and harmonies. "The row provides only a basis, just as key did earlier—strictly to be observed and freely applied," Berg wrote. "The presence of key left to those older composers the element of originality, the purely *personal* element."[40] Despite this statement, in his later twelve-tone music Berg often uses tone rows that are melodious and treated as prominent themes.

In the piano part in the first stanza of "Schließe mir," every note also comes from the basic row, its hexachords reversed so as to begin with the seventh tone and end with the sixth. This rotation—sometimes called a "cyclic permutation" of a row—is a Schoenbergian technique used to create multiple presentations of the full chromatic in both melodic and harmonic dimensions, without repeating or doubling a tone. In mm. 1–3 a twelve-tone line occurs in the voice, another in the piano, and twelve-tone collections (or "aggregates") are formed in the two-dimensional texture. These configurations are shown schematically in Example 7.4.

This multidimensional presentation of twelve-tone lines and fields was basic to Schoenberg's twelve-tone method. A contemporaneous example is found at the beginning of Schoenberg's Waltz from the Piano Pieces, Op. 23 (1923), whose opening four measures are shown in Example 7.5. The basic row is laid out in the right hand while the left-hand accompaniment uses the same row rotated to begin with its sixth tone and end with its fifth. In this way Schoenberg supersaturates the texture with the twelve tones while stressing no one of these notes by repetition or

Example 7.4 "Schließe mir die Augen beide," version of 1925, mm. 1–3

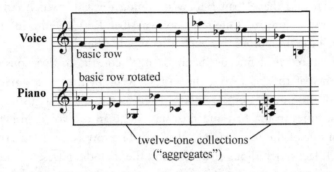

twelve-tone collections
("aggregates")

Example 7.5 Schoenberg, Waltz, Op. 23, no. 5, mm. 1–4

doubling. Later in "Schließe mir" and in subsequent works Berg largely abandons this Schoenbergian technique.

In addition to rotated forms of the basic row in the first stanza of "Schließe mir," there is also one presentation (left hand, mm. 6–8) transposed to the tritone and rotated to begin on the ninth note (A). In a sketch for the song Berg labels this tritone transposition a "dominant" while the untransposed row is a "tonic." These terms were used similarly by Schoenberg in his lectures of 1922–23 on twelve-tone composition and in his sketches for his Piano Suite, Op. 25.[41] The piano music of the second stanza introduces a rotated inversional form of the row (right hand, mm. 11–13) that Klein called its "second form." Otherwise the piano part is largely freed from tone rows until these return in a free reprise in mm. 15–16 that coincides with the final statement of the basic row in the voice. Here fragments from the model alternate with its tritone transposition, and the piece ends by building up a mother chord, from the bass F to the top note B.

Lyric Suite for String Quartet

With the song completed by mid-October 1925, Berg could concentrate on his string quartet, a "return to real composing" as he wrote to Adorno. Berg described his plan for the work in the aforementioned letter of October 12 to Webern: "By the way, it is to be a suite for string quartet with six short movements and more lyric than symphonic in character. It's not going well, but I'm really very weary, not in the very best health."[42] Berg did not mention that the new quartet would, like the Chamber Concerto, be programmatic—a covert representation of his experiences and emotions during his stay with the Fuchs-Robettins during the previous May. He had apparently decided on the overall form of the quartet by the time that he wrote to Webern in mid-October. The *Lyric Suite* builds upon the thematic integration and symmetric design found in all of Berg's instrumental works. In tempo the six movements fan out by alternating fast and slow, each increasing in emotional intensity. The movements also alternate those that are based on twelve-tone tone rows with others that are more freely atonal. Themes and tone rows recur from movement to movement, always with transformations that can suggest dramatic actions.

The history of the *Lyric Suite* is normally dated from the time of Berg's visit to Prague in May 1925, but its prehistory reaches back further, to Berg's encounter with the *Lyric Symphony* by Alexander Zemlinsky. Berg heard Zemlinsky's newly composed and lushly romantic work in December 1922, when Zemlinsky played an early version of it at the piano for a gathering at Schoenberg's Mödling residence. "It made a terrific impression," Webern reported, adding that Berg used the occasion also to show off the newly published piano score of *Wozzeck*.[43] Zemlinsky's *Lyric Symphony* consists of seven orchestral songs, alternating baritone and soprano voices. Its form is more operatic than symphonic, as its movements are irregular in design and connected by common motives, "leitmotives" as Zemlinsky called them.[44] There is a strong suggestion of programmatic content, and although Zemlinsky never spoke out about what that program might contain, the texts suggest a love affair with an unhappy outcome. In his study of the work, Antony Beaumont finds evidence that the *Lyric Symphony* tells of an affair between Zemlinsky—married at the time—and a voice student, Luise Sachsel.[45] The seven songs use love poems by Rabindranath Tagore, laid out symmetrically to trace the rising passion between the two lovers, its consummation, and its ultimate destruction at the hands of fate.

Berg first heard the *Lyric Symphony* in its final form in early June of 1924, when he and Helene traveled to Prague to attend the world premiere of Schoenberg's opera *Erwartung*, conducted by Zemlinsky at the Neues Deutsches Theater. During their stay in Prague Berg also heard the premiere of the *Lyric Symphony*, and after the concert he wrote to Zemlinsky to express his "deep, deep enthusiasm" for the work. Berg continued:

> Even if now I believe that I really know your *Lyric Symphony*, in ten years time I will be forced to admit that today I have only an *inkling* of the score's boundless beauties. But this can do nothing whatsoever to diminish my love, which—since it affects me in a *particularly personal* way—is that true love which overcomes me only in the case of a small, select body of music. . . . With the *Lyric Symphony*—never before was a title so unambiguous and at once so meaningful—a musical child is born, one that contains not one note too many nor indeed one too few.[46]

Berg's remark of 1924 that Zemlinsky's work affected him in a "particularly personal way" is important, as it marks a turning point in the direction that he wanted his music to take from that time forward—deeply personal and emotional and mixed in its compositional means. The *Lyric Symphony* is a tonal composition, in style a throwback to the late romantic idiom of Mahler and Strauss, and Berg's response to it suggests a renewed sympathy for this style despite its conflict with the Schoenbergian ideology of continual evolutionary change in music. Berg's remark suggests a nostalgia for the Tristanesque mood that had engulfed him and inspired him artistically in 1907 upon meeting Helene Nahowski—a state of mind that by 1924 had withered away under the weight of Helene's poor health and long absences, his own asthmatic condition, the couple's childlessness, and his financial struggles.

Berg's glance toward the romantic past would lead him to embrace genres of composition from that period—songs, programmatic instrumental music, and opera. His new disposition explains his readiness to publish the early song "Schließe mir die Augen beide" and the *Seven Early Songs (1907)*. But any overt return to earlier musical styles was impossible for Berg because it would alienate him from Schoenberg, a step that Berg could not and would not take. Instead, he would have to find ways to merge chromatic, dissonant, and now twelve-tone music with the materials and the expressive immediacy of earlier tonal music.

When it was published in 1927, Berg dedicated his *Lyric Suite* to Zemlinsky, a gesture often seen as a smokescreen to divert attention away from its association with Hanna Fuchs. But it is more likely that Zemlinsky's symphony was an indispensable prototype for the *Lyric Suite*. Berg's visits to Prague in 1924 set the stage for him to embark on his *Lyric Suite*: Zemlinsky's *Lyric Symphony* had given him the initial stimulus and conceptual model, and his meeting with Hanna in later 1924 awakened in him an object for the programmatic apparatus that he now needed to propel his creative imagination.

Berg quickly completed the first movement of the quartet in October of 1925, whereupon he put the composition aside until the summer of 1926, during his sojourn in Trahütten. The remainder of the brief six-movement work was completed there on 30 September, according to a note on the manuscript.[47] Revisions followed, and Rudolf Kolisch's Wiener Streichquartett gave the premiere performance in Vienna on 8 January 1927. Berg made additional revisions before the work was published by Universal Edition in summer 1927.

Reviews of early performances of the Suite show that audiences by 1927 were more pleased than ever with Berg's distinctive mixing of atonality with romantic expressivity. Following the premiere performance, a reviewer for the *Neues Wiener Journal* wrote:

> Among partisans of atonal music, the composer—widely known as a Schoenberg student and composer of the opera *Wozzeck*—is the most honest and persuasive. His Suite consists of six movements, with customary Italian tempo designations. It is noteworthy that in addition to these tempi he adds expressive terms. There's an *Allegretto gioviale*, an *Andante amoroso*, an *Allegro misterioso*, even an *Adagio appassionato*, a *Presto delirando*, and a *Largo desolato*. This is especially noteworthy because with Schoenberg and his school until now everything in music suggesting feeling and pathos has been outlawed. . . . The positive side of Berg's talent is most pleasingly apparent in his sonorous inventions. With the strangely whirring sounds from the strings, the Allegro misterioso is highly unusual. The Vienna String Quartet, which is splendidly equipped for playing such compositions, made for themselves and for the composer a great success in the packed hall.[48]

Throughout its early history, the *Lyric Suite* was associated with the Kolisch Quartet.[49] Berg and Universal Edition turned over exclusive performance rights to this ensemble for 1927–28, and they performed the work in fifteen European cities in that season alone, greatly enhancing Berg's international reputation. (From 1930 onward the Quartet played Berg's enormously complex work from memory.) In the spring of 1928, the Quartet gave a private reading of the Suite at Kolisch's Vienna residence for George Gershwin, who was then touring European cities to learn more about modern European music. The meeting was arranged by the pianist and Gershwin's longtime friend Josephine Rosensweet. In 1925 Rosensweet relocated in Vienna, changed her name to Josefa Rosanska, and often performed music by the Viennese modernists. There she met and later married Rudolf Kolisch. She played Berg's Piano Sonata in Berlin with Gershwin in attendance, and a meeting between him and Berg was arranged for 5 May 1928, at Berg's Viennese residence. Gershwin then played for Berg, and he later recalled the meeting as "one of the high spots of my visit." Rosanska arranged for the private performance of the Suite, and Gershwin talked the work up for the remainder of his tour.[50] Gershwin's subsequent interest in Berg's *Wozzeck* has been noted previously.

Shortly after publishing the *Lyric Suite* in July 1927, Emil Hertzka proposed a series of string orchestra arrangements of chamber works by Universal Editions composers. Berg eagerly complied and made an arrangement of the Suite for strings—an abbreviated version limited to movements two, three, and four.[51] The arrangement was published by Universal Edition in 1928 under the title *Three Pieces from the Lyric Suite*, and it was widely performed from that time forward. American audiences first heard the *Lyric Suite* in this orchestral arrangement, in October 1931 with the New York Philharmonic Orchestra, Erich Kleiber conducting. Following the concert Lawrence Gilman wrote about the work in the *New York Herald Tribune*, stressing Berg's expressivity redivivus:

> Apparently Berg has little kinship with those naive prophets of the new day who assure us that music is scarcely respectable unless it is devoting itself to "pure form" disdaining "expression" as a grande dame disdains patchouli. Possibly Berg had not heard of the triumphant announcement made some years ago by a French preacher of the modernist musical evangel who,

introducing a program of contemporary works, proclaimed: "Ladies and gentlemen, we are at last rid of expression! We have returned to Bach!"[52]

The shortened version of the *Lyric Suite* was also taken up by the Kolisch Quartet, which performed it during a residence in Paris in June 1928. During this time the ensemble played primarily in private circumstances where they used the three-movement form that Berg now referred to as the "salon" version.[53]

The *Lyric Suite* has proved to be one of Berg's most admired and often performed compositions. The music has a great and immediate expressivity, ranging from the lighthearted first movement to moments of increasing passion that by the end collapse and dissolve into a bleak emptiness. The composer places musical ideas of the greatest originality beside elements that are traditional, brought forward from tonal music. In some passages he coaxes triadic harmony and diatonic scales out of his tone rows, while in others he brings forth entirely novel sounds from the four stringed instruments. A striking example is in the third movement Allegro misterioso, which so captured the attention of the reviewer for the *Neues Wiener Journal*. Here the four lines mesh into a web of sound in which the individual lines and intervals gradually disappear. The musical effect is similar to the blur of sound that Berg created at the opening of "Seele, wie bist du schöner" from the Altenberg Songs, and it is uncannily similar to the "micropolyphony" used forty years later in works by György Ligeti. In his sketches Berg resorted to arabesque drawings to guide him in shaping these textures.[54]

It is the programmatic dimension of the *Lyric Suite* that has most captured the attention of those who have written about the work. Berg's use of terms like *amoroso* and *appassionato* for movements and an obvious quotation from Wagner's *Tristan und Isolde* in the final movement made plain the presence of a covert program, and Berg freely revealed its details to acquaintances including his students Theodor Adorno and Julius Schloß. "Secret" programs of little secrecy had been favored by many composers of the romantic period including Mahler and Tchaikovsky, and Schoenberg had resorted to secret programs in his early string quartets. Berg evidently wanted the program to be known, at least in general terms. Almost all of the methods that he uses to express it were common in the romantic period: musical quotations and the texts to which they were originally attached, verbal hints in the score, themes symbolizing people, transformations of musical elements to suggest dramatic actions, and themes made from the letters of names. As he did in the Chamber Concerto, Berg also uses the numbers 5, 10, and 23, these having private symbolic meaning, to guide his choice of tempos and formal dimensions.

In a 1937 analysis of the *Lyric Suite*, Adorno—fully aware of the connection of the work to Berg's encounter with Hanna Fuchs—described it as an expression of despair and a "latent opera" whose libretto is missing. "As a latent opera," Adorno explains, "the Suite has the character of an *accompaniment* to a sequence of events that have been largely omitted from it."[55] The description of the work as a "latent opera" has been very influential on later studies of the work. George Perle found in the work "a wholly subjective psychological drama whose protagonist is the composer himself, but which at the same time summarizes the life-experience of everyone."[56] Adorno also astutely compared the *Lyric Suite* to Schoenberg's Second String Quartet (1908). This is another secretly programmatic work relating to Schoenberg's wife, Mathilde, the breakup of Schoenberg's marriage following upon her affair with Richard Gerstl, and the composer's bleak alienation that ensued. The presence of voice in the last two movements of Schoenberg's quartet must have tempted Berg to bring voice into the finale of his own quartet, an option that he ultimately rejected.

Adorno was skeptical about the importance of the Hanna affair for Berg, either personally or musically. It was mere "play acting" on his part, Adorno wrote, with only superficial relevance to the music. In a note from 1955 Adorno discussed the work:

> He [Berg] had numerous affairs, which always turned out unhappily. In some ways the "unhappy ending" was composed in, and one had the feeling that these affairs from their very beginning were bits of play acting which, as the old Austrian joke has it, cause only despair and nothing really serious. . . . He carried out the affair with an endless secrecy, officially so that his wife wouldn't know, probably in truth because secrets gave him pleasure. . . . The *Lyric Suite*, programmatic music with a secret program, was crammed with countless allusions to the whole story without having those allusions—the dedication to Zemlinsky and the quotation from his *Lyric Symphony* among

them—do the slightest harm to its quality. Quite the opposite, this most seductive of works gets its vigorous spirit from just this background.[57]

In his letter to Helene of April 1936, already alluded to, Adorno confesses
his involvement in the Hanna Fuchs affair and offers an insightful explanation of its relevance to the *Lyric Suite*: "One thing was clear to me: that
the H. F. business was *not* paramount for him; that she was not in a position to challenge his relationship with you, and that it was far more a case
of his loving H. F. in order to write the *Lyric Suite* than of his writing the
Lyric Suite out of love." Berg's relationship with Hanna was "dramaturgical," Adorno adds, and in sum "a romantic error."[58]

Helene could never forgive Adorno for his complicity in the affair,
and she harbored a resentment against him from that point forward.
But she also accepted his analysis and repeated it to her closest friends.
To Alma Mahler in November of 1936 she reasserted that her husband
needed "poetic love" and "romantic" fantasy to compose. She continued:

> It was all a flight from reality. This was the only way that the *Lyric Suite* could
> come about. So I can only confirm the meaning of these events—and fall
> silent. And this is why I have not a trace of bitterness, only emotion and mel-
> ancholy. Nothing, nothing at all, can tarnish my love for him. And some day
> I will stand beside her [i.e., Hanna Fuchs] before God [Ich werde einmal mit
> ihr vor Gott stehen].[59]

Berg's compositional manuscripts contain many verbal hints about the
underlying drama that inspired the work.[60] A fuller though superficial
explanation of the covert program is found in Berg's private letters to
Hanna and in annotations that in 1928 he entered for her benefit into
a published study score of the work. Franz Werfel took the score to her,
and Berg's emotion-charged letters and score remained in her possession until her death in 1964, whereupon they were left to her daughter,
Dorothea. These materials were brought into the open in 1977 by George
Perle, acting on information about their existence that he had received
from Hans Redlich.[61] The letters and annotated score were subsequently
purchased by the Austrian National Library.[62]

It would be hasty to assume that Berg's programmatic details written
for Hanna's sake are what the music is really about or how it was created.
A work of such complexity and originality unquestionably goes deeper

than the banal and simplified ideas that Berg presented to her. But Berg's remarks afford, all the same, a starting point for understanding the music. In his comments for Hanna, Berg says that the first movement, Allegretto gioviale, depicts his arrival at the Fuchses. The carefree mood, Berg says, "gives no hint about the tragedy that follows." Berg stresses the presence of diatonic figures in the movement formed from the keys of B major and F major, Hanna's initials. He points also to the presence of his fateful number 23 in the length of the movement—sixty-nine measures, or 3 x 23. Berg is silent about other important aspects of the music. The movement is strictly derived from a twelve-tone row—the same one that he had used in "Schließe mir"—and its design is that of a regular sonata form (without development section). Berg's use of traditional forms steadily erodes as the work progresses.

The second movement, Andante amoroso, is not strictly twelve-tone although twelve-tone rows have an important presence in it. The music depicts Hanna interacting with her children at play. Themes representing Hanna, her son Franz (nicknamed Munzo), and daughter Dorothea (Dodo) recur in a free rondo form in which Hanna's theme repeatedly appears amid the playful interaction of the children. (These themes are shown in Example 7.6.) Dodo's theme is a pun, made from repeating the note C, or "do" in solfege, and Hanna's theme begins with a twelve-note row.

The third movement, Allegro misterioso, returns to a strict use of a tone row and depicts a mysterious whispering that Berg intuited in Hanna's presence. "It was all in secret, even a secret to us," he writes in Hanna's score. Berg also calls attention to the many occurrences of their initials, in the tones A–Bь–B–F (A–B–H–F in German). He adds the date 20.5.1925 (20 May 1925) at the top of the first page of the movement, all numbers that are multiples of 5 and which perhaps mark the occurrence of "that blissful half hour" that Berg recalled in his first private letter to Hanna. In the middle of the movement the whispering is interrupted by a Trio estatico, "the first brief eruption of love," he called it, an outburst to be played as loudly as possible and freed from tone rows. In his score for Hanna, Berg also calls attention to a quotation from Marie's lullaby in Act 1, scene 3, of *Wozzeck*, on the text "Lauter kühle Wein muß es sein" (coolest, purest wine shall it be). The allusion may be to the fine wine that Berg was offered by the Fuchses during his visit.

Example 7.6 *Lyric Suite*, Andante amoroso, symbolic themes

A (Violin I, mm. 1–8): Hanna's theme

B (Violin I, mm. 16–23): Munzo's theme

C (Viola, mm. 56–59): Dodo's theme

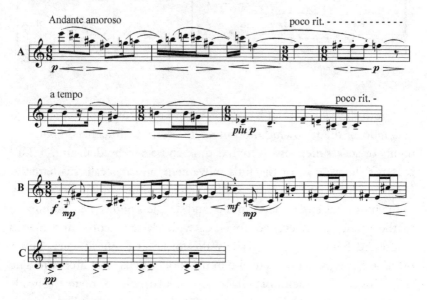

At the end of the ecstatic trio Berg writes "Forget it!" whereupon the opening whispers return in an abbreviated retrograde. But the amorous eruption will not disappear. It returns the next day, portrayed in the fourth movement, Adagio appassionato, again freed from the presence of tone rows. "Only now the initial lightning bolt-like consciousness of love unfolds into a great and limitless love passion," Berg writes. The movement begins with motives from the Trio estatico returning in varied form. The love birds—Berg in the Viola, Hanna in Violin I—then sing rapturously in canon (Example 7.7) while the other parts weave a harp-like accompaniment on triadic harmonies. The love song continues with Berg's viola quoting a figure from the third movement of Zemlinsky's *Lyric Symphony*, the words there "Du bist mein eigen, mein eigen" (you are my own, my own). A few measures later, Hanna answers shyly with the same motive. The music then quickly climbs to a passionate climax filled by the tones A–B–H–F.

Example 7.7 *Lyric Suite*, Adagio appassionato, mm. 24–27 (with Berg's annotations)

"From this all too brief happiness we are torn abruptly by the Presto delirando of the following movement, the fifth, with its hectic pulse, its nights of stale sullenness disrupted time and again by delirium."[63] This is Berg's description of the fifth movement, and it recalls his letter to Hanna on his "night of madness." But in light of the immense originality of the music, his talk of hectic pulses and sleepless nights seems simplistic to the point of irrelevance. Together with Bartók's contemporaneous Third and Fourth String Quartets, the music grips the listener with a breathless energy as nowhere else in the modern chamber literature. The impulsive force of the music effaces any regular pulse or meter, its head-long motion suspended only momentarily by two tension-filled passages marked *tenebroso*. As in the quartets of Bartók, the intensity of the music is heightened by an expanded vocabulary of sounds from the strings. Berg calls for virtually every extended playing technique available to these instruments—harmonics, pizzicato, bowing on the bridge, on the fingerboard, at the frog, with the wood, flautando, tremolo, martellato, and glissando.

Finally, the sixth movement, Largo desolato, maps Berg's "utmost wretchedness and despair" over the hopelessness of their love and the cruelty of fate. In his writings about the work—for one of the few times in his entire oeuvre—Berg could find no presence of a traditional musical form. The music begins with a somber passacaglia-like theme, passes through moments of the greatest contrast in mood and surface design, and dies away at the end in a steady eighth-note motion—reminiscent of the end of *Wozzeck*—during which the instruments drop out one by one.

Berg told Hanna that the movement was a "song without words," guided by Baudelaire's sonnet "De Profundis Clamavi," which Berg knew in Stefan George's German translation:

Zu dir • du einzig teure • dringt mein schrei	To you, my only dear one, I cry out
Aus tiefster schlucht darin mein herz gefallen •	From the deepest pit into which my heart has fallen.
Dort ist die gegend tot • die luft wie blei	All is dead here, the air like lead,
Und in dem finstern fluch und schrecken wallen.	curse and horror seethe in the dark.
Sechs monde steht die sonne ohne warm.	The sun above for six months without warmth.
In sechsen lagert dunkel auf der erde.	Another six with darkness over the land.
Sogar nicht das polarland ist so arm •	Even the polar wastes are not so bleak—
Nicht einmal bach und baum noch feld noch herde.	Here there is no stream, no tree, no field, no flocks.
Erreicht doch keine schreckgeburt des hirnes	No miscarried monster of the brain
Das kalte grausen dieses eis-gestirnes	attains the frigid horror of this frozen moon
Und dieser nacht • ein chaos riesengross!	nor the hideous chaos of the night!
Ich neide des gemeinsten tieres los	I envy the lowest animal
Das tauchen kann in stumpfen schlafes schwindel ..	that can sink into a dull slumber . . .
So langsam rollt sich ab der zeiten spindel!	So slowly unwinds the skein of time!
(freely translated from the French by Stefan George)	

Words and phrases from Baudelaire's text are scattered into the compositional manuscripts, so it is certain that the poem guided Berg in creating the music in song-like fashion. He also wrote out the entire poem in Hanna's score as a text underlay, passing it from instrument to instrument.

Should a voice then be added in the finale to sing this text? This idea was most insistently recommended by George Perle, who created an edition of the work whose finale uses soprano voice.[64] Perle argues that Hanna's score, with its text underlay, makes the vocal version the authentic one, while the version that Berg himself ultimately published—in which he deleted the text presumably for Helene's sake—was in fact an arrangement.

There is widespread disagreement about Perle's conclusion. On the positive side, Arved Ashby writes: "The sketches for the Largo desolato present not only a movement immediately inspired by and based wholly upon Baudelaire's sonnet, in every sense a text-setting that can only be realized through vocal performance."[65] Several recordings of Perle's version, featuring celebrated vocalists including Dawn Upshaw and Renée Fleming, are attractive and have received excellent reviews. Other writers disagree with Perle's theory. Their most persuasive reasoning is that all of the evidence for a vocal part is circumstantial and out of keeping with Berg's insistence on an exact presentation of his artistic ideas. Berg never expressed or intimated that he wanted an actual voice part in the finale or that he suppressed the voice part for practical reasons. Berg made no known hints in this regard to his student Julius Schloß, who worked with the manuscripts and was fully aware of their programmatic background. The voice line that Berg outlined (in red pencil) in the score for Hanna was an artificiality that she could understand, something to simplify the complex and unexplainable relevance of Berg's emotions to the compositional process, something comparable to the F's and H's that the composer so diligently highlighted throughout her score regardless of their significance to the music. It is hard to believe that Berg imagined an actual voice singing a line that spans more than five octaves throughout the music for the quartet. Nick Chadwick writes persuasively:

> The wild despair of the last movement is limited, and possibly cheapened, by the presence of a text, as is the impact of the rest of the work if too much importance is attached to the programme. Also, the almost constant doubling of the voice part in the string writing is not consistent with the practice of Schoenberg in the third and fourth movements of his Second String Quartet, which would have been Berg's chief model.[66]

Berg described the movement as a "Lied ohne Worte," Chadwick concludes, "and as a 'Lied ohne Worte' it should be allowed to remain."

While the programmatic element of the *Lyric Suite* has dominated writings about this work, Berg himself stressed—to everyone except Hanna Fuchs—its structural features. The *Lyric Suite* is Berg's first major twelve-tone composition, and this is the element that he explains in most detail in his writings on the work. Berg's principal analysis of the Suite is an undated, hurriedly written nine-page outline made for the benefit of Rudolf Kolisch, probably drawn up at about the time of the premiere in 1927. Kolisch turned the material over to Willi Reich, who published it in facsimile in 1959 under the title "Neun Blätter zur 'Lyrischen Suite für Streichquartett'" (Nine pages on the *Lyric Suite* for String Quartet).[67] In his notes, Berg goes movement by movement to describe the form, point to thematic connections that link each movement to its neighbors, and explain the presence and application of tone rows in movements one, three, five, and six.

Although Kolisch was aware of the Hanna affair and its connection to the work, Berg makes no reference to any underlying program, except to say that the basic tone row of the first movement changes when it reappears in movements three, five, and six. These changes, Berg continues, are essential to the character of these movements and suggest the "enduring of fate" ("Schicksal erleidend"). Berg places this term in quotation marks, which he almost always does when he draws upon an extraneous source. In this case the term "enduring fate" comes from the 1920 review by Julius Korngold that Berg had ridiculed in his essay "Wiener Musikkritik." In the review Korngold dismissed the atonal style as an empty and artificial language devoid of themes that could express dramatic action. Korngold writes about the atonal style: "There can be no substantial musical episodes within which fate and evolution can take place, because just *that* element is not given shape, cannot be given shape, that can *suffer fate* or evolve—namely, the theme or the basic melodic thought."[68] Korngold's accusation about atonality apparently remained in Berg's mind, and in the *Lyric Suite* he would show that a basic melodic thought—a tone row—can in fact represent the enduring of a fate. He does so by progressively changing the order of tones in the initial row to bring the four notes A–B–F–H closer, then to drive them apart. In the carefree first movement, the basic row is the same one that Berg used in "Schließe mir" (Example 7.8A), and here the lovers (A–B–F–H) are separated. They are brought together in the row of the third movement

Example 7.8 *Lyric Suite*, principal tone rows

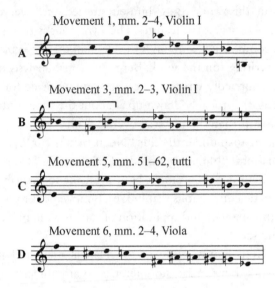

(bracketed in Example 7.8B) by transposing the earlier row up a fourth and switching the position of notes 4 and 10. Berg uses row B in the Allegro misterioso movement only in forms where the four notes remain together as a segment. In the gloomy *tenebroso* passages in the fifth movement additional alterations of the basic row produce row C, in which the lovers' tones are again separated. Berg then extracts widely separated notes from row C to produce row D, and these two rows then alternate in the dreary Largo finale.[69] The changes in the rows also affect the character of the movements in which they appear by moving from a confidently distinctive all-interval content in row A to a drab and near scalar content in row D.

Following the premiere of the *Lyric Suite* in January 1927, Berg again took stock of his future compositional plans. In a letter to Adorno of 25 January 1927, he says that he is uncertain what he will compose next, although an orchestral piece had been in his mind since 1925.[70] A return to operatic composition was for the time stymied by his difficulty in finding a suitable text. Following his trip to Leningrad in June of 1927, Berg and Helene went to Trahütten for their customary summer retreat, but Berg then suffered from an especially serious attack of asthma, and he complained to several friends that he had lost his desire to compose. He wrote to Webern that his summer had become a nightmare:

> Even though I'm better now (except for small relapses) I'm still miserable—like I was suddenly 20 years older, having neither the desire nor the ability to compose. Only the torment of having to work and not being able to do so! I can only lie about . . . and wait.[71]

During this period of doubt, Berg turned his attention to musical theory, to develop and refine the distinctive twelve-tone method of composition that he had begun to use in "Schließe mir" and the *Lyric Suite*. The principal outcome of his theorizing took the form of two large musical tables—Berg dated them 17 July 1927—that show figures that can be derived from a twelve-tone row for use in a composition.[72] The tables begin with the basic row shown in Example 7.9. In some respects the row is similar to Klein's model row that Berg had used in "Schließe mir" and the *Lyric Suite*. The first hexachord (which Berg calls the "antecedent," a term used also by Schoenberg for the first half of a row) has the same white notes C–D–E–F–G–A; the second hexachord (the "consequent") has the black notes plus B, and the contour of the row has an arch shape as does Klein's model. But the row has a far more melodious profile than does Klein's all-interval configuration, suggesting that Berg intended to use the row and its forms to create themes in addition to background sources for harmonies.[73] In his charts Berg writes out the twelve transpositions of the basic form shown in the example and its inversion also in twelve transpositions. From each of the twenty-four forms, he extracts fourteen different configurations of tones that could serve as harmonies or motives. Each of the fourteen has twelve notes, but their order of occurrence is only loosely related or unrelated to that of the basic row. Berg's main intention is apparently to derive harmonies and figures that he had used in his earlier music—triads,

Example 7.9   Row tables of 17 July 1927, basic row

Example 7.10   From the row tables of 17 July 1927

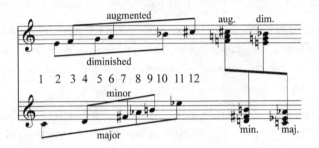

triadic progressions, diatonic scales, whole-tone scales, chains of fourths, and the like—that would exhaust a collection of twelve different notes with none repeated. He also looked for patterns to guide the extraction of these familiar figures from the parent row—choosing every second note or superimposing segments of the parent row, for example—and he often beams notes together as an optical aid for these patterns.

Berg's method for obtaining familiar harmonies from a tone row is illustrated in Example 7.10. Here he finds four triads (augmented, minor, diminished, and major) in the row, which he divides on two staves. In this instance there is no simple pattern by which these chords are drawn from the row—the order of its notes is ignored although Berg keeps all twelve tones together with none repeated. Berg's tables suggest a twelve-tone technique with no persistent element of serialism. Tone rows can be present on the surface of the music as thematic elements, but they can also stand remotely behind the surface of the music, where they are "dissolved"—Berg's term—into familiar harmonic elements. In these ways Berg's twelve-tone method is largely unrelated to Schoenberg's method and more similar to Berg's own earlier composing that freely mixed elements of tonality and atonality.

When he created his large twelve-tone tables in July 1927, Berg first contemplated using them in an orchestral work, a "Romantic Overture," for which he made sketches at about this same time.[74] Typical of his long-standing compositional procedure, Berg first prepared a verbal outline for the overall form of the work. It would be a twelve-tone composition using the materials laid out in his contemporaneous tables, and it would have one movement calling for strings, possibly including harp.

Example 7.11   Romantic Overture, sketch for transition

Its design would be a standard sonata form with exposition, development, and reprise, and it would probably have programmatic content. In one sketch Berg labels the three parts "earth, hell, heaven." Berg also wrote out a melodic sketch, shown in Example 7.11, for the transition section of the exposition, showing how he planned to use elements from his twelve-tone tables. The melody unfolds the triadic harmonies illustrated in Example 7.10. In this transitional passage, Berg also planned to allude to the American popular song "Tea for Two," possibly on account of the program that he had in mind for the work and because he found an analogy in the harmonies of the famous chorus of the song with the minor, diminished, and major chords that he had derived from the tone row. This is Berg's earliest reference in a composition to contemporaneous popular music, something that he would continue in later works.

In August of 1927 the Bergs returned to Vienna from Trahütten. To rekindle his zest for composing Berg abandoned the Romantic Overture and turned his attention back to opera, intensifying his search for a suitable text. This complex undertaking will be described in a later chapter.

The Celebrated Composer, 1928–34

I N 1928 BERG FINALLY CHOSE AS THE SUBJECT OF HIS SECOND OPERA A conflation of two plays by Frank Wedekind, *Erdgeist* (Earth spirit) and its sequel *Die Büchse der Pandora* (Pandora's box). The long and controversial dramas were a daring choice for the opera that Berg titled "Lulu," named after the central character in both plays. The project would occupy the composer for the remainder of his life, posing for him challenges that at times he felt he might not overcome.

When he settled on the Lulu subject in 1928, Berg's outward life had fallen into a measured and largely comfortable routine. He spent the winter and spring months in Vienna, where he taught a few students, attended to correspondence, oversaw business matters, and traveled far and wide in Europe to hear performances of his music. The exhausting trip to Leningrad in June 1927 for *Wozzeck* was mentioned in Chapter 6, and between that year and 1931 he was present in at least eleven cities for local premieres of the opera. He and Helene went to Zurich in March 1927 as guests of the industrialist Werner Reinhart to hear the Chamber Concerto. Then to Paris in March 1928 for the first performance there of the *Lyric Suite*, played by the Kolisch Quartet at the fashionable Salon Jeanne Dubost.

During the winter and spring months Berg also took up new projects. He continued his longtime interest in the analytic study of Schoenberg's music by giving a series of lectures about those works at his Hietzing residence during the spring of 1933.[1] Berg also assisted his student Willi

Berg. Bryan Simms and Charlotte Erwin, Oxford University Press (2021). © Oxford University Press.
DOI: 10.1093/oso/9780190931445.003.0009

Reich in the editing and production of Reich's journal *23: Eine Wiener Musikzeitschrift* (1932–37). Reich's idea for the journal was to imitate the hard-hitting polemical content found in Karl Kraus's *Die Fackel*, and Berg responded enthusiastically: "So a musical *Fackel*! I've wanted this for 25 years, and I'd like to write it myself. But then I'd have to give up composing."[2] Reich's official explanation for the title "23" was that it was the number of the paragraph in Austrian press laws concerning appeals for false statements in newspaper articles, but plainly enough the number was a reference to Berg. "You are the godfather of the journal," Reich admitted.[3] He later added, "Until his death Berg took a passionate interest in *23*. He not only made countless suggestions for editing texts, but he read all of the articles in manuscript and in proofs."[4] Berg's summer months were reserved for composing, and he and Helene regularly traveled to retreats in Styria and Carinthia where Alban could find the isolation he needed to concentrate on creative work.

Prerogatives of Success

With the success of *Wozzeck* and the *Lyric Suite*, Berg had finally established himself internationally as one of the foremost living composers. He soon began to enjoy advantages from his new-found fame. Berg's old friend Hermann Watznauer undertook his first biography, for which Watznauer had preserved notes and correspondence going back to Berg's childhood. Watznauer foresaw an informal memoir, not a published study, and he described the project to Berg:

> I've been struggling with the "Biography" for nearly a year and finally I'm ready to begin writing. I think that the dry chronological material will be more digestible if the form is that of a historical narrative. I'll have to make it into the history of a friendship—and I'll rename Hermann Watznauer "Hermann Herrenried"—to give it more meaning. I won't exaggerate in it, and if you hate it you can always throw it away.[5]

Berg encouraged Watznauer and readily answered his questions about events in his early life and career and about the chronology of his early compositions. In 1929 Watznauer sent Berg a handwritten copy of what he had done, and his recollections informed several later and more extended studies, especially the biographies of Willi Reich, whom Berg subsequently appointed to be his official biographer.[6]

Berg was also named to the boards and juries for numerous musical organizations, including the Allgemeiner Deutscher Musikverein (ADMV), the International Society for Contemporary Music (ISCM), the Österreichischer Komponistenbund (ÖKB), and, in the United States, Henry Cowell's New Music Society and E. Robert Schmitz's Pro Musica. Berg believed in the usefulness of such organizations to promote modern music, and he devoted much time in the late 1920s to studying and evaluating scores so that he could argue for the promotion of music stemming from Schoenbergian principles. Berg also served on the jury for the Kunstpreis der Stadt Wien (in music), after receiving the prize himself as one of six recipients in 1924. In 1930 he was elected an external member of the prestigious Prussian Academy of the Arts in Berlin.

Outwardly Berg's life was good. He was receiving sizeable royalties for *Wozzeck* performances, and he later called the period from 1926 to 1932 his "seven fat years." In 1930 his royalty income was approximately 21,000 schillings, roughly equivalent to $3,000, and this did not include disbursements in dollar denominations from funds that Berg had inherited from his brother and mother and that the Borgfeldt Co. in New York held in trust.[7] In 1930 Berg purchased an automobile, a Ford Model A, for 11,900 schillings—an unheard of luxury at the time for any musician in Schoenberg's circle.[8] Helene's wealth also increased following the death of her father in January 1925 and mother in March 1931. Franz Nahowski's estate, in the form of real property and shares, was valued at 363 million kronen, which with the currency reform of that year became 36,300 schillings.[9] Anna Nahowski's estate value is not recorded, but her assets included cash and substantial shares in the family real estate.[10]

Berg at this time was also keenly interested in receiving an academic appointment to teach composition. The first opportunity arose in 1925, when Franz Schreker offered him an adjunct position to teach music theory at the Berlin Musikhochschule, where Schreker had been director since 1920.[11] Berg turned the offer down, saying that the salary and terms were inadequate.[12] In 1930 Schreker again approached Berg with the opportunity to join Paul Hindemith and himself on the Berlin faculty, now with an adequate monthly salary of 900–1000 deutsche mark (about $225). Schoenberg, who was then teaching a composition class in Berlin at the Akademie der Künste, strongly urged Berg to accept the position, but Berg declined. He explained to Schreker that he had a duty to his profession to work on his new opera, *Lulu*, without interruption through the winter of 1930–31 and bring it to completion at that time.[13] Berg's explanation was plainly disingenuous since he was in no hurry at this time to finish *Lulu*. In Vienna he was making a good income from *Wozzeck* and, despite having little good to say about the musical culture of the city, he was bound to his hometown and to a comfortable life there. Another reason for his declining the position in Berlin was the presence of Schoenberg. Although Berg's belief in Schoenberg's greatness as a composer never wavered, he had long since tired of his teacher's exploitation of him as a person. He enjoyed an occasional meeting with Schoenberg, but he resolutely avoided any longer periods of contact. In 1923 Schoenberg had proposed that the Bergs join him for a summer retreat, and Berg wrote about it to Helene:

> I was speechless! "Well, don't you want to?" "Uh, of course—." But it took a while for me to regain my self-control. What I consider friendship, what it comes down to, is to help, to have an interest in my work. No, *none* of that! Instead just a way of forcing us to be his slaves during the summer. Just imagine it, Pferschi! [14]

Proximity to Schoenberg came up again in 1933, when Berg received his third inquiry about joining the faculty of the Berlin Musikhochschule. Schreker had resigned from the institution in 1932, leaving Paul Hindemith as the most prominent composer on its faculty. On a visit to Vienna in May 1933 for the celebration of Brahms's centenary, Hindemith met Berg at the residence of Egon Wellesz and asked Berg if he was interested in joining the Berlin faculty. There had been tumultuous changes in the Hochschule faculty as a result of the Nazis' Civil Service Restoration Act, passed only weeks before, which demanded the removal of Jews from civil service positions, including those in academia. The purge of Jewish faculty from the Berlin Hochschule began immediately, and even the non-Jewish director Georg Schünemann had lost his job, to be replaced by Fritz Stein, a reliable Nazi. It is questionable that Hindemith could have made good on his offer to Berg, but Berg's comments on the possibility show not only his determination to keep his distance from Schoenberg but also an indifference to Schoenberg's plight. On 15 May he wrote to Helene:

> Even if we are not thinking about accepting such an offer (although it is more arguable now than before since Schoenberg may no longer be in Berlin), it would be a colossal triumph for me to be engaged by the Nazis and for all Austrians—even for Almschi. And I would have something to play off against the Viennese government if they actually come up with an offer [at Vienna's Music Academy], or give them pause if they think I'm not *right* enough for them.[15]

Two days after Berg wrote this letter, Schoenberg and his family left Germany permanently, first for Paris and in October, after he was dismissed from his position at the Akademie der Künste, for the United States.

As he mentioned to Helene in the letter of May 15, Berg was most interested in an appointment closer to home, to the faculty of the Akademie für Musik und Darstellende Kunst in Vienna.[16] For the last ten years of his life he did what he could behind the scenes to obtain a position there, but always in vain. In 1927 an article in a Viennese newspaper announced that Max Springer, the new director of the Academy, was ready to bring Berg aboard: "We understand that the composer Alban Berg, a born Viennese and important student of Schoenberg, will be appointed as instructor of the composition class. Until now the composition class has had no teacher from the ranks of the most modern figures."[17] Berg was skeptical about the information and wrote to Schoenberg, "I don't put much belief in such reports. I think that if it were true, its early announcement would sink the idea because for Springer my appointment would not be really a cherished thought, more a publicity stunt from which he'll be easily dissuaded now that opponents of the idea know of it."[18] At about the time of Hindemith's proposal for him to teach in Berlin, Berg was making another effort for an appointment in Vienna. In May 1933 he met Anton Rintelen, Minister of Education in Austria, at a reception followed by a dinner party given by Alma Mahler. He wrote about it to Helene: "I have this horror of Vienna and these meetings for career purposes. Down deep what I think is important is for me *to work* and *work on* until something good comes of it. *This alone will benefit me and my progress.*"[19]

In 1930 Berg was invited to submit a tribute to the Frankfurt Opera House as part of a celebration of its fifty years of existence. For this homage he composed a four-part canon, "An das Frankfurter Opernhaus" on a text of his own (the only time that he ever set his own words to music):

In deines Lebens	In your life's
fünfzig Jahren	fifty years
hast du erfahren	you've witnessed
viel Freude und Sorgen,	much joy and care;
s'war nicht vergebens,	'twas not in vain,
denn was wert war,	for things with value
bleibt, wie's beschert war,	remain as when bestowed,
von heute auf morgen—	from one day to the next—
in aller Ewigkeit.[20]	to eternity.

Berg's poem says that things of value retain that value permanently, and he cleverly chooses the form of a perpetual canon to capture this idea musically. The beginning of the leading voice of the canon is shown in Example 8.1. In his canon Berg also pays tribute to Schoenberg's opera *Von heute auf morgen*, which earlier in 1930 had its premier performance at the Frankfurt Opera. Berg alludes to Schoenberg's title in his poetic text, and the leading voice in the canon begins by stating a transposed inversion of part of the tone row that begins Schoenberg's opera. Berg's canon is not strictly twelve-tone, and the piece ends on a C-major triad. Schoenberg was delighted with Berg's tribute. "How did you suddenly develop such skill?," he asked Berg jokingly.[21]

Example 8.1   Berg, canon "An das Frankfurter Opernhaus," leading voice, mm. 1–3

Summer Retreats and Family Entanglements

The summer retreat or "Sommerfrische" was an integral part of Berg's composing regimen. Only in the country could he find the energy and inspiration for the new ideas necessary for serious creative work. After the sale of the Berghof in 1920, the Bergs spent their summers at the Nahowskis' rustic villa in the mountain-top village of Trahütten, near the town of Deutschlandsberg in Styria. For years the Bergs had continued to use the villa as a summer residence, sharing it with Helene's sister Anna Lebert and her family. Although Berg was inspired to compose in Trahütten as nowhere else, the arrangement proved unsatisfactory since it lacked the quiet isolation that Berg needed. Additionally, Arthur Lebert suffered from tuberculosis, and Berg was fearful that his asthmatic condition—which always flared up in Trahütten—might make him susceptible to Lebert's disease. So in the spring of 1928 the Bergs found a new but familiar and nostalgic summer home, in a rented cottage called the "Denishube" at the Berghof. They stayed there in August of 1928 and would return every summer through 1932. In November 1932, following the sale of the Trahütten property, the Bergs purchased a small retreat, called the "Waldhaus," on a wooded bluff overlooking the Wörthersee (Figure 8.1). The house was in a dilapidated condition, and in the spring of 1933 Helene traveled there to oversee its renovation. Alban joined her

Figure 8.1 The Waldhaus (photographed in 2017). Collection of the authors

in late May. Despite the lack of conveniences in the house, the Bergs found it to be a refreshing asylum from life in Vienna.

Meanwhile, Berg continued to shoulder the many burdens placed upon him by the Berg and Nahowski families. After the death of Arthur Lebert in 1929 and with the mental illness of Frank Nahowski, Berg found himself to be the only competent male in the Nahowski extended family. This position entailed onerous business and personal responsibilities, and Berg never shirked from fulfilling these duties. One of the most serious family issues was the continuing mental decline of Helene's brother, Frank (Franzl). In August of 1930, on the one hundredth birthday of Emperor Franz Joseph, he used poultry shears to sever the little finger from his left hand, intending to place it on the grave of the emperor, whom he believed to be his father. Frank was then committed to a mental institution, and Berg was subsequently appointed his legal guardian. Berg's time was also consumed by negotiating the sale of the Nahowski family home in Hietzing and later the Trahütten property. These family distractions only increased over the next years and came to include the mounting financial problems of Berg's surviving siblings. The toll that these obligations took on Berg's physical and emotional resources further delayed his progress on the opera *Lulu*.

Flight from Reality

Despite his outward success, Berg's inner life was troubled. Several of the causes are easily identified: his poor health, feelings of anxiety and depression, questions about his accomplishments in life, and other psychological conditions associated with a gathering midlife crisis. His emotional distance from his wife was increased by her illnesses, absences, and jealous attachment to him. An additional factor was Berg's lack of progress on *Lulu*, a difficulty made worse by his grappling with an often unwieldy twelve-tone method and his struggle with the sprawling and complex text. He described his state of mind—his "lack of good spirits"—in a letter of December 1931 to Adorno: "My compositional inactivity of the last 3 months has pulled me down ever further. Most lately to such a degree that I was on the point of despair," Berg wrote.[22]

In the 1930s Berg continued to find an emotional outlet in letters to Hanna Fuchs, averaging one yearly from 1929 to 1934, typically written in December. In these letters he revealed his state of mind, which had become gloomier and more deeply introverted. The theme of madness is replaced by one of living death. He speaks of his life as having ended and its continuation as nothing more than a failed experiment while being buried alive in the Trauttmansdorffgasse (a more than oblique reference to Helene).[23] He reports on "the desolation of my inner self" and the "dreadful diminuendo" and "wretchedness" of his life. Most perceptively and more truthfully, Berg writes about being divided from himself, a process that had in all likelihood begun years earlier, possibly as early as his adolescence. In October of 1931 he writes to Hanna:

> Everything that you may hear, and perhaps even read, about me is generally true, where it is not altogether false—(as, for example, the remark I happened to read today in a Zurich program: "A consummately happy domesticity, with which his wife surrounds him, enables him to work undisturbedly"). But it is true only of a persona that is merely an altogether external layer of me, a part that in the course of the last years has separated from my true self (separated, oh, how painfully!) and formed itself into a rounded-off entity all its own, as which I may appear to my surroundings and the world at large. In that life everything takes place that a normal life brings with it: anger and joy, irritation and jollity, interest and indifference, business and pleasure, art and nature— But believe me, Hanna (and now I can at last address you properly: my one and everlasting beloved), all of that concerns only this outward person whom I am forced to present to my fellow beings and whom you (thank God) have never known—who (to illustrate this characterization) could for a while be filled with the thrill of driving a car but would never be able to compose *Lulu*.[24]

Shortly after writing this letter Berg began several new and simultaneous love fantasies. In late February 1932 he traveled to Brussels for performances of *Wozzeck* and the Chamber Concerto. He stayed for about a week and spent much of his free time with Stefan and Anny Askenase, whom he knew from Vienna. Stefan Askenase (1896–1985) was a gifted pianist and teacher. Born in Lemberg (Polish Galicia, now Lviv in Ukraine), he studied piano in Vienna and performed on one occasion at a concert of the Society for Private Musical Performances. In Vienna he met Anny Lifczis (1904–69), whom he married in 1923. She was the younger sister of Berg's lawyer Otto Lifczis. Berg was presumably acquainted with her before her marriage—he refers in a later letter to having wasted six years of their acquaintance—but in Brussels in 1932 he fell madly in love with her. The "affair," like the prior one with Hanna Fuchs, was carried on in letters, with very little personal contact and certainly without intimate relations. Eighteen letters from Berg to Anny Askenase survive from the years 1932 and 1933, and although he acknowledged receiving several from her, none of these has come to light.[25]

The pianist Martha Argerich gave rare personal information about Anny Askenase in an interview in 1978. In the 1960s Argerich had stopped playing the piano seriously, and in 1964 she went to Brussels to study with Stefan Askenase and to assess her prospects. There she met Anny, who coaxed her back to playing. Argerich recalled Anny's role:

> And then I went to see the Askenases in the morning. My mother said, "Go and see," and she phoned. I met this woman, Stefan's wife, who was extraordinary. Little by little, I started. I went there every day. I was absolutely fascinated by this woman. She had something very special, like a sun. She gave me strength and security. I started to believe again that I could, and little by little I started to play. . . . Because of her I started to play again, and almost immediately I went to the Chopin Competition. It was because of her. Otherwise I couldn't have done it.[26]

Although Argerich encountered Anny Askenase more than thirty years later than Alban Berg, her account points clearly to Anny's personal magnetism, the same that must have drawn Berg to her at a period of stress in his life.

At the time Berg became enamored of Anny, he was beset by creative stagnation and emotional frustration, much as he had been in 1925 at the time he met Hanna Fuchs. There are definite parallels between the two infatuations, and Berg continued to declare his undying love for Hanna as he was also wooing Anny. To compound an already puzzling and provocative situation, he was also writing love letters at the same time to another woman, the actress Edith (Edyth) Edwards. Meanwhile his letters to Helene continue in the same vein as ever, torturing himself over their separations and sending "a thousand little kisses."[27]

Berg's epistolary love-making to four women at once certainly does not speak to his amorous license, rather to its opposite: the tendency, already shown in the Hanna intrigue, to construct imaginary love affairs rather than to carry out real ones. After the meeting in Brussels in February 1932, Berg did not see Anny Askenase for over a year, and when he finally met her again, in April of 1933, the infatuation evaporated in a cloud of romantic despair. Under their fantastic surface, the letters to Anny reveal Berg's continuing struggle with his emotions, and the bleakness he felt about his personal and creative life, in particular as he wrestled with the arduous task of composing Lulu. The elaborate secrecy he practiced with these letters, carefully sending and receiving them in extra envelopes or under false names through his student and amanuensis of the time, Julius Schloß, deceiving Helene every step of the way (or so he thought). All of these machinations appear in a broader context as part of a therapeutic game that Berg devised to come to grips with his emotions and concomitantly with his artistic career.

Unlike Hanna Fuchs, Anny Askenase responded in written form to Berg's advances, but little can be construed from Berg's comments on her letters. She seems to have confided her troubles to him as a younger woman might to an older man. He expresses sympathy for "my poor dear one," while consistently referring to her as a child. Infantilizing her allowed him to play a controlling role, as a middle-aged man to take on the position of advisor and protector rather than dashing young suitor. Nonetheless he does not shy away from lauding her physical charms, imagining himself kissing her on "all, all places of your won-derful body."[28] Echoing Alwa in the love scene with Lulu (Act 2, scene 2, "Wenn deine beiden grossen Kinderaugen nicht wären . . . "), he writes: "These big eyes, in which the beauty of all the world's pain and joy seems captured. . . ."[29]

Many of the themes of the Hanna letters are repeated in those to Anny. Berg is suffering, in despair; their love is a madness. "My outer senses, after these weeks and months of suffering, seem to be more and more confused."[30] He rehearses imaginary future meetings, detailing just how they would have to behave in front of others to disguise their love, as he had also done in Hanna's case. He looks for surrogates—chance meetings with Anny's brother and sister in Vienna when he would be "reminded" of her; a film with Jeanette MacDonald, who resembled Anny, he thought;[31] the performance of Milhaud's Chamber Symphony no. 5 in Vienna, which by chance he had heard with Anny in Brussels—wasn't this fate? Berg also writes—just as he did so poignantly to Hanna—about leading a divided life.

> I live in solitude, sunk into myself. . . . Nothing that really touches me penetrates to the outer world, for there are actually two people that answer to the name A. B. The one is so uninteresting that there is absolutely nothing to be said about him. He vegetates. Concerning the other, you know everything: he loves—and waits.[32]

Berg's flight from reality in these letters increased in direct proportion to the ever greater difficulties he encountered in the real world. As the summer of 1932 wore on, his letters to Anny became more and more despairing, his mood ever darker. He had been unable to see her ("horrible") and he felt trapped by both his marriage and his work: "*Everything else* is horrible enough: the slavery of marriage, from which I've tried (now for 2 or 3 months) to save myself by a flight into the slavery of work. That's *all* that I can tell you about myself."[33]

The summer of 1932 was in all respects a disaster for Berg. The goal of completing *Lulu* seemed ever more distant as at the same time the prospects for the opera's staging looked increasingly dim. In October he wrote to Erich Kleiber to lament his inability to compose amid a whirl of unlucky events.

> This summer there has been no possibility of working as I had hoped. All sorts of unpleasantness (starting small, with two teeth being pulled after days of dental pain, then something really quite dreadful) has kept me from regular and continuous work. Because of the trouble with my mentally ill brother-in-law (I am now his guardian), I lost almost all of July. In August I was ill here with a raging flu-like throat infection that left me bedridden. Then I was assailed by an angry swarm of wasps and bitten 20 or 30 times on the head, throat, neck, arms, and legs so seriously that I was ill for nearly eight days. And finally all of September was taken over by the dreadful occurrence that I mentioned. Due to the carelessness of our house maid, a container of spirits exploded in the kitchen. My wife, who was standing nearby, caught the explosion right in her face. She had the presence of mind to rip the apron off the maid, who was engulfed in flames, but this caused terrible burns to her hands as well. We now have been waiting for 4 or 5 weeks for the effects from this dreadful burn to disappear, which now seems slowly to be happening.[34]

Berg's concern for Helene cannot be doubted, but his reports also betray his concern for himself. Would Helene, always fragile, now finally become incapacitated? What would that mean for him? He turned the accident into a threat against his love affair with Anny. In the fictional world he and she occupy, his slavery is now complete, his life virtually forfeit.

> Yes, my love, worse vexation for our happiness—which in any case has been vexed since our separation at the Brussels train station—could not have occurred than my wife's accident in this otherwise already horrible summer. The last degree of freedom which remained to me in my marriage (you know how small that degree was!) has completely disappeared with this catastrophe. For these 2 months I have existed only as one chained to my wife's fate, *I myself no longer live.*

Berg rages on:

> Everything, everything is destroyed: I can't work, I am indifferent to everything that relates to my existence, I hate mankind—including myself, for whom it would be best to die. Why don't I? Because I still believe that *somewhere* under this mountain of ash [Berg von Asche] in which I am buried there glows a Finale which will light again sometime.[35]

Berg felt the need to spin out the narrative of his wretchedness further in the 1932 fall season. Shortly after writing so desperately to Anny, he wrote again to Hanna—his only letter to her this year—in which he reprised the theme of his undying love.

> Despite this seven-year decrescendo, which must finally end in deathly silence, I cannot, cannot believe that such a "feeling," one transcending any and all "realities," could simply fizzle out. It is there after all, as on the first day, and as long as this certainty does not vanish, I will not only believe and love, but also hope, and hope, and hope again—Help me in that, Hanna![36]

To close out 1932, Berg wrote to the third woman he was pursuing, Edith Edwards (1899–1956). She was a German actress who made her theatrical debut in Berlin in 1924 and had a notable career in film and on the stage. Three love letters from Berg to her survive, and he sent her an autographed photo, taken in 1926.[37] It is not known just how or when he met her, but the surviving letters were written around the same time as those to Anny Askenase, and Berg made Julius Schloß again his postal intermediary. Edith wrote back, although no letters from her have been preserved. Writing on 17 December 1932, Berg recalled his initial infatuation with her followed by resignation: "But with a lingering passion that would blaze into an unquenchable fire if I were to see you again for just one second." He continues with another account of Helene's burn accident:

> If I have been silent recently, it is because I have had an upsetting, even a catastrophic experience. An explosion (in our vacation cottage) resulted in months of serious danger for my wife. Only now can it be said that this danger has been averted. That this is so is a miracle. The thought of you then lay like gentle moonlight over the deep night of that time. This you must believe![38]

Although Helene's burn accident was not in itself the catalyst for Berg's romantic fantasies, his multiple narratives concerning it betray both his self-absorption—the accident becomes something that happened to *him*, as much as to his wife—and his pressing anguish about his situation: fears of increased servitude to Helene's health and more impediments to overcoming his creative impasse.

Berg's epistolary romance with Anny Askenase came to an end in 1933, and with Edith Edwards not long afterwards.[39] At this time, out of necessity, Berg had returned to composing *Lulu*. He never linked Anny to any musical work, as he did so intentionally in the case of Hanna Fuchs and the *Lyric Suite*. Anny for her part preserved a friendship, possibly born out of compassion, for Berg. A letter from Otto Lifczis indicates that he and Anny planned a visit to the Bergs at the Waldhaus in early August of 1935. It is not known if this encounter took place.[40] Berg's last letter to Hanna was written in December 1934, exactly one year before his death. In it he still professes an unchanged and undying love.[41]

It has been noted that letter writing was Berg's favored means of communication, a way of circumventing his natural shyness in personal relations.[42] The love letters to Anny, as well as to Hanna and Edith, are consistent with this observation, but they also represent a special subset of Berg's epistolary writings. They are a search for an erotic stimulation which he did not find elsewhere but which he desired to keep within certain bounds. On another level they have the character of a confessional. Their object is self-revelation directed at an idealized listener but also perhaps at himself. As alluring as the women may have been, the chief character in the drama is always Berg himself with his secret suffering. The private therapeutic act of arranging, analyzing, indulging and eventually mastering his feelings—the end result in all cases is renunciation—ultimately enabled him to persevere in the face of difficulties that would eventually overwhelm him in the last few years of his life.

Berg's Music and the Nazi Threat

Even before the Nazis took over the German government in 1933, a broad reaction against difficult, dissonant music, works thought to be by Jewish composers, and music on violent or erotic texts had spread throughout German lands. Berg had already experienced political opposition to *Wozzeck* in the Prague staging in 1926, but this did not hold back the work's great success. But in the 1930s the mood had changed, and an intolerance for aspects of modern or experimental art became widespread especially in Germany and Austria, an attitude that went hand in hand with the rise of National Socialism. Given his close association with Schoenberg, Berg was increasingly identified in the press as a Jew, perhaps being confused with a popular Austrian singer and actor Armin Berg. Berg's alliance with Schoenberg by itself raised opposition to his music.

Berg willingly and repeatedly sent out documentation showing his Aryan ancestry. Before the premiere of *Wozzeck* at the Landestheater in Braunschweig in 1931, for example, he was asked for such information. He responded:

> On the last point, I have documents proving my Aryan ancestry only back three generations. But I also have family records, which I enclose, that trace my genealogy back to the early 18th century. I would be happy to have the opportunity for these to be officially certified so as to counter the more or less hidden but ever more audible lies that for years have appeared in the newspapers.[43]

Despite such efforts, upcoming performances of *Wozzeck* that were under contract—in Coburg, Mainz, Magdeburg, and elsewhere—were canceled in 1931. Erich Kleiber boldly put on a new staging of *Wozzeck* at the Berlin Staatsoper in November 1932, but its performance a month later in the Czech city of Brno proved to be the last during Berg's lifetime.

Berg received a first-hand taste of Nazi interference in musical culture in February 1933, when he traveled to Munich to participate in
a jury to select works for the forthcoming festival of the Allgemeiner
Deutscher Musikverein (ADMV). "The deference to the Nazis has become so great," he wrote to Helene, "that Schoenberg has been left out,
so too non-German names like Pisk and Jelinek, who *otherwise* would
certainly have been selected. But this is *totally* off the record."[44] Shortly
after the meeting, Joseph Haas, head of the board of directors of the
ADMV, asked for Berg's resignation from the panel. "You, dear Herr
Berg, are an exponent of an artistic direction that is sharply opposed by
the German nationalist movement," Haas wrote. "The board recognizes
your artistic convictions, but there is no possibility that in the future
these can hold sway in the deliberations of the board."[45] Berg complied
with Haas's request, adding:

> Though it is true that I have not a drop of Jewish blood—my family tree goes
> back two centuries (4–5 generations) and shows this—so too for my wife, and
> true also that I have never been politically active and am 5/8 Reichs-German
> and 3/8 German-Austrian in heritage, I understand that in the viewpoint
> of National Socialism the melodies, harmonies, rhythms, musical forms that
> I write are not "German." This is a viewpoint that no one can prove and, by
> the way, would be easy for me to refute. I can fully understand the official
> standpoint of the ADMV, and I take my leave of you, Herr Professor, and
> the gentlemen of the music jury and board in that same personal manner in
> which I have collaborated with you and conducted affairs of the *Allgemeiner
> Deutscher Musikverein* for all these years, in our common interest in a *music* that
> is *German* and therefore—like none other—universally valid. [46]

As Berg's prospects for income from German performances withered,
he and Universal Edition looked hopefully toward other countries for
performances. He had many influential supporters in the United States—
Serge Koussevitzky, Eugene Ormandy, and Leopold Stokowski, among
others—and the spectacular success of *Wozzeck* in Philadelphia and
New York in 1931 made his name known in musical circles throughout
the country. Erich Kleiber conducted Berg's music on visits to America,
and the Kolisch Quartet played the *Lyric Suite* at their first concert
in America in April 1935. Berg's music was also heard in the 1930s in
London, thanks to the support of Edward Clark, program planner for the

BBC from 1927 to 1936, and Adrian Boult, its musical director and conductor of the BBC Symphony.[47] The last performance of *Wozzeck* before the outbreak of World War II was in London, in a broadcast by the BBC Orchestra under Boult, which Berg listened to on the radio. Much to his disappointment, a prospective staging of *Wozzeck* at Covent Garden failed to materialize.

Berg also hoped for performances of his music in fascist Italy, where an openness to modern music remained even through the war years.[48] His works were little known there before January 1933, when Ernest Ansermet conducted the *Wozzeck Fragments* in Rome. Later in that year Berg was invited by Adriano Lualdi to submit a work for performance at the 1934 Venice *Biennale*, during its prestigious Third International Music Festival. Berg at first recommended that the Kolisch Quartet be invited to play the *Lyric Suite*, but when Kolisch played this work in Florence in April 1934, Lualdi announced that Berg's participation in the *Biennale* had been canceled. The bylaws of the festival held that only works not previously performed in Italy were to be scheduled.

Following the cancellation, Berg let his frustrations and paranoia boil over in a letter to Gian Francesco Malipiero, an Italian composer with whom he was on good terms. Berg wrote:

> The damage for me is all the greater because, being officially invited to this international festival, a festival also exceptional for Italy, would have been compensation for me for all the many other wrongs I have been and am suffering in these upsetting times. Imagine! Since the fire in the Berlin Reichstag not a single note of mine has been played in Germany—although I am not a Jew. And in my own country things are not much different—*just because* I am not a Jew. For with the present tendency in Austria to glorify the Jews as martyrs, *I am hardly ever performed*! Hence the disappearance of my name from the program of the Venice Festival will be regarded almost as a confirmation of the measures taken against me in Germany.[49]

Thanks to the support of Malipiero and others, Berg was returned to the *Biennale* program with the scheduling of his concert aria, *Der Wein*, composed in 1929 (to be considered in detail below). The aria was conducted during the festival on 11 September by Hermann Scherchen with Hanna Schwarz, soprano. In the audience was Luigi Dallapiccola, who found in *Der Wein* "an endless sadness." "For the last two days," Dallapiccola wrote to his wife, "I have been humming this agony to myself while I walk in the streets."[50]

The performance of *Der Wein* received polite reviews in the Italian press but predictably dismissive ones in German papers. One that was especially upsetting to Berg was written by the Nazi musicologist Herbert Gerigk. In the October 1934 issue of *Die Musik*—the journal had by then been taken over by the Nazi Kulturgemeinde—Gerigk wrote:

> Alban Berg's concert aria *Der Wein* just as clearly bears the mark of non-music. As the eager student of Schoenberg he has managed to liquidate to its very limits all the basic concepts of music. The music marches along with no regard for the texts of Stefan George-Baudelaire. This work, which has already had several performances, is not helped by repeated hearings. Under the leadership of *Hermann Scherchen* it received a vigorous reading, so much so that one wondered where Berg ended and Scherchen began.[51]

Berg and Gerigk had earlier corresponded, and Berg now asked him for an explanation of the review: "It is not my habit or principle to respond to a 'bad review,'" Berg wrote "since I cannot expect, nor should I expect, that my music will please *everyone*. . . . I ask you only to tell me how my music—composed on these splendid poems solely with the intention of being true to their content—shows no regard for that content."[52] Gerigk responded tersely: "To be brief, I have positive feelings about Alban Berg as a person. But I can find no access to the contemporary expressive means that you use."[53] Malipiero was dismayed by the German reviews. "I've read the German reviews of the Venice music festival," he wrote to Berg. "Outrageous! What's going to happen? Only jackasses are going to rule!"[54] From 1933 onward, Berg's main concern was with the outlook for performances of *Lulu*, a topic to be discussed in the next chapter.

A Musical Digression: *Der Wein*

When Berg returned to his mountain retreat in May of 1929, he had received a lucrative commission that would delay his return to his opera project. Ružena Herlinger, a Viennese soprano who specialized in modern music, had offered him the handsome fee of 5,000 schillings to compose a concert aria for her exclusive use for a period of two years. Berg's decision to accept the commission is odd since at this time he did not especially need the money, and it began a pattern of delays—most of which might have been avoided—in his concentration on the opera.

Herlinger later recalled how the work came about:

I returned to Vienna and Helene Berg prepared for me one of her charming teas, quite intimate, only with the Bergs and me. In the course of our lengthy conversations and after about four cups of tea (one of Berg's favorite drinks) and the splendid brioche that Helene had made, I blurted out: "Tell me, Herr Berg, you say that the Seven Early Songs are not the true Berg. Conductors want orchestra pieces and songs by you, so why not write a large aria or cantata in a modern style, just as Mozart often did?" The conversation continued, and Berg wanted to see how Mozart had composed these arias. So I sent him a large volume with them, and after 8 or 10 days I received another invitation to the Bergs. Then Alban Berg said very shyly: "I have an idea for it, also texts that have long been in my head, but I cannot compose it now because I'm working on *Lulu*. If I delay I won't get my advance from Universal Edition." This matter was arranged, and then there were several wonderful afternoons when I sang for Alban Berg—everything—Mozart, Puccini, Wolf, Brahms, Debussy. He wanted to familiarize himself with all the nuances of my voice. And this is how *Der Wein* came to be.[55]

The Bergs had long known of Ružena Herlinger and her husband, Alfred. They were wealthy socialites admired for their glittering parties, and Alfred, an industrialist, was a major benefactor of Vienna's Volksoper. Frau Herlinger was a recitalist whose repertory included both classic and modern works, and she was often heard in concerts of the Vienna section of the ISCM. Her reviews praise her intelligence and artistry, but some question her lack of a professional's vocal solidity. Following a performance in Berlin in 1926, Otto Steinhagen, critic for the *Signale für die musikalische Welt*, noted: "Her voice reveals good training and temperament but a lack of calm security and of a mastery that is fully pleasing. Her singing has too much jumpiness, and she takes too many chances."[56] In his 1968 memoir *Best Regards to Aida*, Hans W. Heinsheimer recalled her unkindly as "a Viennese lady of Czech descent whose monetary prowess was sadly superior to her vocal excellence."[57] Berg had worked with her in the Paris concert of March 1928 at the Salon Jeanne Dubost, where she sang his Four Songs, Op. 2, and Marie's Lullaby from *Wozzeck*, which Berg accompanied at the piano. After the concert he praised the accuracy of her singing to Schoenberg, so he must have felt reasonably confident in her ability as the interpreter of a new work. This outlook soon faded, and he later said that he would have preferred a tenor as the solo voice.[58]

After arriving at the Berghof in mid-May, Berg composed *Der Wein* hurriedly. He dated the completion of the condensed score 23 July and the full score 23 August, whereupon he returned to work on *Lulu*. Uncertainties about *Der Wein* soon arose. Alfred Herlinger's business had collapsed, and Berg had not been paid his fee. Finally, in late September 1929, the Herlingers came up with the 5,000 schillings, but Frau Herlinger was slow to learn the music and rumors of Berg's unhappiness with her singing began to circulate as the premiere approached, which was set for 18 November in Frankfurt. This performance had to be canceled, and, to make matters still more complicated, Frau Herlinger had apparently fallen in love with the composer.[59] The combination of circumstances cast her into a state of depression, and in the first week of November 1929 she attempted suicide by an overdose of sleeping medication.[60]

Berg found himself in a very delicate situation, especially since Frau Herlinger had two years of exclusive rights to perform *Der Wein*. He wrote to her encouragingly on 13 November, saying that he regretted her "illness" and was aware of its cause. But he denied being the source of rumors about her musical inadequacy. He had created the work to suit her voice, he said, and he was confident in her for the premiere, which was then postponed until the summer of 1930. "But first, dear lady, you must get well, and this means also restoring your emotional balance," Berg advises. "Think no more about this disgusting gossip, which really has nothing to do with our art."[61]

For the texts of his aria Berg returned to the poetry of Charles Baudelaire, which had inspired him during the composition of the *Lyric Suite*. Berg had long admired the writings of Baudelaire, whose mixture of the poetic and mundane appealed to him as it did in the prose poems of Altenberg. For his personal library Berg acquired several volumes of Baudelaire's poetry and essays, including a 1914 version of *Fleurs de mal*, rewritten in German by Stefan George.[62] Berg's edition of the Baudelaire volume contained four related poems under the heading "Wine," and Berg chose three of them as texts for the aria.

Berg had a special attraction to Anacreontic verse—poetry in praise of wine. Two such poems had been used by Mahler in *Das Lied von der Erde*, in which wine rescues the poet from the misery of life. Berg was himself fond of alcohol—wine, Benedictine, and Grand Marnier were his favorite drinks—and he often praised its effect upon his creative imagination. In 1914 he explained this to Helene, who was always critical of her husband's drinking:

I never see things so clearly as in a dream or after enjoying alcohol! If I could capture this state of mind I think I'd be a greater artist, and I understand that Altenberg writes his most beautiful material and thoughts in a twilight state of intoxication and sleep. (They say that Chopin only composed when he was drunk!) But everything has a *limit*! When I'm seriously at work I of course need the clearest head and *greatest sobriety* (also an empty stomach!). But the ideas—those *first* and *last things* without which a work would be *formless*—come to me often in a twilight state produced by sleep or alcohol. And this is *one* reason that I love alcohol.[63]

Baudelaire's "Wine" poetry echoes these sentiments, and the poems that Berg chose also reflect the state of mind expressed in the Hanna letters— the hopeless shabbiness of his everyday life and his desperate search for a higher state in which artistic creativity could again be possible.

In the first poem the spirit of wine speaks to the poet, promising him happiness, courage, and renewed creativity:

Die Seele des Weines	The Spirit of Wine
Des weines geist begann im fass zu singen:	The spirit of wine began to sing within the barrel:
Mensch—teurer Ausgestossener—dir soll	O man, beloved outcast, to you
Durch meinen engen kerker durch erklingen	from out of my narrow cell I bring
Ein lied von licht und bruderliebe voll.	a song of light and brotherly love.
Ich weiss: am sengendheissen bergeshange	Well I know that on the sweltering mountainsides,
Bei schweiss und mühe nur gedeih ich recht—	amid sweat and toil, only there do I grow strong
Da meine seele ich nur so empfange—	and take my spirit unto myself.
Doch bin ich niemals undankbar und schlecht.	But I am never the shameless ingrate.
Und dies bereitet mir die grösste labe	My greatest pleasure comes
Wenn eines arbeit-matten mund mich hält—	when I am brought to weary lips.

Sein heisser schlund wird mir zum süssen grabe	A parched throat is for me a sweet grave
Das mehr als kalte keller mir gefällt.	and all the sweeter than a dank cellar.
Du hörst den sonntagsang aus frohem schwarme?	Do you hear the hymn from the happy throng?
Nun kehrt die hoffnung prickelnd in mich ein:	Then I tingle with hope:
Du stülpst die ärmel—stützest beide arme—	you roll up your sleeves, put your elbows on the table,
Du wirst mich preisen und zufrieden sein.	and then praise me and find contentment.
Ich mache deines weibes augen heiter	I light up the eyes of your lady fair,
Und deinem sohne leih ich frische kraft—	and give your son a new boldness;
Ich bin für diesen zarten lebensstreiter	for those tender contestants in life
Das öl das fechtern die gewandtheit schafft.	I am the oil that makes the fencer nimble.
Und du erhältst von diesem pflanzenseime	And from this vine you will receive
Das Gott—der ewige sämann— niedergiesst	what God, the Eternal Sower, pours down,
Damit in deiner brust die dichtung keime	so that poetry will sprout in your breast,
Die wie ein seltner baum zum himmel spriesst.[64]	and like a rare tree rise toward heaven.

In the second poem—a sonnet that Berg probably associated with thoughts of himself and Hanna Fuchs—the lovers soar freely into a land of dreams, propelled by drink:

Der Wein der Liebenden	The Wine of Lovers
Prächtig ist heute die weite—	Magnificent is the heavenly expanse today,
Stränge und sporen beiseite—	so let us remove the bridle and spurs
Reiten wir auf dem wein	and ride on wine
In den feenhimmel hinein!	into the fairy heaven!
Engel für ewige dauer	Like angels who forever endure
Leidend im fieberschauer—	a feverish madness,

Durch des morgens blauen kristall	we sail through the brilliant blue of morning,
Fort in das leuchtende all!	off toward the radiant all!
Wir lehnen uns weich auf den flügel	Softly we lie on the wings
Des windes der eilt ohne zügel.	of wind racing onward with free rein,
Beide voll gleicher lust	both with the same passion.
Lass schwester uns brust an brust	Away, sister, arm in arm.
Fliehn ohne rast und stand	We take flight with no rest or pause,
In meiner träume land!	into my land of dreams!

Berg's own voice is heard in the third poem, spoken from his state of desolation in an empty and vulgar world. The remedy for his misery is wine, which will raise him to a higher level of being and fulfill the promise made in the first poem:

Der Wein des Einsamen	Wine of the Desolate One
Der sonderbare blick der leichten frauen	The fetching glance of the loose woman,
Der auf uns gleitet wie das weisse licht	lighting upon us like the white light
Des mondes auf bewegter wasserschicht—	of the moon on shimmering water,
Will er im bade seine schönheit schauen—	wanting to behold its beauty there,
Der lezte thaler auf dem spielertisch	The last chip played on the table,
Ein frecher kuss der hageren Adeline	a sultry kiss from the haggard Adeline,
Erschlaffenden gesang der violine	the fiddle's weary tune—
Der wie der menschheit fernes qualgezisch—	all are a distant whimper from mankind:
Mehr als dies alles schätz ich—tiefe flasche—	Better than all this, deep bottle,
Den starken balsam den ich aus dir nasche	is the bracing balm that I draw from you
Und der des frommen dichters müdheit bannt.	to dispel the fatigue of the devout poet.
Du giebst ihm hoffnung liebe jugendkraft	You give him hope, love, the power of youth,
Und stolz—dies erbteil aller bettlerschaft—	and pride—the portion of all beggars—
Der uns zu helden macht und gottverwandt.	which turns us into mighty heroes and the sons of god.

Berg's music for this hedonistic poetry returns to forms familiar from his earlier compositions. Following an orchestral introduction, the three poems are run together to create a symmetrical design in which music for the third poem is an abbreviated and richly varied reprise of that for the first. The symmetry is enhanced in the second poem, whose thirty-measure conclusion (from "Softly we lie on the wings of wind") is immediately repeated in retrograde as an orchestral transition to the third poem. Since the time of Adorno's 1937 discussion of the piece, the design of *Der Wein* has always been called a sonata form, although the analogy is not especially close, and that term was not used by Berg nor is it found in a program note by Willi Reich that was approved by the composer.[65]

The music closely follows the text. The introduction opens in a somber mood in the low woodwinds, depicting, according to Reich's program note, the fermenting of wine in the vat. Gradually the mood lightens as the wine begins to sparkle. Each of the six quatrains of the first poem has a distinctive musical character: the first begins peacefully with tonal harmony (Example 8.2) as the voice ascends a D-minor scale accompanied by seventh chords. Music in the fourth quatrain—where a "hymn" is sung by a happy throng—evokes a jazzy, syncopated tango (Example 8.3).

In the second poem, "Der Wein der Liebenden," the tempo quickens as the lovers soar away toward a brilliant land of dreams. The climax of

Example 8.2   *Der Wein*, mm. 15–16

Example 8.3   *Der Wein*, mm. 39–41

their flight is reached in the sestet of Baudelaire's sonnet (from m. 112), where the voice flies freely by detaching itself metrically from the accompaniment (Example 8.4). The third poem parallels the thoughts of the first, and Berg brings back its themes in a varied reprise.

As he told Frau Herlinger, Berg created the vocal line with her voice in mind. The part provides a bel canto showpiece for the singer, but it also observes certain limits—a regularity in rhythm, a subdued orchestration, and a range that only occasionally rises above A above the staff. The orchestra is moderate in size, with the addition of piano and E♭ saxophone, giving the ensemble a distinctive sound that is related to that of the far larger orchestra in *Lulu* where piano and saxophone also appear prominently. By 1929, saxophones had begun to appear in music for symphonic orchestra, often, as in Milhaud's ballet *La création du monde* (1922) and Gershwin's *An American in Paris* (1928), to suggest jazz or contemporaneous dance music. Berg may have developed a fondness for the expressive and plaintive sound of the instrument after hearing it played by his student Willi Reich, who was an accomplished saxophonist. In the score Berg places the instrument among the woodwinds, but he makes it stand out with lines that are independent of any of the orchestra's choirs.

As he began to compose *Lulu* in 1928, Berg made a careful study of popular American and Latin American dances—loosely called "jazz" by the Europeans—and the makeup of large American dance orchestras like those that toured Europe after World War I. Helene Berg recalled that her husband often listened to dance music on the radio, and he also studied contemporary compositions that used jazz idioms, including

Example 8.4 *Der Wein*, mm. 115–17

Example 8.5   Basic row of *Der Wein*

works by Wilhelm Grosz and Erwin Schulhoff. He also had on hand
Alfred Baresel's *Jazz-Buch*, a manual that discussed jazz dances in their
"musical and psychological aspects."[66]

In *Der Wein* Berg uses a "tempo di tango" in the first poem, on the
words, "Do you hear the hymn from the happy throng?"; it is then repeated
in the third poem on "a sultry kiss from the haggard Adeline." Baresel gives
an example of a syncopated tango rhythm that is close to the one used by
Berg in this passage, and he also calls for a tango tempo of the quarter note
at 46, which approximates Berg's main tempo (quarter at 46–52).

Berg's twelve-tone approach in *Der Wein* builds upon his theorizing from the summer of 1927. The basic row of the work, shown in
Example 8.5, has features familiar from those used earlier. It begins with a diatonic white-note segment whose melodiousness suggests that Berg planned
to use it and its inversions as thematic resources in the foreground of the
music. Allusions to the key of D minor, suggested by the D-minor scale in the
first hexachord of the basic row, occur repeatedly in the music of the aria.[67]

Before he began to compose, Berg placed the basic row for the new
work into a table containing its twelve transpositions and twelve inversions.
Following the procedure that he had used in the row tables dated July 1927,
he dissolved the rows for *Der Wein* into desirable harmonies and harmonic
progressions, often suggesting major or minor keys.[68] He labeled the row
shown in Example 8.5 as the first inversion, but it can be considered the
basic or "prime" form since it appears at the beginning of the work. He
makes no tables for rows in retrograde, and although these occasionally
appear in *Der Wein*, Berg in his twelve-tone works rarely used such rows.[69]

An example of the pattern that guided him in dissolving the row into
pseudo-tonal elements is shown in Figure 8.2. The notes connected by
ascending stems form a minor triad (marked "M," *moll*), a major triad
("D," *dur*), and a major/minor tetrachord ("D–M"), all used prominently
in the music of *Der Wein*. Berg uses upward beams to mark off segments of
the row showing that the minor segment of the row spans five tones, the
major three tones, and the major/minor four tones. The descending stems

Figure 8.2 From Berg's table of tone rows for *Der Wein*

Example 8.6 *Der Wein*, mm. 15–20 (Voice)

show a series of three tritones descending by semitone, with the numbers of notes spanned being 4–3–5, the retrograde of the former numbers.

Berg's use of these rows and their derivatives in the music for *Der Wein* ranges from simple to complex. Straightforward presentations of the basic row, in its various transpositions and inversions, are often found as prominent themes and lines. The opening vocal phrase (Example 8.6) is derived in this way, beginning with the basic row in its prime form followed by an inversion.

In the accompaniment for this opening melodic phrase Berg finds ways to draw familiar chords from his rows that will suggest the "intentional tonality" that he mentioned to Adorno. As shown in Ex. 8.2, the accompaniment in meas. 15–16 begins with a circle of fifths progression D^7–G^7–C^7. Berg obtains these chords by placing an inversion of the basic row in the bass and, in the inner voices, a rotated prime form whose succession of three tritones—F#–C, F–B, E–B♭—is fleshed out as the three seventh chords.[70]

For the publication in 1930 of Erwin Stein's piano-vocal score of *Der Wein*, Berg added Baudelaire's original French text as an alternative to George's German. He probably did so at Frau Herlinger's request, as she may have planned to use the aria for concerts in France. Berg had considerable difficulty in accommodating the French words— the vocal line had to be extensively changed, and George's text is often distant in meaning and syntax from Baudelaire's considerably easier French.

Der Wein has never achieved the success of Berg's other late works. Universal Edition printed its full score only in 1966 (earlier they sent out scores duplicated on Ozalid paper). Even Berg specialists including Theodor Adorno and Mosco Carner have questioned its qualities, and Carner suggests that Berg himself was dissatisfied with it.[71] This assumption is extremely unlikely, as Berg's confidence in his music never wavered, and he expressed no reservations about *Der Wein* in his correspondence other than wanting it sung by an excellent tenor voice. In the 1930s conductors including Hermann Scherchen and Erich Kleiber readily performed the work, but the public response was muted by the somberness of the composition as a whole. Following a performance in Berlin in 1931 by Kleiber and Frau Herlinger, a critic wrote: "The achievement of the noted Viennese singer was admirable. She gave to this artificial concoction—so far as possible—a piece of her soul. But the audience was coolly restrained."[72]

Der Wein was first performed in the United States at a concert of the League of Composers in 1935 in New York, with sparse reaction in the press. After World War II it was revived by conductors including Leonard Bernstein, again with a tepid journalistic response. Following a 1952 performance by Phyllis Curtain and the Boston Symphony Orchestra, Virgil Thomson found the work "in spite of its subject, which was the delights of wine, to be a sober, even sobering, experience. Actually it sounds very much like any other well composed twelve-tone work. Its vocal line is less hysterical than Schoenberg's, but it is jumpy, all the same. . . . The whole piece seemed gloomy and banal to me, its execution careful but far from happy."[73]

With *Der Wein* completed in August 1929, Berg returned to *Lulu* for the remainder of his summer sojourn at the Berghof. His career was flourishing as never before: *Wozzeck* would be premiered in six cities in 1930 alone, including triumphant performances at the Staatsoper in Vienna. His earlier works were now performed worldwide, and he could devote himself to what would prove his greatest artistic challenge— bringing Frank Wedekind's Lulu plays to the operatic stage.

Lulu

B ERG'S DECISION IN 1928 TO COMPOSE HIS SECOND OPERA ON FRANK
Wedekind's Lulu plays—*Erdgeist* and its sequel *Die Büchse der Pandora*—came after five years of uncertainty about where to turn for a subject. He had experienced no such indecision in 1914, when he was immediately gripped by Büchner's *Wozzeck* and certain that it could be made into a successful opera. But the complicated history of Wedekind's works and their outré subject matter posed a new set of problems. In 1928 Berg also had to contemplate new trends in the genre of opera itself. An opera of bleak social criticism like *Wozzeck* ran counter to the works that most attracted attention in the 1920s—operas such as Strauss's *Intermezzo*, Ernst Krenek's *Jonny spielt auf* and Kurt Weill's *Die Dreigroschenoper*—with their satiric texts and light music. Berg would have to choose his subject carefully and rely on his deep understanding of drama to repeat the success of *Wozzeck*.

The Search for Lulu

As he worked from 1923 to 1925 on his tribute to Schoenberg in the Chamber Concerto, Berg's thoughts kept returning to opera. One of his first ideas for a new subject was alliances between artists, somewhat akin to the program underlying the Chamber Concerto but more germane to his conflicted relationship with Schoenberg. Berg was especially fascinated by the rapport between Vincent Van Gogh and Paul Gauguin. After reading a study of Van Gogh by Julius Meier-Graefe, Berg jotted

Berg. Bryan Simms and Charlotte Erwin, Oxford University Press (2021). © Oxford University Press.
DOI: 10.1093/oso/9780190931445.003.0010

down notes for shaping an operatic text about the Dutch artist.[1] In one sketch he refers to an opera titled "Vincent" with four acts in the form of a symphony in four movements subtitled "Arrival," "Quarrel (Adagio)," "Bordello (Ear)," and "Suicide."[2] The terms evidently refer to Van Gogh's arrival in 1888 in Arles where he was joined by Gauguin, who acted as a mentor to the younger artist. As he descended into insanity, Van Gogh quarreled with Gauguin, and Van Gogh then severed his own ear and presented it to a prostitute in a nearby brothel. Shortly thereafter Van Gogh apparently committed suicide.

Berg continued to develop the plan for an opera about artists' relationships in an undated diagram made in 1923 or 1924; see Table 9.1.[3] Here Berg extends the earlier notes for "Vincent" and places them into a plan for his entire future as a composer. The plan is laid out with an eerie symmetry, akin to the palindromic design that the composer was using in the Adagio of the Chamber Concerto to represent Mathilde Schoenberg in the grip of fate. It points again to Berg's belief that his life and affairs were subject to a predetermined destiny adumbrated by mystical numbers, symmetric recurrences, and mirror images. According

Table 9.1   Berg's plan for an operatic triology

Wozzeck Op. 7	*Vincent* Op. 9	*Wolfgang* Op. 11
	The Three W's Trilogy by A[ban] B[erg]	
3 acts of 5 scenes	2 acts of 2, 3 (or 4) scenes	1 act of 3 scenes
15 scenes	6 scenes	3 scenes
Servant	Friend ↑	Master
orch. epilog at the end ↑	orch. interlude between acts 1 and 2	↑ orch. prelude
	1st act | 2nd act = retrograde of 1st act	

↑
Chamber Concerto Op. 8

↑ ↑
Further works: a cappella choruses   last work Op. 12
(Kraus) Op. 10

to the long-range plan, the already completed *Wozzeck* was the first element of a three-part operatic scheme. The next major work, following the Chamber Concerto, was to be "Vincent," in which the servitude of Wozzeck would evolve to the level of a difficult friendship, as between Van Gogh and Gauguin. Certainly Berg's relationship with Schoenberg was in the composer's mind as a model for the underlying drama of both operas. Like the Chamber Concerto and the *Lyric Suite*, "Vincent" was to have a strongly autobiographical dimension.

In April 1924 Berg read an excerpt from Hermann Kasack's play *Vincent*, which seemed promising for his operatic plan.[4] He wrote to the playwright on 25 April asking to see the remainder of Kasack's play:

> After completing my opera *Wozzeck* (Universal Edition)—for several years, that is—I have planned to compose an opera "Vincent," to deal musically not only with the fate of this artist, who for decades has been closest to me, but also (even more) to capture *the drama* of an artistic friendship in general.[5]

A letter exchange ensued between Berg and Kasack, but by 1925 Berg had lost interest in the Vincent idea. Nothing is known of what Berg had in mind for "Wolfgang," although he may have imagined a dramatization of Mozart's relationship with Haydn, as the younger composer achieves a mastery equal to, if not surpassing, that of the older one.

Berg's search for his second operatic subject took on a new intensity after the success of *Wozzeck* in Berlin in December 1925. He dropped his idea of the relationship between artists and looked instead toward the contemporary dramatic literature for a usable text, turning for advice to acquaintances, especially Soma Morgenstern and his precocious student Theodor Adorno. Early in 1926 Morgenstern recommended Gerhart Hauptmann's play *Und Pippa tanzt!* (1906), a work that Berg had long admired and that was often given at Vienna's theaters, including the Burgtheater.[6] *Und Pippa tanzt!* begins in a naturalistic vein, set in winter in a harsh mountainous region of Silesia inhabited by rugged glassblowers, whose craft is depressingly in decline. But the play soon turns toward the folkloric, while at the same time retaining a suppressed erotic impulse. The daughter of a glassblower, Pippa is a delicate, beautiful girl who embodies the *femme fragile*. She is compared repeatedly to a little bird, and the men remark that she seems to have been created in the glass furnace. Several are drawn to her sexually but in the end she is compelled by a strange magic to dance herself to death. The man whose love she has returned, Michel Hellriegel, a strangely muddled idealist, becomes symbolically blind. The meaning of the play is obscure, but Berg was convinced that it had musical possibilities. In a letter from Hauptmann's publisher S. Fischer dated 18 February 1926, Berg learned that he would not be accorded exclusive rights to the play, and his eagerness to undertake the second opera then gradually cooled as his attention was absorbed by the *Lyric Suite* and by his development of the compositional resources of twelve-tone rows.

The idea of using Wedekind's Lulu plays as operatic material probably originated with Berg himself in the fall of 1927, with the encouragement of both Morgenstern and Adorno.[7] It is difficult for us now to imagine more dissimilar plays than the Lulu duo and *Pippa* as material for an opera and baffling that Berg could have long remained equivocal in choosing between them. The mixture of realism and make-believe in *Pippa* is far removed from the explosive concoction of farce, symbolism, myth, sex, and sordid violence in the Lulu plays, a combination that continues to perplex many listeners and offers little similarity to any earlier operatic text.

Berg was keenly aware of the strengths of the Lulu plays as operatic material, and also of their risks. While he found in Lulu an intensification of the hard-hitting drama in *Wozzeck,* he was also concerned that choosing the Lulu plays, which were widely considered pornographic, might limit the acceptability of the opera. The problem with the plays was not the theme of sexuality itself—this had been addressed explicitly in operas from the time of Wagner's *Tristan*, if not before—but that of prostitution and especially the lurid and seemingly gratuitous ending in which two women are stabbed to death by the psychopathic sex murderer Jack the Ripper. In November 1927 Berg explained some of the pros and cons to Morgenstern:

> *For* Lulu: it takes a step beyond *Wozzeck*, something that I and others expect; the *strength* of the play; the fact that I've already revised much of the text and found many good solutions. *Against* Lulu: the daring of the material, which is so great that after years of work I might have something that could only be performed for an invited public. Despite our good ideas for revisions there

remain great difficulties to bring a work with so much dialect like Wedekind's to the operatic stage, where scarcely a word would be understood.[8]

Berg's apprehension about the dangers inherent in the "daring" text later proved accurate.

In early October 1927 Berg wrote to Wedekind's widow, Tilly, to say that he was considering the Lulu plays for operatic treatment, and after receiving a positive reply he began to experiment with ways to merge and to abbreviate Wedekind's texts.[9] Morgenstern was ready to assist in this, and in a letter of November 1927 he asked: "I'm very curious how far your working plan (Lulu) has advanced in the meantime. I've obtained the books and thought a lot about abridgements, condensations, etc. Hopefully I can give you good advice in this (I think I can). Please let me know if you're sticking with it."[10] Later Morgenstern made the startling claim that he had guided Berg's revision of Wedekind's plays to the extent that the composer was ready to split the royalties from the opera with him.[11] Among Berg's large number of sketches and drafts for his text revisions, none was made by Morgenstern.[12]

By late November Berg had narrowed his search to *Pippa* or Lulu, and he reached out again to Morgenstern and Adorno for advice. Morgenstern weighed in on the side of *Pippa*, praising it for its practicality: " I think that you would finish it in (relatively) short order and that the play would be gobbled up by operatic stages."[13] Adorno's response is lost although he later recalled his enthusiasm for Lulu. "I argued with him in favor of *Lulu*," Adorno wrote, "and convinced the theater man in him by pointing out the instability and dramaturgical impracticality of *Pippa*, despite its admittedly ingenious and musical first act. . . . I flatter myself to take the main credit for Berg's choice."[14]

By January 1928 Berg had made his decision: the second opera would be a setting of *Und Pippa tanzt!* Although negotiations with Hauptmann's publisher had not been finalized, Berg let his closest friends know of his plan. On 17 January Webern responded enthusiastically to the news:

What a decision, my dear Alban! My head spins when I think of what will transpire, *must transpire*, between yesterday when you let me know about it and the time when I will see the completed score. I can already imagine the connection between the drama and your music and visualize its outlines. Pippa! Hellriegel! The snowy mountain hut . . . God bless you!![15]

Berg did not consult Schoenberg on his plan for *Pippa* and waited three months to let him know about it, perhaps aware that Schoenberg himself around 1906 had drafted music for the opening of an opera on the *Pippa* text.[16] Berg must have been relieved, all the same, when Schoenberg later responded enthusiastically about the choice of Hauptmann's play. His confidence in his choice of *Pippa* increased after he and Helene met Hauptmann in Rapallo, Italy, in late January 1928, their visit arranged and paid for by Alma Mahler. After their meeting, Berg was reassured that there would be an acceptable agreement with Hauptmann on the division of royalties, and in the spring of 1928 Berg began to make musical sketches for *Pippa* (many of which were subsequently transferred to *Lulu*).[17]

In April of 1928, Berg received additional demands from the S. Fischer Verlag for rights to *Pippa*: 50 percent royalty from performances, 20 percent on the sale of libretti, and 5 percent on the sale of printed scores.[18] By comparison, for *Lulu* Berg and Universal Edition paid 33.5 percent, 15 percent, and 10 percent for the same rights. Berg then realized that he could not continue with his plan, and for financial reasons he was forced to abandon *Pippa* and turn to the Lulu plays. The change was apparently unsettling for him. In a note made in the fall of 1928, he wrote: "The decision not to compose *Pippa* is a crisis comparable only to one of my illnesses."[19]

Much about Wedekind's complex and edgy drama attracted Berg. He had long been enthusiastic about Wedekind's treatment of erotic subjects, spurred on by Karl Kraus's unstinting praise for Wedekind. Far earlier, in 1905, Berg had attended a private staging organized by Kraus of *Die Büchse der Pandora*, in a period when the play was under censorship throughout Germany and Austria. Kraus at this time also delivered a lecture on the play—several times reprinted—that shaped Berg's thinking about the work.[20] In it, Kraus extolled the promiscuous Lulu as a tragic heroine devoted to joy and pleasure but destined to be dragged down by vengeful men and sham morality. For Kraus, Lulu embodies the power of sexuality and a woman's right to express it freely in spite of the repressive attitudes of bourgeois society. Kraus wrote: "The play depicts a woman running the gauntlet: a woman not intended by her Creator to serve the egotism of her possessor, who can only rise to achieve her true worth if allowed her freedom."[21] For Kraus the polygamous female was the ultimate inspiration, the "primal spring" at which man renewed his mind.[22] The evil of prostitution was not sex but the perversion of sex by a hypocritical society.

Kraus was not distracted by the incongruities of the Lulu plays. He explained their ugly grotesquerie as a mask, a dramatic device used by the writer as a vehicle for an underlying idealism. For Wedekind a proper feeling of shame comes not from the overt expression of sexuality, says Kraus, but from observing the persecution of those who express it. Kraus writes about Wedekind:

> His critics mistake the mask for the face, and none has an inkling that the meaning of grotesqueness here is nothing less than a sense of shame on the part of an idealist, one who remains an idealist when he avows in his sublime poem ["Confession"] that he would rather be a whore than the "happiest and most famous of men." That sense of shame reaches to far loftier spheres than the simple prudishness of those who would take offense at his material.[23]

In a letter of 1907 to his friend Frida Semler, Berg echoes Kraus's thoughts by praising the "emphasis on the sensual in modern works." Berg continues:

> This trait is at work in all new art. And I believe it is a good thing. At last we have come to the realization that sensuality is not a weakness, does not mean a surrender to one's own will. Rather is it an immense strength that lies in us—the pivot of all being and thinking. (Yes, all thinking!) In this I am declaring firmly and certainly the great importance of sensuality, for every-thing spiritual. Only through the understanding of sensuality, only through a fundamental insight into the "depths of mankind" (shouldn't it rather be called the "heights of mankind"?) can one arrive at a real idea of the human psyche.[24]

Berg could not have considered taking on such a difficult subject as Lulu without a deep engagement with the elusive central character. As the composer, his authorial voice would ultimately override Wedekind's in the opera. It would be in character with Berg's love of puzzles and ciphers for him to devise a complex musical agenda—mirroring Kraus's distinction of mask and face—through which the obvious, surface aspects of his material turn out not to be "real." What appears repul-sive in Lulu could be made tragic, even sympathetic, by the music. Still,

Berg's celebration of such contradictory characters as Lulu, Countess Geschwitz, and Alwa by music of great passion and beauty caused several early critics of the opera unease. Donald Mitchell wrote in 1954: "Berg himself precipitated a large-scale confusion when basically (either consciously or unconsciously) altering the constitution and character of the opera's Lulu without duly amending the text and dramatic action."[25] For Berg as for Kraus, there was no such confusion about the message of *Lulu*, but it is also the case, as Douglas Jarman writes, that his choice of the Lulu texts was "a deliberate act of subversion and provocation. And this, of course, is part of Berg's plan because it is the hypocrisy of the society represented by the opera's own audience that is the subject of the work."[26] Despite the many ambiguities and conflicts of the text, Berg at the end gives his listeners a choice between understanding what is real and what is "too real." Leaving the audience suspended is not a mark of confusion but rather the type of challenge inherent in the art of modernity where traditional values are intentionally and even violently disrupted. Berg's genius in *Lulu* was the realization of this new level of musical and dramatic complexity on the operatic stage.

To compose Lulu, Berg would also have to grapple with the power of Eros in his own life. Adorno observed that Berg was positively disposed toward the subject of sexuality and candidly observed its role in the lives of others, but in his own life it was a matter of some frustration and sorrow: "Concerning himself, he said that he had never in his life known the full happiness of sexuality, such as he imagined it to be."[27] The erotic element in the Hanna Fuchs affair and later in the flirtations with Anny Askenase and Edith Edwards, Adorno continued, were destined to bring with them the same dejection. Still, like many artists, Berg was inspired by the erotic, and in his personal assimilation of sexual angst, the Hanna affair seems to have been a turning point, an experience that allowed him to unchain something that had built up over time in his psyche, perhaps even from as early as the fathering of his illegitimate daughter, likely his first sexual experience. In the *Lyric Suite*, the lover's program remains hidden; in *Lulu*, it is masked. In both cases, erotic experience becomes for Berg both a spur to creativity and a personal emotional exegesis formed around renunciation. The opera arguably falls into the category of autobiographical works, but on a psychological rather than narrative level. Berg himself betrayed his emotional position in the letter to Hanna in which he remarks on the popular notion of his happy domestic life as that of a man "who might for a time be filled with the thrill of driving a car but would never be able to compose *Lulu.*"[28] It is not just Eros but its suffering that calls forth the composer's genius.

Wedekind's Lulu Plays

In 1894 Frank Wedekind completed a five-act drama, *Die Büchse der Pandora: Eine Monstretragödie*, which he offered for publication in the following year.[29] Out of fear of censorship and to make the play more practical for the stage, he subsequently divided it into two parts, *Der Erdgeist* (later retitled simply "*Erdgeist*") and *Die Büchse der Pandora*, which were published in 1895 and 1902, respectively. Prior to publication, each was augmented by the addition of a new act, bringing the total to seven acts in all. Wedekind later undertook several revisions, finally arriving at definitive versions of the two plays that were then printed in 1913 in his Collected Works.[30]

Earth Spirit begins with a Prologue in which an Animal Tamer, standing before a circus tent, coaxes the passers-by to enter and see his ferocious animals. His "snake" is brought out as the inanimate body of a woman, dressed in a Pierrot costume, who later enacts the role of Lulu. She was created to "murder without leaving a trace," he says. The tangled narrative of the play is gradually told: years earlier, the waif Lulu had been taken in by Dr. Schön, a wealthy newspaper magnate, and became a sister to his son, Alwa. Later, Lulu becomes Schön's mistress, but wishing himself to secure a more respectable alliance, he marries Lulu off to the elderly Dr. Goll. Goll dies of a seizure when he sees Lulu in a compromising situation with Walter Schwarz, who is painting her portrait, and Schön then arranges to have her marry the painter. But when Schön confides to Schwarz about Lulu's dubious past, the painter commits suicide. Schön himself cannot escape Lulu's magnetic attraction. She forces him to break off his newly contracted engagement, and the two are finally married. During Schön's absences, their home is invaded by an odd assortment of Lulu's admirers: the lesbian artist Countess Geschwitz, a schoolboy Hugenberg, a circus performer Rodrigo, and an old beggar, Schigolch, who claims to be Lulu's father. In a madcap finale the visitors scurry about as Schön appears armed with a revolver. He demands that Lulu use the weapon on herself, but when he turns his back to her, she shoots him five times. The police arrive as the curtain ends the play.

Although *Earth Spirit* was found controversial when first staged in 1898, it later proved successful in German theaters. It was almost always assessed as a burlesque or grotesque comedy with lively theater and laughable caricatures of men from different walks of contemporary life—the businessman, the artist, the doctor—each enslaved and driven to the grave by a beautiful *femme fatale*. All the while there are ambiguities that hint at a deeper meaning and disrupt any simple narrative. The dialog is filled with non-sequiturs, contradictions, and absurdities. The characters seem to enact an allegory but its meaning is unclear. Is Lulu a realistic persona, a mythological figure, or a figment of men's imaginations? Is she an innocent victim or a destructive demon? What is the meaning of the differing names given her by the men in the play—Nelly, Eve, and Mignon, in addition to Lulu?

The high-spirited burlesque of *Earth Spirit* dissolves into brutal sordidness in its sequel, *Pandora's Box*. A year has passed with Lulu imprisoned for murder, and the same characters at the end of *Earth Spirit* are still together. Geschwitz succeeds in springing Lulu from prison, and Alwa—a writer, son of the murdered Dr. Schön—is inspired artistically by her beauty and has fallen in love with her. They all escape together from Germany to Paris, where Alwa and Lulu use his inherited money to live lavishly among the demimonde. There Lulu attracts a crowd even more unsavory than before, and soon the money is gone. The pimp Casti-Piani threatens to denounce her to the police if she refuses to be sold to an Egyptian brothel. The pedophile banker Puntschu has sold Alwa and Lulu shares in the Jungfrau Railroad that prove worthless. Schigolch agrees to murder and dispose of Rodrigo, who is also blackmailing Lulu, and news arrives that Hugenberg has committed suicide. Just as the police arrive, Alwa and Lulu escape and flee to London. There Lulu—reunited with Alwa, Schigolch, and Geschwitz but now destitute—turns to prostitution. She attracts a series of men to her shabby garret, one of whom kills Alwa as he attempts to protect her. The last client is identified only as "Jack." He bullies Lulu, who perversely begs and even pays him to stay with her. They go to a moonlit bedroom from which Lulu's death shriek is heard. Jack emerges and stabs Geschwitz. "Lulu, my angel, let me see you once more," pleads the dying Geschwitz, who expires with a curse: "Oh damnation!"

Berg was initially uneasy about the presence in an opera of Wedekind's aberrant characters and especially about the violent, prurient ending. What he had said to Morgenstern, that after years of work he might have an opera that could be performed only for an invited public, probably remained in his mind, all the more as the opera neared completion while prospects for its staging evaporated. In 1931 Leopold Stokowski in Philadelphia backed out of his interest in the opera after learning of the text. Berg's principal text sources were reprintings of *Earth Spirit* and *Pandora's Box* from Wedekind's 1913 Collected Works, but he also considered other, less provocative versions. One was a five-act edition that Wedekind titled *Lulu* and had published in 1913 intending to make the censored play performable.[31] Here the two plays are reunited, the two added acts removed, and the violent ending rewritten. The new conclusion dispenses with Jack; instead, Lulu shoots Geschwitz as the two struggle over a pistol. Lulu leaves to fetch a doctor and is seen no more. As she dies, Geschwitz mutters her own funeral oration, which ends the play.

At some point, probably in 1929 judging from Berg's correspondence with Tilly Wedekind, Berg seriously considered this version as the ending for his opera. He wrote out the complete text of the final engagement between Lulu and Geschwitz from the expurgated *Lulu* and tipped it into one of his printed editions of the plays, and in other sketches he noted that the opera would end with "Geschwitz's poem."[32] But this alternative ending would have disrupted the symmetry of Lulu's victims balanced by her assailants, and it would eliminate the double casting of Schön and Jack that was already being done effectively in stagings of the spoken plays. So Berg ultimately reverted to the better known version with Jack, whom Berg explicitly identifies as Jack the Ripper.

Following the removal of censorship in Germany and Austria after World War I, stagings of Wedekind's plays increased, but the numbers then sharply fell off as a new dramatic style came to dominate German theater during the 1920s. The new movement emphasized contemporaneity through the presentation of modern social or political subjects and productions using new staging techniques and elements of modern culture including jazzy music and new technologies such as film, phonograph, and radio. Plays by Bertolt Brecht such as *Die Dreigroschenoper* (The three-penny opera, 1928) exemplify the new taste. In this work Brecht dispels normal theatric illusion and emotional engagement on the part of the spectator. The audience is entertained instead by the pop songs added by Kurt Weill as they look on dispassionately at a witty, sharp-edged satire of modern society.

While the symbolism and ambiguities in Wedekind's plays were re-mote from the new taste, German directors of the 1920s brought Lulu back to life by freely revising Wedekind's texts and staging the plays in an updated manner. Berg's own adaptation of the Lulu plays looks squarely in this revisionist direction. In a 1926 production of "Lulu" at Berlin's Staatstheater, Erich Engel rewrote and shortened Wedekind's text to pre-serve all seven acts. His version clarified the action and eliminated many ambiguities. Engel double cast the roles of Schön and Jack for the same actor—the celebrated Fritz Kortner—to show that one is the alter ego of the other. Similarly, he clarified the meaning of the circus Prologue by having all of the main characters onstage so that the Animal Tamer could point to them one by one as he enumerates his ferocious beasts. All of Engel's innovations are present, in one manner or another, in Berg's version.

Even more influential for Berg's *Lulu* libretto was a highly successful version created by Otto Falckenberg for the Munich Kammerspiele in 1928.[33] With its use of placards, projections and jazzy music, Falckenberg's staging was in the same mode as Caspar Neher's celebrated and con-temporaneous staging of *Die Dreigroschenoper* in Berlin. Like Engel, Falckenberg keeps all seven acts of the Lulu plays by rewriting and abbreviating Wedekind's text. Like Berg later, he simplifies the action and dialog, doubles additional roles to suggest parallels between characters, and adds popular music to bring the ambience of the play up to date. Falckenberg made use of Wedekind's own cabaret songs in the interludes between acts, as Berg was to do in the opera. Falckenberg's interlude be-fore the Paris act has an especially strong resemblance to Berg's plan for a film clip to fill an interlude that illustrates Lulu's arrest, trial, impris-onment, and escape. Falckenberg's interlude uses a motion-picture-like succession of still images, with train sounds, street noise, and songs added to portray the flight from Germany and arrival in Paris.

Berg's Libretto for *Lulu*

Berg's first step in the creation of his operatic text was to abbreviate Wedekind's seven acts and to arrange them into a large symmetric plan for the entire work, one that would enhance the symmetries implicit in Wedekind's plays and bring out the role of fate in the narrative. Berg made each act into a scene and distributed the scenes into an opera of three acts. He sent an outline of his plan to Schoenberg in a letter of August 1930 (Table 9.2).[34]

The keystone of the symmetric arch is the "large interlude" in the middle of Act 2, which, judging from sketches, Berg foresaw early in his planning as a silent film sequence accompanied by orchestral music, much as he had planned for his operatic project "Nacht" and similar to the interludes in Falckenberg's *Lulu*. In his letter to Schoenberg he also says that his detailed revisions in Wedekind's texts were being carried out

Table 9.2   Berg's plan for the *Lulu* libretto (1930)

THE TWO DRAMAS		THE OPERA
Earth Spirit		
Act 1	Painter's studio in which Dr. Goll, Lulu's husband, suffers a seizure	Act 1 (3 scenes)
Act 2	Lulu's residence and her 2nd husband, the Painter, who kills himself	|
Act 3	Theater dressing room of the dancer Lulu, who pledges to marry Schön	|
Act 4	Residence of Schön, who is murdered by Lulu. She is arrested.	Act 2 (1 stage set divided by a large interlude)
	After a ten-year sentence, Lulu is freed from prison by Alwa (Schön's son) and Geschwitz and she returns . . .	
Pandora's Box		
Act 1	Back in Schön's residence (scenery as before), she becomes Alwa's lover.	|
Act 2	Gaming casino in Paris. Lulu is forced to flee	Act 3 (2 scenes)
Act 3	In the London garret	|

as he composed, just as he had done in *Wozzeck*, and that he was often revising the text to make it fit into predetermined musical forms. Berg extensively abbreviates and simplifies Wedekind's texts, removing many of the digressions, soliloquies, eccentricities in dialog, and even whole scenes to provide the audience with a fast moving and coherent narrative. Taking his cue from Büchner's *Wozzeck*, Berg removes proper names from most of the secondary characters, identifying them instead by occupation: a Medical Specialist (Goll), Painter (Schwarz), Athlete (Rodrigo), School Boy (Hugenberg), Banker (Puntschu), and Marquis (Casti-Piani), among others.

As done earlier by Engel and Falckenberg, Berg assigns two or sometimes three roles to a single performer. This allows him to reinforce a large-scale symmetry in his text and to point to subtle dramatic correspondences underlying certain characters, these correspondences strengthened by having the characters share related music. The most important instances of multiple castings are made by pairing Lulu's three husbands in the first half (Medical Specialist, Painter, and Schön) with her clients in the final scene (a Professor, Negro, and Jack the Ripper). By these doublings, Berg conforms to Kraus's interpretation of the end of the drama. "The great reprisal has begun," Kraus writes, "a men's world is brashly taking revenge for its own guilt."[35] George Perle has found in the multiple casting and recurring music "a sense of *dejà vu*" in the last scene. Perle continues, "in the final scene, the staged events seem to be accompanied by a shadow of themselves in which the first half of the opera, culminating and concluding in the death of Dr. Schön, is reenacted in a nightmarish distortion."[36] In other doublings Berg suggests other more subtle dramatic relationships.

One of Berg's major alterations in Wedekind's text is to make Alwa and Countess Geschwitz more realistic and sympathetic. Berg's *Lulu* is at one level a love story, with a love triangle focused on the passion of Alwa and Geschwitz for Lulu, Schön's helpless attraction to her, and the tragic consequences that intercede in these relationships from the hand of fate. In the plays Alwa is a writer who speaks for Wedekind. In *Pandora's Box*, he says that he wrote a play called *Earth Spirit* in an effort to bring literature closer to real life. Elsewhere in *Pandora*, Alwa is shown in a harsher light: during Lulu's imprisonment he has taken a mistress, his interest in Lulu has become mainly to advance his writing career, and he has contracted venereal disease from Lulu who was infected by Casti-Piani.[37] In the final act of *Pandora* he dissolves in self-pity: consorting with people like Lulu has brought him only disease and failure as a writer, he complains. In his adaptation, Berg identifies himself with Alwa by making him a composer. This was a logical change from Wedekind's text that Berg develops by playful references to and quotations from his music when Alwa mentions his own works. He also makes Alwa more sympathetic by removing most of his self-pitying dialogue in the final scene. We are left with a figure with whom Berg could empathize, one who loves Lulu faithfully, drawn to her by her sensual beauty, which is in turn an inspiration for his creative work.

In Berg's hands Countess Geschwitz undergoes a similar transformation. Wedekind's treatment of Geschwitz stresses her lesbianism and her rejection because of it by those around her. Lulu hurls curses at her, calling her a loathsome pervert. In her final soliloquy Geschwitz declares her satisfaction with her lesbianism, her happiness at being different from other people. "I am not a human being at all," she says with bittersweet satisfaction. Berg removes these passages and leaves Geschwitz as a self-effacing character who, like Alwa, is devoted to Lulu and ready to sacrifice for her.

As he had done in *Wozzeck*, Berg adds many staging instructions to his libretto resembling those found in a director's *Regiebuch*. One example concerns the handling of Lulu's portrait made by the Painter in Act 1. In Berg's libretto it appears in every scene, and his staging instructions heighten its significance beyond Wedekind, where it is at most a silent part of the decor. Wedekind's idea for the painting was probably inspired by Oscar Wilde's novel *The Picture of Dorian Gray*, published shortly before Wedekind began to write the Lulu plays. In the novel, the painting of Dorian Gray ages while Dorian remains young and devoted to a hedonistic life. Wedekind reverses the idea such that the painting remains beautiful during Lulu's decline. Berg calls attention to the painting by having most of the characters repeatedly stare at it and take inspiration from it by the promise and joy that it represents, despite "the sorrow at its unattainable nature," as Adorno wrote.[38] Berg further underscores the importance of the portrait by associating it with one of the opera's most important musical motives.

One staging direction added by Berg to the Paris scene (Act 3, scene 1) proved especially controversial in the later history of the work. The

Banker wins money at the gambling table from the Journalist, who demands that the game must continue using his Jungfrau Railroad shares as collateral. The Banker agrees but tells the Journalist that the Jungfrau shares are now worthless. "You Jewish pig!" screams the Journalist. The term *Saujud* was used by Wedekind and retained by Berg. Berg then sharpens the caricature of the Jewish banker in a way not present in Wedekind by having him continue the exchange using a Yiddish accent that Berg calls "*mauscheln*" in the condensed score and by the synonymous term "*jüdeln*" in his typed text. "This gentleman must pay in cash. Does he think I'm in my bank office?" says the Banker in a speaking voice that rises into the head tones as the orchestra plays a mumbling sixteenth-note ostinato. "You call these shares trash!" responds the Journalist parodying the Banker's Yiddish accent.

The terms "mauscheln" and "jüdeln" were widely used at the time, and Berg occasionally used the word "jüdeln" in his correspondence.[39] Sander Gilman defines *mauscheln* as "a pattern of gestures to represent the spoken language of the Jews. What is stressed is the specifically 'Jewish' intonation, the mode of articulation as well as the semantic context."[40] The terms were generally found insulting to Jews since the Yiddish accent was associated with shady business dealings—exactly how they are applied by Berg in the case of the Banker. Karl Kraus regularly dismissed the Yiddish accent as a symbol of the underhanded business practices of some Jews. In his 1913 article "Er ist doch ä Jude" (He is still a Jew), Kraus wrote:

> I really don't know what Jewish traits are nowadays. If there is something that stands out from things that are better, it is greed and avarice. But I see these equally in all people throughout the Western world, distributed judiciously by the hand of the devil. And if there is one thing more, it would be the singsong intonation in which they conduct and handle business, so I say that the other things relate to this one too, because it is the intonation that happily accompanies the changing of money.[41]

The caricature of the Jewish banker was for Berg a curious and uncharacteristic misstep. The Paris scene was composed and its text written in the late fall of 1933, after the Nazis had taken control of the German government and at a time of widespread persecution of Jews. It is likely that Berg considered the passage to be a harmless and comic parody, in an opera where most of the figures are caricatures. Kraus's lecture on *Pandora* may also have encouraged Berg to heighten the caricature of the Banker, especially since Berg at this time intended to dedicate the opera to Kraus.[42] Kraus wrote in the lecture, "He [the Banker] emerges from the gaming room chuckling impishly over the fact that his Jewish morality is that much more acceptable than the morals of the women clustering around him. Poor girls, they have to pay out their only capital, their bodies, whereas the quick-wittedness of the rogue preserves him intact; and he doesn't need to bathe in eau de Cologne!"[43] Berg apparently discussed the passage with Soma Morgenstern, who did not object to it. Morgenstern later wrote to Helene: "When Alban wrote it, he consulted me, and I told him that I considered the word 'jüdelnd' to be harmless. I still consider it so."[44] The leadership of Universal Edition—Hugo Winter, Alfred Kalmus, and Hans Heinsheimer, all Jews—had seen Berg's text and raised no objections. It would be Arnold Schoenberg who, after Berg's death, took strong exception to Berg's handling of the Banker's character.

Berg did not speak out in detail about his own understanding of the meaning of Wedekind's Lulu plays and their adaptability to opera. As with the text of *Wozzeck*, he was more inclined to point to the ideas of other authorities, especially to Kraus, whose interpretation he fully accepted despite its many implausible aspects. Berg repeatedly argued that the text is not ethically objectionable, but instead a morality play like Mozart's *Don Giovanni*. After typing out the entire text of his version in 1934 to send to Erich Kleiber, he made this comparison:

> Now that I look it over I am all the more convinced that it is a deeply moralistic play. Lulu's rise and fall balance out. In the middle comes the great reversal, until she like Don Giovanni is taken off by the devil. I say this intentionally, like Don Giovanni, not to compare myself with Mozart, for goodness sake, but to equate the two figures: Lulu and Don Giovanni.[45]

Berg may have drawn the comparison between Lulu and Don Giovanni to make the text seem more acceptable, by holding that Lulu, a promiscuous murderer, is "taken off by the devil" in the end. Others found more subtlety in Berg's comparison. Ernst Krenek, in a lecture delivered in 1937 before the Zurich premiere of *Lulu*, explained Berg's analogy by reference to Kierkegaard's essay on *Don Giovanni*, "Die Stadien des unmittelbar Erotischen oder das Musikalisch-Erotische" (The stages of unmediated eroticism, or the musical erotic).[46] For Kierkegaard, Don Giovanni embodies an erotic, amoral force of nature that occupies an "aesthetic" stage of existence. Lulu, Krenek says, is a similar embodiment. All who occupy this stage inevitably fall into doubt and despair when they realize that their existence is empty and meaningless. According to this reading, Don Giovanni and Lulu are comparable allegorical representations of the symmetry of pleasure followed by despair. Berg never mentioned Kierkegaard's essay in his correspondence, although it is plausible that he discussed it with Adorno, who wrote his habilitation thesis in 1931 on Kierkegaard's construction of an aesthetic existence.[47] Willi Reich also states that Berg's comparison of Lulu and Don Giovanni referred to Kierkegaard's interpretation.[48]

Only once did Berg speak up for himself about the essential meaning of the character Lulu and her music. This occurs in his correspondence with Hans W. Heinsheimer of Universal Edition concerning the *Lied der Lulu* (Lulu's song). The *Lied* occurs near the end of *Earth Spirit*, in the deadly confrontation of Schön and Lulu where Schön demands that she shoot herself. Defiantly, Lulu makes a confident and resolute series of assertions about herself—that men including Schön have willingly pursued her for what she is. Berg drew special attention to the *Lied* by placing it at the center of his *Symphonic Pieces from the Opera "Lulu"*, a concert suite to be discussed later in the chapter. If men kill themselves over me, Lulu says, my value is not diminished by their actions. I never pose as other than I am, and this is just what men have understood and wanted. Her proclamations resonate with Kraus's interpretation of her: she does not entice or tempt nor act out of moral choices or responsibilities. Her essential quality, her "innermost secret," as Adorno later wrote paraphrasing Kraus, "is one of tenderness and beauty, and not, as some idiots write, one of 'elemental nature.'"[49] For use in the *Symphonic Pieces* Heinsheimer hoped to persuade Berg to modify the words of the *Lied* to make them less controversial. He wrote: "Don't you think it possible to change the text of the Lulu *Lied*? When taken out of the context of the opera, this text stands out strikingly. Couldn't you revise it to be a bit more general and obliging?"[50] Berg responded quickly to reject Heinsheimer's proposal: "I think that this text itself represents a program for the whole work," he wrote. "In its near philosophical argument about man and woman it has detachment [from the drama] and a generality of meaning—in other words, just what you find missing in it, Herr Doctor."[51]

A Chronology of Composition

Berg began to compose *Lulu* in mid-June 1928, when he arrived in Trahütten to begin his annual summer retreat. He devoted his last seven and one-half years to the creation of the work, but he was never able to bring it fully to completion. Many factors contributed to its prolonged history. *Lulu* is Berg's longest and most complex composition, and during its creation his compositional method underwent important changes. His concentration on the work was interrupted by commissions to compose *Der Wein* and the Violin Concerto, and other minor projects also arose. During the seven-year period his energy was sapped by declining health and personal and financial crises, and it is possible also that Berg was delayed by uncertainty about the poetic material itself—its ambiguous meaning, its appropriateness to musical interpretation, and its acceptability in the highly politicized atmosphere of the 1930s. A major impediment to his progress on the opera arose in the early 1930s as Berg descended into a state of depression during which he questioned his whole direction in life and looked abjectly at the state of his existence. By 1933, faced with financial ruin through growing political repression, he pressed on to complete the opera with a grim necessity that he compared to slavery.

As he began to compose *Lulu* in 1928, Berg had a general idea for reshaping and abbreviating Wedekind's text, a few usable musical sketches that he had made for *Pippa*, and his own twelve-tone method devised during the previous summer. He largely composed the seven acts of Wedekind's text in order, revising and abbreviating it as he created the music. At first he felt no urgency to move his work ahead since *Wozzeck* was flourishing on operatic stages and bringing him ever larger royalties. He devoted more than three years to composing the first act alone, and he pointed to the complex revisions in Wedekind's texts and the limitations of his twelve-tone theory of 1927 as factors that delayed his progress. He reported to Schoenberg in a letter of 1 September 1928 that he had composed 300 measures, and he may have completed the first scene of Act 1 by October 11, when he and Helene returned to Vienna.

Most of the summer of 1929 was taken up by *Der Wein*, and Berg could continue with *Lulu* only from late August of that year to the end of September, when he ended his summer retreat. Although there was limited progress on the opera during these months, Berg at this time—collaborating with his student Willi Reich—revised his twelve-tone method by devising new ways to derive tone rows from the basic row that he had been using to that point. He began to apply his new method, which allowed him better to distinguish or interrelate characters in the drama, when he returned to Act 1, scene 2, upon his return to the Berghof on 10 July 1930. Still, progress was slow, and he may have managed to complete Act 1, scene 2, only by the end of his summer retreat on 28 September 1931.[52] He was pressed by Universal Edition to complete the opera for a premiere in Philadelphia under Leopold Stokowski, but in 1931 Stokowski backed out on account of the text. Berg then wrote to Webern: "So now I'm entirely free from this pressure and I'm composing as usual—slowly!"[53]

On 6 August 1931 Berg reported to Schoenberg that Act 1 was at last finished and that the main impediment—revising the text so that it would fit into preconceived musical forms—had been overcome. In his letter, Berg expresses optimism that *Lulu* could receive its premier performance in the 1932–33 season, although he must have realized that his slow pace of composing—limited to the summer months—plus the distractions from family affairs and personal problems would make this goal impossible to achieve. Berg began to compose Act 2 before ending his summer retreat and returning to Vienna on 28 September. The year 1932 saw even less progress on the opera than before due to mounting stresses in Berg's life. He told Kleiber that he planned to remain at the Berghof through October to work on Act 2, but another year would elapse before it was completed.

The Bergs spent the summer of 1933 in their new summer residence, the "Waldhaus," in an idyllic location overlooking the Wörthersee. They had purchased the property in the previous November, and they remained there through the winter of 1933–34 so that Alban could compose without interruption. They did so despite harsh winter conditions, with no reliable running water and sporadic heating. Act 2 was completed by mid-September 1933 and in late April or early May 1934, after six years, the composition of *Lulu* was essentially complete. (Recall that Berg always considered the composition of a large work to be completed when the condensed score—the *Particell*—was drafted to its end, although revisions and orchestration still remained to be done.) Berg wrote immediately to Kleiber, "It was a difficult piece of work during which I several times thought that it was beyond my powers. But now I've done it and nothing more can happen to me—except starvation."[54] Berg was still apprehensive about the opera being ready for the stage during the 1934–35 season. He wrote about this to Webern:

> Having reached the end of composing *Lulu* did not make me totally as happy as I thought it would. I only *cursorily* sketched some passages toward the end, leaving their working out for later. Also I now have to "overhaul" (as they say about cars) the entire composition. Work that stretched over years and a musical development that *from the start* was not *entirely* foreseen means that I must now go back to make small revisions. This will take me 1 to 3 weeks so that I won't be able to begin the orchestration probably until June, . . . and the time for this (until autumn) is getting ever shorter and my anxiety about it ever larger.[55]

Berg's next step—before he began orchestration or revisions—was to create a concert work out of excerpts from the opera, similar to the *Wozzeck Fragments* that had been so successful in promoting a staging of that work. Berg began to sketch plans for the "suite," as he first called it, in mid-May. At first he contemplated two versions, one short (using voice in one movement, as he had done in the *Wozzeck Fragments*), the other an oversized "Lulu Symphony." At the urging of Heinsheimer, Berg soon dispensed with the larger version and concentrated on the smaller one, which he completed in July 1934 and titled *Symphonische Stücke aus der Oper "Lulu"* (Symphonic pieces from the opera *Lulu*).[56]

After completing the orchestration of the *Symphonic Pieces* in late July, Berg returned to the orchestration of the remainder of *Lulu*, starting from its beginning but again with no special urgency since a staging in the near future seemed a remote possibility.[57] Early in 1935 another project diverted Berg's attention from *Lulu*. In February of that year Berg accepted a commission from the American violinist Louis Krasner for a violin concerto. Krasner offered a fee of $1,500, an offer that Berg could not refuse. The concerto was composed and scored between May and August at the Waldhaus, whereupon Berg again returned to the opera.

Berg's final effort to complete the scoring of *Lulu* ended around the middle of November 1935, when in a precarious state of health he left the Waldhaus for Vienna. He had reached only m. 268 in his orchestration of Act 3, out of a total of 1,326 measures in that act, and he had not fleshed out passages later in the act that he had only sketched earlier nor made the "overhaul" of the entire work that he foresaw in his letter to Webern. Berg died on 24 December, without returning to *Lulu*. With trenchant insight Helene declared that her husband was Lulu's final victim.

The Music of *Lulu*

In a letter of 1934 Berg confidently assured Erich Kleiber that the meaning of Wedekind's problematic plays would be revealed by his music for the opera. Interpretations of the plays, Berg wrote, "will be superfluous for *those* who have heard its *music*."[58] In this music Berg continues to develop the amalgamation of elements of old and new toward which he had moved in the *Lyric Suite* and *Der Wein*. In a review of 1934, H.H. Stuckenschmidt, after hearing excerpts from the opera, focused on this mixed style:

> Berg's essentially synthetic way of thinking combines all the compositional resources of the past and present into a tonal language that bears his unmistakably personal imprint. From a simple C major to twelve-tone harmony, from pure homophony to multi-voice polyphony, from solo violin to orchestral tuttis from whose riot of colors the vibraphone, piano, and alto saxophone stand out. Every musical resource is made to serve an expressive purpose that is dramatic and realistic.[59]

Lulu is also a product of operatic thinking of the 1920s and 1930s, with a return to operatic numbers and styles that allude to the age of Mozart and Rossini. Although there is much use of spoken dialogue and Schoenbergian *Sprechstimme* (speaking voice), *Lulu* is a singer's opera, and the coloratura role of Lulu demands the agility of a Lucia di Lammermoor or, more relevant to the modern period, a Zerbinetta or Fiakermilli. The sextet that comes near the end of Act 1 of *Lulu* will remind many listeners of the ensemble finales of Mozartean opera, as the characters face off against one another, leaving it to the composer to create music that will bring their differences together.

Example 9.1   Cadential chords in *Lulu*

Act 1   Act 2   Act 3

Much of *Lulu* builds upon ideas used in *Wozzeck* that Berg now takes to a higher level of complexity. The sonata-form "jewelry" scene in Act 2 of *Wozzeck*, for example, is a model for the design of the sonata form in Act 1 of *Lulu*, although in *Lulu* it is far longer and further extended by lengthy interruptions. The canons on a rhythmic motive for percussion that follow the death of the Painter in *Lulu* are an extended version of the electrifying rhythmic canon in the interlude following the death of Marie. In *Wozzeck* each act ends on the same harmony, a pseudo-tonic chord according to the composer. The acts of *Lulu* end in a related but more complicated way that is summarized in Example 9.1. Act 1 ends on the chord F–E–A–C♯. Act 2 ends with the same chord except for the top note, which moves down to C natural. In the final three measures of Act 3, these two chords are recapitulated, the top note moving in the final measure down to B, with the empty fifth A–E doubled in the high strings and the dyad B–F reiterated as a pedal point in the harp. This duplicates the motive of Marie's "waiting" that poignantly arises following her death in Act 3 of *Wozzeck*.

Berg did not live to lecture on or give a detailed analytic description of *Lulu* as he did in his "Lecture on *Wozzeck*." The documents closest to such a discussion are writings by his student Willi Reich, whom Berg had chosen as his official biographer and whom he commissioned in the 1930s to express his thoughts in published form, after having himself reviewed and edited all such essays. Reich's writings from this time scrupulously reproduce Berg's ideas as Reich knew them from his discussions with the composer. Reich's most extended study of *Lulu* is found in the article "Alban Berg's *Lulu*," published in *The Musical Quarterly* in 1936 and based on correspondence between Reich and Berg and a close study of the opera made under the composer's supervision.[60]

In the article Reich quotes a letter from Berg in which the composer stresses the formal differences between *Lulu* and *Wozzeck*. In the earlier opera traditional musical forms appear in individual scenes; in *Lulu*, traditional forms are associated instead with a few principal characters, and these forms are spread over whole acts with many interruptions and episodes inserted. Berg also describes the presence in *Lulu* of a general symmetry in the libretto that is reinforced by symmetrical recurrences of whole sections of music and other "subtle musical congruencies." The sectional recurrences are especially pronounced in Act 3, in the music given to characters who are double cast—Schön and Jack, for example—to underscore their dramatic parallelism. The midpoint in the opera's symmetrical arch is the film music interlude in Act 2, whose second half is a scenic and musical retrograde of its first half.

Berg and Reich also note that the seven scenes are each subdivided into a succession of operatic numbers. Berg labels some of these in the score—especially in Act 1, more sparingly in Acts 2, and hardly at all in Act 3. He uses terms that refer mainly to vocal media (e.g., melodramas, ensembles, and duets) and vocal styles (recitative, aria, and the like). These musical numbers are normally set apart from one another by changes in tempo or surface design, sometimes by closed formal patterns. In his letter Berg also comments on his use of specific musical symbols for the characters. These include twelve-tone rows, which derive, he says, from a single basic row (the same one as in the 1927 tables). At times the rows take on a thematic shape in the manner of leitmotives; at other times they occupy a background level more dimly associated with specific characters. Similar associations between characters and music are made by orchestration: Schigolch, for example, is usually accompanied by chamber groups; the Marquis by solo strings. As in *Wozzeck* and even more in *Lulu*, Berg's symbolic association of musical elements with details of the drama often reaches deeply below the surface of the music. Douglas Jarman has aptly commented that in *Lulu* every aspect of the music acts as a leitmotive.[61]

In the survey that follows we will examine the materials and techniques used by Berg to create his multi-layered expressive and formal plan for *Lulu*. The scope and intricacy of Berg's compositional approach will become apparent, as will the manner in which his complex musical thinking coalesces to create a unified work in which his understanding of Wedekind's convoluted drama is realized in musical terms.

PROLOGUE. The first music for *Lulu*, composed in June 1928, was a fragment of the Prologue—fourteen measures of music and a rough sketch for its remaining text—in a version that Berg later discarded.[62] In this fragment and in the other music composed in 1928 (including Act

1, scene 1, and the beginning of Act 1, scene 2) Berg used his method of composing with twelve-tone rows that he had developed during the previous year and drafted in the row tables dated July 1927. Recall from an earlier discussion that these tables show a basic row, its transpositions, and its inversions, each followed by configurations of tones into which each row can be "dissolved" or reassembled. The row derivatives are often harmonies and other figures that Berg had used in his earlier music.

The opening measures of the early Prologue, shown in Example 9.2, illustrate Berg's method as it existed in 1927–28. The music consists of a succession of three phrases (A, B, and C), each containing the twelve tones and each using a transposition of the basic row out of which familiar harmonies are drawn according to patterns constructed for the

Example 9.2   Prologue draft, mm. 1–6 (Percussion omitted)

1927 tables. Phrase A has the simplest derivation. Here notes of the basic row (shown below the example) arise in sustained trills that mass into a twelve-note chord. Phrases B and C present other transpositions of the basic row, in phrase B dissolved into chains of fourths and a diminished chord and in phrase C whole-tone chords.

In April 1934 Berg replaced the provisional draft of the Prologue with new music, the last that he composed for the opera. He keeps some of his earlier materials and formal ideas, but he uses them in a more elaborate way that he had developed during his six long years of composing. An example is the chain-of-fourths motive (phrase B in Example 9.2), a figure that Berg by then had used throughout the opera as a basic unifying figure that often suggests Lulu's primal essence. In a letter to Schoenberg, he called the motive the "Erdgeist fourths."[63] In its first appearance in the revised Prologue the motive calls attention to itself by its sequential repetition in the brass that creates a twelve-tone row (Example 9.3).

In the middle of the 1934 Prologue, the Animal Tamer lists the wild animals that can been seen in his menagerie, and Berg identifies each with a character in the opera by bringing in musical materials—themes, tone rows, and their derivatives—with which these figures are later associated.[64] The tiger is Schön, the worm is Schigolch, the crocodile is Geschwitz, and so on. Finally the snake is brought out for all to see, as the inanimate body of Lulu. The Animal Tamer sings Lulu's theme (Example 9.4) to an accompaniment of sweet triadic harmonies.

Example 9.3 Prologue, mm. 1–4, "Erdgeist fourths"

Example 9.4 Prologue, mm. 46–48: Lulu's theme and row (bracketed)

ACT 1. The first act of *Lulu* consists of a succession of some twenty numbers, divided into three scenes with orchestral interludes between. The first scene is at the studio of the Painter as Alwa arrives, to be greeted by Schön, Lulu, and the Painter. When Alwa compares Lulu to the portrait of her that the Painter has been making, Berg introduces one of the most important motives of the opera, one that returns often when Lulu's portrait is mentioned. Perle calls the motive the "Picture Chords" (Example 9.5)—a succession of four chords, each made from a three-note segment of the basic row or its transposition or inversion.

Left alone with Lulu, the Painter is amorously overcome and chases her around the room to the music of a canon on her theme. Lulu's husband, the Medical Specialist, barges in only to suffer a fatal seizure seeing his wife in a compromising situation with another man. Lulu then sings a "canzonetta" over his body, whose theme (Example 9.6), played delicately by the saxophone, will be heard later following the deaths of the Painter, Schön, and Alwa.

The second scene is set in the Painter's new and lavish studio. He is now married to Lulu, blissfully happy, with his career flourishing thanks to the support of Schön. An old asthmatic beggar, Schigolch, arrives for a semi-comic encounter with Lulu, to a theme that has a low, slithering

Example 9.5   Act 1, scene 1, mm. 93–95, "Picture chords"

Example 9.6   Act 1, scene 1, mm. 258–60, "Canzonetta"

Example 9.7   Act 1, scene 2, mm. 463–64, Schigolch's theme

chromatic profile (Example 9.7). Lulu and Schigolch seem to be longtime acquaintances, and Lulu gives him money while the orchestra sustains a C-major triad, the same harmony used by Berg when Wozzeck gives money to Marie in Act 2, scene 1, of that opera.

To this point in the score Berg had constructed all of the main themes according to his 1927 row charts, using transpositions and inversions of the basic row, divisions of them into familiar harmonies, or reassembling their notes to form new rows. But Berg soon realized that using a single basic tone row would restrict the subtle distinctions that he needed to represent and distinguish among the opera's personae. In September 1929 he mentioned to Webern that he had broadened his twelve-tone method to remedy this shortcoming: "But I think I've recently found a good solution to the *problem* of using only a *single* row in a work of several hours duration (apart from the different row forms that I've already derived)."[65] Berg had discovered that any twelve-tone row, several times reiterated, could produce a new twelve-tone row, with no repeated notes, by selecting every fifth or seventh tone.[66] Berg called the procedures "B5" and "B7," presumably naming them after himself. He used his expanded method from about m. 523 in Act 1, scene 2, onward, but he also revised earlier passages to exploit the new resources.[67] An example of the B7 method is the row that he assigned to Alwa, which uses every seventh note of the repeated row. It is illustrated by its first appearance, which is in Act 1, scene 1 (Example 9.8). Berg was no doubt pleased that rows produced by his B7 and B5 methods retained features of the basic row.[68] For example, Alwa's row preserves the diatonic pitch content that is also present in the first hexachord of the basic row. Berg's new method allowed him better to portray and distinguish the principal characters of the opera by giving them not only different themes but different tone rows that could underlie those themes or stand behind them inconspicuously in the musical background. In his

Example 9.8   Act 1, scene 1, mm. 98–99, Alwa's theme and row

basic row (transposed):

Example 9.9   Act 1, scene 2, mm. 533–34, Dr. Schön's theme and row (bracketed)

own mind at least, Berg could still believe that his method was in line with Schoenberg's twelve-tone idea.

As Schigolch leaves, Schön arrives, there to demand that Lulu cease her visits to him since he is now engaged to a woman from a good family. Berg constructs their tête-à-tête as the first part of a sonata form. It has the familiar Bergian sections: an exposition with main theme, transition, subsidiary, and closing theme (the last labelled "coda" by Berg) followed immediately by a first reprise, just as in the sonata design in *Wozzeck* Act 2, scene 1. The main theme of the sonata is associated with Schön, its underlying tone row being one of the new derivatives created in 1929–30 (Example 9.9).

After Schön tells Lulu that their affair is over, Lulu pours out her heart to him. "If I belong to one man in this world, I belong to you," she laments. You are the only man, she pleads, who has ever truly cared for me. These lines coincide with the closing theme of the exposition (Example 9.10), which is one of the most stirring passages in the opera. Its late-romantic harmonies suggest the key of D♭ major, and the theme recurs poignantly in other crucial moments later in the drama. The melodic line of the closing theme repeatedly states a basic rhythmic motive,

Example 9.10   Act 1, scene 2, mm. 615–19, closing theme and "fate" rhythm

shown below m. 1 in the example, that Berg uses throughout the opera in many varied forms to suggest the power of fate, much as he had done with the basic rhythm in the Adagio of the Chamber Concerto. The composer marks some but not all occurrences of the motive in the score by the abbreviation "RH~" (*Hauptrhythmus*, main rhythm).

The sonata form is then interrupted when Schön takes the Painter aside and tells him about Lulu's debauched past, hoping that the Painter will control her more strictly. In a state of dejection, the Painter rushes off to an adjacent room and commits suicide. Berg calls the music for this lengthy and dramatically gripping number, which extends to the end of the scene, a "Monoritmica." The entire section is an invention on the fate rhythm, which appears continuously in changing shapes and durations. The music moves with growing intensity through short sections that increase in tempo from the eighth note at 76 to the half note at 76. This fastest tempo is reached at m. 833, where the Painter's body is discovered, and from there the tempos gradually slow to their starting rate at the beginning of the interlude before scene 3. The Painter's death, here presented musically as something brutally inescapable, points to the inexorable fate still awaiting the rest of Lulu's lovers.

Example 9.11 Act 1, scene 2, mm. 680–81, "Monoritmica"

Berg brings great artifice to the Monoritmica. An example is the passage when Schön tells the Painter, "I didn't come here to create a scandal, I came to save you from a scandal" (Example 9.11). Schön's first clause uses the notes of his tone row (beginning on B).[69] The second clause reflects his opposing thought by stating the row in retrograde. (Berg rarely uses tone rows in retrograde except, as here, for a special purpose.)[70] The same reversal is found in the accompaniment where an inversion of the row is stated in the first measure, reversed in the second. All the while the fate rhythm is present, in the woodwinds in m. 680, its retrograde in the following measure. After the Painter rushes off, Schön mutters "That was a piece of work!"—a line repeated by Jack after murdering Lulu. Berg then initiates a series of canons on the fate rhythm—at first in the percussion alone—which brings the Monoritmica to a frantic climax.

Scene 3 is set in the dressing room of a theater where Lulu rests between performances as a dancer. She talks with Alwa while the orchestra is heard from the theater playing a ragtime and an "English" (slow) waltz.[71] Alwa's affection for Lulu now awakens, represented by an expressive theme (Example 9.12) partially based on Alwa's tone row. Variants of this "love theme" return ever more insistently in the two scenes of Act 2, as Alwa's love for Lulu intensifies and as he finds in Lulu's beauty a source for his artistic creativity. When Lulu returns to the stage, Alwa thinks to himself about composing an opera about her, whereupon Berg teasingly quotes music from the opening of *Wozzeck*. The first scene of his imaginary opera will be about the death of the Medical Specialist,

Example 9.12 Act 1, scene 3, mm. 1027–33, Alwa's love theme

Example 9.13 Act 1, scene 3, mm. 1143–47 (Voice and solo Strings only)

the second about the Painter's fate, and he can only ponder where it will lead from there.

Just then an African Prince who has proposed marriage to Lulu enters the dressing room and talks to Alwa about her. "She is the embodiment of worldly happiness," he says. "As a wife she would make a man utterly happy." On these words Berg playfully quotes the wedding march from Wagner's *Lohengrin* (Example 9.13). The role of the Prince is triple cast with that of the Servant in Act 2 and the Marquis in Act 3. In a sketch, Berg notes that the three figures participate in leading women "into the slavery of marriage, the household, or the brothel."[72] Accordingly, Berg assigns the three roles to the same "tenor-buffo" performer and gives them related music consisting of variations on a theme that he labels "chorale." Recall that Berg associated this term with any slow-moving theme used as a cantus firmus. In *Wozzeck*, Act 2, scene 4, he used a chorale of this type to accompany "a harmless parody of a sermon," as he explained in the *Wozzeck* Lecture.[73] Berg may have used the term similarly for the Prince's music, as a parody of the character's affected pronouncements.

A bell signals that something is wrong on stage. Lulu has fainted at the sight of Schön and his fiancée in the audience, and in the sextet that follows the characters sing at cross purposes, as in a traditional comic opera finale: "I won't dance for his bride . . . Do your job and dance . . . Let her rest . . . Return to your dancing." Finally, Lulu agrees to return to the stage, but when she is temporarily left alone with Schön they renew their earlier confrontation. Schön at last realizes that he cannot break with her, and Lulu dictates a letter to his fiancée ending their engagement. During their confrontation the sonata movement from the previous scene is completed by a development section and second reprise. "Now comes the execution," Schön confesses at the end, as the closing theme dramatically returns. The curtain falls on the cadential chord for Act 1, repeated over the fate rhythm.

ACT 2 is set in the palatial residence of Schön, now married to Lulu, who entertains a motley crowd of characters during his absences. The painter Countess Geschwitz arrives to invite Lulu to a ball for lady artists, and as she leaves we hear her motive (Example 9.14). The motive has twelve tones and is freely derived from the basic series by Berg's B5 operation. The figure reappears in differing configurations and is most clearly identified by its three components: a sustained fourth (or fifth), a pentatonic scale (bracketed in the example), and the remaining tones usually presented scalewise.

Lulu is briefly left alone with Schön, and to the music of a lighthearted "cavatina" (Example 9.15) she pleads with him to renew his attention to her. "Couldn't you get away this afternoon," she asks, to music that returns pathetically in Act 3 when she asks Jack the Ripper, "Wouldn't you like to spend the whole night here?" Lulu's admirers steal back into Schön's residence, then hide when Alwa arrives. Alwa believes that he and Lulu are alone, and he returns to the love theme from the theater dressing room (Example 9.12) to express his growing passion. The theme returns in a succession of variants separated by comic interruptions from a love-struck Servant, from those hiding in the room, and from Schön,

Example 9.14 Act 2, scene 1, mm. 37–38, Geschwitz's motive

Example 9.15   Act 2, scene 1, mm. 61–62, Cavatina

who glowers down unseen from a gallery with disgust and jealousy at what he witnesses. Alwa finally embraces Lulu and passionately declares, "I love you!" At this moment (m. 336) Berg brings in the *Tristan* chord—a comic touch as with the *Lohengrin* wedding march, especially ludicrous given Lulu's response to Alwa's sweet words: "I poisoned your mother."

The mood then descends further into a dark farce as the hidden admirers spot Schön brandishing a revolver, whereupon all run for cover. In a large five-strophe aria marked *furioso*, Schön demands that Lulu shoot herself to free him from the misery that his attachment to her has caused. Lulu interrupts him to sing her *Lied der Lulu*—her "great aria of self-awareness and justification," as George Perle has aptly termed it.[74] The importance that Berg attached to Lulu's words in her *Lied*—calling them "a near philosophical argument about man and woman"—has been alluded to earlier. Berg attached equal importance to its music, which is extravagantly beautiful, flamboyant in its virtuosity, complete in its self-confidence. As a tribute to Anton Webern on his fiftieth birthday in 1935, Berg arranged to have Universal Edition publish the *Lied* separately, using Erwin Stein's piano-vocal version.[75]

The music of the *Lied* closely mirrors the text. This consists of five sentences, in each of which Lulu first states an accusation against her, then dismisses the accusation by a self-confident rebuttal. "If men have killed themselves over me," she says in the first sentence, "this does not diminish my value." To capture this syntax, Berg inverts the lines used for the accusations in their rebuttals. This relationship for the first sentence is shown in Example 9.16. The orchestra adds relevant materials: the

Example 9.16   Act 2, scene 2, mm. 491–97, "Lied der Lulu"

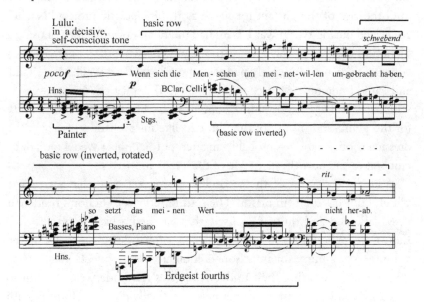

sixteenth-note figure in the first measure refers to the Painter, the one who killed himself over Lulu; the Erdgeist fourths in the second phrase suggest Lulu's primal essence.

Following the *Lied* Schön completes his interrupted aria. As the fate motive grows ever more insistent, Schön is startled and turns his back to Lulu, whereupon she shoots him five times. Lulu pleads with Alwa not to deliver her to the police by singing his own love theme back to him, but as the police pound on the door Alwa pushes her away and opens the door.

The interlude between the two scenes of Act 2 is the midpoint of the opera and its most strictly palindromic passage. Berg planned to have a silent film clip projected during the three-minute interlude whose images would depict aspects of Lulu's arrest, detention, trial, and imprisonment, these images then reversed by parallel events leading to her escape from prison: a revival of her will to live, illness and medical consultation, subsequent isolation, and freedom. In the premiere performance of *Lulu* in its two-act form in Zurich in 1937, a film clip was created and shown, but most observers found the results to be confusing due to the brevity of the interlude. The music itself is a whirlwind ostinato made from the tone rows of several characters, the Erdgeist fourths, and the fate rhythm. The music comes to a pause in the middle at m. 687, then runs in an exact retrograde until the rise of the curtain for scene 2. In his operatic project "Nacht," conceived during World War I, Berg had the highly original idea of using a silent film clip, but by the later 1920s the presence of film in opera had become familiar, used in widely performed works by Kurt Weill, Max Brand, and Paul Hindemith. All such operas were in the spirit of *Zeitoper*—works with banal and satiric portraits of contemporary life. Berg had little affinity for this genre, and his use of the film clip, like his evocation of jazz in the dressing room scene, was probably an attempt to connect Wedekind's difficult text to the new theatric style of the 1920s and 1930s.

With the opening of the second scene of Act 2, a year has passed, which Lulu has spent in prison. The setting returns to Schön's residence, now darkened and dusty. Geschwitz has hatched a bizarre plan to free Lulu from prison, one that reveals her sacrificial devotion to Lulu. She volunteers as a nurse for imprisoned cholera victims, infects herself with the disease by wearing their underwear, gives the underwear to Lulu so that they will both contract the disease, and finally changes clothing with Lulu in their isolation cell so that Lulu can escape. The plan succeeds and Schigolch returns with Lulu to rejoin Alwa and the Athlete.

Following digressions that fill in the plot, Lulu renews her seduction of Alwa, drawing him toward her on a sofa and kissing him passionately. Their twisted love affair intensifies, now to the end of the act with no interruption. The music is a great duet and aria that begins at m. 1059 with Alwa's love theme, as he declares that Lulu's beauty will inspire a dithyramb from him. In an ecstatic variant of the love theme (Example 9.17), as often in the opera, the text refuses to cooperate with the music. "If it were not for your two childlike eyes," Alwa declares, "I should say you were the most designing of whores and bitches who ever inveigled a man to his doom." Lulu enters on a high D to say that she might hope to be just that.

The concluding passage of the love music is an aria for Alwa, marked "Hymn" by Berg. It is a musical high point in the entire work and one of the most brilliant and demanding tenor passages in the entire operatic literature, requiring the strength of a Siegfried with the dramatic complexity of an Otello. Berg probably saw in the Hymn a counterpart to the *Lied der Lulu*: in his correspondence with Universal Edition, he expressed the hope that the Hymn would be published separately, just as was done for the *Lied* in 1935.[76]

Example 9.17   Act 2, scene 2, mm. 1076–87

Alwa's text in his aria is graphically sexual as he again finds artistic inspiration in Eros, albeit in a comically pedantic way. To a distant variant of the love theme, he declares that Lulu's body beneath her dress has musical form. Her ankles are a grazioso, her charming curves a cantabile, her knees a misterioso. Rising to a high C he declares that his lust for her body is an andante. Her two slender rivals (her thighs) nestle quietly together until she awakens and flings them wildly apart. The aria ends somberly over the Erdgeist fourths motive and diminished chords that began the Prologue: "Isn't that the sofa on which your father bled to death?," Lulu asks, in the most devastating of non-sequiturs. "Be quiet! Be quiet!," shouts Alwa as the curtain descends.

ACT 3. In a letter to Webern of 15 September 1933, Berg reported that he had completed Act 2 of the opera and was now setting forth on the most difficult part: "glitter and downfall." The terms refer to the two contrasting scenes of Act 3, the first in a garish salon in Paris and then in a shabby garret in London. Alwa and Lulu have escaped to Paris where Lulu lives as "Countess Adelaide d'Oubra," and in the first scene they entertain a sleazy demimonde: a pedophile Banker, a procurer (the Marquis), and a venal Journalist, among others. Countess Geschwitz, the Athlete, and Schigolch are still on hand. But Alwa's inherited money has now run out except for investments in shares of the Jungfrau Railroad, which have been purchased from the Banker and soon prove worthless.

As the party goes off to play baccarat, the Marquis confronts Lulu, threatening to denounce her to the police unless she agrees to be sold to an Egyptian brothel. She refuses in terms both ambiguous and

Example 9.18   Frank Wedekind, "Konfession" (melody only)

provocative: "I can't sell the one thing that has always been my own."
Their duet consists of twelve "concertante chorale variations" in which
a slow-moving chorale melody supports mincing figures in the solo violin. The variations are soon interrupted by an intermezzo, "The Song
of the Procurer." Here the Marquis describes his work to Lulu in the
most benevolent of terms: he conscientiously places pleasure-loving girls
in situations that will best suit them. He is accompanied by a melody
in the saxophone playing Wedekind's own rough-hewn cabaret tune
"Confession," whose music is shown in Example 9.18, its text as follows.[77]

Freudig schwör'ich es mit jedem Schwure	Joyfully I swear an oath
Vor der Allmacht, die mich züchtigen kann:	before the Almighty, who could strike me down:
Wie viel lieber wär'ich eine Hure	I'd rather be a whore
Als an Ruhm and Glück der reichste Mann!	than in fame and fortune the richest man!
Welt, in mir ging dir ein Weib verloren,	O world, you lost a woman in me,
Abgeklärt und jeder Hemmung bar.	worldly-wise and free from inhibitions.
Wer war für den Liebesmarkt geboren	Who was born for the love market
So wie ich dafür geboren war?	so well as I?

Recall that the text of Wedekind's song had been enthusiastically praised by Kraus in his 1905 lecture on *Pandora's Box*, where Kraus found in its frankness an element of idealism. Berg uses the tune to signal the Marquis's true intentions and, when the tune returns in the final scene, to mark Lulu's progressive descent into squalor, prostitution, and ultimate annihilation.

It is likely that the idea of using a melody by Wedekind in the opera came primarily from Otto Falckenberg's 1928 staging of the spoken play. Falckenberg had characters from the play sing Wedekind's songs during the interludes between acts, their texts commenting on the progress of the play. In Berg's adaptation, the tune returns in variations that form the interlude between the two scenes of Act 3, and these variations return sporadically in the final scene. Following the Marquis's song, Lulu responds by rejecting work in a brothel. She now looks only for the right man, she says, lines that are set to fragments from the *Lied der Lulu*.

The partying in the salon reaches a fevered pitch as everyone wins at the gambling table and the Jungfrau shares continue to climb. But Lulu is now being blackmailed also by the Athlete, and she hatches a plot to be rid of him. She asks Geschwitz to spend the night with him, during which Schigolch will arrive and murder him. For Lulu's sake Geschwitz agrees. Word then arrives that the Jungfrau shares are worthless, and all depart sullenly amid bitter accusations. After exchanging her clothing with a servant, Lulu escapes just as the police arrive and the curtain falls.

In a letter to Schoenberg of January 1934, Berg described the interlude between the two scenes in Act 3 as a "final descent from the false luxury of the former scene to the squalid misery of the latter." Berg continues: "From the false luxury cloaked in an 'orchestrion' scoring to *poly*tonality, to so-called *a*tonality, to *12 tone* variations, finally to the genuinely miserable sound of the tune played by a barrel organ off-stage."[78] Reich describes the interlude similarly as a depiction of Lulu's *via dolorosa*, from the Parisian glitter "so foreign to Lulu's true nature" to the "scene of her deepest debasement."[79] His analysis, approved by Berg, again follows Kraus by portraying Lulu as an innocent victim.

The form of the variations in the interlude is highly unusual. The simple tune itself is placed not at the beginning but at the end, following the rise of the curtain for scene 2. The interlude begins straightaway with the first of four variations, each with a strongly differing

Example 9.19 Act 3, scene 2, mm. 693–98, variation 1 (Horns only)

harmonization and orchestral sound. The tune in the first variation is stated boldly, taken in unison by four horns (Example 9.19). The orchestral lines that harmonize this version of the theme are limited at first to white notes, conforming to the C major, then A minor tonality of the tune. As he told Schoenberg, Berg intended the orchestration of this variation to imitate the sound of a mechanical orchestra, or "orchestrion," which Berg suggests by a sameness of rhythm and lines moving mechanically in thirds.[80]

In the second variation the tune is stated bitonally, in canon at the tritone, with the orchestra similarly divided by the use of diatonic pitch collections a tritone apart. Here the scoring temporarily lightens. The theme is transposed to A major, then F♯ minor in the third variation, marked *funèbre*, where it is harmonized mainly by fourth chords and given a ponderous orchestral sound. The mood darkens further in the fourth variation, with the theme lowered to F♯ major, then D♯ minor. It is divided between Violin II and Cello, both playing pizzicato, and scarcely audible amid shrill outcries in the brass. As the curtain rises, the dreary and impoverished tune emerges in its most unadorned form, played offstage by a barrel organ while Alwa and Schigolch await Lulu's first customer in their dimly lit attic.[81]

Listeners to the final scene of *Lulu* can readily agree with Douglas Jarman's assessment: "The music to which Berg set his closing scene— a music that embodies all his humanity and sympathy for the poor creatures who people his opera—must be amongst the most purely beautiful written by any composer this century."[82] The music traces the final steps in Lulu's relentless descent into darkness that began in the film music interlude at the center of the opera. Much of the music is brought back from Acts 1 and 2: from the sonata's stirring closing theme in which Schön and Lulu confess their hopelessly doomed love, from the canzonetta sung by Lulu over the Painter's body, from Alwa's love music for

Lulu, and from Lulu's cavatina in which she pleads with Schön for his attention. These recapitulations add depth to the drama and reinforce the role of fate and the inevitability of a tragic outcome.

In London, Lulu has become a street walker who intends to bring men to her shabby apartment. The first customer is an eccentric and speechless Professor, double cast as the Medical Specialist. When they retire to an inner room, Alwa and Schigolch ransack his overcoat looking for money, only to find a booklet titled *Exhortations for Pious Pilgrims and Others Who Wish to Become Such*. After his departure, Geschwitz arrives carrying Lulu's portrait, the sight of which infuriates Lulu but reminds Alwa of his earlier passion. A lengthy quartet follows, dominated by Alwa's aria-like praise for Lulu's former beauty.

Lulu soon arrives with her next customer, a Negro, who slays Alwa with a blow to the head when he tries to defend Lulu from him. As the series of bizarre and deadly actions continues to pile up, Lulu again returns to the street, Schigolch leaves (which allows him the mythic outcome of being the only survivor of Lulu's motley entourage), and Countess Geschwitz is left alone in the apartment. The remainder of the opera focuses primarily on her and her desperate and doomed attachment to Lulu. The tempo relentlessly slows—sostenuto, andante, adagio, lento, grave—as fate tightens its grip. At first Geschwitz contemplates suicide, but realizing that this would elicit no pity from Lulu she instead pleads with Lulu's portrait for kindness. Geschwitz's motives now take on a haunted quality with their pentatonic element stated darkly in parallel fifths. Gazing at Lulu's portrait, Geschwitz cries out, "Let me once more, for the last time, speak to your heart!" With this appeal Geschwitz's earlier motive—the sustained fifth, pentatonic segment, and remainder—is transformed into an expressive melodic shape (Example 9.20).

Example 9.20 Act 3, scene 2, mm. 1174–76, Geschwitz's melody

Example 9.21   Act 3, scene 2, mm. 1293–95

Jack and Lulu now arrive. As Lulu tries to arouse Jack's interest, passages from Schön's earlier music return, forging the link between the two characters. Jack follows Lulu into an inner room, and Geschwitz continues her monologue, chanting in a dreamlike manner about a return to Germany to study law and work for women's rights. The music slows and dwindles to nothing, when from within Lulu cries out in a frantic crescendo, "No . . . No . . . No . . . No!" to the fate rhythm and the Erdgeist fourths motive. A blood-curdling shriek—Lulu's scream of death—pierces the tense silence above a twelve-note chord in the full orchestra (Example 9.21). Jack bursts forth from the inner room to music of utter tumult, stabs Geschwitz, then nonchalantly washes his hands to a grotesque return of the circus music of the Prologue. He leaves with a dismissive wave of the hand.

The final twelve-measure *Grave* is Geschwitz's threnody on the melody in Example 9.20, in which she sings of her love for Lulu with the greatest lyric beauty—despite the chaos and horror of this dramatic moment. "I am with you and remain so to eternity." Berg brings the opera to an end (Example 9.22) by quoting the motive heard following the death of Marie in *Wozzeck*, where empty fifths A–E overlay an ostinato tritone B–F. Berg adds multiple, overlapping statements of the fate rhythm, leaving the listener at this poignant moment to ponder the events that brought down Lulu and also Marie: the power of female sexuality, the inescapability of fate, and the ambiguous notions of innocence and sacrifice.

Example 9.22 Act 3, scene 2, mm. 1325–26, end of the opera

Prospects for Staging

To the very end of his life, Berg remained optimistic that *Lulu* could be performed as soon as its orchestration and revision were completed, despite the nearly total absence of his music on programs in Germany and Austria. In mid-March 1934 he sent Erich Kleiber the complete libretto of the work, which was then circulated to officials at the Berlin Staatsoper, including the *Reichsdramaturg* Rainer Schlösser, Wilhelm Furtwängler—recently appointed its Music Director—and Hans Tietjen, the general intendant of all Prussian theaters. Prompted by Heinsheimer, Berg in April wrote to Tietjen (with a copy of his letter sent to Furtwängler) to speak to the appropriateness of his music in the new German Reich:

> Since the Berlin Staatsoper is now considering the premiere of my new opera (whose composition is now completed and whose score will be ready in the fall) this prompts me to bring up an issue that has long been near and dear to me, all the more so now that my friend Kleiber has "turned in" the libretto. This is the complete exclusion of my works from German theaters and concert programs, which for me is a serious grievance. For my whole life I have considered myself to be a German composer, and I have never been taken for anything else. . . . I am justified in calling Germany my musical homeland.[83]

Berg stressed his German heritage and the German character of his music, but in the case of *Lulu* he was arguing the wrong issue. Berg's music by itself might have been acceptable in the Germany of 1934, much as was that of other modernists such as Paul Hindemith. The opera *Der Kreiderkreis* (The Chalk Circle) by Alexander Zemlinsky (who had many Jews among his ancestors) was staged with considerable success at

Berlin's Staatsoper and elsewhere in the Deutsches Reich in 1934. The sticking point with *Lulu* was its text, which was a prime example of the artistic "degeneracy" that was under attack by the Nazis. Even Kleiber, who earlier was enthusiastic about Berg's choice of the Lulu plays, was disturbed when he read Berg's final version. He wrote to Berg:

> I don't know what will happen with the opera in Berlin. I must say that after reading through the libretto I foresee major obstacles in the way, and I hope you won't take it amiss when I tell you that I got goose bumps when I read some passages in this final version. At first I couldn't imagine how you could have composed them. . . . I had foreseen the libretto being much milder when the two parts were put together. But there are secret paths on which we non-creators do not go, and you know best why you had to compose the text as you did. We know that you will have much that is powerful to say to us: of that we are sure and we await it anxiously.[84]

In May Berg heard directly from Furtwängler, who calmly explained that the problem with *Lulu* was not Berg's race, nationality, or allegiance to German culture, instead, its libretto. *Lulu* could not be performed in Germany in the near future:

> It is not necessary for you to identify yourself as a German composer. I know you and have long known your music, and I would have no qualms about accepting *Lulu* were it not for a text that seems to me *for now* quite impossible given the mood in the public sphere here in Germany. This has nothing to do with matters of race—Wedekind was also "Aryan"—but solely that the *Erdgeist* tragedy in the Germany of today absolutely cannot be performed, at least not with any outlook for success. Personally, I regret this all the more since we here in Berlin will for now lose out on one of the few "events" in contemporary music. That you are often described as a Jewish composer— something that you are not—should not surprise you. It comes from your close relationship with Arnold Schoenberg, whose most prominent student you now are. I say this only in passing.[85]

Berg was curiously unable ever to articulate why the opera's text should be accepted, why it was the "deeply moralistic play" that he had described to Erich Kleiber.[86] Karl Kraus had declared that the Lulu plays were works of idealism, and Berg apparently believed that the truth of this interpretation would eventually become apparent.

Berg long intended to dedicate *Lulu* to Kraus. "I dedicate only where my heart dictates," he wrote Willi Reich, "in this long-planned case for the sixtieth birthday of Karl Kraus."[87] But it was also Schoenberg's sixtieth birthday in 1934, and Berg had dedicated a major work to his teacher on his fortieth and fiftieth birthdays. Although Berg's personal estrangement from Schoenberg by this time was pronounced, he could not bring himself to ignore his former teacher—at least not in such an obvious way. Berg wrote to Schoenberg on 28 August 1934 to announce that *Lulu* would be dedicated to him, also sending an autograph fair copy of its Prologue and the opening measures of Act 1.[88] In his letter, Berg's thoughts remained on the German character of the opera, the same that he expressed in his letter of 20 April to Hans Tietjen. "The German world," Berg writes to Schoenberg, "is to recognize in the dedication that this German opera—like all my works—is indigenous to the realm of that most German of music, which will bear your name for all eternity."[89]

That Berg would stress for Schoenberg the German quality of *Lulu* had more than a touch of irony. Recall Schoenberg's bitter rejection of internationalism in music following World War I, when he declared, "When I think of music, I think only of German music!" Surely, Berg realized that declaring oneself "German" in 1934 had taken on a different meaning, a code word that one was Aryan and not Jewish. Schoenberg was very alert to such distinctions, and he waited more than four months to respond to Berg's message. Berg continued to stress his allegiance to German music in a complex acrostic poem on the words "Glaube, Hoffnung und Liebe" (Faith, hope, and love) that he wrote for the festschrift honoring Schoenberg's sixtieth birthday.[90] The poem begins: "Faith, hope—and love *for German music*." Berg then adds that he also has faith, hope, and love for his old teacher.

We can well imagine that Furtwängler's letter was another disheartening blow for Berg. His thoughts must have gone back to what he had written to Morgenstern in 1927, that "after years of work I might have something that could only be performed for an invited public."[91] These fears had now apparently come true. Helene urged Berg to put the orchestration of *Lulu* temporarily aside and turn to other projects. He had been offered a $1,000 commission to write a string quartet for the Library of Congress in America, and he was also tempted by the idea of writing film music.[92] But instead Berg stayed with *Lulu* and contemplated alternative ways that the opera might be brought to the stage.

Symphonic Pieces from the Opera Lulu

The *Symphonic Pieces* that Berg completed in July 1934 to promote an interest in staging the opera proved to be a great success, the last that Berg would live to enjoy. The work had more than ten performances in Europe and America during the last year of Berg's life. Erich Kleiber conducted the premiere at the Berlin Staatsoper on 30 November 1934 after receiving assurances from Hermann Göring that the performance would not be disrupted.[93] The Boston Symphony Orchestra under Serge Koussevitzky gave the American premiere on 22 March 1935. Judging from reviews and reports forwarded to Berg (who did not attend the premiere), Kleiber's Berlin concert was an overwhelming success. The Staatsoper was sold out, and the music was embraced by the audience with only minimal resistance. H.H. Stuckenschmidt wrote for the *B.Z. am Mittag* (Berlin) that "the acclamation was long, spontaneous, and heartfelt." The reviewer for the *Prager Tagblatt* agreed: "Alban Berg's *Lulu* suite, which had its premiere performance in the concert of the orchestra of the Staatsoper under Kleiber, had a strong and indisputable success, which is saying something for Berlin at present."

Despite this success and the high esteem that he enjoyed in Berlin, Kleiber resigned his position at the Staatsoper four days following the concert. He then began the career of a traveling maestro, settled in Argentina in 1936, and conducted orchestras all over the world. He remained a lifelong champion of Berg's music, especially the *Symphonic Pieces*.

There are five movements in the *Symphonic Pieces*:

1. Rondo
2. Ostinato
3. *Lied der Lulu*
4. Variations
5. Adagio

The first movement, Rondo, contains music from two scenes of Act 2 that concern Alwa's growing passion for Lulu. The second movement, Ostinato, is the strictly palindromic film music interlude from the center of the opera in Act 2. Berg places the *Lied der Lulu*, the only movement with obbligato voice, at the center of the *Symphonic Pieces*, a position that underscored its importance to him. The fourth movement, Variations on Wedekind's cabaret song, comes from the interlude between the two scenes of Act 3. The Adagio finale consists of excerpts from the last scene of the opera, ending with Geschwitz's threnody, "Lulu, my angel. Let me see you once again. I am near you—stay with me to eternity!" Berg wanted these words to be sung by the vocalist who had sung the *Lied der Lulu*, although they are shown as optional in the score published by Universal Edition in 1935.[94]

The *Symphonic Pieces* are among Berg's very greatest works. Far from being a mere advertisement for the opera, they form a deeply moving and coherent whole that again shows Berg's profound command of the orchestra and its expressive capacity. The composer's ideas about the *Symphonic Pieces* are most fully recorded in program notes written by Willi Reich for the Berlin premiere in November 1934, notes which Berg himself helped to write and carefully reviewed.[95] Judging from these sources Berg was of two minds about the expressive and formal dimensions of the work. On one hand, he and Reich emphasized that the pieces form a genuine symphony in five movements, a work of absolute music that needs no reference to the opera or its text to be fully understood. In an interview for Radio Vienna on 10 December 1935, the day before the Vienna premiere of the work by the Vienna Symphony Orchestra, Berg explained:

> The introductory Rondo corresponds to the extended first movement of a symphony, the three brief middle movements (film music, song, and variations) are character episodes, as are often found in symphonic works, and the expansive Adagio serves as an appropriately broad finale. This formal shape may be the reason why I readily called my work "Symphony" rather than "Suite."[96]

This absolutist viewpoint was supported by Heinsheimer, who wanted to distance the *Symphonic Pieces* from the opera and its controversial text.

At the same time, Berg and Reich portray the *Symphonic Pieces* as intensely programmatic music whose form and expressive content are generated primarily by topics from the opera. This programmaticism is at its most pronounced in the first and fifth movements and also present in the interlude-like inner movements. The first movement, for example, is not held together by rondo form, which is present only in the most general sense in varied recurrences of the theme shown in Example 9.12. Except for a few fragments the theme disappears entirely in the concluding Hymn, which occupies the last quarter of the movement. The form of the music is governed instead by the absent text, in which Alwa expresses affection, then passion for Lulu and finally acknowledges her power to inspire his creative spirit. Reich writes about the Rondo: "It contains the tender and passionate love scenes of the opera and might well bear the motto, 'how the artist views Lulu.' Berg himself once said that this is how she must be seen if one is to understand why, despite all the horrors that happen because of her, she is still so *beloved*."[97]

The middle three movements are interludes. The palindromic Ostinato movement begins with a tumult of sound that rises to a climax near the middle, then recedes to a fermata at the midpoint, whereupon the music runs in reverse. In the retrograde the brass and strings are muted, symbolizing the beginning of a long transition from light to darkness. The *Lied der Lulu* is a lyric, virtuosic study for the soprano voice, its compass ranging from middle C to D above the staff. The fourth movement is the variations form already described whose unusual form can only be understood in terms of the underlying program. Reich and Berg describe the movement not by reference to classical variations procedures but as a depiction of Lulu's descent from the cheap glitter of Paris to the utter degradation of London.

The Adagio finale of the *Symphonic Pieces* must be counted among the most emotionally laden orchestral character pieces of the twentieth century. It is put together from sections of the opera near the end of Act 3, arranged into a ternary pattern. Programmatically, the Adagio depicts the tragic demise of Countess Geschwitz in the London garret, beginning in the first section with her desperate thoughts of suicide and pathetic appeals to Lulu. Her musical symbols abound, finally emerging in the expressive rather than scalar thematic shape shown in Example 9.20. The middle section of the Adagio comes from the interlude between scenes 2 and 3 of Act 1 (music that is repeated with voices added in Act 3 scene 2). This is the fantasy on the gripping closing theme of the sonata first heard in Act 1, with its powerful late romantic harmony (this theme is shown in Example 9.10). In Act 1 the closing theme depicts the twisted love that connects Schön and Lulu, and here it suggests Geschwitz's hopeless infatuation with Lulu. The music rises to a passionate climax, then subsides ever more in the presence of the fate rhythm. The third section begins with the orchestra's outburst evoking Lulu's death cry and continues from there to the end of the opera, including Countess Geschwitz's threnody in the final twelve bars.

In light of the pathos and beauty of Geschwitz's music, it is curious that Berg confessed to Helene that he had respect but little fondness for the character.[98] George Perle has interpreted Berg's statement as a deception to disguise his personal expression of a hopeless love for Hanna Fuchs, which Perle finds embedded in the conclusion of the opera. An alternative understanding is that Berg was simply telling the truth: Geschwitz did not appeal to him. But her music at the end of the opera—as at the end of the *Symphonic Pieces*—may have become a vehicle by which he could speak directly to the listener. In this interpretation we hear in the closing measures the composer's voice, his "*Lulu* confession," a parallel to the orchestral Epilogue near the end of *Wozzeck*. In *Lulu* the composer does not self-consciously step outside the theatrical action as he did in the *Wozzeck* Epilogue, but he instead inserts himself surreptitiously into it. In this way Geschwitz's music becomes the composer's "appeal to the audience" as Berg designed his *Wozzeck* Epilogue to be. It is a plea for compassion for the desperate failure of humanity that we have just witnessed as well as a lament on the unattainability of beauty. As Berg indicated to Kleiber, *Lulu*'s true meaning could not be readily expressed in words. Rather, it would be fully revealed only through music.

★★★

Berg wrestled with *Lulu* for seven years, and the difficulties posed by the opera did not end with the completion of the *Particell* in May 1934 nor even with the composer's death in the following year. Where and when the opera could be performed, whether it would be accepted by the public in the political atmosphere of the 1930s, whether the orchestration would be completed, and if so, by whom—these questions remained unresolved for many years. Helene Berg introduced an additional level of complexity to the opera's history when she asserted, shortly after Berg died, that higher powers had decreed by Berg's death that *Lulu* was "complete" as a two-act work. We turn to these issues in the following chapters.

Berg's Final Year, 1935

OR ALBAN AND HELENE BERG IN 1935 THE OUTLOOK FOR THE FUTURE
was mixed. A bright note was struck by the recent success in Berlin
of the Lulu *Symphonic Pieces*. Their enthusiastic reception reinforced Berg's
belief that his music could be performed in Nazi Germany—if he could
only stop the repeated statements that he was a Jew. Berg was still optimistic for a staging of *Lulu* during the 1935–36 season—in Prague or elsewhere if not in Berlin. But his finances were increasingly desperate and
his health worse than ever, with repeated asthma attacks, serious flu-like
episodes, and eruptions of boils over his body. In November 1934 Berg
suffered a heart incident at the Waldhaus. He described it to Schoenberg
as "a disturbance of the heart nerves"—later using the term "heart attack" (*Herz-Attacke*)—which was accompanied by persisting chest pain.
His physician in Velden, Dr. Gottfried Engstler, gave him medications to
strengthen and calm the heart and told him to rest and to abstain completely from coffee, tea, alcohol, and nicotine.[1]

A happy moment for Berg was his fiftieth birthday, on 9 February
1935, when his achievements in music were celebrated in concerts,
tributes, and greetings. Hermann Watznauer sent Berg an elaborately
constructed album with photos, handmade illustrations and rhymed
text commemorating their thirty-eight years of friendship.[2] From
California Schoenberg sent a gramophone recording of his spoken
greeting, with a hint that reconciliation among himself, Berg, and
Webern was in order:

Berg. Bryan Simms and Charlotte Erwin, Oxford University Press (2021). © Oxford University Press.
DOI: 10.1093/oso/9780190931445.003.0011

For your fiftieth birthday I wish you continued strength and health, necessities for our struggle. You have been the only one in our cause who has achieved general recognition. It is our common cause. We three will stand and fall together, and over and above our sympathy, friendship, and recognition of the true and the good, our common destiny will by itself insure our mutual fidelity.[3]

Example 10.1 Arnold Schoenberg, Canon for Berg's fiftieth birthday, opening

May I come in? You still ask? Greetings! Bring in greetings, honor and joy!

Schoenberg also sent a witty four-part canon as a birthday tribute (Example 10.1). The canon is based on motives from *Lulu*—the Erdgeist fourths in the bass and the opening motives from Act 1, scene 1, in the canonic voices. Schoenberg had found these materials in the score of the Prologue to *Lulu* that Berg had recently sent him along with the dedication of the opera. Schoenberg's text for the canon answers Berg's question from his letter that accompanied the score. Berg wrote: "I know that you would answer my question 'May I come in?' (which are also Alwa's first words as the curtain rises on the opera *Lulu*): 'Come right on in!'"[4]

Vienna's Verein für Neue Musik organized an all-Berg chamber concert at the Musikverein on the afternoon of Berg's birthday. Rita Kurzmann played the Piano Sonata, Julia Nessy sang a selection of songs, and the Galimir Quartet played the Lyric Suite, among other pieces on the program. Heinrich Jalowetz offered the following encomium before the event:

> Beyond the abundance of music of the most personal nature, full of life, warmth and artful devices, we must thank Alban Berg for the example he has set for an artist's existence, one that is unspoiled by commerce—nearly an anachronism in the present day—and has thus about it the improbability of a romantic phenomenon. We thank him for the exhilarating proof that the path for art and the artist is still towards the realization of the unexpected and unforeseen. At a time when most artists expend their effort for themselves and against others, with him there comes to life a rare image of the pure artist, whose achievement is solely the product of his own essence.[5]

Jalowetz's characterization of Berg as the pure artist, unconcerned with material advancement or profit, ironically came at a time when his financial condition had reached a point of emergency, so dire that it threatened his very life.

Berg's Financial Crisis

Berg's financial plight during his final three years is a subject often addressed in the literature on the composer. He could not complete *Lulu* because of the need to accept commissions, he could not afford adequate medical care despite the decline in his health and strength, he was forced to sell his compositional manuscripts to stay afloat, and he fell ever deeper in debt to his publisher. His financial situation deteriorated relentlessly, and shortly before his death he told Willi Reich that he could survive only one or two more months. He meant "survive" financially, although his words were darkly prophetic.[6] How was it that a composer of international fame had come to such a deplorable state?

The immediate causes are again well known. From early 1933 with Hitler's consolidation of power almost all performances of Berg's works in Germany were curtailed. Other factors abetted his slide into poverty, especially the economic instability that plagued Austria in the interwar years and the international depression of the 1930s. An even more significant factor in Berg's material distress, often overlooked in studies to date, was his complex relationship with both the Berg and Nahowski families that proved to be a burden financially and a distraction artistically. Berg was exceptionally loyal to and generous with his own family and the Nahowskis, although a dispute over money finally produced an intensely embittered break with his siblings Charly and Smaragda.

The decline of family finances had a long history. Earlier, both families were reasonably wealthy, with sizeable investments in real estate and substantial savings. Family money allowed Alban and Helene to live a comfortable existence despite his modest income, even during the postwar period of deprivation and runaway inflation. Adorno commented on their genteel lifestyle: "There are people who have little but leave no impression of poverty," Adorno wrote. "Berg was one of the latter, probably more so than anyone I have ever met. . . . [He and Helene] always maintained an aristocratic atmosphere—if this term is correctly understood. This came, first of all, as a matter of course for those accustomed to the good life, which they both were."[7]

Berg's mother, Johanna, controlled the family purse, which was amply filled by her inheritances. She judiciously distributed this money to her children according to her sense of fairness and their needs. The men, Charly and Alban, needed less, although Alban got a bonus as a musician. Smaragda was in greatest need, and she received the most from her mother. The mutual reliance and sharing of assets by both families gradually descended into bickering and strident accusations, and these increased following the deaths of Johanna Berg in 1926 and Anna Nahowski in 1931. The impoverishment of Helene's sister Anna Lebert following the early death in 1929 of her husband, Artur, imposed an extra burden on the Bergs, who for years gave her a small monthly stipend. (Helene continued this stipend after Berg's death.) Helene's brother, Frank, became an onus on the Bergs as his mental competency worsened. He lived with his mother in Maxingstrasse until 1930, but after a period confined to a mental institution following his self-mutilation (finger amputation) he was returned to the care of his family. In her will of May 1929, Anna Nahowski named Berg the *Kurator* (guardian) of her son after her death, and Berg was legally appointed in this capacity on 24 December 1931.[8] Alban and Helene then became responsible for Frank, and they administered his affairs and contributed financially to his support.

The Maxingstrasse house, Helene Berg's birthplace, symbolized the Nahowski family's rise to the upper-middle class through its historic association with Emperor Franz Joseph's patronage. Its sale took place just prior to Anna Nahowski's death and was planned to provide additional resources for the support of Frank. It was purchased in January 1931 by Martha Schidrowitz, the sister of Erika Stiedry-Wagner, long an acquaintance of the Bergs. Martha Schidrowitz and her husband, Leo, soon defaulted on mortgage payments, leaving Berg with the complex task of initiating legal proceedings. Eventually the house passed into other hands, and the expected income from the sale was received.

As Berg's own financial condition declined, he found himself in a bitter confrontation with his brother Charly. After Charly Berg left the Borgfeldt Co. his business affairs did not prosper and, on the supposition that Alban was financially sound, in October 1932 he sent his son, Erich, with a letter asking for a loan for his father. The figure is not recorded by Charly, but it was over 6,000 schillings.[9] Charly insisted there was no risk, and the loan was scheduled to be paid back in one year. On the back of Charly's letter Helene later wrote: "Charly borrowed our savings, and when Alban no longer had income from his works (Hitler was on the rise), paid nothing back, not even the smallest part."[10] When Alban asked for repayment some months after the term had expired, Charly informed him that he was simply unable to pay.[11]

Charly was not the only person to ask Alban for a loan in these years. In the summer of 1934 Smaragda's companion, May Keller, asked him for 1,000 schillings to help run the Küb house, purchased in 1920 by Johanna Berg for Smaragda's use, as a pension. He declined. Since Smaragda was the titular owner of the house, May owed her income from the pension (they had by now split up), which Keller could not pay with any regularity. Consequently during this summer Smaragda too asked Alban for financial help. From this point on Alban was giving Smaragda between 50 and 100 schillings monthly. May absconded to Switzerland, fleeing debt. The Küb house was sold, but it was heavily mortgaged and did not yield much profit.[12] Smaragda reported to Alban that they were swindled on the sale.[13]

The financial struggle with his family came to a head for Berg in late summer of 1934. Given his ownership of a car and a house in the country, it appeared obvious to Smaragda's friends in Vienna that Alban was doing well financially and should assist his sister more generously. Charly jumped on this bandwagon. He even warned Alban of the rising tide of opinion against him. "I'm against gossip," he wrote disingenuously, "but Smaragda says that all your friends are upset that you don't help [her] sufficiently." He continued:

> It is not true (you realize I'm of course not giving my own opinion here) that you are in trouble, on the contrary, you are in excellent financial shape, and it is your duty, after you've been such a part of everything, to apply your energies to helping your sister. These opinions come partly from your friends in connection to Smaragda, partly presumably from May, who, as I said to you, has openly threatened that she will revenge herself on you, she knows enough about you, etc.[14]

The "friends" mentioned by Charly include Erika Stiedry-Wagner, Hilda Merinsky-Steuermann, and Eugenie Schwarzwald, along with May Keller. It is unclear what May's threats may have amounted to; they were perhaps in connection with Alban's romantic dalliances.

Charly's insinuating letter called forth a long, detailed riposte from Alban, addressed sarcastically to "All those who don't care to understand that—despite auto and villa—one can be in bad financial circumstance."[15] Clearly the automobile and the Waldhaus were the deciding factors in Charly's mind and played a role in the thinking of others that Alban was financially well-off. In fact, Alban had purchased both with his American money—Charly had an equal share of those funds—and Helene was half-owner of the Waldhaus, while Alban's share was paid through a mortgage. In his letter Alban takes great pains to explain and justify both possessions as essential to his career as a composer and to prove further that he and Helene exercise extreme frugality. The letter concludes with a statement of Berg's income sources, which at this time were limited almost entirely to his advance from Universal Edition of 500 schillings monthly. Berg later came back to his carbon copy of the letter to Charly to enter corrections about the sum from Universal, which was reduced in the spring of 1935 to 250 schillings a month, then to nothing beginning in November.[16]

Thus Smaragda became the catalyst for the final break between the Berg brothers. In this last year and a half of Berg's life, her impoverishment only got worse, and her friends thought she might commit suicide. Erika Stiedry-Wagner wrote an impassioned letter to Alban, stating that all of their friends are "astonished" that the two brothers can treat their only sister in such a way. Stiedry wishes to know why a great artist cannot also be a warm-hearted human being.[17] Stung by the moral accusations of Stiedry's letter, Berg replied at length, and he included with his letter a copy of his "To all those . . ." screed to Charly from the previous year to provide further explanation of his financial position. He concludes:

> If you, dear lady, would weigh these circumstances, for which I am truly not
> to blame, and consider that in the time when I *could* help, I gave my brother
> a small capital [loan] without batting an eyelash, thus have *proved* that I can
> be a warm-hearted human being (and my sister is not less close to me than
> my brother). . . . When you consider all of this, you will perhaps see that my
> conduct does not justify my fellow human beings being "astonished," rather
> that the conduct of others who have brought me to this situation could be
> the cause of this moral outrage.[18]

In his correspondence with Erika Stiedry and with his siblings, Berg was open about, in fact stressed, the decline in his monthly advance from Universal Edition, which by the time of his letter to Stiedry had fallen to 250 schillings a month, and was soon scheduled to terminate completely. In his flush days, Berg was receiving payments of 1,000 schillings monthly from Universal, but this sum was reduced in 1933 to 700 and in the next year to 500. As a champion of modern music, Universal was directly affected by the reduction in performances in Germany, so much so that the firm faced bankruptcy. Berg's stipend was progressively reduced, and as royalties and fees from performances disappeared, his advance turned into debt.

Berg was well acquainted with the management of Universal, and he had a special advocate in the person of Yella Hertzka. She was the widow of Emil Hertzka, the director of Universal Edition from 1907 to his death in 1932. Yella Hertzka was a regular benefactor of contemporary music, and she had previously assisted Berg as well as Schoenberg and Ernst Krenek. After her husband's death, Frau Hertzka, as a major stockholder in the firm, continued to have influence at Universal, and Berg turned to her in October 1933 with an emotional appeal for a continuation of his stipend, which had been suspended. Berg estimated that *Lulu* would be completed in six to nine months, and he requested a monthly stipend of 700 schillings for that period.[19] The stipend was renewed at 500 schillings, probably by Frau Hertzka's good offices, but this was not enough to cover his living costs. He again approached Frau Hertzka, this time with a request for a personal loan against the Waldhaus as collateral.[20] Hertzka did not agree to the personal loan, but she suggested Berg apply to his old friend and benefactor, Alma Mahler, and to Dr. Bernhard Panzer, who had also earlier championed Berg's music. Berg did not wish to pursue these avenues, he wrote, but nonetheless Alma sent him money soon afterwards, possibly at the behest of Hertzka.[21]

Berg attempted to enlist Yella Hertzka further in the sale—mediated by Schoenberg in the United States—of the *Wozzeck* autograph score to the Library of Congress, for which the Americans offered $1,000. Universal Edition owned the manuscript by contract, and Berg eventually persuaded the publisher to divide the final purchase price of $1,140 (equivalent to 6,000 schillings) with him. The Library of Congress also offered Berg another $1,000 to compose a string quartet, but when he could not arrange to postpone the commission to a future date, he was forced to decline for lack of time.[22]

The financial and familial strife revealed in Berg's letters during his last years reveals just how tangled the struggle for economic survival had become, as the fragmented political situation in Austria worsened and the country headed towards war. These struggles led to personal controversies: sides were taken, harsh accusations made, and families and friendships irretrievably damaged. The emotional and material toll of these years weighed cruelly on Berg and surely factored into his failure to complete *Lulu* and his early death.

Political Turmoil and Austrofascism

Berg's descent into poverty coincided with a period of intense unrest and instability in Austrian society. "Berg was little concerned with politics," Theodor Adorno recalled, "although he saw himself implicitly as a socialist."[23] The Social Democrats were the dominant political party in Vienna from the founding of Austria's First Republic in 1919. Their archrivals for control of the country's parliament were the more conservative and church-backed Christian Socials. Adorno observed that Berg had benefited directly from socialist policies, including rent control on his Trauttmansdorff apartment, and virtually everyone in Berg's circle had some measure of alliance with the Social Democrats.

Although Berg remained remote from politics, he could not escape the effects of social and political turmoil. Following World War I, Vienna was a hotbed of political division and terror, as paramilitary organizations were formed and went to battle with those of opposing politics. In July 1927 an armed conflict erupted between the *Schutzbund*, the militia of the Social Democrats, and other paramilitary groups allied with Church-backed factions. More than ninty were killed in the incident. By the early 1930s the rising Nazi presence in Austrian politics increased tensions. In the 1932 regional and municipal elections, the Austrian Nazi party won 17 percent of the votes, and, shortly after the election, Engelbert Dollfuss, from the Christian Social party, was named chancellor in a desperate attempt to stem the rising Nazi tide.[24]

Dollfuss was skeptical about the effectiveness of a democratic, parliamentary government for the preservation of Austria's independence and its ability to stop the rise of the Nazis and Marxists. He believed instead in the need for an authoritarian and forceful system, loosely resembling the fascist government led by Mussolini in Italy, to counteract the threat from Nazi Germany. During his two years in office, he bypassed the parliament and ruled Austria largely by emergency decrees that included a return to the death penalty for serious crimes, restrictions on the press, armed intervention against opponents, and finally a banning of all political parties. In their place he created a political organization called the Fatherland Front (*Vaterländische Front*), which he founded in 1933 as a way to unify Austria under the banner of patriotism, German identity, and Christianity. On 25 July 1934 Dollfuss was assassinated by Nazi

terrorists, and he was succeeded by Kurt von Schuschnigg, also from
the Fatherland Front, who remained the head of the Austrian government until the *Anschluß* with Germany in 1938. Given the close alliance
and ideological affinity between the Fatherland Front and Italian fascists
under Mussolini, the term "austrofascism" is often used to describe the
regimes of Dollfuss and Schuschnigg.

Most in Berg's circle who were once Social Democrats had come
to support Dollfuss as the only alternative to the greater evil of Nazi
Germany. Ernst Krenek joined the Fatherland Front and wrote essays
supporting Dollfuss's attempt to unify Austria. Alma Mahler, a personal
friend of Schuschnigg and an enthusiastic supporter of Mussolini, favored authoritarian efforts to thwart the Nazis, and she believed—rightly
as it turned out—that Schuschnigg was too weak to keep the Nazis out.
In June 1934 Erwin Stein wrote approvingly to Schoenberg about the
state of affairs in Vienna:

> Despite everything, we have to be glad that we don't have National
> Socialism, and we definitely would have it if the Social Democrats had
> their way. What we have is really a lesser evil. Anti-Semitism has grown but
> not so openly and brutally as in Germany. Outwardly nothing has changed
> from before.[25]

Berg's student Willi Reich was an admirer of Mussolini and an enthusiastic supporter of Dollfuss's alliance with fascist Italy. At this time
Mussolini was still reasonably popular in Austria. He had promised to
preserve the civil rights of Italian Jews, and he offered armed support to
preserve the independence of Austria in the face of threats from Nazi
Germany. He was said to have wept when he learned of the assassination of Engelbert Dollfuss. For the Swiss publisher Rascher, Reich
translated into German several volumes of the collected speeches and
writings of Mussolini.[26] In a letter to Berg, Reich commented, perhaps
in jest, that he had left his name off the translations because his identity
as an Austrian Jew might have limited the work's sale in Germany. Berg
enthusiastically applauded Reich's project: "I congratulate you with the
greatest enthusiasm for your work. It pleases me immensely. Will you
translate *all* ten volumes?"[27] Following an interview with Mussolini in
Rome in 1934, Reich wrote in the Vienna *Reichspost*:

The pleasure that I took away from our conversation was not just finding that the significance and breadth of his life and work far exceed what I initially knew, but even more the impression that I received from Mussolini, this good and amiable man.[28]

If Berg had any uncertainty about whom to support or about the demise of the Social Democrats, his doubts were removed when Karl Kraus came out strongly in support of Dollfuss. In his lengthy article "Warum die Fackel nicht erscheint" (Why *Die Fackel* does not appear), written just before Dollfuss's assassination in July 1934, Kraus dismissed the political and social idealism of the left:

> I agree completely with Dollfuss. Parliamentarianism is ineffective against the resurrection of Wotan, democracy fails when pitted against the mystery of Blood and Soil, and universal suffrage will not hinder the Elect from being gangsters.[29]

Where did Berg stand in these tumultuous times? He was carefully nonpolitical, in no way an opportunist, and certainly an opponent of Nazi thuggery and anti-Semitism. He believed that his music could and should be performed in Germany, and driven by his dwindling finances he did what he could to promote performances there. He repeatedly stated that he was a German who composed German music, and he readily provided documentation that he was Aryan, not Jewish.

Some at the time may have found a political resonance in his earliest description of the Violin Concerto.[30] When beginning a new work, Berg often jotted down a few isolated words as a starting point for its poetic content or character. He used the terms "earth, hell, heaven" in a sketch for the three sections of his Romantic Overture; for the four parts of the opera "Vincent" he jotted down "arrival, quarrel, bordello, suicide." In a calendar for the year 1935 containing an overview of the form that he initially foresaw for the Violin Concerto, he labeled the four movements with the words "frisch, fromm, fröhlich, frei" (fresh, devout, happy, free); see Table 10.1.[31]

The words were a well-known motto of German and Austrian gymnastics clubs. By the 1930s these groups—like almost all organizations in the German world—had become allied with different political factions, and many excluded Jews. By the 1930s the Deutscher Turnerbund had

Table 10.1   Berg's first outline of the Violin Concerto

The 4 movements	Frisch	Fromm	Fröhlich	Frei
	IV	III	II	I
		Religioso	Ländler	Andante

Nazi associations; a related club, the Christlich-Deutsche Turnerschaft, was allied with the Fatherland Front. Both organizations shared the same four-word motto and virtually the same insignia made from four conjoined F's in the shape of a cross. Berg jotted down a version of this insignia on a sketch page for the Violin Concerto, but it is unlikely that his use of the well-known terms had any political connotation; instead it was a convenient phrase that could capture his initial idea for the sequence of moods that he originally foresaw for the work.

The Violin Concerto

Berg's first idea for the Violin Concerto as something fresh and happy may have come from his intention to appeal to American audiences. The work was commissioned by the American virtuoso Louis Krasner (1903–95), who had a growing reputation as a soloist in cities on the East Coast. Berg planned to devote a whole movement of the concerto to variations on a folk song, something familiar and appealing to American audiences but a type of music explicitly rejected by Schoenberg and out of favor with composers in Schoenberg's circle. Berg chose a Carinthian yodeling song with a saucy, ribald text for this purpose—he may have thought that the Americans would chuckle over it if they discovered the words. Berg also contemplated a "religioso" third movement, this term encountered nowhere else in his music but likely also intended to appeal to American audiences.

Violin concertos were being composed by most of the leading modernist figures during the 1930s. Stravinsky's *Concerto in Re* appeared in 1931, Schoenberg's Violin Concerto in 1936, Bartók's Violin Concerto (no. 2) in 1938, and the violin concertos by Hindemith and Britten in 1939. These works generally fall between two stylistic poles: the neoclassical vs. post-romantic or "symphonic." The neoclassical style is illustrated by Stravinsky's *Concerto in Re* with its motoric rhythms draped over changing meters, diatonic pitch collections that loosely suggest central tonal areas, linearity often taking fugal form, parodies of classical forms, absence of development, and non-emotive tone. The violin concertos by Berg, Schoenberg, and Bartók tend toward the opposite pole: hyperexpressive, chromatic, developmental, with an equal sharing of the expressive burden between the soloist and orchestra.

On 1 March 1935 Krasner signed a contract with Berg and Universal Edition for the new work, for which Berg would receive $1,500 and for which Krasner would have exclusive performing rights through June 1938. The money was a godsend for the composer at this moment, and Krasner would have a major composition by a composer whom he had admired since hearing *Wozzeck* in New York in 1931.

Louis Krasner was born in the Ukraine, grew up in New England, and graduated in 1923 from the New England Conservatory. He continued his violin studies abroad, and in 1928 began a career as a soloist and quartet player, giving concerts in London, Boston, and Vienna that often featured modern music. His interest in Berg's music grew during his periods in Vienna, where he collaborated with the pianist Rita Kurzmann and informally came into contact with Berg's circle. "I participated in discussions and cafe-house meetings with Berg, Webern, and many of the younger twelve-tone followers and enthusiasts," he later recalled.[32] In his memoirs, written forty-five years after the fact, Krasner mentions several meetings with Berg to discuss a concerto, but contemporaneous evidence suggests that the first personal contact between the two was considerably later and that the proposal for the concerto had been made indirectly in February 1935 through mutual acquaintances probably including Kurzmann, David Josef Bach, and officials at Universal Edition. Krasner wrote to Berg from Boston on 5 March 1935:

> Now I am doubly regretful that despite my many stays in Vienna I have still not had an opportunity to get to know you personally. . . . So I am all the happier that with all your other work and issues with health you have decided to write a violin concerto for me. I hope that this means that you are now feeling better and that thinking about the violin and the allure of this instrument may have led you to your decision.[33]

Berg answered Krasner's letter on 28 March to say that he looked forward to meeting him in April in Vienna and that he would begin to compose the concerto, for which he had already done preliminary work, after arriving at the Waldhaus in May.[34]

It is likely that Berg's "preliminary work" included several outlines of the large form and character of the concerto, as he initially contemplated it. The first of these, jotted down on a page of his 1935 musician's calendar, has been shown in Table 10.1. There would be four movements with the moods "free, happy, devout, fresh." On a following page of his calendar he fleshed this idea out, showing movements 1–2 and 3–4 connected into two parts (Table 10.2).[35]

Following a freely rhapsodic and introductory first movement, Berg planned to bring in variations on a Carinthian folk song with a Ländler rhythm in the second movement. His description suggests that he had already chosen the yodeling song "A Vögele af'n Zweschpm-bam" (A birdie on the plum tree), whose opening is shown in Example 10.2.[36]

The third movement would contain variations on a chorale. Berg may have foreseen this third movement as similar to the "concertante chorale variations" of *Lulu* Act 3, also for solo violin and orchestra. The finale would

Table 10.2   Detailed preliminary plan for the Violin Concerto

	Form	
mixed meters	I A Free (Andante ~~Allegro~~) fantasylike	ff
3/4	B Happy (Allegretto) dreamy	a) folk tune, b) yodel ends with a) pp
4/4	IIA Devout (Adagio) chorale	
	Cadenza	
6/8	B Fresh (Rondo) Allegro	ends f (a)
I A	introduction free (rhapsodic)	
I B	a b a (variations on a Carinthian folksong)	
II A	a b a	a = chorale harmonies b = melody as chorale arr. a = chorale & cadenza

Example 10.2 "A Vögele af'n Zweschpm-bam," first phrase

Example 10.3 Violin Concerto, basic row

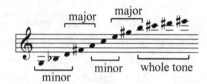

be a rondo in a quick tempo. The calendar pages have a few musical ideas sketched in, although none of these was used later in the concerto itself.

The creation of a tone row for the concerto—shown in Example 10.3 in a transposition beginning on G—was probably Berg's next preliminary step. This row has much in common with the tone rows that Berg used from 1925 onward. It begins by progressing through intervals of the major and minor third, recalling the twelve-tone lines that he had constructed as far back as Act 1, scene 1, of *Wozzeck*. Its first half is diatonic (six tones of a minor scale), and, with its interlocking major and minor triads ended by a segment in whole tones, familiar harmonies and lines could readily be extracted from it. Although the triads contained in the row are its most striking feature, its four-note segments proved to be of nearly equal importance as the work developed. The first two of these tetrachords (both have the form of a minor-major seventh chord) were among Berg's favored atonal harmonies, used prominently in the String Quartet and Clarinet Pieces, as the principal harmonic symbol for the character Wozzeck, and as the chord that ends Act 1 of *Lulu*. The final whole-tone tetrachord would appear throughout the concerto primarily as an independent motive.

Berg's early plans for the concerto and his whole outlook on the work changed radically following the death on 22 April of Manon Gropius, the eighteen-year-old daughter of Alma Mahler and Walter Gropius. The Bergs were greatly attached to Manon, nicknamed "Mutzi," and her death from complications of polio came after a year of great suffering. Helene wrote to Alma immediately following Manon's death:

> Eternally beloved Almschi! Mutzi was not only your child but also mine. We must not lament that God has called her to Him, because she was an *angel*. We must be thankful that she gave us 18 years of her blessings during her sweet earthly existence. She will remain with us in that blessed spirit that came down with her and that we shall never lose.[37]

Despite Helene's thoughtful words, Alma, for weeks after Manon's death, expressed irritable feelings toward the Bergs, whom she accused of abandoning her in her time of need. Alban protested that he had been turned away by servants at Alma's residence in the Hohe Warte. When he began to compose following his arrival at the Waldhaus on 11 May, he had decided to dedicate the concerto to Manon—"to the memory of an angel"—about which he spoke to Alma in an undated letter from about that time:

> My Almschi—I don't know when I'll be seeing you nor when I might express the inexpressible, even if by a wordless embrace. . . . All the same, some day before this terrible year comes to an end, you and Franz [Werfel] will find in a score that is dedicated
> to the memory of an angel
> an echo of what I feel and what I still today cannot express in words. Your Alban.[38]

No longer would the Violin Concerto be a lighthearted work directed at American audiences. Instead it became a profound musical remembrance of Manon, and her suffering, death, and transfiguration. With this idea in mind Berg was inspired to compose, and his work on the concerto advanced with unprecedented speed. He changed his idea for the overall form of the concerto better to accommodate the new program: the first movement probably remained nearly the same as before, but the second movement took on a dance-like, scherzando character in 6/8 and 3/8 that could capture Manon's happy and dreamy naiveté. Berg dispensed with the idea of variations on the ribald folk song but ultimately brought in the tune in an episode toward the movement's end. The third movement with chorale was placed in the fourth movement finale, and a new third movement to depict Manon's suffering was conceived. Berg's correspondence from the summer of 1935 shows that he had changing ideas about the form in the final two movements and settled on a plan for them only as composition was well underway.

Given the elegiac nature of the work, Berg decided to use a true chorale, a German hymn, as the basis for the fourth movement. On 8 June he wrote to Reich requesting from him a score of Bach's *St. Matthew Passion*—a work rich in chorales—and a collection of Bach's chorale harmonizations. "I need a chorale melody for my work—be discreet!," he admonished Reich.[39] Berg selected Johann Rudolf Ahle's chorale "Es ist genug" from the collection that Reich sent him. This was a logical choice since its words, by Franz Joachim Burmeister, are funereal—"It is enough. Lord, when you please, release me . . . "—and it begins with a distinctive whole-tone motion that duplicates the end of the basic tone row that Berg had probably already conceived for the concerto.

Berg completed the condensed score by 15 July, whereupon he wrote to Krasner, "I worked harder than ever before in my life, and in so doing my work brought me ever greater joy."[40] Berg finished the full score by mid-August—well ahead of his contractural deadline of 31 October—and he then returned to the score of *Lulu*, although final refinements in the solo part of the concerto had to await a visit from Krasner to the Waldhaus on 16 September. Rita Kurzmann also traveled to the Waldhaus to discuss her piano arrangement of the work.[41] Berg then looked forward to the ISCM festival in Barcelona in April 1936 as a likely time for the premiere, especially since Anton Webern was on the jury for the Barcelona event. Webern visited the Waldhaus in late August, played through the concerto with Berg, whereupon Berg asked him to conduct the premiere performance.

To repair Alma's wounded feelings and to express his gratitude for her financial support during the previous year, Berg sent her some part of the score for her fifty-sixth birthday on 31 August. Assuming that this was the dedicatory page and opening, Alma would certainly have noticed the references to her birthday, such as the opening tempo of 56 to the quarter note. Alma could also have read further about the concerto in an article by Willi Reich, "Alban Bergs neues Werk: 'Dem Andenken eines Engels,'" published in the *Neues Wiener Journal* on 31 August to coincide with her birthday. Upon receiving the tribute and learning of the dedication of the concerto, Alma telegrammed the Bergs:

> O you uniquely beloved people! By this enormous act of love, you have given me the one birthday present that could still bring me joy. My yearning for you both is unbearably great. Alban, I kiss your blessed hands; Helene I kiss your mouth. Now and forever, your Alma.[42]

In his article on the concerto, Reich had collaborated closely with Berg, with whom he had played through the concerto on a visit to the Waldhaus. Terminology used by Reich in his article often duplicates terms that Berg entered into his compositional manuscripts.[43] Although Reich stresses that the work is both programmatic and absolute, he emphasizes the poetic element. The second movement, Reich writes, conjures a dance-like image of Manon, at one moment dreamy, the next animated by the *Ländler* folk song. The third movement begins with a shrill outcry in the orchestra, then a stormy violin cadenza, followed by muffled groans and shrill cries for help. The finale begins with the violin's somber statement of the chorale, followed by variations on it while the violinist plays a broadly arching obbligato lament. After a last reminiscence of Manon's living image in the folk song and a return of the chorale, the violinist's threnody brings "this deeply sorrowful work to an end."[44]

Berg uses an orchestra of moderate size for the concerto, including E♭ saxophone, harp, and a large battery. Its overall form—four movements in the sequence Andante, Allegretto, Allegro, Adagio—is unusual for Berg and also for the concerto genre in general, but the first three movements individually conform to Berg's predilection for symmetrical designs.[45]

Berg referred to the entire first movement, Andante, as a "Präludium." The music begins with a hushed and pensive introduction in which arpeggios pass between harp and violin. For Rudolf Stephan the opening passage "represents an 'inception,' a rising up of music from a tone whose sound unfolds in fifths, in a process of slow formation, as though of images and memories from the unconscious."[46] The first theme of the movement follows at m. 11 (Example 10.4). It begins with a whispered harmonic progression in the key of G minor followed by the violin's

Example 10.4 Andante, mm. 11–18 (Violas, solo Bass, and solo Violin only)

Table 10.3   Violin Concerto, Allegretto: outline

section	measure	tempo
A	104–	*Scherzando* ♪ = 112 [2 x 56]
Trio I	137–	*Energico*
Trio II	155–	*Meno mosso*
Trio I′	167–	*Energico*
A′	173–	*Tempo Io*
episode	214–	*Pastorale* (folk song quotation)
stretta	240–	*A tempo, ma quasi Stretta*

ascent through the same chords ending with whole tones that complete the basic tone row of the work. The music then comes to life as contrasting thematic ideas appear at mm. 38 (*grazioso*) and 47 (*animato*). The first theme and introductory arpeggios then return to end the movement in symmetrical fashion.

The solo violin takes the leading role in the lively second movement, Allegretto. Berg and Reich describe the movement as a scherzo with connected trios, with its major sections laid out symmetrically (Table 10.3). Near the end of the Allegretto the music drifts off into a pastoral reverie as the horn steals in with the Carinthian folk song. At first the violin seems not to notice, but then joins in dreamily with the "*Überschlag*" (see Example 10.2), which is the yodeler's improvised falsetto line that shadows the tune. At its end the Allegretto dwindles to *pianissimo* and stops on a reiterated chord made from the first four tones of the prime row on G. This chord (G–B♭–D–F♯) refers to a tonal center on G, but, equally important, it is one of the basic atonal harmonies of the concerto.

Example 10.5   Allegro, mm. 1–2

After a pause, Part 2 of the concerto begins in a passionate and improvisatory mood—a sharp contrast with that of Part 1. Here, as often in Berg's music, sections separated by pauses are bridged over by common or related musical materials. The Allegro begins with an orchestral outburst—Berg marked it a "scream" (*Aufschrei*) in one sketch—that is made from the last eight notes of the basic row, the first four having been heard as the cadential chord of the preceding Allegretto. The solo violin then completes the chromatic collection with the arpeggio G–D–B♭–F♯ (Example 10.5).

The entire movement is a virtuosic, cadenza-like study for solo violin. Some of what Berg wrote for the instrument may have been inspired by Krasner's visit to the Waldhaus in June: "I played and played— for hours it seemed—whatever strange figurations, chords, passages, pizzicati and impulsive combinations on the violin—everything that chance brought to my fingers, bow and mind."[47] The movement again has a symmetrical, ABA design. An ostinato begins at m. 24, based on an imperious, asymmetric rhythmic motive (Example 10.6), that Berg labeled *à la marcia* in a sketch. At its first appearance in the winds and brass in m. 23, the figure uses notes from the inverted row on G♯, divided into four-note segments. The last tetrachord—the whole-tone figure—is typically treated separately in the solo violin. Reich aptly described the motive as "an oppressive and persistent rhythm of doom,"

Example 10.6 Allegro, main rhythmic motive (m. 23)

another example, that is, of a fate rhythm found in Berg's music since the Chamber Concerto.[48] The middle section of the movement (mm. 44–95) is slower and more lightly scored, and it brings back motives from the preceding movement. At m. 63 the soloist begins one of the most challenging and treacherous cadenzas in the entire violin literature, culminating in an ingenious four-part canon for solo violin on a motive from the Allegretto. At the reprise from m. 96 the outcry of the movement's opening returns, and the music is again gripped by the fate rhythm and by an unremitting pedal point on the tone F. The music rises to an impassioned climax after which the fate rhythm dissolves, the texture thins, and the head motive of the chorale gradually emerges to forecast Manon's transfiguration.

The fourth movement, Adagio, follows without pause as the chorale melody, long hinted at, enters stoically in the solo violin in the key of B♭ (Example 10.7). Its initial harmonization is ingenious. While the soloist plays the first chorale phrase in B♭, the viola plays the second phrase in E♭, and the bassoon adds a row fragment to complete the prime row form on F♯. Phrases of the chorale played by the violin are then echoed in the clarinets, scored to suggest the sound of a pipe organ and using Bach's harmonization of the chorale from the cantata *O Ewigkeit, du Donnerwort,* BWV 60.

Berg's idea for quoting a Bach chorale harmonization may have come to him from Ferruccio Busoni's Violin Sonata No. 2 (1900). The two works have many similarities. Busoni's sonata, like Berg's concerto, is programmatic and elegiac. In the middle movement, amid music in a dense, late romantic idiom, Busoni brings in Bach's simple chorale-like song

Example 10.7   Adagio, mm. 136–39

Example 10.8   Adagio, mm. 164–70

"Wie wohl ist mir" and its harmonization from the *Notebook for Anna Magdalena Bach* of 1725. The text, which Busoni, like Berg, prints in the score, is a funeral hymn by Wolfgang Christoph Dressler: "How good it is, O friend of souls, when I rest in thy love." As Berg does with "Es ist genug," Busoni forecasts the chorale prior to its outright appearance, and both composers then follow the initial statement with a series of variations.

In Berg's first variation (from m. 158), phrases of the chorale in differing keys are passed from instrument to instrument. As the variation proceeds, the solo violin enters (Example 10.8) with a great soliloquy— Reich termed it a *Klagegesang*, a song of sorrow—which continues to the end of the work. We can well imagine that in this passionate obbligato Berg states a personal lament, uttering "what I feel and what I still today cannot express in words," as he told Alma Mahler.

Example 10.9 Adagio, mm. 178–81

The music relentlessly approaches another climax at m. 186, here marking the catastrophic moment whose meaning is expressed by symbols of death and transfiguration. At m. 170, approaching the climax, Berg instructs the soloist to lead the orchestral strings. "From here the soloist takes over the leadership of the violins and violas, making this *apparent* and audible to the audience," Berg writes in the score. Those instruments gradually respond, falling in line by doubling the soloist's soliloquy, then rising in volume in a passage that Berg marks by the succession of terms *cantabile, amoroso, dolente, appassionato.* Eight measures before the climax a second chorale variation begins with the melody stated by the horns in a grim inversion (Example 10.9). A measure before the climax the tam-tam—the instrument announcing death—enters with a tremolo rising in a great crescendo.

After the climactic *Höhepunkt* all is reversed as the music sinks to the depths of sadness and emptiness: the doublings in the strings gradually drop away and the folk song returns (m. 200), played slowly "as from afar," as though a sad memory. In the Coda (from m. 214), the chorale returns a final time, now *rectus* but harmonized by bitterly dissonant four- and five-note chords drawn from segments of the row (Example 10.10) while the solo violin continues to intone its song of sorrow. The work ends with a calm but empty serenity as the arpeggios from the opening echo from the distance.

In this work Berg frees himself from any systematic application of twelve-tone rows. Complete presentations of rows are confined mainly to isolated passages, especially those that begin structural units. Berg brings forward triadic harmony and tonal harmonic progressions to a greater degree than in any work since his student period. In one sketch

Example 10.10   Adagio, Coda, mm. 214–17 (Orchestra only)

page, headed "Chords and Cadences," he experiments with extracting tonal, triadic progressions from the rows, and he labels these progressions with roman numerals that suggest keys and modulations that pass from key to key.[49] The progressions that he devises are found sporadically in the work itself.

A work of such depth and expressivity can readily suggest a variety of programmatic interpretations. The only one endorsed in any way by Berg is the tribute to Manon Gropius, with references also to Alma Mahler. Given Berg's declining health and his superstitious belief in fate, it is plausible that he may have foreseen the work as his own farewell. This was an idea later expressed by Helene: "The Violin Concerto is Alban Berg's farewell to this world—painful, wistful, and respectful— his last one, directed at everything that was dear to him here, a purely personal confession of his relation to the world, to death, and to God."[50] Webern also embraced this interpretation, as he wrote to Schoenberg:

> At the end the violin plays once more, "*as from a great distance*," on the open strings. How could we fail to see a relationship here? A farewell! And yet, dear friend, *nothing at all* was indicated when last summer, just after the work was completed, I was with Alban, played through it with him, and he told me some things about it, *but nothing even about the dedication!*[51]

Although it is tempting to place the Violin Concerto along-side Mozart's Requiem, Schubert's *Winterreise*, and Mahler's Ninth Symphony as a great last work composed *sub specie mortis*, Berg in 1935 had concrete and optimistic plans for the future. He told Willi Reich about ideas for works following *Lulu*: a third string quartet, chamber music with piano, a symphony, music specifically for radio broadcast,

Table 10.4 Number 23 in the Violin Concerto, Adagio

Measure:	Musical Event	Measures Spanned
136	beginning of the Adagio	23
158	chorale variation 1 begins	23
164	violin *Klagegesang* enters	
186	"*Höhepunkt*" of the Adagio	23
208	return of the folk tune	23
230	final measure of the work	

and film music.[52] Still, his pervasive use of symbolic numbers in the Violin Concerto—especially his own ominous number 23—reinforces the idea that Berg alludes in the work to his personal struggle with fate. Douglas Jarman has pointed to the many occurrences of the number 23, these appearing most prominently in the second part (Allegro-Adagio). The opening tempo of Part 2 has the quarter note at 69 (3 x 23), and, as shown in Table 10.4, the entire part spans 230 measures with junctures often 23 measures apart.[53]

Planning for the premiere of the Violin Concerto at the Barcelona ISCM festival went forward according to Berg's wishes. A preview performance arranged by Universal Edition was given by Krasner and Rita Kurzmann on 8 April 1936 at Vienna's Musikverein, and the Barcelona performance followed on 19 April. Helene Berg and many of the composer's Viennese friends traveled to Spain for the event, although Webern had threatened to back out, only to be convinced by Krasner and others that the Barcelona performance had to go on. When rehearsals in Barcelona began, Webern experienced an emotional crisis and spent most of the allotted rehearsal time on a few measures. Finally, he demanded that the performance be cancelled. Ernst Krenek was present and later described Webern's actions:

> The real torture started when Webern began to rehearse. He seemed to have no working plan and flailed helplessly around, talking to the orchestra in the broadest Austrian dialect that he could muster so that even the few musicians there who had German and who might have acted as translators were unable to explain his tirades to their colleagues.[54]

At Helene's pleading, Webern turned the score over to Hermann Scherchen, who conducted the premiere on a single rehearsal. Later Webern reported to Schoenberg:

> Things went badly for me in Barcelona: I finally had to step aside, and this when I was to give the first performance of Berg's last work. In the end someone else took over. Even though I was able to do the London performance, which I think turned out well, still I lost myself in the terrible conditions in Barcelona. I needed longer to get a grip on things. What anxiety built up while studying the work I am not able to say. I had rehearsed it here [in Vienna] with the violinist, and several times I thought I should bow out. I only hope that I have presented the work as Berg wanted. It was difficult and remains difficult.[55]

As Webern acknowledged, his performance with the BBC Orchestra in London on 1 May, again with Krasner as soloist, was widely praised, a judgment supported by a recording of the performance that was reissued in 1991 as a digital disc.[56]

Krasner then played the work far and wide, eliciting generally positive reviews although many of the early critics seemed confused by the direction taken by Berg in this final composition. Most were uncertain about the mixture of styles—atonality next to Bach, twelve-tone rows beside diatonic scales. What movement in modern music could such a work be part of? Was the mixed style a model for the future or a backward step, a romantic atavism? While most critics heaved a sigh of relief that atonal music could still be movingly expressive, others found in the Violin Concerto a rejection of Schoenberg's influence in favor of a return to Strauss and Mahler. The concerto revealed "a subtilised tonalism with a dash of the atonal," wrote Ernest Newman in the *Sunday Times*, "Berg having simply added a new ingredient to the Strauss-Mahler cup, as Strauss and Mahler had added a new ingredient to the Wagner cup."[57] "History will probably prove that Schönberg's strongest claim to fame will be that he paved the way for Berg," wrote the reviewer for the *Manchester Guardian*.[58]

American audiences were introduced to the Violin Concerto by the Boston Symphony Orchestra under Serge Koussevitzky, who premiered the work in Boston on 6 March 1937 and in New York on 11 March. The American critics were again uncertain about the direction that the concerto represented and many suspected that its apparent mixing of styles was a weakness. Lawrence Gilman found it lacking in the conviction that Berg had shown in *Wozzeck*. "We get for the most part the ancient clichés of atonality and 'twelve-tonalism,'" he wrote in the *New York Herald Tribune*, "the stale odor of spilt modernity, sweetish left-overs from the Schoenbergian pastry shop."[59] Gradually writers abandoned their search for Berg's relevance to stylistic trends in modern music—to its elusive main streams and twisting branches—and accepted the concerto for what it is: a great and unique piece of music, an original creation, and a singular expression of Berg's musical personality and artistic vision. Berg was himself always skeptical about the relevance of stylistic trends in music: "Isn't it enough simply to make beautiful music?" he asked.

Berg did not live to hear an orchestral performance of the Violin Concerto. After his final revisions on the work in September of 1935, he returned to the orchestration of *Lulu*, but his energy was sapped by his bleak financial outlook and the relentless ebbing of his health.

Berg's Final Illness

Berg's heart incident of 1934 was only a single episode in a long chain of ever more serious illnesses that led to his death on 24 December 1935.[60] Although his medical records are only partly preserved and contemporaneous reports about his illnesses are incomplete and often conflicting, we can still piece together a likely series of events and the underlying causes that led to his death at the age of only fifty.

Berg's letters to his wife routinely convey concern for his health, manifested in detailed accounts of his illnesses, his diet, and many treatments. Adorno observed a pronounced hypochrondia in both Berg and his wife. "Part of this hypochondria came from addiction," Adorno wrote. "Berg lived, as he once said, from aspirin and tea, and he probably enjoyed the euphoric aspects of illness."[61] The number of medications he mentions in his letters to Helene, often taken in large quantities, is staggering. In his household budget for December 1934, nearly half of all of his expenditures was for medications.[62] Berg's great fear of asthmatic attack was the original inducement for his over-medication, but gradually his use of drugs became a destructive habit.

In the early twentieth century, great advances were made in the creation of synthetic drugs. Aspirin came to the market around 1900, the sleep medication Veronal in 1904 (it quickly became the suicide drug of choice in Austria), and insulin in 1922. At the same time there were relatively few legal restrictions on the purchase of drugs and little attention to the consequences of excessive or prolonged use. The best-selling synthetic medication during Berg's lifetime was Pyramidon, a trade name for aminopyrine (aminophenazone), marketed by Hoechst AG and used widely for relief from pain and fever. Pyramidon and aspirin were Berg's favorite medications for pain and also for asthma, and he took them in large quantities throughout his life, supplementing them with morphine, cocaine, codeine, chloroform, epinephrine, and a variety of sleep medications.

In all likelihood, Pyramidon had the most damaging long-term effect on Berg's health. He may have been introduced to the drug by Helene, who gave him a sample of it shortly after they met in 1907.[63] Berg's use of this drug is mentioned repeatedly in his correspondence after this time, including just before he was taken on 17 December 1935 to the Rudolfs Hospital, where he would die a week later. Berg was warned about the effects of his overuse of medications. His sister, Smaragda, wrote to him in 1920:

> I plead with you to the extent possible [to stop taking] these poisons Pyramidon, morphine and especially the enormous amount of aspirin that you have been taking for years. You must yourself be aware that one's body and nervous system cannot tolerate these over time. And mentally?[64]

In the later 1930s a connection was established between the use of aminopyrine and agranulocytosis, a condition in which the white blood cell count is significantly lowered. The bone marrow toxicity of aminopyrine is progressive, becoming more acute over time and eventually eliminating the body's ability to fight infections. Aminopyrine also leads to a degeneration of the heart muscle—possibly a factor in Berg's heart incident of 1934—and an enlargement of the spleen, which was noted in Berg's autopsy report. Although Berg's overuse of medication was spurred on by his fear of asthma, this malady in itself was probably independent of the disease from which he died.

Berg fills his correspondence with descriptions of diseases that suggest an increasing lack of resistance to infection. By the 1930s he notes recurring and prolonged cases of flu, periodontal abscesses, gallstone attacks, and, most of all, the repeated appearance of painful furuncles (boils) and carbuncles (large clusters of boils) on his skin, sometimes lasting for weeks or even months. Boils are a common type of staphylococcal skin infection which may have arisen in Berg's case from his lack of personal hygiene (for which he was often criticized by Helene), insect bites, and other such punctures of the skin. There is no evidence (as suggested in the literature) that Berg suffered from the MRSA strain of staph, which is especially resistant to treatment.[65] A typical management of boils is by incision of nodules, draining fluid and pus, and an antiseptic bandaging of the wound. A complication from boils, especially in patients like Berg with a compromised immune response, is for bacteria to enter the blood-stream, leading to blood poisoning (sepsis).

Berg first suffered from furunculosis during his military service in World War I, and he often treated such outbreaks himself. In 1918 he told Helene about one such treatment:

> The carbuncle head came out more quickly than I thought it would yesterday. My treatment was to open the head of the pimple 3 or 4 times, first with a red-hot needle, then today opening it up with benzene cotton swabs so that the hollow would be ever wider without having to squeeze it. Apparently this again proved to be effective. Today a smaller pus head appeared, which readily went away and although the general swelling was rather large, the worst seemed to be over. At least the pain is less than yesterday evening.[66]

The incidence, duration, and severity of Berg's boils increased in the 1920s and 1930s. An especially serious furuncle appeared above the coccyx in the middle of August 1935, which Berg described to his publisher by quoting from Schön's lament in Act 2 of *Lulu*:

> My carbuncle tortures me monstrously. According to the doctor, whom I've now had to consult, it may last weeks! "This in the evening of my life . . . A plague on my house," I groan along with Dr. Schön—a part of *Lulu* that I have just now orchestrated, this taking all my force of will.[67]

Given his dwindling finances Berg turned increasingly to Helene to drain boils in areas, such as the back, that he could not reach himself. In November he wrote to Ignaz Fanzoy, the custodian at the Waldhaus: "[I have] had also a heavy flu and now another boil on my rear. I can scarcely sit. My wife treats me better than Engstler and it costs nothing," he remarked.[68] In his incomplete biography of Berg, Soma Morgenstern makes the accusatory claim that Helene, out of a foolhardy miserliness, drained one of Berg's boils, which caused his fatal sepsis.[69] Many other acquaintances also mention that Helene treated Berg's boils at his request, but assuming that the treatment was done carefully, it is unlikely that it had the fatal consequences that Morgenstern asserts.

Despite complaining of pain from boils, Berg attended the Vienna premiere of the Lulu *Symphonic Pieces* on 11 December 1935, joining friends for a convivial gathering afterward. A few days later, he developed a high fever—105° according to Helene—and on December 17 he was brought to the Rudolfs Hospital (now Vienna's Krankenanstalt Rudolfstiftung). The hospital, which was mainly for indigents, had a bad reputation. Ernst Krenek visited Berg there and was appalled by what he saw. He wrote:

> The building was indescribably filthy and shabby, and it was incredibly disturbing and terrible to realize that one of Austria's greatest composers would have to fight for his life amid such horrible conditions. His struggle did not last very long but certainly too long in light of what he had to undergo.[70]

During his week in the hospital, the nature of his treatment and progress of his disease are known only in general terms from often conflicting recollections by Helene and Berg's close friends, and also from records obtained from the Rudolfs Hospital. The cause of death recorded on his death certificate was "blood poisoning following furunculosis (Pyaemia e furuncolosi [sic])."[71] The complete autopsy report is shown in the Appendix.[72]

Helene believed that negligence by Berg's doctors was to blame for his demise. In 1936 she wrote to Alma Mahler:

> Now to Alban's illness. None of us had any idea of its danger (he had furunculosis four times during our marriage). Dr. [Hermann] Friedmann examined him twice, prescribed this terrible "phlox serum" [Antiphlogestine?] and the third time—the evening when he had the high fever—asserted that the matter was inconsequential, not urgent. The boil would be drained the next day in out-patient care. He said I was "anxious" (I was always that way around Alban, even when he drank too much, because I knew of his delicate health). The doctor assured me during my second telephone call that his fever could be from flu. The next day we went by ambulance to the hospital he had

specified [Rudolfs Hospital], which, as I later learned, had the worst reputation imaginable. Friedmann said that we could return home after he opened
the boil. At the hospital I was told that Alban had to stay overnight for observation, and was placed in the 3d class area because I could not immediately
come up with 200 schillings. That was the beginning of hell for him and for
me. It is really too much, inconceivable. If these frightful events stem from
people and their conduct, they have to be held accountable, and they deserve
a sentence of death.[73]

Helene's accusation of negligence by Berg's physicians is very common
among the bereaved in such situations, and there is no evidence of genuine malpractice on the part of his doctors.

Helene later recorded additional recollections of Berg's final illness,
which she readily sent to those who inquired. These contain a number of
inconsistencies, and she makes no mention of her involvement in treating
her husband's boils. One of the first to inquire about Berg's death was
Dr. Dieter Kerner, a physician known for his studies of illnesses among
the great composers.[74] Helene sent a somewhat more complete statement to Hans Moldenhauer as he prepared his biography of Webern. She
wrote to Moldenhauer:

Alban suffered often in his life with boils, very intensely during the First
World War, and later from time to time in isolated abscesses. (He reported in
detail on these in his letters to me.) In the summer and fall of 1935 he developed a few small boils simultaneously, which were successfully treated by
Dr. Engstler in Velden. Alban was then working feverishly on Lulu and the
Violin Concerto, although he did not feel well. Back in Vienna in November
he had a small heart attack, which Dr. Friedmann remedied within a few
hours. After this Alban swore by his healing ability, and when he got a larger
abscess on the coccyx, Dr. Friedmann treated it with Solux lamp radiation
and pain-killing morphine suppositories.

Suddenly Alban developed a fever of 105°. Dr. Friedmann arrived at 6:00
PM, following a phone call that I made to him at 7:00 AM. He examined
the abscess in the place that he had earlier treated and which was healing and
confirmed that the wound was clean and healing properly. He assumed that
the high fever could not have come from it, instead from some other cause.
I was fearful, while he minimized Alban's condition. He advised me to take
Alban the next day to the hospital where he had a good friend [Dr. Rudolf

Demel] who would "have a look" at him. That night was so bad that at 6:00 AM I called for an ambulance. This was on 17 December. Alban was "thoroughly" examined but no one thought to perform a rectal examination. (He had no pain there due to the morphine suppositories.) After three days incisions as wide as one's hand were made in both of his buttocks (at a red splotch that had apparently come from lying on the hard bed). Nothing at all was found, but Alban had lost so much blood from these unnecessary surgeries that a blood transfusion was urgently needed. So I demanded that a professor [Dr. Leo Hess] be brought in. I was present at his examination. The professor was the first to perform a rectal examination, and he found an abscess in the rectum. But by then it was too late. The poison had spread into the hemorrhoidal blood vessels and from there throughout the entire body. (This last matter was reported to me by our longstanding doctor and friend of the Nahowski family, Dr. [Hans] Martin.) A 24-hour intravenous drip could not save him. Alban insisted that I take a powerful sleep medication in his presence. But I did not sleep and held him in my arms to the end.[75]

Erwin Stein and Anton Webern—Berg's true friends—were regularly at the hospital and later reported in detail on his illness in letters to Schoenberg. "His body was in great distress," wrote Stein. "Helene said that he tore free from his bandages, reared himself up, stretched out his arms and repeatedly cried out, 'Es ist genug!—It is enough!' Poor Helene, to have had to witness this."[76] Webern's report is especially affecting and informative.[77] He visited his friend of thirty years at the hospital virtually every day, and he spoke with him on the afternoon of December 23, the last of Berg's circle to do so.[78] "Very nice, very lovely," were Berg's final words to him. Webern continued:

> Toward evening came new heart attacks. When around 10:00 PM the physician, Dr. Hoess [Hess] was again there, I spoke with him myself, and he had given up all hope. The heart was finished, apparently due to a sepsis. But did this come from the boils or were they only a symptom?

Webern was on the right track with his question. The most likely underlying cause of Berg's fatal sepsis was agranulocytosis, brought on primarily by his use of aminopyrine and possibly heightened by an innate immune deficiency. This diagnosis is consistent with the autopsy findings of staphylococcal septicemia with diffuse parenchymal abscesses of the chest and abdominal organs and accompanying heart failure. By the time that Berg was brought to the hospital on December 17, there was little hope for his survival.

Many anecdotes were told about Berg's final days. Reich contended that Berg's final thoughts were with music, as he muttered "An upbeat, an upbeat!" as his last words. Webern reported that Berg was relieved to be told that the 23rd of the month had passed, assuring those present that now everyone should go to sleep. Reich—someone normally careful with his facts—told the story of Berg thanking the transfusion blood donor, a "genuine, cheerful child of the Viennese folk," Berg then adding, "I hope this won't make an operetta composer out of me!"[79] Reich might have mentioned that the donor was Berg's student Leonhard Märker (later Leonard, or Leo, Marker), who would soon have a great success with his musical revue *Warum lügst du, Chérie?*[80] Soma Morgenstern reported that Berg received extreme unction on his last day, after which he told Morgenstern that the priest "was such a nice person that I couldn't say no to him."[81] Helene and her sister, Anna, were with Berg when the end finally came. "Alban suffered so dreadfully and his death was hard," she later wrote to Schoenberg. "He retained consciousness until the end and his death struggle was frightful. More than 4 hours. I constantly see his desperate face before me and those sad eyes! I constantly ask myself: why not *me*?"[82] Helene told Stein that her husband's last words were "Es ist genug!"

Berg's funeral followed on December 28. The City of Vienna provided an honorary grave site in the Hietzing Cemetery, near the Bergs' apartment on the Trauttmansdorffgasse. A distinguished group of civic and artistic leaders of the city was in attendance, and short statements were read by Ernst Krenek, Egon Wellesz, Willi Reich, and others.[83] Helene did not attend. Berg left behind two wills, the latter and more complete dated 9 September 1934. It begins:

> My testament. I bequeath my entire estate, including my possessions and whatever income should accrue to my musical creations to my wife, Helene Berg. Should she die at the same time as I, this property should go to an "Alban Berg Foundation" that will be created at that time, to which I name Dr. Anton von Webern and Dr. Otto Lifzcis—whom I ask to take on this office—as administrators.[84]

Helene's declaration of the value of her husband's estate reveals his distressing decline into poverty: his half-ownership of the Waldhaus was estimated at 31,500 schillings, although half of this amount was borrowed money. At the time of his death he had 200 schillings in cash, books, music worth 564 schillings, and other items of small value. Knowing that her husband would have wanted it stated, Helene dutifully listed major volumes in Berg's library: the complete works by Ibsen, Rosegger, and Strindberg, among others. The total value of his property was estimated to be 38,114 schillings, or about $6,500. His indebtedness came to approximately the same amount, including a mortgage on the Waldhaus property and a debt to Universal Edition of 14,481 schillings.[85] Certainly other leading composers of the modern period—Bartók and Webern are other examples—suffered from poverty at the end of their lives, but Berg's financial state is exceptional, offering a sobering commentary on the economic condition of one of the great modern composers and the state of musical culture at this point in the twentieth century.

★ ★ ★

The world that inherited Alban Berg's musical legacy had little in common with the one into which he was born fifty years before. In 1885 Vienna was a city of artistic brilliance and opportunity, home to Brahms, Bruckner, Mahler, Wolf, Klimt, and Freud. There was a curiosity and tolerance for new ideas, and a belief in the future that nourished experimentation in the arts. The works of Berg were fostered by this positive atmosphere and by the society in which he lived. All this had changed by 1935. Europe then stood on the precipice of a descent into darkness. An intolerance for the new had come to dominate, pessimism about the future was an accepted view, and an atmosphere of fear and violence was widespread. "Negative emotions cannot produce art," wrote Aaron Copland, referring to the anxiety of American society during the McCarthy era. "You cannot make art out of fear and suspicion; you can make it only out of affirmative beliefs," he continues. "The artist should feel himself affirmed and buoyed up by his community."[86]

The final triumph of Berg's musical legacy could occur only when that spirit of affirmation returned to the world.

Helene Berg and the Management of Berg's Legacy, 1936–76

" I STILL CANNOT BELIEVE THAT ALBAN HAS GONE FOREVER, BUT WHEN such a moment of realization comes I feel as if I were plunging into an abyss."[1] Helene Berg confided these dark thoughts to Arnold Schoenberg as she faced life as a widow. She had good reason to view her future with apprehension. Her financial outlook was clouded, with scant income from her investments and from a few performances of her husband's music abroad. Her refuge at the Waldhaus was in debt, and the sale of her parents' house in the Maxingstrasse had run aground as the buyer defaulted on payments. Additionally, Helene faced emotional distress on several fronts: she learned that her husband was the father of a child, who under Austrian law might claim a part of Berg's property and royalty income. Her friend Alma Mahler accused her of making her husband's life difficult by her penny-pinching, and she was still trying to explain to herself his consorting with other women.[2] Most importantly, what was she to do with the uncompleted *Lulu*, whose near future she in effect controlled?

Helene's spirits must have been buoyed by the lavish praise accorded her husband—both for his music and his person—in the obituaries that appeared in newspapers as far away as Hong Kong. Henry Prunières's tribute in *La revue musicale* was typically reassuring:

> He was a charming soul, a rare mixture of lively intelligence, passionate feeling, freshness, simplicity, kindness, and refined culture; one of those people, finally,

Berg. Bryan Simms and Charlotte Erwin, Oxford University Press (2021). © Oxford University Press.
DOI: 10.1093/oso/9780190931445.003.0012

that you could not admire without also having great fondness. We at *La revue musicale* associate the memory of this man of genius with our recollection of the charming lady who was his intelligent and sensitive companion during his days of pain and joy. We extend to Mme Alban Berg our deepest feelings of respect and sorrow.[3]

A special issue of *23: Eine Wiener Musikzeitschrift* appeared in February 1936 with tributes by Berg's students and close friends: Willi Reich, Soma Morgenstern, Heinrich Jalowetz, Erwin Stein, Theodor Adorno, and Ernst Krenek. One notes the absence of a statement by Anton Webern, whose great emotional distress over Berg's death may have prevented him from speaking out about his departed friend.[4] Among the many letters of condolence that arrived from far and wide, several had special meaning for Helene. The most important of these came from Schoenberg and contained an offer to complete the orchestration of *Lulu*. Helene responded that it was "the first ray of light in my darkness."[5] The matter of *Lulu*—whether the opera should be "completed," and if so, by whom—became in the years following his death the most consuming issue for Berg's musical posterity.

The Completion of *Lulu*

At the time of Berg's death there was much uncertainty—shared by Helene Berg—about the state of completion of *Lulu*. Berg had completed the *Particell* in May 1934, which marked for him the conclusion of the work's compositional phase, despite, in this case, the presence of a few passages in Act 3 that had been composed hurriedly and left in a sketchy state. The creation of the full score of the opera remained to be done, and, after six years of composing, Berg also foresaw the need for an extensive "overhaul," as he termed it, for the entire work. The composer lived to orchestrate all of Acts 1 and 2, the beginning of Act 3 (mm. 1–268 of a total of 1,326 mm.), and about 120 measures later in Act 3 for use in the *Symphonic Pieces*. Additionally, some orchestrated passages in Act 1 could be reused with minor changes in Act 3, such as mm. 958–89 of Act 1, which reappear in the closely related mm. 1235–65 of Act 3 as well as in the final movement of the *Symphonic Pieces*.[6] The extent of Berg's "overhaul" is uncertain. The *Particell* shows revisions entered by Berg at some point in early parts of the opera, and Act 3 records the presence of numerous second thoughts. But passages in Act

3 left as incomplete sketches had not been fleshed out at the time of his death in December 1935.[7]

Universal Edition was heavily invested in *Lulu* and urgently wanted to see it completed and staged as soon as possible. The company itself had for years been in financial straits, and it counted on the success of *Lulu* also to repay the more than 14,000 schillings advanced to the composer. Although it was unlikely that *Lulu* could be performed in Germany, the publisher still hoped for a premiere in some other European country, possibly Czechoslovakia, Switzerland, or Belgium. Performances of the *Symphonic Pieces* from the opera had brought attention to the work, and a piano-vocal score was being made by Erwin Stein to promote interest among conductors and theater directors.

Within days of Berg's death, the directors of Universal Edition contemplated who might complete the score of *Lulu* so that a premiere could take place in the near future. Several names were mentioned in Viennese newspapers, as in *Der Morgen* on 30 December:

> No decision has been reached about the completion of the opera *Lulu*, left behind by Alban Berg. Schoenberg's advice from California is awaited. Apparently Zemlinsky may complete the score, pending the agreement of the widow of the deceased and the directors of Universal Edition. The premiere of *Lulu* will take place in Prague.[8]

Given such reports, it may be that Schoenberg had been sounded out about completing *Lulu* before he contacted Helene Berg on 1 January 1936 in his letter of condolence. At that time he wrote to her: "When I read in a New York paper that the orchestration of *Lulu* is not finished and that Krenek or someone else is to do it, I had the spontaneous idea to ask you whether I should do it. . . . If Alban happened to express the wish that I orchestrate the rest, and if you yourself consider it the best solution, then I would naturally be at your disposal."[9]

Schoenberg's offer was enthusiastically embraced by both Helene Berg and Universal Edition, and the publisher immediately went forward with plans for a premiere. An agreement was reached with the Stadttheater in Zurich for a performance in November 1936. Hugo Winter from Universal Edition wrote to Schoenberg to underscore the narrow timeline:

> We have concluded favorable terms with Zurich. We consider it very impor-
> tant for Frau Berg, for emotional reasons, that the premiere take place as soon

as possible; for her financial condition it is all the more important. We also think that Zurich is a good solution for the premiere in artistic terms since the theater there has an excellent ensemble. . . . The rehearsals are to begin in August, and we have promised to deliver the materials for the first two acts by that time. We must start with the production of materials for Act 3 in early August at latest. We ask you to arrange your work so that we will have the score in hand by August 1.[10]

As is well known, Schoenberg withdrew his offer to complete the score shortly after receiving the *Particell* of Act 3 and the libretto. There were multiple reasons for his decision to back out. His son-in-law, Felix Greissle, told George Perle that the financial arrangements with Universal Edition were insufficient.[11] In a letter to Erwin Stein, Schoenberg observed that Berg had a different approach to twelve-tone composition from his own, often wrote illegibly in the *Particell*, and frequently composed pianistic textures, all of which would slow his task of orchestration.[12] To complete Act 3 would take far longer than the deadline set by Universal Edition. He explained this to Alfred Kalmus:

> I have to return Berg's materials because I am convinced that it would take a year to complete the orchestration. I cannot assume that you would be able to agree to such a prolonged delay in the deadline, especially since Frau Berg needs income as soon as possible. I cannot say that I could keep even to this [later] deadline, since I am often overburdened here with work and often face interruptions. But I imagine that Berg, whose rate of composing was slower than mine, could not have finished it in a shorter time if he also had to earn a living.[13]

Two days before writing to Kalmus, Schoenberg had written to Erwin Stein to give a more private explanation for his withdrawal. He would not complete the orchestration, he told Stein, in light of the parody of the Jewish Banker in Act 3. Recall from an earlier discussion that Berg heightens the caricature of the Banker in his interaction with the Journalist by having him speak and gesture in "*mauscheln*," or "*jüdeln*." "One can't really expect of me," Schoenberg wrote to Stein, "that I should be sufficiently inspired in my orchestration of this passage to give the sharpest characterization to the insult, 'a scoundrel because he's a Jew.'" Schoenberg continued:

I would like to suppose that Berg has done this, difficult as it is to understand, out of thoughtlessness, although in this period of the most extensive persecution of Jews it seems hardly credible that anyone could fail to give thought to something that gives his friends cause for thought. But conceding thoughtlessness, *mauschel* in these days certainly seems to be respectable rather than an indication of knavery since I know so many respectable people who *mauscheln* and since I know of so many who were found worthy of the honor of martyrdom only because of their *mauscheln*. Am I now to be inspired to orchestrate music that is characterized by a special coarseness because this person is a Jew since he speaks *mauschelnd?*[14]

The substance of Schoenberg's letter spread quickly among those in Berg's circle. Several were skeptical about Schoenberg's reasoning. Adorno told Helene that Schoenberg backed out because he was jealous of Berg's success. "I had occasion to observe it [Schoenberg's jealousy] in its basest manifestations, and I have no reservations about claiming that the thought of cutting off Alban's decisive work from posterity through his refusal was a tempting one for him."[15] Ernst Krenek had similar doubts, finding that Schoenberg's letter to Stein introduced "additional ambiguities and contradictions." Krenek's account suggests that Schoenberg had been tipped off in advance about the problematic passage: "It is astonishing that Schoenberg, on the very day that he received the packet from New York [*recte*, two days after], was able to analyze not only the condensed score but also Wedekind's text, volumes that he would have had to acquire, and also on that single day come to the conclusion that he did in the letter."[16]

With Schoenberg's withdrawal, the plan for a November premiere was scrapped and the publisher hatched an alternative strategy to give the premiere as a torso with two acts followed by a symphonic reading of the final two movements from the *Symphonic Pieces*, which used music from Act 3 of the opera. Stein explained this to Schoenberg:

As things stand now, *Lulu* will remain incomplete. We asked Webern and Zemlinsky if they wanted to do the orchestration. Webern has not yet declined and is still dealing with the *Particell*. But I can't imagine that anything will come of it. Zemlinsky—a man of the theater—seemed at first to be very interested. But after two days of study he said no, advising us to perform only what Berg had completed. This is apparently what will happen.

We have proposed to the director of the Zurich theater to stage only the two completed acts and as epilog to perform the purely symphonic Adagio from the *Symphonic Pieces*.[17]

So for the foreseeable future *Lulu* would be a two-act work. With this reality in mind Universal Edition published Stein's piano-vocal score with only those two acts, even though Stein had completed a piano score for all three acts.

The premiere finally took place in the Zurich Stadttheater on 2 June 1937, at the beginning of a festival during which ten operas were staged over an eighteen-day period. The Zurich theater had a reputation for novelties during its yearly festivals. They had staged Shostakovich's *Lady Macbeth of the Mtsensk District* during the previous year and scheduled the world premiere of Hindemith's *Mathis der Maler* in 1938. A prestigious audience from far and wide attended the 1937 festival.[18] At the end of Act 2 of *Lulu*, the director, Karl Schmid-Bloss, came onstage to summarize the action of Act 3, after which the orchestra played the Variations and Adagio from the *Symphonic Pieces*, with scenery and stage actions added and the final music of Countess Geschwitz sung at the end. Most reviewers found the work to be a powerful dramatic success despite its truncated form and the substitute for Act 3 to be effective. Willi Schuh wrote in the *Neue Zürcher Zeitung*:

> The pure and strong effect that came from the performance of the fragments of Act 3 must be especially highlighted. Although the Paris scene was hard to do without, the Variations on Wedekind's lute song ("Confession") was a sturdy replacement, and the Adagio that flowed from there into the discreetly indicated murder scene in the masterful interpretation by [the conductor Robert] Denzler authentically captured this tragedy of beauty in a tightly condensed moment.[19]

Schuh conceded that the film sequence in the middle of Act 2—made especially for the Zurich performance by the local studio "Tempo"—was unsuccessful. He explained: "A virtually insoluble problem arises with the film scene that Berg foresaw at the peripeteia of the drama. Even a less naturalistic film or one that more faithfully followed the instructions of the composer would be a superfluous foreign body at that point for the dramatic action and for its symbolic meaning."[20] The film used in Zurich is now lost except for a few still photographs.[21]

For the subsequent history of *Lulu*, the most important reaction to the Zurich performance came from Helene Berg, who was in attendance as a guest of the theater. In a letter to Alma Mahler written shortly thereafter, she states that the Zurich version of *Lulu* was in fact "complete"—an idea from which she would not deviate after that time. Helene wrote:

> Words alone are inadequate for the music—it must be heard! It has a beauty and truth that effaces all that is ugly and repellent in the text, and only a compellingly great work of art remains. When I heard it for the first time it was as familiar as though it had come from me, like my own words. There are passages which take one out of this world. Alban knew how to capture and express two things to their very depth: love and death, the alpha and omega of our worldly existence. — It was also notable that, despite my being always opposed to this Wedekind, when I heard the music it was different. I have taken Lulu into my heart as I did Wozzeck. I love her and tremble for her as for a child.
>
> The play is terrible and people do not willingly have a light shone on their depravity. But when Alwa sings with tender ecstasy, "a soul that rubs the sleep from its eyes on the other side," I knew then why this drama had to be written, why it has the deepest meaning. That the opera even as a torso was viable onstage does not surprise me. I have learned to trust in the higher powers. Everything happens according to a plan. How could Alban—who had so much to tell and give to us—have been called away when his final work, which should be touched by no other hand, was not in a sense "complete" as he left it! Slowly people will come around, those who today still confront his art without understanding or trust. How far ahead of them he was! In time they will learn who Alban Berg was.[22]

As she does in this letter, Helene calls attention in her private notebooks to Wedekind's line, "A soul that rubs the sleep from its eyes in the other world" (Eine Seele, die sich im Jenseits den Schlaf aus den Augen reibt). These enigmatic, poetic words have a distinctly anthroposophical ring in their evocation of an awakening in a spiritual world. Berg's musical interpretation of them appears to have allayed Helene's doubts about the moral implications of the opera. Set to Berg's music, this phrase conveyed to her a sense of Lulu's spiritual redemption, despite the depravity of the physical world she inhabits.

An event on the day before the Zurich premiere suggests that Helene was at that point still ambivalent on Alban's wishes concerning a completion of *Lulu*. She sought out the advice of Hans Reinhart, a writer and fellow anthroposophist who was the brother of the Swiss music patron Werner Reinhart. He attended the opera rehearsals and had an extended discussion with Helene that he recapitulates in a subsequent letter, written on 1 June. Reinhart was reticent concerning his ability to help her; he found her questions too complex, despite his professed "many years of involvement with anthroposophy." On balance, he appeared to believe that Berg would have better things to do in the afterlife than worry about *Lulu*. He compared Berg to Schiller, who left behind the unfinished play *Demetrius*. Reinhart writes:

> The "I" of your husband, so deeply bound to you in life, freed from the body, must undergo transformations in the interim existence (whose length according to Indian measures cannot be determined here); these transformations will in all probability occur in a wholly other place and in a completely altered time (presumably gender-altered as well) and will present to his new inner eye wholly new tasks, before which former ones will pale and will most likely die down into a distant memory. I believe, I know, that Schiller lives and acts among us in a new incarnation (even very near us), possesses however no urge or "assignment" to complete his "Demetrius" (and what material it is!). I can't imagine that the "I" that once bore the name of Alban Berg, when it is "guided to clarity" (as in the "Prologue to Heaven," Faust Part I) and so achieves higher sight, after these cycles [literally tides: *Gezeiten*] could have the urge to complete musically such time- and sense-bound material as Wedekind's "Lulu" (which appears all too human in the distortion mirror).[23]

With these words of a fellow anthroposophist to reassure her and the evidence of the performance, Helene's idea of the adequacy—even the superiority—of the truncated version of *Lulu* was reinforced to the point of fixity in her mind. From here on she did not waver in her determination to suppress the unfinished third act.

Only months following the Zurich performances of *Lulu*, Austria was annexed into the German Reich. Universal Edition was immediately "Aryanized," and no other possibilities arose for the staging of *Lulu* until after the end of World War II. The question of its completion during these years was deferred. As European operatic culture and interest in

Berg's music revived after the war, Alfred Schlee from Universal Edition reminded Helene that performances of *Lulu* would be limited unless it was presented as a three-act work. Helene then devised a rationale for refusing such requests, which she repeated many times for the rest of her life. If Schoenberg, Webern, and Zemlinsky—composers of eminence who were intimate with Berg—had refused to complete the orchestration of Act 3, then no one else should be entrusted with this task. She explained herself at length in a letter to Hans Redlich:

> I was not opposed in principle to having the instrumentation of *Lulu* completed. There is a confirmation of this, a facsimile of a letter from me to Schoenberg from 1936 in which I thank him for offering to undertake the instrumentation of *Lulu* Act 3. *Unfortunately* he later declined, after looking through it. Afterwards the manuscript went to Zemlinsky, then to Webern, so that they might undertake the work. Here too both men were *opposed*. It was not my choice to deny the completed opera to posterity. But it would have to be done by musicians and composers *of Alban Berg's stature*. I know that he viewed and valued these three friends as "soul mates." Other composers *not to the same degree*. . . . I cannot let something happen that would not be right with Alban. I know of his implacable strictness towards his productions. I also know precisely his views, his unerring judgment in artistic matters, his deep admiration and love for all that is great, genuine, and true—for the highest and most perfect. So I have to insist. It would be for me a sin against the Holy Ghost if I were not always mindful of his convictions.[24]

Surely Helene was aware that her argument was disingenuous. Schoenberg could have completed the orchestration of Act 3 if he had had more time and if the caricature of the Jewish banker had not offended him. Webern long maintained the idea of working on *Lulu*. Alfred Schlee, a close friend of Webern, told Helene about his continuing interest: "It is also not correct that Webern was basically unwilling about the completion. Quite the opposite: in the time shortly before his death he was deeply occupied with the idea of taking on this work, and he even once gave me a firm commitment that he would take it on."[25]

As Schlee predicted, the two-act *Lulu* was far slower to return to the postwar stage than was *Wozzeck*. The first postwar performance was in Vienna in 1949, made for broadcast by Austrian radio (RAVAG), and the first postwar staging was given on 4–5 September 1949 at Venice's Teatro

La Fenice, conducted by Nino Sanzogno. Helene traveled to Venice for the performances, and she was unhappy that the work was not done there in its "complete" form, by which she meant Acts 1 and 2 followed by the movements from the *Symphonic Pieces* at the end. She wrote to an acquaintance about it:

> They stopped at the end of the second act, by which I was appalled. This gave the work an entirely false disposition, and the ending [Adagio from the *Symphonic Pieces*] is also so beautiful and stirring. In Zurich at the premiere it was done that way. I was there only for the final rehearsal and by then nothing could be changed.[26]

The first German postwar staging of *Lulu* was in Essen in 1953, again with Helene Berg in attendance. The reviews were uniformly positive, once more enforcing Helene's belief that the two-act version was how the opera should always be performed. H.H. Stuckenschmidt commented on the Essen production:

> The impression of the evening grew from act to act, from scene to scene. No one who experienced it could be unaffected by the deep artistic serious-ness or the often ingenious inspiration of this score. The total success of the performance and the 20 curtain calls by the performers show that there was more here than discharging some honorary duty.[27]

As interest in *Lulu* again began to stir, a great tug of war erupted among Helene's acquaintances, some trying to convince her to allow the completion of the work, others opposed. Adorno weighed in on the side of completion, stressing that the work could not live on except in its three-act form. He wrote to Helene in 1949:

> Anyone with even the slightest understanding of theatre, which is by its very nature dependent on an audience, knows that an unfinished opera, outside of memorial or festival performances, cannot live. God knows that I honor the idea of the fragment, but in an art form whose aesthetic substance cannot be separated from a certain drastic materiality, a fragmentary reproduction would be an impossibility.[28]

"I do not have the words to express how serious I am about this," Adorno concluded, then suggested René Leibowitz as a qualified person to or-chestrate Act 3. Josef Rufer, Hans Redlich, and Erwin Stein joined with

Adorno in this appeal. Following upon the Hamburg production of *Lulu* in 1957, Erwin Stein wrote to Helene to try to allay her disgust with the text of Act 3:

> I find that the terrible Act 3 is necessary for the musical, dramatic, formal, and moral balance of the work. In "Erdgeist" Lulu atones by her arrest and punishment, that is, through earthly justice. In "Pandora's Box" there is a higher justice in play. In the opera *Lulu*, that is, *in the musical presentation of the drama on stage*, Act 2 ends in a situation that demands a more decisive dramatic atonement.[29]

On the other side of the dispute were some of Helene's most trusted friends. At their head was Erwin Ratz, who shared Helene's involvement with spiritualism and anthroposophy and became one of her most faithful friends and supporters during her widowhood. He was an implacable opponent of the completion of *Lulu*, just as he later was in rejecting all efforts to complete Mahler's Tenth Symphony, efforts that had added weight since Ratz was president of the International Gustav Mahler Society. In his thinking about Mahler's Tenth Symphony, Ratz was supported by Bruno Walter, who wrote to Alma Mahler in 1961:

> No one with even a shred of knowledge about the essence of creativity would dare to complete an incomplete work by a great and creative person. Nothing is so deeply individualized as the creative act, and no other person, even the most gifted, the most humble, the most devoted may attempt to complete what the other and greater individual had begun and was forced to leave unfinished.[30]

Helene Berg often brought forth a copy of Walter's letter to defend her position on *Lulu*. Soma Morgenstern joined in:

> I am happy to hear that you are very much opposed to any attempts at rescue work. There is nothing here to rescue; the work has its full value as it is, and it is your duty to protect it from unprovoked attacks. . . . I am resolutely opposed to have anyone messing around with Alban's works, and it doesn't matter who is doing the messing or who has recommended him.[31]

In his 1937 book on Berg, Willi Reich seemed open to having *Lulu* completed, provided that it was done "by someone intimately acquainted with Berg's way of working." But Reich later joined forces with Helene to oppose any effort to complete the opera. Reich urged Helene to declare mortmain over the work to prevent any future completion. "You should create an unassailable legal order," he advised her, "that sanctions this version and above all strictly forbids any attempt to complete the orchestration. It would be literally tragic if unwarranted hands were to tamper with this marvelous work."[32] Helene attempted to heed Reich's advice by writing in her will dated 23 July 1969: "No one may examine the third act of *Lulu*. Neither may the photocopy in the possession of Universal Edition be examined."[33]

By the time of the Essen performances in 1953, Berg's music had entered a full-fledged international revival. Alfred Schlee realized that Helene Berg would not change her mind about completing *Lulu*, so he chose to work behind her back to have Act 3 orchestrated, even if its use in performance would have to wait for her demise. Schlee's original preference for the composer to oversee its completion was Luigi Dallapiccola, an astute choice. Dallapiccola had a great admiration for and knowledge of the music of Berg, whom he had met in Venice in 1934. Dallapiccola's opera *Il prigioniero* had scored a great success in Florence in 1950, and his approach to twelve-tone composition had much in common with Berg's in *Lulu*. In 1957, Schlee made a formal offer to Dallapiccola to complete *Lulu*, but Dallapiccola declined.[34]

Years elapsed before Schlee moved forward with his plans. In 1962 he turned in a new direction for the completion—not to a prominent composer on the level of a Schoenberg, Webern, or Dallapiccola, nor to a former acquaintance of Berg, nor even to a composer who wrote music like Berg's. Schlee turned instead to a younger and less-known figure—the Viennese composer and professor Friedrich Cerha (b. 1926). By the early 1960s Cerha's music was beginning to attract attention in modern music circles, in the style of emerging postwar modernists such as György Ligeti, Krzysztof Penderecki, and Iannis Xenakis, with clouds of sound and mutating sonorous textures. In style and compositional technique, Cerha's music was not related to that of Berg, although Cerha convinced Schlee of his enthusiasm for and knowledge of Berg's music. Following the first Viennese staged performance of *Lulu*, in June 1962 at the Theater an der Wien, Cerha made his interest in completing Act 3 known to Universal Edition:

While at first I was attracted mainly to the musical and sonorous side, now the structural and formal aspects of the work became the center of my interest, the complex system of relationships that penetrates every corner of the work making it a cohesive, living organism from which nothing can be omitted without brutal damage to and endangerment of the whole.[35]

In 1963 Schlee commissioned Cerha to produce a performing edition of Act 3, a project that covertly occupied Cerha for the next twelve years. During this time the completion of *Lulu* became an international *cause célèbre.* A strategy to force the release of the *Lulu* manuscripts was forged by Hans Redlich in England and George Perle in the United States. Redlich was one of the few outside of Berg's circle to have studied the music for Act 3 of the opera, using Erwin Stein's piano score for that purpose. In his 1957 book on Berg, Redlich analyzed the third act in considerable detail, described the existing materials, and argued persuasively that Act 3 could be readily completed. "The completion of Berg's second dramatic masterpiece, his human and artistic bequest to the world, is an obligation of honor for the epoch in which his greatness has become a lasting possession."[36]

Perle's involvement with *Lulu* had begun in 1959, when he broached his idea for a book on Berg's operas to Redlich.[37] In August 1963 he was finally allowed by Universal Edition to study Berg's manuscripts, after which he stated confidently that *Lulu* was "complete" beyond his most extravagant hopes, and there were no musical reasons why a full, three-act version should not be attainable.[38] But when Schlee indicated that he would not move ahead with a complete edition and performance of *Lulu*, Perle attempted to apply pressure from other leaders in the world of modern music. He asked the American conductor Robert Craft, who in 1963 had conducted *Lulu* at the Santa Fe Opera, to engage Igor Stravinsky to write to Alfred Schlee at Universal Edition urging the completion of *Lulu*. Stravinsky's letter, which was almost certainly written by Craft, states in part:

> I accept, without the slightest hesitation, Dr. Perle's conclusion that no musical problems whatever stand in the way of completing the score in a manner entirely consistent with Berg's intentions, which can be fully deduced from the Particell and from the extensive portions of Act III scored by Berg himself. The evidence presented by Perle is absolutely convincing. . . . One thing

is clear beyond any possible question, and that is that the continued failure to complete the scoring of Act III can no longer be imputed to musical problems. If the problems are legal or financial or a combination of both, then these problems must be plainly formulated and an attempt made to resolve them immediately.[39]

Schlee then confided to Perle that Friedrich Cerha was already at work on a completion of the third act of *Lulu*, but an edition or performance was out of the question given Helene Berg's opposition. Angry letters passed between Schlee and Perle, and Perle developed an animus against Helene Berg that he was never able to put aside. Hans Redlich, keeping a cooler head, meanwhile proposed a less confrontational idea for rescuing Berg's unfinished opera: the establishment of an international Alban Berg Society. He wrote to Perle about it: "In my opinion there is only one way to help Berg and his music:—the foundation of an Alban Berg Society (comparable in scope, duties and aims to the Hugo Wolf and Gustav Mahler Societies) whose chief aim should be:—to publish all music and letters, articles, etc., in a critical edition, not subject to any 'vested interest.'"[40] The proposed new society had a thinly veiled purpose, to secure the release of Berg's unpublished works by marshalling public opinion against Helene Berg's and Universal Edition's prohibition on the *Lulu* materials.

The International Alban Berg Society was formally launched in 1966, and its official goal was "to promote the artistic heritage of Alban Berg and facilitate performances and publications of his works through the fostering of public interest, enlistment of material support and encouragement of relevant research."[41] The presidency of the society was assumed by Stravinsky, with Redlich as vice-president, and the board included an international array of prominent composers: Benjamin Britten, Luigi Dallapiccola, Ernst Krenek, Gian Francesco Malipiero, Darius Milhaud, and Roger Sessions. There was, notably, no one included from Berg's inner circle or, for that matter, from Austria other than Krenek, who had long since emigrated to the United States and was an outspoken proponent of a *Lulu* completion. Redlich wrote politely to Helene to ask for her collaboration, and she replied graciously: "Dear Doctor, The news of the founding of an Alban Berg Society has given me extraordinary pleasure, and I ask you to convey this to the gentlemen of the Society, together with my thanks for the good wishes, which I most sincerely reciprocate. Helene Berg."[42] Despite the pleasantries, Helene understood that the New York-based Society posed a direct challenge to her belief that *Lulu* was complete in its two-act form, and it also constituted a rival to her long-envisioned Alban Berg Foundation in Austria.

The Society founded by Redlich and Perle was unsuccessful in its objective to move forward the publication and performance of a completed *Lulu*. Cerha completed his initial work on Act 3 in 1974, which he later revised for publication by Universal Edition in 1978, shortly after the passing of Helene Berg. Following a legal compromise between Universal Edition and the Alban Berg Foundation, which became the testamentary legatee of Helene Berg, the stage was then set for the first performance of the three-act *Lulu*, at the Paris Opéra on 24 February 1979.

Bereavement, Grief, and Helene Berg's "Eternal Marriage"

The prolonged dispute over the completion of *Lulu* was one of several controversies that haunted Helene Berg in the course of her long widowhood. For her restrictions on Berg's musical legacy, also for her insistence that she was in communication with Alban in the beyond, she was accused—as she was by George Perle—of being "neurotic, superstitious, unbalanced, ignorant."[43] Perle and Erich Berg, Helene's nephew, asserted that she was unhinged with jealousy over Hanna Fuchs, to whom Perle found cryptic references in the *Lulu* score. Perle went so far as to imply that Berg himself during his lifetime was aware of his wife's growing mental instability and promoted the idea of a perfect marriage out of fear of a breakdown. Perle wrote:

> Ought we not to inquire into her mind and character, as well as his, in trying to understand his behavior? For 41 years after his death she persisted in the tragic role of a recently bereaved widow. It is surprising that no-one should have seen—in Freud's own Vienna—anything suspect in her obsessive clinging to this role and to its special privileges.[44]

To inquire into Helene Berg's mind and character, we must bear in mind, first, the wrenching circumstances of Berg's death, which left her in a state of near prostration. Soon after Berg's death she checked into a sanatorium in Hofgastein to cope with her thoughts of plunging into an abyss and described herself to Alma Mahler as "completely shattered."[45]

Alma quickly perceived Helene's dilemma, writing to her confidante Ida Gebauer Wagner: "She has nothing else in the world. She had this husband who was her child, her toy etc.—but she had otherwise no profession, no other opportunity in her life. Now *what* will become of her?"[46] Given the perception of her fragility by Alma and others, was Helene given a pass in "Freud's Vienna," as Perle suggests? And did she unreasonably and extravagantly extend her mourning period?

The idea that mourning should be completed and that the bereaved should "move on" in life was advanced by Freud in 1917, in the context of World War I. Freud proposed that healthy mourning required a conscious severing of psychological connection with the deceased, the so-called "grief work," a view that still had currency at the time of Berg's death.[47] The evolution of grief theory after Freud and especially after World War II has included recognition by psychologists and psychiatrists of grief pathologies, among which is Prolonged Grief Disorder (PGD) in which loss remains unresolved. More recently, contemporary mental health professionals have acknowledged a continuing bond with the dead as something culturally determined and not in itself abnormal. But they note risks of maladaptation to loss associated with a continuing bond that involves illusions and hallucinations concerning the deceased.[48]

Helene Berg chose to deal with her grief by maintaining a continuing bond with her departed husband. Rather than moving beyond her loss as Freud had advocated, she integrated it into a new mode of existence which centered on a continuing marital fidelity and which involved an extraordinary investment of psychological energy in managing her husband's legacy. Her declaration of her "profession" as "composer's widow" (*Komponistenwitwe*) on her passport and other documents signifies her conscious adoption of this new identity.[49] In choosing to nurture a continuing bond with Alban beyond the grave, Helene may have walked a fine line at times between normality and delusion, but there is no evidence that she was functionally impaired, rather the opposite. By virtue of her long study of the ideas of Rudolf Steiner and his anthroposophical movement, she was well equipped to forge her new spiritual marriage. Anthroposophy maintained that there was no barrier between the physical and spiritual world and death was only a transition during which the soul prepared itself for reincarnation. If Helene and Alban were to be reunited in the afterlife, which Helene fervently claimed, then it must follow that they were eternally married. This eternal marriage became the framework upon which Helene hung her bereavement and her grief. She had made clear to Alban on the eve of their marriage that it would be different from the unhappy union of her parents: "I will ever be your companion, lover, and support, from here to eternity."[50]

"Until death us do part" had no place in Helene's marital lexicon. On her thirtieth wedding anniversary, after Berg had been dead for five years, Helene wrote from the Waldhaus to her deceased husband:

> My dearest, eternal one and only! Today is our 30th anniversary. I must tell you again today what I have felt and always will feel, that I am indissolubly bound to you. I am sitting in the Waldhaus in the deep blessed stillness of your room which is exactly as it would be if you had just left the piano to take a moment with me, to step out onto the balcony and—in a deep embrace—to admire our blooming cherry tree and to look at the nearby woods, behind which the snow-capped mountains gleam.[51]

Here the eternal bond is shrouded in a timelessness in which interior and exterior landscapes—both mirroring the psychological terrain—are unchanging. For Helene, time had stopped with Berg's death, and to the extent that she could control it, the external world would also remain static. She would state many times that Alban's room at the Waldhaus was never to be changed. (Likewise *Lulu* was to be understood to be "complete" as Berg left it.) In her writings she often distinguished between "earthly life," a temporary condition in which she now existed, and an afterlife, a *"Jenseits,"* in which her marriage would be eternally fulfilled. Until then, time had little meaning.

The bereaved are known to write letters to the departed, but Helene espoused an even more active connection with her husband for the remainder of her life, routinely speaking and listening to him in the beyond and asking for his advice on worldly matters. This practice is also consistent with Steiner's teachings on communication with the departed as a spiritual exercise. Not long after Berg's death she wrote to Alma Mahler concerning her continuing connection to Alban:

> Life is burdensome and sad—sad in all ways for me. The only ray of light is when Alban is here. And he is often here; he lives with us and we speak to him. His place at the piano and desk, his chair, in which he "knocks out" his

answers. He is punctual in the morning, at midday and in the evening, and at night he is with me and advises me in everything. Nothing more can happen to me. I know that our life here is only an appearance and real life begins with him in the beyond![52]

Helene was not alone in her spiritual thinking and practice. Anthroposophy had many allies among Vienna's artists and intellectuals, as did other occult movements, as has been noted earlier. Schoenberg himself had experimented with theosophy, the parent movement of anthroposophy. Hildegard Jone, known to musical scholars as the author of virtually all of the poetry set by Anton Webern after 1934, submitted works to the anthroposophical journal *Individualität*. In her diaries she recorded "Auditionen" (hearing voices) with spirits and integrated these experiences into her mystical Catholicism.[53] Jone's condolence letter after Berg's death encourages Helene in the notion that Alban was still present:

I would like so very much to tell you, with all the strength of my heart: do not believe that your husband is dead. He is with "the father of heavenly lights," he will come close to you again, he will be wholly with you—this you will experience for certain. You will, when you quietly listen within yourself, perceive his voice and his words. This will not happen right away and perhaps not very soon (at first, you will only feel his having "passed away"), but it will certainly come about.[54]

Jone's letter promotes a positive view of continuing spiritual communication—quite the reverse of maladaptation. Ružena Herlinger also supported Helene when she wrote in 1968 to Hans Redlich: "When I visited Helene Berg I think it was 1956 or 57 . . . [t]he U.E., has told me, she is not normal! She was normal and we understood each other very well."[55] The words of these two women stand in marked contrast to the dismissive attitudes of men such as Perle, Erich Berg, and Alfred Schlee at Universal Edition, suggesting that assessments of Helene's normality sometimes divided along gender lines.

Except for her contact with trusted friends, Helene kept her esoteric spiritual life largely closeted. She did not deposit documentation of her practice with her husband's papers at the Austrian National Library. Most of the sources relating to her anthroposophical study were recovered from the Waldhaus after her death and remain with the Alban Berg Foundation. Open practice of anthroposophy became dangerous after 1935 when the movement was banned by the Nazis.[56] Still, Helene continued to maintain contact with like-minded thinkers.[57]

Underlying Helene's embrace of the eternal bond may be issues of attachment from her childhood which were transferred to her marriage.[58] Her insecure attachment to her father, Franz Nahowski, has been attributed in a prior chapter to the unresolved matter of her paternity. Alban, she once claimed, would fulfill all other male roles in her life—that of the father excepted. She wrote to him during his military service in 1915:

> This terrible loneliness! It is so strange—I have my family—and in spite of that I have no feeling of belonging—I'm always on the outside, alone. I have *only you!* You are my husband, my brother and my child! I want to hold you and protect you forever in my arms . . . I love you so much, *much too much!*[59]

Feelings that Helene may have been astute enough to understand early in her marriage evolved into increasing possessiveness and jealousy over other women, against which Berg came to chafe more and more. Attachment theory may also allow the hypothesis that Helene's ultimate claim to a complete possession of Alban Berg and his musical legacy within the framework of the eternal marriage was the logical outcome of her bereavement.

Helene Berg's Life under the Nazis, 1938–45

In the late 1930s, up to and after the annexation of Austria by Germany in March of 1938, Helene Berg's daily life was focused on survival. In the months following Alban's death she was forced again to accept charity from Alma Mahler.[60] She was determined to hold on to the Waldhaus, which she intended as a memorial site and home for the future Alban Berg Foundation. She also was obligated to contribute to the care of her schizophrenic brother, Frank, and his caregiver, her aunt Barbara Nowak, known as Wetti. She began by reluctantly selling off items of value, as she wrote to Wetti early in 1937: "We have to get our lives in order and I must look into taking a renter, for I can't go on eternally squandering the nice things that have become precious to me."[61] Helene's situation improved somewhat in 1937, when her lawyer, Otto Lifczis, was able to conclude the sale of the Maxingstrasse house. Helene used her portion to pay off the mortgage on the Waldhaus.[62]

Helene also inherited her husband's debt to Universal Edition. The publisher began the process of renegotiating a contract with her in 1936, but with the "Aryanization" of the firm in 1938, her relations with the firm became murky. In 1936 and 1937 Berg's music was still being performed outside Germany and Austria, most frequently the Violin Concerto and the *Lyric Suite*, so some small performance royalties accrued to her, but these soon fell off and ceased to reach her altogether during the war years.

Helene Berg's life under the shadow of the Nazis took a painful turn in 1938, with the mounting in Düsseldorf of the infamous "Entartete Kunst" (Degenerate Art) exhibit. So-called "degenerate art" had a prior history of political repression under the label "cultural bolshevism,"[63] but the Düsseldorf exhibit included a whole new section on "Degenerate Music," organized by Joseph Goebbels. The composers featured most prominently were Schoenberg, Kurt Weill, Ernst Krenek, Paul Hindemith, and Igor Stravinsky, beside figures considered more minor, which included Berg, Josef Matthias Hauer, Ernst Toch, and Webern. The exhibit traveled to Vienna in May 1939. Helene Berg claimed to have visited it every day, meeting there, she wrote, "the best company: those who understand art."[64] Press coverage without exception conformed to Nazi views. According to one reviewer, the Viennese citizen, with his "native understanding of music," would recognize that in the works exhibited "sexual deviance, madness and incompetence are united."[65] A reviewer for the *Wiener neueste Nachrichten* wrote:

> The slogan "absolute polyphony" led him [Schoenberg] into a nihilistic self-renunciation of harmony and to a denial of all laws of sound, which had long been discarded as sterile. In the area of musical drama, this unnatural idea, elevated to the level of principle, reached its gruesome psychoanalytic high point in *Wozzeck* by Alban Berg. This direction soon fizzled out, as we see in the brash curiosity pieces of dilettantes at work in their playgrounds.[66]

Helene challenged the Nazi authorities on Berg's placement in this humiliating exhibition. Writing directly to the organizer of the exhibit, privy councilor and head of the German National Theater Dr. Hans Severus Ziegler, she objected strenuously to Berg's inclusion among Jews and those classed in the exhibit as "petty Bolsheviks": Ernst Toch, Karol Rathaus, Max Brand, and Josef Matthias Hauer. She stressed, as Berg earlier had done, that her husband was not a Jew, and she emphasized his connection to German tradition, asking that a group of experts reevaluate his music in that light. She also asked for a public acknowledgement of Berg's Aryan status.[67] In response Ziegler offered some concessions: he would disassociate Berg's name with anything Jewish and leave his scores without commentary; "there are only a few, anyway," he wrote dismissively. But he could not concede that Berg's music had any artistic merit. This was all because of his association with "the Jew Schoenberg," as Ziegler's virulently anti-Semitic language makes clear:

> Unfortunately this is the bitter truth: "Qui mange du juif, en meure" [He who shall eat of the Jew shall die from it]. So many artists of German blood (Hindemith, for example) have gone along with the Jews through thick and thin, have attached themselves to them as teachers, conductors, virtuosos, as publishers and agents, such that they have become a "meal" for them. Finally they became part of the same movement. Alban Berg, against whom I have and have had no personal prejudice, like von Webern, has attached himself to the Jew Schoenberg as student, and "Wozzeck" is and remains a classic example of atonal music that must be overcome, like the architectural style of Gropius or the painting and sculpture of those well-known to you from the exhibit, "Degenerate Art," created by the Führer himself.[68]

Helene did not get any "reevaluation" of Berg's music nor did she obtain a public *Ariererklärung* (Aryan declaration).

While Helene Berg maintained her Vienna residence on Trauttmansdorffgasse, she spent most of her time after the war broke out at the Waldhaus, despite the difficulty of living there in the winter and the forced billeting there of war workers and later displaced mothers and children. In 1949 she recalled her life during the war to Alfred Schlee at Universal Edition:

> I had a hard enough time in the Nazi period. I certainly couldn't live on STAGMA's monthly beneficence of 33.33 reichsmarks. All those years I couldn't buy a single thing on the black market. I lived by the work of my hands and ate mostly vegetables, which I grew. (And how hard it was: digging, carrying watering cans, pumping water!) And then all the housework, the

laundry and carrying wood from the wood lot. Then the badly paid rentals to the armament workers, 50 cents a bed (every 13 days a new group—fresh bedclothes) until the N.S.V.'s commandeering of the house for mothers and infants put an end to that. These years were a severe toll on my strength. My heart problem, a consequence of constant overexertion, is enough proof, and any doctor can confirm it.[69]

Her postwar account resonates with letters to Alma Mahler from the war period. To her she reports that she had taken in boarders at both her Vienna residence and in the summer at the Waldhaus:

> Last summer I had 7 people [at the Waldhaus], all women between the ages of 50 and 80! It was not easy for me, but if I want to keep the Waldhaus, I have no other choice. My life's goal remains the Alban Berg Foundation. As an *artist* Alban is immortal through his works. *My* task is to do something in memory of this good, noble and generous man. Therefore I work and only in this way can I sustain my life. I still have my monthly STAGMA allowance of RM 33.33. I never worry about how I will get by—oddly, things work out. But in a completely spartan way. I am up at 5 AM and usually still up at 11 PM. I tend two large gardens and Frank, who was sick for a whole year from nerve inflammation and shingles on his face.[70]

Helene's brother Frank and her Aunt Wetti also lived at the Waldhaus at various intervals. Helene became her brother's guardian after Alban's death. Frank died in 1942 of pulmonary disease.[71] After his death, Helene inherited what was left of his money and used it to pay off Alban's debt with Universal Edition.[72] During this time of upheaval, the Waldhaus sustained damage, and in September of 1945 Helene obtained monument protection (*Denkmalschutz*) from the state government of Carinthia for the building and grounds.[73] It took many more years for her to achieve the same protection for Berg's study in Vienna.

In these trying years, Helene sought shelter in her spiritual domain which she inhabited with Alban: "During the terrible time of Nazi rule, Alban's world was my only refuge—I couldn't have lived otherwise. Now the worst is behind us, but I am very tired."[74] Notebooks from the time, most of them written at the Waldhaus, record her private spiritual musings and struggles. These writings frequently take aphoristic form and address anthroposophical themes, such as inner knowledge, listening to one's inner voice, testing and spiritual progress, and being led by heavenly guides. The eternal bond with Alban is often stressed. The importance of both words and music as solace and a means of connection between the physical and the spiritual worlds is reiterated, as in this passage: "Thoughts are power—words (language) the first approach to reality. Music—language from another world, from which you came and to which you returned again."[75] Some of the notebook pages are addressed directly to the departed:

> To Alban: How often in my hard, rough work tears fell from my eyes because my heart burns for you, in longing, love and pain—. Woven into the arduous day-to-day, which *never* was so [arduous] for me when I was still allowed to live with you—I worked then, yes, but your music always, always surrounded me. My sensitive ear missed not a note of your beloved speech. I heard it in the house, in the garden, it grew at the same time into our soul-contact (mine listening, yours sounding [*tönend*]). You felt it too and you were pleased when I was nearby. Sometimes you said: Pferschi, pray! I am stuck! Then we usually took a walk through a favorite landscape, you in front, I behind, silent. Suddenly you pulled your notebook out of your pocket, the solution was found.[76]

Helene's image of herself as the consummate listener, while Alban was the "Tönender," the creator of music, becomes a mystic emblem of their continuing soul-union. She imagines herself waking up in eternity, borrowing her favorite line from *Lulu*: "A soul that rubs the sleep from its eyes in the beyond . . . the most beautiful sentence from the works of Frank Wedekind! Heln. B. Two souls—one making music, the other listening. A. and H.B."[77]

So immersed was Helene in her day-to-day work and in her spiritual exercises that the war seemed remote to her. She again strikes the theme of time standing still.

> Winter 1944–45. A peculiar time. One is pulled so near to eternity—it is almost an unreal feeling. One goes through all that is dreadful as if in a dream.
>
> Summer 1945 (war). Why is everything so strange? In our still house and garden the rude noise of soldiers and the cries of prostitutes. And I, up here in *your* beloved rooms, wander through the sanctuary of your—our world! [78]

While questions about the status of *Lulu* continued to plague her, the war years had given Helene time to refine her thinking about her spiritual state, her continuing connection to Alban, and "his" role in her life of *Komponistenwitwe*. The harsh conditions of her wartime existence hardened her resolve and strengthened her purpose—this in spite of her earlier trope of physical fragility and ill health. She managed to retain possession of the Waldhaus against steep odds, paid off her debts, and clung tenaciously to her vision of a foundation centered at the Waldhaus that would provide a fitting memorial to the man to whom she felt eternally bound. The ups and downs of her stewardship of Berg's legacy must be weighed against her motives and preoccupations which, however eccentric and sometimes misguided, were not the result of mental disorder or malign purposes, despite such charges aimed at her by George Perle and others. She was, on the contrary and by all evidence, fully competent and functional, as Ružena Herlinger attested.

Berg's Musical Manuscripts and Letters

Helene Berg was her husband's sole legatee and administrator of his estate. Although the appraisal of Berg's estate was small, his musical manuscripts had enormous value. Among these documents was the *Particell* of Act 3 of *Lulu*—the sole primary record for this part of his final work. Other manuscripts contained the only records of many of the songs and keyboard pieces from his apprenticeship. Berg's musical sketches and drafts were scarcely less valuable since these contain a unique record of his compositional process and creative thinking. Following the disruption of the war, it would take years for Helene and Universal Edition to sort out the location and rightful ownership of Berg's musical manuscripts. To make such matters more complicated, Helene often gave away pages and even complete works from her store of Berg's manuscripts. Several complete compositions—including unpublished early songs and movements from the still unpublished Altenberg songs, Op. 4—were given to libraries, and pages from drafts and sketches were given to a variety of individuals as mementos. In 1957 Helene began to transfer her remaining manuscripts to the Austrian National Library; those from Universal Edition were also deposited there, and these documents are now open for study and are the basis for the preparation of critical editions of Berg's music and writings under the aegis of the Alban Berg Foundation.[79]

The autograph manuscript of the *Lyric Suite* has an especially complex and controversial history given its connection to Berg's liaison with Hanna Fuchs-Robettin.[80] Berg at first contemplated presenting it to Alexander Zemlinsky, to whom the work is dedicated.[81] But it is unlikely that Berg actually turned it over to Zemlinsky, and there is no evidence that it was ever out of his possession. In March 1935, after the successful sale of the *Wozzeck* autograph, he inquired of both Adorno and Rudolf Kolisch if a buyer for it could be found in England or America, but their inquiries were unsuccessful. After Berg's death the manuscript passed, together with the remainder of his estate, into the possession of Helene Berg, and Alma Mahler urged Helene to give the document to Hanna. News of this possibility spread among Berg's circle, and Adorno spoke up strongly in opposition. He wrote to Helene:

> You are being urged, supposedly in accordance with Alban's wishes, to give it to H. F. I would advise you most urgently, with all my knowledge and all my conscience, not to do so. For all sorts of reasons. I shall name only two. Firstly, Alban had asked me and Kolisch repeatedly and with great urgency to arrange a sale of the manuscript. Would this be conceivable if he had intended for H. F. to receive it at some point? . . . For H. F. it would be a museum piece and a fetish; not only can she not read a bar of it, she probably cannot even understand it. I do not wish to prevent you from sacrificing the score: but from sacrificing it wrongly. It belongs in your hands, under your gaze that brings it to life; it is too precious to satisfy the narcissism of a woman merely bored to death. Forgive me for speaking bluntly; but relinquishing it would immortalize his relationship with H. F. in a way that seems to me, as his friend and yours, an injustice towards him and towards you. The obvious and unprecedentedly barefaced manner in which attempts are being made to snatch the manuscript from you is a further reason not to have anything to do with it.[82]

Despite Adorno's persuasive argument—and perhaps because of Helene's resentment against him for his role in the Hanna affair—she decided to follow Alma's wishes and turn the manuscript over to Hanna. She explained her thinking to Alma:

> As to the gift of the Lyric Suite, now that Alban's plan to sell it has failed I am free to dispose of it as I wish. I have found the following expedient: Frau

Fuchs can have the music for her lifetime. She can put it on her piano for show. But she must pledge that after her death it will be returned to the Alban Berg Foundation, which also will own his collected books and music. This is Alban's wish.[83]

At about this time Helene wrote to the Fuchs-Robettins to offer them the *Lyric Suite* manuscript. Herbert Fuchs-Robettin wrote back declining the offer:

> Dear Helene. Hanna gave me your letter. I readily acknowledge your good will in the fulfillment of the wishes of your unforgettable late husband by your offering me the manuscript of the Lyric Suite under certain conditions. But as a gift from you I plainly cannot accept it and ask you therefore to do with it as you see fit. I sincerely hope that the difficult times that you must now face will be overcome so as to carry out Alban Berg's artistic legacy.[84]

The manuscript remained in Helene's possession and was delivered in 1957, with other Berg manuscripts, to the Austrian National Library, where it has remained ever since.

While researching his 1957 study of Berg, Hans Redlich attempted to locate the *Lyric Suite* manuscript, and following advice given by Universal Edition he stated, incorrectly, that it was then owned by Zemlinsky's heirs. Zemlinsky's widow later informed him that no one in her family had ever been in possession of the document. Redlich explored further and spoke with Hanna Fuchs-Robettin about it, but he received only conflicting evidence on its whereabouts.[85] Based on information from Redlich, George Perle later constructed an often repeated although almost entirely inaccurate narrative filled with insinuations of Helene's duplicity. Perle writes:

> In fact, however, as Mrs. Berg was well aware, her husband had given the manuscript not to its "official" dedicatee but to its "real" dedicatee, Hanna Fuchs-Robettin. After Berg's death, Alma Mahler Werfel prevailed upon her sister-in-law to cede the manuscript to Helene Berg. We do not know why Mrs. Berg did not admit that the autograph was in her own possession, but it is clear that her invention of a fictional account of its history was intended to prevent discovery of its one-time ownership by Hanna Fuchs-Robettin. . . . Mrs. Berg's first response, when she was informed that Mrs. Zemlinsky did

not have the manuscript, was to pretend that, to her great distress, it must be missing. Subsequently, she gave it to the Österreichische Nationalbibliothek.[86]

In addition to his musical manuscripts, Berg's library was also enriched by the letters that he had received throughout his life and his many copies and drafts of his own outgoing letters. Written in the thousands, these documents are vivid records of Berg's inner and outer lives, a window into his mind, as Christopher Hailey and Juliane Brand have remarked.[87] They reveal his personal aspirations and viewpoints and offer unique information about his music and his interpretations of literature, music history, and contemporary culture. To this day, the extent and content of Berg's correspondence to others is not fully known except for letters addressed to a few specific individuals, including his wife, Schoenberg, Adorno, and Erich Kleiber. Letters to other correspondents can sometimes be reconstructed using drafts that Berg was in the habit of making for his more important missives. Often, these drafts are the sole existing record of especially valuable correspondence, such as his letters to Alma Mahler, whose location is now unknown.[88] Beginning in 1923, Berg often made typed carbon copies of his letters.[89] He carefully preserved these materials as he also did the correspondence that he received from others, documents that often speak indirectly about his activities and thoughts.[90] Of unique importance are the hundreds of letters that Berg addressed to his wife during the twenty-nine years of their courtship and marriage.

Helene Berg was highly guarded with her husband's letters, often refusing permission for them to be published except for a few carefully chosen examples. Until the end of her life, she refused all requests to publish a complete letter exchange, fearing that passages might offend those still living and perhaps hesitating to have the real Alban Berg emerge, not the idealized person whose memory she revered. She was especially intent on withholding Berg's intimate letters to Webern, which she knew to be written with great frankness. Despite Helene's scruples, a smattering of Berg's letters appeared in print during her lifetime, most published without her knowledge or permission. An important collection of twenty-one letters to Erwin Schulhoff appeared in 1965, and a few of Berg's letters to Schoenberg, Webern, Adorno, and others were published here and there prior to 1976.[91] Universal Edition planned to publish the Webern–Berg correspondence, with Joseph Polnauer as its editor, but Helene's objections derailed this important project.[92]

During her long widowhood, Helene occupied herself by rereading the hundreds of letters that she had received from her husband from 1907 to 1935. Some of Berg's letters to her were either lost or destroyed. For example, there is no existing correspondence during Berg's weeklong visit to Frankfurt in June 1924. There are no existing letters from either Alban or Helene in 1926, at the height of Berg's infatuation with Hanna Fuchs.

In his letters Berg almost invariably expresses affection for his wife, addressing her by an endless number of childish pet names, showing concern for her well-being and a yearning to be reunited with her. As to be expected in any lengthy correspondence between married couples, the letters also occasionally contain churlish remarks about people and sometimes a sharp criticism of colleagues and family. The letters from 1907 to the early 1920s seem genuinely passionate in their expressions of love, but then they gradually flatten out into records of daily activities, diet, problems with health, and expressions of affection that seem increasingly perfunctory. Very few letters from Helene to Alban remain in the legacy from this later period, and it seems likely that most were discarded by Helene.

Helene at first thought that Berg's letters to her, except for a few samples, were too intimate to publish. Yet by the end of 1954 she had changed her mind and devised a plan to publish an edition solely of her husband's letters to her. In addition to funding the future Alban Berg Foundation, her intention in the project was to create a memorial to the idealized image of her husband and to the perfection of their life together. She knew that only a selection of his letters could be included, and she edited many of these to remove slighting references to people still alive and other controversial statements made by Berg in passing. For example, after returning from a pilgrimage to Bayreuth in 1909, Berg wrote to Helene, "Do you think that Bayreuth could kill Parsifal, or that the hideous army of Jewish homosexual Wagnerians could spoil Wagner for me?"[93] Helene chose to strike only the word "Jewish" from the letter. More extensive editing would be needed for Berg's letters from 1926 onward, in which he repeatedly and falsely attempts to allay Helene's persistent jealousy over his conduct with other women. "For 20 years I have not looked at another woman, let alone touched one or exchanged so much as a word of attraction or love," Berg wrote disingenuously on 9 June 1927 to Helene. "How can I cure you of your delusions?"[94]

Helene's first step in the project was to dictate the letters, almost all handwritten, to a secretary, who typed a transcript that ultimately came to more than 700 dense and single-spaced pages.[95] A book contract with the Munich publisher Albert Langen-Georg Müller was signed by Helene on 23 September 1960, specifying that she would be the work's editor and select which letters to include. Langen could redact the letters with Helene's approval, and an Introduction to the volume would be written either by Helene or by someone appointed by the publisher. Franz Willnauer—a specialist in theater history and the works of Mahler who at the time was working for Universal Edition—was hired as an editorial assistant. Helene worked closely and amicably with Willnauer for more than three years, 1962–65. He spent much time with her at the Waldhaus going over the letter transcripts, even for a time acting as caretaker of the property. Although he was never shown more than a few of the original letters, he believed that the typed transcripts were reasonably faithful to those sources. Based on his conversations with Helene and certainly with her approval, he wrote footnotes and brief headnotes that explained the context of many of the letters, and he also prepared a lengthy introduction to the volume, as prescribed by the contract of 1960.

Yet the letter project was flawed from the very start. Helene had no experience in editorial or publishing practices, and she had little interest in placing Berg's letters within the larger history of music and culture, the things that interested Willnauer. Instead, she most wanted a volume that would show her marriage to be "a paradise of his love," as she put it in her brief introduction to the volume. Helene's deletions from the letters promoted this objective, but her choice of letters was characterized also by what she wanted left in. In her initial selection, she included letters concerning the "Berghof catastrophe" of forty-five years before, even bringing in Berg's letters to his mother and to his brother Herman in which he holds his other brother, Charly, up to ridicule. Plainly, Helene wanted the world to know about the dishonesty of Charly Berg and her disdain for his wife, Stefanie. Helene left in Berg's description of Stefanie as "a woman whose mind is no better than her ugly face."[96]

Finally, relations between Helene and Willnauer soured, and she demanded that his explanatory notes and his name be removed from the volume entirely. In mid-October 1965 Helene received bound copies of the *Briefe an seine Frau*, and she found that some of the passages that she wanted removed were still present. She then sued Langen, demanding that distribution of the book be halted, existing copies retrieved, and 30,000 schillings in damages be paid by the publisher. Langen complied with most of her demands, and the *Briefe* went through three versions in a matter of months. In the first revision, certain lines were blocked out and an explanatory note inserted by the publisher; in a second, larger printing, passages and whole letters were struck, and blank spaces were filled in by artwork.

Langen's accommodations did not end the fiasco. When the letter volume appeared in public, Charly's son, Erich, at last saw his uncle's letters from the time of the Berghof crisis of 1919–20, and he found their publication to be libelous against his father and mother. The ill will between Helene, Erich Berg, Willnauer, and Langen quickly spilled over into the press, dividing those like Willi Reich and Mosco Carner, who wished to remain in Helene's good graces, from others like Hans Redlich, who had long since fallen out of her favor. In their reviews of the edition, Reich and Carner complied with Helene's idea of the letters as a touching memorial to a perfect marriage, and they remained silent on the edition's contorted history and obvious shortcomings.[97] Redlich wrote a more objective review:

> It is regrettable that this first comprehensive publication of Alban Berg's let-
> ters in no way measures up to the editorial standards that can be expected at
> present for the posthumous publication of important documents in the life
> of a great composer of this century. The texts, with their many uncheckable
> ellipses, do not (or only rarely) derive from the autograph sources, and this
> considerably diminishes the documentary value of the collection. The deci-
> sion by the editor and publisher, obviously made at the last minute, to elimi-
> nate almost completely Dr. Willnauer's notes and to suppress his Introduction
> with its discussion of editorial issues, and the merging of an edition originally
> planned for two volumes into a single, overly-thick one may have promoted
> the book's sale but diminished its excellence as an edition. The volume of 655
> printed pages has no table of contents, no index of terms, and no meaningful

division into historical parts. But the many nice pictures of Helene Berg are impressive.[98]

The most widely read and ultimately most embarrassing review of the book was titled "Kusserln vom Floh" (Kisses from the Flea)—the title coming from one of Berg's many complimentary closes in his letters to his wife. The anonymous review, which appeared in the widely read *Der Spiegel*, was based on information provided by Willnauer, and it depicted Helene Berg as a muddled, elderly eccentric. According to the reviewer, the letter edition was based on transcripts "dictated by the eighty-year-old editor to a more-than-eighty-year-old secretary who was hard of hearing." The review continues: "Frau Helene still today has air pumped into the tires of her husband's Ford every year and saves Berg's cigarette butts. Favored visitors receive one as a gift. According to Willnauer, she wanted an 'antiseptic image' of Alban Berg, and the Berg letters are her Berg sermon. Willnauer: 'Her deletions were unrestrained.'"[99] Willnauer later apologized to Helene for the review, saying that he was misquoted.[100]

Despite its shortcomings and thanks largely to Willnauer's contribution and oversight, the *Briefe an seine Frau* proved a valuable addition to a knowledge of Alban Berg, and it remained one of the most often cited sources of information about the composer until superseded in 2012–14 by Herwig Knaus's massive critical edition of the correspondence.[101] But Helene's editorial decisions raised questions about her ability to manage Berg's legacy, just as her restrictions on the completion of the final act of *Lulu* were attracting worldwide attention.

Toward a Berg Biography

As his fame grew in the late 1920s, Berg believed that the time had come to have a study published about his life, works, and artistic achievements. A first step had been made by his childhood friend Hermann Watznauer, who had long been compiling biographical notes about Berg. In 1929 Berg received a copy of Watznauer's handwritten account, which was largely a chronological list of anecdotes, events, and compositions.[102] Berg then wrote to his old friend:

> Your biographical sketch made me *very* happy and was highly interesting to me and Helene. I was really "interested," because you wouldn't believe how much that you say I have long since completely forgotten. In any event, if

the need should ever arise for a biography about me to be written, your records will be the most complete, most reliable, and unique among source materials![103]

By the time that he received Watznauer's sketch, other initiatives for a more formal biography had been made. The Berlin journalist Hermann Rudolf Gail, long a proponent of Berg's music, had informed the composer that he was writing a biography of him, an "appreciative assessment" (*Würdigung*), and Berg willingly communicated information for it. In 1929 Berg sent a draft of the work to his friend Rudolf Ploderer, who gave it a negative report and thereafter Berg lost interest in seeing the project go forward.[104] A more promising initiative came at the same time from Berg's student Willi Reich, who began in 1929 to compile notes for a biography of his teacher, shortly after beginning private lessons with the composer. In the Berlin journal *Die Musik* in February 1930, Reich published a brief life-and-works account of Berg, the first of its kind. Berg was pleased with the result. Reich's article carefully adhered to what Berg wanted said about himself and his music, and in his many later books and articles about his former teacher Reich never deviated from this approach.

Berg soon came to trust in Reich to be his Boswell and commissioned him to write about his new compositions as he himself would have done. According to Reich, Berg later appointed him to be his "authorized" biographer, and for this he turned over to Reich a large trove of manuscript materials—unpublished writings, letters, and musical manuscripts. Reich put these to use in his 1937 book *Alban Berg*, co-authored with Ernst Krenek and Theodor Adorno. This was the earliest published monograph on the composer, and Reich in it again rejected any independent outlook or original analysis. "I have felt bound," he wrote, "solely to carry out Berg's will and to communicate his intentions."[105] Reich drew upon the materials given him by Berg in two later books and some fifty articles about his former teacher.

Helene Berg also contemplated writing a biography of her husband. Alma Mahler had long urged her to do so, to improve upon Willi Reich's slender biographical note in his 1937 *Alban Berg*. "Something quite different must be written about Alban—and will be!," she exclaimed. "I know that you alone, with your powers of love and empathy, can do this exhaustively. Give it a try! You are in a marvelously inward state of mind, so make use of it."[106] Helene began to make notes for just such a biography, which she entered into several notebooks with headings "Alban Berg Biographisches" and "Berg Dokumentation."[107] But her efforts at a narrative biography never progressed beyond repetitive lists of personal facts, dates, and compositions, most information taken from Hermann Watznauer's biography. Helene probably soon recognized that she could not write the sort of reminiscence of her husband that Alma thought she could, and she may also have come to the painful realization that she knew rather little about her husband's inner and creative life.

With the Berg revival in the early 1950s, Universal Edition decided, with Helene Berg's blessing, to publish a new study of the composer's life and music by an author outside of Berg's remaining circle of friends and students. The publisher chose Hans Redlich (1903–68), a prominent scholar of Viennese birth then living in England, for this assignment. Redlich told his friend Egon Wellesz about the project: "The modern reader (especially the German) wants an objective evaluation of Berg and one that is not so tied to a particular period. Those who have originated the idea think that a person like me—who is not a partisan and precisely because I am not a partisan—is the correct one to write such a book."[108]

Not only did Redlich come from outside of the Schoenberg–Berg circle, but his thinking about its music often deviated from established narratives. In his 1934 article "Der große Unzeitgemäße" (The great one out of keeping with his time) Redlich argued that Schoenberg's music was rooted in nineteenth-century romanticism and in its "belief in a permanent artistic progress." By the 1930s Schoenberg's music, Redlich concluded, had lost touch with the society in which it existed. "What could his revelations from a remote world of sound have to do with the marching hordes—youths bedecked with fraternal emblems—or with their march music and communal choruses that accompany the despair over their hopeless future?"[109] The idea that Schoenberg's music was outmoded—although frequently stated in critical writing of the 1920s and 1930s—was bitterly opposed by Schoenberg himself and, accordingly, by his students.[110] That Redlich was chosen to write a large-scale study of Berg was a source of alarm within the composer's circle. Redlich's volume appeared in 1957 in a German edition with detailed

musical analyses followed by a highly condensed English version for general readers.[111]

An especially important and controversial memoir of Berg originating
within his circle of acquaintances is Soma Morgenstern's *Alban Berg und
seine Idole* (Alban Berg and his idols). It was left incomplete at the time
of the author's death in 1976 and published in 1995 in a reconstruction
made from typescripts, related writings, and the existing correspondence between the two.[112] Morgenstern was studying law in Vienna in
1920 when he first encountered the Bergs, and by 1923 he had formed
a close friendship with them that was enriched by lengthy discussions of
literature, theater, and music. From 1928 to 1933 Morgenstern was the
Viennese cultural correspondent for the *Frankfurter allgemeine Zeitung*,
and his critiques reliably supported music by those in Schoenberg's
circle. Berg often consulted Morgenstern on literary questions—his role
in helping Berg to decide between *Und Pippa tanzt!* and the Lulu plays
has been discussed. In 1938 Morgenstern fled the Nazis, first to France
where he spent three harrowing years one step ahead of the Gestapo,
then in 1941 to New York. In the 1950s he began to assemble material
for an autobiography in which a large role would be played by his former
acquaintances—primarily Berg and the writer Joseph Roth, who was
with Morgenstern in his exile in France. He later abandoned the autobiography but extracted the passages about Berg and Roth for separate
books, although he did not live to complete either of them.[113]

Morgenstern's *Alban Berg und seine Idole* cannot be read as an objective or factual memoir about Berg. It is instead a "Romanbericht"—a
"novelesque narrative"—the term used by Morgenstern to describe the
book on Joseph Roth and equally applicable to the one about Berg.[114]
Both books are works of imagination—a mixing of fact and fiction that
the author spins into a discourse on European literature, culture and politics of his time. Morgenstern explains his method:

> Over and over I find that I cannot rely on a recollection except when I allow
> myself a free associational process of thought. The best control over memory
> is to have none at all. You cannot milk a recollection; you can just give it free
> rein. A later recollection will demonstrate that your apparently confused, ap-
> parently accidental impulse almost always had a coherence in which those
> associations are correct.[115]

Berg's role in Morgenstern's narrative is often that of a straight man, an interlocutor whose naive questions trigger lengthy and opinionated narratives by the author. Other passages may come from Morgenstern's recollections of conversations with Berg, although in these there is no effort to distinguish facts from exaggerations, embellishments, and dimly remembered idle chatter.

The villain in Morgenstern's novelesque tale is Helene Berg. She was an illegitimate child, he writes, loose in her morals, perversely cheap, a virulent anti-Semite, and a Nazi supporter who in the end kills Alban Berg. No part of this narrative is true about the real Helene Berg. In a passage that was plainly intended to humiliate Helene, he counts four women with whom Berg had affairs. Berg contemplated—according to Morgenstern—running off with one of them to Latin America.

Morgenstern's disdain for Helene apparently came from a conflicted relationship between the two that arose in the 1920s, briefly bubbled into the open in the 1960s, but all the while was hidden beneath a feigned courtesy on both sides. From the beginning of their acquaintance Morgenstern was clearly attracted to Helene. He writes, "On that day [in 1920] I saw Helene and Alban Berg for the first time. On this first encounter, as with several that came later on Tram 59, the woman interested me far more than the man."[116] Morgenstern then spins a tale about Helene's reciprocal passion:

> The day arrived when you would gladly have heard this little word "love," and just as gladly have heard it coming from me. But as my feelings ripened too early, yours did too late: then I had become a close friend of Alban and you. . . . I had your consent, but I said no. Not because I was prudish; not because I believed in "obsolete taboos." It was just because I was not as free and devoid of jealousy as was Alban.[117]

Morgenstern's titillating story cannot be taken seriously. All that is known about Helene Berg suggests that she was prudish in affairs with men, totally devoted to her marriage, and not in the slightest attracted to Soma Morgenstern. Alban and Helene privately made fun of him, calling him "Finf" (*fünf*) on account of his Yiddish accent. During Berg's trip to Berlin in December 1925 for the *Wozzeck* rehearsals, Morgenstern apparently pestered Helene by his presence. He had arranged to escort her to the Volkstheater on 2 December 1925 but left her in the lurch. She reported this to Alban: "The beast called only at 4:30, not at 2:30, and later I just let the phone ring without answering, so he couldn't pick me up. It was very embarrassing at the theater—neither of us knew what to say. . . . I would not let M[orgenstern] take me home, and I got there rather tired and depressed."[118]

Following Morgenstern's marriage to Ingeborg von Klenau, the two couples renewed their friendship, and following World War II, Morgenstern visited Helene several times in Vienna. In a letter to her of December 1963 he talks about writing a book about Berg, although admits that he has made little progress on it. When *Lulu* was staged at the Vienna Staatsoper in 1968 and 1969, Morgenstern expected that Helene would pay his way to be there, especially since he claimed to have given Berg the idea for the Lulu plays and took credit for creating the libretto for the work. Helene refused to pay, which brought an angry response from him. "It would not have been bad at all if you had taken a small amount from the money you've collected for the Berg Foundation to pay for my travel to Vienna," he snapped.[119] On his letter Helene later noted: "Dr. Morgenstern lies! He never proposed to Alban the idea of setting *Pippa*, nor did *Lulu* come from him. Alban's initial impulse [for Lulu] came instead from his contact with the Karl Kraus circle."[120]

In 1973 Morgenstern sent to Helene excerpts from his still incomplete book on Berg, together with copies of some thirty letters to him written by Berg that Morgenstern had given to relatives for safekeeping before his flight to France in 1938. It is unknown exactly which excerpts he sent, but it is safe to assume that these did not include the many accusatory statements that he had written about her or the remarks about Alban's philandering. She wrote back to Morgenstern to make a few minor corrections in his text and—ironic in light of the volume that appeared in 1995—to thank Morgenstern for his book: "Your kind and so important words about Alban have made me very, very happy. I thank you from the bottom of my heart!"[121]

The Alban Berg Foundation

Helene Berg stated on many occasions after Berg's death that the establishment of an Alban Berg Foundation (*Alban Berg Stiftung*) was her life's goal. Her strongest motivation was sentimental in the broadest sense— the need to create a lasting memorial to her husband. Another impulse was charitable—the desire to help financially struggling composers, among whose ranks Alban Berg had earlier been. Underlying these laudable intentions was the more equivocal purpose of controlling and shaping Berg's legacy according to her personal wishes. As the foundation idea evolved over the course of Helene's widowhood, it shifted between these objectives, finally becoming fixed on the enforcement of Helene's prerogatives.[122]

The idea for a foundation went back to Berg's own lifetime. The earliest recorded idea is in the composer's will dated 9 September 1934, by which Berg leaves everything to his wife Helene unless she and he die together. Then all resources should go to an "Alban Bergstiftung." Any income acquired by this "Stiftung" is designated to support needy composers. There is no mention of any other mission in this document.[123] The creation of the Alban Berg Foundation as a legal and sustainable entity took more than thirty years, until 1967, and the official registration and the first sitting of the board did not take place until early 1969.[124] During this long period Helene made multiple drafts of her foundation plan, the first of which was in the form of a testamentary disposition: the foundation would come into existence following her death. But by the mid-1960s, external pressure coming largely from the United States over the accessibility of Berg's *Lulu* manuscripts compelled her to establish the foundation as a legal entity during her lifetime.

Helene's conception of the foundation was inextricably linked to the Waldhaus. The prospect of a summer escape to the countryside was ingrained in the Viennese middle class, and such a retreat into nature was the ultimate necessity for creative inspiration, as it had been for Berg during his entire lifetime. In the winter of 1946 Helene made her first known written proposal concerning the foundation, in a will whose wording makes the foundation virtually synonymous with the Waldhaus: "It is my last will that the Waldhaus in Auen on the Wörthersee be preserved as the Alban Berg Foundation."[125] As outlined here, the foundation's purpose is consistent with Berg's will of 1934: to provide needy music students a summer stay at the Waldhaus for rest and creative work. Additional stipulations are that Berg's library shall go to the foundation, but his musical manuscripts should be sold to public libraries to provide financial support. Helene further enjoined that Alban's Waldhaus room, as well as hers, must remain unoccupied, and both are to be placed under historic monument protection immediately following her death. In this first iteration of her plan, Helene envisioned the foundation as legatee, a retreat for deserving music students, and a memorial site, all combined into one functional entity.

Helene returned to her foundation plans in earnest in the early 1950s, when the climate of reception of Berg's music had changed significantly. She was by then receiving performance royalties that could fund the foundation into the future. In 1953 Helene wrote another will, to which she appended a four-page document titled "Stiftungsurkunde" (foundation charter). Both documents are signed and dated with Alban's fateful number, 23 July 1953.[126] In this charter the foundation is explicitly named as her legal heir and the beneficiary of specific financial assets including the Waldhaus and all of her remaining assets including copyrights. She calls for an eight-member advisory board, and she reiterates that Alban's manuscripts may be sold if the foundation is short of income, but only to public institutions.

From 1954 to 1966—more than a decade—the Alban Berg Foundation led a ghostly existence, if it could be said to exist at all. No known documentation of personnel, meetings, or decisions was issued. Although the foundation had no legal standing in these years except in Helene Berg's will, Helene took important steps in this period to secure her husband's papers, depositing many of his musical manuscripts in the Music Division of the Austrian National Library, although she deferred an official donation until 1975.[127] Her principal effort continued to be the accumulation of financial assets. In addition to the performance royalties she received from abroad, she arranged to have Universal Edition pay her a monthly stipend, much of which she set aside while continuing to live extremely frugally.[128] The misconceived publication of the *Briefe an seine Frau* was undertaken by Helene in part as a financial venture.

The founding of the International Alban Berg Society in New York in 1966 caused concern among Helene Berg's closest advisors. Willi Reich warned Helene that the Society only intended to force the completion of *Lulu* and the publication of Berg's early songs, both of which Helene opposed.[129] Theodor Adorno flatly declined participation in the new society on the grounds of his close friendship with Helene and also because he foresaw that a competition between New York and Vienna would not serve the purpose of furthering Alban Berg's legacy. "It is surely not to be expected that a Berg Society can have a happy future when from the beginning the key people who preside over the *Nachlass* oppose it," Adorno told Redlich. "I already foresee lawsuits and God knows what else, which can only harm Berg's memory and the transmission of his works."[130] Adorno added that the Society might legitimately devote itself exclusively to a critical edition of Berg's works, like the one being sponsored by the Mahler Society.

Meanwhile, galvanized by events in New York, Helene Berg and others on her behalf began a reassessment of the Berg foundation plan. The first step was to create the foundation immediately, as a legal entity with full powers, as opposed to waiting until Helene's death. For this action a new charter was drafted in 1967 in which the purpose of the foundation was broadened to include the support of performers, scholars, and institutions devoted to Berg's works.[131] Helene's role in the foundation is defined: for her lifetime she will preside at all sittings of the board of directors (*Kuratorium*) and the executive committee (*Arbeitsausschuss*) or send her personal representative. She retains the right to choose board members, and—most important—retains full veto power over all decisions of the foundation's board during her lifetime. By this point the Alban Berg Foundation had evolved from a relatively modest, largely altruistic concept to an instrument for the enforcement of Helene Berg's wishes, first among these the suppression of the third act of *Lulu*. There is little doubt that the formation of the competing International Alban Berg Society in New York precipitated the legal establishment of the Berg Foundation and pushed Helene Berg into her dictatorial position.

Although 1967 is the official founding date of the Berg Foundation, its establishment was not made public for two more years. The board of directors was formed early in 1969. Gottfried von Einem, the most prominent Austrian composer of the time, was named president. For the Viennese he may have represented a counterweight to Stravinsky in the United States. Except for Joseph Polnauer and Erwin Ratz, who had been members of Berg's circle, the remainder of the board members and all of the executive committee were lawyers or officials of one sort or another, putting the face of legal enforcement on the organization. There was no one on the board from outside Austria or even far outside of Berg's or Helene Berg's circle. There was certainly no one who favored a *Lulu* completion.

In her remaining years Helene Berg continued to reiterate her commitment to the foundation and to solidify its finances. In 1969 she turned over 50 percent of her royalties to it. In that summer she wrote out by hand her last will, composed of sixteen pages, carefully excluding all of her relatives from any inheritance, and guaranteeing all royalty income following her death to the foundation. Forcefully maintaining her position of fidelity toward Alban and to his works, she once again, in her last will, expressly forbade examination of the *Lulu* materials and reiterated the reason she had given years previously, invoking the judgment of Schoenberg, Zemlinsky, and Webern. Helene added three codicils to her will, the last one dated six months before her death, in which she bequeathed all musical manuscripts as well as all letters and writings of Berg to the Austrian National Library.[132] The Alban Berg Foundation began to keep official records in 1969. Accounts show that grants were given to individuals and organizations, and the Alban Berg Quartet was founded in 1970 with the foundation's support. In that year the organization's total assets approached 2,700,000 schillings. Income from performance royalties was close to 950,000 schillings.[133]

Helene Berg's Last Years

Helene Berg died on 30 August 1976, at the age of 91, after nearly forty-one years as a faithful *Komponistenwitwe*. Although failing physically she remained lucid and engaged up to the last six months of her life. She continued to divide her time between her Vienna apartment and the Waldhaus until the summer before her death. She was visited by friends and admirers—Berg enthusiasts among them, many from foreign countries. Her calendars in the last years record some of the names of her callers: Gottfried von Einem; Octavian Spitzmüller, a representative of Universal Edition and a devoted friend; Rudolf Kolisch, the violinist and Schoenberg's brother-in-law; and Franz Grasberger, director of the Music Division at the Austrian National Library. Her old friends Eleonore and Bruno Vondenhoff came to see her often in her last years. From the United States, the composer Claudio Spies, professor at Princeton, visited in March of 1976 along with his wife and son, as did Laurence Lyon, a professor of Germanic Languages from the University of California and an early translator of Berg's letters to Schoenberg.[134]

Helene had a devoted friend in Fritzi Schlesinger, whose constant presence in her life in her last decade is apparent from a number of documents.[135] Schlesinger describes Helene's last days in a letter to Claudio Spies.

> The death of Frau Berg was a severe loss for me, although given her age it had to be anticipated. But I have never been so closely bound to anyone and have done everything for her for the last 11 years. Especially in the last year I was with her every day. I have known her much longer, from the time when he [Alban] was still alive. . . . I am happy that you were able to visit her in March. She was especially pleased by the visit and spoke often of you. After April she was bedridden and at Easter she was doing very badly. But she then rallied to the point that in July she was able to spend one or two hours in a wheelchair. On her birthday on July 29 she was even able to spend the whole day in the wheelchair and had a number of visitors. Then her condition deteriorated. She insisted that I take some time off, so I went to Aussee. The nurses called me there regularly (she had nursing care day and night). Then suddenly things got much worse, and I was not there when she died.[136]

Another woman close to Helene Berg at the end of her life was Ida Gebauer Wagner, best known as a confidante and caregiver to Alma Mahler, to whom she was known as "Schulli." A trained nurse, she was hired by Alma Mahler to care for her daughter Manon. Helene's relationship with Wagner was likely cemented around the time of Manon's and Berg's deaths in the same year, 1935, and Helene later referred to Wagner as one of her truest friends.[137] Knowing she would need someone reliable and decisive if she were to die suddenly, Helene in 1965 designated Schulli as her contact person: "To my will: in the event of my sudden death, please call Mrs. Ida Wagner, telephone number 9230083, who will take care of everything. The apartment must be officially sealed (monument protection), and the relatives may not enter."[138] She gave Schulli specific instructions about her documents and the conversion of the Waldhaus property to a memorial site.[139] Finally, Helene requested Schulli to see that she received the "Herzstich"—a knife through the heart, an old Viennese custom—before burial.[140] A doctor would have performed the procedure.

After her death, Helene's detractors gave full vent to their negative opinions. Having been debarred from any role in Helene's estate, Erich

Berg persisted in an accusatory vein that continued the narrative of Helene's illegitimate birth and its supposed evil consequences. He writes:

> It happens frequently in the course of history that behind famous men, politicians, thinkers, artists, there have been strong-willed women who have wished to realize themselves through the work of their husbands. Helene Berg is one of these. . . . She wrote a series of wills in which she consistently emphasized that she as widow regarded herself as the executor of all decisions of Alban Berg that she received from the beyond. I can only explain her testamentary prohibition [against the completion of *Lulu*] as an inborn attitude of mistrust of her surroundings and her advisors inherited from her biological father, Franz Joseph I. As the artist's widow—see above—the one who had a sole voice, she wanted to realize and immortalize herself![141]

From a historical and even more from an artistic perspective, Helene's opposition to the completion of *Lulu* was clearly not in Berg's best interest. But the idea that she wished to immortalize herself is far-fetched at best. She saw herself as a guardian of Berg's life and work, and she used whatever power she had to enable her in this role. She protected herself by weaving a fiction of perfection in her marriage, but this may be seen as a positive instinct. A more balanced and sympathetic assessment of Helene is given by the writer Elias Canetti, who knew the Bergs in Vienna in the 1930s. In his memoirs Canetti writes about Helene:

> Some people ridicule her for "keeping contact" with [Alban] all this time. Even if she was deluding herself, even if he spoke inside her and not from outside, this remains a form of survival that fills me with awe and admiration. I saw her again thirty years later, after a lecture given by Adorno in Vienna. Small and shrunken, she came out of the hall, a very old woman, so absent that it cost me an effort to speak to her. She didn't recognize me, but when I told her my name, she said: "Ah, Herr C.! That was a long time ago. Alban still speaks of you."[142]

Canetti recognized that Helene's immortalization of Alban was a genuine act of love. "It takes a great deal of love to create a dead man who never dies," he adds. Helene's preservation of an enduring emotional bond with her deceased husband is a reminder that a great artistic legacy includes intangibles as well as materials and among the intangibles is the nurturing of memory.

Berg the Outsider

OW SHOULD WE ASSESS ALBAN BERG'S PLACE IN MUSIC OF THE
modern era? In the present day—far more than in the past—the
question defies any broadly acceptable answer. Serious music from Berg's
time to our own has undergone such radical and continuing changes
that any ideology supporting its critical evaluation seems temporary and
arbitrary. The riots that greeted the Altenberg Songs at the Musikverein
in 1913 or the Chamber Concerto in Paris in 1928 are unthinkable at
performances in the present day. Equally unimaginable at present is the
chartering of a train to bring audiences from New York to Philadelphia
to hear a new opera, as happened for the American premiere of *Wozzeck*
in 1931. If he were alive today, Alban Berg would certainly be surprised,
and probably also chagrined, by the twisting course taken by serious
music since his day. He held firmly to a simpler belief, that a single mainstream of modern music, led in his own time by Schoenberg, would
continue to dominate the world of music in the future. In 1924 he wrote
about Schoenberg, "One need be no prophet to say that the works that
he has already sent forth into the world assure the supremacy of his own
art as well as that of German music for the next fifty years."[1]

Berg's narrative concerning modern musical history was shaped at a
time when the hegemony of the German late romantic style associated
with Brahms, Mahler, Strauss, and Schoenberg was unquestioned. Music
of its type was composed by Edward MacDowell and Horatio Parker in
America, by Parker's student Charles Ives, Béla Bartók in Hungary, Jean

Berg. Bryan Simms and Charlotte Erwin, Oxford University Press (2021). © Oxford University Press.
DOI: 10.1093/oso/9780190931445.003.0013

Sibelius in Finland, Edward Elgar in England, and, with a French accent, by Ernest Chausson and César Franck. Berg shared these composers' expressive intensity and readiness to introduce new materials and expand upon traditional rules, and he too was confident in a future understanding for music too difficult, too serious for its own time. Berg saw no possibility that other significant new styles could coexist with or topple this German modernism. When opposing directions in music appeared in the 1920s, Berg dismissed them as flawed and imperfect offshoots of the German mainstream.[2] His self-appointed role was to continue the musical evolution that Brahms, Mahler, and Schoenberg had furthered.

Even during his lifetime, Berg's belief proved unrealistic. The dominance of the German romantic style came to an end in the aftermath of World War I. At that time a new anti-romantic spirit arose in modern music that viewed Berg and others in Schoenberg's circle as passé. The leader in the new musical taste was a not a German or Austrian but the Russian émigré Igor Stravinsky. Stravinsky rejected the heavy emotionalism and appeals for future acceptance of the older style and brought to his music instead a cool objectivity and contemporaneity. "I live neither in the past nor in the future," Stravinsky proclaimed. "I am in the present."[3] With a bit of overstatement he continued, "I consider that music is by its very nature essentially powerless to express anything at all, whether a feeling, an attitude of mind, a psychological mood, a phenomenon of nature, or other."[4] The new music of the 1920s that garnered the most attention was in tune with the temper of the jazz age—something to be heard with a smile on the lips, not with the head in the hands. The new music often called attention to works of the pre-romantic past, especially those of Bach, not by outright quotation as in Berg's Violin Concerto, but instead by parody in which styles of early music were cleverly juggled and reconceived using musical elements both old and new. For many listeners Berg's music was out of touch with this new ethos. Following the riotous reception of Berg's Chamber Concerto in Paris in 1928, Georges Auric spoke for many in France when he wrote that he could find in Berg's work only a "boring scholasticism masked by a lugubrious aestheticism, the polar opposite of the solid and great artistry of a Stravinsky."[5]

Despite such judgments, Berg's music thrived. As *Wozzeck* became known following its premiere in 1925, critics in tune with the neoclassic spirit could only account for its success by placing it among works from a bygone era, while still acknowledging its power. Kurt Weill's assessment of the Berlin premiere of 1925 was typical:

> It is the first attempt to apply Arnold Schoenberg's musical direction, which breaks with everything conventional, to the stage. The result is in itself a unique artwork that is not promising for the future but still a grandiose end-point to a development that leads from Wagner's *Tristan*, through Debussy's *Pelléas et Mélisande* and Strauss's *Elektra*, to this completely negative art. Whatever attitude one takes toward this music, the impartial listener must admit to a powerful impression of a strong musical personality with rare abundance of inspiration and unrivaled craft.[6]

Just as the First World War changed the direction of serious music, so too did World War II. Many observers expected the neoclassical status quo in music to revive following the war and return composers like Stravinsky and Paul Hindemith to positions of leadership. Just the opposite happened, and Berg's music was again under threat of irrelevance. Soon after the war's end many of the younger, rising composers in Europe and America broke with the prewar past and adopted a style that can be termed *postwar modernism*. The new style was abstract and depersonalized, with such heavy emphasis on musical form that form became synonymous with content. References to the musical past were banished, and composition by system and process—at first using approaches that stemmed from Schoenberg's twelve-tone method—became the norm. "I say that any musician who has not experienced the necessity of the twelve-tone language," wrote Pierre Boulez in 1952, "is *useless*, because his whole work is irrelevant to the needs of the age."[7]

The change of orientation brought forth conflicted attitudes about Alban Berg's music, especially its highly personalized *espressivo*, its romantic ethos, explicit references to the past, and a harmonic vocabulary that mixed tonal and atonal elements. Berg's free use of twelve-tone rows seemed perfunctory at a time when composition was moving toward automation. In an article written in 1948, Boulez dismissed the romanticism and sentimentality that he found in Berg's music. Passages of the *Lyric Suite*, he proclaimed, "relate to the most vulgar veristic bombast in Italian opera." The coexistence of serialism and tonality in the Violin Concerto produced only an irreconcilable conflict. "It is necessary to choose one or another of these solutions; not to use them together," he concludes.[8] Hans Keller picked up Boulez's line of thought in a 1951 review of *Wozzeck*: in this opera "there is hardly an untraditional bar," Keller states. The melodies evoke those of Beethoven, Mendelssohn, and Puccini, producing "a *pastiche* that lacks personality."[9]

In later writings Boulez spoke approvingly of the complexity and esoteric character that he found in some of Berg's music, but its use of traditionalisms still made it irrelevant, in his estimation, to the postwar situation. "Attempts to recuperate the past have absolutely no interest for the future."[10] For Boulez as for many of the younger modernists, the more abstract music by Anton Webern was held up as the ideal pre-war model for future development.

Although readers of the present day will readily agree with Boulez when he concedes being "given to exaggeration," his assessment of Berg's music was influential even on conservative writers on the postwar scene.[11] Aaron Copland joined in. "Berg suffered from a failing, if it can be called that, which Robert Craft once cleverly named 'tonal nostalgia,'" Copland wrote. "The composer did not hesitate to choose tone-rows whose succession of notes, as in the Violin Concerto, suggest triadic formations. In effect this practice negates to a certain extent the antitonal basis of the dodecaphonic method. This trait considerably reduces Berg's historical significance."[12]

The Webern craze of the 1950s and 1960s and the outspoken pronouncements of figures like Boulez temporarily diverted attention from Berg's music both in the concert hall and as a point of departure for new works. For some five years after war's end, there were few major performances of Berg's music, and Helene Berg fell into despair thinking that she would have to wait for the afterlife to hear his music again. She wrote bleakly in her notebook:

> 1946–47. Why am I again and again in despair that Alban's work is not played here, that when Austrian composers are numbered in the newspaper and in journals, his name is never mentioned, that his own home has forgotten him? Why do I weep over this appalling injustice that is being done to you? When I cross over into the other world, where your speech, your music will always, always flow to me from your beloved soul— Enough! I will wait, I will hope for *this* happiness.[13]

But despite all, Berg's music again revived. In the early 1950s, it began a great international resurgence that made Boulez's grumbling seem irrelevant. *Wozzeck* led the way in this renewal. Three concert performances in April 1951 by the New York Philharmonic under Dimitri Mitropoulos were a sensation, reminding many of the huge success of *Wozzeck* with American audiences twenty years before. Carnegie Hall was sold out for all three performances, and Columbia Records issued an LP of the production, with Eileen Farrell as Marie and Mack Harrell as Wozzeck. Virgil Thomson—a composer and critic with little affinity for music of the Second Viennese School—wrote glowingly about the recording in terms that Berg himself might have chosen:

> I do not see how anyone can fail to be moved by it. And Alban Berg's music is a powerful agent in the moving. Chromatic almost to the point of atonality, non-thematic to the degree that it gives an effect of constant improvisation; and hence of a constant emotional intensity, it espouses its tale so perfectly that one can almost forget, by moments, that it is there at all. It is a climate rather than an investiture. The story is the rock, and its music the lake in which it bathes.[14]

Berg's growing recognition cast doubt on the value of critical theories like those espoused by Boulez and Keller that found a right and wrong in music based on style. Eric Salzman sneered at such ideas and held that Berg's music was music, not ideology:

> He was certainly precise and fastidious in his musical thought. He worked for top expressive intensity and density and then tried to reconcile this with tonal thinking. Unfortunately, all this quite eliminates him from the small and elect company of ancestors and anticipators of today's avant-garde. . . . Berg may be utterly useless for reconstructing the twentieth century, for showing a direction for young composers to follow or for providing interesting subject matter for metaphysical articles in new-music magazines. But Berg is Berg and his music was made and is. One can perhaps illuminate his work from the viewpoint of the present but in the end it stands or falls on its own soundness and viability.[15]

The Berg revival gained momentum when Karl Böhm led the Vienna Philharmonic Orchestra in a staging of *Wozzeck* in Salzburg in 1951, a production that was repeated in May of 1952 in Paris—its first staging in that city. In the Parisian audience was Igor Stravinsky, to hear *Wozzeck* for the first time. He was accompanied by Robert Craft, who as a conductor would play a large role in the Berg revival. There was much uncertainty about how the French would react to *Wozzeck*, with the riot that accompanied Berg's Chamber Concerto in 1928 remaining in many minds. Olin Downes reported reassuringly from Paris: "*Wozzeck* was given here tonight in the Champs-Elysées Theatre with an effect that left an audience of music lovers and connoisseurs from all parts of the world speechless for a moment after the last note had vanished into silence. Then the audience rocked the theatre with its cheers." Downes continued: "No more significant symbol of recent developments in music could have been offered than Berg's opera. It is far and away the most revolutionary achievement in music drama of the modern age. No work has approached it for dramatic impact and psychology since its premiere in Germany in 1925."[16]

Lulu was far slower to return to operatic stages, and its critical reception at first had little of the enthusiasm that greeted *Wozzeck*. Columbia Records issued the first commercial recording of the two-act work in 1952, and the reviews were mixed: always with praise for the music but with no sympathy for the text. Herbert Kupferberg assessed the recorded work in typical fashion:

> One can admire [Berg's] genius and respect his integrity and yet still conclude that he mistook an obsession with evil for a vision of art. And in so doing, he created in "Lulu" a work which offers exactly the same fascination as a sideshow of freaks, which gives the viewer pleasure only when he leaves it behind him and emerges into the open air.[17]

The first staging of *Lulu* in Germany was in Essen in 1953, whereupon a dissatisfaction with the text persisted in the press. Henry Pleasants reviewed the production for the *New York Times* with little patience for the apologia—somewhat garbled in his rendition—that he had found in long German sentences in the program booklet:

> German Gobbledegook. To this Anglo-Saxon listener, for whom such pseudo-philosophic elucidation [of the character Lulu] as "ein Stück Natur jenseits von Gut und Böse und daher als ein in sich geschlossener Kosmos nur durch die Musik in seinem allen begrifflichen entrückten Zusammenhang zu

enträtseln" elucidates nothing. It is impossible to see in Lulu more than an exceptionally repulsive criminal, or in the play itself more than pretentious sensationalism.[18]

A turning point for the acceptance of *Lulu* was the production created by Günther Rennert for the Hamburg Opera in 1957. Rennert and his stage designer, Teo Otto, used a circus ambience for the entire opera, and they found an effective combination of actions and images to convey the drama of Act 3 during the playing of the Variations and Adagio from the *Symphonic Pieces*. The production helped to establish *Lulu*— including its incomplete Act 3 and text with apparent conundrums— as a mainstay of the modern operatic literature, no longer a flawed masterpiece.

Helene Berg saw the 1957 Hamburg production, which confirmed her earlier viewpoint—that *Lulu* was complete and perfect in its two-act form. She wrote to Erwin Stein:

> Rennert brought off a quite splendid artistic achievement. And the most important thing is that it was not done as a stopgap but in a way in which we see the whole as an organic unity. In its compressed form it made a very, very strong dramatic impression. . . . You can imagine how shaken I was and how happy his solution made me, having been discouraged for years that this work was not properly performed. Now at last we can with assurance send Lulu out into the world![19]

Over the next decade Rennert's production was repeated in cities in Europe and North America: at the Paris Opéra, London Sadler's Wells, Milan La Scala, and New York Metropolitan Opera, among other major theaters. After a performance in Montreal in 1967, Michael Steinberg found the text to be a strength, not a defect, its theatric complexity heightened by Berg's music:

> *Lulu* is perhaps the most vital, certainly the most elemental, of the great 20th century operas. Its ecstasies, Angst, horrors, and humor (sick, but very effective), are felt and experienced with rare fullness, and a remarkable range of characters and milieux is brought to life with assurance and brilliant perception. It is one of the great operas because its music, which goes so far beyond intelligent and effective text setting, succeeds in defining, in creating, a world uniquely that of this particular drama.[20]

The first American staging of *Lulu* was in 1963 at Santa Fe, conducted by Robert Craft. His ghostwritten letters signed by Igor Stravinsky that played a part in the founding of the Alban Berg Foundation and the completion of *Lulu* were noted in the preceding chapter. In these and other matters Craft called on his close relationship with Stravinsky to advance Berg's cause. Before meeting Craft, Stravinsky had little contact with or apparent interest in Berg's music. The two composers had met briefly in Venice during the 1934 *Biennale*, and Craft arranged for Stravinsky to attend the 1952 staging of *Wozzeck* in Paris. While composing *Agon* in 1954, Stravinsky ordered a copy of the score of Berg's Violin Concerto, perhaps curious about Berg's take on the twelve-tone method. Given this slender measure of acquaintance, Stravinsky's detailed remarks on Berg in his 1959 *Conversations with Igor Stravinsky* were startling. There he commented on a wide range of Berg's music, showing an intimate familiarity with even the smallest details. He praised Berg especially for his command of form, the great desideratum of postwar modernist music. Berg is "the most gifted constructor in form of the composers of this century," Stravinsky says.[21]

Gradually it became known that much of what Stravinsky said in the *Conversations*, and probably all of the material on Berg, was entirely written by Robert Craft, with at most a cursory glance by Stravinsky himself.[22] Still, words of praise attributed to the most famous living composer—one who had transformed himself from neoclassicist to postwar modernist—helped to propel Berg's reputation during this period. As a conductor Craft had long been a proponent of Berg's music, as he was also of the music of Schoenberg and Webern. In addition to conducting *Wozzeck* and *Lulu* at Santa Fe, Craft made the first recording, with Bethany Beardslee, of Berg's Altenberg Songs (Columbia Records, 1960), bringing these pieces for the first time to public recognition. Gradually Berg's music became a model for new modernist works. Bernd Alois Zimmermann's *Die Soldaten* and Wolfgang Rihm's *Jakob Lenz* built upon the style of *Wozzeck*. The brilliant virtuosity of Boulez's *Éclat* would have been hard to imagine without the Chamber Concerto, the pathos-laden music of George Rochberg without the Orchestral Pieces, the quotation collages of Luciano Berio and Mauricio Kagel without the Violin Concerto, or the provocative eclecticism of Alfred Schnittke without *Der Wein*.

By the 1970s postwar modernism in music and the doctrinaire critical outlook that supported it came under attack from all sides. Benjamin Britten found much of it to be "pretentious nonsense"; Arvo Pärt compared serialist composers to children playing in a sandbox. The twelve-tone system, Luciano Berio wrote, had become "a brand of fetishism which shares with Fascism and racism the tendency to reduce live processes to immobile, labelled objects."[23] Leonard Bernstein declared, "That year [1966] was for me a low point in the musical course of our century, certainly the lowest I have ever experienced." He explained, "Electronic music, serialism, chance music—they have already acquired the musty odor of academicism."[24]

By the mid-1970s the dogmatic temper of postwar modernism had begun to fade, portending yet another change of direction in the culture for new music in the twentieth century and yet another challenge for the viability of Berg's music. Traditional values in music reappeared as composers reached out for a larger audience. As in earlier changes of style in the century, the new taste was a reaction against what had come before. The older music of modernism was complex and difficult, so the new music was simple and accessible; the older musical culture demanded conformity, so the new was tolerant of any and all approaches to composition. No longer was there a right and wrong in new music.

Again, Berg was the outsider, his music not in line with the new thinking. He was a modernist of an earlier time, his music remote from the pleasing simplicity of new works by Henryk Górecki, the familiar sonority of motets by Arvo Pärt, and the pop music flavor of pieces by Philip Glass. But though Berg remained the outsider, his music thrived. In 1979 audiences heard the complete, three-act *Lulu* for the first time, and the international acclaim for the work again signaled Berg's enduring standing in musical culture.

From his time to our own through the many shifts in taste in modern music, Berg's true eminence in musical history has repeatedly asserted it. His place in music of the modern era comes ultimately from the inherent qualities of the works themselves—their inventiveness, technical ingenuity, and power to touch the imagination. As an artist of the tumultuous twentieth century, Berg grappled with the new demands and materials of modernism and succeeded in combining them with enduring ideas of melody, musical syntax and form. He brought his distinctively wrought language to the expression of emotions ranging from the profoundly beautiful to the most disturbing. The emotional element, so deeply and personally felt, sets the music apart, and this is perhaps the key to its survival: Berg's music, for all its elaborate complexities, speaks with a great and profound sympathy directly to the human heart.

Alban Berg's Autopsy Report

Name: Alban Berg
  Age: 50 years
  Occupation: composer
  Time of death: 24 December 1935, 12:30 AM
  Clinical diagnosis: furunculosis, sepsis, *alveolar pyorrhea*, heart insufficiency, nephritis (paranephritis?)
  Anatomical findings: the body was large, strong, well nourished. In both gluteal regions near the middle (the right side projecting somewhat more than the left) incision wounds into the skin extended lengthwise 6–8 cm with some pussy infiltrations at the sides of the incisions. These incisions extended into the subcutaneous fatty layers. The deep musculature normal.
  Spleen: twice normal size
  Liver: dusky and swollen with yellow spots
  Pancreas: normal
  Adrenal glands: fat deficient
  Kidneys: dusky and swollen, both with small and isolated cortical and medullary abscesses. On the right middle third of the front surface and left front and back subcapsular region is a superficial and protruding cyst filled with watery fluid.
  Bladder: moderately full, contents clear, mucosa pale
  Prostate: moderately enlarged, rough left lobe with a large yellow-brown purulent focus
  Gastrointestinal tract: normal
  Pleural cavities: slight purulent effusion (less than 100cc). Both upper lung lobes softly adherent, otherwise on the pulmonary pleura there is a variable soft fibrin coating. In all lobes of the right lung and also in the upper lobe of the left lung are subpleural cherry-sized abscesses with pleural necrosis. A similar cluster (nearly the size of a child's fist) is in the anterior basal segment of the lower lobe of the right lung.
  Aorta and coronary arteries: almost entirely soft
  Esophagus: dilated by mucous; softened postmortem
  Heart: rather firm, myocardium bright grey-red. On the anterior surface of the right ventricle is a large white patch. On the aortic aspect of the mitral valve leaflet the edge is slightly thickened. There are small bright yellow streaky infiltrates in the myocardium of the anterior septum of the left ventricle near the apex of the heart.

Histology (pancreas and heart): pancreas: well preserved; myocardium: focal prolifer-
ation of the vascular connective tissue without a leukocytic reaction

Pathological-anatomical diagnosis: staphylococcal septicopyemia; metastatic pulmonary
abscesses with pleurisy; multiple renal abscesses; purulent metastases to the prostate; pulmonary edema; acutely enlarged spleen; degeneration of the visceral parenchyma.

Source: Dieter Kerner, *Krankheiten grosser Musiker* (Stuttgard: Friedrich-Karl-Schattauer-
Verlag, 1963), 195–97. Translated by Bryan R. Simms and Cornelia W. Hamilton, M.D.

Notes

Preface

1　Hans W. Heinsheimer, *Best Regards to Aida: The Defeats and Victories of a Music Man on Two Continents* (New York: Alfred A. Knopf, 1968), 47.

2　Theodor Adorno, *Alban Berg: Master of the Smallest Link*, trans. Juliane Brand and Christopher Hailey (Cambridge: Cambridge University Press, 1991), 34.

Introduction

1　See Christopher Hailey, "Die vierte Galerie: Voraussetzungen für die Wiener Avantgarde um 1910," in *Die Wiener Schule in der Musikgeschichte des 20. Jahrhunderts*. Report on the Second Meeting of the International Schoenberg Society, ed. Rudolf Stephan and Sigrid Wiesmann (Vienna: Verlag Elisabeth Lafite, 1986), 242–47.

2　Letter, Giuseppe Verdi to Giuseppe Piroli, 12 June 1875, quoted in Mary Jane Phillips-Matz, *Verdi: A Biography* (Oxford: Oxford University Press, 1993), 614.

3　Stefan Zweig, *The World of Yesterday*, trans. Anthea Bell (Lincoln: University of Nebraska Press, 2009), 40.

4　Leon Botstein, "Time and Memory: Concert Life, Science, and Music in Brahms's Vienna," in *Brahms and His World*, ed. Walter Frisch (Princeton, NJ: Princeton University Press, 1990), 6.

5　Arnold Schoenberg, "New and Outmoded Music, or Style and Idea" (1930), in *Composers on Modern Musical Culture*, ed. Bryan R. Simms (New York: Schirmer Books, 1999), 103.

6　Zweig, *The World of Yesterday*, 43.

7　Edward Timms, *Karl Kraus, Apocalyptic Satirist: Culture and Catastrophe in Habsburg Vienna* (New Haven, CT: Yale University Press, 1986), 7–9.

8　Letter, Arnold Schoenberg to Alban Berg, 13 January 1912, BSB I: 169.

9　Zweig, *The World of Yesterday*, 25.

10　Arnold Schoenberg, *Theory of Harmony*, trans. Roy E. Carter (Berkeley and Los Angeles: University of California Press, 1978), 409.

11　Letter, Franz Liszt to Carolyne von Sayn-Wittgenstein, 18 February 1874, in *Franz Liszts Briefe*, ed. La Mara, vol. 7 (Leipzig: Breitkopf & Härtel, 1902), 57–58.

12　Letter, Johannes Brahms to Otto Grimm, November 1862, in *Johannes Brahms Life and Letters*, ed. Styra Avins, trans. Josef Eisinger and Styra Avins (New York: Oxford University Press, 1997), 248.

13　Letter, Johannes Brahms to Elisabet von Herzogenberg, 12 January 1885, in Max Kalbeck, *Johannes Brahms*, 2nd ed., vol. 3 (Berlin: Deutsche Brahms Gesellschaft, 1913), 408.

14　Richard Wagner, "Ueber die Anwendung der Musik auf das Drama," *Bayreuther Blätter* 2 (November 1879): 318.

15 *Hugo Wolfs musikalische Kritiken*, ed. Richard Batka and Heinrich Werner (Leipzig: Breitkopf & Härtel, 1911), 109–10.

16 See Berg's letter to Erwin Schulhoff of 19 June 1919, in Ivan Vojtěch, "Arnold Schoenberg, Anton Webern, Alban Berg: Unbekannte Briefe an Erwin Schulhoff," *Miscellanea musicologica* 15 (1965): 41–42.

17 Egon Wellesz, "Arnold Schönberg," *Zeitschrift der internationalen Musikgesellschaft* 12 (1911): 347.

18 Arnold Schoenberg, "Composition with Twelve Tones" (1941), in *Style and Idea: Selected Writings of Arnold Schoenberg*, ed. Leonard Stein, trans. Leonard Black (Berkeley and Los Angeles: University of California Press, 1984), 217.

19 Béla Bartók, "The Problem of the New Music" (1920), in *Composers on Modern Musical Culture*, 45.

20 Alban Berg, "What Is Atonal? A Dialogue" (1930), PMPD, 219–27.

21 Ibid., 221.

22 Arnold Schoenberg, "Aesthetic Evaluation of Chords with Six or More Tones" (1911), in *Composers on Modern Musical Culture*, 42.

23 Hans Pfitzner, *Futuristengefahr: Bei Gelegenheit von Busoni's Ästhetik* (Leipzig and Munich: Süddeutsche Monatshefte, 1917), 44.

24 Letter, Alban Berg to Erich Kleiber, 19 February 1925, in *Alban Berg—Erich Kleiber: Briefe der Freundschaft*, ed. Martina Steiger (Vienna: Seifert Verlag, 2013), 42.

Chapter 1

1 "Alban Berg," *Neue Musik-Zeitung* (Stuttgart), 42, no. 20 (21 July 1921): 320. Although the article lacks a byline it was definitely written by Berg, as he told his wife Helene in a letter to her dated 8 June 1921, BW III: 142. Berg's handwritten draft for the article is found in ÖNB, F21.Berg.432.

2 Details of Berg's early life are well represented in the literature. It is surveyed in greatest detail in Rosemary Hilmar, *Alban Berg: Leben und Wirken in Wien bis zu seinen ersten Erfolgen als Komponist* (Vienna: Verlag Hermann Böhlaus Nachf., 1978); "Hermann Watznauer's Biography of Alban Berg," trans. and ed. Nick Chadwick, in *Alban Berg and His World*, ed. Christopher Hailey (Princeton, NJ: Princeton University Press, 2010), 33–90; Herwig Knaus and Wilhelm Sinkovicz, *Alban Berg: Zeitumstände—Lebenslinien* (St. Pölten: Residenz Verlag, 2008); Mosco Carner, *Alban Berg: The Man and The Work*, 2nd ed., rev. (New York: Holmes & Meier Publishers, 1983); and Barbara Meier, *Alban Berg: Biographie* (Würzburg: Königshausen & Neumann, 2018).

3 The Salzgeber family lived above the Bergs in the house at Tuchlauben 8. On Berg's registration of baptism in the parish of St. Peter in Vienna, the only godparent named is Marie von Bareis. Alban von Salzgeber is identified as Berg's godfather by Berg's nephew, Erich Alban Berg, in *Als der Adler noch zwei Köpfe hatte: Ein Florilegium 1858–1918* (Graz: Edition Kaleidoskop, 1980), 39. He died suddenly a year after Alban was born.

4 "Hermann Watznauer's Biography of Alban Berg," 37–38.

5 Letter, Helene Berg to Mosco Carner, 21 November 1968, ÖNB, F21.Berg.1622/261.

6 "Hermann Watznauer's Biography of Alban Berg," 37.

7 ÖNB, F21.Berg.423. The reports are transcribed in Rosemary Hilmar, *Alban Berg*, 168–72.

8 Knaus and Sinkovicz, *Alban Berg*, 10–11.

9 Ernest Newman, *The Life of Richard Wagner* (Cambridge: Cambridge University Press, 1976), I: 45.

10 Settlement for the estate of Conrad Berg was made by Vienna's Handelsgericht, whose proceedings are found in the Archives of the City of Vienna. These documents are cited in Rosemary Hilmar, *Alban Berg*, 16–18.

11 Watznauer's biography of Berg was left incomplete in 1929, when a copy of it was sent to Berg. This copy is now found in the ÖNB, F21.Berg.434, and the original is in the WBR, HIN 204.582. An English translation of the material up to 1906 is found in Chadwick, "Hermann Watznauer's Biography of Alban Berg"; the later entries, very sketchy in nature, are found in Erich Alban Berg, *Der unverbesserliche Romantiker: Alban Berg 1885–1935* (Vienna: Österreichischer Bundesverlag, 1985), 67–106.

12 See Nick Chadwick, "From 'Freund Hein' to Hermann Hesse: Hermann Watznauer and his Friendship with Alban Berg," *Music & Letters* 79 (1998): 396–418.

13 Thirty-eight cards and letters from Berg to Watznauer are found at The Morgan Library & Museum, Mary Flagler Cary Music Collection (MFC), B493.W353.

14 These letter copies are found in WBR, HIN 204.585.

15 A discussion of the topic is found in Erna Furman, *A Child's Parent Dies: Studies in Childhood Bereavement.* (New Haven: Yale University Press, 1974) and summarily in Dora Black, "Coping with Loss: Bereavement in Childhood," *BMJ: British Medical Journal* 316 (1998): 931–33.

16 Copies of Berg's letters to Paul Hohenberg are found in the New York Public Library, JOG 72–82. Some are excerpted in Joan Allen Smith, "The Berg-Hohenberg Correspondence," *Alban Berg Symposion Wien 1980: Tagungsbericht*, ed. Rudolf Klein, ABS 2 (Vienna: Universal Edition, 1981), 189–97.

17 Letter, Alban Berg to Hermann Watznauer, n.d. (20 November 1903), Morgan Library, MFC B493.W353. Berg apparently made no other copy of his improvised song "Hörtest du."

18 The notebooks are found in ÖNB, F21.Berg.100/I–XII. Passages are transcribed in Susanne Rode, *Alban Berg und Karl Kraus: Zur geistigen Biographie des Komponisten der "Lulu"* (Frankfurt: Peter Lang, 1988), and Janet Naudé, "*Lulu*, Child of Wozzeck and Marie: Towards an Understanding of Alban Berg, 'Master of the Smallest Link,' Through his Vocal and Dramatic Music" (PhD diss., University of Cape Town, 1997).

19 The text of the Nora letter is found in Janet Naudé, "'*Lulu*,' Child of Wozzeck and Marie," 371–74.

20 Ibid., 373–74.

21 This aspect of Berg's personality is discussed in Silvio J. dos Santos, *Narratives of Identity in Alban Berg's "Lulu,"* (Rochester, NY: University of Rochester Press, 2014).

22 ÖNB, F21.Berg.3299. The paper on which Berg wrote suggests a date of 1908–10 for the poem.

23 The "Bergwerksdrama" is found in QMG 35: 251–60. Complete translations of this and the poem "Hanna" are in PMPD, 337–68.

24 ÖNB, F21.Berg.1599/7, postcard postmarked 7 June 1899 to Hans Huber. The drawing of Nuremberg is signed "ABerg 99."

25 Letters, Alban Berg to Helene Nahowski, 31 August 1907 and 25 July 1908, BW I: 56, 174–75.

26 Letter, Alban Berg to Helene Nahowski, 13 July 1909, BW I: 317.

27 Letter, Alban Berg to Helene Nahowski, 21–22 July 1909. BW I: 341–43. The menthol dissolved in paraffin oil was used as a nasal remedy. The damaging effect of Pyramidon

is discussed specifically in a later chapter. Arsenferratone was used to treat anemia: see Joseph Price Remington, ed., *The Dispensatory of the United States of America*, 20th ed. (Philadelphia: Lippincott, ca. 1918), 2:1264. Schiffsmumme beer was a sought-after beer produced in Braunschweig. Berg probably drank it to gain weight.

28 Letter, Alban Berg to Helene Nahowski, 21–22 July 1909. BW I: 343.

29 The definitions of somatic symptom disorder and illness anxiety disorder are taken from Mayo Clinic online: www.mayoclinic.org/diseases-conditions. See Theodor W. Adorno, "Im Gedächtnis an Alban Berg" (1955), in Adorno, *Gesammelte Schriften* (Frankfurt: Suhrkamp, 1984), 18: 487–512.

30 On Freud's treatment, see Adorno, "Im Gedächtnis an Alban Berg," 492; and Erich Alban Berg, *Der unverbesserliche Romantiker*, 74. Neither author gives a clear date for this event, but it took place most likely in the summer between the years 1907 and 1909.

31 Letter, Alban Berg to Arnold Schoenberg, 25 July 1912, BSB I: 261–62.

32 Letter, Alban Berg to Helene Nahowski, 23 July 1909, BW I: 346.

33 A.B. Becker, et al. "The bronchodilator effects and pharmokinetics of caffeine in asthma," *New England Journal of Medicine* 310, no. 12 (1984): 743–46; E.J. Welsh et al., "Caffeine for Asthma," *Cochrane Library* 2011, no. 10: 1–34.

34 Letter, Alban to Helene Berg, 12 August 1916, BW II: 334.

35 Letter, Alban Berg to Anton Webern, 9 August 1913, ÖNB, F21.Berg.3270.

36 Adorno, "Im Gedächtnis an Alban Berg," 498.

37 Otto Weininger, *Über die letzten Dinge* (Vienna and Leipzig: Wilhelm Braumüller, 1904), 48. Wolfgang Gratzer dates Berg's reading of this book between 1909 and 1911. See Wolfgang Gratzer, *Zur "wunderlichen Mystik" Alban Bergs: Eine Studie* (Vienna: Böhlau Verlag, 1993), 94–95.

38 The original of this often-reprinted note is found in ÖNB, F21.Berg.474/13. The principal sources of information are Pat Bamford-Milroy, "Alban Berg and Albine Wittula: Fleisch und Blut," *Musical Times*, 134, no. 1881 (2002): 57–62; Erich Alban Berg, *Der unverbesserliche Romantiker*, 144–48; idem, "Bergiana," *Schweizerische Musikzeitung*, 120 (1980): 147–55; Grete Koschier, "Die 'vergessene' Tochter Alban Bergs," *Kleine Zeitung* (Graz), 23 April 2000, 54–55; Rosemary Moravec[-Hilmar] and Hermann Harrauer, "Marie und Albine Scheuchl—Alban Berg und BBC," *Biblos: Beiträge zu Buch, Bibliothek und Schrift* 48, no. 2 (1999): 209–12; "Neues zu Alban Berg: nochmals Albine Scheuchl," *Biblos: Beiträge zu Buch, Bibliothek und Schrift* 49/2 (2000): 243–46; Heinz Sichrovsky, "Alban Bergs uneheliche Tochter (1)," *Arbeiter-Zeitung* (Vienna), 28 April 1979; Jürg Stenzl, "Alban Berg und Marie Scheuchl," *ÖMZ* 40 (1985): 22–30; Christoph Wagner, "Albans Tochter Albine," *Arbeiter-Zeitung*, 5 May 1979, supplement.

39 The letter is found in ÖNB, F21.Berg.474/13 and is transcribed in full in Stenzl, "Alban Berg und Marie Scheuchl," 22–23. It was almost certainly posted to Marie because it was later passed down among Marie's descendants.

40 The present location of Berg's painting is unknown. It is shown in Erich Alban Berg, *Der unverbesserliche Romantiker*, 126.

41 *The Secret Life of Alban Berg / Das andere Leben Alban Bergs* (1992). BBC Symphony Orchestra, Howarth Elgar, conductor; Kristine Ciesinki, narrator. VHS. Princeton: Films for the Humanities & Sciences FFH 10327, 2000. Reissued as DVD, 2004.

42 See Helga Wittula's letters to the ÖNB in Moravec and Harrauer, "Marie und Albine Scheuchl—Alban Berg und BBC," and additional materials from Wittula in Pat Bamford-Milroy, "Alban Berg and Albine Wittula: Fleisch und Blut."

43 A photo of the sculpture is seen in Grete Koschier, "Die 'vergessene' Tochter Alban Bergs."

44 Shown in Pat Bamford-Milroy, "Alban Berg and Albine Wittula: Fleisch und Blut."

45 Douglas Jarman, "Alban Berg, Wilhelm Fliess and the Secret Programme of the Violin Concerto," *Musical Times* 124 (April 1983): 221–22.

46 Card, Helene Berg to Hermann Watznauer, 2 January 1936, WBR, HIN 203.853.

47 Helene Berg's handwritten will, dated 30 January 1946, is located in ÖNB, F21.Berg.1609/8. It is her earliest known will. Later wills by Helene Berg are filed with the Hietzing Bezirksgericht, and copies may be found in the Berg papers with the 1946 document.

48 Rosemary Hilmar, *Alban Berg*, 23.

49 See Semler's informative memoir of those summers in her "1903 and 1904," *International Alban Berg Society Newsletter* 1 (1968): 3–6.

50 Letter, Alban Berg to Hermann Watznauer, 22 August 1904, Morgan Library, MFC B493. W353.

51 See Donald Harris, "Berg and Frida Semler," *International Alban Berg Society Newsletter* 8 (1979): 8–12.

52 Helene and her sisters used the feminine form "Nahowska" in their youth, but Helene later chose Nahowski as the spelling that she preferred. This form will be used here in most cases, and exceptions will be clear from their context.

53 Concerning the affair, see Charlotte Erwin, "A Marital *Ausgleich*: The Affair of Emperor Franz Joseph I and Anna Nahowski," *Journal of Austrian Studies* 51, no. 2 (2018): 1–30.

54 The first diary edition is *Anna Nahowski und Kaiser Franz Joseph: Aufzeichnungen*, ed. Friedrich Saathen (Vienna: Hermann Böhlaus Nachf., 1986). This edition includes one diary only, which according to family nomenclature is Diary 1, although it is chronologically interwoven with Diary 2. The second edition is *Anna Nahowski & Kaiser Franz Josef: Ihr Leben, ihre Liebe, ihre Kinder*, ed. Herwig Knaus (Vienna: Erhard Löcker, 2012). This edition includes both diaries but in conflated form and with a number of omissions. Despite its problematic format, citations will generally be to the Knaus edition. The original diaries may be viewed online through the catalog of the ÖNB, F21. Berg.2490.

55 A recent attempt by the Alban Berg Foundation to retrieve Helene Berg's DNA in order to establish her paternity has been unsuccessful.

56 The divorce was final on 11 February 1879, according to the *Scheidungsurteil* in ÖNB, F21.Berg.1615/8. Newspaper notices about Heuduk's bankruptcies may be found in the *Allgemeine Österreichische Gerichtszeitung*, 10 August 1875, and the *Neue freie Presse*, 20 April 1877.

57 The passport is in ÖNB, F21.Berg.1613/6.

58 Knaus, *Anna Nahowski*, 74. The poem is for New Year's, 1879–80.

59 Ibid. 257.

60 Nahowski's case against the Southern Railway was written up in the *Oesterreichische Zeitung für Verwaltung*, 18 February 1892.

61 Knaus, *Anna Nahowski*, 122, 124.

62 Bruno Walter, "Von Wien nach Kalifornien," *Der Turm: Monatsschrift für österreichische Kultur*, 2, no. 3–4 (December 1946): 114. Helene's letter to the editor of *Der Turm* was published in a February 1947 issue.

63 Letter, Helene Berg to the editors of *Der Turm*, 19 February 1947, ÖNB, F21.Berg.1622/13.

64 Knaus, *Anna Nahowski*, 146.

65 Ibid. 162.

66 Letter, Helene Berg to Franz Nahowski, n.d., ÖNB, F21.Berg.1622/110.

67 Biographical sketch by Helene Berg in one of her notebooks, ÖNB, F21.Berg.1623/181.

68 The source for Carola and Anna's studies is Anna's diary (Diary 1), Saathen, *Anna Nahowski und Kaiser Franz Joseph,* 149. The passage is omitted in the Knaus edition.

69 Notices on the work of Carola Nahowska appear in several Viennese newspapers between 1910–17: *Neuigkeits Welt Blatt, Neues Wiener Tagblatt, Wiener Fremden-Blatt, Arbeiter-Zeitung,* and *Österreichische Illustrierte Zeitung.*

70 Martina Steiger gives Carola's death as 6 June 1946, and a letter from Helene to Alma Mahler confirms the year. See AMB, 537, 601. Herwig Knaus erroneously gives Carola's death year as 1947; see Knaus, *Anna Nahowski,* 373.

71 Helene records her sister Anna's death in an engagement calendar on May 20, 1973, ÖNB, F21.1623/208. Herwig Knaus, in *Anna Nahowski,* gives the year erroneously as 1974. He may also be mistaken in giving the death date of Helene's brother, Frank, as 1943. It is almost certainly 1942.

72 Letter, Helene to Alban Berg, 22 June 1921, BW III: 191.

73 Biographical sketch by Helene Berg in a notebook, ÖNB, F21.Berg.1623/37. The sketch is similar but not identical to F21.Berg.1623/181.

74 See family documents in ÖNB, F21.Berg.429.

75 Letter quoted in full in Knaus and Sinkovicz, *Alban Berg,* 32–35. The passage in quotation marks is from Goethe's Faust I.

76 Letter, Helene Nahowski to Alban Berg, 1 July 1907, BW I: 32–33.

77 The biographical note appears in two slightly varied versions among Helene Berg's notebooks, ÖNB, F.21.Berg.1623/37 and 1623/181. The "jugendlich-dramatisch" characterization applies only to the soprano voice. An alternate classification might be spinto. Helene's own description is supported by a study of her repertoire and of the notices of her public performances by Judith Kopecky, "'So schön habe ich mir Ihre Stimme nicht vorgestellt': Helene Nahowska als Sängerin," in *Erinnerung Stiften: Helene Berg und das Erbe Alban Bergs,* ed. Daniel Ender et al. (Vienna: Universal Edition, 2018), 31–49.

78 See the note by Helene Berg on Brandt, ÖNB, F21.Berg.433/78.

79 Letter of Tony Colbert to Marianne Brandt, undated, but forwarded to Helene Nahowski in a letter postmarked 18 September 1904, ÖNB, F21.Berg.1671.

80 Letter, Mizzi Fink to Helene Nahowski, 21 August 1905, ÖNB, F21.Berg.1748. See also Judith Kopecky, "So schön habe ich mir Ihre Stimme nicht vorgestellt," 40.

81 Letter, Marianne Brandt to Helene Nahowski, 10 February 1904, ÖNB, F21.Berg.1671.

82 Berg mentions Helene's throat operation in his letter to Soma Morgenstern, 11 May 1927, in Morgenstern, *Alban Berg und seine Idole: Erinnerungen und Briefe,* ed. Ingolf Schulte (Berlin: Aufbau Taschenbuch Verlag, 1999), 180.

83 Letter, Marianne Brandt to Helene Nahowski, 26 July 1907, ÖNB, F21.Berg.1671.

84 Letter, Marianne Brandt to Franz Nahowski, 7 March 1906, ÖNB, F21.Berg.1671; published in Knaus, *Anna Nahowski,* 236.

85 In his study "Im serialen Ereignisstrom: Paul Kammerer als Wissenschaftler, Musiktheoretiker und Komponist," *Die Tonkunst Online,*" 2006, p. 3, Stefan Schmidl cites matriculation records from the Vienna Conservatory showing that Kammerer had enrolled in Fuchs's classes from September 1900 to December 1901.

86 Letter, Paul Kammerer to Helene Nahowski, 10 July 1904, ÖNB, F21.Berg.1868.

87 Letter, Paul Kammerer to Helene Nahowski, 18 July 1904, ÖNB, F21.Berg.1868.

88 For more on Kammerer's music, see Bryan R. Simms, "Paul Kammerer and Alban Berg: Rivals in Song," *Music & Letters* 98 (2017): 104–27.

89 Other music by Kammerer is found in the ÖNB and the Alban Berg Stiftung.
90 Letter, Helene Nahowski to Alban Berg, 13 August 1907. BW I: 46–47.
91 Erich Alban Berg, *Als der Adler noch zwei Köpfe hatte*, 95–96.
92 BW I–III, Herwig Knaus and Thomas Leibnitz, eds.
93 See Constantin Floros, *Alban Berg and Hanna Fuchs: The Story of a Love in Letters*, trans. Ernest Bernhardt-Kabisch (Bloomington: Indiana University Press, 2008).
94 George Perle, "The Secret Programme of the Lyric Suite," *Musical Times* 118 (1977): 811.
95 The trip took place August 7–10, and the *Parsifal* performance was on August 8. The plan for the trip is described in a letter to Helene of 30 July 1909, BW I: 383–84.
96 Letter, Alban Berg to Helene Nahowski, 11 August 1909, BW I: 422–23.
97 Letter, Alban Berg to Helene Nahowski, 22 August 1909, BW I: 461.
98 Letter, Alban Berg to Helene Nahowski, 25 August 1909, BW I: 463–65.
99 Knaus and Sinkovicz, *Alban Berg*, 32–35.
100 BW I: 46.
101 Letter, Alban Berg to Helene Nahowski, n.d. (ca. 1907), BW I: 85.
102 Letter, Helene to Alban Berg, 11 July 1914, BW II, 103.
103 BW I: 394.
104 Letter, Helene Nahowski to Alban Berg, undated (ca. January 1909), BW I: 277.
105 Letter, Alban Berg to Franz Nahowski, 28 July 1910, BW I: 547–60.
106 Undated note added by Helene to the end of Berg's letter to her father of 28 July 1910, BW I: 559–60.
107 Letter, Helene Nahowski to Alban Berg, 2 May 1911, BW I: 737.
108 Letter, posthumous, Helene to Alban Berg, 3 May 1940, ÖNB, F21.Berg.1623/192.
109 Letter, Paul Kammerer to Helene Berg, 4 May 1911, ÖNB, F21.Berg.1868.
110 Letter, Alban to Helene Berg, 29 June 1921, BW III: 212–13. Here Berg lists a series of events in Schoenberg's life in 1911 with parallels to those in 1921. "This can't be accidental," he concludes.
111 A sympathetic portrayal of Kammerer's scientific career is given by Arthur Koestler, *The Case of the Midwife Toad* (New York: Random House, 1972). Also see Peter Berz and Klaus Taschwer, Nachwort to Arthur Koestler, *Der Krötenküsser: Der Fall des Biologen Paul Kammerer*, trans. Krista Schmidt (Vienna: Czernin, 2010); and Sander Gliboff, "The Case of Paul Kammerer: Evolution and Experimentation in the Early 20th Century," *Journal of the History of Biology* 39 (2006): 525–63.

Chapter 2

1 "Alban Berg," *Neue Musik-Zeitung* (Stuttgart), 42, no. 20 (21 July 1921): 320. About this article see Chapter 1, note 1.
2 Transcribed in Rosemary Hilmar, *Alban Berg: Leben und Wirken in Wien bis zu seinen ersten Erfolgen als Komponist* (Vienna: Verlag Hermann Böhlaus Nachf, 1978), 173–82.
3 Ibid., 178. Since Mozart's *The Magic Flute* has no overture to Act 2, Berg is probably referring to the "March of the Priests" that begins that act.
4 Willi Reich, "Alban Berg," *Die Musik* 22, no. 5 (1930): 347–48.
5 Arnold Schoenberg, "Für Reich und Wiesengrunds Berg-Buch," in Schönberg, *"Stile herrschen, Gedanken siegen": Ausgewählte Schriften*, ed. Anna Maria Morazzoni, et al. (Mainz: Schott, 2007), 527.

6 Alma Mahler Werfel in collaboration with E.B. Ashton, *And the Bridge Is Love* (New York: Harcourt, Brace, 1958), 180–81.

7 Hans Moldenhauer and Rosaleen Moldenhauer, *Anton von Webern* (New York: Alfred A. Knopf, 1979), 71.

8 Ibid. 147.

9 Egon Wellesz and Emmy Wellesz, *Egon Wellesz: Leben und Werk*, ed. Franz Endler (Vienna: Paul Zsolnay Verlag, 1981), 50.

10 Berg's instruction with Schoenberg is studied by Ulrich Krämer, *Alban Berg als Schüler Arnold Schönbergs: Quellenstudien und Analysen zum Frühwerk*, ABS 4 (Vienna: Universal Edition, 1996); also see Rosemary Hilmar, *Alban Berg*, 32–57.

11 Hugo Riemann, *Katechismus der Kompositionslehre* (Leipzig: Max Hesse's Verlag, 1889), 1: 3.

12 Adolf Bernhard Marx, *Die Lehre von der musikalischen Komposition*, 4 vols. (Leipzig: Breitkopf & Härtel, 1837–47 and many later editions); Johann Christian Lobe, *Lehrbuch der musikalischen Komposition*, 4 vols. (Leipzig: Breitkopf & Härtel, 1850–67); Heinrich Bellermann, *Der Contrapunkt oder Anleitung zur Stimmführung in der musikalischen Composition* (Berlin: Julius Springer, 1862). The theoretical background for Schoenberg's teaching is discussed in Krämer, *Alban Berg als Schüler Arnold Schönbergs*, 38–67, and Robert W. Wason, *Viennese Harmonic Theory from Albrechtsberger to Schenker and Schoenberg* (Rochester, NY: University of Rochester Press, 1985), 132–43. Also see Ulrich Krämer, "Schoenberg's Concepts of *Kompositionslehre* (1904–1911) and the Nineteenth-Century German Tradition," *Revista de musicologia* 16, no. 6 (1993): 3735–53.

13 Berg compiled three notebooks that record Schoenberg's instruction in harmony (ÖNB, F21.Berg.6), which relate closely to Schoenberg's *Harmonielehre*. They were thought by Rosemary Hilmar to date from this earliest period of study (Hilmar, *Alban Berg*, 34–36), but Ulrich Krämer has shown conclusively that they date from 1910–11, after Schoenberg had completed writing his *Harmonielehre*. Berg compiled the notebooks when he audited Schoenberg's harmony lectures at Vienna's Akademie für Musik und Darstellende Kunst. See Krämer, *Alban Berg als Schüler Arnold Schönbergs*, 274.

14 Schoenberg's teaching of species counterpoint for American students of the 1930s is recorded in his *Preliminary Exercises in Counterpoint*, ed. Leonard Stein (New York: St. Martin's Press, 1963).

15 See Ulrich Krämer's edition of selected early compositions from 1901 to ca. 1909, in Berg, *Kompositionen aus der Studienzeit*, 2 vols., Alban Berg Sämtliche Werke (Vienna: Universal Edition, 1998–2007).

16 Arnold Schoenberg, "The Teacher's Testimonial" (1936), in Willi Reich, *Alban Berg*, trans. Cornelius Cardew (New York: Vienna House, 1965), 28.

17 Published in Berg, *Kompositionen aus der Studienzeit*, vol. 2.

18 Schoenberg, "The Teacher's Testimonial," 28.

19 Berg's letters to Frida Semler are in the Library of Congress. This letter is quoted in Rosemary Hilmar, *Alban Berg*, 41.

20 Schoenberg's method was formulated early on and remained intact for his entire teaching career. It is set forth most fully in his *Fundamentals of Musical Composition*, ed. Gerald Strang and Leonard Stein (New York: St. Martin's Press, 1967).

21 Letter, Alban Berg to Helene Nahowski, early May 1907, BW I: 18.

22 Watznauer's dates for Berg's early songs were recorded in his fragmentary biography of the composer. See Nick Chadwick, "Hermann Watznauer's Biography of Alban Berg," in

Alban Berg and His World, ed. Christopher Hailey (Princeton, NJ: Princeton University Press, 2010), 33–90.

23 The music for all of the early songs is found in Alban Berg, *Jugendlieder* . . . , ed. Christopher Hailey, 3 vols. (Vienna: Universal Edition: 1985–2015).

24 ÖNB, F21.Berg.2.

25 Erich Alban Berg, *Der unverbesserliche Romantiker: Alban Berg 1885–1935* (Vienna: Österreichischer Bundesverlag, 1985), 150–51.

26 Editions of Watznauer's biography are found in Erich Alban Berg, *Der unverbesserliche Romantiker,* 9–67, and Nick Chadwick's "Hermann Watznauer's Biography of Alban Berg."

27 A facsimile of the questionnaire is found in Erich Alban Berg, *Der unverbesserliche Romantiker,* 152–53. The original of this document is in the Staatsbibliothek zu Berlin, N. Mus ep 10.

28 Given Helene Berg's restrictions, the early songs were long unpublished and little studied prior to a 1972 Oxford dissertation by Nicholas (Nick) Chadwick, "A Survey of the Early Songs of Alban Berg." Also see Chadwick's article "Berg's Unpublished Songs in the Österreichische Nationalbibliothek," *Music & Letters* 52, no. 2 (April 1971): 123–40, and Sara Adams's "The Development of Alban Berg's Compositional Style: A Study of his 'Jugendlieder' (1901–1908)" (PhD diss., Florida State University, 2008).

29 Several authors speculate that poetry from Berg's early songs around 1903 reflects his depressive moods brought on by the birth out-of-wedlock of his daughter, Albine. See, for example, Jürg Stenzl, "Alban Berg und Marie Scheuchl," *ÖMZ* 40 (1985): 22–30.

30 Schoenberg discusses small ternary form in *Fundamentals of Musical Composition*, 119–20.

31 The partly disassembled presentation copy is found in ÖNB, F21.Berg.67. The document can be seen using a link in the ÖNB catalog record.

32 See George Perle, *The Operas of Alban Berg*, vol. 2, *Lulu* (Berkeley and Los Angeles: University of California Press, 1985), 24–25.

33 See Rudolf Stephan, Preface to Alban Berg, *Sieben frühe Lieder* (Vienna: Philharmonia Partituren, 1997).

34 See Rudolf Stephan, Foreword to *Sieben frühe Lieder*, Alban Berg Sämtliche Werke series 1, part 6 (Vienna: Universal Edition, 1997), xvii–xix.

35 See Berg's letter to Erich Kleiber of 11 September 1928, in *Alban Berg—Erich Kleiber: Briefe der Freundschaft*, Martina Steiger, ed. (Vienna: Seifert Verlag, 2013), 67.

36 BW I: 35.

37 BW I: 50–51.

38 Julius Korngold, *Neue freie Presse,* 10 November 1928.

39 Theodor Adorno, "Alban Bergs frühe Lieder," *Musikblätter des Anbruch* 11 (February 1929): 90.

40 Transcribed by Herwig Knaus in *Alban Berg und Helene Berg: Ein Briefwechsel, 1907–1935* (Wilhelmshaven: Florian Noetzel Verlag, 2015), 35–39.

41 The sketches are found in ÖNB, F21.Berg.9, pp. 67, 70 (online through the ÖNB catalog). As Berg's music moved toward atonality, the composer complied with Schoenberg's practice of placing accidentals on almost all tones. In this book, following the recommendation of George Perle, these redundant accidentals are removed from musical examples. Perle writes: "The convention of supplying these superfluous natural signs, and superfluous repetitions of sharps and flats as well, had a certain usefulness at one time, as a way of keeping the performer's eyes from straying to the left margin of the page in search of a key

signature, but this ceased to be a problem a long time ago." (Perle, *Style and Idea in the Lyric Suite of Alban Berg*, rev. ed. [Hillsdale, NY: Pendragon Press, 2001], 28).

42 See Allen Edwards, *Flawed Words and Stubborn Sounds: A Conversation with Elliott Carter* (New York: W.W. Norton, 1971), 107.

43 See H.H. Stuckenschmidt, "Debussy or Berg? The Mystery of a Chord Progression," *Musical Quarterly* 51 (1965): 453–59.

44 Arnold Schoenberg, *Theory of Harmony*, trans. Roy E. Carter (Berkeley and Los Angeles: University of California Press, 1978), 416.

45 See Berg's letter to Schoenberg of 20 July 1914, BSB I: 491.

46 Willi Reich, *Alban Berg: Mit Bergs eigenen Schriften und Beiträgen von Theodor Wiesengrund-Adorno und Ernst Křenek* (Vienna: Herbert Reichner Verlag, 1937), 30.

47 See David P. Schroeder "Berg, Strindberg, and D Minor," *College Music Symposium* 30, no. 2 (1990): 74–89.

48 Letter, Alban Berg to Anton Webern, mid-August 1911, quoted in Rosemary Hilmar, *Alban Berg*, 53.

49 This idea is put forward by Sara Adams in "The Development of Alban Berg's Compositional Style," 329–30.

50 A selection of these works is found in Ulrich Krämer, ed., *Kompositionen aus der Studienzeit*, vols. 1–2.

51 George Perle, *The Operas of Alban Berg*, vol. 1, *Wozzeck* (Berkeley and Los Angeles: University of California Press, 1980), 2.

52 See the analysis by Ulrich Krämer in *Alban Berg als Schüler Arnold Schönbergs*, 108–22.

53 Review for the *Neues Wiener Journal*, 17 November 1908, reprinted in full in Rosemary Hilmar, *Alban Berg*, 45.

54 Modern editions are found in Ulrich Krämer, ed., *Kompositionen aus der Studienzeit*, vol. 2 and Rudolf Stephan, ed., *Frühe Klaviermusik: Ausgewählte Stücke,* vol. 2 (Vienna: Universal Edition, 1990).

55 See Schoenberg's discussion of the form in his *Fundamentals of Musical Composition*, 167–77.

56 In an often-cited letter to his friend Frida Semler from July 1907, Berg writes, "I am writing a piano sonata for my own benefit." It has been shown conclusively by Ulrich Krämer that this piano piece was not the work that became Op. 1, as is often stated in the literature. See Krämer, *Alban Berg als Schüler Arnold Schönbergs*, 13–14 and passim.

57 Sonatas I–V are published in Ulrich Krämer, ed., *Kompositionen aus der Studienzeit*, vol. 2.

58 Krämer, *Alban Berg als Schüler Arnold Schönbergs*, 171–72.

59 Quoted in Rosemary Hilmar, *Alban Berg*, 48.

60 H. F. Redlich, *Alban Berg: Versuch einer Würdigung* (Vienna: Universal Edition, 1957), 355 n47.

61 Berg's analysis appeared in the *Neue Musik-Zeitung* (Stuttgart) 42, no. 20 (1921): 320. Measure numbers in this discussion begin with the first full measure.

62 See the detailed analysis of the exposition of Op. 1 in Janet Schmalfeldt, "Berg's Path to Atonality: The Piano Sonata, Op. 1," in *Alban Berg: Historical and Analytical Perspectives*, ed. David Gable and Robert Morgan (New York: Oxford University Press, 1991), 79–109.

63 Quoted in Ivan Vojtěch, "Arnold Schoenberg, Anton Webern, Alban Berg: Unbekannte Briefe an Erwin Schulhoff," *Miscellanea musicologica* 15 (1965): 81.

64 Quoted in Volker Scherliess, "Zur Rezeption der Klaviersonata op. 1," in *Alban Berg Symposion Wien 1908: Tagungsbericht*, ed. Rudolf Klein, ABS 2 (Vienna: Universal Edition, 1981), 242.

65 Quoted in Rosemary Hilmar, *Alban Berg*, 49.

66 In a letter to Rudolf Kolisch dated spring 1935, Berg said that he was contemplating the addition of a short third movement to place between the two existing movements of the String Quartet. See Erich Alban Berg, *Der unverbesserliche Romantiker*, 140.

67 Some writers have found central pitch elements in the work. Bruce Archibald holds that the prominent reiteration of the note D is a symbol of Berg's love for Helene. Redlich (*Alban Berg*, English edition p. 52) sees D and F as pseudo-tonics. Jody Rockmaker ("Articulating Form in Alban Berg's String Quartet, Opus 3: An Analysis of the First Movement and the Sketches" [PhD diss., Princeton University, 1989]) finds the tones E and B to be goals of directed motions.

68 Quoted in Vojtěch, "Arnold Schoenberg, Anton Webern, Alban Berg: Unbekannte Briefe an Erwin Schulhoff," 41.

69 Alma Mahler, *Gustav Mahler: Memories and Letters*, 3rd ed., ed. Donald Mitchell, trans. Basil Creighton (Seattle: University of Washington Press, 1975), 112.

70 Bruno Walter, *Von den moralischen Kräften der Musik* (Vienna: Herbert Reichner, 1935), 10.

71 Paul Hindemith, *The Craft of Musical Composition*, revised ed., trans. Arthur Mendel (New York: Associated Music Publishers, 1945), I: 22.

72 Schoenberg, *Theory of Harmony*, 420.

73 Theodor Adorno, in Reich, *Alban Berg* (1937), 35–43. Adorno's discussion is reprinted in his *Alban Berg: Master of the Smallest Link*, trans. Juliane Brand and Christopher Hailey (Cambridge: Cambridge University Press, 1991), 53–62.

74 Letter, Alban to Helene Berg, 3 August 1923, BW III: 358.

75 From an anecdote told to Helene Berg's friend Fritzi Schlesinger-Czapka. See Constantin Floros, *Alban Berg: Musik als Autobiographie* (Wiesbaden: Breitkopf & Härtel, 1992), 154–55.

Chapter 3

1 Letter, Alban Berg to Anton Webern, mid-August 1911, quoted in Rosemary Hilmar, *Alban Berg: Leben und Wirken in Wien bis zu seinen ersten Erfolgen als Komponist* (Vienna: Hermann Böhlaus Nachf., 1978), 53.

2 Cindy Hazan and Phillip Shaver, "Romantic Love Conceptualized as an Attachment Process," *Journal of Personality and Social Psychology*, 52 (1987): 511–24.

3 The circumstances of Schoenberg's departure are described in BSB I: 44 n60.

4 See Berg's letter to Schoenberg, late November 1915, BSB I: 608–17.

5 Furnishings purchased by Anna Nahowski are recorded in ÖNB, F21.Berg.2622.

6 Letter, Alban Berg to Hanna Fuchs-Robettin, n.d. (July 1925), in *Alban Berg and Hanna Fuchs: The Story of a Love in Letters*, ed. Constantin Floros, trans. Ernest Bernhardt-Kabisch (Bloomington: Indiana University Press, 2008), 22.

7 Herwig Knaus and Wilhelm Sinkovicz, *Alban Berg: Zeitumstände - Lebenslinien* (St. Pölten: Residenz Verlag, 2008), 48.

8 BW I–III.

9 See the list given by Knaus and Leibnitz in the Index volume of BW, 149–53. The list is incomplete and not fully accurate, which also characterizes other aspects of the Index.

10 Letter, Helene to Alban Berg, ca. 29 August 1916, BW II: 31. The letter is erroneously dated 1912 in BW; Alban's answer is dated 31 August 1916, BW II: 379–80.

11 See Alban's letter to Helene, 18 May 1910 (BW I: 535) mentioning her use of "Blaud's Pills," an iron supplement.

12 Concerning dysmenorrhea and related gynecological disorders, see Linda Khademol-Reza, "Theories of dysmenorrhea: an historical review from 1850 to 1979," *Journal of the Kansas Medical Society* 84/6 (1983): 335–40, 355–56; and Giuseppe Benagiano et al, "The history of endometriosis: identifying the disease," *Human Reproduction* 6, no. 7 (1991): 963–68. A current clinical study of interest is Giuseppe Benagiano et al., "Adenomyosis: a life-cycle approach," *Reproductive BioMedicine Online* 30 (2015): 220–32. The latter article notes that adenomyosis becomes silent in most cases past menopause.

13 An early use of the term "neurasthenia" was by an American doctor, George Beard. See Beard, "Neurasthenia, or Nervous Exhaustion," *Boston Medical and Surgical Journal* 3, no. 13 (29 April 1869): 217–221. On Krafft-Ebing's view of neurasthenia, see Sabine Wieber, "Sculpting the Sanatorium: Nervous Bodies and Femmes Fragiles in Vienna 1900," in *Women in German Yearbook* 27, ed. Patricia Anne Simpson and Margarete Lamb-Faffelberger (Lincoln: University of Nebraska Press, 2011): 71.

14 A pioneering work on the image of the *femme fragile* is Ariane Thomalla, *Die "femme fragile": Ein literarischer Frauentypus der Jahrhundertwende* (Düsseldorf: Bertelsmann Universitätsverlag, 1972). The visual representation of the femme fragile, in particular its association with the Purkersdorf Sanatorium, is discussed by Sabine Wieber, "Sculpting the Sanatorium," 58–86.

15 Letter, Alban to Helene Berg, 10 March 1914, BW II: 68.

16 Letter, Alban Berg to Franz Nahowski, 28 July 1910, BW I: 553.

17 Letter, Alban to Helene Berg, 20 August 1916, BW II: 346.

18 Letter, Alban to Helene Berg, 8 June 1921, BW III: 144.

19 Letter, Helene to Alban Berg, n.d. (ca. 29 August 1916), BW II: 31.

20 Letter, Alban to Helene Berg, 31 August 1916, ibid., 379.

21 Letter, Alban Berg to Arnold Schoenberg, late November 1915, BSB I: 609.

22 PMPD, 377. The wording of the appeal is often attributed to Berg, but in a letter by Anton Webern to Heinrich Jalowetz dated 19 September 1911, Linke is named as the author. See Webern, *Briefe an Heinrich Jalowetz*, ed. Ernst Lichtenhahn (Mainz: Schott, 1999), 163.

23 Letter, Smaragda Eger-Berg to Alban Berg, 28 June 1915, QMG 35: 210.

24 Letter, Helene to Alban Berg, 19 October 1915, BW II: 248. Also see Helene's scathing remarks about Schoenberg in her letter to Berg of 28 September 1918, BW II: 679–80.

25 Letter, Alban Berg to Arnold Schoenberg, 9 July 1913, BSB I: 423.

26 See Rainer J. Schwob, *Klavierauszug und Klavierskizze bei Alban Berg: Untersuchungen zur Rolle des Klaviers als "Hilfsmittel"* (Anif/Salzburg: Verlag Mueller-Speiser, 2000).

27 Christopher Hailey holds that Wöss was entirely responsible for the piano score of Act 1 of *Der ferne Klang*, but this statement is questioned by Rainer Schwob. See Hailey, *Franz Schreker, 1878–1934: A Cultural Biography* (New York: Cambridge University Press, 1993), 334, and Schwob, *Klavierauszug und Klavierskizze bei Alban Berg*, 83.

28 Quoted in Rosemary Hilmar, *Alban Berg*, 60–61.

29 Ibid. *Alban Berg*, 64.

30 Letter, Arnold Schoenberg to Erhard Buschbeck, 14 December 1912, quoted in Rosemary Ibid. 91–92.

31 BSB I: 337.

32 BSB I: 346.

33 Letter, Alban Berg to Arnold Schoenberg, 17 January 1913, BSB I: 347.

34 There was long uncertainty over which songs from Berg's Op. 4 were performed, but the printed program for the concert (WBR, HIN 204.585, p. 75) shows that these were nos. 2–3.

35 Excerpts from reviews of the concert are found in Walter Szmolyan, "Schönbergs Wiener Skandalkonzert," ÖMZ 31 (1976): 293–304.

36 *Neues Wiener Journal*, 27 April 1913.

37 *Illustriertes Wiener Extrablatt*, 1 April 1913, quoted in Szmolyan, "Schönbergs Wiener Skandalkonzert," 301.

38 Quoted in Rosemary Hilmar, *Alban Berg*, 97.

39 Quoted in Alban Berg's letter to Arnold Schoenberg, 2 April 1913, BSB I: 392.

40 Ibid., 393.

41 In a subsequent interview for *Die Zeit*, Schoenberg remarked that he had performed works by Webern and Berg because they were "highly important talents," not just because they were his students. See Szmolyan, "Schönbergs Wiener Skandalkonzert," 302.

42 Alban Berg, "Arnold Schönbergs Berliner Skandalkonzert," *Neues Wiener Journal*, 6 December 1928.

43 Arnold Schönberg Center (Vienna), Archive, T04.43.

44 Quoted in Rosemary Hilmar, *Alban Berg*, 51.

45 Letter, Alban Berg to Willi Reich, 26 January 1934, Alban Berg/Willi Reich Collection, Library of Congress.

46 Entry for 25 February 1912, Arnold Schönberg, *Berliner Tagebuch* (Frankfurt: Propyläen Verlag, 1974), 31.

47 Letter, Alban Berg to Arnold Schoenberg, 23 November 1912, BSB I: 316–17.

48 Ibid., 325.

49 Quoted in Alban Berg, *Musikalische Schriften und Dichtungen*, ed. Rudolf Stephan and Regina Busch, Alban Berg Sämtliche Werke (Vienna: Universal Edition, 1994), 1: xvii.

50 Letter, Arnold Schoenberg to Alban Berg, 10 March 1913, BSB I: 379.

51 Statistics are given in *Musikalische Schriften und Dichtungen*, 1: xviii–xxv.

52 Ulrich Krämer contends that Berg composed an incomplete orchestral song "Nach einem Regen" on a poem by Richard Dehmel around 1910, but the diatonic and clearly tonal harmonic style in the work points to an earlier date. See Krämer, *Alban Berg als Schüler Arnold Schönbergs: Quellenstudien und Analysen zum Frühwerk*, ABS 4 (Vienna: Universal Edition, 1996), 270–71.

53 The music is found in Berg, *Symphonie-Fragmente*, ed. Rudolf Stephan (Vienna: Universal Edition, 1984). This edition also contains a forty-one-measure fragment of an orchestral piece in a condensed score. On the reverse side of one of its manuscript pages Berg wrote the word "Symphonie," but since Berg several times contemplated writing a symphony between 1911 and 1914, no conclusive date can be given to the fragment. It has no musical connection to the Orchestra Pieces, Op. 6.

54 Letter, Arnold Schoenberg to Alban Berg, 14 February 1912, BSB I: 188.

55 For the English-language reader, Andrew Barker's study of Altenberg, *Telegrams from the Soul: Peter Altenberg and the Culture of fin-de-siècle Vienna* (Columbia, SC: Camden House, 1996), is highly recommended.

56 Peter Altenberg, "Selbstbiographie," in *Was der Tag mir zuträgt*, 2nd ed. (Berlin: Fischer, 1901), 2.

57 Peter Altenberg, "Beschäftigung," *Neues Altes* (Berlin: Fischer, 1911), 203.

58 Rosemary Hilmar, *Alban Berg*, 41.

59 It is unlikely that Altenberg met Helene before 28 July 1909. On that day Berg wrote to her to discuss a passage that Helene had quoted from Altenberg's sketch "Wunsch": "I wish that a lover could look upon a garden flower bed more tenderly and lovingly than upon me . . . " Berg responded: "*If he had known you* [Wenn er aber Dich gekannt hätte] in whom that blending of nature and culture appears in a much more condensed form, he might have written: 'I wish that a lover could look upon the woman Helene more tenderly and lovingly than upon me.—PA'" (emphasis added). The letter is found in BW I: 370.

60 Berg's 1906 Altenberg songs are discussed by Christoph Khittl in "The Other Altenberg Song Cycle: A Document of Viennese Fin-de-Siècle Aesthetics," in *Encrypted Messages in Alban Berg's Music*, ed. Siglind Bruhn (New York: Garland Publishing, 1998), 137–56.

61 Gert Mattenklott, "'Keine Ansiedlungen': Peter Altenbergs Texte der fünf Orchesterlieder Alban Bergs Op. 4," *Hofmannsthal-Blätter* 27 (1983): 74–91.

62 Berg's piano-vocal score of "Hier ist Friede" was published in *Menschen: Zeitschrift neuer Kunst* 4, no. 5–6 (1921): 87–92, reprinted in *Musical Quarterly* 34 (1948): 487–511; the autograph manuscript of Berg's 1917 arrangement of "Hier ist Friede" is found at the Bayerische Staatsbibliothek (Munich), Mus.ms. 17487. A piano-vocal score of the full cycle, edited by Hans E. Apostel, was published by Universal Edition in 1953, the full score in 1966. A critical edition of the full score by Mark DeVoto is found in Alban Berg Sämtliche Werke (Vienna: Universal Edition, 1997).

63 Douglas Jarman, *The Music of Alban Berg* (Berkeley and Los Angeles: University of California Press, 1979), 46.

64 In his article "Reflections upon the Gershwin-Berg Connection," *Musical Quarterly* 83 (1999): 150–68, Allen Forte points to the strongly octatonic opening of the second movement of Berg's *Lyric Suite* and its possible influence on the later harmonic innovations in George Gershwin's music.

65 A detailed analysis of motives and themes in Songs 1 and 5 is found in Mark DeVoto, "Some Notes on the Unknown *Altenberg Lieder*," *Perspectives of New Music* 5 (1966): 37–74.

66 Ferruccio Busoni, *Selected Letters*, trans. and ed. Antony Beaumont (New York: Columbia University Press, 1987), 389.

67 Letter, Alban Berg to Erwin Schulhoff, 24 February 1921 in Ivan Vojtěch, "Arnold Schoenberg, Anton Webern, Alban Berg: Unbekannte Briefe an Erwin Schulhoff," *Miscellanea musicologica* 15 (1965): 63.

68 See Jarman, *The Music of Alban Berg*, 23–25.

69 An explanation of this relationship—often used by Berg—is found in Joseph N. Straus, *Introduction to Post-Tonal Theory* (Englewood Cliffs, NJ: Prentice Hall, 1990), 67–72 and passim. The similarity of the two six-note collections comes from the first being the complement (here transposed) of the second.

70 *Le Ménestrel* 83 (1921), 244.

71 Letter, Alban to Helene Berg, n.d. (ca. 22 June 1921), BW III: 187.

72 Letter, Alban Berg to Arnold Schoenberg, n.d. (late November 1915), BSB I: 608–17.

73 Berg sent his analytic notes to Schüler in a letter of 2 April 1930, and they were used by Fritz Uhlenbruch for the program booklet for the concert. Uhlenbruch's article is found in Reich, *Alban Berg*, trans. Cornelius Cardew (New York: Vienna House, 1965), 115.

74 Letter, Alban to Helene Berg, 11 July 1914, BW II: 100.

75 Letter, Alban Berg to Josef Schmid, 8 August [1914], ÖNB, L6.Alban-Berg-Stiftung.99. See the analysis of pitch cells, motives, and themes in Jarman, *The Music of Alban Berg*, 37–46 and passim.

76 Theodor W. Adorno, *Alban Berg: Master of the Smallest Link*, trans. Juliane Brand and Christopher Hailey (Cambridge: Cambridge University Press, 1991), 22.

77 Compare Tchaikovsky, Symphony No. 6, score (Moscow: P. Jurgenson, n.d. [ca. 1901], Reh. L and Mahler, Symphony No. 6, score (Leipzig: C. F. Kahnt, 1906), Reh. 164.

78 Letter, Alban Berg to Josef Schmid, 8 September [1914], ÖNB, L6.Alban-Berg-Stiftung.99.

79 Mark DeVoto, "Alban Berg's Marche Macabre," *Perspectives of New Music* 22 (1983–84): 442.

80 Walter Schrenk, *Deutsche allgemeine Zeitung* (Berlin), 6 June 1923 (issue 257).

Chapter 4

1 Hermann Bahr, "Gruß an Hofmannsthal," *Neues Wiener Journal*, 26 August 1914.

2 Heinrich Schenker, *Piano Sonata in C Minor, Op. 111. Beethoven's Last Piano Sonatas: An Edition with Elucidation*, trans. John Rothgeb (New York: Oxford University Press, 2015), 3: 2.

3 Alexander Zemlinsky, *Briefwechsel mit Arnold Schönberg, Anton Webern, Alban Berg und Franz Schreker*, ed. Horst Weber (Darmstadt: Wissenschaftliche Buchgesellschaft, 1995), 127.

4 Anton Webern, *Briefe an Heinrich Jalowetz*, ed. Ernst Lichtenhahn (Mainz: Schott, 1999), 317. Lemberg in Galicia had just witnessed a rout of the Austrian army by invading Russian troops.

5 BW II: 189–91.

6 See the English translation, "In These Great Times," by Harry Zohn in *In These Great Times: A Karl Kraus Reader*, ed. Harry Zohn (Montreal: Engendra Press, 1976), 70–83. Concerning Kraus's wartime writings, see Edward Timms, *Karl Kraus, Apocalyptic Satirist: Culture and Catastrophe in Habsburg Vienna* (New Haven: Yale University Press, 1986), 273–303 and passim.

7 Ivan Vojtěch, "Arnold Schoenberg, Anton Webern, Alban Berg: Unbekannte Briefe an Erwin Schulhoff," *Miscellanea musicologica* (Prague) 15 (1965): 31–83.

8 Romain Rolland, "Déclaration de l'indépendance de l'esprit," *L'Humanité*, 26 June 1919. Translation by David James Fisher in *Romain Rolland and the Politics of Intellectual Engagement* (New Brunswick: Transaction Publishers, 2004), 63.

9 Letter, Arnold Schoenberg to Erwin Schulhoff, 20 June 1919, quoted in Vojtěch, "Arnold Schoenberg, Anton Webern, Alban Berg," 36–37.

10 Alban Berg, "Lecture on *Wozzeck*: The Atonal Opera" (1929–30), PMPD, 258.

11 Rosemary Hilmar, *Alban Berg: Leben und Wirken in Wien bis zu seinen ersten Erfolgen als Komponist* (Vienna: Verlag Hermann Böhlaus Nachf, 1978), 119.

12 Letter, Alban Berg to Arnold Schoenberg, 24 June 1918, BSB II: 6. The letter draft to Kraus, dated 28 April 1924, is transcribed in QMG 29: 216.

13 Letter, Alban Berg to August Göttel, 14 April 1916, in *Alban Berg 1885–1935: Ausstellung der Österreichischen Nationalbibliothek* (Vienna: Universal Edition, 1985), 57.

14 The letter is transcribed in BBF, 82.

15 Soma Morgenstern, *Alban Berg und seine Idole: Erinnerungen und Briefe*, ed. Ingolf Schulte (Berlin: Aufbau Taschenbuch Verlag, 1995), 114.

16 See Helene Berg's letters to Alban Berg of 7 and 12 October 1915 in BW II: 231, 234.

17 See Claudia Maurer Zenck, "Zur Vorgeschichte der Uraufführung von Mahlers zehnter Symphonie," *Archiv für Musikwissenschaft* 39 (1982): 245–70.

18 Letter draft, Alban Berg to Alma Mahler, 11 July 1923, AMB, 107.

19 Now located at the Bayerische Staatsbibliothek (Munich), Mus Ms 23463, dated 27 February 1924.

20 Gottfried Kassowitz, "Lehrzeit bei Alban Berg," ÖMZ 23 (1968): 323.

21 Theodor W. Adorno, *Alban Berg: Master of the Smallest Link*, trans. Juliane Brand and Christopher Hailey (Cambridge: Cambridge University Press, 1991), 32–33. Berg's distinction between symphonic composition and character piece is relevant to his Orchestra Pieces, Op. 6.

22 Wolfgang Gratzer explores Berg's interest in mysticism and numerology in *Zur "Wunderlichen Mystik" Alban Bergs: Eine Studie* (Vienna: Böhlau, 1993).

23 Douglas Jarman, "'Man hat auch nur Fleisch und Blut': Towards a Berg Biography," in *Alban Berg: Historical and Analytical Perspectives*, ed. David Gable and Robert P. Morgan (Oxford: Clarendon Press, 1991): 11–23; idem, "'Remembrance of Things That Are to Come': Some Reflections on Berg's Palindromes," in *Alban Berg and His World*, ed. Christopher Hailey (Princeton, NJ: Princeton University Press, 2010), 195–221.

24 Stefan Zweig, *The World of Yesterday*, trans. Anthea Bell (Lincoln: University of Nebraska Press, 2009), 324–25.

25 Letter, Alban to Helene Berg, 11 November 1925, BW III: 427-28. In the letter Berg attempts to dispel Helene's suspicion that he was infatuated with Hanna Fuchs-Robettin.

26 Stefan Zweig, *Three Masters: Balzac, Dickens, Dostoeffsky*, trans. Eden Paul and Cedar Paul (New York: Viking Press, 1930), 16.

27 Quoted in Gratzer, *Zur "Wunderlichen Mystik" Alban Bergs*, 48, from Strindberg's *Ein Blaubuch: Die Synthese meines Lebens,* trans. from Swedish by Emil Schering (Munich: G. Müller, 1908), 2: 774. See also Gratzer, 46-47, including a facsimile page from Berg's copy of *Blaubuch* vol. 2.

28 Gratzer, *Zur "Wunderlichen Mystik" Alban Bergs*, 46. Berg was especially occupied with the *Blaubuch* in July and August of 1909. See BW I: 167, 332, and 445.

29 Ibid. 224. Weininger's "Aphorisms" in *Über die letzen Dinge* include the following: "There is no such thing as chance." See Steven Burns, *A Translation of Weininger's* Über die letzten Dinge *(1904/1907): On Last Things* (Lewiston, NY: Edwin Mellen Press, 2001), 44.

30 See, for example, his letter to Helene, 29 June 1921, BW III: 212–13.

31 Gratzer, *Zur "Wunderlichen Mystik" Alban Bergs*, 155.

32 Letter, Alban to Helene Berg, 27 January 1914, BW II: 62.

33 Berg recalled the year of his first asthma attack as 1900. See his letter to Helene Berg of 2 November 1915, BW I: 265.

34 Wilhelm Fliess, *Vom Leben und vom Tod: Biologische Vorträge* (Jena: Diederich, 1909).

35 Fliess, *Vom Leben und vom Tod*, 1.

36 Ernst Kris, "Wilhelm Fliess's Scientific Ideas," in Sigmund Freud, *The Origins of Psychoanalysis: Letters, Drafts and Notes to Wilhelm Fliess, 1887–1902*, ed. Marie Bonaparte et al., trans. Eric Mosbacher and James Strachey (Garden City, NY: Doubleday, 1954), 7–8. The documents in this publication come from Fliess's papers; no letters from Fliess to Freud are known to exist. A later edition of these letters is *The Complete Letters of Sigmund Freud to Wilhelm Fliess, 1887–1904*, trans. and ed. J.M. Masson (Cambridge, MA: Belknap Press/Harvard University Press, 1985).

37 Peter Gay, *Freud: A Life for Our Time* (New York: Anchor Books, 1989), 56–57.

38 Michael Schröter "Fliess versus Weininger, Swoboda and Freud: The Plagiarism Conflict of 1906 Assessed in the Light of the Documents," *Psychoanalysis and History* 5 (2008): 147–73.

39 Paul Kammerer, "Sexualität und Symmetrie: Ein Beitrag zur Kritik der Periodenlehre von Wilhelm Fließ und Hans Schlieper," *Zeitschrift für Sexualwissenschaft* 5, no. 1-2 (1918): 1–11, 41–54.

40 Letter, Alban Berg to Arnold Schoenberg, 10 June 1915, BSB I: 584.

41 Letter, Arnold Schoenberg to Alban Berg, 15 June 1915, BSB I: 588.

42 Letter, Alban Berg to Arnold Schoenberg, 20 June 1915, BSB I: 589–92.

43 Gratzer, *Zur "Wunderlichen Mystik" Alban Bergs*, 162.

44 Fritz Werle, *Künstlerhoroskope* (Munich: Barth, 1926). Berg's correspondence with Werle on this project can be found in ÖNB, F21.Berg.1524.

45 Marianne Raschig, *Hand und Persönlichkeit. Einführung in das System der Handlehre* (Hamburg: Enoch-Verlag, 1931). A copy of this publication may be found in Berg's library at the Alban Berg Foundation.

46 Helene's occult books are housed at the Alban Berg Foundation.

47 Letter, Günther Marstrand to Alban Berg, 22 September 1929. The eight Marstrand letters to Berg are in ÖNB, F21.Berg.1068/1–8. The Marstrand episode is chronicled in Gratzer, *Zur "Wunderlichen Mystik" Alban Bergs*, 121–41, including transcriptions of all eight letters.

48 Theodor Adorno, "Im Gedächtnis an Alban Berg" (1955), in Adorno, *Gesammelte Schriften* (Frankfurt: Suhrkamp, 1984), 18: 487–88.

49 Douglas Jarman, "'Remembrance of Things That Are to Come,'" 216; Robert P. Morgan, "The Eternal Return: Retrograde and Circular Form in Berg," in *Alban Berg: Historical and Analytical Perspectives*, 146–48.

50 Letter, Johanna Berg to Alban Berg, 5 August 1918, BBF, 67.

51 Stefan Zweig, *The World of Yesterday*, 281.

52 Letter, Alban Berg to Erwin Schulhoff, 27 November 1919, in Vojtěch, "Arnold Schoenberg, Anton Webern, Alban Berg," 53.

53 Quoted in *Arnold Schönberg Gedenkausstellung 1974*, ed. Ernst Hilmar (Vienna: Universal Edition, 1974), 182–83.

54 The first two prospectuses are found in PMPD, 378–86.

55 Prospectus of February 1919, PMPD, 378–83.

56 Letter, Johanna to Alban and Helene Berg, 31 July 1914, BBF, 42–43.

57 Letter, Johanna to Alban Berg, 10 September 1918, BBF, 71.

58 Letters, Helene Berg to Julianne Scheubeutel, 24 October 1919 and undated, WBR, HIN 204.312–13.

59 Letter, Charly to Alban Berg, 12 November 1919, BBF, 82.

60 Letter, Alban to Herman Berg, n.d. (ca. early December 1919), ÖNB, F21.Berg.480/37. The letter is published in QMG 29: 28–29 and excerpted in Herwig Knaus and Wilhelm Sinkovicz, *Alban Berg* (St. Pölten: Residenz Verlag, 2008): 170–71.

61 Letter, Erich to Helene Berg, 16–17 June 1965, WBR, HIN 204.584, p. 93.

62 Letter draft, Alban to Johanna Berg, 29 December 1919, ÖNB, F.21.Berg.468. A sketch of the property made by Berg is also found here.

63 Letter, Alban to Helene Berg, 12–13 January 1920, BW III: 21.

64 QMG 35: 57–63. An abridged copy of the draft letter is in BBF, 97–102.

65 Berg's tax appeal letter may be found in ÖNB, F21.Berg.3010.

66 See Alban's and Helene's drafts, February 1920, BW III: 75–82. Herwig Knaus contends that Alban's wish to speak through Helene was intended to spare his mother his direct criticism, but Helene also wanted an opportunity to defend herself and her family. See Knaus and Sinkovicz, *Alban Berg*, 179–81.

67 BW III: 72 n97.

68 Concerning the purchase of the Küb house, see BBF, 107 and 241 n208.

69 Letter, Alban to Helene Berg, 11 January 1920, BW III: 14.

70 Letter, Alban to Helene Berg, 16 February 1920, BW III: 110.

71 *Arnold Schönberg: Kammersymphonie, Op. 9: Thematische Analyse* (Vienna: Universal Edition, n.d. [1918]).

72 See Steven Vande Moortele, *Two-Dimensional Sonata Form: Form and Cycle in Single-Movement Instrumental Works by Liszt, Strauss, Schoenberg, and Zemlinsky* (Leuven: Leuven University Press, 2009).

73 Letter, Alban Berg to Anton Webern, 16 March 1920, cited in Anna Maria Morazzoni, "Berg, der unverbesserliche Polemiker: Neue Quellen und weitere Implikationen zu Bergs Stellung gegen Pfitzner und Casella," in *Musik zwischen beiden Weltkriegen und Slavko Osterc* (Ljubljana: Festival Ljubljana, 1995), 127.

74 *Pelleas und Melisande (Nach dem Drama von Maurice Maeterlinck). Symphonische Dichtung für Orchester von Arnold Schönberg, Op. 5. Kurze thematische Analyse* (Vienna: Universal Edition, [1920]). The longer guide to *Pelleas* was first published in Alban Berg Sämtliche Werke, series 3, part 1: 97–118, edited by Rudolf Stephan and Regina Busch (Vienna: Universal Edition, 1994). An English translation is in PMPD, 120–42.

75 Berg never settled on a title for the second of these articles. His working titles were "Zwei Feuilletons," "Schönberg und die Kritik," and (finally) "Wiener Musikkritik."

76 Hans Pfitzner, *Die neue Aesthetik der musikalischen Impotenz: Ein Verwesungssymptom?* (Munich: Verlag der Süddeutschen Monatshefte, 1920).

77 Letter, Alban Berg to Helene Nahowski, n.d. (ca. June 1907), BW I: 35.

78 Four drafts of the letter from Berg to Pfitzner are found in QMG 29: 56–57.

79 Hans Pfitzner, *Futuristengefahr: Bei Gelegenheit von Busoni's Ästhetik* (Leipzig and Munich: Süddeutsche Monatshefte, 1917).

80 Ferruccio Busoni, *Entwurf einer neuen Ästhetik der Tonkunst*, 2nd expanded edition (Leipzig: Insel-Verlag [1916]).

81 Arnold Schoenberg, "Falscher Alarm" (ca. 1917), in Schoenberg, *"Stile herrschen, Gedanken siegen": Ausgewählte Schriften*, ed. Anna Maria Morazzoni, et al. (Mainz: Schott, 2007), 367–70.

82 Letter, Helene to Alban Berg, n.d. (ca. 2 February 1920), BW III: 84.

83 Hermann Scherchen, "Zu Hans Pfitzners 'Ästhetik der musikalischen Impotenz,'" *Melos* 1 (1920): 20.

84 Pfitzner, *Die neue Aesthetik* (1920), 125–26.

85 See Bekker's response to Pfitzner's attack in "Impotenz—oder Potenz?," *Frankfurter allgemeine Zeitung*, 15–16 January 1920, reprinted in *Musikblätter des Anbruch* 2, no. 4 (February 1920): 133–41.

86 See the extensive analysis of Berg's reliance on Kraus in Susanne Rode, *Alban Berg und Karl Kraus: Zur geistigen Biographie des Komponisten der "Lulu"* (Frankfurt: Peter Lang, 1988), especially 192–203.

87 Letter, Heinrich Jalowetz to Berg, 1 July 1920, in *Alban Berg 1885–1935: Ausstellung der Österreichischen Nationalbibliothek*, 161.

88 Quoted in Berg's letter to Schoenberg, 21 July 1920, BSB II: 52. See also the draft of Berg's (probably unsent) response to Alma Mahler, AMB, 84–85.

89 Hans Pfitzner, *Gesammelte Schriften* (Augsburg: Benno Filser Verlag, 1926), 2: 130.

90 Letter, Alban Berg to Gottfried Kassowitz, 23 August 1920, in Rosemary Hilmar, *Alban Berg*, 156.
91 Letter, Alban Berg to Arnold Schoenberg, 12 February 1921, BSB II: 117.
92 Berg's notes for the Schoenberg book are discussed by Werner Grünzweig, *Ahnung und Wissen, Geist und Form: Alban Berg als Musikschriftsteller und Analytiker der Musik Arnold Schönbergs*, ABS 5 (Vienna: Universal Edition, 2000), 53–111.

Chapter 5

1 Letter, Alban Berg to Arnold Schoenberg, 6 October 1912, BSB I: 291.
2 Letter, Alban Berg to Helene Nahowski, 2 April 1908, BW I: 118–20.
3 ÖNB, F21.Berg.123. This manuscript can be viewed by a link in the ÖNB catalog record.
4 Gottfried Kassowitz, "Lehrzeit bei Alban Berg," ÖMZ 23 (1968): 325. For a chronology of sketches, see especially Patricia Hall, *Berg's "Wozzeck": Studies in Musical Genesis, Structure, and Interpretation* (New York: Oxford University Press, 2011).
5 In a letter to his wife on 14 August 1915—the day before he began his military service—Berg writes, "I don't have much to report. The swearing in went as usual—a waste of time. Then I went back into town, paid for my books (Büchner). . . ." BW II: 204.
6 Gottfried Kassowitz, "Lehrzeit bei Alban Berg," 326.
7 Letter, Alban to Helene Berg, 27 May 1922, BW III: 247.
8 Letter, Alban Berg to Erhard Buschbeck, ÖNB Handschriftensammlung 982135.
9 See the "Faksimile von 'Nacht (Nokturn)' mit Erläuterung," *Rudolf Stephan zum 80. Geburtstag*, 124–206, ABS 6 (Vienna: Universal Edition, 2008); and Regina Busch, "Alban Bergs Bühnenstück 'Nacht (Nokturn),'" ibid., 96–123. Christopher Hailey's translation of the latter, with additional materials, is found in *Alban Berg and His World*, ed. Christopher Hailey (Princeton, NJ: Princeton University Press, 2010), 91–132.
10 Letter, Alban Berg to Arnold Schoenberg, 13 August 1917, BSB I: 623.
11 Karl Emil Franzos, "Aus Georg Büchner's Nachlaß," *Neue freie Presse*, 3, 5, and 23 November 1875.
12 *Georg Büchner's sämmtliche Werke und handschriftlicher Nachlaß. Erste kritische Gesammt-Ausgabe*, ed. Karl Emil Franzos (Frankfurt: J.D. Sauerländer's Verlag, 1879).
13 Ibid., 204.
14 Georg Büchner, *Wozzeck—Lenz: Zwei Fragmente*. Insel-Bücherei Nr. 92 (Leipzig: Insel-Verlag, n.d. [1913]).
15 See Valeria Lucentini, "Performance as Source: A New Document on the Genesis of Berg's *Wozzeck*," *Schweizer Jahrbuch für Musikwissenschaft* 33 (2013): 171–86.
16 Georg Büchner, *Complete Plays, "Lenz" and Other Writings*, ed. John Reddick (London: Penguin Books, 1993), 202.
17 Ibid., 195–96.
18 A reliable and informative modern resource is Georg Büchner, *Werke und Briefe: Münchner Ausgabe*, ed. Karl Pörnbacher, et al. (Munich: Carl Hanser Verlag, 1988).
19 Clarus's reports are found in ibid., 630–53. Also see the study by Hans Mayer, "Georg Büchners 'Woyzeck': Wirklichkeit und Dichtung," in *Alban Berg "Wozzeck": Texte, Materialien, Kommentare*, ed. Attila Csampai and Dietmar Holland (Reinbeck bei Hamburg: Rohwalt Taschenbuch, 1985), 77–103.
20 Ernst Hilmar, *Wozzeck von Alban Berg: Entstehung—erste Erfolge—Repressionen (1914–1935)* (Vienna: Universal Edition, 1975), 21.

21 ÖNB, F21.Berg.13/II, p. 3. This manuscript can be viewed by a link in the ÖNB catalog record.

22 Letter, Alban to Helene Berg, 7 August 1918, BW II: 599.

23 See the translation of Bieber's article in Douglas Jarman, *Alban Berg "Wozzeck"*, (Cambridge: Cambridge University Press, 1989), 129–32.

24 Georg Witkowski, "Büchners Woyzeck," *Das Inselschiff* 1, no. 1 (October 1919): 20–30.

25 Letter, J.D. Sauerländer to Alban Berg, 2 June 1922, ÖNB, F21.Berg.1289.

26 Letter, Alban Berg to Hanns Heinz Ewers, 21 January 1925, ÖNB, F21.Berg.3272. A draft of the letter is in QMG 29: 68.

27 See Franzos, "Aus Georg Büchners Nachlaß," *Neue freie Presse*, 5 November 1875.

28 Georg Büchner, *Woyzeck*. Nach den Handschriften des Dichters herausgegeben von Georg Witkowski (Leipzig: Insel-Verlag, 1920), 56–57.

29 Letter, Theodor Adorno to Alban Berg, 28 November 1933, in *Theodor W. Adorno and Alban Berg: Correspondence 1925–1935*, ed. Henri Lonitz, trans. Wieland Hoban (Cambridge: Polity, 2005), 202.

30 Letter, Alban Berg to Theodor Adorno, 3 December 1933, in ibid., 204.

31 See Berg's "Lecture on *Wozzeck*: The 'Atonal Opera,'" "The Voice in Opera," "A Few Remarks on Staging the Opera *Wozzeck*," "The Musical Forms in My Opera *Wozzeck*," "With the Composer of *Wozzeck*: A Conversation with Alban Berg," and "A Chat with Alban Berg," in PMPD.

32 Otto Jancke, "A Conversation with Alban Berg," PMPD, 327.

33 Alexander Landau, "Die Musik und das soziale Problem," *Musikblätter des Anbruch* 8 (1926): 275.

34 Letter, Alban Berg to Joseph Lapitzky, 9 August 1927, in Solomon Volkov, "Ein unbekannter Brief Alban Bergs," *ÖMZ* 34 (1979): 559.

35 PMPD, 260. See Otto Brües, "Über Georg Büchner," *Das Nationaltheater* (Berlin), 1929, reprinted in Dietmar Goltschnigg, *Georg Büchner und die Moderne: Texte, Analysen, Kommentar* (Berlin: Erich Schmidt, 2001), 1: 366.

36 Alban Berg, "Lecture on *Wozzeck*: The Atonal Opera" (1929–30), PMPD, 259.

37 Letter, Alban to Helene Berg, 29 March 1923, BW III: 276.

38 From ÖNB, F21.Berg.479/34, transcribed in Hall, *Berg's Wozzeck*, 28–31.

39 See the well-documented chronology in Hall, ibid., Chapters 2–3.

40 ÖNB, F21.Berg.13/II. This sketchbook can be viewed by a link in the ÖNB catalog record.

41 Letter, Alban Berg to Anton Webern, 19 August 1918, in Ernst Hilmar, *Wozzeck von Alban Berg*, 21.

42 See Johanna Berg's letter of 9 May 1922, handwritten in English, to the Borgfeldt Co., ÖNB, F21.Berg.1047.

43 Letter, Arnold Schoenberg to Emil Hertzka, 24 October 1921, BSB II: 153.

44 Letter, Alban Berg to Arnold Schoenberg, 2 June 1922, BSB II: 161.

45 Berg was charged 41,301,000 kronen by Waldheim-Eberle A.-G. to publish 200 copies of the piano-vocal score. See the itemized bill in the Bayerische Staatsbibliothek (Munich), Ana 500.C.

46 See Martina Steiger, "'Achtung Scheck!'—Alma Mahler als Mäzenin von Alban Berg und Arnold Schönberg," *ÖMZ* 63, no. 10 (2008): 17–30.

47 Carl Marilaun, "With the Composer of *Wozzeck*: A Conversation with Alban Berg" (*Neues Wiener Journal*, 20 January 1926), PMPD, 321.

48 Letter draft, Alban Berg to Fritz Heinrich Klein, n.d. (ca. August 1923), QMG 34: 161.

49 Alban Berg, "Lecture on *Wozzeck*: The 'Atonal Opera,'" PMPD, 228–60.

50 A copy of Mahler's scenario is found in the New York Public Library, Hans Redlich Papers.

51 Alban Berg, "The 'Problem of Opera'" (1927–28), PMPD, 217.

52 Alban Berg, "Lecture on *Wozzeck*: The 'Atonal Opera,'" PMPD, 231–32.

53 Ernst Viebig, "Alban Berg's 'Wozzeck': A Contribution to the Problem of Opera" (1923), in Jarman, *Alban Berg "Wozzeck"*, 140, 143.

54 Cited in Hall, *Berg's "Wozzeck"*, 201.

55 Berg's use of harmonic elements to symbolize personae of the opera is studied by Janet Schmalfeldt in *Berg's "Wozzeck": Harmonic Language and Dramatic Design* (New Haven: Yale University Press, 1983) and by Peter Petersen in *Alban Berg "Wozzeck": Eine semantische Analyse unter Einbeziehung der Skizzen und Dokumente aus dem Nachlaß Bergs*, Musik-Konzepte Sonderband (Munich: edition text + kritik, 1985).

56 PMPD, 258. The creation of twelve-tone lines in Act I, scene I, of the opera is described by Petersen in *Alban Bergs "Wozzeck,"* 102–07.

57 Letter, Helene Berg to Hans F. Redlich, 14 September 1954, New York Public Library, Hans Redlich Papers JOB 95–91.

58 Petersen, *Alban Berg "Wozzeck"*, 85.

59 PMPD, 239.

60 Theodor W. Adorno, "Im Gedächtnis an Alban Berg" (1955), in Adorno, *Gesammelte Schriften* (Frankfurt: Suhrkamp, 1984), 18: 501.

61 See Schmalfeldt, *Berg's "Wozzeck"*, 135–41 and passim. Marie's chord A recurs prominently in earlier and later works by Berg. Recall its use (transposed as F♯–G–B–C♯) in the Piano Sonata, and the final chord of the String Quartet, Op. 3, first movement.

62 PMPD, 245.

63 See George Perle, *The Operas of Alban Berg*, vol. 1, *Wozzeck* (Berkeley and Los Angeles: University of California Press, 1980), 169–85; and Petersen, *Alban Berg "Wozzeck"*, 232–37.

64 PMPD, 251.

65 Ulrich Krämer, *Alban Berg als Schüler Arnold Schönbergs: Quellenstudien und Analysen zum Frühwerk*, ABS 4 (Vienna: Universal Edition, 1996), 254–61.

66 PMPD, 251–52.

67 See Perle's detailed analysis, *Wozzeck*, 174–85.

68 PMPD, 258.

69 Letter, Alban Berg to Erich Kleiber, 1 June 1925, in *Alban Berg—Erich Kleiber: Briefe der Freundschaft*, ed. Martina Steiger (Vienna: Seifert Verlag, 2013), 45.

70 PMPD, 261–65.

71 PMPD, 264.

72 Alban Berg, "Should Wagner Stagings Be Modernized?" (1929), PMPD, 392.

73 Arnold Schoenberg, *Theory of Harmony*, trans. Roy E. Carter (Berkeley and Los Angeles: University of California Press, 1978), 420.

Chapter 6

1 Letter, Alban Berg to Emil Hertzka, 29 April 1922, quoted in Ernst Hilmar, *Wozzeck von Alban Berg: Entstehung—erste Erfolge—Repressionen (1914–35)* (Vienna: Universal Edition, 1975), 28.

2 Ernst Viebig, "Alban Berg's 'Wozzeck': A Contribution to the Problem of Opera," in Douglas Jarman, *Alban Berg "Wozzeck"* (Cambridge: Cambridge University Press, 1989), 147, 149.

3 Alban to Helene Berg, 10 April 1923, BW III: 325.

4 Alban to Helene Berg, 13 April 1923, BW III: 328.

5 The contract is transcribed in Ernst Hilmar, *Wozzeck von Alban Berg*, 88.

6 Letter, Alban Berg to Anton Webern, 19 August 1923, from Rosemary Hilmar, *Alban Berg: Leben und Wirken in Wien bis zu seinen ersten Erfolgen als Komponist* (Vienna: Verlag Hermann Böhlaus Nachf., 1978), 164.

7 Letter, Alban to Helene Berg, 13 November 1925, BW III: 431.

8 Hilmar, *Wozzeck von Alban Berg*, 50.

9 Ernst Mandowsky, "Begegnung mit Erich Kleiber," *Neues Wiener Journal*, 14 February 1926.

10 H. H. Stuckenschmidt, *Die Musik eines halben Jahrhunderts, 1925–1975: Essay und Kritik* (Munich, R. Piper, 1976), 337.

11 Konrad Vogelsang, *Dokumentation zur Oper "Wozzeck" von Alban Berg* (Laaber: Laaber-Verlag, 1977), 25.

12 Theodor Adorno, "Im Gedächtnis an Alban Berg" (1955), in Adorno, *Gesammelte Schriften* (Frankfurt: Suhrkamp, 1984), 18:492.

13 See Brian S. Locke, "The '*Wozzeck* Affair': Modernism and the Crisis of Audience in Prague," *Journal of Musicological Research* 27 (2008): 63–93.

14 Emanuel Žák, "Skandál v Národním divadle," *Čech*, 17 November 1926. Translated by Brian S. Locke, "The '*Wozzeck* Affair'," 74.

15 Letter, Alban Berg to Soma Morgenstern, 3 July 1927. In Morgenstern, *Alban Berg und seine Idole: Erinnerungen und Briefe* (Berlin: Aufbau Taschenbuch, 1995), 186.

16 See Shostakovich's recollections of the visit in *Testimony: The Memoirs of Dmitri Shostakovich*, ed. Solomon Volkov, trans. Antonina W. Bouis (New York: Harper & Row, 1979), 43–45.

17 Stein's reduced version is presumably the one still offered by Universal Edition on rental.

18 Julius Korngold, "'Wozzeck', Oper nach Georg Büchners Drama von Alban Berg," *Neue freie Presse*, 1 April 1930.

19 Alban Berg, "Lecture on *Wozzeck*: The 'Atonal Opera,'" PMPD, 228–60.

20 Alban Berg, "What Is Atonal? A Dialogue," PMPD, 219–27.

21 Lawrence Gilman, "New Music from a Remarkable Opera Introduced by the Philharmonic-Symphony," *New York Herald Tribune*, 17 October 1930.

22 Olin Downes, *New York Times*, 20 March 1931.

23 Lawrence Gilman, *New York Herald Tribune*, 20 March 1931.

24 Olin Downes, "Berg's 'Wozzeck' Has New York Premiere—Stokowski Gives Brilliant Performance," *New York Times*, 25 November 1931.

25 Letter draft, Alban to Herman Berg, 24 February 1921, BBF, 111–12.

26 Documents from these sojourns are published in Herwig Knaus, *Anna Nahowski und Kaiser Franz Josef: Ihr Leben—ihre Liebe—ihre Kinder* (Vienna: Erhard Löcker, 2012), 219–21, 238–43.

27 Letters between Alban and Helene in the period of 22 June through 29 August chronicle this long cure, but without significant medical details. See BW I: 141–212.

28 Letter, Helene Nahowski to Alban Berg, 26 August 1908, BW I: 211.

29 A survey of private clinics in the German-speaking world, many aligned with traditional spas, is given by Edward Shorter, "Private Clinics in Central Europe, 1850–1933," *Social History of Medicine* 3, no. 2 (1990): 159–95. A brief overview of European spa culture is

given by David Blackbourn, "Fashionable Spa Towns in Nineteenth-century Europe," and by Jill Steward, "The Culture of the Water Cure in Nineteenth-century Austria, 1800–1914," in *Water, Leisure and Culture: European Historical Perspectives*, ed. Susan C. Anderson and Bruce H. Tabb (New York and Oxford: Berg, 2002), 9–21, 23–35.

30 Helene Nahowski's *Kurordnungsbuch* (Cure program booklet) from the Wildbad Sanatorium Tobelbad is located in ÖNB, F21.Berg.3063. Tobelbad, a well-regarded spa near Graz, is where Alma Mahler met and began her affair with Walter Gropius in the summer of 1910, close to the time of Helene's stay there. See Oliver Hilmes, *Malevolent Muse: The Life of Alma Mahler*, trans. Donald Arthur (Boston: Northeastern University Press, 2015), 65–66.

31 *Zandergymnastik* refers to the physical therapy devised by the Swedish doctor Gustav Zander, who used elaborate mechanical devices to treat specific physical and anatomical problems. See Alfred Levertin, *Dr. G. Zander's Medico-Mechanische Gymnastik: Ihre Methode, Bedeutung und Anwendung, nebst Auszügen aus der einschlägigen Literatur* (Stockholm: Norstedt & Sons, 1892).

32 Letter, Helene to Alban Berg, n.d. (6 June 1921), BW III: 133.

33 Letter, Alban to Helene Berg, 8 June 1921, BW III: 144.

34 Letter, Helene to Alban Berg, n.d. (2 July 1921), BW III: 225.

35 Letter, Helene to Alban Berg, n.d. (17-18 June 1921), BW III: 180. Rudolf Steiner did not consider anthroposophy to be a religion, rather, a practice aimed at increasing the individual's capacity for spiritual knowledge. It is generally considered an esoteric or occult discipline. A useful introduction to Steiner's work is Robert McDermott, *The New Essential Steiner: An Introduction to Rudolf Steiner for the 21st Century* (Great Barrington: Lindisfarne Press, 2009).

36 Letters, Alban to Helene Berg, 27 May 1921 and n.d. (29 May 1921), BW III: 247, 254.

37 Letters, Alban to Helene Berg, 27 March and 1 April 1923, BW III: 267, 287.

38 Herwig Knaus gives Klemperer's first name as "Otto" (BW Index), but this may be confused with the conductor Otto Klemperer. The name may have been Leo Klemperer, who was a *Badearzt* in Karlsbad at this time. No first name for Klemperer appears in the letters.

39 Letter, Helene to Alban Berg, 3 April 1923, BW III: 294.

40 Letter, Helene to Alban Berg, 9 April 1923, BW III: 318.

41 Letter, Alban to Helene Berg, 7 April 1923, BW III: 307.

42 For an analysis of the diaries, see Charlotte Erwin, "A Marital *Ausgleich*: The Affair of Emperor Franz Joseph I and Anna Nahowski," *Journal of Austrian Studies* 51, no. 2 (2018): 1–30.

43 Letter fragment, Alban to Helene Berg, n.d. (6 April? 1923), BW III: 306.

44 Letter, Alban to Helene Berg, 11 April 1923, BW III: 326.

45 See Alexander Carpenter, "'This Beastly Science . . .': On the Reception of Psychoanalysis by the Composers of the Second Viennese School, 1908–1923," *International Forum of Psychoanalysis* 24 (2015): 243–54.

46 Letter, Helene to Alban Berg, n.d. (21-22 November 1923), BW III: 366–70.

47 Letter, Helene to Alban Berg, n.d. (28 November 1923), BW III: 399.

48 Letter, Alban to Helene Berg, 29 November 1923, BW III: 402.

49 Letter, Alban to Helene Berg, 30 November 1923, BW III: 404.

50 This aphorism was published in *Die Fackel* on 30 May 1913. Also see Edward Timms, *Karl Kraus: Apocalyptic Satirist. Culture and Catastrophe in Habsburg Vienna*, Chapter 5: "Sorcerers and Apprentices: The Encounter with Freud" (New Haven, CT: Yale University Press, 1986), 94–114.

51 Letter, Alban Berg to Arnold Schoenberg, 3 October 1913, BSB I: 442.

52 Timms, *Karl Kraus*, 96.

53 Letter, Alban Berg to Arnold Schoenberg, 3 December 1923, BSB II: 215.

54 "Igor Stravinskij über sein Werk und seine Pläne," *Prager Presse*, 13 November 1924.

55 Erich Steinhard, "Tonale, Atonale und antiquierte Musik: Notizen zum Musikfest in Venedig," *Der Auftakt* 5 (1925): 262.

56 Ernst Krenek, "Musik in der Gegenwart," in *25 Jahre neue Musik: Jahrbuch 1926 der Universal Edition*, ed. Hans Heinsheimer and Paul Stefan (Vienna: Universal Edition, 1926), 43–59.

57 See Schoenberg's "Krenek for Light Music" (1926), in *A Schoenberg Reader: Documents of a Life*, ed. Joseph Auner (New Haven, CT: Yale University Press, 2003), 194–96.

58 Arnold Schönberg, *Drei Satiren*, Op. 28 (Vienna: Universal Edition, 1926), 3.

59 Letter, Alban Berg to Anton Webern, 19 August 1923, quoted in Rosemary Hilmar, *Alban Berg*, 164.

60 PMPD, 183–95.

61 PMPD, 194–95.

62 Letter, Alban Berg to Anton Webern, 28 July 1922, quoted in Volker Scherliess, *Alban Berg mit Selbstzeugnissen und Bilddokumenten* (Reinbek bei Hamburg: Rowohlt, 1975), 82.

63 Klein's *Die Maschine* is known in a four-hands arrangement that was published in 1923 (Vienna: Carl Haslinger).

64 There is a small irregularity in the retrograde since tones 6–7–8 in the original are resituated to become tones 1–2–3 in the retrograde. See the example.

65 Berg's longstanding interest in symmetric formations of the chromatic is apparent in a chart containing a symmetric 12 x 12 matrix of tones, a "theoretical trifle" as he called it, sent to Schoenberg in a letter 27 July 1920. See the discussion of it in George Perle, "Berg's Master Array of Interval Cycles," *Musical Quarterly* 63 (1977): 1–30.

66 Letter, Alban to Helene Berg, 31 March 1923, BW III: 286. Berg had a fragmentary copy of typed notes made by an attendee at one of Schoenberg's lectures of 1922 or 1923 on his new compositional method, headed "Komposition mit zwölf Tönen." See ÖNB, F21. Berg.121.

67 Igor Stravinsky [and Alexis Roland-Manuel], *The Poetics of Music in the Form of Six Lessons* (1939–40), trans. Arthur Knodel and Ingolf Dahl (New York: Vintage Books: 1947), 66–67.

68 Alban Berg, "Composition with Twelve-Tone Rows" (ca. 1933), PMPD, 392.

69 On this point see Constantin Floros, "Das Kammerkonzert von Alban Berg: Hommage à Schönberg und Webern," *Musik-Konzepte 9: Alban Berg Kammermuisik II* (1979): 76.

70 "Alban Bergs Kammerkonzert für Geige und Klavier mit Begleitung von dreizehn Bläsern," *Pult und Taktstock* 2, no. 2–3 (February 1925): 23–27; English translation in PMPD, 195–99.

71 PMPD, 198.

72 ÖNB, F21.Berg.74/II, fol. 2. A facsimile of the page is found in Constantin Floros, *Alban Berg: Musik als Autobiographie* (Wiesbaden: Breitkopf & Härtel, 1992), 203.

73 See the discussion of the sketches in Brenda (Barbara) Dalen, "'Freundschaft, Liebe, und Welt': The Secret Programme of the Chamber Concerto," in *The Berg Companion*, ed. Douglas Jarman (Boston, MA: Northeastern University Press, 1989), 141–80.

74 ÖNB, F21.Berg.74/III, fol. 1, cited by Dalen, ibid., 145.

75 The Melisande motive is shown in Berg's *Thematic Analysis* of *Pelleas und Melisande*, PMPD, 122.

76 Letter, Helene to Alban Berg, n.d. (7 February 1920), BW III: 88.

77 Letter, Alban to Helene Berg, 27 January 1920, BW III: 59.

78 Translation from Bryan R. Simms, *The Atonal Music of Arnold Schoenberg* (New York: Oxford, 2000), 215.

79 Ibid., 216.

80 Douglas Jarman, *The Music of Alban Berg* (Berkeley and Los Angeles: University of California Press, 1979), 241; idem, "'Remembrance of Things That Are to Come': Some Reflections on Berg's Palindromes," *Alban Berg and His World*, ed. Christopher Hailey (Princeton, NJ: Princeton University Press, 2010), 207.

81 Theodor W. Adorno, *Alban Berg: Master of the Smallest Link*, trans. Juliane Brand and Christopher Hailey (Cambridge: Cambridge University Press, 1991), 110.

82 Michael Kennedy's term. See Kennedy, *Mahler*, rev. ed. (New York: Schirmer Books, 1990), 140.

83 Constantin Floros, *Alban Berg*, 218.

84 Letter, Anton Webern to Alban Berg, 23 March 1927, quoted in *Anton Webern 1883—1983*, ed. Ernst Hilmar (Vienna: Universal Edition, 1983), 78.

85 *Reichspost* (Vienna), 27 April 1927.

86 Letter, Alban Berg to Daniel Ruynemann, 26 November 1929, in Paul Op de Coul, "Unveröffentlichte Briefe von Alban Berg und Anton Webern an Daniel Ruyneman, *Tijdschrift van de Vereniging voor Nederlandse Muziekgeschiedenis* 22 (1972): 210–11.

87 The manuscript is described by David Congdon in his essay "*Kammerkonzert*: Evolution of the Adagio and the Trio Transcription," in *Alban Berg Symposion Wien 1980: Tagungsbericht*, ed. Rudolf Klein, ABS 2 (Vienna: Universal Edition, 1981), 145–60.

88 In 1953, Hans Redlich asked Hans Apostel about the trio version, to which Apostel responded in a letter of 27 November 1953: "Berg arranged it for violin, clarinet, and piano, that is, with the clarinet part solely apparent as a curved red pencil line that winds through the piano score. At the time I didn't think that the arrangement was especially successful because certain parts given to the clarinet take on excessive weight and many long-held notes in the winds are poorly sustained on the piano. My opinion has been supported since (to my knowledge) except for 3 performances [in 1935 and 1936] interest in the arrangement seems to have disappeared. I don't know where the autograph manu-script is. Whoever has the music is dead or in exile. The war may also have intervened." This letter is found in the Hans Ferdinand Redlich Collection at the New York Public Library. David Congdon, who examined the music with Berg's red-pencil markings, says that the document is in a private American collection (Congdon, "*Kammerkonzert*: Evolution of the Adagio and the Trio Transcription.").

89 Dalen, "'Freundschaft, Liebe, und Welt,'" 179.

90 See Simms, *The Atonal Music of Arnold Schoenberg*, 218.

91 See Constantin Floros, *Alban Berg: Music as Autobiography*, trans. Ernest Bernhardt-Kabisch (Frankfurt: PL Academic, 2014).

92 Theodor Adorno, "Alban Berg" (1956), in Adorno, *Sound Figures*, trans. Rodney Livingstone (Stanford, CA: Stanford University Press, 1999), 76.

Chapter 7

1 The sole exception was a concert of the International Composers' Guild on 13 January 1924, when Greta Torpadie was scheduled to sing Berg's "Spring" ("Warm die Lüfte," Op. 2, no. 4).

2 Letter, Alban to Helene Berg, 15 May 1925, BW III: 416–17.

3   The family also used the spelling "Robetin." The correspondence of twenty-six letters between Alban Berg and the Fuchs-Robettins is published in Constantin Floros, *Alban Berg and Hanna Fuchs: The Story of a Love in Letters*, trans. Ernest Bernhardt-Kabish (Bloomington: Indiana University Press, 2008).

4   Letter, Alban to Helene Berg, 15 May 1925, BW III: 417–18.

5   Letter, Alban Berg to Hanna Fuchs, n.d. (July 1925), in Floros, *Alban Berg and Hanna Fuchs*, 26.

6   See Floros, "The History of an Unhappy Love," in *Alban Berg and Hanna Fuchs*, 65–82; and George Perle, "The Secret Programme of the Lyric Suite," *Musical Times* 118 (1977): 629–32, 709–13, 809–13.

7   Telegram, Alma Mahler to Alban Berg, 9 November 1924, AMB, 124, and commentary, 372–73.

8   Letter, Helene to Alban Berg, n.d. (17? May 1925), BW III: 420.

9   Letter, Alban to Helene Berg, 18 May 1925, BW III: 421.

10 See Theodor W. Adorno, "Im Gedächtnis an Alban Berg," (1955), in Adorno, *Gesammelte Schriften* (Frankfurt: Suhrkam, 1984), 18: 490.

11 Floros, *Alban Berg and Hanna Fuchs*, 18–27. The letter is undated but its content suggests that it was written shortly before 23 July 1925.

12 Floros, *Alban Berg and Hanna Fuchs*, 18–19.

13 Ibid., 26.

14 Letter, Alban to Helene Berg, 11 November 1925, BW III: 426–28. Compare the version in Alban Berg, *Briefe an seine Frau*, ed. Helene Berg (Munich: Albert Langen, 1965), 539–40.

15 BW III: 427–28.

16 See BW III: 457–59, including n2.

17 BW III: 457.

18 Letter, Alban Berg to Hanna Fuchs, n.d. (6–7 November 1926), Floros, *Alban Berg and Hanna Fuchs,* 39–44.

19 Ibid., 39.

20 Letter, Alban Berg to Herbert Fuchs-Robettin, n.d. (ca. 14 November 1926), ibid., 45.

21 Letter, Alban Berg to Hanna Fuchs-Robettin, 16 November 1926, ibid., 49.

22 Ibid., 53.

23 Ibid., 55.

24 Letter, Theodor Adorno to Helene Berg, 16 April 1936, in *Theodor W. Adorno and Alban Berg, Correspondence 1925–1935*, ed. Henri Lonitz, trans. Wieland Hoban (Cambridge, UK: Polity, 2005), 234.

25 Soma Morgenstern, *Alban Berg und seine Idole: Erinnerungen und Briefe*, ed. Ingolf Schulte (Berlin: Aufbau Taschenbuch Verlag, 1995), 307–08.

26 Lesley Fuchs-Robetin [sic], "Hanna Fuchs-Robetin wie ich sie kannte," *Biblos* 48, no. 1 (1999): 57–78.

27 Peter Stephan Jungk, *Franz Werfel: A Life in Prague, Vienna and Hollywood*, trans. Anselm Hollo (New York: Grove Weidenfeld, 1990), 229–30.

28 *Theodor W. Adorno and Alban Berg: Correspondence*, 8.

29 Floros, *Alban Berg and Hanna Fuchs*, 20.

30 Ibid., 20.

31 *Theodor W. Adorno, Alban Berg: Briefwechsel 1925–1935*, ed. Henri Lonitz (Frankfurt: Suhrkamp, 1997), 28.

32 PMPD, 285. Berg's manuscript is now located in New York, The Morgan Library & Museum, B493.S344.

33 Letter, Alban Berg to Anton Webern, 12 October 1925, quoted in H.F. Redlich, *Alban Berg: Versuch einer Würdigung* (Vienna: Universal Edition, 1957), 178.

34 George Perle, *The Operas of Alban Berg*, vol. 2, *Lulu* (Berkeley and Los Angeles: University of California Press, 1985), 10.

35 Letter, Willi Reich to Helene Berg, 8 December 1955, ÖNB, F21.Berg.2040.

36 A facsimile of the Foreword and translation is found in Arved Ashby, "The Development of Berg's Twelve-Tone Aesthetic as Seen in the 'Lyric Suite' and its Sources" (PhD diss., Yale University, 1995), 243–66.

37 Letter, Alban Berg to Theodor Adorno, 21 August 1926, *Theodor W. Adorno, Alban Berg: Briefwechsel*, 74. See also Adorno's letter to Berg of 19 August 1926, ibid., 70–73.

38 Josef Matthias Hauer, *Vom Melos zur Pauke: Eine Einführung in die Zwölftonmusik* (Vienna: Universal Edition, n.d. [1925]), 16. Hauer writes: "Another technique, *sustaining melody tones*, followed shortly. In this way a first step toward polyphony was taken. In my modest array of musical concepts, this style even today has its charms. I think that syncopation and working out the voices touches a bit on artistry."

39 "Advice for Beginners in Composition with Twelve Tones," in *Schoenberg's Program Notes and Musical Analyses*, Schoenberg in Words, vol. 5, ed. J. Daniel Jenkins (New York: Oxford University Press, 2016): 103.

40 See Berg's "Composition with Twelve-Tone Rows" (ca. 1933), PMPD, 392.

41 See transcriptions of Schoenberg's sketches for Op. 25 in Reinhold Brinkmann, Arnold Schönberg Sämtliche Werke, Abt. II, Reihe B, Band 4, 77–85. Schoenberg also discusses "dominant" and "tonic" row forms in his lecture "Komposition mit zwölf Tönen" (ca. 1922–23), in Rudolf Stephan, "Ein frühes Dokument zur Entstehung der Zwölftonkomposition," in *Festschrift Arno Forchert*, ed. Gerhard Allroggen and Detlef Altenburg (Kassel: Bärenreiter, 1986), 296–302. Concerning Berg's use of the terms "tonic" and "dominant," see Arved Ashby, "Of 'Modell-Typen' and 'Reihenformen': Berg, Schoenberg, F.H. Klein, and the Concept of Row Derivation," *Journal of the American Musicological Society* 48 (1995): 92.

42 Redlich, *Alban Berg*, 178.

43 Letter from Anton Webern to Heinrich Jalowetz, 26 December 1922, in Anton Webern, *Briefe an Heinrich Jalowetz*, ed. Ernst Lichtenhahn (Main: Schott, 1999), 523.

44 Alexander Zemlinsky, "Lyrische Symphonie," *Pult und Taktstock* 1, no. 1 (1924): 10–11.

45 In 1930, after the death of his first wife, Ida, Zemlinsky married Luise Sachsel.

46 Quoted in Antony Beaumont, *Zemlinsky* (Ithaca, NY: Cornell University Press, 2000), 322. Beaumont reconstructs Berg's letter from a rough draft.

47 ÖNB, F21.Berg.23/I, fol. 56′. Berg also gave other dates for the completion of the quartet.

48 *Neues Wiener Journal*, 12 January 1927.

49 A detailed history of the Kolisch Quartet is given by Claudia Maurer Zenck, "'Was sonst kann ein Mensch denn machen, als Quartett zu spielen?': Rudolf Kolisch und seine Quartette. Versuch einer Chronik der Jahre 1921–1944," ÖMZ 53, no. 11 (1998): 8–57.

50 First-hand details of the meeting between Gershwin and Berg were recorded in diaries kept by Gershwin's brother Ira, who was present at the meeting. See Howard Pollack, *George Gershwin: His Life and Work* (Berkeley and Los Angeles: University of California Press, 2006), 145. Also see Allen Forte, "Reflections Upon the Gershwin-Berg Connection," *Musical Quarterly* 83 (1999): 150–68, for the influence that the *Lyric Suite* may have had on Gershwin's later compositions.

51 See Berg's letter to Webern of 10 August 1927 asking for advice about this selection of movements, quoted in Ursula Rauchhaupt, *Schönberg, Berg, Webern: Die Streichquartette der Wiener Schule: Eine Dokumentation* (Munich: Ellermann, 1972).

52 Lawrence Gilman, "From Berg to Schumann at the Philharmonic Concert Under Kleiber," *New York Herald Tribune*, 23 October 1931.

53 See Berg's letter to Helene, 17 June 1928, BW III: 488.

54 See the illustrations in Constantin Floros, *Alban Berg: Musik als Autobiographie* (Wiesbaden: Breitkopf & Härtel, 1992): 277–78.

55 Willi Reich, *Alban Berg: Mit Bergs eigenen Schriften und Beiträgen von Theodor Wiesengrund-Adorno und Ernst Křenek* (Vienna: Herbert Reichner Verlag, 1937), 93.

56 Perle, *Lulu*, 12.

57 Theodor Adorno, "Im Gedächtnis an Alban Berg," 490–91.

58 *Theodor W. Adorno and Alban Berg: Correspondence 1925–1935*, 234.

59 Letter, Helene Berg to Alma Mahler, 28 November 1936, AMB, 518.

60 The sketches are found in ÖNB, F21.Berg.76/I–XV, and their content is surveyed by Constantin Floros, *Alban Berg: Musik als Autobiographie*, 241–91. Also see Arved Ashby, *The Development of Berg's Twelve-Tone Aesthetic*, Chapter 6 and Appendix 6.

61 See Perle, "The Secret Programme of the Lyric Suite."

62 The annotated study score is found in the ÖNB, F21.Berg.3437, and it can be viewed by a link in the ÖNB catalog record.

63 Letter, Alban Berg to Hanna Fuchs, 23 October 1926, Floros, *Alban Berg and Hanna Fuchs*, 38.

64 *Lyric Suite: The Secret Vocal Part*, ed. George Perle (Vienna: Universal Edition, 1999). Perle explains the thinking behind his edition in his book *Style and Idea in the "Lyric Suite" of Alban Berg*, rev. ed. (Hillsdale, NY: Pendragon Press, 2001), 49–56.

65 Ashby, *The Development of Berg's Twelve-Tone Aesthetic*, 286.

66 Nick Chadwick, review of Perle, *Style and Idea in the "Lyric Suite" of Alban Berg*, *Music & Letters* 77 (1996): 480.

67 See Reich's *Alban Berg: Bildnis im Wort* (Zurich: Die Arche, 1959), 45–54. Translation in PMPD, 206–214. Reich discussed his acquisition of Berg's notes in a letter to Kolisch dated 10 January 1960, ÖNB, F21.Berg.2040.

68 Julius Korngold, "Feuilleton. Musik," *Neue freie Presse*, 17 July 1920.

69 For an extended analysis of Berg's twelve tone method in the *Lyric Suite*, see Douglas Jarman, *The Music of Alban Berg* (Berkeley and Los Angeles: University of California Press, 1979), 125–29 and passim, and George Perle, *Style and Idea in the "Lyric Suite" by Alban Berg*.

70 Letter, Alban Berg to Theodor Adorno, 21 September 1925, *Theodor W. Adorno and Alban Berg: Correspondence 1925–1935*, 17.

71 Letter, Alban Berg to Anton Webern, 13 July 1927. Quoted in Thomas Ertelt, *Alban Bergs "Lulu": Quellenstudien und Beiträge zur Analyse*, ABS 3 (Vienna: Universal Edition, 1993), 47.

72 ÖNB, F21.Berg.28/L. The documents are discussed in Volker Scherliess, "Alban Bergs analytische Tafeln zur *Lulu*-Reihe," *Die Musikforschung* 30 (1977): 452–64.

73 This is also the basic row of *Lulu*, leading many to see the documents as intended for that work. Thomas Ertelt gives persuasive evidence that the tables originated earlier. See his *Alban Bergs "Lulu"*, 39–49.

74 See the detailed discussion of the sketches for the Romantic Overture in ibid.

Chapter 8

1 Berg describes the lectures in his letter to Schoenberg of 8 March 1933, BSB II: 504. Berg's notes for the lectures are discussed and transcribed in Werner Grünzweig, *Ahnung und Wissen, Geist und Form: Alban Berg als Musikschriftsteller und Analytiker der Music Arnold Schönbergs*, ABS 5 (Vienna: Universal Edition, 2000), 161–93, 274–82.

2 Letter, Alban Berg to Willi Reich, 12 September 1931, Library of Congress, Alban Berg/ Willi Reich Collection.

3 Letter, Willi Reich to Alban Berg, 4 June 1933, ibid.

4 Willi Reich, "Dokumentarische Einleitung," reprint of *23: Eine Wiener Musikzeitschrift* (Vienna: Verlag O. Kerry, 1971).

5 Letter, Hermann Watznauer to Alban Berg, 12 February 1927, ÖNB, F21.Berg.1504.

6 Watznauer's handwritten biography is found in the WBR, HIN 204.582; a copy is in the ÖNB, F21.Berg.434. An English translation of the material up to 1906 is given by Nick Chadwick, "Hermann Watznauer's Biography of Alban Berg," in *Alban Berg and His World*, ed. Christopher Hailey (Princeton, NJ: Princeton University Press, 2010), 33–90; the later entries, very sketchy in nature, are found in Erich Alban Berg, *Der unverbesserliche Romantiker: Alban Berg 1885–1935* (Vienna: Österreichischer Bundesverlag, 1985), 67–106.

7 See Herwig Knaus and Wilhelm Sinkovicz, *Alban Berg: Zeitumstände—Lebenslinien* (St. Pölten: Residenz Verlag, 2008), 333.

8 See Daniel Ender, "Der '. . . Erfolg, der ja in dem Luxus unseres Wagerls' gipfelt. . . ,'" in Wolfgang M. Buchta et al., eds., *Alban Berg und der Blaue Vogel: Eine Auto-Biographie* (Vienna: Alban Berg Stiftung, 2017), 26–65.

9 Herwig Knaus, *Anna Nahowski und Kaiser Franz Josef: Ihr Leben—ihre Liebe—ihre Kinder* (Vienna: Erhard Löcker, 2012), 312. The figure is found in notes by Alban Berg titled "Erbschaft Papa Nahowski," ÖNB, F21.Berg.473/2.

10 Concerning Anna Nahowski's assets, see Knaus and Sinkovicz, *Alban Berg*, 341–42.

11 See Christopher Hailey, *Franz Schreker: A Cultural Biography* (Cambridge: Cambridge University Press, 1993), 112–31, for a description of Schreker's work at the Berlin Musikhochschule.

12 Letter, Alban to Helene Berg, 2 December 1925, BW III: 442.

13 Letter, Alban Berg to Franz Schreker, 8 May 1930, QMG 34: 185.

14 Letter, Alban to Helene Berg, 8 April 1923, BW III: 310.

15 Letter, Alban to Helene Berg, n.d. (15 May 1933), BW III: 664.

16 On this issue see Berg's letters to Theodor Adorno, 2 May 1927 and 19 February 1935, in *Theodor W. Adorno and Alban Berg: Correspondence 1925–1935*, ed. Henri Lonitz, trans. Wieland Hoban (Cambridge: Polity, 2005), 103, and Berg's letter to Schoenberg, 6 August 1931, BSB II: 435.

17 "Direktor Springer beruft Alban Berg an die Kompositionsklasse der Akademie," *Die Stunde* (Vienna), 8 February 1927.

18 Letter, Alban Berg to Arnold Schoenberg, 16 February 1927, BSB II: 291.

19 Letter, Alban to Helene Berg, 14 May 1933, BW III: 660.

20 Berg's canon was published in the festschrift *50 Jahre Opernhaus: 1880–1930. Festwoche vom 10.–16. Oktober*, ed. Friedrich Ammermann (Frankfurt a.M., 1930); an edition of the music is found in Willi Reich, *Alban Berg: Mit Bergs eigenen Schriften und Beiträgen von Theodor Wiesengrund-Adorno und Ernst Křenek* (Vienna: Herbert Reichner Verlag, 1937), musical supplement 16.

21 Letter, Arnold Schoenberg to Alban Berg, 12 September 1930, BSB II: 418.

22 Letter, Alban Berg to Theodor Adorno, 24 December 1931, in *Theodor W. Adorno and Alban Berg: Correspondence*, 188.

23 Letter, Alban Berg to Hanna Fuchs, 20 December 1928, in *Alban Berg and Hanna Fuchs: The Story of a Love in Letters*, ed. Constantin Floros, trans. Ernest Bernhardt-Kabisch (Bloomington: Indiana University Press, 2008), 55.

24 *Alban Berg and Hanna Fuchs*, 58–59.

25 Fifteen letters from Berg to Anny Askenase are located at the BStaB, Manuscripts Division, Fasc. germ. 90; two letters are found at the ÖNB, F21.Berg.3275, and one other letter is in a private collection. Three of the letters are published in *Altenberg bis Zuckerkandl: Briefe an Alban Berg, Liebesbriefe von Alban Berg*, ed. Herwig Knaus and Thomas Leibnitz (Vienna: Erhard Löcker, 2009): 210–22.

26 "The Mercurial Martha Argerich: An Interview," in Dean Elder, *Pianists at Play: Interviews, Master Lessons, and Technical Regimes* (Evanston, IL: The Instrumentalist Company, 1982), 153.

27 The letters to Anny Askenase span the period from 1 March 1932 to spring (probably late April) 1933. Only one of Berg's three known letters to Edith Edwards is dated (17 December 1932); one other may have preceded those to Anny and another may have been written as late as 1935.

28 Letter, Alban Berg to Anny Askenase, 1 April 1932, BStaB, Manuscripts Division, Fasc. germ. 90.4.

29 Letter, Alban Berg to Anny Askenase, undated [early March], 1932, BStaB, Manuscripts Division, Fasc. germ. 90.11.

30 Letter, Alban Berg to Anny Askenase, 27 April 1932, BStaB, Manuscripts Division, Fasc. germ. 90.7.

31 The film, in English, starring Maurice Chevalier, was titled *One Hour with You* (1932).

32 Letter, Alban Berg to Anny Askenase, 11 April 1932, BStaB, Manuscripts Division, Fasc. germ. 90.13.

33 Letter, Alban Berg to Anny Askenase, n.d. (July–August? 1932), in *Altenberg bis Zuckerkandl*, 220–21.

34 Letter, Alban Berg to Erich Kleiber, 5 October 1932, in *Theodor W. Adorno and Alban Berg Correspondence*, 100–01. Helene's accident happened around the beginning of September. Also see Berg's description of the accident in his letter to Schoenberg of 10 September 1932, BSB II: 485.

35 Letter, Alban Berg to Anny Askenase, 27 October 1932, BStaB, Manuscripts Division, Fasc. germ. 90.09. By the time Berg wrote this letter to Anny, Helene was well on the way to recovery.

36 Letter, Alban Berg to Hanna Fuchs, November 1932, in Constantin Floros, *Alban Berg and Hanna Fuchs*, 61–62.

37 The letters, now in ÖNB, F21.Berg.3274, are published in *Altenberg bis Zuckerkandl*, 223–28.

38 Letter, Alban Berg to Edith Edwards, 17 December 1932, ibid., 227.

39 The last letter to Anny is undated but written after an encounter around Easter (16 April) 1933. The latest to Edith is dated February 1935, although this date may be questioned since it refers to the possibility of Berg's spending the winter in Carinthia, which he did in 1933–34. See *Altenberg bis Zuckerkandl*, 228.

40 A letter from Otto Lifczis to Berg proposing the visit and asking Berg to make a hotel reservation is found in ÖNB, F21.Berg.1034.

41 Floros, *Alban Berg and Hanna Fuchs*, 63–64.

42 This point is made by Christopher Hailey and Juliane Brand, "Vorwort" to BSB I: xxiii–xxiv.

43 Letter, Alban Berg to Thur Himmighoffen, 28 November 1930. In Ernst Hilmar, *Wozzeck von Alban Berg: Entstehung—erste Erfolge—Repressionen (1914–1935)* (Vienna: Universal Edition, 1975), 66.

44 Letter, Alban to Helene Berg, 28 February 1933, BW III: 607.

45 Letter, Joseph Haas to Alban Berg, 9 May 1933, in *Alban Berg 1885–1935: Katalog zur Ausstellung der Österreichischen Nationalbibliothek* (Vienna: Universal Edition, 1985), 188.

46 Letter, Alban Berg to Joseph Haas, 17 May 1933, ibid., 188.

47 See Nick Chadwick, "Alban Berg and the BBC," *British Library Journal* (1985): 46–59.

48 See Anna Maria Morazzoni, "Berg and Italy in the Thirties," *Alban Berg Society Newsletter* 13 (1985): 10–31; and Mosco Carner, "The Berg Affair, Venice 1934," *Musical Times* 110 (1969): 1129–31.

49 Letter, Alban Berg to Gian Francesco Malipiero, 17 July 1934, in Morazzoni, "Berg and Italy in the Thirties," 15.

50 Ibid., 18.

51 Herbert Gerigk, "Musikfestdämmerung," *Die Musik* 27 (October 1934): 48.

52 Letter, Alban Berg to Herbert Gerigk, QMG 34: 47.

53 Letter quoted in Knaus and Sinkovicz, *Alban Berg*, 404.

54 Letter, Gian Francesco Malipiero to Alban Berg, 26 September 1934, in Morazzoni, "Berg and Italy in the Thirties," 30.

55 From an undated letter from Ružena Herlinger to Konrad Vogelsang. See Vogelsang's *Alban Berg: Leben und Werk* (Berlin: Max Hesses Verlag, 1959), 41.

56 Otto Steinhagen, *Signale für die musikalische Welt*, 1 December 1926.

57 Hans W. Heinsheimer, *Best Regards to Aida* (New York: Alfred A. Knopf, 1968), 50.

58 Berg wrote to Erich Kleiber on 10 April 1933 about a singer for *Der Wein:* "Even more a tenor, with a nice, sweet, bright voice (it's basically a *man's* song)." See *Alban Berg—Erich Kleiber: Briefe der Freundschaft,* ed. Martina Steiger (Vienna: Seifert Verlag, 2013), 107.

59 The Bergs' housekeeper Anna Lenz Lauritsch, later recalled: "Herr Berg composed something for a singer (the wine aria), and the lady was also much in love with Herr Berg. Frau Berg upbraided him for this." Quoted in Erich Alban Berg, *Der unverbesserliche Romantiker: Alban Berg 1885–1935* (Vienna: Österreichischer Bundesverlag, 1985), 170.

60 Herlinger's suicide attempt was recounted in detail in the *Neues Wiener Journal* (28 November 1929) in an article "Sensationeller Selbstmordversuch."

61 QMG 34: 59.

62 Charles Baudelaire, *Die Blumen des Bösen: Umdichtungen von Stefan George* (Berlin: Georg Bondi, 1914).

63 Letter, Alban to Helene Berg, 29 December 1914, BW II: 181.

64 Berg makes several minor changes in George's text to clarify its meaning, and for these he was indebted to Soma Morgenstern. See Herwig Knaus, "Alban Bergs Skizzen und Vorarbeiten zur Konzertarie *Der Wein,*" in *Festschrift Othmar Wessely zum 60. Geburtstag,* ed. Manfred Angerer et al. (Tutzing: Hans Schneider, 1982), 357.

65 Adorno's analysis is found in Willi Reich, *Alban Berg: Mit Bergs eigenen Schriften und Beiträgen von Theodor Wiesengrund-Adorno und Ernst Křenek* (Vienna: Herbert Reichner Verlag, 1937), 101–06. Reich's often republished program note was written for the premiere performance in Königsberg in 1930 and first published in the *Signale für die musikalische Welt* 88, no. 22 (28 May 1930): 679–80. It contains several musical examples provided by Berg to illustrate aspects of his use of tone rows.

66 Alfred Baresel, *Das Jazz-Buch* (Berlin: Zimmermann, 1925).

67 Concerning the allusion to the key of D minor in the row, see David Schroeder, "Berg, Strindberg, and D Minor," *College Music Symposium* 30, no. 2 (1990): 74–89; and Douglas Jarman, *The Music of Alban Berg* (Berkeley and Los Angeles: University of California Press, 1979), 101–02, 131–33.

68 The tables are found in ÖNB, F21.Berg.80/IV.

69 On this point see Douglas Jarman, *The Music of Alban Berg*, 107 and passim.

70 A detailed explanation of this passage is found in George Perle, *The Operas of Alban Berg*, vol. 2, *Lulu* (Berkeley and Los Angeles: University of California Press, 1985), 30; Jarman, *The Music of Alban Berg*, 108; and Anthony Pople, "In the Orbit of *Lulu*: The Late Works," *Cambridge Companion to Berg*, ed. Anthony Pople (Cambridge: Cambridge University Press, 1997), 217.

71 Mosco Carner, *Alban Berg: The Man and the Work*, 2nd ed. (New York: Holmes & Meier Publishers, 1983), 82, 112.

72 Hugo Engelbrecht, *Wiener Zeitung*, 4 January 1931.

73 Virgil Thomson, *New York Herald Tribune*, 16 March 1952.

Chapter 9

1 Julius Meier-Graefe, *Vincent van Gogh; mit vierzig Abbildungen und dem Faksimile eines Briefes* (Munich: R. Piper, 1910).

2 ÖNB, F21.Berg.98/I, fol. 17. A facsimile of the page and discussion of its contents are found in Julia Wechsler (Veksler), "'Die drei W': Zu einem Opernplan Alban Bergs," *Jahrbuch des Staatlichen Instituts für Musikforschung Preussischer Kulturbesitz* (2000), 247 and passim.

3 Based on ÖNB, F21.Berg.70/I, fol. 2. A facsimile of the page is found in Wechsler, ibid., 236.

4 Hermann Kasack, *Vincent: Schauspiel in fünf Akten* (Potsdam: Gustav Kiepenheuer Verlag, 1924).

5 Wechsler, "Die drei W," 248.

6 Letter, Alban Berg to Theodor Adorno, 11 January 1926, in *Theodor W. Adorno and Alban Berg: Correspondence 1925–1935*, ed. Henri Lonitz, trans. Wieland Hoban (Cambridge: Polity, 2005), 42.

7 Soma Morgenstern later claimed that he gave Berg the idea for an opera on Lulu, but there is no support for this assertion anywhere in Berg's writings. See Joan Allen Smith, "Sprechstimmen-Geschichte: An Oral History of the Twelve-Tone Idea," (PhD diss., Princeton University, 1977), 286.

8 Letter, Alban Berg to Soma Morgenstern, 27 November 1927, in Morgenstern, *Alban Berg und seine Idole: Erinnerungen und Briefe*, ed. Ingolf Schulte (Lüneburg: Dietrich zu Klampen, 1995), 194–95.

9 Excerpts from Tilly Wedekind's letters to Berg in 1927 are found in Susanne Rode, *Alban Berg und Karl Kraus: Zur geistigen Biographie des Komponisten der "Lulu"* (Frankfurt: Peter Lang, 1988), 230 and passim.

10 Letter, Soma Morgenstern to Alban Berg, 11 November 1927, in *Alban Berg und seine Idole*, 192–93.

11 Letter, Soma Morgenstern to Helene Berg, 20 May 1969, ÖNB, F21.Berg.1961. On the letter Helene Berg writes, "Dr. Morgenstern lügt!" (Dr. Morgenstern lies!)

12 An analysis of the sketches made by Berg that document his text revisions is found in Rosemary Hilmar, "Die Bedeutung der Textvorlagen für die Komposition der Oper *Lulu* von Alban Berg," in *Festschrift Othmar Wessely zum 60. Geburtstag*, ed. Manfred Angerer, et al. (Tutzing: Hans Schneider, 1982), 265–93; and Susanne Rode, *Alban Berg und Karl Kraus*. Berg's revisions are assessed in detail in Kordula Knaus, *Gezähmte "Lulu": Alban Bergs Wedekind-Vertonung im Spannungsfeld von literarischer Ambition, Opernkonvention und "absoluter Musik"* (Freiburg im Breisgau: Rombach Verlag, 2004).

13 Morgenstern, *Alban Berg und seine Idole*, 201–02. Also see Theodor Adorno's negative assessment of *Pippa* in his letter to Berg of 30 January 1926, in *Theodor W. Adorno and Alban Berg: Correspondence 1925–1935*, 46–47.

14 Theodor Adorno, "Im Gedächtnis an Alban Berg" (1955), in Adorno, *Gesammelte Schriften*, (Frankfurt: Suhrkamp, 1984), 18: 503.

15 Quoted in Thomas Ertelt, *Alban Bergs "Lulu": Quellenstudien und Beiträge zur Analyse*, ABS 3 (Vienna: Universal Edition, 1993), 30.

16 The fragments are published in Arnold Schönberg Sämtliche Werke, B/6/2, ed. Ullrich Scheideler (Mainz: Schott, 2005).

17 See Thomas Ertelt, *Alban Bergs "Lulu"*, 11–24.

18 Letter, Alban Berg to Arnold Schoenberg, 10 April 1928, BSB II: 320.

19 QMG 34: 314. The note is dated 26 October 1928 after a meeting with Tilly Wedekind.

20 Kraus published the lecture "Die Büchse der Pandora" in *Die Fackel* no. 182 (June 1905): 1–14, and (revised) in his *Literatur und Lüge* (Vienna: Verlag "Die Fackel," 1929). The later version is translated ("*Pandora's Box*") by Celia Skrine in Douglas Jarman, *Alban Berg "Lulu"* (Cambridge: Cambridge University Press, 1991), 102–12.

21 Kraus, "Die Büchse der Pandora," in Jarman, *The Music of Alban Berg*, 104.

22 Karl Kraus, "Der Prozess Riehl," from *Die Fackel* 211: 27–28, quoted in Edward Timms, *Karl Kraus, Apocalyptic Satirist* (New Haven, CT: Yale University Press): 84. The same sentiment is expressed in an aphorism by Kraus, "The sensuality of woman is the primal spring at which the intellectuality of man finds renewal" (from Kraus, *Sprüche und Widersprüche* [Munich: Albert Langen, 1909], 1).

23 Karl Kraus, "Die Büchse der Pandora," *Die Fackel* 182 (June 1905): 11–12.

24 Letter, Alban Berg to Frida Semler [Seabury], 18 November 1907, quoted in Willi Reich, *Alban Berg*, trans. Cornelius Cardew (New York: Vienna House, 1965), 22–23.

25 Donald Mitchell, "The Character of Lulu: Wedekind's and Berg's Conceptions Compared," *Music Review* 15 (1954): 274.

26 Douglas Jarman, "A Suggested Interpretation," in *Alban Berg: "Lulu"*, 99.

27 Theodor Adorno, "Im Gedächtnis an Alban Berg," 490–91.

28 Alban Berg to Hanna Fuchs, October 1931, in Constantin Floros, *Alban Berg and Hanna Fuchs: The Story of a Love in Letters*, trans. Ernest Bernhardt-Kabisch (Bloomington: Indiana University Press, 2008), 58–59.

29 Frank Wedekind, *Die Büchse der Pandora: Eine Monstretragödie*, in *Werke, Kritische Studienausgabe*, ed. Hartmut Vinçon, 3, no. 1 (Darmstadt: Jürgen Hausser, 1996), 319–400.

30 Frank Wedekind, *Gesammelte Werke* (Munich: Georg Müller, 1913), vol. 3. Margaret Notley closely studies early versions of Wedekind's Lulu plays in *"Taken by the Devil": The Censorship of Frank Wedekind and Alban Berg's "Lulu"* (New York: Oxford University Press, 2020).

31 Frank Wedekind, *Lulu: Tragödie in fünf Akten mit einem Prologue* (Munich: Georg Müller, 1913).

32 See Rode, *Alban Berg und Karl Kraus*, 287–93, and Ertelt, *Alban Bergs "Lulu"*, 174–77.

33 *Lulu: Schauspiel in sieben Bildern von Frank Wedekind, autorisierte Bühneneinrichtung von Otto Falckenberg* (Berlin: Drei Masken-Verlag, n.d. [ca. 1928]).

34 Letter, Alban Berg to Arnold Schoenberg, 7 August 1930, BSB II: 408.

35 Karl Kraus, "Pandora's Box," in Jarman, *Alban Berg "Lulu"*, 103. Concerning the dramatic and formal effect of the multiple casting, see Patricia Hall, *A View of Berg's "Lulu" Through the Autograph Sources* (Berkeley and Los Angeles: University of California Press, 1996), 61–88.

36 George Perle, *The Operas of Alban Berg*, vol. 2, *Lulu* (Berkeley and Los Angeles: University of California Press, 1985), 60.

37 ALWA: Who but my wife sent me to my sickbed? LULU. Am I ill? [. . .] ALWA. She gave it to me from that Casti-Piani of hers. She's way beyond getting it herself. From Wedekind, *Gesammelte Werke (Die Büchse der Pandora)*, 3: 175.

38 On this subject see Silvio José dos Santos, "Ascription of Identity: The *Bild* Motif and the Character of Lulu," *Journal of Musicology* 21 (2004): 267–308.

39 In his letter to Helene of 15 September 1919, Berg writes, "In the coffee house I met Hugo Heller, who sat by me and talked to me—or should I say *jüdelte*—for a whole hour, which became quite disgusting." BW II: 706. The phrase containing "jüdelte" was removed by Helene Berg from the letter in her 1965 edition of Berg's *Briefe an seine Frau* (Munich: Albert Langen-Georg Müller), 410.

40 Sander Gilman, *Jewish Self-Hatred: Anti-Semitism and the Hidden Language of the Jews* (Baltimore, MD: The Johns Hopkins University Press, 1986), 139.

41 Karl Kraus, "Er ist doch ä Jude," *Die Fackel* 386 (1913): 3.

42 See Berg's letter to Willi Reich, 6 October 1933, Library of Congress, Alban Berg/Willi Reich Collection.

43 Karl Kraus, "Pandora's Box," in Jarman, *Alban Berg "Lulu"*, 108.

44 Letter, Soma Morgenstern to Helene Berg, 29 November 1973, ÖNB, F21.Berg.1961.

45 Letter, Alban Berg to Erich Kleiber, 21 March 1934, in *Alban Berg—Erich Kleiber: Briefe der Freundschaft*, ed. Martina Steiger (Vienna: Seifert Verlag, 2013), 118.

46 Søren Kierkegaard, in *Entweder/Oder: Ein Lebensfragment* part 1 (1843), in Kierkegaard, *Gesammelte Werke* vol. 1, ed. Viktor Eremita [pseud. for Kierkegaard] (Jena: Eugen Diederich, 1922), 41–123.

47 Theodor Adorno, *Kierkegaard: Konstruktion des Ästhetischen* (Tübingen: Mohr, 1933).

48 Letter, Willi Reich to "Meister Rutz," 24 April 1967, ÖNB F21. Berg.1318–21. Concerning the relation of Lulu to Kierkegaard's essay, see Ulrich Schreiber, "Hetzjagden bis in den Tod," in *Alban Berg "Lulu": Texte, Materialien, Kommentare*, ed. Attila Csampai and Dietmar Holland (Reinbek bei Hamburg: Rowohlt, 1985), 282–91.

49 Letter, Theodor Adorno to Alban Berg, 23 March 1935, in *Theodor W. Adorno and Alban Berg: Correspondence 1925–1935*, 221–22.

50 Letter, Hans Heinsheimer (Universal Edition) to Alban Berg, 26 June 1934, WBR (UE-Archiv).

51 Letter, Alban Berg to Hans Heinsheimer, 28 June 1934, WBR (UE-Archiv).

52 See the chronology in Hall, *A View of Berg's "Lulu" Through the Autograph Sources*, 40–60 and passim.

53 Letter, Alban Berg to Anton Webern, 22 June 1931, ÖNB, F21.Berg.3270.

54 Letter, Alban Berg to Erich Kleiber, 20 April 1934, *Alban Berg—Erich Kleiber: Briefe der Freundschaft*, 120.

55 Letter, Alban Berg to Anton Webern, 6 May 1934, in Willi Reich, "Aus unbekannten Briefen von Alban Berg an Anton Webern," *Schweizerische Musikzeitung* 93 (1953): 52.

56 The history of the *Symphonic Pieces* is studied by Margaret Notley in "Berg's Propaganda Pieces: The 'Platonic Idea' of *Lulu*," *Journal of Musicology* 25 (2008): 95–142.

57 Helene Berg, in a letter to Alma Mahler dated 24 March 1934, stressed that Berg was then under no deadline for the completion of *Lulu*. See AMB, 224–25.

58 Letter, Alban Berg to Erich Kleiber, *Alban Berg—Erich Kleiber: Briefe der Freundschaft*, 119.

59 H.H. Stuckenschmidt, review of the premier performance of the Lulu *Symphonic Pieces*, *B. Z. am Mittag* (Berlin), 1 December 1934.

60 Willi Reich, "Alban Berg's *Lulu*," *Musical Quarterly* 22 (1936): 383–401.

61 Jarman, *Alban Berg "Lulu"*, 66.

62 ÖNB, F21.Berg.80/VII, dated 23 June 1928. The draft can be viewed by a link in the ÖNB catalog record. Also see Douglass Green, "A False Start for *Lulu*: An Early Version of the Prologue," in *Alban Berg: Historical and Analytical Perspectives*, ed. David Gable and Robert P. Morgan (Oxford: Clarendon Press, 1991), 203–13; and Thomas Ertelt, "'Hereinspaziert . . .': Ein früher Entwurf des Prologues zu Alban Bergs *Lulu*," ÖMZ 41 (1986): 15–25.

63 Letter, Alban Berg to Arnold Schoenberg, 9 February 1935, BSB II: 559.

64 These associations are enumerated in Douglas Jarman, *The Music of Alban Berg* (Berkeley and Los Angeles: University of California Press, 1979), 216.

65 Letter, Alban Berg to Anton Webern, 20 September 1929, ÖNB, F21.Berg.3270.

66 See Hall, *A View of Berg's "Lulu*," 109–27.

67 Ibid., 122.

68 See Berg's letters to Willi Reich of 20 and 21 September 1929, Library of Congress, Alban Berg/Willi Reich Collection.

69 The 1936 piano-vocal score of these measures has a number of errors in pitch. These are corrected in the Apostel-Cerha score (Universal Edition No. 13640a, 1985).

70 On Berg's use of rows in retrograde, see Jarman, *The Music of Alban Berg*, 107 and passim.

71 Concerning Berg's use of jazzy styles in *Lulu*, see especially Albrecht Dümling, "Symbol des Fortschritts, der Dekadenz und der Unterdrückung: Zum Bedeutungswandel des Jazz in den zwanziger Jahren," in *Angewandte Musik, 20er Jahre: Exemplarische Versuche gesellschaftsbezogener musikalischer Arbeit für Theater, Film, Radio, Massenveranstaltung*, ed. Dietrich Stern (Berlin: Argument-Verlag, 1977), 81–100.

72 See Hall, *A View of Berg's "Lulu"*, 71–73.

73 PMPD, 251.

74 Perle, *Lulu*, 81.

75 Alban Berg, *Lied der Lulu aus der gleichnamigen Oper nach den Tragödien "Erdgeist" und "Büchse der Pandora" von Frank Wedekind*, piano-vocal arr. by Erwin Stein (Vienna: Universal Edition, 1935).

76 See Berg's letter to Universal Edition, 7 July 1934, quoted in Margaret Notley, "Berg's Propaganda Pieces," 108, 141.

77 From Frank Wedekind, *Lautenlieder: 53 Lieder mit eigenen und fremden Melodien* (Berlin: Drei-Masken Verlag, 1920). This was Berg's source for the tune.

78 Letter, Alban Berg to Arnold Schoenberg, 17 January 1934, BSB II: 525–26.

79 Reich, "Alban Berg's *Lulu*," 399.

80 In a letter to Adrian Boult of 19 February 1935, Berg described this passage: "This first variation is genuinely a 'variation'! Thus the 'theme' in the 4 horns is not the main element

but must merely enter very distinctly and then be present after that, not drown everything! The main element in the whole of this first variation is the descant melody with its harmonic thickening (to which the horn part also belongs!)—in other words from bars [693–94] all the strings, oboes, and clarinets, later also flutes, and all this up to the end of the first variation. Thus the horn part has not to dominate but simply to be clear and to adapt itself to the top part, which leads throughout." From Nick Chadwick, "Alban Berg and the BBC," *British Library Journal* 11, no. 1 (1985): 53.

81 In Friedrich Cerha's orchestration of the opening of the final scene the tune is given to the woodwinds, but it is likely that Berg intended it to be played by an actual barrel organ offstage.

82 Jarman, *Alban Berg "Lulu"*, 81.

83 Letter, Alban Berg to Hans Tietjen, 20 April 1934, in *Alban Berg—Erich Kleiber: Briefe der Freundschaft*, 275–77.

84 Letter, Erich Kleiber to Alban Berg, 30 April 1934, ibid., 121.

85 Letter, Wilhelm Furtwängler to Alban Berg, 23 May 1934, ibid., 278.

86 Letter, Alban Berg to Erich Kleiber, 21 March 1934, ibid., 118.

87 Letter, Alban Berg to Willi Reich, 6 October 1933, Library of Congress, Alban Berg/Willi Reich Collection.

88 Now in the British Library (London), Zweig MS 17.

89 Letter, Alban Berg to Arnold Schoenberg, 28 August 1934, BSB II: 531–32.

90 The festschrift was published in the September 1934 issue of *Anbruch: Monatsschrift für moderne Musik* (formerly *Musikblätter des Anbruch*); see the translation of Berg's poem in PMPD, 309–10.

91 Letter, Soma Morgenstern to Alban Berg, 11 November 1927, in Morgenstern, *Alban Berg und seine Idole*, 192–93.

92 See the letter (draft) from Helene Berg to Alma Mahler, 24 March 1934, AMB, 224–25.

93 The story of Ruth Kleiber's meeting with Göring to discuss the performance is told by John Russell, *Erich Kleiber: A Memoir* (London: Andre Deutsch, 1957), 146. Presumably Russell learned of the encounter from conversations with Mrs. Kleiber herself.

94 Alban Berg, *Symphonische Stücke aus der Oper "Lulu"* (Vienna: Universal Edition, 1935).

95 No copy of the program notes has come to light, but Reich used their content in a series of contemporaneous articles concerning the *Symphonic Pieces*. See especially Reich's "Alban Berg und seine Musik zu Wedekinds *Lulu*-Tragödie," *Schweizerische Musikzeitung* 75 (1935): 81–85.

96 Alban Berg, "We Spoke Today with Alban Berg," PMPD, 331.

97 Reich, "Alban Berg's *Lulu*," 203.

98 Letter, Alban to Helene Berg, 9 March 1934, BW III: 716.

Chapter 10

1 Letters, Alban Berg to Arnold Schoenberg, 4 November 1934 and 27 December 1934, BSB II: 536, 548.

2 The album is found at the Alban Berg Stiftung. Watznauer's greeting is discussed in Nick Chadwick, "From 'Freund Hein' to Hermann Hesse: Hermann Watznauer and his Friendship with Alban Berg," *Music & Letters* 79 (1998): 410.

3 Letter, Arnold Schoenberg to Alban Berg, 22 January 1935, BSB II: 554.

4 Letter, Alban Berg to Arnold Schoenberg, 28 August 1934, BSB II: 531.

5 Heinrich Jalowetz, "Alban Berg," *Der Auftakt* 15 (1935): 117. The complete text of Jalowetz's talk is in ÖNB, F21.Berg.2488.

6 Letter, Alban Berg to Willi Reich, 4 November 1935, Library of Congress, Alban Berg/ Willi Reich Collection.

7 Adorno, "Im Gedächtnis an Alban Berg" (1955), in Adorno, *Gesammelte Schriften* (Frankfurt: Suhrkamp, 1984), 18: 496.

8 Anna Nahowski's will consists of a handwritten document titled "Mein Testament," signed and dated 29 May 1929, plus a typed copy of the same with three codicils, the first two dated 18 September 1929, the last undated. ÖNB, F21.Berg.1612.

9 In his request to Yella Hertzka for a loan of 6,000 schillings, Berg noted that his brother owed him "far more than this amount." A draft of this letter of 4 March 1934 is published in QMG 29: 93–94.

10 Letter, Charly to Alban Berg, 20 October 1932, ÖNB, F21.Berg.548/123. The letter and Helene's annotation are reproduced in facsimile in BBF, 205.

11 Letter, Charly to Alban Berg, 27 February 1934, found in part in BBF, 209–10.

12 See Herwig Knaus and Wilhelm Sinkovicz, *Alban Berg: Zeitumstände – Lebenslinien* (St. Pölten: Residenz Verlag, 2008), 399, 439 n62.

13 Smaragda Eger-Berg to Alban Berg, 8 July 1934, excerpt in BBF, 212–13.

14 Letter, Charly to Alban Berg, 26 August 1934, ÖNB, F21.Berg.548, excerpt in BBF, 217–19.

15 See the typed draft of the letter, undated, shown in facsimile in BBF, 220–21.

16 Ibid., 220–21.

17 Letter, Erika Stiedry-Wagner to Alban Berg, 23 September 1935, ÖNB, F21.Berg.1412, in *Altenberg bis Zuckerkandl: Briefe an Alban Berg*, ed. Herwig Knaus and Thomas Leibnitz (Vienna: Erhard Löcker, 2009), 160–61.

18 Letter, Alban Berg to Erika Stiedry-Wagner, late September 1935, in QMG 34: 204–05.

19 Letter, Alban Berg to Yella Hertzka, 11 October 1933, in *Alban Berg, 1885-1935: Austellung der Österreichischen Nationalbibliothek* (Vienna: Universal Edition, 1985), 193.

20 Letter draft, Alban Berg to Yella Hertzka, undated, in QMG 29: 93–94.

21 See letter, Alma Mahler to Alban Berg, undated but probably early April 1934, AMB, 226–27, and editorial commentary, 473.

22 The figure for the final sale of the *Wozzeck* autograph score is taken from BSB II: 523 n991. Drafts of Berg's long letters arguing the case for his claim to the *Wozzeck* manuscript are to be found in ÖNB, F21.Berg.3055 and ÖNB, F21.Berg.480/160/1–9 (the latter transcribed in QMG 29: 94–96).

23 Theodor Adorno, "Im Gedächtnis an Alban Berg," 502. In a letter to Helene of 8 March 1934, Berg writes, "Gerhart Hauptmann is writing his memoirs (Neue Rundschau) and says that in his youth, 'though I stood close to socialism I never thought of myself as a Social Democrat.' He states this viewpoint with wonderful simplicity, and it serves for me as well." BW III: 712.

24 Informative histories of Austria during this period include Francis L. Carsten, *Fascist Movements in Austria: From Schönerer to Hitler* (London: Sage Publications, 1977); and Jürgen Gehl, *Austria, Germany and the Anschluss, 1931–1938* (Westport, CT: Greenwood Press, 1979).

25 Letter, Erwin Stein to Arnold Schoenberg, 23 June 1934, in Thomas Brezinka, *Erwin Stein: Ein Musiker in Wien und London* (Vienna: Böhlau Verlag, 2005), 123.

26 Benito Mussolini, *Schriften und Reden*, 4 vols. of 8 planned (Zurich: Rascher, 1934–37). The German edition was a translation of Mussolini's *Scritti e discorsi*, vols. 1–10 (Milan: Ulrico Hoepli Editore, 1933).

27 Letter, Alban Berg to Willi Reich, 3 November (*recte* 3 December) 1933, Library of Congress, Alban Berg/Willi Reich Collection.

28 Willi Reich, "Mussolini und sein Uebersetzer," *Reichspost* (Vienna), 4 October 1934.

29 Karl Kraus, "Warum die Fackel nicht erscheint," *Die Fackel* 890–905 (July 1934): 276–77. Berg was so impressed by Kraus's article that he sent a copy of it to Schoenberg in California.

30 See Rudolf Stephan, "Von der Planung zum musikalischen Kunstwerk: Über Alban Bergs Komponieren," in *Vom Einfall zum Kunstwerk: Der Kompositionsprozeß in der Musik des 20. Jahrhunderts*, ed. Hermann Danuser and Günter Katzenberger (Laaber: Laaber-Verlag, 1993), 253–72; and Douglas Jarman, "'Frisch, Fromm, Fröhlich, Frei.' The Deutscher Turnerbund and the Berg Violin Concerto," *Musicologica austriaca*, 2017, no pagination.

31 From ÖNB, F21.Berg.432/31, p. 159. The page can be viewed by a link in the ÖNB online catalog record.

32 Louis Krasner, "The Origins of the Alban Berg Violin Concerto," in *Alban Berg Symposion Wien 1980: Tagungsbericht*, ed. Rudolf Klein, ABS 2 (Vienna: Universal Edition, 1982), 109.

33 Letter, Louis Krasner to Alban Berg, 5 March 1935, in *Altenberg bis Zuckerkandl*, 33.

34 Letter, Alban Berg to Louis Krasner, 28 March 1935, in [Willi Reich], "Zur Entstehung des Violin-Konzertes von Alban Berg," *Anbruch* 18 (1936): 197.

35 From ÖNB, F21.Berg.432/31, p. 161.

36 From *Wulfenia-Blüten: Einige fünfzig Lieder und Jodler aus Kärnten*, ed. Karl Liebleitner (Vienna: Universal Edition-Dr. Johannes Perschul, n.d. [1932]). This was Berg's source for the tune.

37 Letter draft, Helene Berg to Alma Mahler, 23 April 1935, AMB, 231.

38 From Berg's undated letter draft, AMB, 234. Given the content of the letter, it was likely written in mid-May, shortly after the Bergs arrived at the Waldhaus.

39 Letter, Alban Berg to Willi Reich, 8 June 1935, Library of Congress, Alban Berg/Willi Reich Collection.

40 Letter, Alban Berg to Louis Krasner, 16 July 1935, in "Zur Entstehung des Violin-Konzertes von Alban Berg," 196.

41 The score published by Universal Edition in 1936 has a number of questionable and erroneous readings. The critical edition by Douglas Jarman in Alban Berg Sämtliche Werke (Vienna: Universal Edition 18115b, 1996) is recommended. Rita Kurzmann's piano-violin arrangement was published by Universal Edition in 1938 with Kurzmann's name omitted for political reasons.

42 Telegram, Alma Mahler to Alban and Helene Berg, 31 August 1935, AMB, 240.

43 See Constantin Floros, *Alban Berg: Musik als Autobiographie* (Wiesbaden: Breifkopf & Härtel, 1992), 327 and passim.

44 Willi Reich, "Alban Bergs neues Werk: Dem andenken eines Engels," *Neues Wiener Journal*, 31 August 1935. Reich made minor revisions in his description of the work and added a formal analysis (written under the guidance of Anton Webern) in a series of later articles. See Reich, "Alban Bergs neuestes Werk," *Schweizerische Musikzeitung* 75 (1935): 735–37, reprinted under the title "Requiem für Manon" in *Anbruch* 17 (1935): 250–52. Also see Reich's analysis of the Violin Concerto in his *Alban Berg: Mit Bergs eigenen Schriften und Beiträgen von Theodor Wiesengrund-Adorno und Ernst Křenek* (Vienna: Herbert Reichner Verlag, 1937), 126–33.

45 In a letter to Otto Jokl of 25 June 1935 (BStaB, Ana 500), Berg described the form of the chorale variations in the finale also as "symmetric."

46 Rudolf Stephan," *Alban Berg: Violinkonzert (1935)* (Munich: Wilhelm Fink Verlag, 1988), 21.

47 Krasner, "The Origins of the Alban Berg Violin Concerto," 111.

48 Reich, *Alban Berg* (1937), 128.

49 ÖNB, F21.Berg.85/I, fol. 6. A discussion of Berg's sketches is found in Constantin Floros, "Die Skizzen zum Violinkonzert von Alban Berg," in *Alban Berg Symposion Wien 1980*, 118–35.

50 From a letter, Helene Berg to Universal Edition, 14 August 1958, ÖNB, F21.Berg.2160.

51 Letter, Anton Webern to Arnold Schoenberg, 9 March 1936, Library of Congress, Arnold Schoenberg Collection.

52 Willi Reich, *Alban Berg* (1937), 17.

53 Adapted from Douglas Jarman, "The Secret Programme of the Violin Concerto," *Musical Times* 124 (April 1983): 221.

54 Ernst Krenek, *Im Atem der Zeit: Erinnerungen an die Moderne*, English to German trans. by Friedrich Saathen and Sabine Schulte (Hamburg: Hoffmann und Campe, 1998), 921.

55 Letter, Anton Webern to Arnold Schoenberg, 18 January 1936, Library of Congress, Arnold Schoenberg Collection.

56 Compact disc, Continuum SBT 1004, 1991.

57 Ernest Newman, "Alban Berg's Violin Concerto: Tonality and Atonality," *Sunday Times* (London), 10 May 1936. See also Willi Reich's response to Newman's column, "An Ernest Newman," *23: Eine Wiener Zeitschrift* 28–30 (November 1936): 20–28.

58 W.L., "Alban Berg's Violin Concerto, *Manchester Guardian*, 10 December 1936.

59 Lawrence Gilman, "Alban Berg's Memorial Concerto for Violin Heard at Boston Symphony Concert," *New York Herald Tribune*, 12 March 1937.

60 The authors thank Paul Z. Bodnar, M.D. and Cornelia W. Hamilton, M.D., for their review and analysis of Berg's medical history.

61 Theodor Adorno, "Im Gedächtnis an Alban Berg," 498.

62 Knaus and Sinkovicz, *Alban Berg*, 410.

63 Berg writes in a letter to Helene, ca. 1 May 1907, "Until now I have only had that Pyramidon powder as a sacred memento from you. Now with your card I am all the richer." BW I: 17.

64 Letter, Smaragda Eger-Berg to Alban Berg, 14 September 1920, in BBF, 108–09.

65 Pat Bamford-Milroy, "Fatal Abscess," *Musical Times* 140 (1999): 3–4.

66 Letter, Alban to Helene Berg, 12 July 1918, BW II: 591–92.

67 Letter, Alban Berg to Universal Edition, 21 August 1935, quoted in Volker Scherliess, *Alban Berg* (Reinbek bei Hamburg, Rowohlt, 1975), 133.

68 Letter, Alban Berg to Ignaz Fanzoy, 23 Nov 1935, ÖNB, F21.Berg.3295/8. Gottfried Engstler was the Bergs' physician in Velden, near the Waldhaus.

69 Soma Morgenstern, *Alban Berg und seine Idole: Erinnerungen und Briefe*, ed. Ingolf Schulte (Lüneburg: Dietrich zu Klempen Verlag, 1995), 376–84.

70 Krenek, *Im Atem der Zeit*, 916.

71 Cited in *Alban Berg—Erich Kleiber: Briefe der Freundschaft*, ed. Martina Steiger (Vienna: Seifert Verlag, 2013), 327, based on a document in the Wiener Stadt- und Landesarchiv.

72 The autopsy report was obtained by Dr. Dieter Kerner and published in his book *Krankheiten grosser Musiker* (Stuttgart: Friedrich-Karl-Schattauer-Verlag, 1963), 195–97. Kerner also corresponded with Helene Berg about her husband's final illness.

73 Letter, Helene Berg to Alma Mahler, 28 November 1936, in AMB, 516.

74 See Dieter Kerner, *Krankheiten grosser Musiker*, and Kerner, "Alban Bergs Ende," *Hessisches Ärzteblatt* 21 (1960): 610–12, reprinted in *Melos* 29 (1962): 112–13.

75 ÖNB, F21.Berg.1622/101 (n.d.).

76 Letter, Erwin Stein to Arnold Schoenberg, 17 January 1936, Library of Congress, Arnold Schoenberg Collection.

77 Letter, Anton Webern to Arnold Schoenberg, 23 January 1936, ibid. An unnamed reporter for the *Neues Wiener Journal*, who was present on the last evening, wrote "Alban Berg gestorben: Der bedeutende Komponist," *Neues Wiener Journal*, 25 December 1935.

78 Based on a communication from Joseph Polnauer to Hans Moldenhauer. See Hans Moldenhauer and Rosaleen Moldenhauer, *Anton von Webern: A Chronicle of His Life and Work* (New York: Alfred A. Knopf, 1979), 452.

79 Willi Reich, "An der Seite von Alban Berg," *Melos* 27 (1960): 42.

80 Konrad Vogelstein first identified Marker as the donor (*Alban Berg: Leben und Werk* [Berlin: Max Hesses Verlag, 1959], 54). Marker mentions the blood transfusions in his article "Portrait of Berg," *New York Times*, 30 March 1952, although he does not say that he was the donor.

81 Soma Morgenstern, *Alban Berg und seine Idole*, 370.

82 Letter, Helene Berg to Arnold Schoenberg, 14 January 1936, BSB II: 581.

83 The graveside statements by Hugo Winter, Ernst Krenek, and Willi Reich were published in *23: Eine Wiener Musikzeitschrift: Alban Berg zum Gedenken* 24–25 (February 1936). See the translation by Mark DeVoto, "Alban Berg zum Gedenken: The Berg Memorial Issue of *23: A Viennese Music Journal*, in *Alban Berg and His World*, ed. Christopher Hailey (Princeton, NJ: Princeton University Press, 2010), 285–86.

84 AMB, 591–92.

85 Documents concerning the settlement of Berg's estate are found in ibid., 590–94.

86 Aaron Copland, *Music and Imagination* (New York: Mentor Books, 1959), 117–18.

Chapter 11

1 Letter, Helene Berg to Arnold Schoenberg, 14 January 1936, BSB II: 581.

2 See Helene Berg's letter to Alma Mahler, n.d. (ca. April–May 1936), AMB, 510–12.

3 Henry Prunières. Nécrologie—Alban Berg, *La Revue musicale*, 17/162 (1 January 1936), 80.

4 See the account in Hans Moldenhauer and Rosaleen Moldenhauer, *Anton von Webern: A Chronicle of His Life and Work* (New York: Alfred A. Knopf, 1979), 452–54.

5 Letter, Helene Berg to Arnold Schoenberg, 14 January 1936, BSB II: 581.

6 These measure numbers are taken from the score edition of Friedrich Cerha (Vienna: Universal Edition, 1978). They differ from the numbers in earlier sources, including the score of the *Symphonische Stücke* (Vienna: Universal Edition, 1935).

7 See Friedrich Cerha, *Arbeitsbericht zur Herstellung des 3. Akts der Oper "Lulu" von Alban Berg* (Vienna: Universal Edition, 1979) for a detailed discussion of the incomplete portions of the *Particell* of Act 3. A facsimile of Berg's *Particell* for Act 3 is found in *Particell des III. Aktes: (Faksimile)*, Alban Berg Sämtliche Werke, Abteilung 1, vol. 2 (Lulu Supplement) (Vienna: Universal Edition, 2013).

8 "Zemlinsky vollendet Alban Bergs 'Lulu,'" *Der Morgen* (Vienna), 30 December 1935.

9 Letter, Arnold Schoenberg to Helene Berg, 1 January 1936, BSB II: 580. The newspaper article mentioning Krenek that Schoenberg read was "Alban Berg Dead; Modern Composer," *New York Times*, 25 December 1935.

10 Letter, Hugo Winter to Arnold Schoenberg, 19 February 1936, Arnold Schönberg Center (Vienna).

11 Letter, George Perle to Robert Craft, 27 September 1963, New York Public Library, George Perle Papers.

12 Letter, Arnold Schoenberg to Erwin Stein, 9–11 March 1936, in Walter Szmolyan, "Zum III. Akt von Alban Bergs 'Lulu,'" ÖMZ 32 (1977): 398–400.

13 Letter, Arnold Schoenberg to Alfred Kalmus (Universal Edition), 13 March 1936, Arnold Schönberg Center (Vienna).

14 Schoenberg's complete letter is found in Walter Szmolyan, "Zum III. Akt von Alban Bergs 'Lulu,'" 396–401. This translation is based on the one found in George Perle, *The Operas of Alban Berg*, vol. 2, *Lulu* (Berkeley and Los Angeles: University of California Press, 1985), 283–84.

15 Letter, Theodor Adorno to Helene Berg, 23 November 1949, in *Theodor W. Adorno and Alban Berg: Correspondence 1925–1935*, ed. Henri Lonitz, trans. Wieland Hoban (Malden, MA: Polity, 2005), 239.

16 Ernst Krenek, "Zur Vollendung von Alban Bergs 'Lulu'-Fragment," *Musica* 31 (1977): 403.

17 Letter, Erwin Stein to Arnold Schoenberg, 30 April 1936, Library of Congress, Arnold Schoenberg Collection. A copy can be viewed on the website of the Arnold Schönberg Center (www.schoenberg.at).

18 See Norbert Graf, "'Generöse Weltliebe' oder 'schwüle Erotik'?—Kunstpatriotismus auf einer neutralen Bühne. Zur Uraufführung von Alban Bergs *Lulu* 1937 in Zürich," *Archiv für Musikwissenschaft*, 60 (2003): 236–61.

19 Willi Schuh, "Alban Bergs 'Lulu,'" *Neue Zürcher Zeitung*, 4 June 1937.

20 Ibid.

21 Four of these photographs are shown in Melissa Ursula Dawn Goldsmith, *Alban Berg's Filmic Music: Intentions and Extensions in the Film Music Interlude in the Opera "Lulu"* (PhD diss. Louisiana State University, 2002), 49–52.

22 Letter, Helene Berg to Alma Mahler, 24 June 1937, AMB, 521–22.

23 Letter, Hans Reinhart to Helene Berg, 1 June 1937, WBR, HIN 203.774.

24 Letter, Helene Berg to Hans Redlich, 14 September 1954, New York Public Library, Hans Redlich Papers.

25 Letter, Alfred Schlee (Universal Edition) to Helene Berg, 5 January 1949, ÖNB, F21. Berg.2160/42–43.

26 Letter, Helene Berg to Ida Gebauer Wagner, ÖNB, F21.Berg.3279/1.

27 H.H. Stuckenschmidt, "Opern-Tragödie der Schönheit: Alban Bergs 'Lulu' als deutsche Erstaufführung," newspaper clipping of unknown origin from a copy in the New York Public Library, Hans Redlich Papers.

28 Letter, Theodor Adorno to Helene Berg, 23 November 1949, in *Theodor W. Adorno and Alban Berg: Correspondence*, 239–40.

29 Letter, Erwin Stein to Helene Berg, 30 July 1957, ÖNB, F21.Berg.2116/34.

30 Letter, Bruno Walter to Alma Mahler, 14 March 1961, in *Bruno Walter Briefe 1894–1962*, ed. Lotte Walter Lindt (Frankfurt: S. Fischer 1969), 371–72.

31 Letter, Soma Morgenstern to Helene Berg, 10 February 1951, ÖNB, F21.Berg.1961.

32 Letter, Willi Reich to Helene Berg, 30 April 1957, ÖNB, F21.Berg.2010.

33 Quoted in Walter Szmolyan, "Helene Bergs Vermächtnis," ÖMZ 32, no. 4 (1977): 170.

34 Dallapiccola's letter of 19 June 1957 to Schlee is cited in Anna Maria Morazzoni, "Berg and Italy in the Thirties," *International Alban Berg Society Newsletter* 13 (1985): 20, 24 n73.

35 Cerha, *Arbeitsbericht*, 2.

36 H.F. Redlich, *Alban Berg: Versuch einer Würdigung* (Vienna: Universal Edition, 1957), 267.

37 Perle, *Lulu*, 260–95.

38 Ibid.

39 Copy of letter, typed signature, Igor Stravinsky to Alfred Schlee, 21 October 1963, New York Public Library, George Perle Papers. By this period, almost all of Stravinsky's communications were handled by Craft. See Stephen Walsh, *Stravinsky: The Second Exile. France and America, 1934–1971* (New York: Alfred A. Knopf, 2006), 482: "The idea of Stravinsky—no lover of the Bergian *Jugendstil* and a sworn enemy of tamperers—going into battle for a scholarly completion of a post-Romantic Viennese masterpiece is so implausible that one wonders how much thought he gave as he appended his signature."

40 Letter (aerogramme), Hans Redlich to George Perle, 9 March 1965, New York Public Library, George Perle Papers.

41 Copy of letter, Hans Redlich to Helene Berg, 28 October 1955.

42 *International Alban Berg Society Newsletter*, no. 1 (December 1968).

43 Letter, George Perle to Hans Redlich, 15 October 1963, New York Public Library, Hans Redlich Papers.

44 George Perle, "The Secret Programme of the Lyric Suite," *Musical Times* 118 (1977): 812.

45 Letter, Helene Berg to Alma Mahler, 19 June 1936, AMB, 513.

46 Letter, Alma Mahler to Ida Gebauer Wagner, 15 January 1936, ÖNB, Sig. 1314/5–11. Erwin Stein also expressed his concern about Helene in a letter to Arnold Schoenberg, 17 January 1936, Arnold Schönberg Center, Vienna.

47 Freud's seminal essay on grief is "Trauer und Melancholie" (published 1917). For the English version, see "Mourning and Melancholia," in *The Standard Edition of the Complete Psychological Works of Sigmund Freud*, ed. James Strachey et al. (London: The Hogarth Press, 1966), 14: 243–58.

48 Nigel P. Field et al., "Continuing Bonds, Risk Factors for Complicated Grief, and Adjustment to Bereavement," *Death Studies* 34 (2010): 1–2.

49 See Melanie Unseld, "Erinnerung stiften. Voraussetzungen und Handlungsspielräume der Komponistenwitwe Helene Berg," in *Erinnerung stiften: Helene Berg und das Erbe Alban Bergs, Bericht zur internationalen Tagung am 16. und 17. März 2017* (Vienna: Alban Berg Stiftung & Universal Edition, 2018), 9–30.

50 Letter, Helene Nahowski to Alban Berg, 2 May 1911, BW I: 737.

51 Notebook, Helene Berg, passage dated 3 May 1940, ÖNB, F21.Berg.1623/192.

52 Letter, Helene Berg to Alma Mahler, 19 June 1936, AMB, 513.

53 Thomas Reinecke, *Hildegard Jone (1891–1963): Untersuchungen zu Leben, Werk und Veröffentlichungskontexten* (Frankfurt: Peter Lang, 1999), 103.

54 Quoted in Moldenhauer, *Anton von Webern*, 452. The original letter is in ÖNB, F21.Berg.2311.

55 Card, Ružena Herlinger to Hans Redlich (in English), Christmas 1968, New York Public Library, Hans Redlich Papers.

56 For a history of the Nazi persecution of anthroposophists, see Uwe Werner and Christoph Lindenberg, *Anthroposophen in der Zeit des Nationalsozialismus (1933–1945)* (Munich: Verlag R. Oldenberg, 1999).

57 See letter, Gerti Müller to Helene Berg, 24 February 1950, ÖNB, F21.Berg.1963/15. Müller had emigrated to New York from Vienna in 1939 and from there she wrote to Helene: "When I have the money, I like to go to the medium, mainly to talk to the departed. Many Viennese come, but Alban hasn't been there."

58 A succinct overview of attachment theory and grief may be found in E.A. Doughty, A. Wissel, and C. Glorfield (2011), *Current Trends in Grief Counseling*. Retrieved from http://counselingoutfitters.com/vistas11/Article_94.pdf.

59 Letter, Helene to Alban Berg, 17 October 1915, BW II: 243.

60 Letter, Helene Berg to Alma Mahler, 19 June 1936, AMB, 512.

61 Letter, Helene Berg to Barbara Nowak, 25 February 1937, AMB, 589. Barbara Nowak was Anna Nahowski's younger sister who lived with the Nahowski family and was always referred to as "Wetti" or "Tante."

62 Ibid., 589.

63 Eckard John, *Musikbolschewismus: Die Politisierung der Musik in Deutschland, 1918–1938* (Stuttgart: J. B. Metzler, 1994), 367.

64 Helene Berg, notebook, ÖNB, F21.Berg.433/35'. This note is among Helene's sketches for a biography of Berg.

65 Unsigned review, *Neues Wiener Tagblatt*, May 28, 1939.

66 Hermann Hibler, "'Entartete Musik': Sonderschau in der Ausstellung 'Entartete Kunst,'" *Wiener neueste Nachrichten*, 23 May 1939.

67 Draft of letter, Helene Berg to Hans Severus Ziegler, June 1939, ÖNB, F21. Berg.1622/194.

68 Letter, Hans Severus Ziegler to Helene Berg, 23 August 1939, ÖNB, F21.Berg.2207/3.

69 Letter, Helene Berg to Alfred Schlee, 14 February 1949, ÖNB, F21.Berg.2217. STAGMA (Staatlich genehmigte Gesellschaft zur Verwertung musikalischer Aufführungsrechte) was the music performing rights collection society under the Nazi regime. The N.S.V. refers to the Nationalsozialistische Volkswohlfahrt, a German welfare organization under the Nazis that among other things oversaw the removal of children from cities and areas of danger.

70 Letter, Helene Berg to Alma Mahler, 29 May 1941, AMB, 534.

71 Letter, Helene Berg to Alma Mahler, 6 July 1946, AMB, 538. The date given in this letter for Frank's death, 1943, is probably an error, since elsewhere Helene gives his death date in full as 16 June 1942. No official record of Frank Nahowski's death has been located.

72 Letter, Helene Berg to Alfred Schlee, 14 February 1949, ÖNB, F21.Berg.2217.

73 See the draft of a letter by Helene Berg dated 8 December 1945 from the Waldhaus confirming the *Denkmalschutz* agreement. The letter is inserted into a volume of Rudolf Steiner's lectures, *Über Schicksalsbildung* (1915) with Alice Wengraf's owner's mark, now located in the Alban Berg Foundation.

74 Letter, Helene Berg to Alma Mahler, 4 May 1946, AMB, 535.

75 Notebook, Helene Berg, ÖNB, F21.Berg.1623/176.

76 Notebook, Helene Berg, ÖNB, F21.Berg.1623/188.

77 Notebook, Helene Berg, ÖNB, F21.Berg.1623/194.

78 Notebook, Helene Berg, ÖNB, F21.Berg.1623/188.

79 Alban Berg Sämtliche Werke (Vienna: Alban Berg Stiftung and Universal Edition, 1984–). This critical edition of Berg's works consists of published musical works (Abteilung 1), works left in manuscript (Abteilung 2), and writings (Abteilung 3). Commentaries are planned for each volume.

80 This is an eighty-page engraver's copy now located in the ÖNB, F21.Berg.23/II.

81 A note in Berg's contract with Universal Edition concerning the work states that the manuscript had been presented to Zemlinsky. See the letter from Alfred Schlee to Helene Berg, 16 February 1953, ÖNB, F21.Berg.2160.

82 Letter, Theodor Adorno to Helene Berg, 16 April 1936, in *Theodor W. Adorno and Alban Berg: Correspondence*, 234–35.

83 Letter, Helene Berg to Alma Mahler, n.d. (ca. April–May 1936), AMB, 511.

84 Letter, Herbert and Hanna Fuchs-Robettin to Helene Berg, 11 June 1936, ÖNB, F21. Berg. 2267. Helene added a note to this letter: "The conditions were that Fr. Fuchs would sell the manuscript only to a public collection."

85 See Redlich's letters to Helmut Hoever (6 October 1961), to Universal Edition (15 February 1962), and the letter from Otto Lifczis (Liff) to Helene Berg (28 October 1962), New York Public Library, Hans Redlich Collection.

86 Perle, *Lulu*, 27.

87 Christopher Hailey and Juliane Brand, "Vorwort," BSB I: xxiii.

88 Many of these drafts are transcribed in QMG 29 and QMG 35.

89 Many of the typed carbon copies are given in facsimile in QMG 34.

90 A selection of such letters can be found in *Altenberg bis Zuckerkandl: Briefe an Alban Berg, Liebesbriefe von Alban Berg*, ed. Herwig Knaus and Thomas Leibnitz (Vienna: Erhard Löcker, 2009).

91 "Arnold Schoenberg, Anton Webern, Alban Berg: Unbekannte Briefe an Erwin Schulhoff," ed. Ivan Vojtěch, *Miscellanea musicologica* (Prague) 15 (1965): 31–83.

92 The complete existing correspondence between Berg and Webern has been announced for future publication by Schott in the Briefwechsel der Wiener Schule series.

93 Letter, Alban to Helene Nahowski, 22 August 1909, BW I: 462.

94 BW III: 465.

95 ÖNB, F21.Berg.1581. In a letter of late November 1939 (AMB, 531), Helene tells Alma Mahler that she had then reread Berg's letters to her, sorted them by date, and begun to type them out.

96 Letter, Alban Berg to Helene Nahowski, 25 August 1908, BW I: 209. The sentence was deleted following the initial printing of the volume.

97 Willi Reich, "Von zu Haus und unterwegs: Briefe Alban Bergs an seine Braut und Gattin Helene," *Forum: Österreichische Monatsblätter für kulturelle Freiheit* 12 (1965): 140–41; Mosco Carner, "Alban Berg in His Letters to His Wife," *Music & Letters* 50 (1969): 365–75.

98 Hans Ferdinand Redlich, "Bergs Briefe an seine Frau," ÖMZ 21 (1966): 342.

99 "Berg-Briefe: Kusserln vom Floh," *Der Spiegel*, 17 January 1966.

100 Letter, Franz Willnauer to Helene Berg, 22 December 1967, ÖNB, F21.Berg.2194.

101 *Briefwechsel Alban Berg–Helene Berg: Gesamtausgabe*, ed. Herwig Knaus and Thomas Leibnitz, 3 vols. (Wilhelmshaven: Florian Noetzel Verlag, 2012–14). An abbreviated English version of the 1965 *Briefe*, titled *Alban Berg Letters to His Wife*, was translated and edited by Berg's former student Bernard Grun (New York: St. Martin's Press, 1971). Grun's edition is far less reliable than Willnauer's, as he often deletes important text and makes many errors in his footnotes.

102 Copies are found in ÖNB, F21.Berg.424 and WBR, HIN 204.582.

103 Letter, Alban Berg to Hermann Watznauer, 22 April 1929, Morgan Library, MFC B493. W353 (31).

104 See Ploderer's letter to Berg, 23 February 1929, in ÖNB, F21.Berg.1159.

105 Willi Reich, *Alban Berg. Mit Bergs eigenen Schriften und Beiträgen von Theodor Wiesengrund-Adorno und Ernst Křenek* (Vienna: Herbert Reichner Verlag, 1937): 206.

106 Letter, Alma Mahler to Helene Berg, 6 January 1938, AMB, 523.

107 ÖNB, F21.Berg.433; also F21.Berg.1622–23.

108 Letter, Hans Redlich to Egon Wellesz, 27 January 1952, ÖNB, F13.Wellesz.1515.

109 Hans Redlich, "Der große Unzeitgemäße (Gedanken zu Arnold Schönbergs 60. Geburtstag)," *23: Eine Wiener Musikzeitschrift* 15–16 (October 1934): 7.

110 See Schoenberg's essay "New Music and Outmoded Music, or Style and Idea," in *Composers on Modern Musical Culture: An Anthology of Readings on Twentieth-Century Music*, ed. Bryan R. Simms (New York: Schirmer Books, 1999), 96–107.

111 H.F. Redlich, *Alban Berg: Versuch einer Würdigung* (Vienna: Universal Edition, 1957); idem, *Alban Berg: The Man and his Music* (London: John Calder, 1957).

112 Soma Morgenstern, *Alban Berg und seine Idole: Erinnerungen und Briefe*, ed. Ingolf Schulte (Lüneburg: Dietrich zu Klampen, 1995).

113 Soma Morgenstern, *Joseph Roths Flucht und Ende: Erinnerungen*, ed. Ingolf Schulte (Cologne: Kiepenheuer & Witsch, 2008).

114 See Ingolf Schulte, "Soma Morgenstern: Der Autor als Überlebender," in ibid., 363.

115 Morgenstern, *Alban Berg*, 46.

116 Ibid., 46.

117 Ibid., 376–77.

118 Letter, Helene to Alban Berg, 3 December 1925, BW III: 447.

119 Letter, Soma Morgenstern to Helene Berg, 20 May 1969, ÖNB, F21.Berg.1961.

120 Ibid. Berg's correspondence with Morgenstern shows that Morgenstern did, in fact, give Berg the idea for using *Pippa* as an opera text. See Morgenstern's letter to Berg, 30 November 1927, in Morgenstern, *Alban Berg*, 201.

121 Letter, Helene Berg to Soma Morgenstern, 14 March 1974, ÖNB, F21.Berg.1622/289.

122 For a complete overview of the genesis and establishment of the Alban Berg Foundation, see Charlotte E. Erwin, "Helene Berg and the Creation of the Alban Berg Stiftung," in *Erinnerung stiften: Helene Berg und das Erbe Alban Bergs, Bericht zur internationalen Tagung am 16. und 17. März 2017* (Vienna: Alban Berg-Stiftung and Universal Edition, 2018), 154–69.

123 A certified copy of Alban Berg's will may be found in the Wiener Stadt- und Landesarchiv, Hauptarchiv-Akten-Persönlichkeiten, A1: B19. A transcription is published by Martina Steiger in AMB, 591–92.

124 A discussion of the foundation's establishment in 1967 is presented in Franz Willnauer, "Wie frei wird Alban Berg? Das Ende der Schutzfrist—und die (möglichen) Folgen," ÖMZ 60, no. 12 (2005): 14–29. Supporting documents are located in ÖNB, F21. Berg.1629. Willnauer does not cover the pre-1967 history of the foundation.

125 The original eight-page 1946 will in Helene Berg's hand is located in ÖNB, F21. Berg.1609/8.

126 Helene made a habit of dating her wills and other significant documents with the number 23 in deference to Alban. The 1953 will drafts and the dated version, along with the 1953 *Stiftungsurkunde*, are located in the files of the Hietzing Bezirksgericht as UV 301/77, UV 299/77 and UV 298/77 respectively. The authors wish to acknowledge the kind assistance of Dr. Daniel Ender of the Alban Berg Stiftung in obtaining copies of these documents.

127 *Alban Berg 1885–1935: Ausstellung der Österreichischen Nationalbibliothek* (Vienna: Universal Edition, 1985), 203.

128 Letter, Helene Berg to Alma Mahler, 28 July 1956, AMB, 571.

129 Letter, Willi Reich to Helene Berg, 6 March 1967, ÖNB, F21.Berg.2040.

130 Letter, Theodor Adorno to Hans Redlich, 22 June 1964, copy in New York Public Library, George Perle Papers.

131 Excerpts from the charter are transcribed in *Alban Berg 1885–1935: Ausstellung der Österreichischen Nationalbibliothek*, 204–05. Also see the letter from lawyer Hans Wolfgang Ploderer to Adolf Streuli, 8 July 1966, ÖNB, F21.Berg.1629/59.

132 Walter Szmolyan, "Helene Bergs Vermächtnis," *ÖMZ* 32, no. 4 (April 1977): 169–79. Helene Berg's will of 1969 and related documents may be found in ÖNB, F21.Berg.1609.

133 Financial reports of the Alban Berg Foundation may be found in ÖNB, F21.Berg.1629/ 58.

134 Helene Berg's engagement calendars are grouped together under the signature F21. Berg.1623 in the ÖNB. Laurence Gill Lyon was a professor at UCLA from 1974 to 1980. He is acknowledged as the translator of Berg's letters to Schoenberg cited in the article by Donald Harris, "Some Thoughts on the Teacher-Student Relationship between Arnold Schoenberg and Alban Berg," *Perspectives of New Music* 15, no. 2 (Spring–Summer 1977): 133–44.

135 Fritzi (Friederike) Schlesinger had a family connection to the Czapka piano firm and sometimes signed her name Schlesinger-Czapka. Schlesinger was an accomplished painter and costume designer. Some of her work may be found in ÖNB, F21.Berg.1599 and F21. Berg.3111.

136 Letter, Fritzi Schlesinger to Claudio Spies, 21 September 1976, Library of Congress, Claudio Spies Papers, box 1, folder 21.

137 Letter, Helene Berg to Ida Gebauer Wagner, 23 August 1955, ÖNB, F21.Berg.3279/3.

138 Handwritten note by Helene Berg, ÖNB, F21.Berg.3567/2.

139 Letters, Helene Berg to Ida Gebauer Wagner, 12 August and 18 October 1966, ÖNB, F21. Berg.3279/12–13.

140 Handwritten note signed by Helene Berg and Ida Wagner. Helene states: "I would like to request the knife in the heart before I am buried. Vienna, 3 March 1965, Helene Berg." On the back of the note: "Accepted at the wish of Mrs. Alban Berg. Ida Wagner. 14 April 65." ÖNB, F21.Berg.3278/16.

141 Typescript, two pages, signed by Erich Alban Berg, ÖNB, F21.Berg.3567/3.

142 Elias Canetti, *The Memoirs of Elias Canetti* (New York: Farrar, Straus and Giroux, 1999), 763.

Epilogue

1 Alban Berg, "Why Is Schoenberg's Music So Difficult to Understand?" (1924), PMPD, 195.

2 Ibid., 194.

3 Igor Stravinsky, *An Autobiography* (1936; repr. New York: Norton, 1962), 176.

4 Ibid., 153.

5 Georges Auric, "L'Apothéose d'Igor Stravinsky," *Les annales politiques et littéraires*, no. 2305 (1 March 1928): 233.

6 Kurt Weill, "Alban Berg, *Wozzeck*," *Der Deutsche Rundfunk* 3 (1925): 3422.

7 Pierre Boulez, "Eventually . . ." (1952), in *Notes on an Apprenticeship*, trans. Herbert Weinstock (New York: Alfred A. Knopf, 1968), 148.

8 Pierre Boulez, "Present-Day Encounters with Berg" (1948), in ibid., 235–41.

9 Hans Keller, "First Performances: The Eclecticism of *Wozzeck*," *Music Review* 12 (1951): 314.

10 Pierre Boulez, *Conversations with Célestin Deliège* (London: Eulenburg Books, 1976), 25.

11 Boulez's assessment is summarized in Ibid., 25.

12 Aaron Copland, *The New Music 1900–1960*, rev. ed. (New York: W.W. Norton, 1968), 89.

13 ÖNB, F21.Berg.1623/188, p. 4.

14 Virgil Thomson, *New York Herald Tribune*, 13 January 1952.

15 Eric Salzman, "New Look at Berg," *New York Times*, 25 March 1962.

16 Olin Downes, "Paris Fete Offers Berg's 'Wozzeck,'" *New York Times*, 2 May 1952.

17 Herbert Kupferberg, "Alban Berg's Menagerie," *New York Herald Tribune*, 28 September 1952.

18 Henry Pleasants, "Alban Berg's 'Lulu' Has Premiere in Germany," *New York Times*, 19 April 1953. The quotation in the 1953 program book was taken from Willi Reich's 1937 book on Berg (p. 110), where it reads: ". . . ein Stück Natur jenseits von Gut und Böse und daher als ein in sich geschlossener Kosmos nur durch die Musik in seinem, allem Begrifflichen entrückten Zusammenhang zu enträtseln" (A piece of nature beyond good and evil and, as such, in a world unto itself, only to be deciphered, in its coherence conceptually detached from everything else, by music). The sentence is mangled in Pleasants's citation. Reich says that the statement came from a 1934 Prague critique of the Lulu *Symphonic Pieces*.

19 Letter (draft), Helene Berg to Erwin Stein, n.d. (ca. May 1957), ÖNB F21.Berg.1622/205.

20 Michael Steinberg, "'Lulu': Pain, Ecstasy of a Literal Femme Fatale," *Boston Globe*, 19 June 1967.

21 Igor Stravinsky and Robert Craft, *Conversations with Igor Stravinsky* (1959; repr. Berkeley and Los Angeles: University of California Press, 1980), 71–73 and passim.

22 On this matter see Stephen Walsh, *Stravinsky: The Second Exile, France and America, 1934–1971* (New York: Alfred A. Knopf, 2006), 287 and passim.

23 Luciano Berio, "The Composer and His Work," *Christian Science Monitor*, 15 July 1965.

24 Leonard Bernstein, *The Unanswered Question: Six Talks at Harvard* (Cambridge, MA, 1976), 419; Bernstein, *The Infinite Variety of Music* (New York: Simon and Schuster, 1966), 10.

Selected Bibliography

For a comprehensive bibliography and catalogue raisonné of writings about Alban Berg to 2016 see Bryan R. Simms, *Alban Berg: A Research and Information Guide*, 3rd edition (New York: Routledge, 2018).

Adorno, Theodor W. "Im Gedächtnis an Alban Berg." In Adorno, *Gesammelte Schriften*, vol. 18, 487–512. Frankfurt: Suhrkamp, 1984.

Alban Berg and His World. Edited by Christopher Hailey. Princeton, NJ: Princeton University Press, 2010.

Alban Berg—Erich Kleiber: Briefe der Freundschaft. Edited by Martina Steiger. Vienna: Seifert Verlag, 2013

Altenberg bis Zuckerkandl: Briefe an Alban Berg. Liebesbriefe von Alban Berg aus den Beständen der Österreichischen Nationalbibliothek. Edited by Herwig Knaus and Thomas Leibnitz. Vienna: Erhard Löcker, 2009.

AMB. *"Immer wieder werden mich thätige Geister verlocken": Alma Mahler-Werfels Briefe an Alban Berg und seine Frau*. Edited by Martina Steiger. Vienna: Seifert Verlag, 2008.

BBF. Alban Berg. *Briefwechsel mit seiner Familie*. Edited by Herwig Knaus. Wilhelmshaven: Florian Noetzel Verlag, 2016.

Berg, Alban. *Sämtliche Werke*. Edited by Rudolf Stephan and Regina Busch. Vienna: Universal Edition for the Alban Berg Stiftung, 1984–.

BSB. *Briefwechsel Arnold Schönberg—Alban Berg*. Edited by Juliane Brand, Christopher Hailey, and Andreas Meyer. 2 vols. Mainz: Schott, 2007.

BW. *Briefwechsel Alban Berg—Helene Berg: Gesamtausgabe*. Edited by Herwig Knaus and Thomas Leibnitz. 3 vols. and index vol. Wilhelmshaven: Florian Noetzel Verlag, 2012–14.

The Cambridge Companion to Berg. Edited by Anthony Pople. Cambridge: Cambridge University Press, 1997.

Carner, Mosco. *Alban Berg*. 2nd, revised edition. New York: Holmes & Meier Publishers, 1983.

Floros, Constantin. *Alban Berg: Music as Autobiography*. Translated by Ernest Bernhardt-Kabisch. Frankfurt: PL Academic Research, 2014.

Hall, Patricia. *Berg's "Wozzeck"*. New York: Oxford University Press, 2011.

Headlam, Dave. *The Music of Alban Berg*. New Haven, CT: Yale University Press, 1996.

Hilmar, Rosemary. *Alban Berg: Leben und Wirken in Wien bis zu seinen ersten Erfolgen als Komponist*. Wiener Musikwissenschaftliche Beiträge, vol. 10. Vienna: Verlag Hermann Böhlaus Nachf., 1978.

Jarman, Douglas. *The Music of Alban Berg*. Berkeley and Los Angeles: University of California Press, 1979.

Knaus, Herwig. *Anna Nahowski und Kaiser Franz Josef: Ihr Leben—Ihre Liebe—Ihre Kinder*. Vienna: Erhard Löcker, 2012.

Knaus, Herwig, editor. *Alban Berg: Handschriftliche Briefe, Briefentwürfe und Notizen aus den Beständen der Musiksammlung der Österreichischen Nationalbibliothek.* Quellenkataloge zur Musikgeschichte, vol. 29. Wilhelmshaven: Florian Noetzel, 2004.

Knaus, Herwig, and Thomas Leibnitz, eds. *Alban Berg: Briefentwürfe, Aufzeichnungen, Familienbriefe, das "Bergwerk" aus den Beständen der Musiksammlung der Österreichischen Nationalbibliothek.* Quellenkataloge zur Musikgeschichte, vol. 35. Wilhelmshaven: Florian Noetzel, 2006.

Knaus, Herwig, and Thomas Leibnitz, eds. *Alban Berg: Maschinenschriftliche und handschriftliche Briefe, Briefentwürfe, Skizzen und Notizen aus den Beständen der Musiksammlung der Österreichischen Nationalbibliothek.* Quellenkataloge zur Musikgeschichte, vol. 34. Wilhelmshaven: Florian Noetzel, 2005.

Knaus, Herwig, and Wilhelm Sinkovicz. *Alban Berg: Zeitumstände—Lebenslinien.* St. Pölten and Salzburg: Residenz Verlag, 2008.

Krämer, Ulrich. *Alban Berg als Schüler Arnold Schönbergs: Quellenstudien und Analysen zum Frühwerk.* Alban Berg Studien, vol. 4. Vienna: Universal Edition, 1996.

Meier, Barbara. *Alban Berg: Biographie.* Würzburg: Königshausen & Neumann, 2018.

Morgenstern, Soma. *Alban Berg und seine Idole.* Edited by Ingolf Schulte. Lüneburg: Dietrich zu Klampen Verlag, 1995.

Notley, Margaret. *"Taken by the Devil": The Censorship of Frank Wedekind and Alban Berg's "Lulu".* New York: Oxford University Press, 2020.

Perle, George. *The Operas of Alban Berg.* 2 vols. (1 *"Wozzeck"*; 2 *"Lulu"*). Berkeley and Los Angeles: University of California Press, 1980–85.

PMPD. *Pro Mundo—Pro Domo: The Writings of Alban Berg.* Edited with commentaries by Bryan R. Simms. New York: Oxford University Press, 2014.

Redlich, H[ans] F[erdinand]. *Alban Berg: Versuch einer Würdigung.* Vienna: Universal Edition, 1957.

Reich, Willi. *Alban Berg.* Translated by Cornelius Cardew. New York: Vienna House, 1965.

Rode, Susanne. *Alban Berg und Karl Kraus: Zur geistigen Biographie des Komponisten der "Lulu."* Frankfurt: Peter Lang, 1988.

Santos, Silvio J. dos. *Narratives of Identity in Alban Berg's "Lulu."* Eastman Studies in Music. Rochester: University of Rochester Press, 2014.

Schmalfeldt, Janet. *Berg's "Wozzeck": Harmonic Language and Dramatic Design.* New Haven, CT: Yale University Press, 1983.

Seminara, Graziella. *Alban Berg.* Palermo: L'Epos, 2012.

Theodor W. Adorno and Alban Berg: Correspondence 1925–1935. Edited by Henri Lonitz. Translated by Wieland Hoban. Cambridge, UK: Polity, 2005.

Index

Institutions are found following the city of their location